TEST PREP 2018

Study & Prepare

Pass your test and know what is essential to become a safe, competent pilot—from the most trusted source in aviation training

Instructor

Aviation Supplies & Academics, Inc.
Newcastle, Washington

Instructor Test Prep
2018 Edition

Aviation Supplies & Academics, Inc.
7005 132nd Place SE
Newcastle, Washington 98059-3153
425.235.1500
www.asa2fly.com

Important: This Test Prep should be sold with and used in conjunction with *Airman Knowledge Testing Supplement for Flight Instructor, Ground Instructor, and Sport Pilot Instructor* (FAA-CT-8080-5G).

ASA reprints the FAA test figures and legends contained within this government document, and it is also sold separately and available from aviation retailers nationwide. Order #ASA-CT-8080-5G.

ASA-TP-CFI-18
ISBN 978-1-61954-526-7

Printed in the United States of America

2018   2017   5   4   3   2   1

Stay informed of aviation industry happenings

Website www.asa2fly.com
Updates www.asa2fly.com/testupdate
Twitter www.twitter.com/asa2fly
Facebook www.facebook.com/asa2fly
Blog www.learntoflyblog.com

About the Contributors

Charles L. Robertson
Associate Professor, UND Aerospace
University of North Dakota

Charles Robertson as ground and flight instructor, ATP, associate professor and manager of training at UND Aerospace, contributes a vital and substantial combination of pilot and educator to ASA's reviewing team. After graduating with education degrees from Florida State University in 1967, and Ball State University in 1975, he began his twenty-year career in the United States Air Force as Chief of avionics branch, 58th Military Airlift Squadron, and went on to flight instruction, training for aircraft systems, and airport managing, while gaining many thousands of hours flying international passenger and cargo, aerial refueling and airlift missions. As Division Chief in 1988, Robertson directed the USAF Strategic Air Command's "Alpha Alert Force" and coordinated its daily flight training operations.

Jackie Spanitz
Director of Curriculum Development
Aviation Supplies & Academics, Inc.

As Director of Curriculum Development for Aviation Supplies & Academics, Jackie Spanitz oversees maintenance and development of more than 750 titles and pilot supplies in the ASA product line and integration of these products into new and existing curricula. Ms. Spanitz has worked with airman training and testing for more than 20 years, including participation in the ACS development committees. Jackie holds a Bachelor of Science degree in aviation technology from Western Michigan University, a Masters degree from Embry Riddle Aeronautical University, and Instructor and Commercial Pilot certificates. She is the author of *Guide to the Flight Review*, and the technical editor for ASA's *Test Prep* and *FAR/AIM* series.

Paul Hamilton
Sport Pilot and Light-Sport Aircraft Expert
Adventure Productions

Flight instructor, FAA Designated Examiner, and Sport/Ultralight Pilot for more than 30 years, Paul contributed Light-Sport Aircraft and Sport Instructor information.

About ASA: Aviation Supplies & Academics, Inc. (ASA) has been providing trusted aviation training products for more than 75 years to flight instructors, aviation maintenance technicians, air traffic controllers, career aviators, students, remote pilots and drone operators. ASA's pilot supplies, software, and publications are supported with integrity, consistency, superior quality, and the best customer service in the industry. Aviators are invited to visit **www.asa2fly.com** for a free copy of our catalog.

Contents

Preface

Welcome to ASA's Test Prep Series. ASA's test books have been helping pilots prepare for the FAA Knowledge Tests for more than 60 years with great success. We are confident that with proper use of this book, you will score very well on any of the flight instructor certificate tests.

Begin your studies with a classroom or home-study ground school course, which will involve reading a comprehensive textbook. Fundamentals of Instructing (FOI) applicants should thoroughly review the most current edition of the *Aviation Instructor's Handbook* (FAA-H-8083-9). Conclude your studies with this Test Prep or comparable software. Read the question, select your choice for the correct answer, then read the explanation. Use the Learning Statement Codes and references that conclude each explanation to identify additional resources if you need further study of a subject. Upon completion of your studies, take practice tests at www.prepware.com (see inside front cover for your free account).

The FAA Flight Instructor questions have been arranged into chapters based on subject matter. Topical study, in which similar material is covered under a common subject heading, promotes better understanding, aids recall, and thus provides a more efficient study guide. Study and place emphasis on those questions most likely to be included in your test (identified by the aircraft above each question). For example: a candidate preparing for the Flight Instructor–Airplane test would focus on the questions marked "ALL" and "AIR," and a candidate preparing for the Flight Instructor–Rotorcraft test would focus on the questions marked "ALL" and "RTC." Those preparing for the add-on tests (people who hold a Flight Instructor certificate in one category and are transitioning to another) would focus on the questions marked with that category (AIR, RTC, GLI, LSA, WSC, or PPC). Ground Instructors are responsible for all aircraft categories, and therefore need to study all the questions in the database (other than Chapter 1, Fundamentals of Instructing — this is a separate test).

It is important to answer every question assigned on your FAA Knowledge Test. If in their ongoing review, the FAA authors decide a question has no correct answer, is no longer applicable, or is otherwise defective, your answer will be marked correct no matter which one you chose. However, you will not be given the automatic credit unless you have marked an answer. Unlike some other exams you may have taken, there is no penalty for "guessing" in this instance.

The FAA exams are "closed tests" which means the exact database of questions is not available to the public. The question and answer choices in this book are based on our extensive history and experience with the FAA testing process. You might see similar although not exactly the same questions on your official FAA exam. Answer stems may be rearranged from the A, B, C order you see in this book. Therefore, be careful to fully understand the intent of each question and corresponding answer while studying, rather than memorize the A, B, C answer. You may be asked a question that has unfamiliar wording; studying and understanding the information in this book and the associated references will give you the tools to answer question variations with confidence.

If your study leads you to question an answer choice, we recommend you seek the assistance of a local instructor. We welcome your questions, recommendations or concerns:

Aviation Supplies & Academics, Inc.
7005 132nd Place SE   Voice: 425.235.1500   Fax: 425.235.0128
Newcastle, WA 98059-3153   Email: cfi@asa2fly.com Website: www.asa2fly.com

The FAA appreciates testing experience feedback. You can contact the branch responsible for the FAA Knowledge Exams at:

Federal Aviation Administration
AFS-630, Airman Testing Standards Branch
PO Box 25082, Oklahoma City, OK 73125
Email: afs630comments@faa.gov

Updates and Practice Tests

Free Test Updates for the One-Year Life Cycle of Test Prep Books

The FAA rolls out new tests as needed throughout the year; this typically happens in June, October, and February. The FAA exams are "closed tests" which means the exact database of questions is not available to the public. ASA combines more than 60 years of experience with expertise in airman training and certification tests to prepare the most effective test preparation materials available in the industry.

You can feel confident you will be prepared for your FAA Knowledge Exam by using the ASA Test Preps. ASA publishes test books each June and keeps abreast of changes to the tests. These changes are then posted on the ASA website as a Test Update.

Visit the ASA website before taking your test to be certain you have the most current information. While there, sign up for ASA's free email Update service. We will then send you an email notification if there is a change to the test you are preparing for so you can review the Update for revised and/or new test information.

www.asa2fly.com/testupdate

We invite your feedback. After you take your official FAA exam, let us know how you did. Were you prepared? Did the ASA products meet your needs and exceed your expectations? We want to continue to improve these products to ensure applicants are prepared, and become safe aviators. Send feedback to: **cfi@asa2fly.com**

Description of the Tests

All applicants seeking initial flight or ground instructor certification must successfully complete a fundamentals of instructing knowledge test. However, a person holding a current teacher's certificate at the junior or senior high school level or who is an instructor at a college or university can receive credit for this test.

Fundamentals of instructing, flight instructor, and ground instructor test results expire at the end of 24 months after the month in which the test was taken.

All test questions are the objective, multiple-choice type, with three choices of answers. Each question can be answered by the selection of a single response. Each test question is independent of other questions, that is, a correct response to one does not depend upon, or influence the correct response to another.

Refer to the following table, placing emphasis on those questions most likely to be included on your test (identified by the aircraft category above each question number).

Test Code	Test Name	Test Prep Study	Number of Questions	Min. Age	Allotted Time (hrs)	Passing Score
FOI	Fundamentals of Instructing	FOI	50	16	1.5	70
BGI	Ground Instructor — Basic	ALL, AIR, RTC, GLI, LTA, LSA, WSC, PPC	80	16	2.5	70
AGI	Ground Instructor — Advanced	ALL, AIR, RTC, GLI, LTA, LSA, WSC, PPC	100	16	2.5	70
FIA	Flight Instructor — Airplane	ALL, AIR	100	16	2.5	70
FRH	Flight Instructor — Helicopter	ALL, RTC	100	16	2.5	70
FRG	Flight Instructor — Gyroplane	ALL, RTC	100	16	2.5	70
FIG	Flight Instructor — Glider	ALL, GLI	100	16	2.5	70
AFA	Flight Instructor — Airplane (Added Rating)	AIR	25	16	1.0	70
HFA	Flight Instructor — Helicopter (Added Rating)	RTC	25	16	1.0	70
GFA	Flight Instructor — Gyroplane (Added Rating)	RTC	25	16	1.0	70
AFG	Flight Instructor — Glider (Added Rating)	GLI	25	16	1.0	70
MCI	Military Competency Instructor	FOI, ALL, MCI	125	16	3.0	70

Note: Unlike Flight Instructor Certificates, Ground Instructor Certificates are not category-specific. In other words, it is not possible to get a Ground Instructor Certificate with an Airplane Rating. Although the emphasis of the tests is "Airplane," applicants will be tested on all questions in all aircraft categories. Therefore, applicants need to study all questions in Chapters 2 through 10.

Sport Pilot Instructor continues on the next page...

The Sport Pilot test is found in the Private Pilot Test Prep book (ASA-TP-P) and Prepware software (ASA-TW-PVT). Applicants seeking initial flight or ground instructor certification must successfully complete a Fundamentals of Instructing (FOI) test. However, a person holding a current teacher's certificate at the junior or senior high school level, an instructor at a college or university level, or an Ultralight Instructor who already took this test can receive credit for it.

Test Code	Test Name	Test Prep Study	Number of Questions	Min. Age	Allotted Time (hrs)	Passing Score
SPORT PILOT INSTRUCTOR						
FOI	Fundamentals of Instructing	FOI	50	16	1.5	70
SIA	Flight Instructor Sport Airplane	ALL, LSA	70	16	2.5	70
SIB	Flight Instructor Sport Balloon	ALL, LTA	70	16	2.5	70
SIG	Flight Instructor Sport Glider	ALL, GLI	70	16	2.5	70
SIL	Flight Instructor Sport Lighter-than-Air (Airship)	ALL, LTA	70	16	2.5	70
SIP	Flight Instructor Sport Powered Parachute	ALL, PPC	70	16	2.5	70
SIW	Flight Instructor Sport Weight-Shift Control	ALL, WSC	70	16	2.5	70
SIY	Flight Instructor Sport Gyroplane	ALL, RTC	70	16	2.5	70

Knowledge Test Eligibility Requirements

If you are pursuing an instructor certificate, you should review Title 14 of the Code of Federal Regulations (14 CFR) Part 61, §61.23 "Medical Certificates: Requirement and Duration," 14 CFR §61.35 "Knowledge Test: Prerequisites and Passing Grades," and 14 CFR §61.65 "Instrument rating requirements."

You must pass the Fundamentals of Instructing Knowledge Test and a Flight or Ground Instructor Knowledge Test specific to the instructor rating sought. You may take these tests on the same day, and you do not have to take them in any particular order. When applying for any additional instructor rating, you are not required to take the Fundamentals of Instructing Knowledge Test again. Once you have acquired a flight instructor certificate, you are eligible to give ground instruction required for a pilot or instructor certificate or rating, based on the ratings on your flight instructor certificate. Because of this, it is not necessary to obtain a separate ground instructor certificate since you would already have these privileges.

Process for Taking a Knowledge Test

The FAA has designated holders of airman knowledge testing (AKT) organization designation authorization (ODA). These AKT-ODAs sponsor hundreds of knowledge testing center locations. The testing centers offer a full range of airman knowledge tests including: Aircraft Dispatcher, Airline Transport Pilot, Aviation Maintenance Technician, Commercial Pilot, Flight Engineer, Flight Instructor, Flight Navigator, Ground Instructor, Inspection Authorization, Instrument Rating, Parachute Rigger, Private Pilot, Recreational Pilot, Sport Pilot, Remote Pilot, and Military Competence. Contact information for the AKT-ODA holders is provided at the end of this section.

The first step in taking a knowledge test is the registration process. You may either call the testing centers' 1-800 numbers or simply take the test on a walk-in basis. If you choose to use the 1-800 number to register, you will need to select a testing center, schedule a test date, and make financial arrangements for test payment. You may register for tests several weeks in advance, and you may cancel your appointment according to the AKT-ODA holder's cancellation policy. If you do not follow the AKT-ODA holder's cancellation policies, you could be subject to a cancellation fee.

The next step in taking a knowledge test is providing proper identification. Although no prior authorization is necessary, except in the case of failure, to take any flight or ground instructor knowledge test, proper identification is required. Testing center personnel will not begin the test until your identification is verified. Sport pilot flight instructors must have a test authorization (endorsement).

Acceptable Forms of Authorization

Flight and Ground Instructor

1. Requires *no* instructor endorsements or other form of written authorization.
2. Failed, passing or expired Airman Knowledge Test Report, provided the applicant still has the *original* test report in his/her possession. (*See* Retesting explanation.)
3. Sport Pilot Flight Instructor applicants must present a ground school certificate or FAA Knowledge Exam endorsement from an authorized ground or flight instructor.

Test-Taking Tips

Prior to launching the actual test, the AKT-ODA holder's testing software will provide you with an opportunity to practice navigating through the test. This practice (or tutorial) session may include a "sample" question(s). These sample questions have no relation to the content of the test, but are meant to familiarize you with the look and feel of the system screens, including selecting an answer, marking a question for later review, time remaining for the test, and other features of the testing software.

Follow these time-proven tips, which will help you develop a skillful, smooth approach to test-taking:

1. Be careful to fully understand the intent of each question and corresponding answer while studying, rather than memorize the A, B, C answer choice — answer stems may appear in a different order than you studied.
2. Take with you to the testing center a photo I.D., the testing fee, calculator, flight computer (ASA's E6-B or CX-2 Pathfinder), plotter, magnifying glass, and a sharp pointer, such as a safety pin.
3. Your first action when you sit down should be to write on the scratch paper the weight and balance and any other formulas and information you can remember from your study. Remember, some of the formulas may be on your E6-B.
4. Answer each question in accordance with the latest regulations and guidance publications.
5. Read each question carefully before looking at the possible answers. You should clearly understand the problem before attempting to solve it.
6. After formulating an answer, determine which answer choice corresponds the closest with your answer. The answer chosen should completely resolve the problem.
7. From the answer choices given, it may appear that there is more than one possible answer. However, there is only one answer that is correct and complete. The other answers are either incomplete, erroneous, or represent popular misconceptions.
8. If a certain question is difficult for you, it is best to mark it for REVIEW and proceed to the other questions. After you answer the less difficult questions, return to those which you marked for review and answer them. Be sure to untag these questions once you have answered them. The review marking

procedure will be explained to you prior to starting the test. Although the computer should alert you to unanswered questions, make sure every question has an answer recorded. This procedure will enable you to use the available time to the maximum advantage.

9. Perform each math calculation twice to confirm your answer. If adding or subtracting a column of numbers, reverse your direction the second time to reduce the possibility of error.

10. When solving a calculation problem, select the answer nearest to your solution. The problem has been checked with various types of calculators; therefore, if you have solved it correctly, your answer will be closer to the correct answer than any of the other choices.

11. Remember that information is provided in the FAA Figures.

12. Remember to answer every question, even the ones with no completely correct answer, to ensure the FAA gives you credit for a bad question.

13. Take your time and be thorough but relaxed. Take a minute off every half-hour or so to relax the brain and the body. Get a drink of water halfway through the test.

14. Your test will be graded immediately upon completion. You will be allowed 10 minutes to review any questions you missed. You will see the question only; you will not see the answer choices or your selected response. This allows you to review the missed areas with an instructor prior to taking the Practical exam.

Test Reports

Your test will be graded immediately upon completion. You will be allowed 10 minutes to review any questions you missed. You will see the question only; you will not see the answer choices or your selected response. This allows you to review the missed areas with an instructor prior to taking the Practical exam. After this review period you will receive your Airman Test Report, with the testing center's embossed seal, which reflects your score.

Validity of Airman Test Reports

Airman Test Reports are valid for the 24-calendar month period preceding the month you complete the practical test. If the Airman Test Report expires before completion of the practical test, you must retake the knowledge test.

Test Reports and Learning Statement Codes

The Airman Test Report lists the learning statement codes for questions answered incorrectly. The total number of learning statement codes shown on the Airman Test Report is not necessarily an indication of the total number of questions answered incorrectly. Study these knowledge areas to improve your understanding of the subject matter. See the Learning Statement Code/Question Number Cross-Reference in the back of this book for a complete list of which questions apply to each learning statement code.

Your instructor must provide instruction on each of the knowledge areas listed on your Airman Test Report and complete an endorsement of this instruction. You must present the Airman Test Report to the examiner prior to taking the practical test. During the oral portion of the practical test, the examiner is required to evaluate the noted areas of deficiency.

If you wish to have your test hand-scored (if you believe a question or your score are in error), you must submit a request, in the form of a signed letter, to the Airman Testing Standards Branch, AFS-630. The request must be accompanied by a copy of your Airman Knowledge Test Report and a legible photocopy of a government issued identification with your photograph and signature. Mail or fax this information to (e-mail requests are not accepted due to security issues): FAA, AFS-630, PO Box 25082, Oklahoma City, OK 73125 or fax to 405-954-4748.

Should you require a duplicate Airman Test Report due to loss or destruction of the original, send a signed request accompanied by a check or money order for $12 payable to the FAA. Your request should be sent to the Federal Aviation Administration, Airman Certification Branch, AFS-760, P.O. Box 25082, Oklahoma City, OK 73125.

Airman Knowledge Testing Sites

The following airman knowledge testing (AKT) organization designation authorization (ODA) holders are authorized to give FAA knowledge tests. This list should be helpful in case you choose to register for a test or simply want more information. The latest listing of computer testing center locations is available on the FAA website at **http://www.faa.gov/pilots/testing**, under "Knowledge Testing" select "Commercial Testing Center List" and a PDF will download automatically.

Computer Assisted Testing Service (CATS)
Applicant inquiry and test registration: 800-947-4228 or 650-259-8550
www.catstest.com

PSI Computer Testing
Applicant inquiry and test registration: 800-211-2753 or 360-896-9111
www.psiexams.com

Use of Test Aids and Materials

Airman knowledge tests require applicants to analyze the relationship between variables needed to solve aviation problems, in addition to testing for accuracy of a mathematical calculation. The intent is that all applicants are tested on concepts rather than rote calculation ability. It is permissible to use certain calculating devices when taking airman knowledge tests, provided they are used within the following guidelines. The term "calculating devices" is interchangeable with such items as calculators, computers, or any similar devices designed for aviation-related activities.

Guidelines for Use of Test Aids and Materials

The applicant may use test aids and materials within the guidelines listed below, if actual test questions or answers are not revealed.

1. Applicants may use test aids, such as scales, straightedges, protractors, plotters, navigation computers, log sheets, and all models of aviation-oriented calculating devices that are directly related to the test. In addition, applicants may use any test materials provided with the test.

2. Manufacturer's permanently inscribed instructions on the front and back of such aids listed in 1(a), e.g., formulas, conversions, regulations, signals, weather data, holding pattern diagrams, frequencies, weight and balance formulas, and air traffic control procedures are permissible.

3. The test proctor may provide calculating devices to applicants and deny them use of their personal calculating devices if the applicant's device does not have a screen that indicates all memory has been erased. The test proctor must be able to determine the calculating device's erasure capability. The use of calculating devices incorporating permanent or continuous type memory circuits without erasure capability is prohibited.

4. The use of magnetic cards, magnetic tapes, modules, computer chips, or any other device upon which prewritten programs or information related to the test can be stored and retrieved is prohibited. Printouts of data will be surrendered at the completion of the test if the calculating device used incorporates this design feature.

5. The use of any booklet or manual containing instructions related to the use of the applicant's calculating device is not permitted.

6. Dictionaries are not allowed in the testing area.

7. The test proctor makes the final determination relating to test materials and personal possessions that the applicant may take into the testing area.

Testing Procedures For Applicants Requesting Special Accommodations

If you are an applicant with a learning or reading disability, you may request approval from the local FSDO or FAA International Field Office (IFO) to take an airman knowledge test, using the special accommodations procedures outlined in the most current version of FAA Order 8080.6 "Conduct of Airman Knowledge Tests."

Prior to approval of any option, the FSDO or IFO Aviation Safety Inspector must advise you of the regulatory certification requirement of being able to read, write, speak, and understand the English language.

Retesting Procedures

Flight and Ground Instructor

Applicants retesting *after failure* are required to submit the applicable score report indicating failure, along with an endorsement (on the test report) from an authorized instructor who gave the applicant the additional training, and certifying the applicant is competent to pass the test. The original failed test report (with retest endorsement) presented as authorization shall be retained by the proctor and attached to the applicable sign-in/out log. The latest test taken will reflect the official score.

Applicants retesting *in an attempt to achieve a higher passing score* may retake the same test for a better grade after 30 days. The latest test taken will reflect the official score. Applicants are required to submit the *original* applicable score report indicating previous passing score to the testing center prior to testing. Testing center personnel must collect and destroy this report prior to issuing the new test report.

Note: The testing centers require a wait period of 24 hours before any applicant may retest.

Cheating or Other Unauthorized Conduct

Computer testing centers must follow strict security procedures to avoid test compromise. These procedures are established by the FAA and are covered in FAA Order 8080.6, Conduct of Airman Knowledge Tests. The FAA has directed testing centers to terminate a test at any time a test proctor suspects a cheating incident has occurred. An FAA investigation will then be conducted. If the investigation determines that cheating or unauthorized conduct has occurred, then any airman certificate or rating that you hold may be revoked, and you will be prohibited for 1 year from applying for or taking any test for a certificate or rating under 14 CFR Part 61.

Eligibility Requirements for the Flight Instructor Certificates

The Flight Instructor Certificate

To be eligible for a flight instructor certificate, a person must:

1. Be at least 18 years old.

2. Read, speak, write, and understand the English language.

3. Hold a current FAA Medical Certificate (unless exercising privileges of a glider or balloon rating).

4. Hold either a Commercial or Airline Transport Pilot Certificate with appropriate aircraft rating.

5. Hold an instrument rating if applying for either airplane or instrument instructor.

6. Pass an FAA Knowledge Exam on the Fundamentals of Instructing after satisfactory completion of a ground instruction or home study course.

7. Pass an FAA Knowledge Exam on the appropriate flight instruction subjects after satisfactory completion of a ground instruction or home study course.

8. Obtain an instructor logbook endorsement or certificate of satisfactory knowledge of subject areas where questions were missed as listed on the FAA airman test reports.

9. Receive flight instruction and training and obtain an instructor logbook endorsement or certificate of competence in the appropriate flight training procedures and maneuvers.

10. Pass an oral and flight test on the subjects and maneuvers in the appropriate flight instructor practical test standards:

    | ASA-8081-6 | Airplane Single-Engine or Multi-Engine |
    | ASA-8081-7 | Helicopter/Rotorcraft |
    | ASA-8081-9 | Instrument Airplane & Helicopter |

Eligibility Requirements for Sport Pilot Instructors

Always check the current 14 CFR Part 61 for pilot certificate requirements. To be eligible for a Flight Instructor Certificate with a Sport Pilot Rating a person must:

1. Be at least 18 years old.

2. Be able to read, speak, write, and understand English or have a limitation placed on the certificate.

3. Hold at least a current and valid Sport Pilot Certificate with category and class ratings or privileges, as applicable, that are appropriate to the flight instructor privileges sought.

4. Score at least 70 percent on the required FAA Knowledge Test.

5. Pass a practical test on the subjects and maneuvers outlined in the Sport Pilot practical test standards (ASA-8081-SPORT — Fixed Wing, Weight-Shift Control and Powered Parachute).

6. The following table explains the aeronautical experience you must have to apply for a Sport Pilot Certificate:

If you are applying for a flight instructor certificate with a sport pilot rating for...	Then you must log at least...	Which must include at least...
(a) Airplane category and single-engine class privileges,	(1) 150 hours of flight time as a pilot,	(i) 100 hours of flight time as pilot in command in powered aircraft, (ii) 50 hours of flight time in a single-engine airplane, (iii) 25 hours of cross-country flight time, (iv) 10 hours of cross-country flight time in a single-engine airplane, and (v) 15 hours of flight time as pilot in command in a single-engine airplane that is a light-sport aircraft.
(b) Glider category privileges,	(1) 25 hours of flight time as pilot in command in a glider, 100 flights in a glider, and 15 flights as pilot in command in a glider that is a light-sport aircraft, or (2) 100 hours in heavier-than-air aircraft, 20 flights in a glider, and 15 flights as pilot in command in a glider that is a light-sport aircraft.	
(c) Rotorcraft category and gyroplane class privileges,	(1) 125 hours of flight time as a pilot,	(i) 100 hours of flight time as pilot in command in powered aircraft, (ii) 50 hours of flight time in a gyroplane, (iii) 10 hours of cross-country flight time, (iv) 3 hours of cross-country flight time in a gyroplane, and (v) 15 hours of flight time as pilot in command in a gyroplane that is a light-sport aircraft.
(d) Lighter-than-air category and airship class privileges,	(1) 100 hours of flight time as a pilot,	(i) 40 hours of flight time in an airship, (ii) 20 hours of pilot in command time in an airship, (iii) 10 hours of cross-country flight time, (iv) 5 hours of cross-country flight time in an airship, and (v) 15 hours of flight time as pilot in command in an airship that is a light-sport aircraft.
(e) Lighter-than-air category and balloon class privileges,	(1) 35 hours of flight time as pilot-in-command,	(i) 20 hours of flight time in a balloon, (ii) 10 flights in a balloon, and (iii) 5 flights as pilot in command in a balloon that is a light-sport aircraft.
(f) Weight-shift-control aircraft category privileges,	(1) 150 hours of flight time as a pilot,	(i) 100 hours of flight time as pilot in command in powered aircraft, (ii) 50 hours of flight time in a weight-shift-control aircraft, (iii) 25 hours of cross-country flight time, (iv) 10 hours of cross-country flight time in a weight-shift-control aircraft, and (v) 15 hours of flight time as pilot in command in a weight-shift-control aircraft that is a light-sport aircraft.
(g) Powered-parachute category privileges,	(1) 100 hours of flight time as a pilot,	(i) 75 hours of flight time as pilot in command in powered aircraft, (ii) 50 hours of flight time in a powered parachute, (iii) 15 hours of cross-country flight time, (iv) 5 hours of cross-country flight time in a powered parachute, and (v) 15 hours of flight time as pilot in command in a powered parachute that is a light-sport aircraft.

The Ground Instructor Certificate

To be eligible for a ground instructor certificate, a person must:

1. Be at least 18 years old.
2. Read, speak, write, and understand the English language.
3. Pass an FAA Knowledge Exam on the Fundamentals of Instructing.
4. Pass an FAA Knowledge Exam on the required flight instruction subjects.

There are three levels of ground instructor certificate:

A. **Basic Ground Instructor.** A basic ground instructor may instruct on subjects related to the sport, private and recreational pilot certificates. The FAA Knowledge Exam questions are included in this Certified Flight Instructor test book. A basic ground instructor may endorse a logbook to authorize Sport, Private and Recreational FAA Knowledge Exams.

B. **Advanced Ground Instructor.** An advanced ground instructor may instruct on all subjects related to any certificate or rating, except for the aeronautical knowledge areas required for an instrument rating. The FAA Knowledge Exam questions are included in this Certified Flight Instructor test book. An advanced ground instructor may endorse a logbook to authorize these FAA Knowledge Exams.

C. **Instrument Ground Instructor.** An instrument ground instructor may instruct and endorse logbooks on all subjects related to instrument procedures and operations at all levels. The FAA Knowledge questions for instrument ground instructor are included in the ASA Test Prep for the Instrument Rating (not this book).

Note: *Since the Knowledge Test questions for the Basic Ground Instructor, the Advanced Ground Instructor and the Certified Flight Instructor all come from the same body of questions, we recommend that a person taking the Ground Instructor Exam study for and take the Advanced Ground Instructor examination.*

We also recommend that a person studying for the Certified Flight Instructor Knowledge Test take the Advanced Ground Instructor exam at the same time since the material is the same for both tests. There is no medical or flight test required for a Basic or Advanced ground instructor certificate. The Fundamentals of Instructing Knowledge Test is required for all ground and flight instructor certificates, unless you hold a teacher's certificate at the high school level or higher.

Knowledge Exam References

The FAA references the following documents to write the FAA Knowledge Exam questions. You should be familiar with all of these as part of your ground school studies, which you should complete before starting test preparation:

FAA-G-8082-7 *Flight and Ground Instructor Test Guide*

FAA-H-8083-9 *Aviation Instructor's Handbook*

FAA-H-8083-25 *Pilot's Handbook of Aeronautical Knowledge*

FAA-H-8083-2 *Risk Management Handbook*

FAA-H-8083-3 *Airplane Flying Handbook*; FAA-H-8083-13 *Glider Flying Handbook*;
    FAA-H-8083-21 *Helicopter Flying Handbook*; FAA-H-8083-11 *Balloon Flying Handbook*;
    FAA-H-8083-5 *Weight-Shift Control Handbook*; FAA-H-8083-29 *Powered Parachute Handbook*

FAA-H-8083-1 *Aircraft Weight and Balance Handbook*

FAA-H-8083-15 *Instrument Flying Handbook*

FAA-S-8081-6 *Flight Instructor Airplane Practical Test Standards*;
    FAA-S-8081-29 *Sport Instructor Airplane Practical Test Standards*; or
    FAA-S-8081-7 *Flight Instructor Helicopter Practical Test Standards*

FAA-S-ACS-6 *Private Pilot Airplane Airman Certification Standards*

FAA-S-ACS-7 *Commercial Pilot Airplane Airman Certification Standards*; or
    FAA-S-8081-16 *Commercial Pilot Helicopter Practical Test Standards*

Chart Supplements U.S. (previously Airport/Facility Directory or A/FD)

Sectional Aeronautical Chart (SAC)

AC 00-6 *Aviation Weather*

AC 00-45 *Aviation Weather Services*

AC 20-43 *Aircraft Fuel Control*

AC 61-65 *Certification: Pilots, Flight and Ground Instructors*

AC 61-67 *Stall and Spin Awareness Training*

AC 61-107 *Operations of Aircraft at Altitudes Above 25,000 MSL*

AC 90-48 *Pilots' Role in Collision Avoidance*

AC 91-13 *Cold Weather Operation of Aircraft*

AC 91-43 *Unreliable Airspeed Indications*

AC 91-51 *Effect of Icing on Aircraft Control and Airplane Deice and Anti-Ice Systems*

Aeronautical Information Manual (AIM)

14 CFR Parts 1, 43, 61, 71, 91, 121

49 CFR Part 830

Visit the ASA website for these and many more titles and pilot supplies for your aviation endeavors: **www.asa2fly.com**

ASA Test Prep Layout

The sample FAA questions have been sorted into chapters according to subject matter. Within each chapter, the questions have been further classified and all similar questions grouped together with a concise discussion of the material covered in each group. This discussion material of "Chapter text" is printed in a larger font and spans the entire width of the page. Immediately following the sample FAA Question is ASA's Explanation in *italics*. The last line of the Explanation contains the Learning Statement Code and further reference (if applicable). *See* the EXAMPLE below.

Figures referenced by the Chapter text only are numbered with the appropriate chapter number, i.e., "Figure 1-1" is Chapter 1's first chapter-text figure.

Some Questions refer to Figures or Legends immediately following the question number, i.e., "6201. (Refer to Figure 14.)." These are FAA Figures and Legends which can be found in the separate booklet: *Airman Knowledge Testing Supplement* (CT-8080-XX). This supplement is bundled with the Test Prep and is the exact material you will have access to when you take your computerized test. We provide it separately, so you will become accustomed to referring to the FAA Figures and Legends as you would during the test.

Figures referenced by the Explanation and pertinent to the understanding of that particular question are labeled by their corresponding Question number. For example: the caption "Questions 6245 and 6248" means the figure accompanies the Explanations for both Question 6245 and 6248.

Answers to each question are found at the bottom of each page.

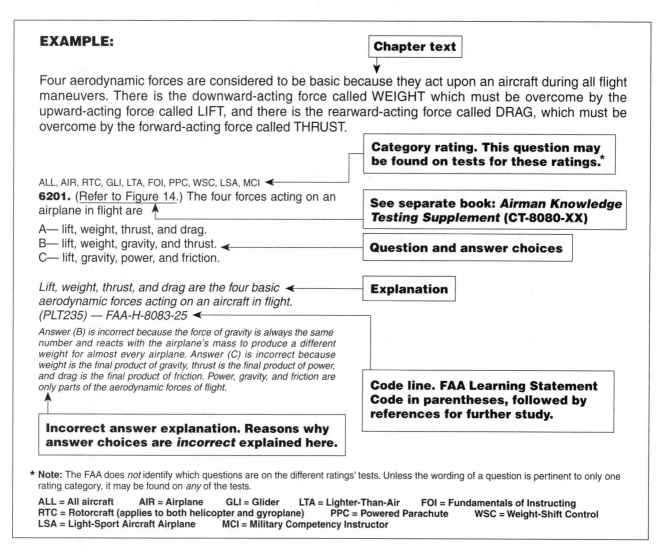

EXAMPLE:

Chapter text

Four aerodynamic forces are considered to be basic because they act upon an aircraft during all flight maneuvers. There is the downward-acting force called WEIGHT which must be overcome by the upward-acting force called LIFT, and there is the rearward-acting force called DRAG, which must be overcome by the forward-acting force called THRUST.

Category rating. This question may be found on tests for these ratings.*

ALL, AIR, RTC, GLI, LTA, FOI, PPC, WSC, LSA, MCI

6201. (Refer to Figure 14.) The four forces acting on an airplane in flight are

See separate book: *Airman Knowledge Testing Supplement* (CT-8080-XX)

A— lift, weight, thrust, and drag.
B— lift, weight, gravity, and thrust.
C— lift, gravity, power, and friction.

Question and answer choices

Lift, weight, thrust, and drag are the four basic aerodynamic forces acting on an aircraft in flight. (PLT235) — FAA-H-8083-25

Explanation

Answer (B) is incorrect because the force of gravity is always the same number and reacts with the airplane's mass to produce a different weight for almost every airplane. Answer (C) is incorrect because weight is the final product of gravity, thrust is the final product of power, and drag is the final product of friction. Power, gravity, and friction are only parts of the aerodynamic forces of flight.

Code line. FAA Learning Statement Code in parentheses, followed by references for further study.

Incorrect answer explanation. Reasons why answer choices are *incorrect* explained here.

* **Note:** The FAA does *not* identify which questions are on the different ratings' tests. Unless the wording of a question is pertinent to only one rating category, it may be found on *any* of the tests.

ALL = All aircraft	AIR = Airplane	GLI = Glider	LTA = Lighter-Than-Air	FOI = Fundamentals of Instructing
RTC = Rotorcraft (applies to both helicopter and gyroplane)		PPC = Powered Parachute	WSC = Weight-Shift Control
LSA = Light-Sport Aircraft Airplane		MCI = Military Competency Instructor

Chapter 1
Fundamentals of Instructing

The Learning Process

Learning is a change in the student's behavior as a result of experience. The amount of learning is controlled by the student's desires. The behavior change can be physical and overt, or it can be intellectual or attitudinal and not easily detected. Yet almost everyone has a set of goals in life, and he/she learns best those things which apply directly to these goals.

All learning involves experience. To be effective, instructors must provide experiences the student can identify as steps toward attaining his/her personal goals. The learning process involves several types of learning: verbal, conceptual, perceptual, motor, problem solving, and emotional. Learning is complex, and while working to learn one thing, something else may be learned. This additional learning is called **incidental learning**.

The basis of all learning is one's **perceptions**, which are directed to the brain from one or more of five senses: sight, hearing, touch, smell, and taste. Perception results when a person gives meaning to sensations being experienced. The ability to perceive is affected by:

1. The **physical organism** which is the vehicle by which we become aware of, and operate in, the world of which we are a part.

2. Our **basic need**, which is to enhance our own organized self.

3. Our **goals and values**, which color every experience we have.

4. Our **self-concept**, which is the way we picture ourselves, is a powerful determinant in learning. A positive self-concept enhances our perception, but a negative self-concept inhibits the perceptual processes. It introduces psychological barriers which prevent our perceiving.

5. **Time and opportunity**, which are needed in order to provide the experiences necessary to perceive. Instruction by the use of a properly planned training syllabus is far superior to learning by trial and error, because it allows the instructor to teach the relationship of perceptions as they occur.

6. Recognition of the **element of threat**. Fear adversely affects our perception by narrowing our perceptual field.

Insights involve the grouping of perceptions into meaningful wholes. Instructors must point out to the student the way details work together to form complete ideas and concepts. A student is able to tie experiences together and develop insights when there is no threat, and when he/she has a favorable self-concept, or self-image. A negative self-concept prevents a student from being receptive to new experiences and causes him/her to reject additional training.

Motivation is possibly the most important force which governs the student's progress and ability to learn. Motivations can be tangible or intangible, and they may be obvious, or subtle and difficult to identify. The desire for personal gain, either the acquisition of objects or position, is a basic positive motivation for all human endeavor, and helps a student learn. Negative motivation engenders fear and is perceived by the student as a threat. Negative motivation seldom promotes effective learning. The use of negative motivation is discouraged, but carefully used reproof often produces desired results with students who are overconfident and impulsive.

There are several principles that break down and explain the process of learning. The **principle of readiness** says that individuals learn best only when they are ready to learn. If they see no reason for learning, it is likely they will not learn. The **principle of exercise** explains that those things most often repeated are best remembered. This is the reason for practice and drill. The **principle of primacy** shows that instructors must teach all facts correctly the first time. The **principle of effect**, which is based on the emotional reaction of the learner, explains that a person learns best when the experience is pleasant and satisfying. Learning is weakened if the experience is unpleasant. The **principle of intensity** says that a student will learn more from the real thing than from a substitute. The **principle of recency** says that the things most recently learned will be the things best remembered. This is the reason for post flight critiques and lesson summaries.

There are four levels of learning. **Rote** is the lowest level and provides the ability to repeat back something which has been taught, without understanding or being able to apply what has been learned. **Understanding** is the basis of effective learning. A person with understanding knows the reason for a sequence of events and knows the relationship between related objects and actions. **Application** is the development of the skills needed to apply what is being taught. **Correlation** is the highest level of learning, and with correlation a student is able to associate an element which has been learned with other segments or "blocks" of learning or accomplishment.

Besides the four basic levels of learning, educational psychologists have developed several additional levels. These classifications consider what is to be learned. Is it knowledge only, a change in attitude, a physical skill, or a combination of knowledge and skill? One of the more useful categorizations of learning objectives includes three domains: **cognitive domain** (knowledge), **affective domain** (attitudes, beliefs, and values), and **psychomotor domain** (physical skills). Each of the domains has a hierarchy of educational objectives. The listing of the hierarchy of objectives is often called a **taxonomy**. A taxonomy of educational objectives is a systematic classification scheme for sorting learning outcomes into the three broad categories (cognitive, affective, and psychomotor) and ranking the desired outcomes in a developmental hierarchy from least complex to most complex.

During the learning experience, a student may be aided or hindered by things previously learned. If the learning of one thing aids the learning of something else, positive transfer occurs. But, if the learning of one thing hinders the learning of something else, negative transfer occurs. For example, positive transfer allows proficiency in flying rectangular patterns to aid in learning to correctly fly traffic patterns.

The formation of correct habits is essential for further learning and for correct performance after the completion of training. The most acceptable way of forming correct habits is by using the **building block method of instruction**. Each simple task is performed acceptably and correctly before the next learning task is introduced.

There are several reasons people forget. The most common of these are:

- **Fading.** A person forgets those things which are not used.
- **Interference.** People forget a thing because a certain experience has overshadowed it, or because the learning of similar things has intervened.
- **Repression** or **suppression.** Things that are unpleasant or that produce anxiety may be relegated to the unconscious mind and are thus forgotten.

Material that is thoroughly learned is highly resistant to forgetting. Rote learning is superficial and is not easily retained, but meaningful learning goes deep, because it involves principles and concepts anchored in the student's own experience. The following principles have a direct application to recall:

- **Praise,** which is a response that produces a pleasurable feeling and stimulates remembering. Negativism makes recall less likely.
- **Recall is promoted by association.** Each bit of information or action which is associated with something to be learned tends to facilitate its later recall.
- **Favorable attitudes aid retention.** People learn and remember only the things they wish to know.
- **Learning with all the senses is most effective.** When several senses respond together, fuller understanding and greater chance of recall is achieved.
- **Meaningful repetition aids recall.** Each repetition gives the student an opportunity to gain a clearer and more accurate perception of the subject being learned. Practice provides an opportunity for learning, but it is not a direct cause of learning.

Skills, both motor and mental, are best taught by providing the student with a clear, step-by-step example. This gives the student a correct idea of what to do and helps him/her understand each step in the sequence. Learning a skill does not progress along a straight upward path. The performance increases rapidly at first, then levels off for a time before it begins to increase again; this is called a **learning plateau**. The students must be made aware of it so they will not become discouraged at the seeming cessation of progress. One primary consideration in developing a skill is the length of time devoted to practice. A student reaches a point at which additional practice is not only unproductive, but is actually harmful. When the student tires, errors increase and motivation declines.

Memory is an integral part of the learning process. Although there are several theories of how the memory works, a widely accepted view is the multi-stage concept which states that memory includes three parts: sensory register, working or short-term, and long-term systems. The **sensory register** receives input from the environment and quickly processes it according to the individual's preconceived concept of what is important.

Several common steps help retention in the **short-term memory**. These include rehearsal or repetition of the information, and sorting or categorization into systematic chunks, a process called "coding." Methods of coding vary with subject matter, but typically they include some type of association; also, use of rhymes or mnemonics is common. Variations of the coding process are practically endless. They may consist of the use of acronyms, the chronology of events, images, semantics, or an individually developed structure based on the person's past experiences. In addition, the coding process may involve "recoding" to adjust the information to individual experiences — this is when actual learning begins to take place. Therefore, recoding may be described as a process of relating incoming information to concepts or knowledge already in memory.

Long-term memory is where information is stored for future use. For the stored information to be useful, some special effort must have been expended during the coding process of the working or short-term memory. The coding should have provided meaning and connections between old and new information. If initial coding was not properly accomplished, recall will be distorted and it may be impossible. The more effective the coding process, the easier the recall. However, it should be noted that the long-term memory is a reconstruction, not a pure recall of information or events.

Fatigue is one of the most treacherous hazards to flight safety because it might not be discernible to a pilot until serious errors are made. Fatigue can be either acute (short-term) or chronic (long-term). Acute fatigue, a normal occurrence of everyday living, is the tiredness felt after long periods of physical and mental strain, including strenuous muscular effort, immobility, heavy mental workload, strong emotional pressure, monotony, and lack of sleep. Chronic fatigue occurs when there is not enough time for a full recovery from repeated episodes of acute fatigue. The underlying cause of chronic fatigue is generally not "rest-related" and may have deeper points of origin.

Fatigue is the primary consideration in determining the length and frequency of flight instruction periods. Flight instruction should be continued only as long as the student is alert, receptive to instruction, and performing at a level consistent with experience.

FOI

6001. A change in behavior as a result of experience can be defined as

A— learning.
B— knowledge.
C— understanding.

Learning is defined as a change in behavior as a result of experience. (PLT308) — FAA-H-8083-9

Answer (B) is incorrect because even though knowledge is a result of experience, it does not necessarily cause a change in behavior. Answer (C) is incorrect because understanding is merely one of the four levels of learning.

FOI

6002. The learning process may include some elements such as verbal, conceptual, and

A— habitual.
B— experiential.
C— problem solving.

The learning process includes these elements:
* *verbal*
* *conceptual*
* *perceptual*
* *motor*
* *problem solving*
* *emotional*

(PLT308) — FAA-H-8083-9

FOI

6002-1. Learning can be classified by different types, such as verbal, conceptual, and

A— cognitive.
B— experiential.
C— emotional.

The learning process may include verbal, conceptual, perceptual, emotional, and problem-solving elements all taking place at once. (PLT308) — FAA-H-8083-9

FOI

6003. While learning the material being taught, students may be learning other things as well. This additional learning is called

A— residual.
B— conceptual.
C— incidental.

When students learn other things in addition to the material being taught, the learning is called incidental learning. (PLT306) — FAA-H-8083-9

Answer (A) is incorrect because residual is not a definition of a type of learning. Answer (B) is incorrect because conceptual learning is part of the process of learning the main subject being taught.

FOI

6014. Which factor affecting perception has a great influence on the total perceptual process?

A— Self-concept.
B— Goals and values.
C— Time and opportunity.

Among the factors that affect an individual's ability to perceive are:

1. *Physical organism*
2. *Basic need*
3. *Goals and values*
4. *Self-concept*
5. *Time and opportunity*
6. *Recognition of the element of threat*

Self-concept, how one pictures oneself, is a most powerful determinant in learning. Self-image has a great influence on the total perceptual process. (PLT308) — FAA-H-8083-9

FOI

6015. Perceptions result when a person

A— gives meaning to sensations being experienced.
B— is able to discern items of useful information.
C— responds to visual cues first, then aural cues, and relates these cues to ones previously learned.

Perceptions result when a person gives meaning to sensations. Actions are based on the way we perceive, or believe, things to be. (PLT308) — FAA-H-8083-9

Answer (B) is incorrect because when they are able to discern items of useful information a person has learned (not simply perceived). Answer (C) is incorrect because this is an example of a person demonstrating rote learning.

Answers

| 6001 [A] | 6002 [C] | 6002-1 [C] | 6003 [C] | 6014 [A] | 6015 [A] |

FOI

6021. Insights, as applied to learning, involve a person's

A— association of learning with change.
B— grouping of associated perceptions into meaningful wholes.
C— ability to recognize the reason for learning a procedure.

Insights involve the grouping of perceptions into meaningful wholes. When an instructor organizes the instructional material into blocks, it enables the student to gain insights. (PLT308) — FAA-H-8083-9

Answer (A) is incorrect because change in behavior as a result of learning is part of the broad definition of learning itself, whereas gaining "insight" is a specific process in learning. Answer (C) is incorrect because the ability to recognize the reason for learning a procedure is a feature of the principle of readiness.

FOI

6011. What is the basis of all learning?

A— Perception.
B— Motivation.
C— Positive self-concept.

Perception is the basis of all learning. Everything we know comes to our brain through one of our five senses: sight, hearing, touch, smell, and taste. (PLT308) — FAA-H-8083-9

Answer (B) is incorrect because motivation is the force that governs the student's progress and ability to learn. Answer (C) is incorrect because positive self-concept affects an individual's ability to learn, but is not the basis of all learning.

FOI

6016. The factor which contributes most to a student's failure to remain receptive to new experiences and which creates a tendency to reject additional training is

A— basic needs.
B— element of threat.
C— negative self-concept.

A negative self-concept keeps the student from being receptive to new experiences. This reluctance keeps the student from perceiving and learning. (PLT308) — FAA-H-8083-9

Answer (A) is incorrect because fulfillment of basic needs can be used to promote learning. Answer (B) is incorrect because an element of threat will cause attention to be limited to the threatening object or condition, but the student will still be able to learn.

FOI

6022. Which statement is true concerning motivations?

A— Motivations must be tangible to be effective.
B— Motivations may be very subtle and difficult to identify.
C— Negative motivations often are as effective as positive motivations.

Motivation is the dominant force that governs a student's ability to learn. Some motivations may be subtle and difficult to identify, but they are important. (PLT308) — FAA-H-8083-9

Answer (A) is incorrect because both intangible and tangible motivations can be effective. Answer (C) is incorrect because negative motivations can discourage the student.

FOI

6023. Motivations that cause a student to react with fear and anxiety are

A— tangible.
B— negative.
C— difficult to identify.

Negative motivations are those that cause a student to react with fear and anxiety. Negative motivations are seldom the best way to help a student learn. (PLT490) — FAA-H-8083-9

Answer (A) is incorrect because tangible and intangible motivations can be both positive or negative. Answer (C) is incorrect because motivations that are difficult to identify can be either positive or negative.

FOI

6024. For a motivation to be effective, students must believe their efforts will be rewarded in a definite manner. This type of motivation is

A— subtle.
B— negative.
C— tangible.

Tangible motivation ensures the students that their efforts in learning will be suitably rewarded. These rewards must be apparent to the student throughout the learning process. (PLT490) — FAA-H-8083-9

Answer (A) is incorrect because subtle motivation can cause the student to feel unrewarded. Answer (B) is incorrect because negative motivations are not as effective as positive motivations.

Answers

| 6021 | [B] | 6011 | [A] | 6016 | [C] | 6022 | [B] | 6023 | [B] | 6024 | [C] |

FOI

6019. In the learning process, fear or the element of threat will

A— narrow the student's perceptual field.
B— decrease the rate of associative reactions.
C— cause a student to focus on several areas of perception.

The negative motivation of fear and threat keeps students from learning by narrowing their perceptual field. (PLT308) — FAA-H-8083-9

Answer (B) is incorrect because the element of threat will increase the rate of associative reactions. Answer (C) is incorrect because the element of threat will cause attention to be limited to the threatening object or condition.

FOI

6012. A basic need that affects all of a person's perceptions is the need to

A— maintain and enhance the organized self.
B— accomplish a higher level of satisfaction.
C— avoid areas that pose a threat to success.

One of our most basic needs is that of maintaining and enhancing our own organized self. All of our perceptions are affected by this need. (PLT308) — FAA-H-8083-9

Answer (B) is incorrect because accomplishing a higher level of satisfaction refers to a goal, not a basic need. Answer (C) is incorrect because avoiding areas that pose a threat to success is a defense mechanism.

FOI

6030. At which level of learning do most instructors stop teaching?

A— Application.
B— Correlation.
C— Understanding.

The ability to understand and perform a particular skill is known as application. It is at this level of learning where many instructors stop teaching. (PLT306) — FAA-H-8083-9

Answer (B) is incorrect because correlation is the highest level of learning and many instructors skip other levels to go straight to this goal. Answer (C) is incorrect because understanding is the second level of learning and instructors continue to teach through this level.

FOI

6025. Which is generally the more effective way for an instructor to properly motivate students?

A— Maintain pleasant personal relationships with students.
B— Provide positive motivations by the promise or achievement of rewards.
C— Reinforce their self-confidence by requiring no tasks beyond their ability to perform.

The instructor produces maximum learning when the positive goal of rewards based on achievement is kept before the student. (PLT490) — FAA-H-8083-9

Answer (A) is incorrect because maintaining a pleasant personal relationship is not the most effective way for an instructor to motivate students. Answer (C) is incorrect because requiring no tasks beyond a student's ability will not motivate the student.

FOI

6026. Motivations in the form of reproof and threats should be avoided with all but the student who is

A— overconfident and impulsive.
B— avidly seeking group approval.
C— experiencing a learning plateau.

The negative motivation gained by reproof and threats seldom produces effective learning, but it may sometimes be useful with students who are overconfident and impulsive. (PLT490) — FAA-H-8083-9

Answer (B) is incorrect because student's avid seeking of group approval is a strong motivating factor; therefore, instructors should not use threats or reproofs against this factor. Answer (C) is incorrect because a student experiencing a learning plateau will remain at that level if reproofs and threats are used.

FOI

6017. The mental grouping of affiliated perceptions is called

A— insights.
B— association.
C— conceptualization.

Insights involve the grouping of affiliated perceptions into meaningful wholes. The best teaching results when an instructor organizes the material to be taught into related blocks so the student will relate these things in his/her mind. (PLT308) — FAA-H-8083-9

Answer (B) is incorrect because although association is part of the process, it is not the final product of this mental grouping of perceptions. Answer (C) is incorrect because conceptualization is the formation of individual ideas.

Answers

6019 [A]	6012 [A]	6030 [A]	6025 [B]	6026 [A]	6017 [A]

FOI

6018. An instructor may foster the development of insights by

A— helping the student acquire and maintain a favorable self-concept.

B— pointing out the attractive features of the activity to be learned.

C— keeping the rate of learning consistent so that it is predictable.

We learn best when we have a positive self-image, or self-concept. An instructor who helps a student acquire and maintain a good self-concept helps the student understand the relationship of the facts being taught. (PLT308) — FAA-H-8083-9

Answer (B) is incorrect because pointing out the attractive features of the activity is a factor of increasing motivation. Answer (C) is incorrect because the rates of learning should vary in accordance with each lesson.

FOI

6020. Name one way an instructor can help develop student insights.

A— Provide a secure and nonthreatening environment in which to learn.

B— Point out various items to avoid during the learning process.

C— Keep learning blocks small so they are easier to understand.

We learn best when we have a secure and non-threatening environment in which to learn. An instructor who provides a safe environment for learning helps the student understand the relationship of the facts being taught. (PLT308) — FAA-H-8083-9

Answer (B) is incorrect because the instructor should point out such items as they occur in practice, not while just talking about them. Answer (C) is incorrect because insights develop when a student's perceptions increase in number and are assembled into larger blocks of learning.

FOI

6020-1. As perceptions increase in number, the student develops insight by

A— assembling them into larger blocks of learning.

B— unassociated perceptions.

C— organizing demonstrations and explanations.

Insight involves the grouping of perceptions into meaningful wholes. As perceptions increase in number, the student develops insight by assembling them into larger blocks of learning. As a result, learning becomes more meaningful and more permanent. (PLT308) — FAA-H-8083-9

Answer (B) is incorrect because insight requires the grouping of perceptions into meaningful wholes. Answer (C) is incorrect because this describes the instructor's responsibility for fostering insight.

FOI

6013. Which factor affecting perceptions is based on the effectiveness of the use of a properly planned training syllabus?

A— Basic need.

B— Time and opportunity.

C— Goals and values.

It takes time and opportunity to perceive. The effectiveness of the use of a properly planned training syllabus is proportional to the consideration it gives to the time and opportunity factor in perception. (PLT308) — FAA-H-8083-9

FOI

6004. Individuals make more progress learning if they have a clear objective. This is one feature of the principle of

A— primacy.

B— readiness.

C— willingness.

The principle of readiness states that students make more progress if they have a clear objective. (PLT308) — FAA-H-8083-9

Answer (A) is incorrect because the principle of primacy states that first experiences often create a strong, almost unshakable impression. Answer (C) is incorrect because "willingness" is not a defined principle as stated in the reference.

Answers

| 6018 [A] | 6020 [A] | 6020-1 [A] | 6013 [B] | 6004 [B] |

FOI

6005. Providing opportunities for a student to practice and then directing this process towards a goal is the basis of the principle of

A— exercise.
B— learning.
C— readiness.

The principle of exercise states that the instructor must provide opportunities for students to practice and see that this process is directed towards a goal. (PLT308) — FAA-H-8083-9

Answer (B) is incorrect because learning is defined as a change of behavior as a result of experience. Answer (C) is incorrect because the principle of readiness states that individuals learn best when they are ready to learn.

FOI

6005-1. Drill and practice method of training delivery is based on the learning principle of

A— intensity.
B— recency.
C— exercise.

A time-honored training delivery method, drill and practice is based on the learning principle of exercise, which holds that connections are strengthened with practice. (PLT308) — FAA-H-8083-9

FOI

6006. The principle that is based on the emotional reaction of the learner is the principle of

A— effect.
B— primacy.
C— intensity.

The principle of effect is based on the emotional reaction of the learner. (PLT308) — FAA-H-8083-9

Answer (B) is incorrect because the principle of primacy states that a strong, almost unshakable impression is created by first experiences. Answer (C) is incorrect because the principle of intensity states that vivid, dramatic, or exciting learning experience teaches more than a routine or boring experience.

FOI

6008. Which principle of learning implies that a student will learn more from the real thing than from a substitute?

A— Principle of effect.
B— Principle of primacy.
C— Principle of intensity.

Students almost always learn more from the real thing than they do from a substitute. This is in accordance with the principle of intensity. (PLT308) — FAA-H-8083-9

Answer (A) is incorrect because the principle of effect states that learning is strengthened when accompanied by a pleasant or satisfying feeling, and weakened when associated with an unpleasant feeling, and these experiences may result from either the real thing or a substitute. Answer (B) is incorrect because the principle of primacy states that a strong, almost unshakable impression is created by first experiences, which may result from either the real thing or a substitute.

FOI

6009. Which principle of learning often determines the sequence of lectures within a course of instruction?

A— Principle of primacy.
B— Principle of recency.
C— Principle of intensity.

The principle of recency often determines the sequence of lectures within a course of instruction. (PLT308) — FAA-H-8083-9

Answer (A) is incorrect because the principle of primacy tells instructors that they must teach all facts correctly the first time. Answer (C) is incorrect because the principle of intensity explains that a student will learn more from the real thing than from a substitute.

FOI

6010. Which principle of learning often creates a strong almost unshakable impression?

A— Principle of primacy.
B— Principle of intensity.
C— Principle of readiness.

Primacy, the state of being first, often creates a strong, almost unshakable impression. This is the basis for the principle of primacy. (PLT308) — FAA-H-8083-9

Answer (B) is incorrect because the principle of intensity explains that a student will learn more from the real thing than from a substitute. Answer (C) is incorrect because the principle of readiness says that individuals learn best only when they are ready to learn.

Answers

| 6005 [A] | 6005-1 [C] | 6006 [A] | 6008 [C] | 6009 [B] | 6010 [A] |

FOI

6007. Things most often repeated are best remembered because of which principle of learning?

A— Principle of effect.
B— Principle of recency.
C— Principle of exercise.

The principle of exercise explains that the things most often repeated are the things that are best remembered. (PLT308) — FAA-H-8083-9

Answer (A) is incorrect because the principle of effect, which is based on the emotional reaction of the learner, explains that a person learns best when the experience is pleasant and satisfying. Answer (B) is incorrect because the principle of recency refers to the things most recently learned.

FOI

6027. What level of knowledge is being tested if asked, "What is the maneuvering speed of the aircraft listed in the owner's manual?"

A— Rote.
B— Application.
C— Understanding.

The answer to this question can be learned and repeated back by rote. Rote is the lowest level of learning. It is the level at which a person can repeat back something which has been taught, without understanding or being able to apply what has been learned. (PLT306) — FAA-H-8083-9

Answer (B) is incorrect because application involves the development of skills need to apply what is being taught. Answer (C) is incorrect because understanding happens when the reason for a sequence of events, and the relationship between related objects and actions is known, and this question challenges none of these areas.

FOI

6027-1. A rote question is not represented by

A— Multiple-choice questions.
B— True-false questions.
C— Supply-type questions.

Closed-ended questions tend to evaluate the student's understanding only at the rote level of learning. Closed-ended questions can be answered by "yes" or "no." When used in a multiple-choice scenario, closed-ended questions have a finite set of answers from which the respondent chooses. Supply type test items require the learner to furnish a response in the form of a word, sentence, or paragraph. (PLT306) — FAA-H-8083-9

FOI

6027-2. Which of the following is an example of a rote question?

A— Multiple-choice.
B— True-false.
C— Supply-type.

Closed-ended questions tend to evaluate the student's understanding only at the rote level of learning. Closed-ended questions can be answered by "yes" or "no." When used in a multiple-choice scenario, closed-ended questions have a finite set of answers from which the respondent chooses. Supply-type test items require the learner to furnish a response in the form of a word, sentence, or paragraph. (PLT306) — FAA-H-8083-9

FOI

6027-3. Which is true regarding overlearning knowledge?

A— Overlearning can result in automatic responses that are undesirable.
B— Overlearning is helpful to increase student proficiency of a subject.
C— Overlearning is part of acquiring higher-order thinking skills.

Overlearning is the continued study of a skill after initial proficiency has been achieved. In some cases, the overlearning of knowledge has the advantage of making application of knowledge more streamlined and efficient. In other cases, the development of automated routines can lead to problems. For example, a verbal checklist procedure becomes so automatic that a streamlined recitation of checklist items becomes decoupled from the thoughts and actions the checklist items are intended to trigger. In this case, the pilot or mechanic might not stop to consider each item. (PLT306) — FAA-H-8083-9

FOI

6027-4. What type of test promotes guessing?

A— Multiple choice.
B— Supply type.
C— Selection type.

The chief disadvantage of a selection type test (such as one that includes true-false questions) is that it creates the greatest probability of guessing. (PLT306) — FAA-H-8083-9

Answer (A) is incorrect because when properly devised and constructed, multiple choice items offer several advantages that make this type more widely used and versatile than other selection type tests. Answer (B) is incorrect because supply type tests require the learner to furnish a response in the form of a word, sentence, or paragraph, which eliminates a lot of guesswork.

Answers

6007 [C]	6027 [A]	6027-1 [C]	6027-2 [B]	6027-3 [A]	6027-4 [C]

FOI

6027-5. Which is true regarding the overlearning of knowledge?

A— An advantage of overlearning is the eventual replacement of basic knowledge or concepts with automated skills.

B— Overlearning almost always makes the application of knowledge less streamlined and less efficient.

C— Overlearning sometimes occurs when knowledge used frequently begins to take on the properties of a skill.

Overlearning is the continued study of a skill after initial proficiency has been achieved. Practice proceeds beyond the point at which the act can be performed with the required degree of excellence. The phenomenon of overlearning sometimes occurs when knowledge used frequently begins to take on the properties of a skill. (PLT306) — FAA-H-8083-9

Answer (A) is incorrect because this describes a disadvantage to overlearning. Answer (B) is incorrect because in some cases, the overlearning of knowledge has the advantage of making application of knowledge more streamlined and efficient.

FOI

6028. During the flight portion of a practical test, the examiner simulates complete loss of engine power by closing the throttle and announcing "simulated engine failure." What level of learning is being tested?

A— Application.
B— Correlation.
C— Understanding.

When the applicant develops the ability to associate all elements learned, the skills and knowledge, and brings them all together in order to perform correctly, he/she has achieved correlation. (PLT481) — FAA-H-8083-9

Answer (A) is incorrect because application is the development of the ability to understand a particular procedure, after having seen it demonstrated and practiced it until consistency has been achieved. Answer (C) is incorrect because understanding refers to knowing the reason for a sequence of events, and the relationship between related objects and actions.

FOI

6029. When asking a student to explain how gross weight affects maneuvering speed, what level of learning is being tested?

A— Application.
B— Correlation.
C— Understanding.

A person understands a concept when they know the reason for a sequence of events and know the relationship between related objects and actions. The student at this learning level will be able to explain how gross weight affects maneuvering speed. (PLT306) — FAA-H-8083-9

Answer (A) is incorrect because the application level refers to the student's ability to apply the knowledge. Answer (B) is incorrect because the correlation level refers to the student's ability to relate maneuvering speed with other concepts.

FOI

6039-1. The performance of rectangular patterns helps a student fly traffic patterns. What type transfer of learning is this?

A— Lateral.
B— Positive.
C— Deliberate.

Positive transfer of learning occurs when a student applies something he/she already knows to a task that is being learned. A positive transfer of learning occurs between the performance of rectangular patterns and the correct flying of a traffic pattern. (PLT306) — FAA-H-8083-9

Answers (A) and (C) are incorrect because the transfer of learning is either positive or negative.

FOI

6039-2. Which memory system processes input from the environment?

A— Long-term.
B— Working.
C— Sensory register.

The sensory register receives input from the environment and quickly processes it according to the individual's preconceived concept of what is important. (PLT307) — FAA-H-8083-9

Answers

6027-5 [C]	6028 [B]	6029 [C]	6039-1 [B]	6039-2 [C]

FOI

6039-3. The use of some type of association, such as rhymes or mnemonics is best suited to which memory system?

A— Short-term.
B— Sensory.
C— Long-term.

Several common steps help retention in the short-term memory, including rehearsal or repetition of the information and sorting or categorization into systematic chunks. Variations of the coding process include the use of associations, mnemonic devices, and acronyms. (PLT307) — FAA-H-8083-9

FOI

6039-4. How can recoding be described?

A— The relating of incoming information to concepts or knowledge already in memory.
B— The initial storage of information in short-term memory.
C— The selective process where the sensory register is set to recognize certain stimuli.

Recoding may be described as a process of relating incoming information to concepts or knowledge already in memory. (PLT307) — FAA-H-8083-9

FOI

6039-5. Where is information for future use stored?

A— Short-term memory.
B— Sensory register.
C— Long-term memory.

Long-term memory is where information is stored for future use. (PLT307) — FAA-H-8083-9

FOI

6039-7. Which is true regarding long term memory?

A— It allows the ability to instinctively perform certain maneuvers or tasks, allowing more time to concentrate on other duties such as navigation, communications, and visual scanning for other aircraft.
B— It is the part of the memory system that receives initial stimuli from the environment and processes them according to the individual's preconceived concept of what is important.
C— It has three basic operations: iconic memory, acoustic memory, and working memory.

Long term memory (LTM) is relatively permanent storage of unlimited information and it is possible for memories in LTM to remain there for a lifetime. Memory also applies to psychomotor skills, allowing for execution with very little thought. (PLT307) — FAA-H-8083-9

Answer (B) is incorrect because this describes sensory memory. Answer (C) is incorrect because this describes short-term memory.

FOI

6039-8. Which memory system can be enhanced by practice and repetition?

A— Short-term.
B— Long-term.
C— Sensory register.

Short-term memory is the part of the memory system where information is stored for roughly 30 seconds, after which it may rapidly fade or be consolidated into long-term memory, depending on the individual's priorities. Several common steps help retention in STM, including rehearsal or repetition of the information, and sorting or categorization into systematic chunks. (PLT307) — FAA-H-8083-9

FOI

6039-9. The use of some type of association such as rhymes or word patterns to assist in remembering information is called

A— association.
B— mnemonics.
C— transfer.

A mnemonic uses a pattern of letters, ideas, visual images, or associations to assist in remembering information. Mnemonics include but are not limited to acronyms, acrostics, rhymes, and chaining. (PLT307) — FAA-H-8083-9

Answers

| 6039-3 [A] | 6039-4 [A] | 6039-5 [C] | 6039-7 [A] | 6039-8 [A] | 6039-9 [B] |

FOI
6039-10. Describe precoding.

A— The selective process where the sensory register is set to recognize certain stimuli.
B— The initial storage of information in short-term memory.
C— The relating of incoming information to concepts or knowledge already in memory.

Precoding is a selective process where the sensory register is set to recognize certain stimuli and immediately transmit them to the short-term memory (STM) for action. An example of sensory precoding is recognition of a fire alarm: no matter what is happening at the time, when the sensory register detects a fire alarm, the working memory is immediately made aware of the alarm and preset responses begin to take place. (PLT307) — FAA-H-8083-9

FOI
6039-11. Short-term memory (STM) is time limited, and has a capacity limited

A— to usually seven bits of chunks of information.
B— to usually nine bits or chunks of information.
C— by the rate at which chunks are recorded to individual experiences.

The STM is not only time limited, it also has limited capacity, usually about seven bits or chunks of information. (PLT307) — FAA-H-8083-9

FOI
6038. Which transfer of learning occurs when the performance of a maneuver interferes with the learning of another maneuver?

A— Adverse.
B— Positive.
C— Negative.

Negative transfer of learning occurs when something we already know interferes with learning another task. (PLT295) — FAA-H-8083-9

Answer (A) is incorrect because the transfer of learning is either positive or negative. Answer (B) is incorrect because the performance of a maneuver interfering with the learning of another maneuver is a hindrance, and therefore a negative transfer of learning.

FOI
6040-1. To ensure proper habits and correct techniques during training, an instructor should

A— use the building block technique of instruction.
B— repeat subject matter the student has already learned.
C— introduce challenging material to continually motivate the student.

The building block technique of instruction is one of the most basic and successful methods of teaching. It ensures that the student will learn proper habits and correct techniques. (PLT228) — FAA-H-8083-9

Answer (B) is incorrect because repeating subject matter the student has already learned will produce boredom. Answer (C) is incorrect because introducing challenging material prematurely will produce frustration.

FOI
6040-2. Which domain of learning deals with knowledge?

A— Affective.
B— Cognitive.
C— Psychomotor.

The cognitive domain contains additional levels of knowledge and understanding. (PLT308) — FAA-H-8083-9

Answer (A) is incorrect because the affective domain deals with attitudes, beliefs and values. Answer (C) is incorrect because the psychomotor domain deals with physical skills.

FOI
6040-3. Affective domain relates to

A— physical skills.
B— knowledge.
C— attitudes, beliefs, and values.

The affective domain is concerned with a student's attitudes, personal beliefs, and values. (PLT308) — FAA-H-8083-9

Answer (A) is incorrect because this is in the psychomotor domain. Answer (B) is incorrect because this is in the cognitive domain.

Answers
6039-10 [A]   6039-11 [A]   6038 [C]   6040-1 [A]   6040-2 [B]   6040-3 [C]

FOI

6040-4. The educational objective levels for the cognitive domain are

A— receiving, responding, valuing, organization, and characterization.

B— perception, set, guided response, mechanism, complex overt response, adaptation, and origination.

C— knowledge, comprehension, application, analysis, synthesis, and evaluation.

In aviation, educational objectives in the cognitive domain refer to knowledge which might be gained as a result of attending school, reading, listening, reviewing, or taking part in training. The educational objectives include knowledge, comprehension, application, analysis, synthesis, and evaluation. (PLT308) — FAA-H-8083-9

Answer (A) is incorrect because these are the educational objectives for the affective domain. Answer (B) is incorrect because these are the educational objectives for the psychomotor domain.

FOI

6040-5. The listing of the hierarchy of objectives is often referred to as a

A— taxonomy.

B— skill.

C— domain.

The listing of the hierarchy of objectives is often referred to as a taxonomy. (PLT306) — FAA-H-8083-9

FOI

6040-6. The most complex outcome in the affective domain is

A— organization.

B— characterization.

C— valuing.

In order from least to most complex, the educational objectives in the affective domain are receiving, responding, valuing, organization, and characterization. (PLT306) — FAA-H-8083-9

FOI

6040-7. The least complex outcome in the psychomotor domain is

A— adaptation.

B— mechanism.

C— perception.

In order from least to most complex, the educational objectives in the psychomotor domain are perception, set, guided response, mechanism, complex overt response, adaptation, and origination. (PLT306) — FAA-H-8083-9

FOI

6040-8. Which skill is an example of psychomotor domain of learning?

A— Flying the airplane.

B— Asking a question after the instructor tunes the GPS.

C— Signing an endorsement in a logbook.

The psychomotor domain is skill-based and includes physical movement, coordination, and use of the motor-skill areas. (PLT306) — FAA-H-8083-9

Answer (B) is incorrect because this is an example of the affective domain which includes feelings, values, enthusiasms, motivations and attitudes. Answer (C) is incorrect because this is an example of the cognitive domain which includes remembering specific facts (content knowledge) and concepts that help develop intellectual abilities and skills.

FOI

6040-9. Which skill involves the cognitive domain of learning?

A— Understanding how the flight controls should be positioned during a turn.

B— A positive reception for learning new skills.

C— Performing a short-field approach and landing to Practical Test Standards.

The cognitive domain includes remembering specific facts (content knowledge) and concepts that help develop intellectual abilities and skills. (PLT306) — FAA-H-8083-9

Answer (B) is incorrect because this is an example of the affective domain, which includes feelings, values, enthusiasms, motivations and attitudes. Answer (C) is incorrect because this is an example of the psychomotor domain, which is skill-based and includes physical movement, coordination, and use of the motor-skill areas.

Answers

6040-4 [C]	6040-5 [A]	6040-6 [B]	6040-7 [C]	6040-8 [A]	6040-9 [A]

FOI

6040-10. Which is an example of the affective domain?

A— Reacting to an instructor's question.
B— Answering an instructor's question.
C— Demonstrating a skill to the instructor.

The affective domain addresses a learner's emotions toward the learning experience. It includes feelings, values, enthusiasms, motivations, and attitudes. (PLT306) — FAA-H-8083-9

Answer (B) is incorrect because this is an example of the cognitive domain, which includes remembering specific facts (content knowledge) and concepts that help develop intellectual abilities and skills. Answer (C) is incorrect because this is an example of the psychomotor domain, which is skill-based and includes physical movement, coordination, and use of the motor-skill areas.

FOI

6040-11. Which domain of learning requires remembering specific facts and concepts?

A— Cognitive.
B— Affective.
C— Comprehensive.

One of the best known educational domains, the cognitive domain includes remembering specific facts (content knowledge) and concepts that help develop intellectual abilities and skills. (PLT308) — FAA-H-8083-9

FOI

6040-13. An example of a skill involving the psychomotor domain would be

A— learning to correctly evaluate a flight maneuver.
B— determining the temperature at a specific altitude using standard lapse rate.
C— programming a global positioning satellite (GPS) receiver.

The psychomotor domain is skill-based and includes physical movement, coordination, and use of the motor-skill areas. Development of these skills requires repetitive practice and is measured in terms of speed, precision, distance, and techniques; examples include learning to fly a precision instrument approach procedure, programming a GPS receiver, or using sophisticated maintenance equipment. (PLT306) — FAA-H-8083-9

FOI

6040-12. An example of a skill involving the cognitive domain would be

A— programming a global positioning satellite (GPS) receiver.
B— making a logbook entry.
C— learning to fly a precision approach procedure.

Cognitive domain includes remembering specific facts (content knowledge) and concepts that help develop intellectual abilities and skills. As physical skills and equipment become more complex, the requirement for integration of cognitive and physical skills increases. (PLT306) — FAA-H-8083-9

FOI

7320. What are the educational levels of the cognitive domain?

A— rote, understanding, application and correlation
B— recall, response, application, analysis, and evaluation.
C— knowledge, comprehension, conceptualization, application, and correlation.

The cognitive domain includes remembering specific facts (content knowledge) and concepts that help develop intellectual abilities and skills. There are six major categories, starting from the simplest behavior (recalling facts) to the most complex (evaluation). (PLT306) — FAA-H-8083-9

FOI

6034. According to one theory, some forgetting is due to the practice of submerging an unpleasant experience into the subconscious. This is called

A— blanking.
B— immersion.
C— repression.

Repression is a way of submerging unpleasant experiences into the subconscious. This causes the unpleasant experience to be forgotten. (PLT307) — FAA-H-8083-9

Answer (A) is incorrect because blanking is the temporary inability to remember. Answer (B) is incorrect because immersion is not a definition in the theory of forgetting.

Answers

6040-10 [A]	6040-11 [A]	6040-13 [C]	6040-12 [C]	7320 [B]	6034 [C]

FOI

6035. When the learning of similar things overshadows other learning experiences, it is called

A— suppression.
B— correlation.
C— interference.

Interference is the process that allows an experience to overshadow that which we are trying to learn. (PLT306) — FAA-H-8083-9

Answer (A) is incorrect because suppression is not a definition in the theory of forgetting. Answer (B) is incorrect because correlation is the highest level of learning, not a theory of forgetting.

FOI

6035-1. When new events displace something that had been previously learned, it is called

A— displacement.
B— interference.
C— repression.

Interference theory suggests that people forget something because a certain experience has overshadowed it, or that the learning of similar things has intervened. This theory might explain how the range of experiences after graduation from school causes a person to forget or to lose knowledge. In other words, new events displace many things that had been learned. (PLT306) — FAA-H-8083-9

FOI

6036. When a person has difficulty recalling facts after several years, this is known as

A— fading.
B— repression.
C— poor retention.

The theory of fading or decay suggests that a person forgets information that is not used for an extended period of time, that it fades away or decays. (PLT307) — FAA-H-8083-9

Answer (B) is incorrect because repression is the theory that things which are unpleasant or produce anxiety may be relegated to the unconscious mind and are thus forgotten. Answer (C) is incorrect because poor retention is the result of forgetting, due to disuse, interference, or repression.

FOI

6037. Responses that produce a pleasurable return are called

A— reward.
B— praise.
C— positive feedback.

Praise is a response that gives a pleasurable return, and stimulates learning. (PLT306) — FAA-H-8083-9

Answer (A) is incorrect because rewards are motivators, not a response. Answer (C) is incorrect because positive feedback is part of the learning, not retention, process.

FOI

6031. The best way to prepare a student to perform a task is to

A— explain the purpose of the task.
B— provide a clear, step-by-step example.
C— give the student an outline of the task.

The best way to prepare a student to perform a task is to provide a clear, step-by-step example. It is the instructor's responsibility to provide this example. (PLT487) — FAA-H-8083-9

Answers (A) and (C) are incorrect because explaining the purposes and providing an outline of the task is not as useful as a clear, step-by-step example.

FOI

6032. A primary consideration in planning for student performance is the

A— student's motivational level.
B— student's intellectual level.
C— length of the practice session.

The instructor must carefully watch the length of practice sessions given to a student. Beginning students can take in only so much instruction at a time. Attempts to force instruction on a student will not only be unproductive, they may even be harmful. (PLT487) — FAA-H-8083-9

Answers

| 6035 [C] | 6035-1 [B] | 6036 [A] | 6037 [B] | 6031 [B] | 6032 [C] |

FOI

6033. A learning plateau may be defined as the

A— point in the learning curve at which skill proficiency retrogresses.
B— normal leveling-off of an individual's learning rate.
C— achievement of the highest possible level of competence for a particular individual.

Graphs of the progress of an individual's learning rate usually follow the same pattern. There is rapid improvement in early trials, then the curve levels-off and may stay level for significant periods of effort. Such a development is called a learning plateau. (PLT308) — FAA-H-8083-9

FOI

6033-1. Fatigue can be either

A— physiological or psychological.
B— physical or mental.
C— acute or chronic.

Fatigue can be either acute (short-term) or chronic (long-term). Acute fatigue, a normal occurrence of everyday living, is the tiredness felt after long periods of physical and mental strain, including strenuous muscular effort, immobility, heavy mental workload, strong emotional pressure, monotony, and lack of sleep. Chronic fatigue occurs when there is not enough time for a full recovery from repeated episodes of acute fatigue. (PLT308) — FAA-H-8083-9

FOI

6033-2. A CFI can detect fatigue by noting these characteristics in the student:

A— Nervous laughter.
B— Loss of accuracy and control, and irritability.
C— Poor performance and macho attitude.

It is important for a CFI to be able to detect fatigue, both in assessing a student's substandard performance early in a lesson, and also in recognizing the deterioration of performance. The following deficiencies are apparent to others before the individual notices any physical signs of fatigue. Acute fatigue is characterized by: inattention, distractibility, errors in timing, neglect of secondary tasks, loss of accuracy and control, lack of awareness of error accumulation, irritability. (PLT308) — FAA-H-8083-9

FOI

6033-3. Chronic fatigue can be defined as

A— a combination of both physiological problems and psychological issues.
B— a result of continuous stress.
C— a normal occurrence of everyday living.

Chronic fatigue is a combination of both physiological problems and psychological issues. Psychological problems such as financial, home life, or job-related stresses cause a lack of qualified rest that is only solved by mitigating the underlying problems before the fatigue is solved. Without resolution, human performance continues to fall off, and judgment becomes impaired so that unwarranted risks may be taken. Unless adequate precautions are taken, personal performance could be impaired and adversely affect pilot judgment and decision-making. (PLT308) — FAA-H-8083-9

FOI

6033-4. Acute fatigue is characterized by

A— errors in timing and neglect of secondary tasks.
B— a combination of both physiological problems and psychological issues.
C— a lack of physical robustness or mental acuity.

Acute fatigue is characterized by: inattention, distractibility, errors in timing, neglect of secondary tasks, loss of accuracy and control, lack of awareness of error accumulation, irritability. (PLT308) — FAA-H-8083-9

Answer (B) is incorrect because this describes chronic fatigue. Answer (C) is incorrect because acute fatigue is not necessarily a function of physical robustness or mental acuity.

FOI

7319. Fatigue is one of the most treacherous hazards to flight safety

A— because it results in slow performance.
B— as it may not be apparent to a pilot until serious errors are made.
C— as it may be a function of physical robustness or mental acuity.

Fatigue is one of the most treacherous hazards to flight safety as it may not be apparent to a pilot until serious errors are made. (PLT308) — FAA-H-8083-9

Answers

| 6033 [B] | 6033-1 [C] | 6033-2 [B] | 6033-3 [A] | 6033-4 [A] | 7319 [B] |

FOI

6033-5. Which is true regarding learning plateaus?

A— Learning plateaus result from poor instruction.
B— Learning plateaus are a normal part of the learning process and are usually temporary.
C— Learning plateaus result from lack of practice.

Learning plateaus are a normal part of the learning process and tend to be temporary, but instructors and students should be prepared for them. If the student is aware of this learning plateau, frustration may be minimized. (PLT306) — FAA-H-8083-9

Answer (A) is incorrect because learning plateaus are a normal part of the process and not necessarily a reflection of the quality of instruction. Answer (C) is incorrect because learning plateaus can result from over-practice.

FOI

6033-6. How can instructors help students through a learning plateau?

A— Continue practicing until the progress is made.
B— Assume the student has reached his/her potential for that skill.
C— Move to a different place in the curriculum.

Instructors can help students who fall into a learning plateau by moving the student to a different place in the curriculum and giving the current task a break. (PLT306) — FAA-H-8083-9

Answer (A) is incorrect because learning plateaus can result from over-practice. Answer (B) is incorrect because although the student may have reached his or her current capability limit at that time, instructors should not assume this is the student's maximum potential for the skill but instead take a break from it and return later.

FOI

6033-7. Which stage of skill acquisition is characterized by a student who is able to assess personal progress and adjust performance accordingly?

A— Cognitive stage.
B— Associative stage.
C— Automatic response stage.

Students make their way from beginner to expert via three stages of skill knowledge acquisition, which helps them transition from beginner to expert. The development of any skill acquisition (or the learning process) has three characteristic stages: cognitive, associative, and automaticity. An instructor must learn to recognize each stage in student performance in order to assess student progress. During the associative stage, the storage of a skill via practice continues. The student learns to associate individual steps in performance with likely outcomes. The student no longer performs a series of memorized steps, but is able to assess his or her progress along the way and make adjustments in performance. (PLT306) — FAA-H-8083-9

Answer (A) is incorrect because the cognitive stage is based in factual knowledge and in memorized performance of a skill. Answer (C) is incorrect because the automatic response stage involves multi-task demonstrations but with less understanding of the individual skills required for a given task.

FOI

6033-8. Which stage of skill acquisition is characterized by a student who is able to perform a procedure rapidly and smoothly while simultaneously performing other tasks?

A— Cognitive stage.
B— Associative stage.
C— Automatic response stage.

Students make their way from beginner to expert via three stages of skill knowledge acquisition, which helps them transition from beginner to expert. The development of any skill acquisition (or the learning process) has three characteristic stages: cognitive, associative, and automaticity. An instructor must learn to recognize each stage in student performance in order to assess student progress. During the automatic response stage, procedures become automatic; less attention is required to carry them out, so it is possible to do other things simultaneously, or at least do other things more comfortably. By this stage, student performance of the skill is rapid and smooth. The student devotes much less deliberate attention to performance, and may be able to carry on a conversation or perform other tasks while performing the skill. (PLT306) — FAA-H-8083-9

Answer (A) is incorrect because the cognitive stage is based in factual knowledge and in memorized performance of a skill. Answer (B) is incorrect during the associative stage the student is able to assess his or her progress along the way and make adjustments in performance but may not be able to multi-task seamlessly.

Answers

6033-5 [B]	6033-6 [C]	6033-7 [B]	6033-8 [C]

FOI

6033-9. Which stage of skill acquisition is characterized by student entering a steep turn with the proper power and pitch trim but unable to hold the correct control inputs?

A— Cognitive stage.
B— Associative stage.
C— Automatic response stage.

Students make their way from beginner to expert via three stages of skill knowledge acquisition, which helps them transition from beginner to expert. The development of any skill acquisition (or the learning process) has three characteristic stages: cognitive, associative, and automaticity. An instructor must learn to recognize each stage in student performance in order to assess student progress. During the cognitive stage, students are often learning without any basis in factual knowledge. Since the student has no prior knowledge of flying, the instructor first introduces a basic skill. The student then memorizes the steps required to perform the skill. As the student carries out these memorized steps, he or she is often unaware of progress, or may fixate on one aspect of performance. Performing the skill at this stage typically requires all the student's attention; distractions introduced by an instructor often cause performance to deteriorate or stop. (PLT306) — FAA-H-8083-9

Answer (B) is incorrect because during the associative stage the student no longer performs a series of memorized steps, but is able to assess his or her progress along the way and make adjustments in performance. Answer (C) is incorrect because the automatic response stage involves multi-task demonstrations but with less understanding of the individual skills required for a given task.

FOI

6033-10. Studies suggest a student achieves better results if distractions are avoided during what type of practice?

A— Deliberate practice.
B— Blocked practice.
C— Random practice.

There are three types of practice, each of which yields particular results in acquiring skills: deliberate, blocked, and random. During deliberate practice, the student practices specific areas for improvement and receives specific feedback after practice. Studies of skill learning suggest a student achieves better results if distractions are avoided during deliberate practice. (PLT306) — FAA-H-8083-9

Answer (B) is incorrect because blocked practice is practicing the same drill until the movement becomes automatic; distractions are helpful during this type of practice. Answer (C) is incorrect because

random practice mixes up the skills to be acquired throughout the practice session; distractions can help make the learning more meaningful.

FOI

6033-11. What type of practice includes repeating the same drill or task until the movement becomes automatic?

A— Deliberate practice.
B— Blocked practice.
C— Random practice.

There are three types of practice, each of which yields particular results in acquiring skills: deliberate, blocked, and random. Blocked practice is practicing the same drill until the movement becomes automatic. (PLT306) — FAA-H-8083-9

Answer (A) is incorrect because during deliberate practice, the student practices specific areas for improvement and receives specific feedback after practice. Answer (C) is incorrect because random practice mixes up the skills to be acquired throughout the practice session.

FOI

6033-12. What type of practice mixes up the skills to be acquired throughout the practice session?

A— Deliberate practice.
B— Blocked practice.
C— Random practice.

There are three types of practice, each of which yields particular results in acquiring skills: deliberate, blocked, and random. Random practice mixes up the skills to be acquired throughout the practice session. This type of practice leads to better retention because by performing a series of separate skills in a random order, the student starts to recognize the similarities and differences of each skill which makes it more meaningful. The learner also is able to store the skill more effectively in the long-term memory. (PLT306) — FAA-H-8083-9

Answer (A) is incorrect because during deliberate practice, the student practices specific areas for improvement and receives specific feedback after practice. Answer (B) is incorrect because blocked practice is practicing the same drill until the movement becomes automatic.

Answers

6033-9 [A]   6033-10 [A]   6033-11 [B]   6033-12 [C]

ALL, FOI

7317. What is the best way to teach students how to multi-task while flying?

A— Help students develop both types of multitasking abilities, including attention switching and simultaneous performance.

B— Help students develop attention switching skills.

C— Offer distractions while a student is learning a skill so they understand how to sequence the task.

Since doing several things at once is a natural part of aviation, instructors need to help students develop both types of multi-tasking abilities: attention switching and simultaneous performance. Before students are asked to perform several tasks at once, instructors should ensure that the student has devoted enough time to study and practice such that the individual tasks can be performed reasonably well in isolation. (PLT306) — FAA-H-8083-9

FOI

6033-13. Chronic fatigue

A— occurs when there is not enough time for a full recovery from repeated episodes of acute fatigue.

B— is the tiredness felt after long periods of physical and mental strain and lack of sleep.

C— impairs performance and ability but not judgment.

Chronic fatigue occurs when there is not enough time for a full recovery from repeated episodes of acute fatigue. The underlying cause of chronic fatigue is generally not "rest-related" and may have deeper points of origin. Therefore, rest alone may not resolve chronic fatigue. (PLT306) — FAA-H-8083-9

Answer (B) is incorrect because this describes acute fatigue. Answer (C) is incorrect because chronic fatigue could impair personal performance and adversely affect pilot judgment and decision-making.

FOI

6033-14. Chronic fatigue may be evidenced by a student pilot's apparent

A— increase in knowledge and skill retention.

B— need for sleep.

C— acceptance of unwarranted risks.

Recovery from chronic fatigue requires a prolonged and deliberate solution. Without resolution, human performance continues to fall off, and judgment becomes impaired so that unwarranted risks may be taken. (PLT306) — FAA-H-8083-9

Answer (A) is incorrect because chronic fatigue often results in a decrease of knowledge and skill. Answer (B) is incorrect because chronic fatigue's underlying cause is generally not "rest-related" and may have deeper points of origin.

FOI

6033-15. Acute fatigue may be evidenced by a student pilot's apparent

A— increase in attention to detail.

B— neglect of secondary tasks.

C— acceptance of unwarranted risks.

A CFI who is familiar with the signs indicative of acute fatigue will be more aware if the student is experiencing them. Acute fatigue is characterized by inattention, distractibility, errors in timing, neglect of secondary tasks, loss of accuracy and control, lack of awareness of error accumulation, and irritability. (PLT306) — FAA-H-8083-9

Answer (A) is incorrect because this is acute fatigue is often characterized by inattention. Answer (C) is incorrect because this is an indicator of chronic fatigue.

Answers

7317 [A]	6033-13 [A]	6033-14 [C]	6033-15 [B]

Human Behavior

The pyramid of human needs suggested by Professor Maslow lists five levels of needs. The lower level must be satisfied before a level above it can be satisfied. The levels of needs, beginning with the most basic, are:

Physical — includes the need for food, rest, exercise, and protection from the elements. Another term used for physiological needs is "biological needs."

Safety — includes protection against danger, threat, and deprivation. These are also called security needs.

Social — the need to belong, to associate, and to give and receive friendship and love.

Egoist — the needs related to one's self-esteem and reputation, including the need for self-confidence, independence, achievement, competence, knowledge, status, recognition, appreciation, and the deserved respect of one's fellows.

Self-fulfillment — the highest level, which can be met only after all lower levels have been satisfied. This is the need for realizing one's own potentialities, for continued development, and for being creative in the broadest sense of that term.

Human needs that must be met to encourage learning include physiological, security, belonging, esteem, cognitive and aesthetic, and self-actualization.

There are certain behavior patterns students use to soften the feeling of failure, to alleviate feelings of guilt, and to protect their feeling of personal worth and adequacy. These are called **defense mechanisms**, and while they can serve a useful purpose, they can also be a hindrance because they involve some self-deception and distortion of reality:

Repression — the defense mechanism whereby a person places uncomfortable thoughts into inaccessible areas of the unconscious mind.

Denial — a refusal to accept external reality because it is too threatening.

Compensation — a process of psychologically counterbalancing perceived weaknesses by emphasizing strength in other areas.

Projection — occurs when an individual places his or her own unacceptable impulses onto someone else.

Rationalization — a subconscious technique for justifying actions that otherwise would be unacceptable.

Reaction formation — faking a belief opposite to one's true belief because the true belief causes anxiety.

Fantasy — occurs when a student engages in daydreams about how things should be rather than doing anything about how things are.

Displacement — an unconscious shift of emotion or desire from the original object to a more acceptable, less threatening substitute.

The relationship between an instructor and his/her students has a profound impact on how much the students learn. Students expect the instructor to exercise certain controls, and they recognize and submit to authority as a valid means of control. A good instructor directs and controls the behavior of the students, guiding them and helping them accomplish their goals.

Students learn more from wanting to learn than from being forced to learn. One basic function of an instructor is to help the student want to learn. Seven ways of encouraging a student to want to learn are:

Keep students motivated — when students see the benefits or purpose of a lesson, their enjoyment and efforts will increase.

Keep students informed — students feel insecure and lose enthusiasm when they do not know what is expected of them. Not knowing their progress causes students to not want to accept further instruction.

Approach students as individuals — when instructors limit their thinking to the whole group without considering the individuals who make up that group, their effort is directed at an average personality which really fits no one.

Give credit when due — students become frustrated if no praise or recognition is given for a job well done. Praise should be given carefully; if it is given too freely, it becomes meaningless.

Criticize constructively — when a student makes an error, he/she should be made aware of what has been done wrong and shown how to prevent repetition of the error. Pointing out an error without explaining how to correct it causes frustration.

Be consistent — students want to please their instructor. The instructor must let the student know what is expected by being consistent in his/her actions and philosophy.

Admit errors — We all make mistakes, and if instructors try to cover up or bluff, the students will be quick to sense it. This leads to destruction of student confidence in the instructor.

FOI
6043. Which of the student's human needs offer the greatest challenge to an instructor?

A— Physiological.
B— Psychological.
C— Self-actualization.

Self-actualization needs of a student are the most important, yet the most difficult for an instructor to recognize and guide in their achievement. Only after the instructor has helped the student satisfy all of the lesser needs do self-actualization needs become apparent. (PLT270) — FAA-H-8083-9

Answer (A) is incorrect because physiological needs are fulfilled by the students on their own. Answer (B) is incorrect because self-actualization needs are more difficult for the instructor than psychological needs.

FOI
6042. After individuals are physically comfortable and have no fear for their safety, which human needs become the prime influence on their behavior?

A— Belonging.
B— Self-actualization.
C— Esteem.

The next need, after a student has met the basic physical and safety needs, is the social need. Students need to belong, to associate, to give and receive friendship and love. (PLT270) — FAA-H-8083-9

Answer (B) is incorrect because self-actualization is the last human need to be met. Answer (C) is incorrect because this is the fourth level, and the question is seeking the third level of human needs.

FOI
6041. Before a student can concentrate on learning, which human needs must be satisfied?

A— Safety.
B— Physiological.
C— Security.

The most basic of human needs is the physical need. Until the physical needs are satisfied, at least to a reasonable degree, the student cannot concentrate on what is to be learned. (PLT270) — FAA-H-8083-9

Answers (A) and (C) are incorrect because physical needs must be met before safety and security needs (which are on the same level) can be tended to.

Answers

6043 [C]   6042 [A]   6041 [B]

FOI

6041-1. Before a student can concentrate on learning, which human needs must be satisfied?

A— Aesthetic.
B— Biological.
C— Psychological.

Unless the biological needs are met, a person cannot concentrate fully on learning, self-expression, or any other tasks. (PLT270) — FAA-H-8083-9

FOI

6045. Although defense mechanisms can serve a useful purpose, they can also

A— provide feelings of adequacy.
B— alleviate the cause of problems.
C— involve some degree of self-deception and distortion of reality.

Even though defense mechanisms can sometimes serve a useful purpose, they can also be a hindrance because they involve some self-deception and distortion of reality. Defense mechanisms do not help students solve problems. (PLT269) — FAA-H-8083-9

Answer (A) is incorrect because defense mechanisms are used as a mask to protect a person's feelings of self worth and adequacy. Answer (B) is incorrect because defense mechanisms alleviate symptoms of problems, not causes.

FOI

6046. When a student presents beliefs opposite to what they truly believe, it usually is an indication of the defense mechanism known as

A— fantasy.
B— reaction formation.
C— displacement.

In reaction formation a person fakes a belief opposite to the true belief because the true belief causes anxiety. (PLT269) — FAA-H-8083-9

Answer (A) is incorrect because fantasy occurs when a student engages in daydreams about how things should be rather than doing anything about how things are. Answer (C) is incorrect because displacement results in an unconscious shift of emotion or desire from the original object to a more acceptable, less threatening substitute.

FOI

6047. Fantasy is a defense mechanism students use when they

A— want to escape from frustrating situations.
B— cannot accept the real reasons for their behavior.
C— lose interest during the advanced stages of training.

The defense mechanism of fantasy is often used by students when they want to escape from their frustrations. A good instructor tries to help the student face and overcome the frustrations instead of running from them. (PLT269) — FAA-H-8083-9

Answer (B) is incorrect because if a person isn't facing the true reasons for his/her actions, the common effect is one of rationalization and finding excuses, rather than running away. Answer (C) is incorrect because this describes the defense mechanism of projection.

FOI

6044. When a student uses excuses to justify inadequate performance, it is an indication of the defense mechanism known as

A— fantasy.
B— displacement.
C— rationalization.

When students use excuses to try to justify inadequate performance, they are using the defense mechanism of rationalization. (PLT233) — FAA-H-8083-9

Answer (A) is incorrect because fantasy refers to the daydreaming that allows students to escape from frustrating situations. Answer (B) is incorrect because displacement is an unconscious shift of emotion or desire from the original object to a more acceptable, less threatening substitute.

FOI

6044-1. A student pilot blames the failure of a Practical Exam on an unfair evaluation by the examiner. This demonstrates the defense mechanism known as

A— rationalization.
B— projection.
C— denial.

Through projection, an individual places his or her own unacceptable impulses onto someone else. A person relegates the blame for personal shortcomings, mistakes, and transgressions to others or attributes personal motives, desires, characteristics, and impulses to others. The student pilot who fails a flight exam and says, "I failed because I had a poor examiner" believes the failure was not due to a lack of personal skill or knowledge. This student projects blame onto an "unfair" examiner. (PLT306) — FAA-H-8083-9

Answers

6041-1 [B]	6045 [C]	6046 [B]	6047 [A]	6044 [C]	6044-1 [B]

Answer (A) is incorrect because rationalization is a subconscious technique for justifying actions that otherwise would be unacceptable. Answer (C) is incorrect because denial is a refusal to acknowledge what has happened, is happening, or will happen.

FOI

6048. When students subconsciously use the defense mechanism called rationalization, they

A— use excuses to justify acceptable behavior.
B— cannot accept the real reasons for their behavior.
C— fake a belief opposite to their true belief because the true belief causes anxiety.

Students often use the defense mechanism of rationalization, sometimes subconsciously, when they cannot accept the real reason for their behavior. (PLT269) — FAA-H-8083-9

Answer (A) is incorrect because when students use rationalization, they use excuses to justify unacceptable or inadequate behavior. Answer (C) is incorrect because this describes reaction formation.

FOI

6051. The process of psychologically counterbalancing perceived weaknesses by emphasizing strength in other areas is

A— projection.
B— compensation.
C— rationalization.

Compensation is a process of psychologically counterbalancing perceived weaknesses by emphasizing strength in other areas. (PLT269) — FAA-H-8083-9

Answer (A) is incorrect because through projection, an individual places his or her own unacceptable impulses onto someone else. Answer (C) is incorrect because rationalization is a subconscious technique for justifying actions that otherwise would be unacceptable.

FOI

6051-1. When a student attempts to disguise a weak or undesirable quality by emphasizing a more positive one, this is a defense mechanism in the form of

A— rationalization.
B— submission.
C— compensation.

Compensation is a process of psychologically counterbalancing perceived weaknesses by emphasizing strength in other areas. Through compensation, students often attempt to disguise the presence of a weak or undesirable quality by emphasizing a more positive one. (PLT269) — FAA-H-8083-9

FOI

6049. When students display the defense mechanism called repression, they

A— refuse to accept reality.
B— place uncomfortable thoughts into inaccessible areas of the unconscious mind.
C— attempt to justify actions by asking numerous questions.

Repression is the defense mechanism whereby a person places uncomfortable thoughts into inaccessible areas of the unconscious mind. (PLT233) — FAA-H-8083-9

Answer (A) is incorrect because this describes the defense mechanism denial. Answer (C) is incorrect because this describes the defense mechanism rationalization.

FOI

6049-1. When students display the defense mechanism of denial they

A— become visibility angry, upset, or childish.
B— may attempt to minimize the situation.
C— attempt to justify actions by asking numerous questions.

Denial is a refusal to accept external reality because it is too threatening. It is the refusal to acknowledge what has happened, is happening, or will happen. It is a form of repression through which stressful thoughts are banned from memory. Related to denial is minimization. When a person minimizes something, he or she accepts what happened, but in a diluted form. (PLT233) — FAA-H-8083-9

FOI

6049-2. A student who has a hidden fear of flying that inhibits learning during training is displaying the defense mechanism of

A— flight.
B— repression.
C— resignation.

Repression is the defense mechanism whereby a person places uncomfortable thoughts into inaccessible areas of the unconscious mind. For example, a student pilot may have a repressed fear of flying that inhibits his or her ability to learn how to fly. (PLT233) — FAA-H-8083-9

FOI

6050. When a student engages in daydreaming, it is the defense mechanism of

A— compensation.
B— fantasy.
C— denial.

Fantasy occurs when a student engages in daydreams about how things should be rather than doing anything about how things are. Daydreaming is a defense mechanism used by students when they take mental flight to escape from the problems that face them. (PLT269) — FAA-H-8083-9

Answer (A) is incorrect because compensation is a process of psychologically counterbalancing perceived weaknesses by emphasizing strength in other areas. Answer (C) is incorrect because denial is a refusal to accept external reality because it is too threatening.

FOI

6052. Which would more likely result in students becoming frustrated?

A— Giving the students meaningless praise.
B— Telling students their work is unsatisfactory with no explanation.
C— An instructor freely admitting mistakes causing lack of trust.

It is extremely important when evaluating unsatisfactory performance for the instructor to explain the reason it is unsatisfactory and to show the student the best way to make it satisfactory. (PLT482) — FAA-H-8083-9

Answer (A) is incorrect because giving students meaningless praise has no value, but does not result in frustration. Answer (C) is incorrect because the instructor can win the respect of students by honestly acknowledging mistakes.

FOI

6053. When students are unable to see the benefits or purpose of a lesson, they will

A— be less motivated.
B— not learn as quickly.
C— be expected to increase their efforts.

When students are unable to see the benefits or purpose of a lesson as it relates to their goals, they will become less motivated. (PLT490) — FAA-H-8083-9

Answer (B) is incorrect because the speed of learning is not necessarily affected by this. Answer (C) is incorrect because students' efforts will decrease without a known goal.

FOI

6054. When the instructor keeps the student informed of lesson objectives and completion standards, it minimizes the student's feelings of

A— insecurity.
B— resignation.
C— aggressiveness.

Insecurity is minimized by an instructor keeping the student informed of the lesson objectives and the standards that are to be used in evaluating the lesson or project. (PLT490) — FAA-H-8083-9

Answer (B) is incorrect because resignation refers to what happens when the student completes the early phase of training without understanding the fundamentals. Answer (C) is incorrect because aggression is a defense mechanism used when the student feels insecure.

FOI

6054-1. If a lesson objective is not clearly stated, the student will become

A— apathetic.
B— motivated to see the big picture.
C— less motivated.

Clearly defined training objectives that the student understands naturally lead him or her to be motivated. This is essential to the teaching process regardless of the teaching method used. (PLT490) — FAA-H-8083-9

Answer (A) is incorrect because students may experience uncertainty and frustration without a clearly stated objective, but not necessarily become apathetic. Answer (B) is incorrect because students need a clearly stated lesson objective for any kind of motivation to occur.

FOI

6055. Student confidence tends to be destroyed if instructors

A— bluff whenever in doubt about some point.
B— continually identify student errors and failures.
C— direct and control the student's actions and behavior.

Students must have confidence in their instructor. An instructor who bluffs when uncertain about some point or when unable to correctly answer a question destroys this confidence. (PLT419) — FAA-H-8083-9

Answers (B) and (C) are incorrect because identifying student errors and failures, and directing and controlling the student's actions and behavior are responsibilities of the instructor.

Answers

| 6050 [B] | 6052 [B] | 6053 [A] | 6054 [A] | 6054-1 [C] | 6055 [A] |

FOI

6055-1. Students who recognize that the instructor is inadequately prepared can become

A— assertive.
B— apprehensive.
C— apathetic.

Students can become apathetic when they recognize that the instructor has made inadequate preparations for the instruction being given, or when the instruction appears to be deficient, contradictory, or insincere. To hold the student's interest and to maintain the motivation necessary for efficient learning, well-planned, appropriate, and accurate instruction must be provided. (PLT419) — FAA-H-8083-9

Effective Communications

Effective communication is measured by the similarity between the idea transmitted and the idea received. Effective communication requires three elements: the source (the instructor), the symbols (the words or signs used to convey the message), and the receiver (the student). These elements interrelate dynamically and reciprocally in the complex, two-way process of communication.

The instructor should have a positive attitude toward himself/herself, toward the material being presented, and toward the student. For effective communication, the instructor should select symbols that are meaningful to the student. This is best done by the instructor speaking or writing from a broad background of accurate, up-to-date, stimulating material. The most effective communication uses a variety of symbols that use the channels of hearing and seeing and, when appropriate, of feeling. Effective communication takes place only when the students react with understanding and change their behavior accordingly. The three basic **barriers to effective communication** are:

Lack of common core of experience — this is the greatest single barrier to successful communication. Communication can be effective only to the extent that the experiences — physical, mental, or emotional — of the people involved are similar. Words never carry precisely the same meaning from the mind of the communicator to the mind of the receiver. Experiences of the receiver add meaning to the words that are heard.

Confusion between the symbol and the thing symbolized — communicators must be careful to differentiate between the symbols and the things they represent.

Overuse of abstractions — concrete words refer to objects that can be experienced directly. Abstract words stand for ideas that cannot be directly experienced, that do not put specific mental images in the mind of the receiver. When using abstractions, the communicator does not necessarily evoke in the receiver's mind the specific items of experience he/she intends. The communicator can main-tain control of the image produced in the mind of the listener or reader by using more concrete terms than abstractions.

FOI

6056. The effectiveness of communication between instructor and student is measured by the

A— degree of dynamic, interrelated elements.
B— similarity between the idea transmitted and the idea received.
C— relationship between communicative and dynamic elements.

Instructors know they are getting through to the student when the idea the student receives is the same idea that was transmitted. (PLT204) — FAA-H-8083-9

Answer (A) is incorrect because this is merely part of the process of communication, not a degree of effectiveness. Answer (C) is incorrect because it is the relationship between communicative elements that is dynamic.

Answers

6055-1   [C]   6056   [B]

FOI

6057. To be more likely to communicate effectively, an instructor should speak or write from a background of

A— technical expertise.
B— knowing the ideas presented.
C— up-to-date, stimulating material.

Successful communicators speak or write from a background of up-to-date, stimulating material. (PLT204) — FAA-H-8083-9

Answer (A) is incorrect because relying only on technical language may impede effective communication. Answer (B) is incorrect because success requires more effort than simply knowing the ideas presented.

FOI

6039-6. When has instruction taken place?

A— When a procedure has been explained, and the desired student response has occurred.
B— When the student hears what is presented.
C— When all the required material has been presented.

Instruction has taken place when the instructor has explained a particular procedure and subsequently determined that the desired student response has occurred. (PLT419) — FAA-H-8083-9

FOI

6058. To communicate effectively, instructors must

A— recognize the level of comprehension.
B— provide an atmosphere which encourages questioning.
C— reveal a positive attitude while delivering their message.

The attitude of the instructor is extremely important. He/she must reveal a positive and confident attitude while delivering the message. (PLT204) — FAA-H-8083-9

Answer (A) is incorrect because recognizing the level of comprehension can take place in the application step of the teaching process. Answer (B) is incorrect because, while it is important to provide an atmosphere which encourages questioning, students must exercise their participation in the exchange to communicate effectively.

FOI

6059. Effective communication has taken place when, and only when, the

A— information is transmitted and received.
B— receivers react with understanding and change their behavior accordingly.
C— receivers have the ability to question and comprehend ideas that have been transmitted.

Effective communication has taken place when, and only when, the receivers react with understanding and change their behavior accordingly. (PLT204) — FAA-H-8083-9

Answer (A) is incorrect because information can be transmitted and received without achieving effective communication. Answer (C) is incorrect because receivers must change their behavior accordingly, in addition to the ability to question and comprehend ideas, in order to achieve effective communication.

FOI

6060. In the communication process, the communicator will be more successful in gaining and retaining the receiver's attention by

A— being friendly and informative.
B— using a varied communicative approach.
C— using a variety of audiovisual aids in class.

Variety of presentation helps an instructor reach all of the students. The communicator will be more successful in gaining and retaining the receiver's attention by using a varied communicative approach. (PLT204) — FAA-H-8083-9

Answers (A) and (C) are incorrect because being friendly and informative, and simply using a variety of audiovisual aids in class aids the learning atmosphere, but does not guarantee attention and the most effective communication process.

Answers

| 6057 [C] | 6039-6 [A] | 6058 [C] | 6059 [B] | 6060 [B] |

FOI

6061. By using abstractions in the communication process, the communicator will

A— bring forth specific items of experience in the minds of the receivers.

B— be using words which refer to objects or ideas that human beings can experience directly.

C— not evoke in the listener's or reader's mind the specific items of experience the communicator intends.

Abstractions should be avoided in the process of teaching. Abstract words stand for ideas that cannot be directly experienced, so they may not cause the student to have the mental image the communicator (instructor) intended. (PLT204) — FAA-H-8083-9

Answer (A) is incorrect because abstract words do not bring forth specific items of experience in the minds of the receivers. Answer (B) is incorrect because concrete words (not abstract) refer to objects or ideas that human beings can experience directly.

FOI

6062. The danger in using abstract words is that they

A— sum up vast areas of experience.

B— call forth different mental images in the minds of the receivers.

C— will not evoke the specific items of experience in the listener's mind that the communicator intends.

Abstract words do not evoke the specific items of experience in the listener's mind that the communicator (instructor) intends. (PLT204) — FAA-H-8083-9

Answer (A) is incorrect because the purpose (not danger) of abstract words is to sum up vast areas of experience. Answer (B) is incorrect because abstract words represent ideas that do not put specific mental images in the hearer's mind; many hearers may receive different images, yet to be most effective, the instructor needs to convey specific mental images.

FOI

6063. Probably the greatest single barrier to effective communication in the teaching process is a lack of

A— respect for the instructor.

B— personality harmony between instructor and student.

C— a common experience level between instructor and student.

Probably the greatest single barrier to effective communication in the teaching process is a lack of a common experience level between the instructor and the student. (PLT204) — FAA-H-8083-9

Answers (A) and (B) are incorrect because although lack of respect and personality harmony are a hindrance to communication, they are not as great a barrier as a common experience level.

FOI

6064. A communicator's words cannot communicate the desired meaning to another person unless the

A— words have meaningful referents.

B— words give the meaning that is in the mind of the receiver.

C— listener or reader has had some experience with the objects or concepts to which these words refer.

For successful learning to take place, the instructor and the student must have a common ground. The instructor's words cannot communicate the desired meaning to the student unless the student has had some experience with the words or concepts to which the instructor's words refer. (PLT204) — FAA-H-8083-9

Answer (A) is incorrect because the words must have the same meaningful referents. Answer (B) is incorrect because the interpretation of the meaning of the words depends on the receiver's common ground of experience with the communicator.

Answers

| 6061 | [C] | 6062 | [C] | 6063 | [C] | 6064 | [C] |

The Teaching Process

Logical steps for teaching new material are:

1. **Preparation** — this includes making a written lesson plan which defines the material to be covered, outlines the lesson objectives, clearly states the goals to be attained, makes certain that all necessary supplies and equipment are readily available, and the equipment is operating properly.

2. **Presentation** — the instructor must determine which method of presentation is best suited for the information to be conveyed. Some of these methods are: lecture method, and the demonstration/performance method.

3. **Application** — this gives the student an opportunity to apply what is being taught. By allowing the student to apply the newly gained knowledge early in the learning process, faulty habits can be prevented.

4. **Review and evaluation** — students should be evaluated on their performance and on the attainment of the stated objectives and goals at the end of each step in the learning process. Deficiencies and faults should be carefully noted and steps taken to remedy them.

FOI

6070. To enhance a student's acceptance of further instruction, the instructor should

A— keep the student informed of the progress made.
B— continually prod the student to maintain motivational levels.
C— establish performance standards a little above the student's actual ability.

Students perform best when they know the progress they are making. Instructors may enhance the students' acceptance of further instruction by keeping them informed of their progress. (PLT482) — FAA-H-8083-9

Answer (B) is incorrect because continuously prodding the student will decrease the motivational level and therefore decrease the student's acceptance of further instruction. Answer (C) is incorrect because establishing performance standards a little above the student's actual ability will cause frustration and decrease their acceptance of further instruction.

FOI

6065. When teaching new material, the teaching process can be divided into which steps?

A— Preparation, presentation, application, and review and evaluation.
B— Preparation, demonstration, practice, and review.
C— Explanation, demonstration, practice, and evaluation.

The steps in the learning process are: preparation, presentation, application, and finally, review and evaluation. (PLT481) — FAA-H-8083-9

FOI

6069. Evaluation of student performance and accomplishment during a lesson should be based on

A— objectives and goals established in the lesson plan.
B— performance of each student compared to an objective standard.
C— each student's ability to make an objective evaluation of their own progress.

The basis for the evaluation of student performance and accomplishment during a lesson should be the objectives and goals that were established in the lesson plan. (PLT211) — FAA-H-8083-9

Answer (B) is incorrect because the performance of each student compared to an objective standard is a critique (not an evaluation). Answer (C) is incorrect because the student's evaluation of his/her own progress is subjective (not objective).

FOI

6067. Which statement is true regarding student evaluation?

A— The student's own evaluations can only be objective.
B— Evaluation of the student's learning should be an integral part of each lesson.
C— If deficiencies or faults not associated with the present lesson are revealed, they should be corrected immediately.

Keeping the student fully informed of his/her progress by evaluation of the student's learning should be an integral part of each lesson. (PLT482) — FAA-H-8083-9

Answer (A) is incorrect because the student's own evaluations can only be subjective. Answer (C) is incorrect because if deficiencies or faults not associated with the present lesson are revealed, they should be noted and pointed out, not necessarily corrected immediately.

Answers

6070 [A]   6065 [A]   6069 [A]   6067 [B]

Teaching Methods

There are three main teaching methods: the **lecture** method, **guided discussion** method, and **demonstration/performance** method.

The **lecture** method is used primarily to introduce students to a new subject, but it is also a valuable method for summarizing ideas, showing relationships between theory and practice, and re-emphasizing main points. Lectures are the most effective way of presenting a large number of ideas in a short time. Lectures may be given to either small or large groups and may be used to introduce a complete training program or a unit of instruction. They may be combined with other teaching methods to give added meaning and direction. The first step in organizing a lecture is to establish the objective and identify the desired outcome. The entire lecture should be directed toward these goals. There are several types of lectures; among them are:

- The *illustrated talk*, in which the instructor relies heavily on visual aids.

- The *briefing*, which presents a concise array of facts without elaboration or supporting material.

- The *formal speech*, whose purpose is to inform, persuade, or entertain.

- The *teaching lecture*, which is an oral presentation designed to help the student reach a desired learning outcome.

The teaching lecture is one of the most widely used methods of teaching, but requires a high degree of organization and skill in presentation. There is very little direct student feedback, so the instructor must be on the watch for subtle responses to determine whether or not the students are assimilating the material. When presenting a teaching lecture, the instructor should be confident, relaxed, and in complete control of the situation. The lecture is best delivered in an extemporaneous manner, using a mental or written outline. But the material should not be read directly from notes nor recited from memory; it should be delivered in a relaxed way to help put the students at ease.

Substandard English and vulgarisms should never be used; they detract from an instructor's dignity and reflect upon the intelligence of the students. Lectures need not be formal. The use of well-formulated and directed questions during an informal lecture encourages active student participation and allows the instructor to get immediate feedback. Questioning allows the instructor to determine the experience and background of the students, to add variety and stimulate interest, and to check student understanding.

One of the oldest and most effective teaching methods is that of the **guided discussion**. By the skillful use of questioning, the instructor directs the class and keeps everyone working toward the goals and objectives of the lesson, to develop an understanding of the subject. The more intense the discussion and the greater the participation, the more effective the learning will be. Guided discussion requires a high degree of skill on the part of the instructor. The instructor must encourage questions, exercise patience and tact, and comment on all responses. Sarcasm and ridicule must never be used. A guided discussion must be carefully planned, with attention paid to the following topics:

1. *Select a topic* the students can profitably discuss. Very little learning can take place unless all of the students have some knowledge to exchange with each other.

2. Establish a *specific lesson objective* and desired learning outcome. Guided discussions are most useful when the objective is stated at least at the understanding level of learning. Guided discussions are of little use when teaching at the rote level.

3. *Conduct adequate research* to become familiar with the topic. The instructor must have such complete knowledge of the subject that he or she can turn a wrong answer into a springboard to develop further meaningful discussion.

Continued

4. *Organize the main and subordinate points* of the lesson in a logical sequence. A guided discussion consists of three main parts:

   a. Introduction. This gains the attention of the student, provides motivation, and presents an overview of the lesson.

   b. Discussion. The instructor guides the discussion so that all of the main points are discussed and the lesson progresses logically to the objective.

   c. Conclusion. This consists of a summary, remotivation, and closure.

5. Plan at least one *lead-off question* for each desired learning outcome. The purpose of a lead-off question is to get the discussion started, not to seek a specific answer. Lead-off questions should not have a short answer, but should begin with such words as "how" or "why" to encourage discussion.

Questions used in guided discussion may be classified as:

Overhead — these questions are directed at the entire group to stimulate thought and response from each group member. Overhead questions are normally used as leadoff questions.

Rhetorical — the rhetorical question is also used to stimulate thought, but it is normally answered by the instructor.

Direct — a direct question is used to get specific information from an individual member of the class.

Reverse — a reverse question is used as an answer to a student's question. Rather than giving the student a direct answer, the instructor leads the student to provide the answer.

Relay — a relay question is similar to a reverse question except that it is redirected to the group, rather than to the student who asked the question.

When it appears that the students have discussed the ideas that support the particular part of the lesson, the instructor should summarize what the students have accomplished. In a discussion lesson, the interim summary is one of the most effective tools available to the instructor.

Such skills as cross-country flight planning are best taught by the **demonstration/performance** method. Demonstration/performance instruction has five essential phases:

1. *Explanation.* The instructor explains to the student the precise actions to be performed. Explanation must be clear, detailed, and pertinent to the objectives of the lesson.

2. *Demonstration.* The instructor shows the student the correct way to perform the task.

3. *Student performance.* The student performs the task.

4. *Instructor supervision.* Concurrent with the student performance is supervision by the instructor.

5. *Evaluation.* The instructor judges the performance. This gives the instructor the opportunity to correct any misunderstandings the student might have.

Regardless of the teaching method used, the instructor should organize the material in a way that will produce the most learning. One effective organization is:

Introduction. The introduction sets the stage for learning. It establishes a common ground between the instructor and the students to capture and hold the attention of the group. It indicates what is to be covered during the presentation and relates this coverage to the entire course. Finally, it establishes a receptive attitude toward the subject and leads into the lesson development. The introduction should contain these features:

1. Attention. This allows the instructor to gain the attention of the class and focus it on the subject.

2. Motivation. This appeals to each student personally and accentuates the desire to learn.

3. Overview. This is a clear, concise presentation of the objectives of the lesson and the key ideas give the students a road map of the route to be followed.

Development. The instructor organizes the material in a manner that shows the relationship between the main points:

1. From the past to the present.

2. From the simple to the complex.

3. From the known to the unknown. This allows the instructor to use the previous knowledge and experience of the student.

4. From the most frequently used to the least frequently used.

Conclusion. This retraces the important elements of the lesson and relates them to the objective. All pertinent points are reviewed in order to reinforce them in the student's memory.

FOI

6068. In the teaching process, which method of presentation is suitable for presenting new material, for summarizing ideas, and for showing relationships between theory and practice?

A— Lecture method.
B— Integrated instruction method.
C— Demonstration/performance method.

The lecture is the best teaching method for presenting new material, for summarizing ideas, and for showing the relationships between theory and practice. (PLT488) — FAA-H-8083-9

Answer (B) is incorrect because the integrated instruction method is used to teach flight maneuvers. Answer (C) is incorrect because the demonstration/performance method is used to teach skills.

FOI

6076. The first step in preparing a lecture is to

A— research the subject.
B— develop the main ideas or key points.
C— establish the objective and desired outcome.

The logical steps in the preparation of a lecture are, in their proper sequence:

1. *Establishing the objective and the desired outcome.*

2. *Researching the subject.*

3. *Organizing the material.*

4. *Planning productive classroom activities.*

(PLT488) — FAA-H-8083-9

FOI

6079. What is one advantage of a lecture?

A— Uses time economically.
B— Excellent when additional research is required.
C— Allows for maximum attainment of certain types of learning outcomes.

A lecture is a convenient method of instructing large groups, of introducing new material, and of presenting many ideas in a relatively short time. (PLT488) — FAA-H-8083-9

Answer (B) is incorrect because the lecture method does not require students to do additional research. Answer (C) is incorrect because lecturing does not allow for maximum learning attainment in, for example, the area of motor skills. You don't learn motor skills by listening to a lecture.

FOI

6080. An instructor can inspire active student participation during informal lectures through the use of

A— questions.
B— visual aids.
C— encouragement.

The most effective tool an instructor can use to inspire active student participation in an informal lecture is the use of skillfully chosen questions. (PLT488) — FAA-H-8083-9

Answer (B) is incorrect because visual aids enhance the lecture but will not necessarily get students actively involved. Answer (C) is incorrect because encouragement aids learning but does not necessarily get students actively involved.

Answers

6068 [A]   6076 [C]   6079 [A]   6080 [A]

FOI

6081. The distinguishing characteristic of an informal lecture is the

A— use of visual aids.
B— student's participation.
C— requirement for informal notes.

Student participation is the distinguishing characteristic of an informal lecture. Students learn best when they are free to actively participate in a friendly, relaxed atmosphere. (PLT488) — FAA-H-8083-9

Answers (A) and (C) are incorrect because visual aids and informal notes are not distinguishing characteristics of an informal lecture since they may or may not be used in both formal and informal lectures.

FOI

6082-1. Which teaching method is most economical in terms of the time required to present a given amount of material?

A— Briefing.
B— Teaching lecture.
C— Demonstration/performance.

The lecture is the most time-effective teaching method for introducing new material to a student, for summarizing ideas, and for showing the relationship between theory and practice. When a lecture is efficiently used, more information can be presented in a shorter period of time than with any other teaching method. (PLT488) — FAA-H-8083-9

Answer (A) is incorrect because a briefing is used to present facts to listeners without elaboration or supporting material. Answer (C) is incorrect because the demonstration/performance method is the least economical in terms of time required to present a given amount of material.

FOI

6082-2. The most significant characteristic of group learning is that it

A— continually requires active participation of the student.
B— continually requires active participation of both the student and the instructor.
C— usually requires passive participation of the student.

The most significant characteristic of group learning is that it continually requires active participation of the student in the learning process. (PLT488) — FAA-H-8083-9

FOI

6082-3. The main advantage(s) with heterogeneous groups are that students tend to

A— think for themselves since they are in a group of dissimilar students.
B— interact and achieve in ways and at levels that are rarely found with other instructional strategies.
C— interact and achieve since they are in a group of similar students.

The main advantages with heterogeneous groups are that students tend to interact and achieve in ways and at levels that are rarely found with other instructional strategies. They also tend to become tolerant of diverse viewpoints, to consider the thoughts and feelings of others, and to seek more support and clarification of various opinions. (PLT488) — FAA-H-8083-9

FOI

6082-4. The main reason that students are put in cooperative learning groups is so they

A— learn and help each other.
B— can individually achieve greater success than if they were to study alone.
C— learn that teamwork is essential if all members are to learn equally well.

The main reason students are put in cooperative learning groups is so they can individually achieve greater success than if they were to study alone. (PLT488) — FAA-H-8083-9

FOI

6082-5. An instructional strategy which organizes students into small groups so that they can work together to maximize their own and each other's learning is called

A— workshop learning.
B— heterogeneous group learning.
C— cooperative or group learning.

Cooperative or group learning is an instructional strategy which organizes students into small groups so they can work together to maximize their own and each other's learning. (PLT488) — FAA-H-8083-9

Answers

6081 [B]	6082-1 [B]	6082-2 [A]	6082-3 [B]	6082-4 [B]	6082-5 [C]

FOI

6077. Which is a true statement regarding the teaching lecture?

A— Delivering the lecture in an extemporaneous manner is not recommended.

B— Instructor receives direct feedback from students which is easy to interpret.

C— Instructor must develop a keen perception for subtle responses and be able to interpret the meaning of these reactions.

Effective teaching lectures demand much of an instructor. He/she must develop a keen perception for subtle responses and must be able to interpret the meaning of these reactions. (PLT488) — FAA-H-8083-9

Answer (A) is incorrect because the lecture should be delivered from an outline but with the flexibility to vary the material, in order to personalize and suit different audience moods. Answer (B) is incorrect because the feedback is not as direct as other teaching methods and is therefore harder to interpret.

FOI

6077-1. In the teaching lecture,

A— simple rather than complex words should be used whenever possible.

B— slang and colloquialisms should be avoided.

C— use substandard English to add variety and vividness.

In the teaching lecture, simple rather than complex words should be used whenever possible. Good newspapers offer examples of the effective use of simple words. (PLT488) — FAA-H-8083-9

Answer (B) is incorrect because if they suit the subject, these can add variety and vividness to a teaching lecture. Answer (C) is incorrect because substandard English should never be used.

FOI

6088. When it appears students have adequately discussed the ideas presented during a guided discussion, one of the most valuable tools an instructor can use is

A— a session of verbal testing.

B— a written test on the subject discussed.

C— an interim summary of what the students accomplished.

In the guided discussion method of teaching, when the students have adequately discussed the ideas that have been presented, the instructor should summarize what the students have just learned. (PLT488) — FAA-H-8083-9

Answer (A) is incorrect because a session of verbal testing is contradictory to the intention of the guided discussion, which is to keep the discussion open, and draw out what the students know. Answer (B) is incorrect because in a guided-discussion situation, a written test on the subject discussed would test opinions and experiences rather than facts.

FOI

6078. During a teaching lecture, what would detract from an instructor's dignity and reflect upon the student's intelligence?

A— Use of figurative language.

B— Errors in grammar and use of vulgarisms.

C— Using picturesque slang and colloquialisms.

For a lesson to be successful, the students must have respect for the instructor. To gain this respect, the instructor must guard against the use of substandard English. Errors in grammar and vulgarisms detract from the instructor's dignity and authority and reflect upon the intelligence of the students. (PLT488) — FAA-H-8083-9

Answers (A) and (C) are incorrect because figurative language, picturesque slang, and colloquialisms can enhance the lecture when used correctly.

FOI

6084. Which statement about the guided discussion method of teaching is true?

A— The lesson objective becomes apparent at the application level of learning.

B— Students without a background in the subject can also be included in the discussion.

C— Unless the students have some knowledge to exchange with each other, they cannot reach the desired learning outcomes.

While guided discussions are an excellent teaching method, they do have limitations. Unless the students have some knowledge to exchange with each other, they cannot reach the desired learning outcomes. (PLT488) — FAA-H-8083-9

Answer (A) is incorrect because the lesson objectives should be known during the preparation level, not the application level of learning. Answer (B) is incorrect because students without some background in the subject will not be able to contribute to the discussion.

Answers

6077 [C]	6077-1 [A]	6088 [C]	6078 [B]	6084 [C]

FOI

6087. In a guided discussion, leadoff questions should usually begin with

A— why.
B— what.
C— when.

Leadoff questions usually begin with "how" or "why." (PLT488) — FAA-H-8083-9

Answers (B) and (C) are incorrect because questions beginning with "what" and "when" tend to prompt short answers and may not encourage discussion.

FOI

6086. Which question would be best as a leadoff question for a guided discussion on the subject of torque?

A— Does torque affect an airplane?
B— How does torque affect an airplane?
C— What effect does torque have on an airplane in a turn?

A leadoff question is used to bring about discussion, not merely to get an answer. The question "How does torque affect an airplane?" opens the class for discussion and gives the instructor a subject on which to build. (PLT488) — FAA-H-8083-9

Answers (A) and (C) are incorrect because these types of leadoff questions would prompt yes/no or short answers, and would not encourage a discussion.

FOI

6085. In a guided discussion, learning is achieved through the

A— skillful use of questions.
B— use of questions, each of which contains several ideas.
C— use of reverse questions directed to the class as a whole.

Skillfully chosen questions are used in a guided discussion to produce learning. (PLT488) — FAA-H-8083-9

Answer (B) is incorrect because questions used in a guided discussion should each contain one idea. Answer (C) is incorrect because questions directed to the class as a whole are called relay questions.

FOI

6083. A question directed to an entire group to stimulate thought and response from each group member is identified as

A— Relay.
B— Overhead.
C— Rhetorical.

One of the best ways to lead off a guided discussion is by asking an overhead question. The overhead question is directed toward the entire class rather than an individual student, and it does not require a specific answer. An overhead question centers the thoughts of the entire class around the subject being taught. (PLT488) — FAA-H-8083-9

Answer (A) is incorrect because a relay question is the instructor's response to a student's question that redirects it back to the rest of the group. Answer (C) is incorrect because rhetorical questions are more commonly used in lectures, not guided discussions.

FOI

6066. Which method of presentation is desirable for teaching a skill such as ground school lesson on the flight computer?

A— Presentation/practice.
B— Demonstration/performance.
C— Lecture/application.

Skills requiring the use of tools, machines, and equipment are particularly well suited to the demonstration-performance method. (PLT487) — FAA-H-8083-9

FOI

6090. In the demonstration/performance method of instruction, which two separate actions are performed concurrently?

A— Instructor explanation and demonstration.
B— Student performance and instructor supervision.
C— Instructor explanation and student demonstration.

The critical parts of the demonstration/performance method of teaching are the student performance and instructor supervision. These two phases are separate actions, but they are performed concurrently. (PLT487) — FAA-H-8083-9

Answers

6087 [A]   6086 [B]   6085 [A]   6083 [B]   6066 [B]   6090 [B]

FOI

6091-1. What is the last step in the demonstration/performance method?

A— Summary.
B— Evaluation.
C— Student performance.

The demonstration/performance method of instruction consists of five essential steps:

1. Explanation

2. Demonstration

3. Student performance

4. Instructor supervision

5. Evaluation

(PLT487) — FAA-H-8083-9

FOI

6091-2. Which statement is true concerning computer-based training (CBT)?

A— The instructor need not be actively involved with the students when using instructional aids.
B— CBT may be used by the instructor as stand-alone training.
C— One of the major advantages of CBT is that students can progress at a rate which is comfortable for them.

One of the major advantages of CBT is that students can progress at a rate which is comfortable for them. The students also are often able to access the CBT at their own convenience rather than that of the instructor. (PLT505) — FAA-H-8083-9

FOI

6091-3. Some of the more advanced computer-based training (CBT) applications allow students to progress through a series of interactive segments where the presentation varies as a result of their

A— training.
B— responses.
C— needs.

Some of the more advanced computer-based training (CBT) applications allow students to progress through a series of interactive segments where the presentation varies as a result of their responses. (PLT505) — FAA-H-8083-9

FOI

6091-4. The major advantage of computer-based training (CBT) over other forms of instruction is that it is interactive — the computer responds in different ways, depending on the student's

A— background.
B— input.
C— training.

The major advantage of computer-based training (CBT) over other forms of instruction is that it is interactive—the computer responds in different ways, depending on the student's input. (PLT505) — FAA-H-8083-9

FOI

6091-5. How is learning enhanced by electronic-based learning?

A— Instructors can control what is learned and how fast students learn it.
B— Less time can be spent on instruction compared to traditional classroom training.
C— Peer interaction and personal feedback are limited resulting in a more efficient training program.

Electronic learning or e-learning has become an umbrella term for any type of education that involves an electronic component such as the Internet, a network, a stand-alone computer, CD/DVDs, video conferencing, websites, or e-mail in its delivery. Due to the active nature of e-learning, the overall learning process is enhanced in several ways. Well-designed programs allow students to feel as if they are in control of what they are learning and how fast they learn it. The main advantages are less time spent on instruction compared to traditional classroom training, and higher levels of mastery and retention. (PLT306) — FAA-H-8083-9

Answer (A) is incorrect because instructors may have a more difficult time controlling the learning situation. Answer (C) is incorrect because lack of peer interaction and personal feedback is a disadvantage of e-learning.

FOI

6091-6. What type of training aids are interactive?

A— Interactive video.

B— Web-based instruction with email discussions and assignments.

C— Multi-media presentations.

"Interactive" refers broadly to computer software that responds quickly to certain choices and commands by the user. Interactive training aids include those that directly involve the student in the learning process, including a varying response depending on student input. As a result, each student receives a customized learning experience. (PLT505) — FAA-H-8083-9

Answers (A) and (C) are incorrect because these are passive training aids as they do not change with student input.

FOI

6089. What are the essential steps in the demonstration/performance method of teaching?

A— Demonstration, practice, and evaluation.

B— Demonstration, student performance, and evaluation.

C— Explanation, demonstration, student performance, instructor supervision, and evaluation.

The demonstration/performance method of instruction consists of five essential steps. These are:

1. *Explanation*

2. *Demonstration*

3. *Student performance*

4. *Instructor supervision*

5. *Evaluation*

(PLT487) — FAA-H-8083-9

FOI

6073. The method of arranging lesson material from the simple to complex, past to present, and known to unknown, is one that

A— creates student thought pattern departures.

B— shows the relationships of the main points of the lesson.

C— requires students to actively participate in the lesson.

Each lesson should build on the preceding lessons, and lesson materials should be arranged to go from the simple to the complex, from the past to the present,

and from the known to the unknown. This arrangement shows the relationships of the main points of the lesson. (PLT491) — FAA-H-8083-9

FOI

6071. The proper sequence for the subparts of an introduction is

A— attention, motivation, and overview.

B— attention, development, and overview.

C— overview, motivation, and conclusion.

The introduction of all lessons should include some device to gain the attention of the students, motivation for the students to get and use the material being presented, and an overview to allow the students to check that they have received the information the instructor prepared for them. (PLT491) — FAA-H-8083-9

FOI

6074. When teaching from the known to the unknown, an instructor is using the student's

A— current knowledge of the subject.

B— previous experiences and knowledge.

C— previously held opinions, both valid and invalid.

When instructors teach from the known to the unknown, they build on the student's previous experiences and knowledge. (PLT489) — FAA-H-8083-9

FOI

6072. In organizing lesson material, which step sets the stage for everything to come?

A— Overview.

B— Conclusion.

C— Introduction.

The introduction should establish a common ground between the instructor and the students, and it should capture and hold the attention of the group. It should show how the material to be covered relates to the entire course, and should point out specific benefits the students can expect from learning this material. The introduction should be presented in such a way that it will cause the students to have a receptive attitude toward the subject. (PLT491) — FAA-H-8083-9

Answer (A) is incorrect because the overview includes the material covered during the period of instruction, not how it relates to the entire course. Answer (B) is incorrect because the conclusion includes the important material of the lesson and relates it to the lesson objective, not the entire course.

Answers

| 6091-6 [B] | 6089 [C] | 6073 [B] | 6071 [A] | 6074 [B] | 6072 [C] |

FOI

6075. In developing a lesson, the instructor should organize explanations and demonstrations to help the student

A— achieve the desired learning outcome.
B— acquire a thorough understanding of the material presented.
C— acquire new concepts, generally progressing from the known to the unknown.

In developing a lesson, the instructor's main objective is to organize the explanations and demonstrations to help the student achieve the desired learning outcome. (PLT491) — FAA-H-8083-9

Answer (B) is incorrect because the ability to acquire a thorough understanding of the material presented is dependent on more than the organization of the material. Answer (C) is incorrect because progressing from the known to the unknown shows the relationships of the main points, but is not the intent of developing a lesson.

The Instructor as a Critic

An instructor has the unique responsibility of criticizing the actions of a student in order to help the students evaluate their own performance. A critique is not part of the evaluating process, it is part of the learning process, and is not necessarily negative. A critique considers the positive aspects of the performance as well as the negative.

A **critique** may be either oral, written, or both, and it should come immediately after the student's individual or group performance. At this time, the details of the performance are easy to recall. A critique should improve the student's performance and provide something constructive from which to work, and upon which the student can build. It should provide direction and guidance to raise his or her level of performance. An effective critique should be:

- objective
- flexible
- acceptable
- comprehensive
- constructive
- well organized
- thoughtful
- specific

FOI

6092. Which statement is true about an instructor's critique of a student's performance?

A— Praise for praise's sake is of value.
B— It should be constructive and objective.
C— It should treat every aspect of the performance in detail.

A critique should provide the students with something constructive upon which they can work or build. It should provide direction and guidance to raise their level of performance. (PLT482) — FAA-H-8083-9

Answer (A) is incorrect because praise for praise's sake is of no value. Answer (C) is incorrect because a comprehensive critique is not necessarily a long one, nor must it treat every aspect of the performance in detail.

FOI

6092-1. Which statement is true about an instructor's assessment of a student's performance?

A— Instructor comments and recommendations should be based on the performance as it should have been.
B— The critique should always be conducted in private.
C— It is a step in the learning process, not just in the grading process.

Assessment is an essential and continuous (ongoing) component of the teaching and learning processes. (PLT482) — FAA-H-8083-9

Answer (A) is incorrect because if an assessment is to be objective, it must be honest; it must be based on the performance as it was, not as it could have been. Answer (B) is incorrect because only negative feedback should be restricted to a private exchange.

Answers

6075 [A]	6092 [B]	6092-1 [C]

FOI

6094. When an instructor critiques a student, it should always be

A— done in private.
B— subjective rather than objective.
C— conducted immediately after the student's performance.

For a critique to be most effective, it should be done immediately after the student's performance. The student's actions and the reason for the actions are fresh in his/her mind, and the instructor can identify the areas of weakness. This helps the student to overcome these weaknesses. (PLT482) — FAA-H-8083-9

Answer (A) is incorrect because a critique may be done in private or before the entire class. Answer (B) is incorrect because a critique should be objective.

FOI

6093. Which statement is true about instructors' critiques?

A— Instructors should rely on their personality to make a critique more acceptable.
B— A comprehensive critique should emphasize positive aspects of student performance.
C— Before students willingly accept their instructor's critique, they must first accept the instructor.

An instructor's critique of a student's performance can only be effective when the student accepts the instructor. When instructors do not prepare their lesson material, or when they present it in an unprofessional manner, the students do not respect the instructor, and therefore will not value the critique. (PLT482) — FAA-H-8083-9

Answer (A) is incorrect because an instructor's critique should be based on student performance and not reflect the personality of the instructor. Answer (B) is incorrect because a comprehensive critique should include both the positive and negative aspects of the student's performance.

FOI

6095. An instructor's critique of a student's performance should

A— treat every aspect of the performance in detail.
B— be private so that the student is not embarrassed.
C— provide direction and guidance to improve performance.

The purpose of a critique is to help a student learn, and an effective critique provides direction and guidance to improve performance. (PLT482) — FAA-H-8083-9

Answer (A) is incorrect because the critique should cover the details pertinent to the improvement of the performance, but does not have to treat every aspect in detail. Answer (B) is incorrect because the critique may be done before the entire class if it can be beneficial to everyone.

FOI

6096. Which statement is true about an instructor's critique of a student's performance?

A— Praise for praise's sake is of value.
B— It should be constructive and objective.
C— It should treat every aspect of the performance in detail.

For a critique to be most effective, it must be constructive and objective. (PLT482) — FAA-H-8083-9

Answer (A) is incorrect because praise for praise's sake is of no value to the student's performance. Answer (C) is incorrect because the critique should only cover those aspects of the performance which will benefit future student performance.

FOI

6097. To be effective, a critique should

A— not contain negative remarks.
B— treat every aspect of the performance in detail.
C— be flexible enough to satisfy the requirements of the moment.

An effective critique is not just a criticism. It is an individual, specific, objective, comprehensive, well-organized discussion of the student's performance. To be effective, it must be flexible enough to satisfy the requirements of the moment. (PLT482) — FAA-H-8083-9

Answers

6094 [C]   6093 [C]   6095 [C]   6096 [B]   6097 [C]

Evaluation

The most practical means of evaluation is direct or indirect **oral questioning** of the student. Oral questions can be divided into two categories: fact and thought. Fact questions are based on memory or recall. Thought questions require the student to combine knowledge of facts with the ability to analyze situations, solve problems, and arrive at conclusions.

Some of these desirable results of proper quizzing are as follows: it can reveal the effectiveness of the instructor's training procedures, and check the student's retention of what has been learned. It not only reviews material already covered by the student, but can be used to retain the student's interest and stimulate thinking. Proper oral questioning emphasizes the important points of the training, and identifies points which need more emphasis. Finally, it checks the student's comprehension of what has been learned, and promotes active student participation.

Effective questions used in oral quizzing have some general characteristics. There is only one correct answer to each question, but that answer may be expressed in a variety of ways. The answer should be easily evaluated by the instructor. Effective questions must apply to the subject being taught, and they should be brief, concise, clear, and definite. They must be adapted to the ability, experience, and stage of training of the students. They must center on only one idea; one idea = one question. The questions must present a challenge to the students. They must be difficult for the student at that particular stage of training. And finally, effective questions demand and deserve the use of good English.

Before attempting to answer a student's question, the instructor must clearly understand the question. After the question is answered, the instructor must determine whether or not the student is satisfied with the answer.

The skill of the test writer determines the validity of a written test as an evaluator of a student's knowledge. The characteristics of a good written test are:

- **Reliability.** A written test should yield consistent results each time it is used.

- **Validity.** A written test should actually measure what it is supposed to measure, and nothing else.

- **Usability.** A written test should be easy to give and easy to grade.

- **Comprehensiveness.** A written test should sample liberally whatever is being measured.

- **Discrimination.** A written test should be able to detect small differences: There should be a wide range of scores. All levels of difficulty should be included in the test, and each item should distinguish between the students who are low and those who are high in achievement of the course objectives.

There are two basic types of written tests: **supply-type** and **selection-type** tests. A supply-type test requires the students to organize their knowledge, and demands an ability to express ideas in written form. A supply-type test is valuable for measuring the students' generalized understanding of a subject. The main disadvantage of this type of test is the difficulty and lack of uniformity in grading. The same test graded by different instructors will likely be scored differently. Selection-type tests are highly objective and can be scored the same, regardless of the student taking the test or the person grading it. Selection-type tests, which include multiple-choice and true/false tests, make it possible to directly compare the accomplishment of students within the same or different classes.

True-False tests are well adapted to testing knowledge of facts and details, especially in cases where there are only two possible answers. The chief disadvantage of true-false tests is the probability of the student guessing the answer.

Continued

Multiple-choice tests may be used to determine student achievement, ranging from acquisition of facts to understanding, reasoning, and the ability to apply what has been learned. Multiple-choice tests are appropriate when these conditions exist:

- Test item has a built-in or unique solution.
- Test item is clearly limited by the wording so that the student must choose the best of several offered solutions.
- Test item has several options that are plausible, or even scientifically accurate, but the student is asked to identify the one that is clearly correct. This type of question measures achievement at a high level of learning.
- Test item has several pertinent solutions, and the student is asked to identify the most appropriate solution.

There are three major difficulties encountered in constructing multiple-choice test items. These are:

1. The item stem of the question must be expressed clearly and without ambiguity.
2. The answer must be stated in such a way that it cannot be refuted.
3. The lures, or distracters, must be attractive to those students who do not possess the knowledge or understanding necessary to recognize the correct answer.

FOI
6098-1. Which is a valid reason for the use of proper oral quizzing during a lesson?

A— Promotes active student participation.
B— Identifies points that need less emphasis.
C— Helps the instructor determine the general intelligence level of the students.

A basic premise of learning is that students learn best by doing. For this reason, effectively conducted oral quizzes enhance the learning process by promoting active student participation. (PLT482) — FAA-H-8083-9

Answer (B) is incorrect because proper oral quizzing identifies which points need more emphasis. Answer (C) is incorrect because proper oral quizzing checks comprehension of what has been learned (not the general intelligence level).

FOI
6098-2. Practical tests for pilot certification are

A— evaluation-referenced.
B— norm-referenced.
C— criterion-referenced.

Practical tests for maintenance technicians and pilots are criterion-referenced tests. The practical tests are criterion-referenced because the objective is for all successful applicants to meet the high standards of knowledge, skill, and safety required by the Federal Aviation Regulations. (PLT211) — FAA-H-8083-9

FOI
6124-3. A pretest constructed to measure knowledge and skills necessary to begin a course is referred to as a

A— virtual-reality test.
B— norm-referenced test.
C— criterion-referenced test.

A pretest is a criterion-referenced test constructed to measure the knowledge and skills necessary to begin the course. Pretests also may be used to determine the student's current level of knowledge and skill in relation to the material that will be presented in the course. (PLT211) — FAA-H-8083-9

FOI
6098-3. The objective of the Practical Test Standards (PTS) and Airman Certification Standards (ACS) is to ensure the certification of pilots at a high level of performance and proficiency, consistent with

A— the time available.
B— safety.
C— their abilities.

The purpose of the ACS and PTS is to delineate the standards by which FAA inspectors and designated pilot examiners conduct tests for ratings and certificates. The objective of the ACS and PTS is to ensure the certification of pilots at a high level of performance and proficiency, consistent with safety. (PLT481) — FAA-H-8083-9

Answers

6098-1   [A]   6098-2   [C]   6124-3   [C]   6098-3   [B]

FOI

6098-9. During a flight training course, when is it appropriate to introduce the students to the acceptable standards for passing the practical test?

A— At the beginning of each flight lesson.
B— Not until 3 hours before the practical test preparation instruction required by regulation.
C— During phase/stage check to assess a student's progression at strategic course transitions.

Instructors should not introduce the minimum acceptable standards for passing the check ride when introducing lesson tasks. The minimum standards to pass the check ride should be introduced during the "3 hours of preparation" for the check ride. Keep the PTS in the proper perspective, with increasing emphasis on the Practical Test Standard (PTS) later in the training. (PLT481) — FAA-H-8083-9

FOI

6098-4. The Practical Test Standards and Airman Certification Standards is to be used

A— for flight training only.
B— for flight training and tests.
C— for testing only.

The Practical Test Standards and Airman Certification Standards hold an important position in aviation training curricula because they supply the instructor with specific performance objectives based on the standards that must be met for the issuance of a particular aviation certificate or rating. (PLT270) — FAA-H-8083-9

FOI

6098-5. The Practical Test Standards (PTS) and Airman Certification Standards (ACS) are an example of

A— criterion referenced tests.
B— formative assessments.
C— summative assessments.

The practical tests, defined in the Practical Test Standards (PTS) and Airman Certification Standards (ACS), are criterion referenced because the objective is for all successful applicants to meet the high standards of knowledge, skill, and safety required by the regulations. (PLT270) — FAA-H-8083-9

FOI

6098-6. As a professional pilot, you know that

A— the FAA practical test standards and airman certification standards should only be used for testing purposes.
B— the FAA practical test standards and airman certification standards are objective-based and should be used for training and testing purposes.
C— the FAA practical test standards and airman certification standards are standards-based and should be used as a primary aid to instruction as well as for testing.

These important documents should be used for both training and testing. (PLT270) — FAA-H-8083-9

Answer (A) is incorrect because the PTS and ACS should be used for both training and testing. Answer (C) is incorrect because the PTS and ACS are objective-based.

FOI

6098-7. The FAA practical test standards and airman certification standards

A— are criterion-based and should be used for testing purposes only.
B— are objective-based and should be used for training and testing purposes.
C— are standards-based and contain additional tasks that go beyond those required under 14 CFR Part 61.

These important documents should be used for both training and testing. (PLT270) — FAA-H-8083-9

Answer (A) is incorrect because the PTS should be part of the training process as well as for testing. Answer (C) is incorrect because the PTS and ACS are in accordance with the requirements of 14 CFR Parts 61, 65, 91 and other FAA publications including the AIM, pertinent advisory circulars, and handbooks.

FOI

6098-8. When should an instructor introduce the practical test standards and airman certification standards?

A— During the 3-hour practical exam prep.
B— At instructor's discretion.
C— At the introduction of each new maneuver.

CFIs should encourage each student to learn as much as he or she is capable of and keep raising the bar. When introducing lesson tasks, flight instructors should not introduce the minimum acceptable standards for passing the checkride. The overall focus of flight training should be on education, learning, and understanding why the standards are there and how they were set.

Continued

Answers

6098-9 [B]	6098-4 [B]	6098-5 [A]	6098-6 [B]	6098-7 [B]	6098-8 [A]

The minimum standards to pass the checkride should not be emphasized until the 3 hours of preparation for the checkride. (PLT270) — FAA-H-8083-9

Answers (B) and (C) are incorrect because the Aviation Instructor's Handbook states the PTS and ACS should not be introduced until the 3 hours of preparation for the checkride.

FOI

6101. During oral quizzing in a given lesson, effective questions should

A— be brief and concise.
B— provide answers that can be expressed in a variety of ways.
C— divert the student's thoughts to subjects covered in previous lessons.

To be effective, oral quizzes used during a lesson should be brief and concise. Since oral quizzes are used to check the progress of the learning plan, the questions should be short and require only a few words to answer. The questions should be carefully chosen to show the instructor whether or not the students have an adequate grasp of the material that is being taught. (PLT482) — FAA-H-8083-9

Answer (B) is incorrect because effective oral questions have only one correct answer. Answer (C) is incorrect because effective oral questions must apply to the subject at hand.

FOI

6102. Regarding oral quizzes, what kind of question would be answered based on memory or recall?

A— A fact question.
B— A provocative question.
C— A thought question.

The answer to a fact question is based on memory or recall. This type of question usually concerns who, what, when, and where. (PLT482) — FAA-H-8083-9

FOI

6099. Proper oral quizzing by the instructor during a lesson can have which result?

A— Promotes effective use of available time.
B— Identifies points which need more emphasis.
C— Permits the introduction of new material not covered previously.

The main reason for quizzing a student during a lesson is to identify any points or areas that need more emphasis. (PLT482) — FAA-H-8083-9

Answer (A) is incorrect because lesson plans promote effective use of available time. Answer (C) is incorrect because the introduction of new material not covered previously should be done in the presentation step of the teaching process.

FOI

6100. One desirable result of proper oral quizzing by the instructor is to

A— reveal the effectiveness of the instructor's training procedures.
B— fulfill the requirements set forth in the overall objectives of the course.
C— reveal the essential information from which the student can determine progress.

One desirable result of an oral quiz is to reveal to the instructor the effectiveness of his/her training procedures. (PLT482) — FAA-H-8083-9

Answer (B) is incorrect because quizzing is a measure of progress toward, not the fulfillment of, objectives of the course. Answer (C) is incorrect because this is what a critique does.

FOI

6103. To be effective in oral quizzing during the conduct of a lesson, a question should

A— be of suitable difficulty for that stage of training.
B— include a combination of where, how, and why.
C— divert the student's thoughts to subjects covered in other lessons.

Effective questions used in oral quizzing must be adapted to the ability, experience, and stage of training of the students. (PLT482) — FAA-H-8083-9

Answer (B) is incorrect because effective questions should not include a combination, but be limited to who, what, when, where, how, or why. Answer (C) is incorrect because effective questions should focus on the subject at hand.

FOI

6103-1. The most common means of assessment is

A— indirect or direct oral questioning of the student by the instructor.
B— written testing.
C— authentic.

The most common means of assessment is direct or indirect oral questioning of students by the instructor. These questions can be either fact-based or involve high-order thinking skills (or, HOTS). The answer to a fact question is based on memory or recall of who, what, when, and where. HOTS questions involve why or how, and require the student to combine knowledge of facts with an ability to analyze situations, solve problems, and arrive at conclusions. (PLT482) — FAA-H-8083-9

Answers

| 6101 [A] | 6102 [A] | 6099 [B] | 6100 [A] | 6103 [A] | 6103-1 [A] |

FOI

6103-2. Criterion-referenced tests

A— include norm-based objectives.
B— include performance-based objectives.
C— are subjective.

In criterion-referenced testing, students are graded against a carefully written, measurable standard or criterion rather than against each other. This includes defined performance-based objectives. (PLT482) — FAA-H-8083-9

FOI

6103-3. What are the desirable results of oral quizzing?

A— Identifies points that need more emphasis.
B— Provides medium to test a combination of ideas in one question.
C— A solid yes/no response to ensure the knowledge is complete.

Proper quizzing by the instructor can have a number of desirable results: reveals the effectiveness of the instructor's training methods; checks student retention of what has been learned; reviews material already presented to the student; can be used to retain student interest and stimulate thinking; emphasizes the important points of training; identifies points that need more emphasis; checks student comprehension of what has been learned; and promotes active student participation, which is important to effective learning. (PLT306) — FAA-H-8083-9

Answer (B) is incorrect because oral questioning should center on only one idea, not a combination. Answer (C) is incorrect because effective oral quizzing should not include yes/no questions.

FOI

6103-4. During oral quizzing in a given lesson, effective questions should

A— start with why, how, what, where, when, or a combination of these.
B— should be related to the desired outcome of the lesson.
C— be brief and concise.

To be effective, questions must be brief and concise. (PLT482) — FAA-H-8083-9

Answer (A) is incorrect because questions should center on only one idea and not a combination. Answer (B) is incorrect because questions should apply to the subject of the instruction but may not be directly related to the desired lesson outcome.

FOI

6104. To answer a student's question, it is most important that the instructor

A— clearly understand the question.
B— have complete knowledge of the subject.
C— introduce more complicated information to partially answer the question, if necessary.

It is important that an instructor clearly understand a student's question before he/she attempts to answer it. The instructor must be sure that the question is completely answered to the satisfaction of the student. (PLT482) — FAA-H-8083-9

Answer (B) is incorrect because instructors will not have complete knowledge of all subjects, but can use resources to track down the correct answer. Answer (C) is incorrect because introducing more complicated information to partially answer the question will cause confusion and frustration.

FOI

6110. Which type of test item creates the greatest probability of guessing?

A— True-false.
B— Supply-type.
C— Multiple choice.

Since there are only two possible choices for the correct answer to a true/false question, this type of question provides the student the greatest temptation to guess the answer. (PLT482) — FAA-H-8083-9

FOI

6111. Which is the main disadvantage of supply-type test items?

A— They cannot be graded with uniformity.
B— They are readily answered by guessing.
C— They are easily adapted to statistical analysis.

Essay questions (supply-type questions) are used to measure the generalized understanding of a subject. The main disadvantage is the difficulty of grading them with uniformity. (PLT482) — FAA-H-8083-9

Answer (B) is incorrect because true/false tests are readily answered by guessing. Answer (C) is incorrect because selection-type tests are easily adapted to statistical analysis.

Answers

6103-2 [B]	6103-3 [A]	6103-4 [C]	6104 [A]	6110 [A]	6111 [A]

FOI

6107. The characteristic of a written test, which measures small differences in achievement between students, is its

A— validity.
B— reliability.
C— discrimination.

Discrimination is the characteristic of a written test that measures small differences in achievement between students. (PLT482) — FAA-H-8083-9

Answer (A) is incorrect because validity refers to when a written test measures what it is supposed to and nothing else. Answer (B) is incorrect because reliability refers to when a written test yields consistent results.

FOI

6105. A written test has validity when it

A— yields consistent results.
B— samples liberally whatever is being measured.
C— measures what it is supposed to measure.

The validity of a written test is its ability to measure what it is supposed to measure. (PLT482) — FAA-H-8083-9

Answer (A) is incorrect because reliability refers to when a test yields consistent results. Answer (B) is incorrect because comprehensiveness means that a test samples liberally whatever is being measured.

FOI

6117. In a written test, which type of selection-type test items reduces the probability of guessing correct responses?

A— Essay.
B— Matching.
C— Multiple-choice.

Matching-type test items are particularly good for measuring students' ability to recognize relationships and make associations. In addition, as compared to multiple-choice type questions, they reduce the probability of guessing correct responses. (PLT482) — FAA-H-8083-9

Answer (A) is incorrect because essay questions are a supply-type test item. Answer (C) is incorrect because multiple-choice questions do not reduce the probability of guessing correct responses as much as matching-type test items can.

FOI

6112. What is a characteristic of supply-type test items?

A— They are easily adapted to testing of knowledge facts and details.
B— Test results would be graded the same regardless of the student or the grader.
C— The same test graded by different instructors would probably be given different scores.

One main problem with supply-type (essay) test items is the difficulty of uniform grading. If the same test is graded by different instructors, the scores will probably be different. (PLT482) — FAA-H-8083-9

Answer (A) is incorrect because this is a characteristic of true-false tests. Answer (B) is incorrect because this is a characteristic of selection-type tests.

FOI

6108. A written test having the characteristic of discrimination will

A— be easy to give and easily graded.
B— include a representative and comprehensive sampling of the course objectives.
C— distinguish between students both low and high in achievement.

Discrimination is the degree to which a test distinguishes the difference between students. When a test is constructed to have the characteristic of discrimination it will have three features:

1. *There is a wide range of scores.*

2. *All levels of difficulty are included.*

3. *Each item distinguishes between the students who are low and those who are high in achievement of the course objectives.*

(PLT482) — FAA-H-8083-9

FOI

6109. A written test is said to be comprehensive when it

A— includes all levels of difficulty.
B— samples liberally whatever is being measured.
C— measures knowledge of the same topic in many different ways.

A comprehensive test is one that liberally samples whatever it is that is being measured. (PLT482) — FAA-H-8083-9

Answers (A) and (C) are incorrect because a test shows discrimination when it includes all levels of difficulty and measures knowledge of the same topic in many different ways.

Answers

6107 [C]	6105 [C]	6117 [B]	6112 [C]	6108 [C]	6109 [B]

FOI

6106. A written test that has reliability

A— yields consistent results.
B— measures small differences in the achievement of students.
C— actually measures what it is supposed to measure and nothing else.

A written test that produces consistent results has reliability. (PLT482) — FAA-H-8083-9

Answer (B) is incorrect because a written test that measures small differences in the achievement of students shows discrimination. Answer (C) is incorrect because this demonstrates the validity, not the reliability, of the test.

FOI

6113. One of the main advantages of selection-type test items over supply-type test items is that the selection-type

A— decreases discrimination between responses.
B— would be graded objectively regardless of the student or the grader.
C— precludes comparison of students under one instructor with those under another instructor.

The main reason selection-type (multiple-choice) tests are used rather than supply-type (essay) tests is that multiple-choice tests can be graded objectively regardless of the student or the grader. (PLT482) — FAA-H-8083-9

Answer (A) is incorrect because selection-type test items increase discrimination between responses. Answer (C) is incorrect because with selection-type test items, you can compare students under one instructor with those under another instructor.

FOI

6116. Which statement is true relative to effective multiple-choice test items?

A— Negative words or phrases need not be emphasized.
B— Items should call for abstract background knowledge.
C— Keep all alternatives of approximately equal length.

When making up a multiple-choice test, instructors should try to keep all of the alternatives to approximately the same length. This helps discourage guessing. (PLT482) — FAA-H-8083-9

Answer (A) is incorrect because negative words or phrases should be emphasized, as they are easy to skip over while reading during a test. Answer (B) is incorrect because items should call for essential knowledge.

FOI

6114. Which is one of the major difficulties encountered in the construction of multiple-choice test items?

A— Adapting the items to statistical item analysis.
B— Keeping all responses approximately equal in length.
C— Inventing distractors which will be attractive to students lacking knowledge or understanding.

One of the hardest things about making a good multiple-choice test is inventing distractors which will be attractive to students who lack knowledge or understanding. All distractors should be logical, and they should appear to be correct to one who lacks knowledge, but they should be definitely wrong. A distractor should not be correct under any condition at all. (PLT482) — FAA-H-8083-9

FOI

6115. Which statement is true about multiple-choice test items that are intended to measure achievement at a higher level of learning?

A— It is unethical to mislead students into selecting an incorrect alternative.
B— Some or all of the alternatives should be acceptable but only one should be clearly better than the others.
C— The use of common errors as distracting alternatives to divert the student from the correct response is ineffective and invalid.

Multiple-choice test items that are designed to measure achievement at a higher level of learning should have some alternatives that are nearly correct, but only one that is clearly correct. (PLT482) — FAA-H-8083-9

Answer (A) is incorrect because it is not unethical to mislead students into selecting an incorrect alternative, but only one answer should be clearly correct. Answer (C) is incorrect because this is an effective and valid method of discouraging students from guessing the answers.

FOI

6118. Which type test is desirable for evaluating training that involves an operation, procedure, or process?

A— Oral.
B— Performance.
C— Proficiency.

A performance test is the best type for evaluating training that involves an operation, procedure, or process. A performance test involves the actual performance of an operation. (PLT482) — FAA-H-8083-9

Answers

6106 [A]   6113 [B]   6116 [C]   6114 [C]   6115 [B]   6118 [B]

Instructional Aids

Instructional aids are used to secure and hold the attention of the students. When properly used, they enhance learning, but it is extremely easy to misuse them. These guidelines will help prevent misuse of instructional aids:

1. Clearly establish the lesson objective before deciding on the use of instructional aids.

2. Gather the necessary data by researching the available support material.

3. Organize the material into an outline or lesson plan that includes all key points to be presented.

4. The instructional aids should be chosen only after all the previous steps are complete. The aids should concentrate on the key points.

Instructional aids should be simple and compatible with the learning outcomes to be achieved. They should never be used by the instructor as a crutch.

FOI

6119. Which is a true statement concerning the use of instructional aids?

A— Instructional aids should be designed to cover the key points in a lesson.
B— Instructional aids ensure getting and holding the student's attention.
C— Instructional aids should not be used simply to cover a subject in less time.

Instructional aids are devices that assist an instructor in the teaching–learning process. They should be designed to cover the key points and concepts. (PLT504) — FAA-H-8083-9

FOI

6120. Instructional aids used in the teaching/learning process should be

A— self-supporting and require no explanation.
B— compatible with the learning outcomes to be achieved.
C— selected prior to developing and organizing the lesson plan.

All instructional aids used in the teaching/learning process should be simple and should be compatible with the learning outcomes that are to be achieved. (PLT505) — FAA-H-8083-9

Answer (A) is incorrect because instructional aids are not self-supporting and will require explanation. Answer (C) is incorrect because instructional aids should be chosen after developing and organizing the lesson plan.

FOI

6121. Instructional aids used in the teaching/learning process should not be used

A— as a crutch by the instructor.
B— for teaching more in less time.
C— to visualize relationships between abstracts.

It is important that an instructor not use instructional aids as a crutch. There are no instructional aids that can replace careful lesson preparation by an instructor. (PLT505) — FAA-H-8083-9

FOI

6122. The use of instructional aids should be based on their ability to support a specific point in the lesson. What is the first step in determining if and where instructional aids are necessary?

A— Organize subject material into an outline or a lesson plan.
B— Determine what ideas should be supported with instructional aids.
C— Clearly establish the lesson objective, being certain what must be communicated.

Instructional aids should not be chosen until the lesson objectives are clearly established. When the instructor knows exactly what is to be communicated to the student, then instructional aids that support specific points in the lesson can be chosen. (PLT505) — FAA-H-8083-9

Answers

6119　[A]　　　　6120　[B]　　　　6121　[A]　　　　6122　[C]

FOI

6122-1. A disadvantage of using commercially produced study material is that

A— students may learn to pass a given test.
B— students use rote learning to remember key knowledge.
C— students often exhibit a lack of knowledge during oral questioning.

Test preparation materials are effective in preparing students for FAA tests. However, students relying on study materials as the exclusive source of study may learn to pass a given test, but fail to learn other critical information essential to safe piloting and maintenance practices. In addition, FAA inspectors and designated examiners have found student applicants sometimes exhibit a lack of knowledge during oral questioning, even though they excelled on the FAA knowledge test. Test preparation materials emphasize rote learning, which is one element of learning, but does not provide comprehensive training. Test preparation publications are not designed as stand-alone learning tools. They should supplement instructor-led training and other ground training resources. (PLT482) — FAA-H-8083-9

FOI

6122-2. Computer-assisted learning (CAL)

A— eliminates the need for instructor-led training.
B— encourages rote learning.
C— couples the personal computer with multimedia software to create a training device.

CAL is the combination of a PC and multimedia software, as a training device. When using CAL, the instructor should remain actively involved with the students by using close supervision, questions, examinations, quizzes, or guided discussions on the subject matter to constantly assess student progress. (PLT482) — FAA-H-8083-9

FOI

6122-3. Commercially-developed test preparation material

A— replaces instructor-led training.
B— teaches higher-order thinking skills.
C— places emphasis on rote learning over the more advanced learning levels.

Test preparation publications are not designed as stand-alone learning tools. They should be considered as a supplement to instructor-led training or comprehensive ground school. Question and answer study aids emphasize rote learning over the more advanced learning levels or higher-order thinking skills (HOTS). (PLT505) — FAA-H-8083-9

FOI

6122-4. Which of the following is true concerning the use of instructional aids?

A— Instructional aids often fail to evoke the image of the symbol in the minds of the receivers.
B— Instructional aids can lead to confusion between the symbol and idea.
C— Instructional aids can be used to show the physical relationship between material objects or concepts.

Another use for instructional aids is to clarify the relationships between material objects and concepts. When relationships are presented visually, they often are much easier to understand. (PLT505) — FAA-H-8083-9

Answer (A) is incorrect because this is often the result of poor communication or word choice. Answer (B) is incorrect because good instructional aids should clarify the symbol and idea.

FOI

6122-5. Commercially-developed test preparation material is

A— FAA approved for knowledge tests only.
B— designed to be used as a stand-alone method of study.
C— intended to be used as a supplement to instructor-led training and materials.

Test preparation publications are not designed as stand-alone learning tools. They should be considered as a supplement to instructor-led training or comprehensive ground school. (PLT505) — FAA-H-8083-9

Answers

| 6122-1 | [C] | 6122-2 | [C] | 6122-3 | [C] | 6122-4 | [C] | 6122-5 | [C] |

Flight Instructor Characteristics and Responsibilities

The requirements for a flight instructor include **professionalism** which relates to the instructor's public image. The characteristics of an instructor's professionalism include:

1. **Sincerity.** Any facade of instructor pretentiousness, whether it be real or mistakenly assumed by the student, will immediately cause the student to lose confidence in the instructor, and little learning will be accomplished. Anything less than sincere performance destroys the effectiveness of the professional instructor.

2. **Acceptance of the student.** The professional relationship between the instructor and the student should be based on a mutual acknowledgment that both the student and the instructor are important to each other, and both are working toward the same objectives. Under no circumstances should an instructor do anything which implies degradation of the student.

3. **Personal appearance and habits.** A flight instructor who is rude, thoughtless, and inattentive cannot hold the respect of the students, regardless of his/her piloting ability.

4. **Demeanor.** The instructor should avoid erratic movements, distracting speech habits, and capricious changes in mood.

5. **Safety practices and accident prevention.** A flight instructor must meticulously observe all regulations and recognized safety practices during all flight operations.

6. **Proper language.** The use of profanity and obscene language leads to distrust, or at best, to a lack of complete confidence.

7. **Self-improvement.** Professional flight instructors must never become complacent or satisfied with their own qualifications and ability.

An effective instructor maintains a high level of student motivation by making each lesson a pleasurable experience. The instructor must realize that people are not always attracted to something because it is easy. Most people will devote the required effort to things which bring such rewards as self-enhancement and personal satisfaction.

The instructor should make learning to fly interesting by keeping the students apprised of the course and lesson objectives. Not knowing the objectives leads the student to confusion, disinterest, and uneasiness. The instructor should guide the students in exploration and experimentation, to help them develop their own capabilities and self-confidence.

For instruction to produce the desired results, an instructor must carefully and correctly analyze the personality, thinking, and ability of each student. Students who have been incorrectly analyzed as slow thinkers may actually be quick thinkers, but act slowly or at the wrong time because of lack of confidence. Slow students can often be helped by assigning subgoals which are more easily attainable than the normal learning goals. This allows the student to practice elements of the task until confidence and ability is gained.

Apt students also create problems. Because they make less mistakes, they may assume that the correction of errors is unimportant. Such overconfidence results in faulty performance. A good instructor will constantly raise the standard of performance demanded of apt students and will demand greater effort.

Flight instructors fail to provide competent instruction when they permit their students to get by with a substandard performance, or without learning thoroughly some item of knowledge pertinent to safe piloting. The positive approach to flight instruction points out to the student the pleasurable features of aviation before the unpleasant possibilities are discussed. One example of a positive approach is to include in the first instructional flight a normal round-trip flight to a nearby airport.

Anxiety, or fear, is probably the most significant psychological factor affecting flight instruction. The responses to anxiety vary greatly, ranging from hesitancy to act, to the impulse "to do something even if it's wrong." Some students may freeze in place and do nothing, while others may do unusual things without rational thought or reason. Normal reaction to anxiety can be countered by reinforcing the student's enjoyment of flying, and by teaching them to treat fear as a normal reaction rather than ignoring it. Normal individuals react to stress by responding rapidly and exactly, within the limits of their experience and training. Abnormal reactions to stress are evidenced by:

- Autonomic responses, such as sweating, rapid heart rate, paleness, etc.

- Inappropriate reactions, such as extreme overcooperation, painstaking self-control; inappropriate laughter or singing, very rapid changes in emotions, and motion sickness under stress

- Marked changes in mood on different lessons, such as excellent morale followed by deep depression

- Severe anger at the flight instructor, service personnel, or others.

FOI

6123-1. Which statement is true regarding true professionalism as an instructor?

A— Anything less than sincere performance destroys the effectiveness of the professional instructor.
B— To achieve professionalism, actions and decisions must be limited to standard patterns and practices.
C— A single definition of professionalism would encompass all of the qualifications and considerations which must be present.

The professionalism of an instructor is based on straightforwardness and honesty. Anything less than sincere performance destroys the effectiveness of the professional instructor. When a student loses confidence in his or her instructor, little learning will be accomplished. (PLT229) — FAA-H-8083-9

Answer (B) is incorrect because professionalism requires good judgment and cannot be limited to standard patterns and practices. Answer (C) is incorrect because professionalism cannot be encompassed by a single definition.

FOI

6123-2. Aviation instructors should be constantly alert for ways to improve the services they provide to their students, their effectiveness, and their

A— appearance.
B— qualifications.
C— demeanor.

Professional aviation instructors must never become complacent or satisfied with their own qualifications and abilities. They should be constantly alert for ways to improve their qualifications, effectiveness, and the services they provide to students. (PLT229) — FAA-H-8083-9

FOI

6123-3. True performance as a professional is based on study and

A— perseverance.
B— research.
C— attitude.

Included in the definition of professionalism, true performance as a professional is based on study and research. (PLT229) — FAA-H-8083-9

FOI

6124-1. An instructor can most effectively maintain a high level of student motivation by

A— making each lesson a pleasurable experience.
B— relaxing the standards of performance required during the early phase of training.
C— continually challenging the student to meet the highest objectives of training that can be established.

Student motivation can be kept at a high level by making each lesson a pleasurable experience. (PLT490) — FAA-H-8083-9

Answer (B) is incorrect because relaxing the standards will reduce student motivation. Answer (C) is incorrect because performance standards must be based on the individual students' potential.

Answers

6123-1   [A]   6123-2   [B]   6123-3   [B]   6124-1   [A]

FOI

6124-2. Confusion, disinterest, and uneasiness on the part of the student could happen as a result of not knowing the

A— importance of each period of instruction.
B— objective of each period of instruction.
C— subject of each period of instruction.

Students feel insecure when they do not know what is expected of them or what is going to happen to them. Instructors can minimize feelings of insecurity by telling students the objective of each period of instruction. (PLT211) — FAA-H-8083-9

FOI

6126. What should an instructor do with a student who assumes that correction of errors is unimportant?

A— Divide complex flight maneuvers into elements.
B— Try to reduce the student's overconfidence to reduce the chance of an accident.
C— Raise the standard of performance for each lesson, demanding greater effort.

Apt students can be a challenge to an instructor. Because they make less mistakes, they may assume that the correction of errors is unimportant. When dealing with this type of student, the instructor should raise the standard of performance for each lesson, demanding greater effort. (PLT232) — FAA-H-8083-9

Answer (A) is incorrect because this is a method to teach students whose slow progress is due to a lack of confidence, not for the overconfident student. Answer (B) is incorrect because reducing the student's overconfidence will not provide motivation for the student.

FOI

6127. Which statement is true regarding the achievement of an adequate standard of performance?

A— A flight instructor should devote major effort and attention to the continuous evaluation of student performance.
B— Flight instructors can affect a genuine improvement in the student/instructor relationship by not strictly enforcing standards.
C— Flight instructors fail to provide competent instruction when they permit students to partially learn an important item of knowledge or skill.

Students normally achieve more when high standards are expected of them. Flight instructors fail to provide competent instruction when they accept substandard performance or permit their students to only partially learn an important item of knowledge or skill. (PLT211) — FAA-H-8083-9

Answer (A) is incorrect because instructors should devote major effort and attention to all areas of the teaching process. Answer (B) is incorrect because instructors must strictly enforce standards to have a genuine affect on student performance.

FOI

6128. Which statement is true regarding positive or negative approaches in aviation instructional techniques?

A— A student with normal abilities should not be affected by an instructor who emphasizes emergency procedures early in training.
B— A positive approach, to be effective, will point out the pleasurable features of aviation before the unpleasant possibilities are discussed.
C— The introduction of emergency procedures before the student is acquainted with normal operations is likely to be neither discouraging nor affect learning.

Students learn best from positive motivations. To be effective, a positive approach will point out the pleasurable features of aviation before the unpleasant possibilities are discussed. (PLT230) — FAA-H-8083-9

Answers (A) and (C) are incorrect because introducing emergency procedures early in training will have a negative effect, regardless of the student's abilities.

FOI

6129-1. Which is an example of a positive approach in the first flight lesson of a student with no previous aviation experience?

A— Conducting a thorough preflight.
B— A normal flight to a nearby airport and return.
C— Instruction in the care which must be taken when taxiing an airplane.

An example of a positive approach to learning is a first flight which consists of a normal round-trip to a nearby airport. Emphasis should be placed on the ease and enjoyment of the flight. (PLT232) — FAA-H-8083-9

Answers (A) and (C) are incorrect because a thorough preflight and lesson on taxiing an airplane are examples of a negative approach.

Answers

6124-2 [B]	6126 [C]	6127 [C]	6128 [B]	6129-1 [B]

FOI

6129-2. Evaluation of demonstrated ability during flight instruction must be based upon

A— the instructor's background and experience relating to student pilots at this stage of training.
B— the progress of the student, considering the time and experience attained since beginning training.
C— established standards of performance, suitably modified to apply to the student's experience.

Evaluation of demonstrated ability during flight instruction must be based upon established standards of performance, suitably modified to apply to the student's experience and stage of development as a pilot. The evaluation must consider the student's mastery of the elements involved in the maneuver, rather than merely the overall performance. (PLT211) — FAA-H-8083-9

FOI

6129-3. Evaluation of demonstrated ability during flight instruction must be based upon

A— the progress of the student.
B— the instructor's opinion concerning the maneuver(s).
C— established standards of performance.

Evaluation of demonstrated ability during flight instruction must be based upon established standards of performance, suitably modified to apply to the student's experience and stage of development as a pilot. The evaluation must consider the student's mastery of the elements involved in the maneuver, rather than merely the overall performance. (PLT211) — FAA-H-8083-9

FOI

6129-4. In evaluating student demonstrations of piloting ability, it is important for the flight instructor to

A— remain silent and observe.
B— keep the student informed of progress.
C— explain errors in performance immediately.

In evaluating student demonstrations of piloting ability, it is important for the flight instructor to keep the student informed of progress. This may be done as each procedure or maneuver is completed or summarized during postflight critiques. (PLT230) — FAA-H-8083-9

FOI

6129-5. The student should be capable of handling problems that might occur, such as traffic pattern congestion, change in active runway, or unexpected crosswinds prior to

A— the first solo cross-country flight.
B— initial solo.
C— being recommended for a Recreational or Private Pilot Certificate.

Before endorsing a student for solo flight, the instructor should require the student to demonstrate consistent ability to perform all of the fundamental maneuvers. The student should also be capable of handling ordinary problems that might occur, such as traffic pattern congestion, change in active runway, or unexpected crosswinds. (PLT230) — FAA-H-8083-9

FOI

6129-6. Before endorsing a student for solo flight, the instructor should require the student to demonstrate consistent ability to perform

A— all maneuvers specified in the Student Pilot Guide.
B— all of the fundamental maneuvers.
C— slow flight, stalls, emergency landings, takeoffs and landings, and go-arounds.

Before endorsing a student for solo flight, the instructor should require the student to demonstrate consistent ability to perform all of the fundamental maneuvers. The student should also be capable of handling ordinary problems that might occur, such as traffic pattern congestion, change in active runway, or unexpected crosswinds. (PLT230) — FAA-H-8083-9

FOI

6129-7. Examples of all common endorsements can be found in the current issue of

A— AC 61-67, Appendix 1.
B— AC 91-67, Appendix 1.
C— AC 61-65, Appendix 1.

Examples of all common endorsements can be found in the current issue of AC 61-65, Certification: Pilots and Flight Instructors, Appendix 1. (PLT230) — FAA-H-8083-9

Answers

6129-2 [C]   6129-3 [C]   6129-4 [B]   6129-5 [B]   6129-6 [B]   6129-7 [C]

FOI

6129-8. Which type of assessment is desirable for evaluating a student's ability to use critical thinking skills in performing real-world tasks?

A— Authentic assessment.
B— Traditional assessment.
C— Practical assessment.

Authentic assessment requires the student to demonstrate not just rote and understanding, but also the application and correlation levels of learning. Authentic assessment generally requires the student to perform real-world tasks, and demonstrate a meaningful application of skills and competencies. (PLT230) — FAA-H-8083-9

Answer (B) is incorrect because traditional assessment involves written testing (e.g., multiple choice, matching) and grading. Answer (C) is incorrect because this is not one of the types of assessment.

FOI

6129-9. Which statement is true regarding assessment of student learning?

A— Assessment should be a formal process and results recorded so the students are continually aware of their progress.
B— Assessment of student learning should be an integral part of each lesson.
C— If deficiencies or faults not associated with the present lesson are revealed, they should be corrected immediately.

Summative assessments are used periodically throughout the training to measure how well learning has progressed to that point. For example, a chapter quiz or an end-of-course test can measure the student's overall mastery of the training. These assessments are an integral part of the lesson, as well as the course of training. (PLT230) — FAA-H-8083-9

Answer (A) is incorrect because assessments can be both formal or informal. Answer (C) is incorrect because while it's important to identify weaknesses, it may not be appropriate to address all faults until the student is ready to start that lesson.

FOI

6129-10. What type of assessment focuses on real-world skills?

A— Collaborative.
B— Authentic.
C— Traditional.

By using open-ended questions and established performance criteria, authentic assessment focuses on the learning process, enhances the development of real-world skills, encourages higher order thinking skills (HOTS), and teaches students to assess their own work and performance. (PLT230) — FAA-H-8083-9

FOI

6125. Faulty performance due to student overconfidence should be corrected by

A— increasing the standard of performance for each lesson.
B— praising the student only when the performance is perfect.
C— providing strong, negative evaluation at the end of each lesson.

Overconfidence can be controlled in many students by increasing the standard of performance required for each lesson. (PLT232) — FAA-H-8083-9

Answers (B) and (C) are incorrect because students need consistent, fair evaluations.

FOI

6130. When under stress, normal individuals usually react

A— by showing excellent morale followed by deep depression.
B— by responding rapidly and exactly, often automatically, within the limits of their experience and training.
C— inappropriately such as extreme overcooperation, painstaking self-control, and inappropriate laughing or singing.

When under stress, normal individuals begin to respond rapidly and exactly, within the limits of their experience and training. (PLT231) — FAA-H-8083-9

Answers

6129-8 [A]	6129-9 [B]	6129-10 [B]	6125 [A]	6130 [B]

FOI

6131. One possible indication of a student's abnormal reaction to stress would be

A— a hesitancy to act.
B— extreme overcooperation.
C— a noticeable lack of self-control.

Abnormal reactions to stress often show up as extreme overcooperation, painstaking self-control, inappropriate laughter or singing, rapid changes in emotions, and motion sickness. (PLT231) — FAA-H-8083-9

Answer (A) is incorrect because a hesitancy to act is an indication of anxiety. Answer (C) is incorrect because a noticeable lack of self-control is a normal reaction to stress.

FOI

6132. The instructor can counteract anxiety in students by

A— teaching students to cope with their fears.
B— avoiding anxiety-causing lessons.
C— explaining how these maneuvers are necessary for safe flight.

Anxiety can be countered by reinforcing the students' enjoyment of flying and by teaching them to cope with their fears. (PLT231) — FAA-H-8083-9

Answers (B) is incorrect because this will not aid students in overcoming anxiety. Answer (C) is incorrect because an explanation may not aid students in overcoming anxiety; they may instead need to be able to cope with their fears.

FOI

6132-1. An instructor can help a student cope with fear or anxiety by

A— emphasizing the benefits and pleasurable experiences from flying.
B— discontinuing the lesson or maneuver and moving them to another part of the curriculum.
C— repeating the lesson or maneuver until the anxiety goes away.

Anxiety can be countered by reinforcing the students' enjoyment of flying and by teaching them to cope with their fears. Student anxiety can be minimized throughout training by emphasizing the benefits and pleasurable experiences that can be derived from flying, rather than by continuously citing the unhappy consequences of faulty performances. (PLT231) — FAA-H-8083-9

FOI

6133. How does a student who is responding abnormally react to stress?

A— Inadequate or completely absent response.
B— By responding rapidly and exactly often automatically within the limits of their experience.
C— Slow learning.

Reactions to stress may produce abnormal responses in some people. With them, response to anxiety or stress may be completely absent or at least inadequate. Their responses may be random or illogical, or they may do more than is called for by the situation. (PLT231) — FAA-H-8083-9

Answer (B) and (C) are incorrect because these both describe normal reactions to stress.

FOI

6133-1. Which would most likely be an indication that a student is reacting normally to stress?

A— Slow learning.
B— Inappropriate laughter or singing.
C— Automatic response to a given situation.

When dealing with stress, normal individuals begin to respond rapidly and exactly, within the limits of their experience and training. Many responses are automatic, highlighting the need for proper training in emergency operations prior to an actual emergency. The affected individual thinks rationally, acts rapidly, and is extremely sensitive to all aspects of the surroundings. (PLT231) — FAA-H-8083-9

Answers

6131 **[B]**	6132 **[A]**	6132-1 **[A]**	6133 **[A]**	6133-1 **[C]**

FOI

6133-2. A student demonstrates a specific flight maneuver correctly; however, the instructor believes the student does not understand the fundamentals of the maneuver. What should the instructor do?

A— Ask the student to orally explain the maneuver.
B— Ask the student to demonstrate a different maneuver which uses the same fundamentals.
C— Ask the student to demonstrate the same maneuver again.

Students may perform a procedure or maneuver correctly but not fully understand the principles and objectives involved. If the instructor suspects this, students should be required to vary the performance of the maneuver or procedure slightly. The maneuver or procedure may also be combined with other operations, or the same elements could be applied to the performance of other maneuvers or procedures. Students who do not understand the principles involved will probably not be able to successfully complete the revised maneuver or procedure. (PLT491) — FAA-H-8083-9

FOI

6133-3. Which of the following is a risk element of ADM?

A— The aircraft.
B— The amount of fuel on board.
C— Any passengers.

*During each flight, decisions must be made regarding events involving interactions between the four risk elements—**P**ilot-in-command, **A**ircraft, en**V**ironment, and **E**xternal pressures. The four risk elements can be remembered with the acronym PAVE. (PLT231) — FAA-H-8083-9*

Answer (B) and (C) are incorrect because while these are important risk factors, they are not part of the ADM mnemonic device PAVE this question is asking about.

FOI

6133-4. If a pilot wants to mitigate risk during a cross-country flight in marginal VFR conditions, the pilot could

A— take a pilot who is IFR-rated.
B— continue the flight as planned.
C— stay out of controlled airspace.

Risk assessment is only part of the equation. After determining the level of risk, the pilot needs to mitigate the risk. For example, the pilot flying a cross-country in MVFR conditions has several ways to reduce risk: wait for the weather to improve to good visual flight rules (VFR) conditions; take a pilot who is rated as an IFR pilot; delay the flight; cancel the flight; or drive. (PLT231) — FAA-H-8083-9

Answer (B) is incorrect because this would be accepting the risk, not mitigating it. Answer (C) is incorrect because this could potentially increase risk, not mitigate it.

FOI

6133-5. A pilot's experience in direct crosswinds greater than 10 knots is an example of which of the fundamental risk elements?

A— The aircraft.
B— The pilot in command.
C— The external pressures.

The pilot is one of the risk factors in a flight. The pilot must ask, "Am I ready for this trip?" in terms of experience, currency, physical and emotional condition. (PLT231) — FAA-H-8083-9

Answer (A) and (C) are incorrect because while these are both part of the PAVE risk elements, they are not related to the pilot's experience with crosswinds.

Answers

6133-2 [B]   6133-3 [A]   6133-4 [A]   6133-5 [B]

Techniques of Flight Instruction

Flight instruction is normally done by the **demonstration/performance** method. The steps in this method of instruction are:

1. Instructor tells — instructor does.

2. Student tells — instructor does.

3. Student tells — student does.

4. Student does — instructor evaluates.

Integrated flight instruction is when students are taught to perform flight maneuvers, from the first time each maneuver is introduced, by both outside visual references and reference to the flight instruments. The first instruction on the function of the flight controls includes the expected instrument indications as well as the outside references used in attitude control. The objective of integrated flight instruction is to help the student form firm habits of observing and relying on flight instruments from his/her very first piloting experience. It is important that the students develop, from the start of their training, the habit of looking for other air traffic at all times when they are not operating under simulated instrument conditions.

The most commonly recognized obstacles to learning during flight instruction are:

Feeling of unfair treatment — student motivation declines when a student believes the instructor is making unreasonable demands for performance and progress.

Impatience to proceed to more interesting operations — student impatience is a greater deterrent to learning pilot skills than is generally recognized. It can be corrected by the instructor presenting the necessary preliminary training one step at a time, with clearly stated goals for each step.

Worry or lack of interest — students who are worried or emotionally upset do not learn well, and they derive little benefit from any practice performed.

Physical discomfort, illness, or fatigue — these factors slow the rate of learning during both classroom instruction and flight training. Students who are uncomfortable and not completely at ease cannot learn at the normal rate. Fatigue is the primary consideration in determining the length and frequency of flight instruction periods.

Apathy, fostered by poor instruction — students quickly become apathetic when they recognize that the instructor has made inadequate preparation for the instruction being given, or when the instruction appears to be deficient, contradictory, or insincere.

Anxiety — anxiety may place additional burdens on the instructor, and it limits the students' perceptive ability and retards the development of insights. The student must be comfortable, confident in the instructor and the airplane, and at ease for effective learning to occur.

Successful instructors teach their students not only "how," but also "why" and "when." By incorporating ADM and risk management into each lesson, the aviation instructor helps the student learn, develop, and reinforce the decision-making process which ultimately leads to sound judgment and good decision-making skills. Risk management, ADM, automation management, situational awareness, and controlled flight into terrain (CFIT) awareness are the skills included under higher order thinking skills (HOTS). HOTS should be taught throughout the curriculum from simple to complex and from concrete to abstract.

FOI
6134. The basic demonstration/performance method of instruction consists of several steps in proper order. They are

A— instructor tells–student does; student tells–student does; student does–instructor evaluates.
B— instructor tells–instructor does; student tells– instructor does; student does–instructor evaluates.
C— instructor tells–instructor does; student tells– instructor does; student tells–student does; student does–instructor evaluates.

The steps in the learning technique of demonstration/ performance are:

1. Instructor tells—instructor does

2. Student tells—instructor does

3. Student tells—student does

4. Student does—instructor evaluates

(PLT487) — FAA-H-8083-9

FOI
6135. Integrated flight instruction has many benefits but, the main objective is to

A— develop the student's ability to fly the aircraft during inadvertent IMC.
B— ensure the student is not overly dependent on instruments during VFR flight.
C— help the student develop habit patterns for observance of and reference to flight instruments.

The objective of integrated flight instruction is the formation of firm habit patterns for the observation of and reference to flight instruments from the student's first piloting experience. (PLT227) — FAA-H-8083-9

FOI
6136. The primary objective of integrated flight instruction is the

A— formation of firm habit patterns for observing and relying on flight instruments.
B— difference in the pilot's operation of the flight controls during both VMC and IMC.
C— developing of the habit of occasionally monitoring their own and the aircraft's performance.

The objective of integrated flight instruction is the formation of firm habit patterns for observing and relying

on flight instruments from the student's first piloting experience. (PLT227) — FAA-H-8083-9

FOI
6137. Which is an acceptable procedure when using the integrated method of flight instruction?

A— Use alternate and distinct periods devoted entirely to instrument flight or to visual flight.
B— Prior to the first flight, clearly explain the differences in the manipulation of flight controls for maintaining aircraft control when under simulated instrument conditions and when using references outside the aircraft.
C— Include in the student's first instruction on the function of flight controls the instrument indication to be expected, as well as the outside references used in attitude control.

In the integrated method of flight instruction, the instructor should include, in the student's first briefing on the function of the flight controls, the instrument indications to be expected, as well as the outside references that should be used to control the attitude of the airplane. (PLT227) — FAA-H-8083-9

Answer (A) is incorrect because integrated flight instruction simultaneously uses instrument and outside visual references. Answer (B) is incorrect because this stated difference does not exist.

FOI
6138. During integrated flight instruction, the instructor must be sure the student

A— develops the habit of looking for other traffic.
B— is able to control the aircraft for extended periods under IMC.
C— can depend on the flight instruments when maneuvering by outside references.

In the process of using the integrated method of flight instruction, the instructor must be sure that the students develop, from the start of their training, the habit of looking for other air traffic at all times when they are not operating under simulated instrument conditions. If the students are allowed to believe that the instructor assumes all responsibility for avoiding other traffic, they cannot develop the habit of keeping a constant watch, which is essential to safety. (PLT227) — FAA-H-8083-9

Answer (B) is incorrect because it is not the objective of integrated flight instruction to control the aircraft for extended period under IMC. Answer (C) is incorrect because the student should keep a diligent look out for other traffic, not focus attention on the flight instruments.

Answers

6134	[C]	6135	[C]	6136	[A]	6137	[C]	6138	[A]

FOI

6138-1. For the integrated method of flight instruction to be fully effective, the use of instrument reference should begin

A— after the student has mastered the elements of using visual references.
B— only after collision avoidance scanning techniques have been developed.
C— the first time each new maneuver is introduced.

Integrated flight instruction is flight instruction during which students are taught to perform flight maneuvers both by outside visual references and by reference to flight instruments. For this type of instruction to be fully effective, the use of instrument references should begin the first time each new maneuver is introduced. (PLT227) — FAA-H-8083-9

FOI

6140. Which obstacle to learning is a greater deterrent to learning pilot skills than is generally recognized?

A— Anxiety.
B— Impatience.
C— Physical discomfort.

Impatience is a greater deterrent to learning flying skills than is generally recognized. In a flight student, this may take the form of a desire to make an early solo flight or to set out on cross-country flights before the basic elements of flight have been learned. (PLT295) — FAA-H-8083-9

FOI

6140-1. A method for correcting student impatience is for the instructor to

A— present the necessary preliminary training one step at a time, with clearly stated goals for each step.
B— key the instruction to use the interests and enthusiasm students bring with them.
C— avoid assigning impossible or unreasonable goals for the student to accomplish.

Impatience is a greater deterrent to learning pilot skills than is generally recognized. For a student, this may take the form of a desire to make an early solo flight, or to set out on cross-country flights before the basic elements of flight have been learned. The instructor can correct student impatience by presenting the necessary preliminary training one step at a time, with clearly stated goals for each step. (PLT306) FAA-H-8083-9

Answer (B) is incorrect because this describes a method to combat worry or lack of interest, not impatience. Answer (C) is incorrect because this describes a method to combat a student's feeling of unfair treatment.

FOI

6141. What is the primary consideration in determining the length and frequency of flight instruction periods?

A— Fatigue.
B— Mental acuity.
C— Instructor preparation.

Fatigue is the primary consideration in determining the length and frequency of flight instruction periods. The amount of training which can be absorbed by one student without incurring fatigue does not necessarily indicate the capacity of another student. (PLT295) — FAA-H-8083-9

FOI

6142. Students quickly become apathetic when they

A— realize material is being withheld by the instructor.
B— understand the objectives toward which they are working.
C— recognize that the instructor is not adequately prepared.

The responsibility of an instructor is to present the material in the most professional way he/she can. Students quickly become apathetic when they recognize that the instructor has made inadequate preparation for the instruction being given, or when the instructor appears to be deficient, contradictory, or insincere. (PLT295) — FAA-H-8083-9

Answer (A) is incorrect because a student's reaction is to lose respect for the instructor, if he/she realizes material is being withheld. Answer (B) is incorrect because this situation would encourage motivation, not apathy.

Answers

| 6138-1 | [C] | 6140 | [B] | 6140-1 | [A] | 6141 | [A] | 6142 | [C] |

FOI

6139. Students who grow impatient when learning the basic elements of a task are those who

A— are less easily discouraged than the unaggressive students.

B— should have the preliminary training presented one step at a time with clearly stated goals for each step.

C— should be advanced to the next higher level of learning and not held back by insisting that the immediate goal be reached before they proceed to the next level.

Some students grow impatient with the basic elements of learning a task. When this occurs, the instructor should present the necessary preliminary training one step at a time, with clearly stated goals for each step. (PLT295) — FAA-H-8083-9

Answer (A) is incorrect because impatient students are more easily discouraged than unaggressive students. Answer (C) is incorrect because students should be held back until the whole task is accomplished, before progressing to the next level.

FOI

6139-1. Assignment of goals the student considers difficult

A— usually provides a challenge and promotes learning.

B— may discourage the student and retard learning.

C— is usually appropriate for only highly motivated students.

Assignment of goals the student considers difficult, but possible, usually provides a challenge and promotes learning. In a typical flight lesson, reasonable goals are listed in the lesson objectives and the desired levels of proficiency for the goals are included in statements that contain completion standards. (PLT295) — FAA-H-8083-9

FOI

6143. Which is one of the ways in which anxiety will affect a student?

A— Anxiety may limit the student's ability to learn from perceptions.

B— Anxiety will speed up the learning process for the student if properly controlled and directed by the instructor.

C— Anxiety causes dispersal of the student's attention over such a wide range of matters as to interfere with normal reactions.

Anxiety and apprehension frequently limits the student's perceptive ability and retards the development of insights. (PLT295) — FAA-H-8083-9

Answer (B) is incorrect because perceptions blocked by anxiety will slow the learning process. Answer (C) is incorrect because anxiety narrows a student's attention.

FOI

6143-1. The accurate perception and understanding of all the factors and conditions within the four fundamental risk elements that affect safety is called

A— aeronautical decision making.

B— Single Pilot Resource Management.

C— situational awareness.

Situational awareness is the accurate perception and understanding of all the factors and conditions within the four fundamental risk elements (PAVE: pilot, aircraft, environment, external pressures) that affect safety before, during, and after the flight. (PLT231) — FAA-H-8083-9

Answer (A) is incorrect because ADM is a systematic approach to the mental process used by aircraft pilots to consistently determine the best course of action in response to a given set of circumstances. Answer (B) is incorrect because SRM is the art and science of managing all resources (both onboard the aircraft and from outside sources) available to a single pilot (prior and during flight) to ensure the successful outcome of the flight.

FOI

6143-2. What systematic approach to the mental process does the pilot consistently apply to take the best course of action in a given situation?

A— Aeronautical decision making.

B— Pilot judgment chain.

C— Crew resource management.

Aeronautical decision making (ADM) is a systematic approach to the mental process used by aircraft pilots to consistently determine the best course of action in response to a given set of circumstances. (PLT231) — FAA-H-8083-9

Answers

6139 [B]	6139-1 [A]	6143 [A]	6143-1 [C]	6143-2 [A]

Planning Instructional Activity

Before any instruction can begin, a determination of **standards and objectives** must be made. Training for piloting an aircraft requires the development and assembly, into their proper relationships, of many segments or "**blocks of learning**." A student can master these segments of the overall pilot perfor-mance requirements individually, and can progressively combine them with other related segments until their sum meets the final objective.

After the overall training objectives have been established, the next step is the identification of the blocks of learning which constitute the necessary parts of the total objective. Extraneous blocks of instruction are expensive frills, especially in flight instruction, and detract rather than assist in the completion of the final objectives.

The form of the **syllabus** may vary, but it is always an abstract or digest of the course of training. It consists of the blocks of learning to be completed in the most efficient order. Any practical training syllabus must be flexible, and should be used primarily as a guide.

When an instructor must depart from the order prescribed by the syllabus, he/she must consider the relationships of the blocks of learning affected. When a scheduled lesson must be postponed, it is often preferable to skip to a completely different part of the syllabus, rather than proceeding to the next block in which performance may depend on skills to be developed during the lesson that is being postponed. Each lesson in a training syllabus includes an objective, content, and completion standards.

A **lesson plan** is an organized outline or "blueprint" for a single instructional period and should be prepared in written form for each ground school and flight period, regardless of the instructor's experience. Lesson plans help instructors keep a constant check on their own activity, as well as that of their students. An adequate lesson plan, when properly used, should:

1. Ensure a wise selection of material and the elimination of unimportant details;
2. Make certain that due consideration is given to each part of the lesson;
3. Aid the instructor in presenting the material in a suitable sequence for efficient learning;
4. Provide an outline for the teaching procedure to be used;
5. Serve as a means of relating the lesson to the objectives of the course of training;
6. Give confidence to an inexperienced instructor;
7. Promote uniformity of instruction regardless of the instructor or the date the lesson is given.

In a well-planned lesson, each lesson is a unified segment of instruction, and each lesson contains new material that is related to lessons previously presented. Each lesson should be reasonable in scope, planned practically in terms of the conditions under which the training is to be conducted. The lesson should be planned and taught so its relation to the course objectives are clear to each student. And every lesson, when adequately developed, falls logically into the four steps of the teaching process: presentation, application, review, and evaluation.

FOI

6145. Which statement is true concerning extraneous blocks of instruction during a course of training?

A— They are usually necessary parts of the total objective.

B— They detract from the completion of the final objective.

C— They assist in the attainment of the lesson's objective.

Extraneous blocks of instruction are expensive frills, especially in flight instruction, and detract from, rather than assist in, the completion of the final objective. (PLT295) — FAA-H-8083-9

FOI

6146. Development and assembly of blocks of learning in their proper relationship will provide a means for

A— both the instructor and student to easily correct faulty habit patterns.

B— challenging the student by progressively increasing the units of learning.

C— allowing the student to master the segments of the overall pilot performance requirements individually and combining these with other related segments.

Developing and assembling blocks of learning in their proper relationship allows the student to master individually the segments of the overall pilot performance requirements, and then combine these with other related segments. (PLT491) — FAA-H-8083-9

Answer (A) is incorrect because the development and assembly of block of learning will prevent the formation of faulty habit patterns. Answer (B) is incorrect because progressively increasing the units of learning will cause frustration and deter the student's progress.

FOI

6144. In planning any instructional activity, the first consideration should be to

A— determine the overall objectives and standards.

B— establish common ground between the instructor and student.

C— identify the blocks of learning which make up the overall objective.

The first consideration in planning any instructional activity is to determine the overall objectives and standards. (PLT491) — FAA-H-8083-9

Answer (B) is incorrect because establishing common ground between the instructor and student is part of introduction. Answer (C) is incorrect this is the second consideration in planning instructional activity.

FOI

6144-1. Performance-based objectives consist of which elements?

A— Flight training scenarios, judgment assessment, and maneuver assessment.

B— Cognitive skills, affective skills, and psychomotor skills.

C— Description of the skill or behavior, conditions, and criteria.

Aviation training involves two types of objectives: performance based and decision based. Performance-based objectives are used to set measurable, reasonable standards that describe the desired performance of the student and consist of three elements: description of the skill or behavior, conditions, and criteria. Each part is required and must be stated in a way that leaves every reader with the same picture of the objective, how it is performed, and to what level of performance. (PLT306) — FAA-H-8083-9

Answer (A) is incorrect because these are decision-based objective elements. Answer (B) is incorrect because these are the domains of learning, not elements of performance-based objectives.

FOI

6144-2. An aviation instructor should write performance-based objectives

A— to fit the desired outcome of the lesson.

B— that match the practical test standards.

C— that also work with decision-based objectives.

An instructor should write performance-based objectives to fit the desired outcome of the lesson. (PLT228) — FAA-H-8083-9

Answer (B) is incorrect because the PTS criteria might not always be specific enough for a particular lesson. Answer (C) is incorrect because instructors should shift from performance-based to decision-based objectives over time but most likely, these will not coincide.

FOI

6147. In planning instructional activity, the second step is to

A— develop lesson plans for each period or unit of instruction.

B— identify blocks of learning which constitute the necessary parts of the total objective.

C— develop a training syllabus that will serve as a guide for conducting training at each level of learning.

Answers

| 6145 | [B] | 6146 | [C] | 6144 | [A] | 6144-1 | [C] | 6144-2 | [A] | 6147 | [B] |

After the overall training objectives have been established, the next step is the identification of the blocks of learning which constitute the necessary parts of the total objective. (PLT295) — FAA-H-8083-9

Answer (A) is incorrect because the instructor must first determine the overall objectives and then identify the blocks of learning necessary to meet those objectives. Answer (C) is incorrect because a syllabus will be developed after the blocks have been identified.

FOI

6148. Each lesson of a training syllabus includes

A— attention, motivation, and overview.
B— introduction, development, and conclusion.
C— objective, content, and completion standards.

Each lesson in a training syllabus includes:

1. The objective

2. The content

3. The completion standards

(PLT228) — FAA-H-8083-9

FOI

6149. When it is impossible to conduct a scheduled lesson, it is preferable for the instructor to

A— review and possibly revise the training syllabus.
B— proceed to the next scheduled lesson, or if this is not practical, cancel the lesson.
C— conduct a lesson that is not predicated completely on skills to be developed during the lesson which was postponed.

The material presented in a lesson should build upon material that has been mastered in previous lessons. When it is impossible to conduct a scheduled lesson, it is preferable for the instructor to conduct a lesson that is not predicated completely on the skills to be developed during the lesson which was postponed. (PLT228) — FAA-H-8083-9

Answer (A) is incorrect because the training syllabus does not necessarily need to be reviewed or revised when a scheduled lesson is postponed. Answer (B) is incorrect because the current lesson needs to be accomplished before proceeding to the next one, since the next lesson may need skills that would have been learned in the postponed lesson.

FOI

6150-1. Which statement is true regarding lesson plans?

A— Lesson plans should not be directed toward the course objective; only to the lesson objective.
B— A well-thought out mental outline of a lesson may be used any time as long as the instructor is well prepared.
C— Lesson plans help instructors keep a constant check on their own activity as well as that of their students.

Lesson plans help instructors keep a constant check on their own activity, as well as that of their students. The development of lesson plans by instructors signifies, in effect, that they have taught the lessons to themselves prior to attempting to teach the lessons to students. (PLT228) — FAA-H-8083-9

Answer (A) is incorrect because lesson plans should be directed to both the lesson objective and the course objective. Answer (B) is incorrect because a lesson plan needs to be in written form, regardless of the instructor's level of preparation.

FOI

6150-2. Every lesson, when adequately developed, falls logically into the four steps of the teaching process—

A— preparation, introduction, presentation, and review and evaluation.
B— preparation, introduction, presentation, and review and application.
C— preparation, presentation, application, and review and evaluation.

Every lesson, when adequately developed, falls logically into the four steps of the teaching process—preparation, presentation, application, and review and evaluation. (PLT228) — FAA-H-8083-9

FOI

6150-3. The main concern in developing a lesson plan is the

A— format.
B— content.
C— student.

The main concern in developing a lesson plan is the student. With this in mind, it is apparent that one format does not work well for all students, or for all training situations. Because of the broad range of aviation training requirements, a variety of lesson plans and lesson plan formats is recommended. (PLT228) — FAA-H-8083-9

Answers

| 6148 | [C] | 6149 | [C] | 6150-1 | [C] | 6150-2 | [C] | 6150-3 | [C] |

FOI

6151. With regard to the characteristics of a well-planned lesson, each lesson should contain

A— new material that is related to the lesson previously presented.
B— one basic element of the principle, procedure, or skill appropriate to that lesson.
C— every bit of information needed to reach the objective of the training syllabus.

A well-planned lesson should include new material that relates to the lessons which have been previously presented. (PLT228) — FAA-H-8083-9

Answer (B) is incorrect because all of the elements necessary to learn the principle, procedure, or skill should be presented. Answer (C) is incorrect because each lesson should contain every bit of information needed to reach its own objective, not that of the entire training syllabus.

FOI

6152. Which statement is true about lesson plans?

A— Lesson plans should follow a prescribed format.
B— Standard prepared lesson plans are effective for teaching all students.
C— The use of standard lesson plans may not be effective for students requiring a different approach.

A lesson plan may need to be adjusted to be effective for students requiring a different approach. (PLT228) — FAA-H-8083-9

Answer (A) is incorrect because lesson plans should be tailored for the individual students, yet still contain certain items. Answer (B) is incorrect because standard lesson plans may need to be adjusted to be effective for certain students.

FOI

6153. A lesson plan, if constructed properly, will provide an outline for

A— proceeding from the unknown to the known.
B— the teaching procedure to be used in a single instructional period.
C— establishing blocks of learning that become progressively larger in scope.

A properly constructed lesson plan is a necessary guide for the instructor, in that it tells what to do, in what order to do it, and what procedure to use in teaching the material for a single instructional period. (PLT228) — FAA-H-8083-9

Answer (A) is incorrect because a lesson plan will proceed from the known to the unknown. Answer (C) is incorrect because a syllabus (not lesson plan) will establish blocks of learning that become progressively larger in scope.

FOI

6153-1. A properly developed lesson plan should

A— be an organized written outline that can be used for multiple instructional periods.
B— promote uniformity of instruction regardless of the instructor using it.
C— be a mental outline of a lesson for a single instructional period.

A lesson plan should be put into writing. Another instructor should be able to take the lesson plan and know what to do in conducting the same period of instruction. (PLT228) — FAA-H-8083-9

Answer (A) is incorrect because a lesson plan is an organized outline for a single instructional period. Answer (C) is incorrect because a mental outline of a lesson is not a lesson plan; a lesson plan should be put into writing.

FOI

6160. (Refer to Figure 1.) Section F is titled:

A— Student's Actions.
B— Understanding.
C— Application.

In the lesson plan, section F is the student's actions. (PLT228) — FAA-H-8083-9

Answers (B) and (C) are incorrect because understanding and application are not title sections of a lesson plan.

FOI

6154. (Refer to Figure 1.) Section A is titled:

A— Overview.
B— Introduction.
C— Objective.

In the lesson plan, section A is the lesson objective. (PLT228) — FAA-H-8083-9

Answers (A) and (B) are incorrect because overview and introduction are not title sections of a lesson plan.

FOI

6155. (Refer to Figure 1.) Section B is titled:

A— Elements.
B— Course of Training.
C— Content.

In the lesson plan, section B is titled "Content." (PLT228) — FAA-H-8083-9

Answer (A) is incorrect because this is the name used in an integrated flight/ground training lesson. Answer (B) is incorrect because Course of Training is not a lesson plan title section.

Answers

| 6151 | [A] | 6152 | [C] | 6153 | [B] | 6153-1 | [B] | 6160 | [A] | 6154 | [C] |
| 6155 | [C] | | | | | | | | | | |

FOI

6156. (Refer to Figure 1.) Section G is titled:

A— Summary.
B— Completion Standards.
C— Evaluation.

In the lesson plan, section G is the completion standards. (PLT228) — FAA-H-8083-9

Answers (A) and (C) are incorrect because summary and evaluation are not title sections of a lesson plan.

FOI

6157. (Refer to Figure 1.) Section E is titled:

A— Instructor's Actions.
B— Discussion.
C— Content.

In the lesson plan, section E is the instructor's actions. (PLT228) — FAA-H-8083-9

Answers (B) and (C) are incorrect because discussion and content are not title sections of a lesson plan.

FOI

6158. (Refer to Figure 1.) Section C is titled:

A— Overview.
B— Training Schedule.
C— Schedule.

In the lesson plan, section C is the schedule for the lesson. (PLT228) — FAA-H-8083-9

Answers (A) and (B) are incorrect because overview and training schedule are not title sections of a lesson plan.

FOI

6159. (Refer to Figure 1.) Section D is titled:

A— Instructor's Actions.
B— Content.
C— Equipment.

In the lesson plan, section D is the equipment required for the lesson. (PLT228) — FAA-H-8083-9

Answer (A) is incorrect because Instructor's Actions is Section E. Answer (B) is incorrect because content is not a title section of a lesson plan.

Answers

| 6156 | [B] | 6157 | [A] | 6158 | [C] | 6159 | [C] |

Chapter 2
Aerodynamics and the Principles of Flight

The Axes of an Aircraft

A fixed-wing aircraft has three axes which are perpendicular to each other. These axes intersect at the center of gravity of the aircraft.

- The **longitudinal axis**, also called the **roll axis**, or X-axis, extends lengthwise through the fuselage. The ailerons cause rotation about the longitudinal axis.

- The **lateral axis** extends across the aircraft from wing tip to wing tip and is called the **pitch**, or Y-axis. Movement of the elevators causes the aircraft to rotate about the lateral axis.

- The **vertical axis**, also called the **yaw**, or Z-axis, extends vertically through the center of gravity, and movement of the rudder causes rotation about the vertical axis.

AIR, GLI, LSA, WSC, PPC, MCI
6505. The three axes of an aircraft intersect at the

A— center of gravity.
B— center of pressure.
C— midpoint of the mean chord.

The three axes of rotation of an aircraft intersect at the center of gravity. (PLT234) — FAA-H-8083-25

AIR, GLI, LSA, WSC, PPC, MCI
7283. Action of the elevators moves the plane on its

A— lateral axis.
B— longitudinal axis.
C— vertical axis.

The elevators rotate the plane about its lateral axis to produce pitch. (PLT095) — FAA-H-8083-25

Answer (B) is incorrect because ailerons move the plane on its longitudinal axis. Answer (C) is incorrect because rudders move the plane on its vertical axis.

AIR, GLI, LSA, WSC, PPC, MCI
7284. Aileron deflection moves the airplane about its

A— lateral axis.
B— longitudinal axis.
C— vertical axis.

The ailerons rotate the plane about its longitudinal axis to produce roll. (PLT095) — FAA-H-8083-25

Answer (A) is incorrect because elevators move the plane on its lateral axis. Answer (C) is incorrect because rudders move the plane on its vertical axis.

AIR, LSA, MCI
7285. If the pilot applies right rudder to a stable airplane, the

A— tail deflects right and the nose moves right.
B— tail deflects left and the nose moves right.
C— tail deflects right and the nose moves left.

When pressure is applied to the right rudder pedal, the tail deflects left and the airplane's nose moves (yaws) to the right in relation to the pilot. (PLT244) — FAA-H-8083-25

Answers

6505 [A]   7283 [A]   7284 [B]   7285 [B]

Airfoils and Aerodynamic Shapes

An airfoil is a specially shaped surface, designed to produce aerodynamic lift as air flows over it. For an airfoil to produce lift, the wind must strike it at an angle, called the angle of attack. *See* Figure 2-1.

When the air, which is a viscous fluid, strikes an airfoil, it adheres to the surface and splits, some passing over the top and the rest passing below it. The top of the airfoil drops away from the air flowing over it, and the air speeds up, just as water speeds up as it flows down a hill. The lower surface of the airfoil rises into the path of the air flowing below it, and the air slows down just as water slows down when it is forced over a rise.

Bernoulli's principle explains the relationship between pressure and velocity in the air flowing over the wing. If no energy is added to or taken from the air as it flows over an airfoil, the pressure will decrease as the velocity increases and will

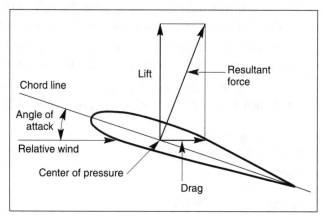

Figure 2-1. Angle of attack

increase as the velocity decreases. When the air flowing over the top of the wing speeds up, its pressure drops and air above it is pulled down to fill this low pressure. Since for every action there is an equal and opposite reaction, the force with which the wing pulls the air down is exactly balanced by a force which pulls the wing up. The air below the wing is slowed down, and its pressure increases, forcing air away from it. The same force that pushes the air away pushes the wing up. The result of the air being pulled down to the top and pushed away from the bottom causes the air flowing over the wing to be forced down at an angle called the downwash angle. The weight of the air forced down is exactly the same as the lift causing the airplane to be forced up. It is determined by five factors:

1. The cross-sectional shape of the airfoil

2. The surface area of airfoil

3. The angle the air strikes the airfoil (angle of attack)

4. The speed of the air moving over the airfoil

5. The density of the air

Some terms that are associated with airfoils:

Chord Line — A line that passes through an airfoil from the leading edge to the trailing edge.

Leading Edge — The front of an airfoil, the portion that passes through the air first.

Trailing Edge — The rear of an airfoil, the portion that passes through the air last.

Center of Pressure — The point on the chord line of an airfoil at which all the aerodynamic forces are thought to be concentrated.

Relative Wind — The direction from which the wind is moving when it reaches the airfoil.

Downwash Angle — The angle the air is flowing when it leaves the airfoil.

Angle of Attack — The angle between the chordline of an airfoil and the relative wind. The angle of attack varies in flight.

Angle of Incidence — The angle between the chordline of an airfoil and the longitudinal axis of an aircraft. The angle of incidence is fixed.

Upper Camber — The contour of the top surface of an airfoil.

Lower Camber — The contour of the bottom surface of an airfoil.

Mean Camber — A line drawn from the leading edge to the trailing edge of an airfoil, equidistant at all points from the upper and lower cambers. The shape of the mean camber line determines the aerodynamic characteristics of a wing.

See Figure 2-2.

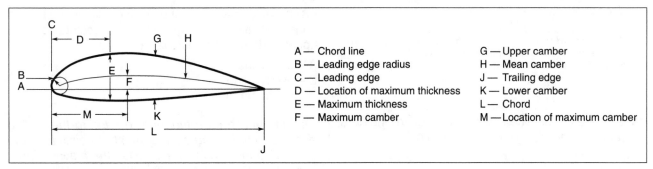

A — Chord line
B — Leading edge radius
C — Leading edge
D — Location of maximum thickness
E — Maximum thickness
F — Maximum camber
G — Upper camber
H — Mean camber
J — Trailing edge
K — Lower camber
L — Chord
M — Location of maximum camber

Figure 2-2. Airfoil nomenclature

The angle of attack directly controls the distribution of the pressures above and below the wing. As the angle of attack is increased, the pressure differential becomes greater until the stalling angle of attack is reached. At this time, the smooth airflow over the top of the wing breaks away and the air becomes turbulent. This lowers the pressure differential.

An asymmetrical airfoil is one in which the upper camber and lower cambers are different, and a symmetrical airfoil is one whose upper and lower cambers are the same on either side of the chord line. Because of the shape of an asymmetrical airfoil, air flowing over the wing directly in line with the chord line (at zero angle of attack) will still produce a pressure on the upper surface that is lower than that of the surrounding air.

Air flowing over a symmetrical airfoil at zero angle of attack will not produce a pressure differential across the airfoil. The location of the **center of pressure** in a symmetrical airfoil remains relatively constant as the angle of attack changes, but in an asymmetrical airfoil, the center of pressure moves forward as the angle of attack increases and rearward as the angle of attack decreases. The changes in the center of pressure affect the aerodynamic balance and controllability of the aircraft. *See* Figure 2-3.

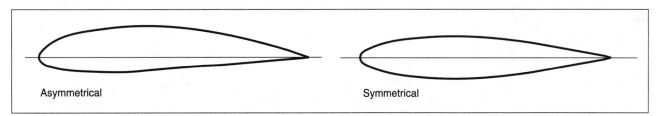

Asymmetrical

Symmetrical

Figure 2-3. Airfoil shapes

ALL

6514. The angle between the chord line of the wing and the longitudinal axis of the aircraft is known as

A— dihedral.
B— the angle of attack.
C— the angle of incidence.

The acute angle between the chord line of the wing and the longitudinal axis of the aircraft is the angle of incidence. (PLT235) — FAA-H-8083-25

Answer (A) is incorrect because dihedral is the amount the wings are slanted upward from the root to the tip. Answer (B) is incorrect because the angle of attack is between the chord line of the wing and the direction of the relative wind.

ALL

6515. The angle between the chord line of an airfoil and the relative wind is known as the angle of

A— lift.
B— attack.
C— incidence.

The angle of attack is the acute angle between the chord line of the wing and the direction of the relative wind. (PLT168) — FAA-H-8083-25

Answer (A) is incorrect because the angle of lift is not an aerodynamic term used in aviation. Answer (C) is incorrect because the angle between the chordline of an airfoil and the longitudinal axis of an aircraft is known as the angle of incidence.

ALL

6516. A line drawn from the leading edge to the trailing edge of an airfoil and equidistant at all points from the upper and lower contours is called the

A— chord line.
B— camber line.
C— mean camber line.

The line drawn from the leading edge to the trailing edge of an airfoil and equidistant at all points from the upper and lower contours is called the mean camber line. (PLT235) — FAA-H-8083-25

Answer (A) is incorrect because the chord line is a straight line connecting the leading edge and the trailing edge of the airfoil. Answer (B) is incorrect because the camber line is the curvature of the upper and lower surface of the airfoil.

The Aerodynamic Forces

A fixed-wing aircraft in flight is acted on by four basic forces:

Lift — an aerodynamic force produced by an airfoil which acts perpendicular to the relative wind. Lift is concentrated at the center of pressure.

Weight — acts vertically downward toward the center of the earth, and is concentrated at the center of gravity.

Thrust — is produced by the engine or engine-propeller combination. It acts forward parallel to the axis of the engine.

Drag — is a combination of forces that acts rearward, parallel to the relative wind. Total drag is made up of induced drag, caused by the production of lift, and parasite drag, caused by the friction of the air passing over the aircraft surface.

See Figure 2-4.

The two lift variables the pilot has at his/her control are the **airspeed** and the **angle of attack**. To maintain level flight at a lower airspeed, the pilot must increase the angle of attack. To prevent the aircraft climbing when the speed is increased, the angle of attack must be reduced.

The amount of lift increases as the angle of attack is increased until the angle of attack becomes so great that the air flowing over the surface breaks away and burbles. This is the **critical angle of attack**.

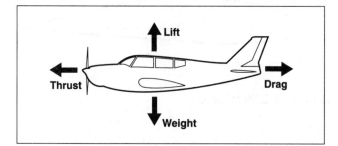

Figure 2-4. The four forces in flight

Answers

6514 [C]   6515 [B]   6516 [C]

The actual weight of an aircraft is caused by gravity, and it always acts directly toward the center of the earth. The tail load of a normal aircraft acts downward, and must be overcome by lift in the same way as weight. The apparent weight of an aircraft is the increase in weight caused by acceleration. In a coordinated steep turn with a bank angle of 60°, there is an acceleration force of 2 Gs. A 3,600-pound airplane in a 2-G turn has an apparent weight of 7,200 pounds. It is the apparent weight that causes an airplane to stall at a higher than normal airspeed when in a high-G turn.

There are two basic types of drag: induced and parasite.

Induced drag is caused by the production of lift and it is affected by the same factors which affect lift.

Induced drag is greatly affected by the airspeed. It varies inversely as the square of the airspeed. If the airspeed is reduced to one-half its original value, the induced drag increases 4 times. In order for an aircraft to fly slowly, its angle of attack must be high, and a high angle of attack produces a large amount of induced drag.

Parasite drag is caused by the friction of the air flowing over the aircraft, and it is not related to the production of lift. Parasite drag increases proportional to the square of the airspeed.

Parasite drag can be further classified into:

Form drag — caused by the frontal area of the aircraft.

Profile drag — caused by the viscous nature of the air passing over the aircraft's surfaces.

Interference drag — caused by interference of the airflow between adjacent parts of the aircraft.

Because induced drag decreases as airspeed increases and parasite drag increases as airspeed increases, there is an airspeed and an angle of attack at which the induced and parasite drag are the same. This is the airspeed at which the total drag is the least and the lift-to-drag ratio is maximum (L/D$_{MAX}$). At airspeeds above that for L/D$_{MAX}$, the total drag increases due to the increase in parasite drag, and at airspeeds below that for L/D$_{MAX}$, the total drag increases because of the increase in induced drag. *See* Figure 2-5.

Thrust is a force which imparts a change in the velocity of a mass. Thrust, produced by a turbojet engine or an engine-propeller combination, provides the force used to move an aircraft through the air. Thrust acts forward, in line with the propeller shaft. If the engine is mounted well below or well above the longitudinal axis of the aircraft, a change in power will produce a rotational force about the aircraft's lateral axis. If the thrust line is below the longitudinal axis, an increase in power will produce a nose-up rotational force.

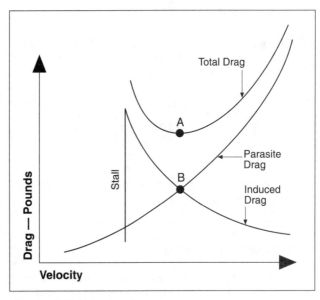

Figure 2-5. Drag vs. airspeed

ALL

6504. Why does increasing speed also increase lift?

A— The increased velocity of the relative wind overcomes the increased drag.
B— The increased impact of the relative wind on an airfoil's lower surface creates a greater amount of air being deflected downward.
C— The increased speed of the air passing over an airfoil's upper surface increases the pressure, thus creating a greater pressure differential between the upper and lower surface.

An increase in the velocity of the air passing over the wing increases lift and drag. Lift is increased because (1) the increased impact of the relative wind on the wing's lower surface creates a greater amount of air being deflected downward; (2) the increased speed of the relative wind over the upper surface creates a lower pressure on top of the wing (Bernoulli's principle); and (3) a greater pressure differential between the upper and lower wing surface is created. (PLT237) — FAA-H-8083-25

Answer (A) is incorrect because thrust overcomes increased drag as speed increases. Answer (C) is incorrect because the increased speed of air passing over an airfoil's upper surfaces decreases the pressure.

ALL

6512. The point on an airfoil through which lift acts is the

A— center of gravity.
B— center of pressure.
C— midpoint of the chord.

All of the upward lift forces on a wing can be considered to be concentrated at the center of pressure of the airfoil. (PLT236) — FAA-H-8083-25

Answer (A) is incorrect because the center of gravity is the point at which all weight is considered to be concentrated. Answer (C) is incorrect because the midpoint of the chord is the midpoint between the leading edge and the trailing edge of the airfoil.

ALL

6513. Lift produced by an airfoil is the net force developed perpendicular to the

A— chord.
B— relative wind.
C— longitudinal axis of the aircraft.

Lift produced by an airfoil always acts perpendicular to the direction of the relative wind. (PLT242) — FAA-H-8083-25

ALL

6520. Which statement relates to Bernoulli's principle?

A— For every action there is an equal and opposite reaction.
B— An additional upward force is generated as the lower surface of the wing deflects air downward.
C— Air traveling faster over the curved upper surface of an airfoil causes lower pressure on the top surface.

Bernoulli's principle states in part that the internal pressure of a fluid (liquid or gas) decreases at points where the speed of the fluid increases. In other words, high-speed flow is associated with low pressure and low-speed flow with high pressure. Air traveling faster over the curved upper surface of an airfoil causes lower pressure on the top surface. (PLT025) — FAA-H-8083-25

Answers (A) and (B) are incorrect because these refer to Newton's Third Law of Motion.

ALL

6521. An aircraft wing is designed to produce lift resulting from

A— negative air pressure below the wing's surface and positive air pressure above the wing's surface.
B— positive air pressure below the wing's surface and negative air pressure above the wing's surface.
C— a larger center of pressure above the wing's surface and a lower center of pressure below the wing's surface.

Aerodynamic lift is produced by an airfoil as a result of the difference in air pressure above and below the wing. There is a relatively positive air pressure below the wing's surface and a relatively negative air pressure above the wing's surface. As a result of this pressure differential, air flowing over the wing is deflected downward. Downward deflection of the air produces an upward force, which is aerodynamic lift. (PLT242) — FAA-H-8083-25

Answer (A) is incorrect because the pressure is positive below the wing and negative above the wing. Answer (C) is incorrect because the larger center of pressure is above the wing.

Answers

6504   [B]   6512   [B]   6513   [B]   6520   [C]   6521   [B]

ALL
6522. During flight with zero angle of attack, the pressure along the upper surface of a wing would be

A— equal to atmospheric pressure.
B— less than atmospheric pressure.
C— greater than atmospheric pressure.

Because of the shape of an asymmetrical airfoil, even at 0° angle of attack, the pressure along the upper surface of the wing will be less than that of the surrounding atmosphere. (PLT235) — FAA-H-8083-25

ALL, GLI
6533. The angle of attack of a wing directly controls the

A— angle of incidence of the wing.
B— amount of airflow above and below the wing.
C— distribution of positive and negative pressure acting on the wing.

The angle of attack is the acute angle between the chord line of the wing and the direction of the relative wind. Changing the angle of attack directly controls the pressure distribution between the top and bottom of the wing. (PLT168) — FAA-H-8083-25

Answer (A) is incorrect because the angle of incidence is a fixed angle determined by the aircraft design. Answer (B) is incorrect because the amount of airflow above and below the wing is controlled by airspeed.

ALL
6523. That portion of the aircraft's total drag created by the production of lift is called

A— induced drag, and is not affected by changes in airspeed.
B— induced drag, and is greatly affected by changes in airspeed.
C— parasite drag, and is greatly affected by changes in airspeed.

Induced drag is that portion of the aircraft's total drag that is produced by the same factors that produce lift. Induced drag increases as the airspeed decreases. A decrease in airspeed requires an increased angle of attack to produce the same amount of lift, and the increased angle of attack increases the induced drag. Induced drag increases in proportion to the square of the decrease in airspeed. (PLT241) — FAA-H-8083-25

ALL
6524. As airspeed increases in level flight, total drag of an aircraft becomes greater than the total drag produced at the maximum lift/drag speed because of the

A— increase in induced drag.
B— decrease in induced drag.
C— increase in parasite drag.

Parasite drag increases as the square of the airspeed. As the airspeed decreases to near the stalling speed, the total drag becomes greater, due mainly to the sharp rise in induced drag. Similarly, as the airspeed increases beyond that which produced the maximum L/D ratio, the total drag again increases, this time because of parasite drag. (PLT237) — FAA-H-8083-25

Answer (A) is incorrect because induced drag decreases as airspeed increases above the maximum L/D ratio. Answer (B) is incorrect because the decrease in induced drag is less than the increase in parasite drag.

ALL
6525. As airspeed decreases in level flight, total drag of an aircraft becomes greater than the total drag produced at the maximum lift/drag speed because of the

A— decrease in induced drag.
B— increase in induced drag.
C— increase in parasite drag.

Induced drag increases with a decrease in airspeed because of the increased angle of attack needed to produce the required lift at the lower speed. (PLT241) — FAA-H-8083-25

Answer (A) is incorrect because induced drag increases as airspeed decreases below the maximum L/D ratio. Answer (C) is incorrect because parasite drag decreases as airspeed decreases below the maximum L/D ratio.

ALL, GLI
6526. The resistance, or skin friction, due to the viscosity of the air as it passes along the surface of a wing is called

A— form drag.
B— profile drag.
C— parasite drag.

Profile drag is the resistance, or skin friction, due to viscosity (stickiness) of the air as it passes along the surface of the wing. (PLT237) — FAA-H-8083-25

Answer (A) is incorrect because form drag is caused by the frontal area of the aircraft. Answer (C) is incorrect because parasite drag includes both form drag and profile drag.

Answers

| 6522 | [B] | 6533 | [C] | 6523 | [B] | 6524 | [C] | 6525 | [B] | 6526 | [B] |

ALL

6527. Which relationship is correct when comparing drag and airspeed?

A— Induced drag increases as the square of the airspeed.
B— Induced drag varies inversely as the square of the airspeed.
C— Profile drag varies inversely as the square of the airspeed.

The induced drag varies inversely as the square of the airspeed. If the airspeed is decreased to one half of its original value, the induced drag will increase four times. (PLT241) — FAA-H-8083-25

Answer (A) is incorrect because induced drag varies inversely with airspeed. Answer (C) is incorrect because profile drag is parasite drag, which varies directly as the square of the airspeed.

ALL

6559. (Refer to Figure 20.) At the airspeed represented by point A, in steady flight, the aircraft will

A— have its maximum lift/drag ratio.
B— have its minimum lift/drag ratio.
C— be developing its maximum coefficient of lift.

Point "A" on the Drag Chart represents the point of lowest total drag. The lowest total drag occurs at the angle of attack that produces the maximum lift over drag ratio (L/D$_{MAX}$). (PLT046) — FAA-H-8083-25

ALL

6560. (Refer to Figure 20.) At an airspeed represented by point B, in steady flight, the pilot can expect to obtain the aircraft's

A— maximum coefficient of lift.
B— minimum coefficient of lift.
C— maximum glide range in still air.

Point "B" on the Drag Chart indicates the airspeed that will allow a pilot to glide for the greatest distance in still air. This is the airspeed for the lowest total drag and it occurs at the angle of attack which produces the maximum lift over drag ratio (L/D$_{MAX}$). (PLT046) — FAA-H-8083-25

ALL

6517. The force which imparts a change in the velocity of a mass is called

A— work.
B— power.
C— thrust.

Thrust is the force which imparts a change in the velocity of a mass. (PLT241) — FAA-H-8083-25

AIR, LSA

6571. If an increase in power tends to make the nose of an airplane rise, this is the result of the

A— line of thrust being below the center of gravity.
B— center of lift being ahead of the center of gravity.
C— center of lift and center of gravity being collocated.

The point of application of the force that pulls an air-plane through the air is its thrust line. If the thrust line is below the center of gravity of the airplane an increase in power will produce a rotational force that tends to cause the nose to rise. (PLT240) — FAA-H-8083-25

Answers

| 6527 [B] | 6559 [A] | 6560 [C] | 6517 [C] | 6571 [A] |

The Balance of Forces

When an airplane, weight-shift control or powered parachute is flying at a steady speed, is not rising or descending, and is not speeding up or slowing down, all of the forces are in balance. The upward force of lift is exactly the same as the down-ward forces of weight and the aerodynamic load on the tail. Thrust is exactly the same as drag.

Some form of energy must be expended to cause an aircraft to rise. Chemical energy is converted into mechanical energy in the engine; this in turn is converted into thrust to pull the aircraft through the air so aerodynamic lift can be produced. When the engine power is increased in an aircraft trimmed for straight-and-level, unaccelerated flight, these things happen:

1. The additional power produces more thrust.

2. The additional thrust causes the aircraft to begin to accelerate. For an airplane, this increases the downward tail load which increases the angle of attack. The airplane begins to increase its altitude.

3. The increased angle of attack increases the drag until the new drag force balances the increased thrust, and the acceleration stops with the airplane flying at the same airspeed it had before the power was increased.

4. The upward force of lift is equal to the combined downward force of weight and tail load, and the airplane climbs at a steady speed.

During a steady climb, the **rate of climb** for an airplane, weight-shift control and powered parachute is determined by the difference between the power available and the power required. The more excess power available, the greater the rate of climb. The **angle of climb** is determined by the difference between the available thrust and the drag. The greater the thrust, the greater the angle of climb.

Since an aircraft is held at altitude by an expenditure of energy, it will descend if the energy being expended is decreased. If the power is slightly decreased on an airplane cruising at altitude in straight-and-level, unaccelerated flight, these things will happen:

1. The reduction in power decreases the thrust.

2. The decreased thrust causes a momentary deceleration. For an airplane, the upward lift and down-ward tail load both decrease and the nose drops, and the airplane begins to descend and accelerate.

3. As the airplane descends, the forward vector of the descent angle acts as thrust to make up for the propeller thrust reduction.

4. The airspeed builds up enough to increase the tail load, and the nose rises enough to hold the air-speed the same as it was before the power was reduced. The drag is now the same as the engine thrust plus the thrust vector from the descent angle, and all acceleration stops.

5. The upward force of lift is now equal to the combined downward force of weight and tail load, and the airplane descends at a constant power and constant airspeed.

The climbing and descending of weight-shift control and powered parachute is similar, but the trim generally maintains the aircraft at a constant airspeed with smooth and gradual throttle advances and reductions in power.

An aircraft turns when the lift vector is tilted and the **horizontal component of the lift** pulls the nose around in a curved path. In straight-and-level flight, lift acts upward and balances the weight of the aircraft. When the airplane is banked, the lift vector tilts and the vertical component is no longer equal to the weight, and the aircraft begins to descend. To complicate this, the centrifugal force caused by the turn increases the apparent weight of the aircraft. To prevent the aircraft descending in this turn, the tilted lift vector must be increased enough to equal the resultant of the weight and the centrifugal force. This is done by increasing the angle of attack. *See* Figure 2-6.

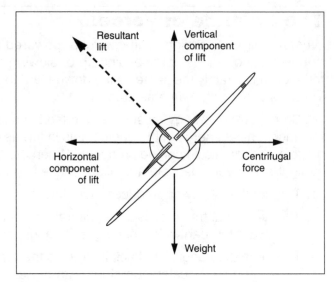

Figure 2-6. Forces in a turn

All aircraft turn by banking, but an airplane rudder is still an important flight control for the airplane. When turning an airplane to the right, the left aileron is lowered and the right aileron is raised. The lift and induced drag on the left wing both increase at the same time the lift and induced drag on the right wing decrease. The increased induced drag causes the nose to momentarily yaw to the left before the wing rises enough to bank the aircraft and produce a horizontal component of the lift to pull the nose around to the right. This momentary yawing to the left is called **adverse yaw**. Adverse yaw is minimized by differential aileron movement. The aileron moving upward travels farther than the one moving downward. This causes the upward-moving aileron to produce enough parasite drag to counter the induced drag produced by the downward-moving aileron. When rolling out of a steep-banked turn, the slower airspeed, higher angle of attack, and higher wing loading require a greater aileron deflection than when rolling into the turn. This produces adverse yaw, but this time the yaw is in the direction of the turn, and it requires more rudder pressure to counteract it.

The weight-shift control has a slight amount of adverse yaw when a bank is started, but the nose angle quickly stabilizes the wing to track directly into the relative wind for a coordinated turn.

A powered parachute is designed to track directly into the wind with no noticeable adverse yaw while banking.

The rate of turn at any given airspeed depends on the amount of the sideward force causing the turn, that is, the horizontal lift component. The horizontal lift component varies in proportion to the amount of bank. The rate of turn at a given airspeed increases as the angle of bank is increased. On the other hand, when a turn is made at a higher airspeed at a given bank angle, the inertia is greater, and the centrifugal force created by the turn becomes greater, causing the turning rate to become slower. Therefore, at a given angle of bank, a higher airspeed will make the radius of the turn larger because the airplane will be turning at a slower rate.

ALL

6510. How can a pilot increase the rate of turn and decrease the radius at the same time?

A— Shallow the bank and increase airspeed.
B— Steepen the bank and decrease airspeed.
C— Steepen the bank and increase airspeed.

The rate of turn is dependent on the horizontal component of lift. The radius of turn is dependent on airspeed. To increase the rate of turn and decrease the radius at the same time, the bank should be steepened and the airspeed decreased. (PLT248) — FAA-H-8083-3

ALL

6530. As the angle of bank is increased, the vertical component of lift

A— increases and the sink rate increases.
B— decreases and the sink rate increases.
C— increases and the sink rate decreases.

In a turn, the total lift is separated into two components: the horizontal component pulls the aircraft around in the turn, and the vertical component opposes the weight. If the turn is made with no increase in the angle of attack, the total lift will remain constant, and as the angle of bank is increased, the vertical component of lift will decrease, and the sink rate will increase. (PLT248) — FAA-H-8083-25

Answer (A) is incorrect because the vertical component of lift decreases when the angle of bank is increased. Answer (C) is incorrect because the vertical component of lift decreases and the sink rate increases.

ALL

6532. What action is necessary to make an aircraft turn?

A— Yaw the aircraft.
B— Change the direction of lift.
C— Change the direction of thrust.

A turn is started by banking the aircraft. This bank changes the direction of lift from vertical to angled, and the angled lift has a horizontal component. It is the horizontal component of lift which brings the nose of the aircraft around in a turn. (PLT248) — FAA-H-8083-25

Answer (A) is incorrect because yawing rotates the aircraft about the vertical axis. Answer (C) is incorrect because the direction of thrust cannot be changed in propeller-driven aircraft while in flight.

AIR, LSA, WSC, PPC

6507. When considering the forces acting upon an airplane in straight-and-level flight at constant airspeed, which statement is correct?

A— Weight always acts vertically toward the center of the Earth.
B— Thrust always acts forward parallel to the relative wind and is greater than drag.
C— Lift always acts perpendicular to the longitudinal axis of the wing and is greater than weight.

The relationship between the forces acting on an aircraft in straight-and-level flight at a constant airspeed are:

1. *Thrust acts parallel to the center line of the propeller shaft.*

2. *Drag acts parallel to the relative wind, in the direction opposite that of thrust.*

3. *Lift acts perpendicular to the relative wind.*

4. *Weight, which is caused by gravity, always acts vertically toward the center of the earth.*

(PLT242) — FAA-H-8083-25

Answer (B) is incorrect because thrust and drag are equal during straight-and-level flight at a constant airspeed. Answer (C) is incorrect because lift and weight are equal during straight-and-level flight at a constant airspeed.

AIR, LSA, WSC, PPC

6518. During a steady climb, the rate of climb depends on

A— excess power.
B— excess thrust.
C— thrust available.

During a steady climb, the rate of climb depends upon excess power. (PLT246) — FAA-H-8083-25

Answer (B) is incorrect because the angle of climb depends upon excess thrust. Answer (C) is incorrect because thrust available does not contribute to the rate of climb.

Answers

6510 [B]	6530 [B]	6532 [B]	6507 [A]	6518 [A]

AIR, LSA, WSC, PPC

6519. During a steady climb, the angle of climb depends on

A— excess thrust.
B— power available.
C— thrust required.

During a steady climb, the angle of climb is a function of excess thrust. (PLT246) — FAA-H-8083-25

Answer (B) is incorrect because power available does not contribute to the angle of climb. Answer (C) is incorrect because excess thrust determines the angle of climb.

AIR, LSA, WSC, PPC

6529. Which statement is true regarding the forces acting on an airplane in a steady-state climb?

A— The sum of all forward forces is greater than the sum of all rearward forces.
B— The sum of all upward forces is greater than the sum of all downward forces.
C— The sum of all upward forces is equal to the sum of all downward forces.

During a steady-state climb, the sum of all upward forces is equal to the sum of all downward forces. (PLT246) — FAA-H-8083-25

AIR, LSA, WSC, PPC

6528. Which statement describes the relationship of the forces acting on an aircraft in a constant-power and constant-airspeed descent?

A— Thrust is equal to drag; lift is equal to weight.
B— Thrust is equal to drag; weight is greater than lift.
C— Thrust is greater than drag; weight is greater than lift.

When the nose of an aircraft pitches down, the angle of attack decreases and the lift produced by the wing is momentarily reduced. This imbalance between lift and weight causes the airplane to start a descending flight path with respect to the horizontal. The opposing forces are equal to each other during a steady climb, descent, or straight-and-level flight: thrust is equal to drag; lift is equal to weight. (PLT247) — FAA-H-8083-25

AIR, GLI, LSA

6508. Adverse yaw during a turn entry is caused by

A— increased induced drag on the lowered wing and decreased induced drag on the raised wing.
B— decreased induced drag on the lowered wing and increased induced drag on the raised wing.
C— increased parasite drag on the raised wing and decreased parasite drag on the lowered wing.

When the ailerons are moved to cause an aircraft to bank, one aileron moves down, and the other moves up. As the aileron moves down, it increases the camber, the lift, and the induced drag on its wing, and the wing moves up. As the aileron moves up, it decreases the camber, the lift, and the induced drag on its wing, and the wing moves down. The increased induced drag on the rising wing causes the nose of the airplane to momentarily yaw in the direction opposite to the direction of the desired turn. This is called adverse yaw. (PLT235) — FAA-H-8083-25

Answer (A) is incorrect because induced drag is decreased on the lowered wing and increased on the raised wing. Answer (C) is incorrect because parasite drag is affected by airspeed.

AIR, GLI, LSA

6509. When rolling out of a steep-banked turn, what causes the lowered aileron to create more drag than when rolling into the turn?

A— The wing's angle of attack is greater as the rollout is started.
B— The wing being raised is traveling faster through the air than the wing being lowered.
C— The wing being lowered is traveling faster through the air and producing more lift than the wing being raised.

When rolling out of a steep-banked turn, the yaw effect will often be more apparent than when rolling into the turn. This is caused by the higher angle of attack, the higher wing loading and the slower airspeed which exists when the rollout is started. (PLT248) — FAA-H-8083-3

Answer (B) is incorrect because the wing being raised is traveling slower than the wing being lowered. Answer (C) is incorrect because the wing being raised is producing more lift than the wing being lowered.

Answers

| 6519 | [A] | 6529 | [C] | 6528 | [A] | 6508 | [B] | 6509 | [A] |

Maneuverability, Controllability, and Stability

Maneuverability is the quality of an aircraft that permits it to be maneuvered easily and to withstand the stresses imposed by maneuvers. **Controllability** is the capability of an aircraft to respond to the pilot's control, especially with regard to flight path and attitude. **Stability** is the inherent quality of an air-craft to correct for conditions that may disturb its equilibrium, and to return or continue on the original flight path. An aircraft can have two basic types of stability: **static** and **dynamic**, and three conditions of each type of stability: **positive**, **neutral**, and **negative**.

Positive static stability is the condition of stability in which restorative forces are set up that will tend to return the aircraft to its original condition anytime it is disturbed from a condition of straight-and-level flight. If an aircraft has **negative static stability**, anytime it is disturbed from a condition of straight-and-level flight, forces are set up that will tend to cause it to depart further from its original condition. Negative static stability is a highly undesirable characteristic as it can cause loss of control. An aircraft with neutral static stability produces neither forces that tend to return it to its original condition, nor cause it to depart further from this condition. *See* Figure 2-7.

Positive dynamic stability is a condition in which the forces of static stability decrease with time. Positive dynamic stability is desirable. **Negative dynamic stability** causes the forces of static stability to increase with time. Negative dynamic stability is undesirable. **Neutral dynamic stability** causes an aircraft to hunt back and forth around a condition of straight-and-level flight, with the corrections getting neither larger or smaller. Neutral dynamic stability is also undesirable. *See* Figure 2-8.

An aircraft is longitudinally stable if it returns to a condition of level flight after the control wheel is momentarily moved forward and then released. The location of the center of pressure relative to the center of gravity determines the **longitudinal stability**, and thus the controllability of an aircraft. An aircraft is given positive longitudinal stability by locating the center of gravity ahead of the center of pressure, and balancing this nose-down moment with a nose-up moment caused by the downward aerodynamic tail load. Negative longitudinal static stability would result if the center of pressure were forward of the center of gravity, the aircraft would have a tendency to nose up and enter a stalled condition. The amount of downward tail load is determined by the airspeed. When the nose momentarily drops, the airspeed increases and the tail load increases enough to return the nose to level flight. When the nose momentarily rises, the airspeed decreases and the tail load decreases enough for the nose to drop back to level flight attitude.

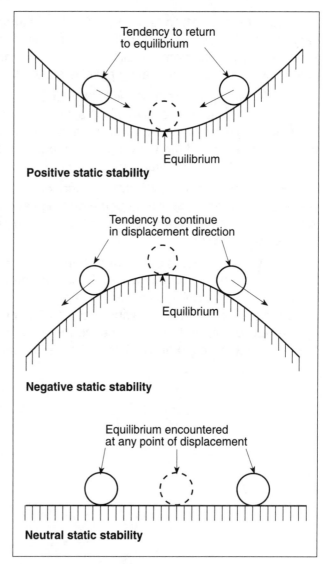

Figure 2-7. Static stability

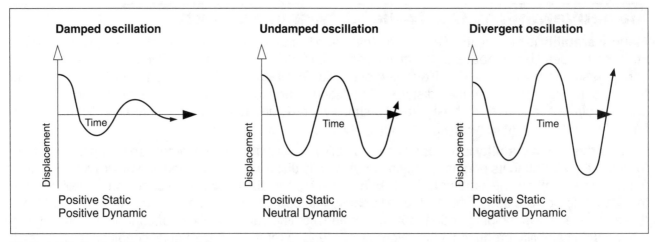

Figure 2-8. Static and dynamic stability

Phugoid oscillation is a long-period oscillation in which the pitch attitude, airspeed, and altitude vary, but the angle of attack remains relatively constant. It is a gradual interchange of potential and kinetic energy about some equilibrium airspeed and altitude. An aircraft experiencing longitudinal phugoid oscillation is demonstrating positive static stability, and it is easily controlled by the pilot.

An aircraft will return to level flight after a wing drops if it has **positive lateral stability**. The wings of most aircraft have a positive dihedral angle. This is the angle produced by the wing tips being higher than the wing roots. If the left wing drops in flight, the aircraft will momentarily begin to slip to the left, and the angle of attack of the left wing will increase and the angle of attack of the right wing will decrease. The increased angle of attack will cause the left wing to rise back to level-flight attitude.

Directional stability, which is the tendency of the nose of an aircraft to turn into the relative wind, is achieved by the vertical area of the fuselage and vertical tail surfaces behind the center of gravity. If a wing drops and the aircraft begins to slip to the side, the directional stability will cause the nose to yaw into the relative wind.

Dihedral effect rights an aircraft when a wing drops, and directional stability causes the nose to yaw into the direction of the low wing. These two forces oppose each other, and an aircraft with a strong static directional stability and weak dihedral effect will have spiral instability. When the wing drops, the nose will yaw toward the low wing and the airplane will begin to turn. The increased speed of the wing on the outside of the turn will increase the angle of bank, and the strong directional stability will force the nose to a low pitch angle. This will cause the aircraft to enter a descending spiral.

ALL

6502. The tendency of an aircraft to develop forces which restore it to its original condition, when disturbed from a condition of steady flight, is known as

A— stability.
B— controllability.
C— maneuverability.

Stability is the inherent quality of an aircraft to correct for conditions that may disturb its equilibrium, and to return to or continue on the original flight path. Stability is primarily an aircraft design characteristic. (PLT480) — FAA-H-8083-25

Answer (B) is incorrect because controllability is the capability of an aircraft to respond to the pilot's control, especially with regard to flight path and attitude. Answer (C) is incorrect because maneuverability is the quality of an aircraft that permits it to be maneuvered easily and to withstand the stresses imposed by maneuvers.

ALL

6566. The quality of an aircraft that permits it to be operated easily and to withstand the stresses imposed on it is

A— stability.
B— maneuverability.
C— controllability.

Maneuverability is the quality of an aircraft that permits it to be maneuvered easily and to withstand the stresses imposed by maneuvers. (PLT214) — FAA-H-8083-25

Answer (A) is incorrect because stability is the inherent quality of an aircraft to correct for conditions that may disturb its equilibrium, and to return or to continue on the original flight path. Answer (C) is incorrect because controllability is the capability of an aircraft to respond to the pilot's control, especially with regard to flight path and attitude.

ALL

6567. The capability of an aircraft to respond to a pilot's inputs, especially with regard to flightpath and attitude, is

A— response.
B— controllability.
C— maneuverability.

Controllability is the capability of an aircraft to respond to the pilot's control, especially with regard to flight path and attitude. (PLT244) — FAA-H-8083-25

Answer (A) is incorrect because response is how the aircraft reacts to the pilot's inputs. Answer (C) is incorrect because maneuverability is the quality of an aircraft that permits it to be maneuvered easily and to withstand the stresses imposed by maneuvers.

ALL

6563. The initial tendency of an aircraft to develop forces that further remove the aircraft from its original position, when disturbed from a condition of steady flight, is known as

A— negative static stability.
B— dynamic instability.
C— positive static stability.

Negative static stability is an inherent quality of an aircraft that causes it to deviate further from a condition of steady flight once it is disturbed from such a condition. An aircraft has negative static instability if, when the nose drops in flight, no restorative force is supplied by the horizontal tail and the nose continues to drop. (PLT480) — FAA-H-8083-25

Answer (B) is incorrect because dynamic instability is the tendency for oscillations to increase. Answer (C) is incorrect because positive static stability is the tendency for an aircraft to return to its original position once disturbed.

ALL

6564. If the aircraft's nose initially tends to return to its original position after the elevator control is pressed forward and released, the aircraft displays

A— positive static stability.
B— neutral dynamic stability.
C— negative dynamic stability.

An aircraft has positive static stability if there is an initial tendency for it to return to its original state of equilibrium after being disturbed. The nose of an aircraft with positive static stability will tend to return to its original position after the elevator control is pressed forward and released. (PLT480) — FAA-H-8083-25

Answer (B) is incorrect because neutral dynamic stability is the tendency for oscillations to continue at the same rate. Answer (C) is incorrect because negative dynamic stability is the tendency for oscillations to increase once they start.

ALL

6565. If the aircraft's nose initially tends to move farther from its original position after the elevator control is pressed forward and released, the aircraft displays

A— negative static stability.
B— positive static stability.
C— positive dynamic stability.

Negative static stability is the tendency for an aircraft to deviate further from its original state of equilibrium after being disturbed. The nose of an aircraft with negative static stability will tend to continue to go down after the elevator control is pressed forward and released. (PLT480) — FAA-H-8083-25

Answer (B) is incorrect because positive static stability is the tendency for the aircraft to return to its original position. Answer (C) is incorrect because positive dynamic stability is the tendency for oscillations to decrease.

ALL

6568. If the aircraft's nose remains in the new position after the elevator control is pressed forward and released, the aircraft displays

A— neutral static stability.
B— negative static stability.
C— positive static stability.

Neutral static stability is the initial tendency for an aircraft to remain in a new condition after its equilibrium has been disturbed. An aircraft demonstrates neutral static stability if its nose remains in its new position when the elevator control is pressed forward and released. (PLT480) — FAA-H-8083-25

Answer (B) is incorrect because negative static stability is the tendency for the aircraft to move further from the original position. Answer (C) is incorrect because positive static stability is the tendency for the aircraft to return to its original position.

ALL

6562. The most desirable type of stability for an aircraft to possess is

A— neutral static stability.
B— positive static stability.
C— positive dynamic stability.

Positive static stability is the initial tendency for an aircraft to return to the original state of equilibrium after being disturbed. Positive dynamic stability is the most desirable type of stability for an aircraft to posses. (PLT236) — FAA-H-8083-25

ALL

6569. If the airspeed increases and decreases during longitudinal phugoid oscillations, the aircraft

A— will display poor trimming qualities.
B— is maintaining a nearly constant angle of attack.
C— is constantly changing angle of attack making it difficult for the pilot to reduce the magnitude of the oscillations.

When the airspeed increases and decreases as an aircraft experiences phugoid oscillations (long-period longitudinal oscillations), the aircraft is demonstrating positive static stability and is maintaining a nearly constant angle of attack. (PLT095) — FAA-H-8083-25

Answer (A) is incorrect because phugoid oscillations can usually be trimmed out. Answer (C) is incorrect because the angle of attack remains constant as the airspeed changes.

ALL

6570. If an aircraft has negative dynamic and positive static stability, this will result in

A— undamped oscillations.
B— divergent oscillations.
C— convergent oscillations.

An aircraft having positive static stability will tend to return to its condition of steady flight after it has been disturbed. But, if it has negative dynamic stability, the static corrections will increase and result in divergent oscillations. (PLT236) — FAA-H-8083-25

Answer (A) is incorrect because undamped oscillations are the result of neutral dynamic stability. Answer (C) is incorrect because convergent oscillations are the result of positive dynamic stability.

Answers

6565 [A]   6568 [A]   6562 [C]   6569 [B]   6570 [B]

AIR, LSA, WSC

6506. An airplane would have a tendency to nose up and have an inherent tendency to enter a stalled condition when the center of pressure is

A— below the center of gravity.
B— aft of the center of gravity.
C— forward of the center of gravity.

For longitudinal stability in an airplane, the center of pressure of the wing is located behind the center of gravity, where it produces a downward pitching moment. This downward pitching moment is balanced by a downward aerodynamic force on the horizontal tail, which causes the nose to pitch up. When the nose pitches up, the airspeed drops off, and the aerodynamic down-load on the tail decreases. The nose drops and returns the airplane to level flight. If the airplane is loaded in such a way that the center of gravity is behind the center of pressure, the airplane will be unstable. When it pitches upward, the pitch will increase, and the airplane will tend to enter into a stalled condition. (PLT477) — FAA-H-8083-25

AIR, LSA

6576. A sweptwing airplane with weak static directional stability and increased dihedral causes an increase in

A— Mach tuck tendency.
B— Dutch roll tendency.
C— longitudinal stability.

When the dihedral effect is large in comparison with static direction stability, the dutch roll motion has weak dampening and is increased. (PLT214) — FAA-H-8083-25

Answer (A) is incorrect because Mach tuck tendency occurs when going through the sound barrier. Answer (C) is incorrect because longitudinal stability is not affected by directional stability or dihedral.

AIR, GLI, LSA, WSC

6531. Changes in the center of pressure of a wing affect the aircraft's

A— lift/drag ratio.
B— lifting capacity.
C— aerodynamic balance and controllability.

The center of pressure of an asymmetrical airfoil moves forward as the angle of attack is increased, and backward as the angle of attack is decreased. This backward and forward movement of the point at which lift acts, affects the aerodynamic balance and the controllability of the aircraft. (PLT236) — FAA-H-8083-25

Answer (A) is incorrect because the lift/drag ratio is determined by the angle of attack. Answer (B) is incorrect because lifting capacity is determined by angle of attack and airspeed.

AIR, GLI, LSA, WSC

6575. The purpose of aircraft wing dihedral angle is to

A— increase lateral stability.
B— increase longitudinal stability.
C— increase lift coefficient of the wing.

Dihedral, the acute angle between the lateral axis of an aircraft and a line that passes through the center of the wing, is used to increase the lateral stability of the aircraft. When a wing drops, the angle of attack and the lift of the dropping wing are increased. At the same time, the angle of attack and the lift of the rising wing are decreased, and the aircraft returns to level flight. (PLT214) — FAA-H-8083-25

Answers (B) and (C) are incorrect because longitudinal stability and lift coefficient of the wing is not affected by wing dihedral.

AIR, GLI, LSA, WSC

6561. Which aircraft characteristics contribute to spiral instability?

A— Weak static directional stability and weak dihedral effect.
B— Strong static directional stability and weak dihedral effect.
C— Weak static directional stability and strong dihedral effect.

Strong static directional stability and weak dihedral effect contribute to spiral instability. When the lateral equilibrium of an aircraft is disturbed by a gust of air and a sideslip is introduced, the strong directional stability tends to yaw the nose into the resultant relative wind, while the comparatively weak dihedral lags in restoring the lateral balance. Due to this yaw, the wing on the outside of the turn travels forward faster than the inside wing, and as a consequence, its lift becomes greater. This action produces an overbanking tendency which, if not corrected by the pilot, will result in the bank angle becoming steeper and steeper. At the same time, the strong directional stability which yaws the aircraft into the relative wind is actually forcing the nose to a lower pitch attitude. This is the start of a downward spiral which, if not counteracted by the pilot, will gradually increase into a steep spiral dive. (PLT244) — FAA-H-8083-25

Answers (A) and (C) are incorrect because spiral instability occurs with strong static directional stability and weak dihedral effect.

Answers

6506 [C]	6576 [B]	6531 [C]	6575 [A]	6561 [B]

Aerodynamic Efficiency

The efficiency of a wing is shown by the relationship between the lift and the drag produced at any given angle of attack. The Angle of Attack Chart shows the important relationships between the coefficient of lift C_L, the coefficient of drag C_D, and the lift over drag ratio L/D.

1. The C_L increases smoothly with the angle of attack until the stalling angle of attack is reached at 20°. Beyond this angle of attack the lift drops off totally.

2. The C_D increases steadily with the angle of attack.

3. The L/D curve increases with the angle of attack until the L/D_{MAX} is reached; then it decreases. The L/D_{MAX} is the most efficient angle of attack to fly. At L/D_{MAX} the airfoil produces the greatest lift for the least drag, and this is the angle of attack at which the aircraft will travel the maximum horizontal distance for each foot of altitude lost. In FAA Figure 19, L/D_{MAX} is reached at an angle of attack of 6°.

4. At angles of attack below that which provides L/D_{MAX}, the majority of the drag is parasite drag, and at angles of attack above that which produces L/D_{MAX}, the majority of the drag is induced drag. Flight at any airspeed other than that which produces L/D_{MAX} will cause the total drag for the lift to increase.

The Drag Chart shows the relationship between parasite drag, induced drag, and total drag for any airspeed, and thus at any angle of attack. The velocity increases from left to right, but the angle of attack increases from right to left. Induced drag increases as the angle of attack increases, and parasite drag increases as the angle of attack decreases. The least total drag is produced at the airspeed at which the induced and parasite drag are equal, and this is the airspeed at which the airplane has the highest lift over drag ratio, L/D_{MAX}, and it is the airspeed at which the aircraft will have its maximum glide range in still air. *See* Figure 2-9.

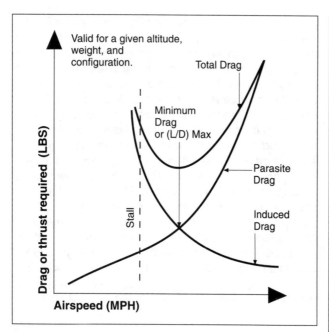

Figure 2-9. Drag vs. airspeed

ALL
6814. Maximum gliding distance of an aircraft is obtained when

A— parasite drag is the least.
B— induced drag and parasite drag are equal.
C— induced drag equals the coefficient of lift.

L/DMAX occurs at the airspeed where parasite drag and induced drag are equal. If the aircraft is operated in steady flight at L/DMAX, the total drag is at a minimum. Maximum gliding distance of the aircraft will be obtained at this airspeed. (PLT237) — FAA-H-8083-25

ALL
6556. (Refer to Figure 19.) The lift/drag at 2° angle of attack is approximately the same as the lift/drag for

A— 9.75° angle of attack.
B— 10.5° angle of attack.
C— 16.5° angle of attack.

In the Angle of Attack Chart, follow a vertical line upward from the 2° angle of attack until it intersects the L/D curve. From this point of intersection, follow a line horizontally to the right until it again intersects the L/D curve. From

Answers

6814   [B]   6556   [C]

this point, follow a line downward until it reaches the angle of attack scale. This line intersects the scale at 16.5°. (PLT046) — FAA-H-8083-25

AIR, WSC, LSA

6555. (Refer to Figure 19.) Which statement is true regarding airplane flight at L/D$_{MAX}$?

A— Any angle of attack other than that for L/D$_{MAX}$ increases parasite drag.

B— Any angle of attack other than that for L/D$_{MAX}$ increases the lift/drag ratio.

C— Any angle of attack other than that for L/D$_{MAX}$ increases total drag for a given airplane's lift.

The L/D curve peaks at the point of L/D$_{MAX}$. This occurs at an angle of attack of 6°. Flight at any other angle of attack results in a lower L/D, because the total drag increases for a given amount of lift. If the angle of attack is increased, the induced drag increases, and if the angle

of attack is decreased, the airspeed increases and the parasite drag increases. (PLT046) — FAA-H-8083-25

Answer (A) is incorrect because parasite drag changes with speed, not angle of attack. Answer (B) is incorrect because any angle of attack other than that for L/D$_{MAX}$ decreases the L/D ratio.

AIR, WSC, LSA

6557. (Refer to Figure 19.) At which angle of attack does the airplane travel the maximum horizontal distance per foot of altitude lost?

A— 6°.

B— 12.3°.

C— 20°.

An airplane travels the greatest horizontal distance per foot of altitude lost when it is flying at an angle of attack which produces the maximum L/D ratio (L/D$_{MAX}$). The chart shows that this is an angle of attack of 6°. (PLT018) — FAA-H-8083-25

Load Factors and Maneuvering Speed

Load factor is the ratio of the amount of load imposed on an aircraft structure to the weight of the structure itself. Load factors imposed on an aircraft in flight are measured by accelerometers and are expressed in G-units. A 1-G load factor is one in which the load on the structure is equal to the weight of the structure. An aircraft resting on the ground imposes a 1-G load on its landing gear.

When an aircraft is maneuvered in flight, the inertia forces increase its apparent weight, and the structure must support a weight greater than that of the airplane at rest. If an accelerometer in an airplane weighing 2,675 pounds indicates 2.5 in a steep turn, the wings are supporting a load of 2.5 × 2,675, or 6,687.5 pounds. An aircraft stalls when its wing reaches a **critical angle of attack**, regardless of its airspeed.

The load factor increases in a coordinated banked turn because of the centrifugal force acting on the aircraft as it is pulled around in the turn. The increased load factor requires a higher angle of attack to provide the needed lift, and as a result, there is a correlation between the angle of bank, the load factor, and the increase in stall speed.

When an airplane is flying in a coordinated 60°-banked level turn, the load factor is 2, and the stall speed has increased by approximately 40%. If the airplane normally stalls at 60 knots, it will stall at 84 knots in a coordinated 60°-banked turn. This is the reason it is so important to teach students to recognize the onset of an accelerated stall.

By using FAA Figure 18, it is found that an airplane with a normal stalling speed of 62 knots can be forced into an accelerated stall at 124 knots (an increase of 100%). This will occur at a bank angle of 75°, and at this bank angle the load factor is 4 Gs.

Continued

Answers

6555　[C]　　　　6557　[A]

The **design maneuvering speed** (V_A) of an aircraft is the maximum airspeed at which an aircraft may be safely stalled. This airspeed is not marked on the airspeed indicator, but it is found in the Pilot's Operating Handbook (POH). For aircraft that do not have a POH, this speed is approximately 1.7 times the normal stalling speed. When flying into severe turbulence, the pilot should reduce the airspeed to the maneuvering speed.

Airplanes certified in the normal category can tolerate a load factor of +3.8 and -1.52. Airplanes certified in the utility category can tolerate load factors of +4.4 and -1.76.

A Load Factor Chart, or V-g Diagram shows the relationship between airspeed and load factor for all types of operations. *See* FAA Figure 17.

1. Point A is the normal wings-level stall speed of this airplane. This is the airspeed at which the 1-G horizontal line crosses the dashed maximum-lift capability curve.

2. Point C is the design maneuvering airspeed, V_A. This is the highest airspeed the airplane can be stalled without exceeding the 3.8-G load factor.

3. Point D is the maximum structural cruising airspeed, V_{NO}. This is marked on the airspeed indicator as the upper limit of the green arc or the bottom of the yellow arc.

4. Point E is the never-exceed airspeed, V_{NE}. This is marked on an airspeed indicator with a red radial line.

5. The horizontal dashed line between points A and C show the positive limit load factor, which for this airplane is 3.8 Gs.

6. The red-shaded area all around the outside of the V-g diagram shows the airspeeds and load factors that will cause structural damage.

7. The darker shaded area is the caution speed range, and is the limiting speed for flight in which abrupt maneuvers may be executed, or in which turbulent air may be encountered.

8. The straight lines marked -30 fps, -15 fps. +15 fps, and +30 fps are the lines showing the load factors produced at the various indicated airspeeds by sharp-edged wind gusts of 30 and 15 feet per second positive and 15 and 30 feet per second negative.

AIR, WSC, LSA, PPC

6541. If severe turbulence is encountered, the aircraft's airspeed should be reduced to

A— maneuvering speed.
B— normal structural cruising speed.
C— the minimum steady flight speed in the landing configuration.

If severe turbulence is encountered in flight, the aircraft's airspeed should be reduced to the design maneuvering speed. This speed is not marked on the airspeed indicator, but it is found in the Pilot's Operating Handbook (POH). (PLT120) — FAA-H-8083-25

AIR, WSC, LSA, PPC

6542. If an airplane's gross weight is 3,250 pounds, what is the load acting on this airplane during a level 60° banked turn?

A— 3,250 pounds.
B— 5,200 pounds.
C— 6,500 pounds.

A coordinated, level 60° banked turn subjects an airplane to a load factor of 2 Gs. This means that if the airplane has a gross weight of 3,250 pounds, the wings will have to support 3,250 x 2 or 6,500 pounds in a coordinated 60° banked turn. (PLT309) — FAA-H-8083-25

Answers

6541   [A]   6542   [C]

AIR, WSC, LSA

6543. An airplane has a normal stalling speed of 60 knots but is forced into an accelerated stall at twice that speed. What maximum load factor will result from this maneuver?

A— 4 G's.
B— 2 G's.
C— 1 G.

An accelerated stall is one that occurs at a higher than normal airspeed, and this often occurs in a steep-banked turn. An airplane that normally stalls at 60 knots can be forced into an accelerated stall at 120 knots. This is a 100% increase in stalling speed. In FAA Figure 18 we see that the stalling speed increases 100% in a 75° bank. We also see that a coordinated 75° bank subjects the airplane to a load factor of 4 Gs. (PLT477) — FAA-H-8083-25

AIR, WSC, LSA, PPC

6550. (Refer to Figure 18.) What increase in load factor would take place if the angle of bank were increased from 60° to 80°?

A— 2 G's.
B— 3 G's.
C— 4 G's.

In a coordinated 60° banked turn, the load factor is 2 Gs. In a coordinated 80° banked turn, the load factor is 6 Gs. This is an increase of 4 Gs. (PLT074) — FAA-H-8083-25

AIR, WSC, LSA

6544. (Refer to Figure 17.) A positive load factor of 4 at 140 knots would cause the airplane to

A— stall.
B— break apart.
C— be subjected to structural damage.

The horizontal line for a load factor of 4 crosses the vertical line for 140 knots in the shaded area, indicating possible structural damage. (PLT074) — FAA-H-8083-25

AIR, WSC, LSA

6545. (Refer to Figure 17.) What load factor would be created if positive 30 feet per second gusts were encountered at 130 knots?

A— 3.8.
B— 3.0.
C— 2.0.

Follow the slanted line for +30 fps gusts until it crosses an imaginary vertical line for 130 knots (midway between 120 and 140 knots). This intersection falls on the horizontal line for a load factor of 3.0. (PLT074) — FAA-H-8083-25

AIR, WSC, LSA

6546. (Refer to Figure 17.) The horizontal dashed line from point C to point E represents the

A— positive limit load factor.
B— airspeed range for normal operations.
C— maximum structural cruise airspeed range.

The horizontal dashed line between points C and E represents the positive limit load factor. For this airplane, which is licensed in the normal category, the limit load factor is 3.8 Gs. (PLT074) — FAA-H-8083-25

AIR, WSC, LSA

6546-1. (Refer to Figure 17.) The airspeed indicated by point A is

A— maneuvering speed.
B— normal stall speed.
C— maximum structural cruising speed.

The airspeed indicated by point A is the normal stall speed. The aircraft in Figure 17 is capable of developing no more than +1G at 65 knots, the wings-level stall speed of the aircraft. (PLT074) — FAA-H-8083-25

Answer (A) is incorrect because maneuvering speed is indicated by point B. Answer (C) is incorrect because maximum structural cruising speed is indicated by point C.

AIR, WSC, LSA

6547. (Refer to Figure 17.) The airspeed indicated by point C is

A— maneuvering speed.
B— never-exceed speed.
C— maximum structural cruising speed.

The airspeed indicated by point C is V_A, the design maneuvering airspeed. This is the maximum airspeed recommended for flight into turbulence. (PLT074) — FAA-H-8083-25

Answer (B) is incorrect because V_{NE} is indicated by point E. Answer (C) is incorrect because V_{NO} is indicated by point D.

Answers

6543 [A]	6550 [C]	6544 [C]	6545 [B]	6546 [A]	6546-1 [B]
6547 [A]					

AIR, WSC, LSA

6548. (Refer to Figure 17.) The airspeed indicated by point E is

A— maneuvering speed.
B— never-exceed speed.
C— maximum structural cruising speed.

The airspeed indicated by point E is never-exceed speed (V_{NE}). (PLT074) — FAA-H-8083-25

Answer (A) is incorrect because V_A is indicated by point C. Answer (C) is incorrect because V_{NO} is indicated by point D.

AIR, WSC, LSA

6549. (Refer to Figure 17.) The airspeed indicated by point D is

A— maneuvering speed.
B— never-exceed speed.
C— maximum structural cruising speed.

The airspeed indicated by point D is V_{NO}, the maximum structural cruising speed. (PLT074) — FAA-H-8083-25

Answer (A) is incorrect because V_A is indicated by point C. Answer (B) is incorrect because V_{NE} is indicated by point E.

Stalls and Spins

A **stall** is a flight condition that occurs when the angle of attack becomes so high that the air flowing over the top of the wing can no longer flow smoothly and it breaks away. This disturbs the low pressure and causes the wing to lose lift. A wing does not stall because of low airspeed or high gross weight, but it stalls when a specific angle of attack is reached, regardless of the speed or weight. This is the reason it is important to teach accelerated stalls and approach to landing stalls.

By using the Load Factor/Stall Speed Chart in FAA Figure 18, we can determine the percent increase in stall speed and the load factor produced by any degree of bank in a coordinated turn. To use this chart, follow the vertical line upward from 60° bank angle until it intersects the Load-Factor Curve, and then project a line horizontally to the left until it intersects the Load Factor Index at 2-G. Follow the vertical line upward from the 60° bank angle until it intersects the Stall-Speed-Increase Curve, then project a line horizontally to the left until it intersects the Percent Increase in Stall Speed Index at 40%. A 60° banked coordinated turn will produce a 2-G load factor, and it will cause a 40% increase in the aircraft's stall speed.

A **spin** is a flight condition in which one wing is more stalled than the other. A spin is entered by increasing the angle of attack until the aircraft stalls. At this instant the rudder is deflected and the aircraft yaws about its vertical axis. Yawing causes the outside wing to speed up and come out of the stall a little, while the inside wing is driven deeper into the stall. The lift produced by the outside wing has a forward component which causes the aircraft to rotate as it descends in a nose-down attitude at a slow airspeed.

AIR, PPC, WSC, LSA, MCI

6534. The angle of attack at which an airplane stalls

A— increases with an increase in engine power.
B— remains constant regardless of gross weight.
C— varies with gross weight and density altitude.

An aircraft wing stalls when the air can no longer flow smoothly over the surface. At the critical angle of attack, the airflow breaks away and burbles. The stall always occurs at the same angle of attack, regardless of the gross weight. (PLT168) — FAA-H-8083-3

Answers (A) and (C) are incorrect because the airplane stalls at a constant angle of attack.

AIR, PPC, WSC, LSA, MCI

6748. As altitude increases, the indicated airspeed at which a given airplane stalls in a particular configuration will

A— remain the same as at low altitude.
B— decrease as the true airspeed increases.
C— increase because the air density decreases.

An airplane of given weight and configuration requires the same dynamic pressure to maintain flight at a given angle of attack at any altitude. The airspeed indicator is affected by the dynamic pressure in the same way as the airfoil. Thus, the airplane at altitude will stall at the same indicated airspeed as at sea level, but because of the reduced air density, the true airspeed will be greater. (PLT127) — FAA-H-8083-25

Answers

6548 [B]	6549 [C]	6534 [B]	6748 [A]

AIR, PPC, WSC, LSA, MCI

6551. (Refer to Figure 18.) What is the stall speed of an airplane under a load factor of 4 if the unaccelerated stall speed is 70 knots?

A— 91 knots.
B— 132 knots.
C— 140 knots.

The stall speed of an airplane increases as the square root of the load factor. An airplane with a stalling speed of 70 knots will stall at 140 knots under a load factor of 4. The stall speed increases as the square root of the load factor, but it can also be found by using the Load Factor/Stall Speed Curve. Draw a line to the right from the load factor of 4 until it intersects the Load Factor Curve. From this point, draw a line upward until it intersects the Stall-Speed-Increase Curve. From this point of intersection, draw a line to the left until it intersects the Percent-Increase-In-Stall-Speed Index. This intersection is at 100%. When this airplane is in a flight condition that increases its load factor to 4 GS, the stalling speed will increase by 100% to 140 knots. (PLT018) — FAA-H-8083-25

AIR, PPC, WSC, LSA, MCI

6551-1. (Refer to Figure 18.) What is the stall speed of an airplane in a 30 degree bank turn if the level stall speed is 100 knots?

A— 100 knots.
B— 102 knots.
C— 108 knots.

The stall speed can be found by using the Load Factor/ Stall Speed Curve. Starting at the bottom 30-degree mark, move up to the stall speed increase line, then move to the left to find an 8% increase. When this airplane is in a 30° bank, the stall speed will increase by 8% to 108 knots. (PLT018) — FAA-H-8083-25

AIR, PPC, WSC, LSA

6552. (Refer to Figure 18.) If, during a steady turn with a 50° bank, a load factor of 1.5 were imposed on an airplane which has an unaccelerated stall speed of 60 knots, at what speed would the airplane first stall?

A— 68 knots.
B— 75 knots.
C— 82 knots.

Draw a line to the right from the load factor of 1.5 until it intersects the Load Factor Curve (this intersection is at a 50° bank angle). Draw a line upward until it intersects the Stall-Speed-Increase Curve. From this point of intersection, draw a line to the left until it intersects the Percent-Increase-In-Stall-Speed Index. This intersection is at 25%. When this airplane is in a flight condition that increases its load factor to 1.5 Gs, the stalling speed will increase to 25% of 60 knots, or 75 knots. (PLT018) — FAA-H-8083-25

AIR, PPC, WSC, LSA

6553. (Refer to Figure 18.) A 70 percent increase in stalling speed would imply a bank angle of

A— 67°.
B— 70°.
C— 83°.

Follow a horizontal line to the right from the 70% Increase-In-Stall-Speed Index until it intersects the Stall-Speed-Increase Curve. This intersection is on the vertical line for 70°. When an airplane is in a coordinated 70° bank, its stall speed increases by 70%. (PLT074) — FAA-H-8083-25

AIR, PPC, WSC, LSA

6554. (Refer to Figure 18.) What is the stall speed of an airplane under a load factor of 2 if the unaccelerated stall speed is 100 knots?

A— 115 knots.
B— 129 knots.
C— 140 knots.

Draw a line to the right from the load factor of 2 until it intersects the Load Factor Curve (this intersection is at a 60° bank angle). Draw a line upward from this point until it intersects the Stall-Speed-Increase Curve. From this point of intersection, draw a line to the left until it intersects the Percent-Increase-In-Stall-Speed Index. This intersection is at 40%. When this airplane is in a flight condition that increases its load factor to 2 Gs, the stalling speed will increase to 140% of 100 knots, or 140 knots. (PLT018) — FAA-H-8083-25

Answers

| 6551 [C] | 6551-1 [C] | 6552 [B] | 6553 [B] | 6554 [C] |

AIR, GLI, PPC, WSC, LSA, MCI

6535. Which statement is true relating to the factors which produce stalls?

A— The critical angle of attack is a function of the degree of bank.
B— The stalling angle of attack depends upon the speed of the airflow over the wings.
C— The stalling angle of attack is independent of the speed of airflow over the wings.

An aircraft wing stalls at the same angle of attack, regardless of the gross weight or the speed of the air over the surface. The constant regarding a stall is the angle of attack. An airfoil stalls when the angle of attack becomes great enough that the air can no longer flow smoothly over its upper surface. (PLT168) — FAA-H-8083-3

AIR, GLI, PPC, WSC, LSA, MCI

6536. The critical angle of attack at which a given aircraft stalls is dependent on the

A— gross weight.
B— design of the wing.
C— attitude and airspeed.

Each aircraft has a particular angle of attack where the airflow separates from the upper surface of the wing and the stall occurs. This critical angle of attack varies from 16° to 20° depending on the aircraft's design. But each aircraft has only one specific angle of attack where the stall occurs. (PLT168) — FAA-H-8083-25

AIR, GLI, PPC, WSC, LSA, MCI

6558. Which action will result in a stall?

A— Flying at too low an airspeed.
B— Raising the aircraft's nose too high.
C— Exceeding the critical angle of attack.

A given aircraft will always stall at the same angle of attack regardless of airspeed, weight, load factor, or density altitude. Each aircraft has a particular angle of attack where the airflow separates from the upper surface of the wing and the stall occurs. This critical angle of attack varies from 16° to 20°, depending on the aircraft design, but each aircraft has only one critical angle of attack where the stall occurs. (PLT168) — FAA-H-8083-25

AIR, GLI, PPC, WSC, LSA, MCI

6511. Which statement is true concerning the aerodynamic conditions which occur during a spin entry?

A— After a full stall, both wings remain in a stalled condition throughout the rotation.
B— After a partial stall, the wing that drops remains in a stalled condition while the rising wing regains and continues to produce lift, causing the rotation.
C— After a full stall, the wing that drops continues in a stalled condition while the rising wing regains and continues to produce some lift, causing the rotation.

When an aircraft is fully stalled and one wing drops, the nose yaws in the direction of the low wing. If this yawing is not corrected, the low wing will go lower, and its angle of attack will increase beyond its stalling angle and keep the low wing stalled. As the high wing rises, its angle of attack decreases and it regains some lift, pulling the aircraft around into the spin. The aircraft descends vertically, rolling and yawing. (PLT245) — FAA-H-8083-3

Answer (A) is incorrect because the high wing regains some lift. Answer (B) is incorrect because a spin occurs after a full stall.

AIR, GLI, PPC, WSC, LSA, MCI

6806. Which characteristic of a spin is not a characteristic of a steep spiral?

A— Stalled wing.
B— High rate of rotation.
C— Rapid loss of altitude.

A spin results when a sufficient degree of rolling or yawing control input is imposed on an aircraft in the stalled condition. Without at least one wing stalled, a spin cannot occur. (PLT245) — FAA-H-8083-3

Answers

| 6535 | [C] | 6536 | [B] | 6558 | [C] | 6511 | [C] | 6806 | [A] |

Wing Shapes

It is desirable for a wing to stall in the root area before it stalls near the tips. This provides a warning of an impending stall and allows the ailerons to be effective during the stall. A **rectangular wing** stalls in the root area first. The stall begins near the tip and progresses inboard on a highly tapered wing, or a wing with sweepback. *See* Figure 2-10.

An **elliptical wing** produces the best lift coefficient and a minimum of induced drag for a given aspect ratio, but an elliptical wing does not have aileron effectiveness during the stall. The main disadvantage of an elliptical wing for general aviation aircraft, however, is its high production cost.

The wings of most modern high-performance airplanes are swept back. Sweepback increases the **critical Mach number**, the airspeed at which there is the first indication of air flowing over the surface at the speed of sound. By increasing the critical Mach number, sweepback delays the onset of compressibility effects. One major disadvantage of a sweptback wing is that it increases the dutch roll tendencies of the airplane. **Dutch roll** is a coupled lateral-directional oscillation which is usually dynamically stable, but it is objectionable in an airplane because of its oscillatory nature. Dutch roll is normally prevented by the use of yaw dampers in the flight control system.

Aspect ratio is the ratio of the span of an aircraft wing to its mean, or average, chord. Generally speaking, the higher the aspect ratio, the more efficient the wing. But for practical purposes, structural considerations normally limit the aspect ratio for all except high-performance sailplanes. A high-aspect-ratio wing has a low stall speed, and at a constant air velocity and high angle of attack, it has less drag than a low-aspect-ratio wing.

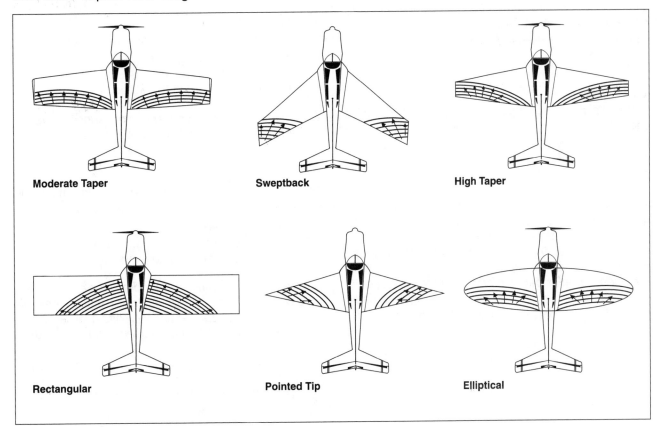

Figure 2-10. Stall progression patterns based on different wing shapes.

Continued

Considering the wings described in FAA Figure 21, we see the following relationships:

Aircraft 1 has an aspect ratio of 40/6 or 6.7.

Aircraft 2 has an aspect ratio of 35/5 or 7.

Aircraft 3 has an aspect ratio of 48/6 or 8.

Aircraft 3 has the highest aspect ratio of those in FAA Figure 21. If we consider only the aspect ratio, this wing will generate the greatest lift of all those given here.

Aircraft 4 has an aspect ratio of 30/6 or 5.

Aircraft 4 has the lowest aspect ratio of those given here. If we consider only the aspect ratio, this wing will have the greatest drag of all those given in the FAA figure.

AIR, PPC, WSC, LSA

6574. A rectangular wing, as compared to other wing planforms, has a tendency to stall first at the

A— wingtip providing adequate stall warning.
B— wing root providing adequate stall warning.
C— wingtip providing inadequate stall warning.

The rectangular wing planform, in addition to being easiest and least costly to build, has the advantage of the stall beginning at the wing root and progressing toward the tip. This provides good stall warning and allows aileron control to be effective well into the stall. (PLT214) — FAA-H-8083-25

Answers (A) and (C) are incorrect because the wing root stalls first with a rectangular wing.

AIR, PPC, WSC, LSA

6572. Which subsonic planform provides the best lift coefficient?

A— Tapered wing.
B— Elliptical wing.
C— Rectangular wing.

The elliptical wing is the ideal subsonic planform. The normal distribution of lift along the span of a wing matches an elliptical planform, and each square foot of area produces the same lift pressure. The induced downflow caused by the wing is uniform throughout the span. An elliptical planform produces the best lift coefficient and a minimum of induced drag for a given aspect ratio. (PLT214) — FAA-H-8083-25

AIR, PPC, WSC, LSA

6573. On which wing planform does the stall begin at the wingtip and progress inward toward the wing root?

A— Sweepback wing.
B— Rectangular wing.
C— Moderate taper wing.

On a sweptback wing, the stall begins at the tips and progresses inward to the wing root. (PLT214) — FAA-H-8083-25

AIR, GLI, PPC, WSC, LSA

6577. Aspect ratio of a wing is defined as the ratio of the

A— wingspan to the wing root.
B— wingspan to the mean chord.
C— square of the chord to the wingspan.

Aspect ratio is the ratio of the span of a wing to its mean (average) chord. (PLT238) — FAA-H-8083-25

AIR, GLI, PPC, WSC, LSA

6578. A wing with a very high aspect ratio (in comparison with a low aspect ratio wing) will have

A— a low stall speed.
B— increased drag at high angles of attack.
C— poor control qualities at low airspeeds.

A high-aspect-ratio wing has less drag than a low-aspect-ratio wing, especially at high angles of attack. Generally speaking, a high-aspect-ratio wing has a lower stalling speed than a wing with a low aspect ratio. (PLT238) — FAA-H-8083-25

Answer (B) is incorrect because a high-aspect-ratio wing de-creases drag at higher angles of attack. Answer (C) is incorrect because control qualities at low airspeeds are better with a high-aspect-ratio wing.

Answers

6574 [B]   6572 [B]   6573 [A]   6577 [B]   6578 [A]

AIR, GLI, PPC, WSC, LSA

7329. (Refer to Figure 21.) Of aircraft 1, 2, or 3, which has the lowest aspect ratio?

A— 1.
B— 2.
C— 3.

Aspect ratio is the ratio of the wing span to the average wing chord.

Aircraft 1 has an aspect ratio of 6.7 (40 ÷ 6).

Aircraft 2 has an aspect ratio of 7 (35 ÷ 5).

Aircraft 3 has an aspect ratio of 8 (48 ÷ 6).

(PLT238) — FAA-H-8083-25

AIR, GLI, PPC, WSC, LSA

6579. At a constant velocity in airflow, a high aspect ratio wing will have (in comparison with a low aspect ratio wing)

A— increased drag, especially at a low angle of attack.
B— decreased drag, especially at a high angle of attack.
C— increased drag, especially at a high angle of attack.

A wing with a high aspect ratio will have less drag, especially at a high angle of attack, than a wing with a lower aspect ratio. (PLT238) — FAA-H-8083-25

AIR, GLI, PPC, WSC, LSA

6580. (Refer to Figure 21.) Which aircraft has the highest aspect ratio?

A— 2.
B— 4.
C— 6.

Aspect ratio is the ratio of the wing span to the average wing chord.

Aircraft 2 has an aspect ratio of 7 (35 ÷ 5).

Aircraft 4 has an aspect ratio of 5 (30 ÷ 6).

Aircraft 6 has an aspect ratio of 9 (36 ÷ 4).

(PLT238) — FAA-H-8083-25

AIR, GLI, PPC, WSC, LSA

6581. (Refer to Figure 21.) Which aircraft has the lowest aspect ratio?

A— 8.
B— 10.
C— 12.

Aspect ratio is the ratio of the wing span to the average wing chord.

Aircraft 8 has an aspect ratio of 9 (36 ÷ 4).

Aircraft 10 has an aspect ratio of 12.7 (57 ÷ 4.5).

Aircraft 12 has an aspect ratio of 25 (75 ÷ 3).

(PLT238) — FAA-H-8083-25

AIR, GLI, PPC, WSC, LSA

6582. (Refer to Figure 21.) Consider only aspect ratio (other factors remain constant). Which aircraft will generate greatest lift?

A— 13.
B— 15.
C— 16.

Aspect ratio is the ratio of the wing span to the average wing chord.

Aircraft 13 has an aspect ratio of 14.75 (59 ÷ 4).

Aircraft 15 has an aspect ratio of 9 (117 ÷ 13).

Aircraft 16 has an aspect ratio of 6.4 (32 ÷ 5).

With all other considerations the same, the wing with the highest aspect ratio will generate the greatest lift. (PLT238) — FAA-H-8083-25

AIR, GLI, PPC, WSC, LSA

6583. (Refer to Figure 21.) Consider only aspect ratio (other factors remain constant). Which aircraft will generate greatest drag?

A— 2.
B— 4.
C— 6.

Aspect ratio is the ratio of the wing span to the average wing chord.

Aircraft 2 has an aspect ratio of 7 (35 ÷ 5).

Aircraft 4 has an aspect ratio of 5 (30 ÷ 6).

Aircraft 6 has an aspect ratio of 9 (36 ÷ 4).

With all other considerations the same, the wing with the lowest aspect ratio will generate the greatest drag. (PLT238) — FAA-H-8083-25

Answers

7329 [A]	6579 [B]	6580 [C]	6581 [A]	6582 [A]	6583 [B]

High-Lift Devices

An aircraft wing stalls at a specific angle of attack, but the stalling angle of attack can be increased by the use of high-lift devices such as **flaps**, **slots**, and **slats**. High-lift devices allow a wing to fly at a higher angle of attack before it stalls; therefore, these devices allow lift to be produced at slower airspeeds than would be possible without them.

Slots are fixed ducts between the bottom and the top of the leading edge of a wing ahead of the aileron. At high angles of attack, high-pressure air from below the wing is ducted back over the top of the wing. Here, its high velocity creates the needed low pressure that holds the air against the surface and prevents it from burbling until a much higher angle of attack is reached. Allowing a higher angle of attack before the stall occurs allows the aircraft to land at a slower airspeed.

Flaps, which are the most widely used high-lift devices on general aviation aircraft, modify the airfoil shape by increasing the camber of the wing. This increases both the lift and the drag produced by the wing. It is common practice in airplanes, on takeoff, to lower the flaps less than half way. This increases the lift more than it increases the drag, and the airplane is able to take off in a shorter distance than it could without the use of flaps. For landing, the flaps can be fully extended. This increases the drag more than the lift, and the aircraft can descend at a steep approach angle without building up excessive airspeed. The most commonly used flaps are seen in FAA Figure 23.

1. The plain, or simple, flap is a hinged portion of the wing trailing edge inboard of the ailerons. This is the least effective type of flap, but its economy of construction makes it popular on light airplanes.

2. The split trailing edge flap creates a large amount of drag and produces the least change in pitching moment.

3. The slotted flap produces a gap between the wing and the flap leading edge. High-energy air from below the wing flows through this gap and accelerates the air on the upper surface of the flap. This delays flow separation over the flap.

4. The Fowler flap extends out from the rear of the wing on tracks, and increases the area of the wing as well as changing its camber. The Fowler flap produces the largest increase in lift coefficient with the smallest increase in drag, and it causes the greatest change in pitching moment of all of the flaps listed here.

AIR, LSA

6501. The use of a slot in the leading edge of the wing enables an airplane to land at a slower speed because it

A— changes the camber of the wing.
B— delays the stall to a higher angle of attack.
C— decelerates the upper surface boundary layer air.

A fixed slot in a wing conducts the flow of high-energy air into the boundary layer on the upper surface and delays airflow separation to a higher angle of attack and lift coefficient. (PLT305) — FAA-H-8083-25

Answer (A) is incorrect because flaps change the wing camber. Answer (C) is incorrect because a slot accelerates the upper surface boundary layer of air.

AIR, GLI, LSA

6688. (Refer to Figure 23.) Which is a fowler flap?
A— 2.
B— 3.
C— 4.

Flap 4 is a Fowler flap. A Fowler flap moves out of the trailing edge of the wing on tracks and increases both the wing area and the amount of camber. (PLT473) — FAA-H-8083-25

Answer (A) is incorrect because flap 2 is a split flap. Answer (B) is incorrect because flap 3 is a slotted flap.

Answers

6501 [B]   6688 [C]

AIR, GLI, LSA

6689. (Refer to Figure 23.) Which is a slotted flap?

A— 1.
B— 3.
C— 4.

Flap 3 is a slotted flap. When the flap is lowered, a slot is formed between the leading edge of the flap and the flap well in the wing. (PLT473) — FAA-H-8083-25

Answer (A) is incorrect because flap 1 is a plain flap. Answer (C) is incorrect because flap 4 is a Fowler flap.

AIR, GLI, LSA

6690. (Refer to Figure 23.) Which is a split flap?

A— 2.
B— 3.
C— 4.

Flap 2 is a split flap. Split flaps consist of a hinged plate that deflects downward from the lower surface of the wing. (PLT473) — FAA-H-8083-25

Answer (B) is incorrect because flap 3 is a slotted flap. Answer (C) is incorrect because flap 4 is a Fowler flap.

AIR, GLI, LSA

6691. Which type of flap creates the greatest change in pitching moment?

A— Plain.
B— Split.
C— Fowler.

The Fowler flap is characterized by the largest increase in CL_{MAX} with the least changes in drag. The Fowler flap also creates the greatest change in pitching moment. (PLT473) — FAA-H-8083-25

AIR, GLI, LSA

6692. Which type of flap creates the least change in pitching moment?

A— Split.
B— Fowler.
C— Slotted.

The split flap produces the least change in the pitching moments of a wing when it is lowered. (PLT305) — FAA-H-8083-25

AIR, GLI, LSA

6693. Which type of flap is characterized by large increases in lift coefficient with minimum changes in drag?

A— Split.
B— Fowler.
C— Slotted.

The Fowler flap is characterized by large increases in CL_{MAX} with minimum changes in drag. (PLT473) — FAA-H-8083-25

Ground Effect

An aircraft can be flown just clear of the ground at a slightly slower airspeed than is required to sustain level flight at higher altitude because of a phenomenon known as ground effect. **Ground effect** is caused by the ground interfering with the pattern of the air flowing over the aircraft wing.

When the aircraft is flown at an altitude of less than one half of its wing span above the surface, the aerodynamic characteristics of the wing change. As an aircraft is flown into ground effect, the air spilling over the wing tips is reduced. This changes the spanwise flow of air, which lowers the induced angle of attack and decreases the induced drag without increasing the parasite drag. With decreased drag, less thrust is required in ground effect than out of ground effect.

The lift coefficient for a given angle of attack is higher in ground effect, and as a result, the wing produces more lift at the same angle of attack in ground effect than out of ground effect. If a constant

Answers

| 6689 [B] | 6690 [A] | 6691 [C] | 6692 [A] | 6693 [B] |

angle of attack is held as an aircraft enters ground effect, the lift will increase and the induced drag will decrease. There will be no increase in the total drag. When an aircraft leaves ground effect on takeoff, the following occurs:

1. A greater angle of attack is required to maintain the same lift coefficient.

2. The aircraft experiences an increase in induced drag and thrust required, in a powered aircraft.

3. The aircraft experiences a decrease in stability and has a nose-up pitching moment.

4. There is a reduction in static pressure in the pitot-static system which increases the indicated airspeed.

AIR, PPC, WSC, LSA, MCI

6539. An airplane leaving ground effect will

A— experience a decrease in thrust required.
B— experience a decrease in stability and a noseup change in moments.
C— require a lower angle of attack to attain the same lift coefficient.

An airplane leaving ground effect will:

1. Require an increase in angle of attack to maintain the same lift coefficient.

2. Experience an increase in induced drag and thrust required.

3. Experience a decrease in stability and a nose-up change in moments.

4. Produce a reduction in static source pressure and an increase in indicated airspeed.

(PLT131) — FAA-H-8083-3

AIR, PPC, WSC, LSA, MCI

6540. An airplane is usually affected by ground effect at what height above the surface?

A— Three to four times the airplane's wingspan.
B— Twice the airplane's wingspan above the surface.
C— Less than half the airplane's wingspan above the surface.

The height above the surface determines the amount of ground effect. For practical purposes, ground effect occurs up to a height equal to 1/2 of the airplane's wingspan. (PLT131) — FAA-H-8083-3

AIR, GLI, PPC, WSC, LSA, MCI

6537. If the same angle of attack is maintained in ground effect as when out of ground effect, lift will

A— increase, and induced drag will decrease.
B— decrease, and parasite drag will increase.
C— decrease, and parasite drag will decrease.

If the same angle of attack is maintained in ground effect as when out of ground effect, lift will increase due to the decreased loss of energy by the wing-tip vortices. The decrease in the effect of the wing-tip vortices changes the spanwise lift distribution and reduces the angle of attack, thus decreasing the induced drag. (PLT131) — FAA-H-8083-3

Answers (B) and (C) are incorrect because lift increases, and parasite drag is not affected by ground effect.

AIR, GLI, PPC, WSC, LSA, MCI

6538. It is possible to fly an aircraft just clear of the ground at a slightly slower airspeed than that required to sustain level flight at higher altitudes. This is the result of

A— interference of the ground surface with the airflow patterns about the aircraft in flight.
B— a cushioning effect of the air as it is trapped between the ground and the descending aircraft.
C— ground interference with the static pressure system which produces false indications on the airspeed indicator.

An aircraft can fly in ground effect at a slower airspeed than it can outside of ground effect because of the increased aerodynamic efficiency. Ground effect is due to the interference of the ground (or water) surface with the patterns of airflow about an airplane in flight. While the aircraft is in ground effect, the wing-tip vortices are altered, and the decrease in their effect changes the spanwise lift distribution, allowing an increase in lift with no increase in the angle of attack. (PLT131) — FAA-H-8083-3

Answer (B) is incorrect because ground effect is caused by the change in the wing upwash, downwash, and vortices near the surface. Answer (C) is incorrect because although this is true, it is not the reason aircraft fly at a slightly lower airspeed in ground effect.

Answers

6539 [B]	6540 [C]	6537 [A]	6538 [A]

Principles of Rotorcraft Flight

Dissymmetry of lift is the difference in lift that exists between the two halves of a helicopter rotor disc in forward flight. The advancing blade (the blade whose tip is moving in the same direction as the helicopter) has an airspeed equal to the tip speed plus the forward speed of the helicopter. The airspeed of the retreating blade (the blade whose tip is moving in the direction opposite to that of the helicopter) is equal to its tip speed minus the forward speed of the helicopter. Since lift is a function of the airspeed, the lift on the side of the advancing blade is greater than the lift on the side of the retreating blade.

Dissymmetry of lift is compensated for by allowing the blades to flap. As the lift of the advancing blade increases, the blade flaps upward, decreasing its angle of attack. At the same time, the retreating blade flaps downward, increasing its angle of attack. The changes in the lift caused by the differences in angle of attack counteract the changes in lift caused by the differences in airspeed.

During forward cruising flight, the individual blades operate at unequal airspeeds and unequal angles of attack, but with equal lift moments.

The forward speed of a rotorcraft is restricted primarily by dissymmetry of lift. As the forward speed increases, the difference in the speeds of the advancing and retreating blades becomes greater. At a high forward speed, the slow airspeed of the retreating blade causes it to have such a high angle of attack that it stalls. The stall begins at the tip and spreads inboard as forward airspeed increases.

A helicopter can maintain a constant altitude as long as the vertical component of lift equals its weight. When a helicopter makes a banked turn, the lift must be increased. The **total lift vector** is always a bisector of the coning angle, and when the disc is tilted, the total lift vector tilts so that it has both vertical and horizontal components. The total lift vector must be increased enough so it is equal to the helicopter weight plus the additional load caused by centrifugal force in the turn.

On the ground with the engine not running, rotor blades are acted on only by gravity. When they are spinning, but producing no lift, centrifugal force holds them out flat. When they are producing lift, they try to rise, but the balance of centrifugal force and lift cause them to assume an upward angle, called the **coning angle**.

Thrust produced by the tail rotor of a single-rotor helicopter will cause the helicopter to drift. To compensate for this drift, some helicopters have their mast rigged slightly away from the vertical position. This offset gives the lift produced by the main rotor a slight horizontal component.

As the blades of a helicopter rotor flap upward, the center of mass of the blades shifts in closer to their center of rotation, their mass-arm shortens. This shift, called the Coriolis effect, causes the blades to try to increase their rotational velocity.

RTC

6597-1. When the angle of attack of a symmetrical airfoil is increased, the center of pressure will

A— remain unaffected.
B— have very little movement.
C— move aft along the airfoil surface.

On a symmetrical airfoil, center of pressure movement is very limited. (PLT236) — FAA-H-8083-21

RTC

6597-2. In a helicopter, drag is a force parallel to the

A— rotor blade plane of rotation due to coning angle.
B— relative wind and perpendicular to lift.
C— angle of incidence and perpendicular to lift.

Drag is the force that tends to resist movement of the airfoil through the air—the retarding force of inertia and wind resistance. Drag acts parallel and in the opposite direction to the movement of the airfoil or in the same direction as the relative wind, and acts perpendicular to lift. (PLT470) — FAA-H-8083-21

Answers
6597-1　[B]　　　6597-2　[B]

RTC
6599-1. During flight, if you apply cyclic control pressure which results in a decrease in pitch angle of the rotor blades at a position approximately 90° to your left, the rotor disc will tilt

A— aft.
B— left.
C— right.

If cyclic input is made to decrease the pitch angle of a blade on the pilot's left, due to gyroscopic precession the maximum downward deflection occurs 90 degrees later when the blade reaches the aft position. Simultaneously, maximum upward deflection of the opposite blade in the forward position occurs, resulting in aft tilt of the rotor disk. (PLT199) — FAA-H-8083-21

RTC
6599-2. Tip path plane may be described as

A— meaning the same as rotor disc.
B— being proportional to disc loading.
C— the longitudinal axis of the rotor disc in horizontal flight.

The tip path plane is the imaginary circular plane outlined by the rotor blade tips in making a cycle of rotation. The area within the tip path plane of the main rotor is known as the disc area or rotor disc. (PLT470) — FAA-H-8083-21

RTC
6600. The lift differential that exists between advancing and retreating main rotor blades is known as

A— translational lift.
B— dissymmetry of lift.
C— translating tendency.

The lift differential that exists between the advancing and retreating main rotor blades is known as dissymmetry of lift. At the 90° position on right side, the advancing blade has combined speed of blade velocity plus helicopter's speed. At the 90° position on left side, the retreating blade speed is the blade velocity minus the helicopter's speed. (PLT470) — FAA-H-8083-21

RTC
6601-1. Rotor blade flapping action is

A— an undesirable reaction to changes in airspeed and blade angle of attack.
B— an aerodynamic reaction to high speed flight and cannot be controlled by the pilot.
C— a design feature permitting continual changes in the rotor blade angle of attack, compensating for dissymmetry of lift.

Blade flapping compensates for dissymmetry of lift in a helicopter rotor system when the helicopter is in forward flight. The advancing blade has a greater airspeed than the retreating blade, and therefore it produces a greater lift. The increased lift causes it to rise, and as it rises, its angle of attack and lift decrease. The retreating blade has a slower airspeed and produces less lift, so it flaps downward. Its angle of attack increases and its lift increases. (PLT470) — FAA-H-8083-21

RTC
6601-2. Flapping of rotor blades is the result of

A— dissymmetry of lift.
B— retreating blade stall.
C— transverse flow effect.

Blade flapping compensates for dissymmetry of lift in a helicopter rotor system when the helicopter is in forward flight. The advancing blade has a greater airspeed than the retreating blade, and therefore it produces a greater lift. The increased lift causes it to rise, and as it rises, its angle of attack and lift decrease. The retreating blade has a slower airspeed and produces less lift, so it flaps downward. (PLT470) — FAA-H-8083-21

RTC
6607-1. In forward flight and with the blade-pitch angle constant, the increased lift on the advancing blade will cause it to

A— flap up, causing a decrease in the angle of attack.
B— flap up, causing an increase in the angle of attack.
C— flap down, causing a decrease in the angle of attack.

In forward flight, the advancing blade has a greater airspeed than the retreating blade. If the blade angle of the advancing blade is held constant, it will produce a greater lift and flap upward. As it rises, its angle of attack decreases. (PLT470) — FAA-H-8083-21

Answers

6599-1 [A]   6599-2 [A]   6600 [B]   6601-1 [C]   6601-2 [A]   6607-1 [A]

RTC

6607-2. During an autorotation, more forward cyclic is required than during powered flight in order to

A— attain an airspeed that will enable the rotor system to reach its equilibrium RPM.
B— neutralize the anti-autorotative forces.
C— allow aerodynamic force vectors to accelerate the rotor to normal RPM.

Rotor RPM stabilizes when the autorotative forces (thrust) of the "driving region" and the antiautorotative forces (drag) of the "driven region" and "stall region" are equal. Assume that rotor RPM has been increased by entering an updraft; a general lessening in angle of attack will follow along the entire blade. This produces a change in aerodynamic force vectors which results in an overall decrease in the autorotative forces and the rotor tends to slow down. If rotor RPM has been decreased by entering a downdraft, autorotative forces will tend to accelerate the rotor back to its equilibrium RPM. (PLT175) — FAA-H-8083-21

RTC

6607-3. (Refer to Figure 37A). The area of a rotor blade area contributing most during an autorotation is

A— 70-100 percent area, known as the stall region.
B— 0-25 percent area, known as the driven region.
C— 25-70 percent area, known as the driving region.

The portion of the rotor blade that produces the forces that cause the rotor to turn when the engine is no longer supplying power to the rotor is that portion between approximately 25–70% of the radius outward from the center. This portion is often referred to as the "autorotative or driving region." (PLT175) — FAA-H-8083-21

RTC

6607-4. (Refer to Figure 37A). During an autorotation, which portion of the rotor blades provides the thrust required to maintain rotor RPM?

A— Inner or stall.
B— Middle or autorotative.
C— Outer or propeller.

The portion of the rotor blade that produces the forces that cause the rotor to turn when the engine is no longer supplying power to the rotor is that portion between approximately 25–70% of the radius outward from the center. This portion is often referred to as the "autorotative or driving region," and is the middle portion of the rotor blade. (PLT470) — FAA-H-8083-21

RTC

6604. The forward speed of a rotorcraft is restricted primarily by

A— dissymmetry of lift.
B— transverse flow effect.
C— high-frequency vibrations.

The forward speed of a rotorcraft is restricted primarily by dissymmetry of lift. As the forward speed increases, the difference in the speeds of the advancing and retreating blades becomes greater. At a high forward speed, the slow airspeed of the retreating blade gives it such a high angle of attack that it stalls. (PLT470) — FAA-H-8083-21

RTC

6605. What is dissymmetry of lift?

A— The difference in lift that exists between the advancing blade half and the retreating blade half of the disc area.
B— The difference in lift that exists between the rearward part and the forward part of the rotor disc during forward flight.
C— A term used to differentiate between air flowing downward through the rotor in powered flight and upward through the rotor in autorotative flight.

Dissymmetry of lift is the difference in lift that exists between the two halves of a helicopter rotor disc in forward flight. The advancing blade has an airspeed equal to the tip speed plus the forward speed of the helicopter and the retreating blade has a speed equal to the tip speed minus the forward speed. Since lift is a function of the blade airspeed, the lift produced by the advancing blade is greater than that produced by the retreating blade. (PLT242) — FAA-H-8083-21

RTC

6606. During forward cruising flight at constant airspeed and altitude, the individual rotor blades, when compared to each other, are operating at

A— unequal airspeed, equal angles of attack, and unequal lift moment.
B— unequal airspeed, unequal angles of attack, and equal lift moment.
C— constant airspeed, unequal angles of attack, and unequal lift moment.

Because of dissymmetry of lift, the individual blades operate during forward cruising flight at unequal airspeeds and unequal angles of attack, but with equal lift moments. (PLT470) — FAA-H-8083-21

Answers

6607-2 [A]	6607-3 [C]	6607-4 [B]	6604 [A]	6605 [A]	6606 [B]

RTC

6616. When a rotorcraft transitions from straight-and-level flight into a 30° bank while maintaining a constant altitude, the total lift force must

A— increase, and the load factor will decrease.
B— increase, and the load factor will increase.
C— remain constant, and the load factor will increase.

A helicopter can maintain a constant altitude as long as the vertical component of lift equals its weight. The total lift vector is always a bisector of the coning angle, and when the disc is tilted, the total lift vector tilts so it has both vertical and horizontal components. When a helicopter makes a banked turn, the lift must be increased enough to be equal to the helicopter weight plus the additional load caused by centrifugal force caused by the turn. (PLT235) — FAA-H-8083-21

RTC

6609. In certain single-rotor helicopters, the mast is rigged away from the vertical position by approximately 1°. This slight vertical offset is primarily for the purpose of counteracting

A— yaw.
B— drift.
C— torque.

The offset of the rotor mast gives the main-rotor lift a slight horizontal component to compensate for the drift caused by the tail rotor thrust. (PLT470) — FAA-H-8083-21

RTC

6611. The tendency of a helicopter to drift in the direction of tail rotor thrust during a hover is called

A— Coriolis force.
B— translating tendency.
C— transverse flow effect.

The entire helicopter has a tendency to move in the direction of tail rotor thrust when hovering. This is called translating tendency. (PLT470) — FAA-H-8083-21

RTC

6612. When a helicopter experiences a translating tendency, it

A— moves in the direction of tail rotor thrust.
B— gains increased rotor efficiency as air over the rotor system reaches approximately 15 knots.
C— tends to dip slightly to the right as the helicopter approaches approximately 15 knots in a take-off.

Translating tendency is the tendency to move in the direction of the tail rotor thrust (to the right) when hovering. (PLT470) — FAA-H-8083-21

RTC

6613-1. Most helicopters tend to drift to the right when hovering. What is done to counteract this?

A— The mast is rigged slightly to the left.
B— The direction of tail rotor thrust can be changed by using anti-torque pedals.
C— The cyclic pitch system is rigged forward, and along with gyroscopic precession, this tendency is corrected.

Translating the tendency or drift is when the entire helicopter has the tendency to move in the direction of the tail rotor thrust (to the right) when hovering. To counteract this drift, the rotor mast in some helicopters is rigged slightly to the left side so that the tip-path plane has a built in tilt to the left, thus producing a small sideward thrust. (PLT244) — FAA-H-8083-21

RTC

6613-2. Transverse flow effect is caused by

A— increased downwash velocity of air flowing over the rear portion of the rotor disc.
B— disturbed flow of air due to gyroscopic precession.
C— air flowing through the rotor system opposite the direction of forward flight.

In forward flight, air passing through the rear portion of the rotor disc has a higher downwash velocity than air passing through the forward portion. This is because the air passing through the rear portion has been accelerated for a longer period of time than the air passing through the forward portion. This increased downwash velocity at the rear of the disc decreases the angle of attack and blade lift, hence in combination with gyroscopic precession, causes the rotor disc to tilt to the right (the

Answers

| 6616 [B] | 6609 [B] | 6611 [B] | 6612 [A] | 6613-1 [A] | 6613-2 [A] |

advancing side). The lift on the forward part of the rotor disc is greater than on the rearward part. According to the principle of gyroscopic precession, maximum deflection of the rotor blades occurs 90° later in the direction of rotation. This means that the rotor blades will reach maximum upward deflection on the left side and maximum downward deflection on the right side. This transverse flow effect is responsible for the major portion of the lateral cyclic stick control required to trim the helicopter at low speed. (PLT470) — FAA-H-8083-21

RTC

6613-3. Effective translational lift is that point during helicopter flight when

A— hovering flight may be maintained.
B— additional lift is obtained from increased airflow through the rotor disc.
C— the increased groundspeed provides additional performance required to transition from a hover.

Translational lift is that additional lift obtained when entering horizontal flight, due to the increased efficiency of the rotor system. The rotor system produces more lift in forward flight because the higher inflow velocity supplies the rotor disc with a greater mass of air per unit time upon which to work than it receives while hovering. Translational lift is present with any horizontal movement although the increase will not be noticeable until airspeed reaches approximately 15 miles per hour. The additional lift available at this speed is referred to as "effective translational lift" and is easily recognized in actual flight by the increased performance of the helicopter. (PLT242) — FAA-H-8083-21

RTC

6613-4. The vibration that you notice in a helicopter when entering translational lift is a result of a condition called

A— advancing blade compressibility.
B— transverse flow effect.
C— dissymmetry of lift.

The vibration encountered when entering translational lift is a result of transverse flow effect. (PLT472) — FAA-H-8083-21

RTC

6602-1. The combination of lift and centrifugal force produces

A— coning.
B— flapping.
C— Coriolis effect.

Coning is upward bending of the blades caused by combined forces of lift and centrifugal force. (PLT470) — FAA-H-8083-21

RTC

6602-2. With the rotor turning at normal operating RPM, blades will bend upward due to

A— lift being greater than centrifugal force.
B— centrifugal force being greater than lift.
C— lift being greater than drag.

Coning is the upward bending of the blades caused by the combined forces of lift and centrifugal force. Increasing lift or decreasing centrifugal force increases coning. (PLT470) — FAA-H-8083-21

RTC

6603-1. What will cause an increase in coning?

A— Increase in lift; increase in centrifugal force.
B— Increase in lift; decrease in centrifugal force.
C— Decrease in lift; decrease in centrifugal force.

When a vertical takeoff is made, two major forces act at the same time: centrifugal force acting perpendicular and lift acting upward. Increasing lift or decreasing centrifugal force increases coning. (PLT470) — FAA-H-8083-21

RTC

6608-1. The purpose of lead-lag (drag) hinges on a three-bladed, fully articulated rotor system is to compensate for

A— Coriolis effect.
B— dissymmetry of lift.
C— blade flapping tendency.

The acceleration and deceleration actions of the rotor blades are absorbed by either damper or blade structure itself. The purposes of this system is to compensate for Coriolis effect. (PLT470) — FAA-H-8083-21

Answers

| 6613-3 [B] | 6613-4 [B] | 6602-1 [A] | 6602-2 [A] | 6603-1 [B] | 6608-1 [A] |

RTC
6608-2. Coriolis effect causes rotor blades to

A— vary the angle of attack.
B— accelerate and decelerate.
C— precess 90 degrees in the direction of rotation.

The tendency of a rotor blade to increase or decrease its velocity in its plane of rotation due to mass movement is known as Coriolis effect. (PLT197) — FAA-H-8083-21

RTC
6608-3. The purpose of a horizontal stabilizer on a helicopter is to provide

A— a fixed surface to improve speed in flight.
B— sufficient controllability of the aerodynamic pitching moment of the fuselage.
C— adequate cyclic control travel when operating at or near CG limits.

The purpose of a horizontal stabilizer on a helicopter is to level the fuselage and decrease drag. (PLT470) — FAA-H-8083-21

Answer (A) is incorrect because not all stabilizers are fixed. Answer (C) is incorrect because the down force would restrict the forward cyclic even more, especially when the CG is in the aft range.

RTC
6610-1. As each blade flaps up and down, it produces a shift of the center of its mass. When the blade flaps up, the CG moves closer to its axis of rotation, giving that blade a tendency to

A— accelerate its rotational velocity; this tendency is known as Coriolis effect.
B— stabilize its rotational velocity, thus compensating for dissymmetry of lift.
C— decelerate its rotational velocity; this tendency is known as translating tendency.

As the blades of a helicopter rotor flap upward, the center of mass of the blades shifts in closer to their center of rotation, and the blades try to speed up. This is called the Coriolis effect. (PLT470) — FAA-H-8083-21

Gyroplane Aerodynamics

Rotation of the blades of a gyroplane rotor is produced by the horizontal component of the rotor lift. In flight, air flows upward through the rotor disc and causes the blades to produce lift that acts at right angles to the direction of the air through the rotor disc.

Drag acts parallel to the wind through the rotor, and the resultant of the lift and drag forces lies at a slight angle ahead of the axis of rotation of the rotor. This is called the **autorotation angle**.

An autorotative force, perpendicular to the axis of rotation, causes the blades of a gyroplane to rotate with no power applied to them. The driving force for the rotors of a gyroplane is caused by air flowing upward through its rotors, and is not affected by the movement of the gyroplane over the ground.

A gyroplane can safely descend vertically or move backward with respect to ground references as long as air is moving upward through its rotors.

RTC
6503. Rotor blade rotation during powered flight in a gyroplane is produced by the

A— horizontal component of rotor lift.
B— interaction between engine propeller thrust and rotor blade drag.
C— transfer of engine power through the clutch to the rotor shaft.

Rotation of the blades of a gyroplane rotor is produced by the horizontal component of the rotor lift. (PLT470) — FAA-H-8083-21

Answers

6608-2 [B]   6608-3   [B]   6610-1   [A]   6503   [A]

RTC

6614. In preparing to take off in a gyroplane, your student engages the clutch and prerotates the rotor to takeoff RPM. If brakes are released prior to disengaging the clutch, the gyroplane will turn

A— left because of rotor torque.
B— right because of rotor torque.
C— right because of engine propeller torque.

The unpowered rotors of a gyro produce no torque except during prerotation prior to takeoff. Therefore, the gyroplane will turn right because of rotor torque. (PLT470) — FAA-H-8083-21

RTC

6615-1. What changes take place regarding lifting force and load factor produced by the rotor system when a gyroplane goes from straight and level flight into a 45° banked turn while maintaining constant altitude?

A— Total lift must increase; load factor will increase.
B— Total lift must increase; load factor will remain constant.
C— Total lift will remain constant; load factor will increase.

Load factor increases in a 45° bank and additional lift is required to maintain altitude. (PLT235) — FAA-H-8083-21

RTC

6615-2. Removing the rotor force on a gyroplane can lead to

A— a power push over.
B— increased rotor RPM.
C— pilot induced oscillation.

The stability of a gyroplane is greatly influenced by rotor force. If rotor force is rapidly removed, some gyroplanes have a tendency to pitch forward abruptly. This is often referred to as a forward tumble, buntover or power pushover. Removing the rotor force is often referred to as unloading the rotor, and can occur if pilot-induced oscillations become excessive, if extremely turbulent conditions are encountered, or the nose of the gyroplane is pushed forward rapidly after a steep climb. (PLT235) — FAA-H-8083-21

RTC

6618. Longitudinal and lateral control of a gyroplane in flight are affected by

A— antitorque pedals.
B— tilting the plane of rotation of the rotor in the direction that control is desired.
C— adjusting the pitch of the rotor blades to the angle and direction that control is desired.

The control stick tilts the rotor blades in relation to the airframe to move the gyroplane longitudinally and laterally. (PLT095) — FAA-H-8083-21

RTC

6618-1. In order to maintain level flight (laterally) as airspeed increases on climbout after takeoff in a gyroplane, the pilot will need to increase

A— rudder pressure to the left.
B— cyclic pressure to the right.
C— rudder and cyclic pressure to the left.

The pilot will need to increase cyclic pressure to the right toward the advancing blade. The pitch cone coupling found in some gyroplanes with the fully articulated rotor system requires a cyclic position change as airspeed increases due to fluctuation in gyroscopic precession. (PLT222) — FAA-H-8083-21

RTC

6620. A gyroplane will have the greatest tendency to roll during

A— horizontal flight at high speed.
B— climbing flight in which forward airspeed decreases.
C— descending flight in which forward airspeed decreases.

As forward speed increases, dissymmetry of lift created by horizontal flight causes roll. (PLT470) — FAA-H-8083-21

RTC

6699-1. A one-per-revolution vibration in a gyroplane indicates which condition?

A— Rotor blades out of balance.
B— One rotor blade out of track.
C— Possible onset of retreating blade stall.

A one-to-one vibration indicates one rotor blade out of track. (PLT472) — FAA-H-8083-21

Answers

6614 [B]	6615-1 [A]	6615-2 [A]	6618 [B]	6618-1 [B]	6620 [A]
6699-1 [B]					

RTC
6699-2. What should help prevent aircraft induced oscillation on a gyroplane?

A— Adding a horizontal stabilizer.
B— Increasing cyclic control sensitivity.
C— Lowering the center of gravity below the thrust line.

Porpoising can be caused by an unstable aircraft due to a weak design, no horizontal stabilization, an out-of-balance or wrongly-loaded aircraft, or too much play in the control system. (PLT213) — FAA-H-8083-21

Answer (B) is incorrect because cyclic control sensitivity needs to be reduced rather than increased. Answer (C) is incorrect because the center of gravity is already below the center of thrust and will increase the initial pitch-down tendency if it is lowered even more.

RTC
7093-1. Which statement is true concerning a gyroplane?

A— Rotor RPM will remain constant during changes in airspeed while descending.
B— A gyroplane is capable of getting into a settling-with-power situation much the same way as a helicopter.
C— A gyroplane can safely descend vertically or move backward with respect to ground references during a descent if altitude permits.

A gyroplane lift is produced by air flowing upward through its rotors, and a gyroplane can safely descend vertically or move backward with respect to ground references as long as air is moving upward through its rotors. (PLT260) — FAA-H-8083-21

RTC
7093-2. Which is true concerning operation of a gyroplane?

A— Like a helicopter, vertical descents to a safe landing are possible.
B— Altitude permitting, flying behind the power curve is not a problem.
C— Rotor RPM remains constant during changes in airspeed while descending.

Altitude permitting, flying behind the power curve is not a problem. (PLT260) — FAA-H-8083-21

RTC
7095. In which takeoff situation would a gyroplane with jump takeoff capability have an advantage?

A— Soft field.
B— Short field.
C— High elevation.

The autogyro can execute a vertical takeoff like a helicopter if the rotorblades are engaged by a mechanical device and pitch of the blades is increased. Even though the aircraft will handle a rough runway very well, it is a good idea to spend as little time on it as possible, especially at takeoff speeds. (PLT260) — FAA-H-8083-21

Answers (B) and (C) are incorrect, assuming there is adequate runway for takeoff with and without jump takeoff capability. Since acceleration to best climb speed prior to gaining altitude is necessary in order to obtain some margin of safety, the advantage of having a jump takeoff capability is nullified. However, the jump takeoff capability will allow a shorter runway for the short field and high elevation takeoff where the extra margin of safety is not required.

RTC
7097-1. Rotor torque is a concern in gyroplanes only during

A— prerotation or clutch engagement.
B— maneuvers requiring high rotor RPM.
C— maximum performance climbs and go-arounds requiring higher engine RPM.

If you use too much pressure when first engaging the pre-rotator, it will cause chattering at the head and undue stress and wear on the system. (PLT470) — FAA-H-8083-21

Answers (B) and (C) are incorrect because rotor is free-spinning or autorotating.

RTC
7097-2. What should be the first step in correcting pilot induced oscillation in a gyroplane?

A— Reduce power.
B— Establish a climb.
C— Apply positive forward cyclic.

If pilot-induced oscillation is encountered, reduce the throttle at once. Neutralize the stick, establish a smooth glide, and then advance the throttle slowly to maintain airspeed. (PLT208) — FAA-H-8083-21

Answers (B) and (C) are incorrect because you should establish a descent and neutralize the stick.

Answers

6699-2 [A]	7093-1 [C]	7093-2 [B]	7095 [A]	7097-1 [A]	7097-2 [A]

RTC
7097-3. Which pilot action will help reduce pilot induced oscillation in a gyroplane?

A— Avoid flight at high speeds.
B— Increase power if nose pitches down.
C— Prior to a climb, increase pitch attitude before increasing power.

Higher airspeeds can aggravate oscillations and speed is where a pilot gets into trouble. (PLT208) — FAA-H-8083-21

Answer (B) is incorrect because the power must be decreased when the nose pitches down. Answer (C) is incorrect because the power should be adjusted prior to changing the pitch attitude. Increase power before initiating a climb and decrease power prior to starting a descent.

RTC
7097-4. What should be the first action taken if a gyroplane begins to oscillate in flight?

A— Reduce power.
B— Unload rotor system.
C— Apply aft cyclic pressure to increase pitch and reduce airspeed.

If you notice a GIO and the resulting pitching down of the nose, reduce power. If the gust was violent, cut power. This takes the life out of the porpoise. (PLT208) — FAA-H-8083-21

Answer (B) is incorrect because this will cause the power push over. Answer (C) is incorrect because only slight aft cyclic pressure should be applied when a gust causes the nose to go down; however, your first action should be to reduce power.

RTC
7097-5. Which will help prevent pilot induced oscillation in a gyroplane?

A— Adding a horizontal point of reference.
B— Decreasing loading on the rotor blades.
C— Raising the center of thrust above the center of fuselage drag.

It helps if the pilot can see some part of the gyroplane near the horizon. By comparing the part of the gyro with the horizon, the pilot can have a more critical way to determine how the machine is moving in pitch; that is, nose-up or nose-down. (PLT112) — FAA-H-8083-21

Answer (B) is incorrect because reducing the rotor blade loading will cause a power push over, while reducing power or flying slower would help. Answer (C) is incorrect because raising the center of thrust will make the problem worse with a greater pitching tendency.

RTC
6603-2. Gyroplanes that use small wings will cause rotor drag to do what at higher cruise airspeeds?

A— Increase.
B— Decrease.
C— Remain the same.

The faster you fly, the smaller the angle of attack of the rotordisc becomes, to produce the same amount of lift at lower speeds. This causes the rotor drag to decrease with increasing speed. (PLT470) — FAA-H-8083-21

RTC
6610-2. What type of stability does the horizontal stabilizer provide during flight?

A— Airspeed.
B— Longitudinal.
C— Lateral.

A horizontal stabilizer helps in longitudinal stability, with its efficiency greater the further it is from the center of gravity. (PLT240) — FAA-H-8083-21

RTC
6621-2. When is rotor downwash most prevalent in certain gyroplanes?

A— During all surface movement.
B— Immediately prior to touchdown after a steep approach.
C— During a vertical takeoff when rotor blades are in a propeller state.

Answer (C) is the most correct of the choices provided. While very few gyroplanes are capable of a vertical takeoff, it is possible during prerotation and a jump takeoff. (PLT470) — FAA-H-8083-21

Answers

7097-3 [A]   7097-4 [A]   7097-5 [A]   6603-2 [B]   6610-2 [B]   6621-2 [C]

RTC
6700-2. Low speed blade flap on a gyroplane is a result of

A— taxiing too fast.
B— rotor blade pitch set too high.
C— the rotor blades being too heavy.

If too much wind gets into the rotor before it is up to speed, it will flap and hit the ground if allowed to continue. The pilot should get the stick forward and slow down. (PLT260) — FAA-H-8083-21

Answer (B) is incorrect because this conduction should cause a high speed flap. Answer (C) is incorrect because too-heavy rotor blades may droop more.

RTC
6827-2. How does a negative G maneuver affect a gyroplane's rotor RPM?

A— Increases rapidly.
B— Remains the same.
C— Decreases rapidly.

Negative Gs will cause the rotors to lose so much speed that it can start flapping (buffeting) if airspeed is gained again. (PLT470) — FAA-H-8083-21

RTC
6833-2. Which may lead to a power push-over in a gyroplane?

A— Low speed.
B— Rotor force is removed.
C— Decreasing power too quickly.

A power push over can happen not only as a result of PIO, but also if the rotor force is removed. (PLT244) — FAA-H-8083-21

RTC
6835-2. Which maneuver would cause the unloading the rotor system, and result in a possible power pushover?

A— During a steep descent.
B— After a pushover from a steep climb.
C— Just prior to landing

Removing the rotor force is often referred to as unloading the rotor, and can occur if pilot-induced oscillations become excessive, if extremely turbulent conditions are encountered, or the nose of the gyroplane is pushed forward rapidly after a steep climb. (PLT244) — FAA-H-8083-21

RTC
6835-3. If the gyroplane's CG is below the propeller thrust line, which direction will the application of power cause the nose to move?

A— The nose will pitch up.
B— The nose will pitch down.
C— The nose will not move.

Manufacturers use a combination of the various stability factors to achieve a trimmed gyroplane. For example, if you have a gyroplane where the CG is below the propeller thrust line, the propeller thrust gives your aircraft a nose down pitching moment when power is applied. To compensate for this pitching moment, the CG, on this type of gyroplane, is usually located behind the rotor force line. This location produces a nose up pitching moment. (PLT240) — FAA-H-8083-21

Answers

6700-2 [A]   6827-2 [C]   6833-2 [B]   6835-2 [B]   6835-3 [B]

Glider Aerodynamics

Almost all gliders use an asymmetrical airfoil in which the upper camber is greater than the lower camber. This characteristic of an airfoil section produces good lift at slow airspeeds.

The minimum drag and the highest L/D ratio (L/D$_{MAX}$) of a glider occur at the angle of attack and airspeed where the parasite drag and the induced drag are the same.

A glider will travel the maximum distance through the air when it is operating at an airspeed that produces the L/D$_{MAX}$.

The L/D ratio of a glider is an index of its performance, and it is an aerodynamic function. For a given airfoil section, the L/D$_{MAX}$ is determined only by the angle of attack and is not affected by the weight of the glider. The L/D$_{MAX}$ always occurs at the same angle of attack.

A glider carrying water ballast can increase its lift by flying faster, rather than by increasing its angle of attack.

A higher airspeed is required for a heavy glider to obtain the same glide ratio it would have when it is lightly loaded.

GLI

6622. Which statement is generally true regarding wing camber of a glider's airfoil?

A— There is no camber on either the upper or lower surface of the wing.

B— The camber is the same on both the upper and lower surface of the wing.

C— The camber is greater on the upper wing surface than it is on the lower surface of the wing.

Almost all gliders use an asymmetrical airfoil in which the upper camber is greater than the lower camber. This characteristic of an airfoil section produces good lift at slow airspeeds. (PLT236) — FAA-H-8083-13

GLI

6623. When a slight upward or negative flap deflection is used, the result is

A— increased drag.

B— decreased drag.

C— decreased lift.

Upward or negative flap deflection reduces drag at high speed by allowing the wing to remain at its most efficient angle of attack. (PLT257) — FAA-H-8083-13

GLI

6624. When a glider is turning in flight, the force that opposes the inward turning force is called

A— adverse yaw.

B— resultant force.

C— centrifugal force.

Centrifugal force acting outward is opposite and equal to the inward turning force. (PLT236) — FAA-H-8083-13

GLI

6625. At what bank angle will the resultant of gravity and centrifugal force equal twice a glider's weight?

A— 30°.

B— 45°.

C— 60°.

The load factor for any airplane in a 60° bank is 2 Gs. Therefore, in a 60° bank the resultant of gravity and centrifugal force equals twice the glider weight. (PLT309) — FAA-H-8083-13

GLI

6715. The primary purpose of spoilers on gliders is to

A— decrease lift.

B— decrease stall speed.

C— control speed at steep glide angles.

The primary purpose of spoilers is to break up the smooth flow of air over a portion of the wing, "spoiling" the lift. (PLT473) — FAA-H-8083-13

Answers

| 6622 | [C] | 6623 | [B] | 6624 | [C] | 6625 | [C] | 6715 | [A] |

GLI

6836. The best lift/drag ratio of a glider occurs when parasite drag is

A— equal to total drag.
B— equal to induced drag.
C— less than induced drag.

The minimum drag and the highest L/D ratio (L/D$_{MAX}$) of a glider occur at the angle of attack and airspeed where the parasite drag and the induced drag are equal. A glider will travel the maximum distance through the air when it is operating at an airspeed that produces the L/D$_{MAX}$. (PLT303) — FAA-H-8083-13

GLI

6837. The best lift/drag ratio of a glider is a value that

A— varies depending upon the weight being carried.
B— remains constant regardless of airspeed changes.
C— remains constant and is independent of the weight being carried.

The L/D ratio of a glider is an aerodynamic function that is determined by the angle of attack and is not affected by the weight of the glider. The L/D$_{MAX}$ always occurs at the same angle of attack. (PLT054) — FAA-H-8083-13

GLI

6838. Which is true about the effect on a glider's performance by the addition of ballast or weight?

A— The glide ratio at a given airspeed will increase.
B— A higher airspeed is required to obtain the same glide ratio as when lightly loaded.
C— The heavier the glider is loaded, the less the glide ratio will be at all airspeeds.

The L/D ratio of a glider is an index of its performance, and it is an aerodynamic function. For a given airfoil section, the L/D$_{MAX}$ is determined only by the angle of attack. It is not affected by the weight of the glider. A glider carrying water ballast can increase its lift by flying faster, rather than by increasing its angle of attack. A higher airspeed is required for a heavy glider to obtain the same glide ratio it would have when it is lightly loaded. (PLT328) — FAA-H-8083-13

GLI

6840. (Refer to Figure 38.) A glider is flying from A to C. With a normal L/D ratio of 20:1 and a constant airspeed of 40 MPH, what minimum altitude AGL is needed at B to arrive over C at 800 feet AGL with no sinking air?

A— 3,520 feet.
B— 4,320 feet.
C— 6,080 feet.

By using the following formula, it can be determined that an aircraft with a normal glide ratio of 20:1 would have a new glide ratio of 30:1 when flying with a 20 mph tail wind.

Consider that your Glide Angle over the Ground (GAG), is your new glide ratio under a given set of circumstances, and that your Glide Angle in the Air (GAA) is the given glide ratio of the aircraft, in this case 20. If there is a headwind, you will need to subtract it from the airspeed. If there is a tailwind, you will need to add it to the airspeed. In this example, there is a 20 mph tailwind.

GAG = GAA (airspeed ± wind) ÷ airspeed
GAG = 20 x (40 + 20) ÷ 40
GAG = 1,200 ÷ 40
GAG = 30

With this wind condition, your aircraft now has a glide ratio of 30:1.

Dividing the number of feet in a mile by 30 gives the number of feet the aircraft will descend per mile:

5,280 ÷ 30 = 176

It is 20 miles from point B to point C:

20 x 176 = 3,520

This means you would need to be at an altitude of 3,520 feet to travel 20 miles. However, you must add 800 feet to satisfy the desired altitude upon reaching point C:

3,520 + 800 = 4,320

(PLT012) — FAA-H-8083-13

GLI

7191. While maintaining the best glide speed, a glider pilot may expect the

A— fastest cross country speed.
B— longest cross country flight.
C— loss of the least amount of altitude.

Best glide speed results in the flattest glide angle and longest distance in still air. (PLT303) — FAA-H-8083-13

Answers

6836 **[B]**   6837 **[C]**   6838 **[B]**   6840 **[B]**   7191 **[B]**

Balloon Aerodynamics

LTA

6626. Which will improve the response time of a hot air balloon?

A— Increased weight.
B— Less-dense ambient air.
C— Increased fuel flow through burner.

Increased temperature reduces the time needed to maneuver. (PLT177) — Balloon Digest

LTA

6627. The term 'weigh-off' as used in ballooning means to determine the

A— standard weight and balance of the balloon.
B— static equilibrium of the balloon as loaded for flight.
C— amount of fuel required for ascent to a preselected altitude.

A weigh-off is used to determine the static equilibrium of the balloon. (PLT267) — Powerline Excerpts

LTA

6628. The lifting force acting on a hot air balloon is primarily the result of the interior envelope temperature being

A— equal to ambient temperature.
B— greater than ambient temperature.
C— less than surrounding air temperature.

The lifting forces which act on a hot air balloon causing the balloon to rise are primarily the result of the interior air temperature of the envelope being greater than the ambient temperature. (PLT183) — Balloon Ground School

LTA

6629. The part of a balloon that bears the weight of the balloon and its payload is the

A— load tapes.
B— load cables.
C— envelope material.

The load tape supports the weight of the balloon and minimizes the strain on the envelope fabric. (PLT179) — Balloon Ground School

LTA

6630. What causes false lift which sometimes occurs during a balloon launch?

A— Venturi effect of wind on the envelope.
B— Closing the maneuvering vent too rapidly.
C— Excessive temperature within the envelope.

False lift is created when there is a wind blowing across the top of an inflated envelope creating a venturi effect. This lowers the pressure above the balloon, creating a dynamic lifting force. As the balloon is accelerated by the wind, this force decreases. (PLT180) — Balloon Ground School

LTA

6631. In ballooning, when can false lift occur?

A— During launches near obstacles.
B— Just after a balloon begins to accelerate during initial ascent.
C— When a balloon lifts off and the relative wind suddenly increases.

False lift is created when there is a wind blowing across the top of an inflated envelope creating a venturi effect. This lowers the pressure above the balloon, creating a dynamic lifting force. As the balloon is accelerated by the wind, this force decreases. (PLT180) — Balloon Ground School

LTA

7201. What is the relationship of false lift to the wind? False lift

A— exists only if the surface winds are calm.
B— increases if the vertical velocity of a balloon increases.
C— decreases as the wind accelerates a balloon to the same speed as the wind.

False lift is caused by the "venturi effect" produced by wind blowing across the inflated but stationary envelope. When the balloon is released, the relative wind decreases as the balloon accelerates to the wind's speed and false lift decreases. (PLT180) — Powerline Excerpts

Answers

| 6626 | [C] | 6627 | [B] | 6628 | [B] | 6629 | [A] | 6630 | [A] | 6631 | [A] |
| 7201 | [C] | | | | | | | | | | |

LTA

7202. Why is false lift dangerous?

A— Pilots are not aware of its effect until the burner sound changes.
B— To commence a descent, the venting of air will nearly collapse the envelope.
C— When the balloon's horizontal speed reaches wind speed, the balloon could descend into obstructions downwind.

False lift is caused by the "venturi effect" produced by wind blowing across the inflated but stationary envelope. When the balloon is released, the relative wind decreases as the balloon accelerates to the wind's speed and false lift decreases. (PLT180) — Powerline Excerpts

LTA

6632. What causes a gas balloon to start a descent if a cold air mass is encountered and the envelope becomes cooled?

A— Contraction of the gas.
B— A temperature differential.
C— A barometric pressure differential.

As the gas is cooled, it contracts and becomes more dense and so displaces less air. (PLT183) — How to Fly a Balloon

LTA

6850. Burner efficiency of a hot air balloon decreases approximately what percent for each 1,000 feet above MSL?

A— 4 percent.
B— 8 percent.
C— 15 percent.

A pilot flying at high altitudes should remember that burner efficiency decreases approximately 4% for each 1,000 feet above MSL (mean sea level). (PLT253) — Balloon Ground School

LTA

6854. Below pressure height, each 5°F of positive superheat amounts to approximately

A— 1 percent of net lift.
B— 1 percent of static lift.
C— 2 percent of gross lift.

Below pressure height, each 5°F of positive superheat amounts to approximately 1 percent of static lift. (PLT153) — Goodyear Airship Operations Manual

LTA

6855. The difference between the weight of the air being displaced and the weight of the lifting gas is

A— gross lift.
B— useful lift.
C— design lift.

The difference between the weight of the air being displaced and the weight of the lifting gas is gross lift. (PLT030) — Goodyear Airship Operations Manual

LTA

6638. An airship with a small fineness ratio has a hull form that will introduce

A— greater nose pressures.
B— lower pressure variations from nose to tail.
C— more frictional drag due to the plump shape of the hull.

Fineness ratio is the ratio of the length to the maximum diameter. A plump-shaped hull would have a small ratio. (PLT153) — Goodyear Airship Operations Manual

LTA

6634. An airship will float in the air when buoyant force

A— equals horizontal equilibrium existing between propeller thrust and airship drag.
B— equals the difference between airship weight and the weight of the volume of air being displaced.
C— is less than the difference between airship weight and the weight of the air volume being displaced.

A lighter-than-air craft is in equilibrium when buoyancy equals weight. The buoyant force is equal to the weight of the air volume displaced. (PLT153) — Goodyear Airship Operations Manual

---

Answers

7202 [C]	6632 [A]	6850 [A]	6854 [B]	6855 [A]	6638 [C]
6634 [B]					

LTA

6633. During flight in an airship, vertical equilibrium is established when

A— pressure height is reached.
B— buoyancy equals airship weight.
C— buoyancy is greater than airship weight.

When buoyancy equals weight the airship is in equilibrium. (PLT153) — Goodyear Airship Operations Manual

LTA

6635. If an airship is either light or heavy in flight, the unbalanced condition must be overcome

A— by valving air.
B— aerodynamically.
C— by releasing ballast.

A light or heavy condition must be overcome aerodynamically. (PLT153) — Goodyear Airship Operations Manual

LTA

6636. An airship descending through a temperature inversion will

A— become heavier as superheat is lost.
B— show no change in superheat as altitude is lost.
C— become progressively lighter and increasingly more difficult to drive down.

As superheat (temperature of gas in envelope warmer than the surrounding air) is lost, the airship becomes heavier. (PLT153) — Goodyear Airship Operations Manual

LTA

6637. The four principal forces acting on an airship in flight are

A— buoyancy, drag, gravity, and thrust.
B— lift, drag, temperature, and pressure.
C— gravity, compression, buoyancy, and equilibrium.

The famous four forces are: Lift (in the form of buoyancy), gravity, thrust, and drag. (PLT239) — Goodyear Airship Operations Manual

LTA

6639. What are the two most significant effects of positive superheat?

A— Improved fineness ratio and pressure height.
B— Increased static lift and decreased pressure height.
C— Increased dynamic lift and decreased ballonet capacity.

Positive superheat results in increased dynamic lift and results in decreased air capacity in ballonets. (PLT160) — Goodyear Airship Operations Manual

LTA

6640. Critical factors affecting flight characteristics and controllability of an airship are

A— lift and drag.
B— static and dynamic trim.
C— temperature and atmospheric density.

Critical factors affecting the characteristics and controllability of an airship are lift and drag. (PLT153) — Goodyear Airship Operations Manual

LTA

6731. The main advantage of internal suspension in an airship is that it

A— increases stability.
B— provides better load distribution.
C— absorbs side and longitudinal forces.

The main advantage of internal suspension in an airship is that it provides better load distribution. (PLT114) — Goodyear Airship Operations Manual

LTA

6732. When operating an airship with the ballonet air valves in the automatic forward position, the aft valve lock should not be engaged with either aft damper open because

A— ballonet over-inflation and rupture could occur.
B— the airship will enter an excessive nose-high attitude.
C— envelope pressure will increase, causing possible damage to the air lines.

Under the conditions described, the aft ballonet could inflate, causing a nose-high condition. (PLT304) — Goodyear Airship Operations Manual

Answers

| 6633 | [B] | 6635 | [B] | 6636 | [A] | 6637 | [A] | 6639 | [C] | 6640 | [A] |
| 6731 | [B] | 6732 | [B] | | | | | | | | | | |

LTA
6733. If the gas in an airship envelope shows a steady loss of purity and the percentage of fullness in the envelope increases, what is, most likely, the problem?

A— Rip in a ballonet.
B— Defective helium valve.
C— Small rip in bottom of envelope.

A leaking ballonet will reduce the percent of helium contained in the envelope. (PLT153) — Goodyear Airship Operations Manual

LTA
6734. What is one indication of a serious envelope rip in an airship?

A— Drop in air pressure.
B— Increase in gas pressure.
C— Difficulty in controlling altitude.

A serious rip would result in loss of gas pressure and altitude. (PLT208) — Goodyear Airship Operations Manual

LTA
6735. To prevent loss of air from ballonets when airspeed and engines are inadequate to maintain pressure, the

A— pilot should close dampers.
B— pilot should turn on electric blowers.
C— airship is equipped with check valves in the air scoops to maintain pressure.

Air entering through the damper valves will result in air being released from the ballonets. (PLT153) — Goodyear Airship Operations Manual

LTA
6851. How does an airship pilot know when pressure height has been reached?

A— Liquid in the gas and air manometers will rise above normal levels.
B— Liquid in the gas manometer will rise and liquid in the air manometer(s) will fall below normal levels.
C— Liquid in the gas manometer will fall and liquid in the air manometer(s) will rise above normal levels.

The pilot will know when pressure height has been reached when the liquid in the gas manometer will rise and the liquid in the air manometer will fall below normal levels. (PLT158) — Goodyear Airship Operations Manual

LTA
6852. When an airship is at pressure height and super-heat increases, constant pressure must be maintained by valving

A— gas from the envelope.
B— air from the envelope.
C— air from the ballonets.

At pressure the ballonets are empty. Gas must be released from the envelope. (PLT160) — Goodyear Airship Operations Manual

LTA
6853. The maximum altitude an airship can reach under any given atmospheric condition and return safely to the surface is determined by

A— ballonet capacity.
B— the disposable weight.
C— ballonet capacity and disposable weight.

The maximum altitude would be reached when ballonets are deflated. (PLT153) — Goodyear Airship Operations Manual

LTA
7215. If all engine power is lost during flight, an airship should be

A— brought to a condition of equilibrium as soon as possible and free-ballooned.
B— trimmed nose-heavy to use the airship's negative dynamic lift to fly the airship down to the landing site.
C— trimmed nose-light to use the airship's positive dynamic lift to control the angle and rate of descent to the landing site.

An airship without engine power must be flown as a free balloon. (PLT208) — Goodyear Airship Operations Manual

LTA
7216. Under which condition is maximum headway possible in an airship?

A— Slightly nosedown.
B— Flying at equilibrium.
C— Slightly heavy and with dynamically positive force.

Flying in equilibrium will produce the smallest frontal area and least drag. (PLT156) — Goodyear Airship Operations Manual

Answers

6733 [A]	6734 [C]	6735 [A]	6851 [B]	6852 [A]	6853 [A]
7215 [A]	7216 [B]				

LTA

7217. To land an airship that is 250 pounds heavy when the wind is calm, a wheel landing should be made with the airship

A— in trim.
B— tail heavy, up to 5°.
C— approximately 5° nose heavy.

A heavy airship should be landed tail heavy. (PLT221) — Goodyear Airship Operations Manual

LTA

7218. What action is required to dynamically trim an airship that is in even static trim and equilibrium during a weigh-off?

A— Transfer air aft.
B— Increase airspeed.
C— Transfer air forward.

To overcome the climbing tendency, air must be ballasted forward. (PLT153) — Goodyear Airship Operations Manual

LTA

7219. Dampers should normally be kept closed during a climb to altitude because any air blown into the system would

A— decrease the volume of gas within the envelope.
B— increase the amount of air to be valved, resulting in a slower rate of ascent.
C— increase the amount of gas to be valved, preventing the airship from ascending too fast.

Air entering through the damper valves would have to be exhausted as well as the air in the ballonets. (PLT157) — Goodyear Airship Operations Manual

LTA

7220. When checking pressure height of an airship during a climb, the dampers should be

A— opened.
B— closed.
C— opened aft and closed forward.

Any ram pressure will keep the ballonet pressure too high, and prevent deflation at pressure height. (PLT153) — Goodyear Airship Operations Manual

LTA

7221. Which action is necessary in order to perform a normal descent in an airship?

A— Valve gas from the envelope.
B— Take air into the aft ballonet.
C— Valve air from the forward ballonet.

An airship is normally flown heavy and so a decrease in power will result in a descent. (PLT125) — Goodyear Airship Operations Manual

LTA

7222. The purpose of a ground weigh-off for an airship is to determine

A— available lift.
B— static and/or trim condition.
C— trim angle necessary to make an up-ship takeoff.

The purpose of the ground weigh-off is to determine the static condition of the airship and the condition of the trim. (PLT154) — Goodyear Airship Operations Manual

Answers

7217 [B]	7218 [C]	7219 [B]	7220 [B]	7221 [A]	7222 [B]

LTA

7223. Which takeoff procedure is considered to be most hazardous for an airship?

A— Not using an up-ship takeoff when the airship is more than 200 pounds heavy.

B— Maintaining 50 percent of the maximum permissible positive angle of inclination.

C— Maintaining a negative angle of inclination during a wheel takeoff after elevator response is adequate for controllability.

The most hazardous takeoff condition would be maintaining a negative angle of inclination during takeoff, after elevator response is adequate for stability. (PLT221) — Goodyear Airship Operations Manual

LTA

7224. A heavy airship, flying dynamically with air ballasted forward to overcome a climbing tendency and slowed down for a weigh-off prior to landing, will be very nose heavy. This condition can be corrected prior to landing by

A— ballasting air aft.

B— discharging forward ballast.

C— dumping fuel from the forward tanks.

Air must be ballasted aft to overcome the bow heavy condition. (PLT170) — Goodyear Airship Operations Manual

Weight-Shift Control Aerodynamics

The explanations for the answers given describe the concepts that should be understood before taking the test. Many of these questions are based on older weight-shift and PPC designs and unique characteristics of specific designs. The answers given are the best of the choices provided.

WSC

7273. As a weight shift aircraft wing approaches a stall, the wing tips

A— decrease the wing's angle of attack.

B— act in much the same way as ailerons on a three-axis aircraft.

C— increase the wing's angle of attack.

As the angle of attack of the wing is increased, the nose is at a higher angle of attack and therefore stalls first while the tips keep flying. This drops the nose and as a result, decreases the wing's angle of attack. (PLT114) — Trikes, the Flex-Wing Flyers, Chapter 3

Answer (B) is incorrect because the wing tips act the same way ailerons do while flying normally and while approaching a stall. Answer (C) is incorrect because the tips only increase the wing's angle of attack when the wing is at a low angle of attack, far from a stall.

WSC

7274. During a wing stall, the wing tips of a weight shift aircraft are

A— ineffective for stall recovery.

B— effective for stall recovery.

C— effective only when combined with maximum engine output.

Since the wing tips are at a lower angle of attack, they do not normally stall when the rest of the wing is stalled. They keep flying, creating an up-force in back of the CG—causing the nose to rotate down and decrease the angle of attack of the wing—therefore they are very effective for stall recovery. (PLT242) — Trikes, the Flex-Wing Flyers, Chapter 3

Answer (A) is incorrect because the tips are very effective for stall recovery, allowing the nose to fall through. Answer (C) is incorrect because the tips have more effect for stall recovery than the engine power.

WSC

7275. The crosstube is positioned by

A— a quick release pin.

B— self-locking bolts.

C— restraining cables attached to the rear of the keel.

The crossbar is pulled back to tension the airframe into the sail with the crossbar cables. These are attached to a connection point on the rear of the keel. (PLT114) — Trikes, the Flex-Wing Flyers, Chapter 3

Answers (A) and (B) are incorrect because these are fasteners and would only make smaller variations in the crossbar position if these fasteners were adjusted to different settings.

Answers

7223   [C]   7224   [A]   7273   [A]   7274   [B]   7275   [C]

WSC

7276. On some trikes, the hang point is part of

A— a variable trim arrangement that allows the pilot to adjust the aircraft center of gravity during flight to obtain the most favorable aircraft performance.

B— an adjustable trim arrangement that allows the pilot to adjust the aircraft center of gravity during flight to obtain the most favorable aircraft performance.

C— an adjustable trim arrangement that allows the center of gravity to shift fore and aft along the wing's keel.

Most trikes have an adjustment to move the position on the keel fore and aft on the ground. This is a common way to adjust the trim speed and bar position of the wing. (PLT114) — Trikes, the Flex-Wing Flyers, Chapter 3

Answers (A) and (B) are incorrect because although this is a viable design concept that has been and may be used for trikes, not many incorporate the complexity of a variable CG during flight.

WSC

7277. The keel pocket's purpose is to

A— act as a longitudinal stabilizer, keeping the wing from wandering left and right.

B— act as a roll stabilizer, keeping the wing from wandering left and right.

C— act as a yaw stabilizer, keeping the wing from wandering left and right.

The most significant effect a keel pocket could have on stability would be for yaw. This was an early design concept used in the development of the flex wing. Today, the wing sweep, washout, and airfoil shape are designed to optimize the tracking (yaw) for the vertical axis. Keel pockets today are a fabric channel in the sail material the keel is inserted into, to hold the keel in place at the root of the wing. (PLT114) — Trikes, the Flex-Wing Flyers, Chapter 3

Answers (A) and (B) are incorrect because the keel pocket does not supply this stability.

WSC

7278. How does the wing design feature "washout" affect the production of lift?

A— The wing tips continue producing lift when the main body of the wing is not producing lift.

B— The main body of the wing continues to produce lift when the wing tips are not producing lift.

C— The center of lift moves from the trailing edge of the wing, to the leading edge of the wing, as the wing begins to stall.

The washout/twist in the wing, starts with a high angle of attack at the root/nose, and decreases the angle of attack as the you approach each tip. This washout/twist, sweep, and airfoil shape is designed into the wing to make the nose lose lift first while the tips keep flying at high angles of attack. (PLT114) — Trikes, the Flex-Wing Flyers, Chapter 3

Answer (B) is incorrect because this happens only when the wing is at very low angles of attack where the wing is not near the critical angle of attack to stall. Answer (C) is incorrect because this is not the design of any trike wing and would produce a wing that would be unstable near the stall.

WSC

7279. The wing of a weight-shift aircraft twists so that the angle of attack

A— from the center of the wing to the wing tip is variable and can be adjusted by the pilot in flight to optimize performance.

B— changes from a low angle of attack at the center of the wing, to a high angle of attack at the tips.

C— changes from a high angle of attack at the center of the wing, to a low angle of attack at the tips.

The fundamental design of the flex wing is for the wing to twist from a high angle of attack at the nose, to a lower angle of attack at the tips. (PLT114) — Trikes, the Flex-Wing Flyers, Chapter 3

Answer (A) is incorrect because this would provide a wing that would be unstable and dangerous. Flex wings are not designed this way. Answer (B) is incorrect because this only applies for some wing designs but not all. Varying the twist in the wing is common to most high performance hang gliders in flight and used as one method to trim weight-shift wings as well.

Answers

7276 [C]   7277 [C]   7278 [A]   7279 [C]

Powered Parachute Aerodynamics

PPC

7245. During flight, advancing thrust will

A— increase airspeed.
B— cause the aircraft to climb.
C— cause the aircraft to increase airspeed and climb.

Throttle controls vertical speed in a PPC. Advancing the throttle will produce decreased descent rates or increased climb rates. Speed in a PPC is controlled by the weight and not the throttle. (PLT125) — FAA-H-8083-29

Answers (A) and (C) are incorrect because throttle does not affect airspeed.

PPC

7246. The torque effect of an engine that rotates clockwise in a powered parachute is counteracted by

A— increasing the length of the right and decreasing the length of the left riser cables.
B— decreasing the length of the left riser cables.
C— decreasing the length of right riser cables.

A clockwise or right-turning propeller when viewed from the rear creates an opposite reaction to turn the undercarriage aircraft to the left. Therefore, a slight right-hand turn needs to be built into the aircraft to accommodate for this torque. Many designs are used by manufacturers to accomplish this. Decreasing the length of the right-hand riser will accomplish this by bringing the right side of the wing down. (PLT114) — FAA-H-8083-29

Answers (A) and (B) are incorrect because they would create a turn in the wrong direction.

PPC

7247. The steering bars

A— are used during taxi operations with the parachute stowed.
B— control the outboard trailing edge of the parachute.
C— control the main landing gear brakes.

The steering bars are the main control to turning in flight. Pushing on the right-hand steering bar will pull the right control line, lower the trailing edge of the right wing, create more drag on the right side and turn the aircraft to the right. (PLT346) — FAA-H-8083-29

Answers (A) and (C) are incorrect because the steering bars control the wing and are not used for ground operations.

PPC

7264. The center of gravity tube is

A— lengthened for heavier pilots.
B— shortened for lighter pilots.
C— lengthened for lighter pilots.

The lighter the pilot, the more rearward the wing attachment should be for the hanging airframe to be balanced properly. Most modern designs have a number of hook-in points fore and aft on the airframe. For the tube CG adjustment system, lengthening the CG tube moves the wing hang point back to account for the lightweight person in the front. (PLT114) — FAA-H-8083-29

Answer (A) is incorrect because this would balance the airframe with the nose wheel too low. Answer (B) is incorrect because this would move the CG forward and the front wheel would be too high.

PPC

7265. The fan guard surrounds the propeller and

A— increases aerodynamic efficiency.
B— reduces "P" factor.
C— protects the parachute suspension lines from damage.

The purpose of the fan guard is to protect the parachute lines from hitting the prop. (PLT114) — FAA-H-8083-29

Answers (A) and (B) are incorrect because the fan guard reduces performance and has no effect on P factor.

PPC

7266. Cross ports in the parachute ribs aid in

A— weight reduction of the canopy.
B— the pressurization of the neighboring cells.
C— drying of the canopy.

Cross ports in the wing ribs allow air to flow sideways from cell to cell, called "cross flow" in the wing. This causes the cells next to each other to transfer pressure inside the wing and cells to pressurize neighboring cells. (PLT114) — FAA-H-8083-29

Answers

7245   [B]   7246   [C]   7247   [B]   7264   [C]   7265   [C]   7266   [B]

PPC

7267. Splicing severed suspension lines

A— is permissible if using the same size material as the original line.

B— is a very dangerous practice.

C— is an acceptable field repair.

Splicing lines is dangerous because you can change the airfoil; the lines could come loose and go through the prop. (PLT114) — FAA-H-8083-29

Answers (A) and (C) are incorrect because it is a dangerous practice.

PPC

7268. Tying a severed suspension line

A— will change the shape of the wing and is not permissible.

B— is permissible if it is shortened no more than six inches.

C— is an acceptable field repair.

Tying a severed suspension line would shorten it and create a discontinuity in the wing shape and is not acceptable. (PLT114) — FAA-H-8083-29

Answers (B) and (C) are incorrect because it is a dangerous practice.

PPC

7268-1. What gives your powered parachute wing/canopy its airfoil shape?

A— The risers because, by decreasing the length of the right riser you will get the precise airfoil shape.

B— The suspension lines as they are precisely measured and fitted to a specific location.

C— The air as it enters the cell openings on the leading edge of the airfoil.

The precise lengths of the suspension lines determine the bottom shape of the airfoil. Airfoil-shaped ribs attached to the bottom of the airfoil where the suspension lines are attached define the top shape of the airfoil. (PLT114) — FAA-H-8083-29

Answer (A) is incorrect because the decreased length of the right riser is used to counteract torque on some designs, thus causing a turn. Answer (C) is incorrect because the air inflates the canopy to whatever airfoil shape the suspension lines and ribs define.

PPC

7269. Swapping wings from one brand or type of powered parachute to another is

A— permissible as long as the basic shape of the parachutes are similar.

B— dangerous since every wing is designed for a specific aircraft.

C— permissible if the overall area of the parachutes is the same.

Every wing is designed for a specific airframe configuration, engine torque and weight. (PLT114) — FAA-H-8083-29

Answers (A) and (C) are incorrect because there can be a different length in the lines between the right and left, which has nothing to do with the shape and area of the wing.

PPC

7270. Degradation of the parachute's protective polyurethane coating results in

A— increased takeoff distances, decreased maximum gross weight, and increased fuel consumption.

B— reduced takeoff distances, increased maximum gross weight, and reduced fuel consumption.

C— increased takeoff distances, increased maximum gross weight, and increased fuel consumption.

A degradation of the fabric results in air leaking through the fabric and a loss in performance since this creates more drag. (PLT114) — FAA-H-8083-29

Answers (B) and (C) are incorrect because there is no increased gross weight.

PPC

7272. Flaring allows the pilot to touchdown at a

A— higher rate of speed and a slower rate of descent.

B— lower rate of speed and a higher rate of descent.

C— lower rate of speed and a lower rate of descent.

Flaring slows you down and decreases your descent rate for a soft and slow landing. (PLT346) — FAA-H-8083-29

Answers (A) and (B) are incorrect because flaring does not produce a higher rate of speed or a higher rate of descent.

Answers

7267 [B]	7268 [A]	7268-1 [B]	7269 [B]	7270 [A]	7272 [C]

PPC
7281. Flaring during a landing

A— decreases the powered parachute's speed due to increased drag.

B— increases the powered parachute's speed due to reduced drag.

C— decreases the powered parachute's drag due to increased speed.

Flaring or pulling down on the trailing edge creates more drag and slows the aircraft similar to a flap on an airplane. (PLT346) — FAA-H-8083-29

Answers (B) and (C) are incorrect because flaring does not increase the speed of a PPC.

Answers

7281   [A]

Chapter 3
Aircraft Systems

Magnetic Compass

The most basic instrument required for flight is the magnetic compass. The compass consists of a float which is free to turn on a hardened steel pivot that rides in a glass bearing. There are two small bar magnets attached to the bottom of the float, and a calibrated card is mounted around the float. The float assembly rides in a bowl of compass fluid, which is a highly refined kerosene-type liquid. The calibrated card is visible to the pilot through the glass front of the bowl, and the direction the aircraft is headed is read on the card opposite the vertical lubber line just behind the glass. The magnetic compass is subject to several errors and limitations:

Variation — This is the error caused by the compass pointing toward the magnetic north pole, while the aeronautical charts are oriented to the geographic north pole. Variation is not affected by changes in heading, but it does change with the location on the earth's surface. Aeronautical charts show the amount of variation to be applied.

Deviation — This is the error caused by local magnetic fields produced by certain metals and the electrical systems in the aircraft. Deviation error is corrected for by "swinging" the compass. The aircraft is aligned with the directional marks on a compass rose on the airport, and the small magnets inside the compass housing are rotated to minimize the error between the compass reading and the direction of the mark with which the aircraft is aligned. Corrections are made on the four cardinal headings, and the errors are read every 30°. A compass correction card is made and installed near the compass to show the pilot the compass heading to fly for each magnetic heading.

Magnetic dip error — This error is caused by the compass magnets pointing downward as they align with the earth's magnetic field. This downward pointing is caused by the vertical component of the field, and is greatest near the magnetic poles.

Northerly turning error — This error is caused by the vertical component of the earth's magnetic field. When flying in the northern hemisphere, on a northerly heading, and banking in either direction to start a turn, the vertical component of the magnetic field pulls on the north-seeking end of the magnets and rotates the compass card in the direction opposite that of the turn being started. When flying on a southerly heading, and banking in either direction to start a turn, the vertical component pulling on the magnets rotates the card in the same direction as the turn is being made. The card moves in the correct direction, but at a rate greater than the actual rate of turn.

Acceleration error — This error is caused by the center of gravity of the compass float being below its pivot. When the aircraft is flying in the northern hemisphere on an easterly or westerly heading and accelerates, the rear end of the float tips upward, and the magnetic pull on the compass magnets causes the card to rotate and indicate a turn toward the north. When the aircraft decelerates on an easterly or westerly heading, the rear end of the float dips down and the magnet is pulled in the direction that rotates the card to indicate a turn toward the south. A memory device to help remember the effect of acceleration error is the word "ANDS": **A**ccelerate **N**orth, **D**ecelerate **S**outh. There is no acceleration error when accelerating or decelerating on a northerly or southerly heading.

When making turns by reference to the magnetic compass, these corrections should be made:

1. If you are on a northerly heading and start a turn to the east or west, the indication of the compass lags or shows a turn in the opposite direction.

2. If you are on a southerly heading and start a turn to the east or west, the indication of the compass leads the turn, showing a greater amount of turn than is actually being made.

3. The amount of lead or lag depends upon the latitude at which you are flying. For all practical purposes, the lead or lag is equal to approximately 1° for each degree of latitude.

4. When rolling out of a turn, using a coordinated bank, the rollout should be started before the desired heading is reached by an amount that is equal to approximately one-half of the bank angle being used.

ALL

6672. Deviation error of the magnetic compass is caused by

A— northerly turning error.
B— certain metals and electrical systems within the aircraft.
C— the difference in location of true north and magnetic north.

Deviation is a compass error caused by local magnetic disturbances produced by certain metals and electrical systems in the aircraft. (PLT215) — FAA-H-8083-25

Answer (A) is incorrect because northerly turning error is caused by magnetic dip. Answer (C) is incorrect because this defines magnetic variation.

ALL

6675. Which statement is true about magnetic deviation of a compass?

A— Deviation is the same for all aircraft in the same locality.
B— Deviation varies for different headings of the same aircraft.
C— Deviation is different in a given aircraft in different localities.

The compass needles are affected not only by the earth's magnetic field, but also by magnetic fields generated when the aircraft's electrical equipment is operated, and by metal components in the aircraft. These magnetic disturbances within the aircraft deflect the compass needles from alignment with magnetic north. This error is called deviation. Deviation varies according to the electrical components in use, and the magnetism changes with jolts from hard landings and installation of additional radio equipment, and is different on each heading flown. (PLT215) — FAA-H-8083-25

Answers (A) and (C) are incorrect because they both apply to variation, not deviation.

ALL

6670. In the Northern Hemisphere, a magnetic compass will normally indicate a turn toward the north if

A— a left turn is entered from a west heading.
B— an aircraft is decelerated while on an east or west heading.
C— an aircraft is accelerated while on an east or west heading.

In the Northern Hemisphere, a magnetic compass will momentarily indicate a turn toward the north when the aircraft is accelerated while flying on either an easterly or a westerly heading. (PLT215) — FAA-H-8083-25

Answer (A) is incorrect because turning errors do not occur from west headings. Answer (B) is incorrect because the compass would indicate a turn to the south if an aircraft is decelerated while on an east or west heading.

ALL

6671. In the Northern Hemisphere, if an aircraft is accelerated or decelerated, the magnetic compass will normally indicate

A— a turn momentarily, with changes in airspeed on any heading.
B— a turn toward the south while accelerating on a west heading.
C— correctly when on a north or south heading while either accelerating or decelerating.

The compass card in a magnetic compass is weighted to compensate for magnetic dip. The inertia of this weight causes the compass to momentarily indicate a turn to the north when accelerating on either an easterly or a westerly heading, and to indicate a turn to the south when decelerating on either of these headings. The compass has no appreciable acceleration error when accelerating or decelerating on a northerly or southerly heading. (PLT215) — FAA-H-8083-25

Answer (A) is incorrect because acceleration and deceleration errors only occur on east and west headings. Answer (B) is incorrect because the compass will normally indicate a turn toward the north while accelerating on a west heading.

Answers

6672	[B]	6675	[B]	6670	[C]	6671	[C]

ALL

6673. In the Northern Hemisphere, which would be correct about starting the rollout from a turn using a magnetic compass? Start the rollout

A— after the compass indication passes south by a number of degrees approximately equal to the latitude minus the normal rollout lead.

B— before the compass indication reaches south by a number of degrees approximately equal to the latitude over which the turn is made plus the pilot's normal lead.

C— after the compass indication passes south by a number of degrees approximately equal to the magnetic variation of the area over which the turn is made plus the pilot's normal lead.

The dip compensation weight on the card of a magnetic compass causes an error called the northerly turning error. When rolling out of a turn on a southerly heading, start the rollout after the compass indication passes south by a number of degrees approximately equal to the latitude, minus the normal rollout lead (one half of the bank angle). (PLT215) — FAA-H-8083-25

ALL

6674. What should be the indication on the magnetic compass as you roll into a standard rate turn to the right from a south heading in the Northern Hemisphere?

A— The compass will initially indicate a turn to the left.

B— The compass will indicate a turn to the right, but at a faster rate than is actually occurring.

C— The compass will remain on south for a short time, then gradually catch up to the magnetic heading of the airplane.

If you are on a southerly heading and roll into a standard-rate turn to the right, the compass will immediately indicate a turn toward the west (to the right), because of the northerly turning error. During the first part of the turn, it will show a faster rate of turn than you are actually making. (PLT215) — FAA-H-8083-25

Answer (A) is incorrect because the compass will initially indicate a turn to the left when rolling into a standard rate turn from a north heading in the Northern Hemisphere. Answer (C) is incorrect because the compass indication will lead the turn when rolling into a standard-rate turn from a south heading in the Northern Hemisphere.

Pitot-Static Instruments

The **altimeter**, **airspeed indicator**, and **vertical speed indicator** are important flight instruments that are operated by air pressure. All three of these instruments receive their static pressure from the static air ports located on the side of the fuselage or the vertical tail surface.

When flying at high angles of attack, such as when practicing power-off stalls with flaps down, the air flowing around the aircraft is disturbed to the extent that the air pressure at the static ports is no longer that of undisturbed air. The indicated airspeed at the moment of the stall will likely be lower than that indicated by the white arc on the airspeed indicator. This erroneous airspeed indication is caused by an installation error in the static system, called position error. An airspeed correction table is often included in the Pilot's Operating Handbook to show the airspeed correction to be applied when flying with flaps down. Pitot-static system errors caused by position error are generally the greatest at low airspeed.

The airspeed indicator is a differential pressure indicator that measures the difference between the static air pressure and the ram air pressure caused by the movement through the air. The airspeed indicator is connected to both the static ports and the pitot tube which is an open-end tube that points directly into the airstream and picks up the ram pressure of the air. If both the ram-air input and the drain hole in the pitot tube become blocked, there will be no variations in the airspeed indication in level flight even if large power changes are made. There will, however, be changes in the airspeed indication if the aircraft changes altitude with the pitot pressure inlet blocked.

Continued

Answers

6673 [A]   6674 [B]

The airspeed indicator is color-coded to help the pilot immediately recognize the important airspeeds and ranges of airspeed. The color codes are:

White arc — Flap operating speed. The bottom of this arc is at the power-off stall speed with the gear and flaps down, V_{SO}. Where the green arc meets the white arc (bottom of green arc), is the power-off stall speed with flaps and gear up, V_{S1}. The top of the white arc is at V_{FE}.

Green arc — Normal operating range. The top of the green arc is the maximum structural cruising speed, V_{NO}.

Yellow arc — Caution range. The aircraft should not be flown in this speed range in rough air. This arc extends from the top of the green arc to the never-exceed red line.

Red radial line — This is the never-exceed speed, V_{NE}.

Blue radial line — This is the best rate-of-climb speed for a twin-engine airplane with one engine inoperative.

The **design maneuvering speed (V_A)** of an aircraft, which is the maximum speed at which the aircraft can be safely stalled, is not color-coded on the airspeed indicator. This maneuvering speed is noted in the Aircraft Flight Manual and is often marked on a placard on the instrument panel. If V_A for an aircraft is not known, a generally accepted rule of thumb for a safe maneuvering speed is 1.7 times the normal stalling speed. *See* Figure 3-1.

The altimeter is an absolute pressure indicator that measures the static pressure of the air surrounding the aircraft. This pressure is referenced from the appropriate level and is indicated on the instrument dial in units of feet. If the barometric pressure in the window is set to standard sea level pressure of 29.92 inches of mercury or 1013.2 millibars, the altimeter will indicate pressure altitude. If the pressure in the window is set to the existing altimeter setting, the altimeter will indicate indicated altitude.

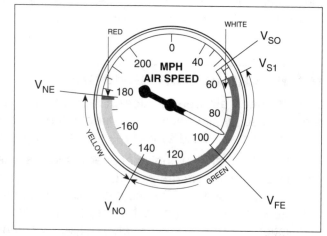

Figure 3-1. Airspeed indicator

The altimeter is connected to the static port for its normal operation, and in the event the static port ices over, an alternate static air source valve may be opened to allow the altimeter to take its static pressure from inside the aircraft. If the alternate static air pressure valve in an unpressurized aircraft is opened in flight, the altimeter will likely indicate higher than that actually being flown. The air flowing over the fuselage speeds up and its pressure drops. This causes the pressure of the air inside the cabin to be lowered enough to give a slightly inaccurate indication on the altimeter. If the static system of a pressurized aircraft should leak and allow pressurized air to enter the system while flying at high altitude, the altimeter will read the cabin altitude, which is lower than the actual flight altitude.

The altimeter measures the absolute pressure of the air to indicate the altitude. Temperature affects the density and thus the pressure of the air, and correction must be made to the air pressure to find the true altitude. If you fly into an area where the temperature is colder than standard, the air will be denser than standard air, and the pressure levels will be closer together. This will cause the aircraft to be lower than the altimeter indicates. If, on the other hand, you fly into an area where the temperature is warmer than standard, the air will be less dense than standard air, and the pressure levels will be farther apart. The aircraft will be higher than the altimeter indicates. *See* Figure 3-2.

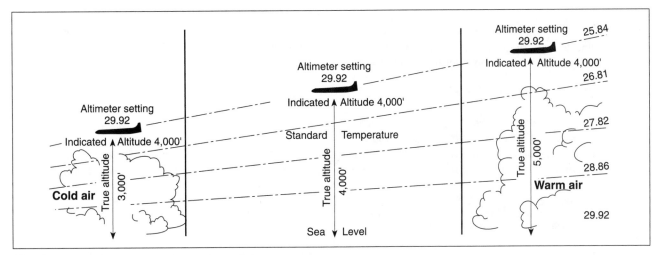

Figure 3-2. Temperature vs. altimeter indication

ALL

6681. Which statement is true about the effect of temperature changes on the indications of a sensitive altimeter?

A— Warmer-than-standard temperatures will place the aircraft lower than the altimeter indicates.

B— Colder-than-standard temperatures will place the aircraft lower than the altimeter indicates.

C— Colder-than-standard temperatures will place the aircraft higher than the altimeter indicates.

Cold air is more dense than warm air, and an altimeter is affected by air density. When flying in an area where the air is colder and more dense than standard, the pressure levels are closer together, and the aircraft will be lower than the altimeter indicates. (PLT165) — FAA-H-8083-25

Answer (A) is incorrect because warmer-than-standard temperatures raise the pressure levels, and therefore will place the aircraft higher than the altimeter indicates. Answer (C) is incorrect because colder-than-standard temperatures lower the pressure levels, and therefore will place the aircraft lower than the altimeter indicates.

ALL

7282. What is true altitude?

A— The vertical distance of the aircraft above sea level.

B— The vertical distance of the aircraft above the surface.

C— The height above the standard datum plane.

True altitude is the vertical distance of the airplane above sea level—the actual altitude. It is often expressed as feet above mean sea level (MSL). Airport, terrain, and obstacle elevations on aeronautical charts are true altitudes. (PLT023) — FAA-H-8083-25

Answer (B) is incorrect because the vertical distance above the surface is absolute altitude. Answer (C) is incorrect because the height above the standard datum plane is pressure altitude.

ALL

7287. Under what condition is indicated altitude the same as true altitude?

A— If the altimeter has no mechanical error.

B— When at sea level under standard conditions.

C— When at 18,000 feet MSL with the altimeter set at 29.92.

On a standard day (29.92" Hg and +15°C) at sea level, pressure altitude, indicated altitude, and density altitude are all equal. Any variation from standard temperature or pressure will have an effect on the altimeter. (PLT023) — FAA-H-8083-25

Answer (A) is incorrect because mechanical error does not apply to true altitude. Answer (C) is incorrect because when the altimeter is set to 29.92, it indicates pressure altitude.

Answers

6681   [B]   7282   [A]   7287   [B]

ALL

7288. What is absolute altitude?

A— The altitude read directly from the altimeter.
B— The vertical distance of the aircraft above the surface.
C— The height above the standard datum plane.

Absolute altitude is height above the surface. This height may be indicated directly on a radar altimeter. Absolute altitude may be approximately computed from indicated altitude and chart elevation data. (PLT023) — FAA-H-8083-25

Answer (A) is incorrect because the altitude read from the altimeter is indicated altitude. Answer (C) is incorrect because the height above the standard datum plane is pressure altitude.

AIR

6680. If the static pressure tubes are broken inside a pressurized cabin during a high-altitude flight, the altimeter would probably indicate

A— sea level.
B— lower than actual flight altitude.
C— higher than actual flight altitude.

If the static pressure tubes are broken inside a pressurized cabin, the altimeter will sense the cabin altitude, rather than flight altitude. In high-altitude flight, the cabin altitude is lower than the flight altitude. (PLT337) — FAA-H-8083-25

AIR, RTC, LSA, WSC

6677. Pitot-static system errors are generally the greatest in which range of airspeed?

A— Low airspeed.
B— High airspeed.
C— Maneuvering speed.

When the aircraft is at high angle-of-attack flight, the air does not strike the pitot tube at the correct angle, and pitot-static system errors are greatest at low airspeeds. (PLT337) — FAA-H-8083-25

Answer (B) is incorrect because high airspeed flight occurs at a normal angle-of-attack, when the pitot tube is facing directly into the relative wind. Answer (C) is incorrect because flight at maneuvering speed does not cause pitot-static system errors.

AIR, RTC, LSA, WSC

6679. If a pitot tube is clogged, which instrument would be affected?

A— Altimeter.
B— Airspeed indicator.
C— Vertical speed indicator.

The airspeed indicator picks up its pressures from both the pitot tube and the static ports. Therefore, if the pitot tube was clogged, the airspeed indicator would have erroneous indications. (PLT337) — FAA-H-8083-25

Answers (A) and (C) are incorrect because the vertical speed indicator and the altimeter are connected only to the static ports.

ALL

7289. The pitot system provides impact pressure for which instrument?

A— Altimeter.
B— Vertical-speed indicator.
C— Airspeed indicator.

The pitot tube provides input for the airspeed indicator only. (PLT337) — FAA-H-8083-25

Answer (A) is incorrect because the altimeter and vertical speed indicator operate off of the static system. Answer (B) is incorrect because the altimeter and vertical speed indicator operate off of the static system.

AIR, RTC, LSA, WSC

6712. If both the ram-air input and drain hole of the pitot system are blocked, what airspeed indication can be expected?

A— Decrease of indicated airspeed during a climb.
B— Zero indicated airspeed until blockage is removed.
C— No variation of indicated airspeed in level flight even if large power changes are made.

When both the ram-air inlet of the pitot tube and its drain hole are plugged, the airspeed indicator cannot sense the existing ram-air pressure, and there will be no variation in the indicated airspeed in level flight even if large power changes are made. (PLT337) — AC 91-43

Answer (A) is incorrect because indicated airspeed would increase in a climb. Answer (B) is incorrect because the airspeed would indicate zero only if the ram-air input was blocked while the drain hole remained open.

Answers

7288 [B]	6680 [B]	6677 [A]	6679 [B]	7289 [C]	6712 [C]

ALL

6736-1. What airspeed indicator marking identifies the maximum structural cruising speed of an aircraft?

A— Red radial line.
B— Upper limit of the green arc.
C— Upper limit of the yellow arc.

The maximum structural cruising speed of an aircraft (V_{NO}) is identified by the upper limit of the green arc on the airspeed indicator. (PLT278) — FAA-H-8083-25

Answer (A) is incorrect because the red radial line indicates the never-exceed speed (V_{NE}). Answer (C) is incorrect because the lower (not upper) limit of the yellow arc indicates the maximum structural cruising speed (V_{NO}).

AIR, RTC, LSA, WSC

6739. Which airspeed is identified by color coding on an airspeed indicator?

A— Design maneuvering speed.
B— Maximum structural cruising speed.
C— Maximum gear operation or extended speed.

The maximum structural cruising speed (V_{NO}) is identified on an airspeed indicator by the upper limit of the green arc. (PLT088) — FAA-H-8083-25

Answers (A) and (C) are incorrect because these speeds are not color-coded.

AIR, RTC, LSA, WSC

6740. What is an important airspeed limitation not color coded on airspeed indicators?

A— Maneuvering speed.
B— Never-exceed speed.
C— Maximum flaps-extended speed.

The design maneuvering speed (V_A) of an aircraft is not color-coded on the airspeed indicator. It is noted in the Aircraft Flight Manual and is often marked on a placard on the instrument panel. (PLT088) — FAA-H-8083-25

Answer (B) is incorrect because the never-exceed speed (V_{NE}) is indicated by the red line at the upper limit of the yellow arc. Answer (C) is incorrect because the maximum flaps-extended speed (V_{FE}) is indicated by the upper limit of the white arc.

AIR, LSA

6678. During power-off stalls with flaps full down, the stall occurs and the pointer on the airspeed indicator shows a speed less than the minimum limit of the white arc on the indicator. This is most probably due to

A— a low density altitude.
B— a malfunction in the pitot-static system.
C— installation error in the pitot-static system.

During high-angle-of-attack flight, such as power-off stalls with flaps full down, the ram air does not strike the pitot tube directly, and the airspeed indicator generally indicates a much slower airspeed than is actually being flown. This error is due to installation error in the pitot-static system. (PLT337) — FAA-H-8083-25

AIR, LSA

6682. A possible result of using the emergency alternate source of static pressure inside the cabin of an unpressurized airplane is the

A— airspeed indicator may indicate less than normal.
B— altimeter may indicate an altitude lower than the actual altitude being flown.
C— altimeter may indicate an altitude higher than the actual altitude being flown.

The use of the alternate static air source in an unpressurized airplane can result in an altimeter indication that is higher than the aircraft is actually flying. When an aircraft is flying, the air flowing around the fuselage speeds up, and in accordance with Bernoulli's principle, the pressure of the air entering the cabin is slightly lower than that of the surrounding air. The altimeter sensing this lowered cabin pressure through the alternate static source will indicate higher than the airplane is actually flying. (PLT167) — FAA-H-8083-25

AIR, GLI, LSA

6737. What does the lower limit of the white arc on an airspeed indicator represent?

A— Minimum controllable airspeed with flaps extended.
B— Power-off stall speed in a landing configuration.
C— Power-off stall speed in a specified configuration.

The lower limit of the white arc on an airspeed indicator is the power-off stall speed (V_{SO}), with the wing flaps and landing gear in the landing position. (PLT088) — FAA-H-8083-25

Answers

6736-1 [B]	6739 [B]	6740 [A]	6678 [C]	6682 [C]	6737 [B]

AIR, GLI, WSC, LSA

6738. What does the lower limit of the green arc on an airspeed indicator represent?

A— Power-off stall speed in a landing configuration.
B— Power-off stall speed in a specified configuration.
C— Minimum controllable airspeed with gear and flaps retracted.

The lower limit of the green arc on an airspeed indicator is the power-off stall speed (V_{S1}), in a specified condition. (PLT088) — FAA-H-8083-25

RTC

6736-2. How does temperature and weight affect the V_{NE} of a helicopter?

A— V_{NE} increases as temperature and weight increase.
B— V_{NE} decreases as temperature and weight increase.
C— V_{NE} decreases as temperature increases and weight decreases.

High temperature contributes to high density altitude, which lessens helicopter performance. Also, the heavier the gross weight, the greater the power required to hover and for flight in general, and the poorer the performance of the helicopter since less reserve power is available. Therefore, V_{NE} decreases as temperature and weight increase. (PLT123) — FAA-H-8083-21

Gyroscopic Instruments

Gyroscopic flight instruments are divided into two categories; **attitude indicators** and **rate indicators**. The attitude indicators are the directional gyro, gyro horizon, and horizontal situation indicator. The rate indicators are the turn and slip indicator and the turn coordinator.

Gyroscopic instruments can be operated either electrically or pneumatically. As a safety feature, airplanes that have pneumatically-operated attitude indicators often have electrically-operated rate indicators. Pneumatically-operated instruments can be connected to the airplane's vacuum system or to the pressure air system. Instruments connected to the vacuum system are actually driven by air pressure flowing into the instrument to fill the case that has been evacuated by the vacuum pump.

AIR, RTC, LSA, MCI

6676. Which instrument would be affected by excessively low pressure in the airplane's vacuum system?

A— Heading indicator.
B— Airspeed indicator.
C— Pressure altimeter.

Pneumatic heading indicators are vacuum-driven gyro instruments and are affected by excessively low pressure in the airplane's vacuum system. Low pressure (insufficient vacuum) is unable to draw enough air into the instrument housing for the rotor to reach its required speed, and the gyro will not be rigid enough to avoid excessive drift. (PLT118) — FAA-H-8083-25

Answers (B) and (C) are incorrect because the airspeed indicator and pressure altimeter are part of the pitot-static system and are not affected by the vacuum system.

Answers

6738   [B]   6736-2   [B]   6676   [A]

Automation Management

Automation management is the demonstrated ability to control and navigate an aircraft by means of the automated systems installed in the aircraft. It is one of the components associated with single pilot resource management: aeronautical decision making and risk management, automation management, task management, situation awareness, and controlled flight into terrain (CFIT) awareness. In advanced avionics aircraft, proper automation management requires a thorough understanding of how the autopilot interacts with the other systems. An advanced avionics safety issue identified by the FAA concerns pilots who develop an unwarranted overreliance in their avionics and the aircraft, believing that the equipment compensates for pilot shortcomings. Advanced avionics should be used to increase safety, not risk.

ALL

7322. When a pilot believes advanced avionics enable operations closer to personal or environmental limits,

A— greater utilization of the aircraft is achieved.
B— risk is increased.
C— risk is decreased.

Advanced avionics can sometimes have a negative effect on pilot risk-taking behavior, where more information results in pilots taking more risk than they might be willing to accept without the information. Advanced avionics should be used to increase safety, not risk. (PLT104) — FAA-H-8083-6

ALL

7323. Automation in aircraft has proven

A— to present new hazards in its limitations.
B— that automation is basically flawless.
C— prevent accidents.

Advanced avionics were designed to increase safety as well as the utility of the aircraft. However, the systems are not infallible. While automation does help prevent many existing types of errors, it has also created new kinds of errors. (PLT104) — FAA-H-8083-6

ALL

7324. The lighter workloads associated with glass (digital) flight instrumentation

A— are useful in decreasing flightcrew fatigue.
B— have proven to increase safety in operations.
C— may lead to complacency by the flightcrew.

Risk management is the last of the three flight management skills needed for mastery of the advanced avionics aircraft. The enhanced situational awareness and automation capabilities offered by a glass flight deck vastly expand its safety and utility, especially for personal transportation use. At the same time, there is some risk that lighter workloads could lead to complacency. (PLT104) — FAA-H-8083-2

Answers

7322	[B]	7323	[A]	7324	[C]

The Electrical System

Most large aircraft use alternating current (AC) electrical systems as their main source of electrical power. But because of the ease of storing direct current (DC) electricity for starting the engine, almost all small airplanes use DC systems. When AC is needed for instruments, an inverter is used to change DC into AC.

A typical light airplane electrical system uses a battery to start the engine. It uses a generator or alternator to supply all of the electrical needs when the engine is running and to keep the battery charged.

Most older airplanes have **generators**, but almost all of the newer airplanes use **alternators**. One of the basic differences between a generator and an alternator is the number of magnetic poles used to produce the electricity. Generators normally have 2 or 4 poles, while alternators have between 8 and 14 poles. The larger number of poles allows an alternator to produce its electrical power at a lower engine RPM than a generator.

The **ignition system** in an aircraft engine is entirely separate from the aircraft electrical system. The engine can operate normally with the electrical system turned off. The only time the engine needs the electrical system is to turn the starter.

If an aircraft electrical system should fail in flight, the ignition system will not be affected, but the fuel quantity indicators, aircraft lighting system, avionics equipment, and all instruments that require outside electrical power would be inoperative.

AIR, RTC, WSC, PPC, LSA

6668. Concerning the advantages of an aircraft generator or alternator, select the true statement.

A— A generator always provides more electrical current than an alternator.

B— An alternator provides more electrical power at lower engine RPM than a generator.

C— A generator charges the battery during low engine RPM; therefore, the battery has less chance to become fully discharged, as often occurs with an alternator.

One of the basic differences between a generator and an alternator used on an aircraft engine is the number of magnetic poles used to produce the electricity. Generators normally have 2 or 4 poles, while alternators have between 8 and 14 poles. Because of the greater number of poles, an alternator can provide more electrical power at a lower engine RPM than a generator. (PLT207) — FAA-H-8083-25

AIR, RTC, WSC, PPC, LSA

6705. An electrical system failure (battery and alternator) occurs during flight. In this situation, you would

A— experience avionics equipment failure.

B— probably experience failure of the engine ignition system, fuel gauges, aircraft lighting system, and avionics equipment.

C— probably experience engine failure due to the loss of the engine-driven fuel pump and also experience failure of the radio equipment, lights, and all instruments that require alternating current.

If you experience an in-flight electrical system failure, you have an avionics equipment failure and cannot use your electrical fuel boost pump. (PLT207) — FAA-H-8083-15

Answer (B) is incorrect because the ignition system of an aircraft reciprocating engine is powered by two self-contained magnetos that are not dependent upon the aircraft electrical system. Answer (C) is incorrect because the engine-driven fuel pumps are mechanical and not dependent on the electrical system.

Answers

6668   [B]   6705   [A]

Oxygen Systems

Modern aircraft that fly at high altitudes are equipped with oxygen systems to supply the occupants with supplemental oxygen when there is not enough outside air pressure to force the required oxygen into the lungs.

Most general aviation aircraft oxygen systems carry gaseous oxygen in either installed or portable high-pressure steel bottles. These systems must be serviced with "Aviators Breathing Oxygen" which meets Federal Specification BB-O-925A, Grade A or equivalent. Hospital or industrial oxygen must never be used.

The high pressure of the oxygen is reduced with a regulator and fed to the masks at the pressure needed to allow the oxygen to flow into the user's lungs. The more complex oxygen systems use demand-type regulators that meter the oxygen to the user only during inhalation.

The simpler systems use a continuous flow of oxygen into a rebreather-type mask. In this mask, the air exhaled from the lungs flows into a flexible bag where it mixes with oxygen. When the wearer inhales, fresh oxygen and some of the exhaled air is taken into the lungs. This type of mask conserves oxygen.

AIR, RTC, LTA, GLI, MCI

6707. What precautions should be taken with respect to aircraft oxygen systems?

A— Ensure that only medical oxygen has been used to replenish oxygen containers.
B— Prohibit smoking while in an aircraft equipped with a portable oxygen system.
C— Ensure that industrial oxygen has not been used to replenish the system.

When servicing an aircraft oxygen system, be sure that industrial oxygen is not used. Only oxygen marked "Aviators Breathing Oxygen" which meets Federal Specification BB-O-925A, Grade A or equivalent may be used. (PLT438) — AC 61-107

Answer (A) is incorrect because aviation breathing oxygen must be used. Answer (B) is incorrect because smoking is prohibited when using oxygen, but not necessarily on aircraft equipped with oxygen systems.

AIR, RTC, LTA, GLI, MCI

6708. What type of oxygen system is most commonly found in general aviation aircraft?

A— Demand.
B— Continuous flow.
C— Pressure demand.

Basic continuous flow systems are used in general aviation. (PLT326) — AC 61-107

Answer (A) is incorrect because the demand system is used for operations up to altitudes of 40,000 feet. Answer (C) is incorrect because the pressure demand system is used for operations above 40,000 feet.

AIR, RTC, LTA, GLI, MCI

6709. What type of oxygen should be used to replenish an aircraft oxygen system?

A— Medical.
B— Aviation.
C— Industrial.

When servicing an aircraft oxygen system, be sure that industrial oxygen is not used. Only oxygen marked "Aviators Breathing Oxygen" which meets Federal Specification BB-O-925A, Grade A or equivalent may be used. (PLT326) — AC 61-107

AIR, RTC, LTA, GLI, MCI

6718. What is the purpose of the rebreather bag on an oxygen mask in a continuous-flow system?

A— Helps to conserve oxygen.
B— Allows excess oxygen to be expelled during use.
C— Controls amount of oxygen that each individual breathes through the mask.

The rebreather bag used on the mask in a continuous-flow oxygen system helps conserve oxygen. Oxygen from the regulator flows into the bottom of the bag, and when the wearer of the mask exhales, the air fills the rebreather bag. Some of the air, that which was in the lungs longest, spills out of the bag. When the user inhales, the used air in the bag mixed with the oxygen that flowed into the bottom of the bag is breathed in. (PLT326) — FAA-H-8083-25

Answers

| 6707 | [C] | 6708 | [B] | 6709 | [B] | 6718 | [A] |

Cold Weather Operation

When an aircraft has been exposed to extreme cold for any length of time, extra care should be taken when preparing the aircraft for flight. Check all drain valves, oil tank sumps, oil drains, fuel strainers, vent lines and all main and auxiliary control hinges and surfaces for the existence of ice or hard snow. Check the crankcase breather line to be sure that it is not plugged with ice.

When possible, the aircraft should be preheated, with heat applied to the following sections or parts of the aircraft: accessory section, nose section, Y-drain valve, all oil lines, oil tank sump, starters, instruments, tires, cockpits and elevator trim tabs.

ALL

6710. Which statement is true regarding preheating of an aircraft during cold-weather operations?

A— The cockpit, as well as the engine, should be preheated.

B— The cockpit area should not be preheated with portable heaters.

C— Hot air should be blown directly at the engine through the air intakes.

When conditions warrant, preheating is used on the following sections or parts of the aircraft: accessory section, nose section, Y-drain valve, all oil lines, oil tank sump, starters, instruments, tires, cockpits, and elevator trim tabs. (PLT126) — AC 91-13

AIR, RTC, LSA, WSC, PPC

6711. During preflight in cold weather, crankcase breather lines should receive special attention because they are susceptible to being clogged by

A— ice from crankcase vapors that have condensed and subsequently frozen.

B— congealed oil from the crankcase.

C— moisture from the outside air which has frozen.

It is possible for a crankcase breather line to become plugged with ice so it cannot vent the crankcase. This line must be checked during a preflight inspection to be sure that it is clear. (PLT324) — AC 91-13

The Powerplant

Most of the smaller general aviation airplanes are powered by four-stroke-cycle reciprocating engines that operate on the following principle:

1. On the **intake** stroke, the piston is moving inward, the intake valve is open, and the gaseous fuel-air mixture is pulled into the cylinder.

2. On the **compression** stroke, the piston moves outward with both valves closed. The fuel-air mixture is compressed. Near the top of the compression stroke, the spark plugs ignite the mixture and it begins to burn.

3. On the **power** stroke, the burning and expanding gases force the piston inward, doing work. Near the end of the power stroke, the exhaust valve opens so the burned gases can begin to leave the cylinder.

4. On the **exhaust** stroke, the piston moves outward and forces the burned gases out of the cylinder.

   See Figure 3-3.

An engine can be operated efficiently only when the pilot monitors all conditions and keeps them within the allowable ranges. Aircraft engines are highly susceptible to damage if the oil temperature and cylinder head temperature are allowed to exceed their allowable limits. Excessively high temperatures can cause a power loss, excessive oil consumption, and permanent damage to the engine. Damaging high temperatures can be caused by operating the engine at a power output that is too high, or with a fuel-air mixture that is too lean for the power being developed.

Answers

6710　[A]　　　　6711　[A]

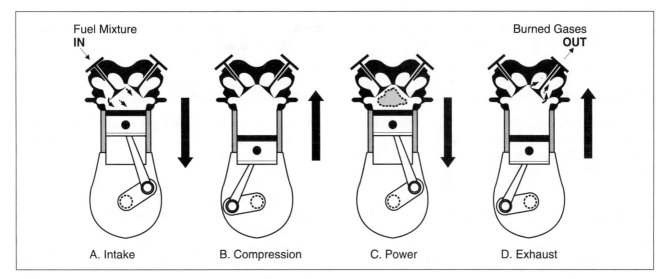

Figure 3-3. Four-stroke cycle

AIR, RTC, WSC, PPC, LSA

6667. During which stroke of a reciprocating engine is the gaseous mixture expanding within the cylinder?

A— Power.
B— Intake.
C— Compression.

Work is done inside a reciprocating engine only during the power stroke when the burning and expanding gases force the piston inward. (PLT343) — FAA-H-8083-25

AIR, RTC, WSC, PPC, LSA

6641. Excessively high engine temperatures, either in the air or on the ground, will

A— not appreciably affect an aircraft engine.
B— cause damage to heat-conducting hoses and warping of cylinder cooling fans.
C— cause loss of power, excessive oil consumption, and possible permanent internal engine damage.

Operating the engine at higher than designed temperatures can cause a loss of power, excessive oil consumption and detonation. Excessive operating temperatures will also lead to serious permanent engine damage, such as scored cylinder walls, damaged pistons and rings, and burned and warped valves. (PLT343) — FAA-H-8083-25

AIR, RTC, WSC, PPC, LSA

6642. If the engine oil temperature and cylinder head temperature gauges have exceeded their normal operating range, you may have been

A— operating with the mixture set too rich.
B— using fuel that has a higher-than-specified fuel rating.
C— operating with too much power and with the mixture set too lean.

Overheating an aircraft engine is indicated by the oil temperature and cylinder head temperature exceeding their normal operating range. Overheating can be caused by allowing the engine to produce too much power, and by operating with a mixture that is too lean for the power being produced. (PLT343) — FAA-H-8083-25

Answer (A) is incorrect because operating with the mixture set too rich tends to cause the engine to operate at lower temperatures. Answer (B) is incorrect because using fuel that has a higher-than-specified fuel rating tends to lower the engine operating temperatures.

Answers

6667   [A]   6641   [C]   6642   [C]

AIR, RTC, WSC, PPC, LSA

7293. What action can a pilot take to aid in cooling an engine that is overheating during a climb?

A— Reduce rate of climb and increase airspeed.
B— Reduce climb speed and increase RPM.
C— Increase climb speed and increase RPM.

To avoid excessive cylinder head temperatures, a pilot can open the cowl flaps, increase airspeed, enrich the mixture, or reduce power. Any of these procedures will aid in reducing the engine temperature. Establishing a shallower climb (increasing airspeed) increases the airflow through the cooling system, reducing high engine temperatures. (PLT342) — FAA-H-8083-25

Answer (B) is incorrect because reducing airspeed hinders cooling, and increasing RPM will further increase engine temperature. Answer (C) is incorrect because increasing RPM will increase engine temperature.

AIR, RTC, WSC, PPC, LSA

7299. What should be the first action after starting an aircraft engine?

A— Adjust for proper RPM and check for desired indications on the engine gauges.
B— Place the magneto or ignition switch momentarily in the OFF position to check for proper grounding.
C— Test each brake and the parking brake.

As soon as the engine starts, check for unintentional movement of the aircraft and set power to the recommended warm-up RPM. The oil pressure should then be checked to determine that the oil system is functioning properly with pressure at recommended levels within the manufacturer's time limit. (PLT479) — FAA-H-8083-25

Answer (B) is incorrect because this is usually done at the end of the flight. Answer (C) is incorrect because brakes are checked when beginning to taxi.

AIR, RTC, WSC, PPC, LSA

7306. An abnormally high engine oil temperature indication may be caused by

A— operating with a too high viscosity oil.
B— the oil level being too low.
C— operating with an excessively rich mixture.

The oil pressure indication varies inversely with the oil temperature. High temperature and low pressure usually indicate low oil level. (PLT324) — FAA-H-8083-25

AIR, RTC, WSC, PPC, LSA

7307. For internal cooling, air cooled engines are especially dependent on

A— a properly functioning thermostat.
B— air flowing over the exhaust manifold.
C— the circulation of lubricating oil.

Oil, used primarily to lubricate the moving parts of the engine, also cools the internal parts of the engine as it circulates. (PLT324) — FAA-H-8083-25

Answer (A) is incorrect because most air-cooled aircraft engines do not have thermostats. Answer (B) is incorrect because, although air-cooling is important, internal cooling is more reliant on oil circulation. Air cools the cylinders, not the exhaust manifold.

Answers

7293 [A]   7299 [A]   7306 [B]   7307 [C]

The Ignition System

The ignition system of an aircraft reciprocating engine is a dual, self-contained electrical system. Two magnetos produce high-voltage AC electricity and direct it to spark plugs in each cylinder so that a spark will ignite the fuel-air mixture inside the cylinders at the proper time.

Magnetos are electrical generators that produce AC electricity when they are rotated. To turn a magneto OFF, its output is directed to ground (the engine structure) through the ignition switch. If the ground wire between the magneto and the ignition switch becomes disconnected, the engine cannot be shut down by turning the switch to the OFF position.

Dual ignition provides a safety factor in case one system should fail, but more importantly, having two spark plugs in each cylinder provides better combustion. The fuel-air mixture inside the cylinder is ignited at two places, so that it requires only half the time to completely burn the charge inside the cylinder.

If one ignition system should fail, or if one spark plug becomes fouled, the mixture is ignited at only one point, and the time required for complete combustion allows the unburned mixture to become so hot it explodes, or detonates. Detonation produces enough heat and pressure to seriously damage the engine.

Spark plugs can become so fouled they cannot ignite the mixture, if the engine is operated with an excessively rich fuel-air mixture, or if the fuel used in the engine has a lead content greater than that recommended for the engine.

AIR, RTC, WSC, PPC, LSA

6646. Which statement is true regarding fouling of the spark plugs of an aircraft engine?

A— Spark plug fouling results from operating with an excessively rich mixture.
B— Carbon fouling of the spark plugs is caused primarily by operating an engine at excessively high cylinder head temperatures.
C— Excessive heat in the combustion chamber of a cylinder causes oil to form on the center electrode of a spark plug and this fouls the plug.

When an engine is operated with an excessively rich fuel-air mixture, the mixture burns with a lower than normal temperature and carbon is left inside the cylinder. This carbon collects in the firing end of the spark plug in the form of black, conductive soot which provides a conductive path for the high voltage, and no spark jumps the gap to ignite the fuel-air mixture in the cylinder. (PLT253) — FAA-H-8083-25

Answer (B) is incorrect because carbon fouling of the spark plugs is caused by operating at low cylinder head temperatures. Answer (C) is incorrect because excessive heat is caused by too lean a mixture, which does not cause spark plug fouling.

AIR, RTC, WSC, PPC, LSA

7297. Fouling of spark plugs is more apt to occur if the aircraft

A— gains altitude with no mixture adjustment.
B— descends from altitude with no mixture adjustment.
C— throttle is advanced very abruptly.

If the fuel/air mixture is too rich, excessive fuel consumption, rough engine operation, and appreciable loss of power will occur. Because of excessive fuel, a cooling effect takes place which causes below normal temperatures in the combustion chambers. This cooling results in spark plug fouling. Unless the mixture is leaned with a gain in altitude, the mixture becomes excessively rich. (PLT478) — FAA-H-8083-25

Answer (B) is incorrect because descending without a mixture adjustment (operating with an excessively lean mixture) would result in overheating, rough engine operation, a loss of power, and detonation. Answer (C) is incorrect because advancing the throttle abruptly may cause the engine to hesitate or stop.

Answers

6646   [A]   7297   [A]

AIR, RTC, WSC, PPC, LSA
6687. In addition to an added safety factor, dual ignition systems also provide

A— better combustion.
B— increased spark plug life.
C— shorter engine warmup periods.

For the fuel-air mixture to burn inside an engine cylinder most efficiently, it must be ignited at two places at the same time. Dual ignition (two spark plugs in each cylinder) not only provides additional safety in the event of the failure of one system, it also provides more efficient combustion. (PLT478) — FAA-H-8083-25

AIR, RTC, WSC, PPC, LSA
6669. If the ground wire between the magneto and the ignition switch becomes disconnected, the most noticeable result will be that the engine

A— will run very rough.
B— cannot be started with the switch in the ON position.
C— cannot be shut down by turning the switch to the OFF position.

If the ground wire between a magneto and the ignition switch becomes disconnected, the primary current cannot be directed to ground, and the engine cannot be shut down by turning the switch to the OFF position. (PLT478) — FAA-H-8083-25

AIR, RTC, WSC, PPC, LSA
7300. If the ground wire between the magneto and the ignition switch becomes disconnected, the engine

A— will not operate on one magneto.
B— cannot be started with the switch in the on position.
C— could accidentally start if the propeller is moved with fuel in the cylinder.

If the magneto switch ground wire is disconnected, the magneto is ON even though the ignition switch is in the OFF position. The engine could fire if the propeller is moved from outside the airplane. (PLT478) — FAA-H-8083-25

Answer (A) is incorrect because both magnetos remain on when the ground wire is disconnected. Answer (B) is incorrect because the engine can still be started, and the magnetos cannot be turned off.

Fuel Systems

It is important that aircraft engines be adequately supplied with the **proper grade of fuel**, free from water or other contaminants. Aviation gasoline (100LL Avgas) is rated according to its ability to resist detonation, and it contains dye to identify its grade. It is extremely important that only the proper grade fuel be used in an aircraft engine. If too high a grade of fuel is used, there is a possibility that the excess lead will foul the spark plugs. If too low a grade of fuel is used, there is the extreme danger of detonation which will seriously damage the engine. Many light-sport aircraft are designed to run on auto gas. If the correct grade of fuel is not available, it is generally permissible to use the next higher grade of fuel until the proper grade can be obtained. No fuel should ever be used that is not approved for use in the engine.

Water in the fuel can cause engine failure, and any water that has collected in the tanks must be removed before flight. In order to purge all of the liquid water from the fuel system, the fuel strainer drain and the sumps in all of the tanks must be drained. Water condenses inside a partially full fuel tank when the air temperature drops. Some water is absorbed into the fuel and the rest collects in the bottom of the tank. The amount of water the fuel can absorb is determined by the temperature of the fuel. The warmer the fuel, the more water it can hold. When the fuel is cooled, the water condenses out.

Since many light-sport aircraft use auto fuel which contains alcohol, this can absorb water and run it through the system harmlessly. However, if Avgas is used for systems designed for auto gas, additional precautions must be taken since fuel drains may not be present and the additional lead in the Avgas requires maintenance. Consult the POH for details on fuel use.

Absorbed water is a greater problem with turbine-powered aircraft than it is with reciprocating engine-powered airplanes because of the lower atmospheric temperatures at which turbine engines operate:

Answers

6687 [A]   6669 [C]   7300 [C]

the water condenses out of the fuel and freezes on the fuel filters. To properly remove all water from an aircraft fuel system, fuel must be drained from every one of the fuel tank sumps and the main fuel strainer, until fuel that is free from any indication of water, flows from them.

Aircraft fuel systems normally consist of more than one tank, as well as the proper selector valves, pumps, and strainers needed to supply the correct volume of clean, contamination-free fuel to the carburetor or fuel injection system on the engine.

All fuel tanks have a vent that allows air to enter the tank and take the place of fuel as it is used. It is important that the vent be open, and it should be checked on the preflight inspection. If the vent becomes plugged, the air pressure above the fuel will become too low to force a steady flow of fuel to the fuel pump or carburetor.

Vapor lock is a condition in which fuel vapors form in the fuel line between the tank and the engine. The pressure of the vapor is high enough that it prevents liquid fuel from flowing to the engine, and the engine dies of fuel starvation. Vapor lock is most likely to form on hot days when the engine is operated for a long time on the ground. The danger of vapor lock can be minimized by using the fuel boost pump, if installed, to maintain a positive pressure on the fuel in the lines between the tank and the engine. Vapor can also be introduced into the fuel line by running one tank dry before selecting a full tank. This happens when the engine-driven fuel pump or electric boost pump draws air into the fuel lines, causing a vapor lock that prevents fuel reaching the carburetor or fuel injection system.

Static electricity, formed by the flow of fuel through the hose and nozzle, creates a fire hazard during refueling. To guard against the possibility of a spark igniting the fuel fumes, a ground wire should be attached to the aircraft before the cap is removed from the tank. The refueling nozzle should be grounded to the aircraft before refueling is begun and throughout the refueling process. The fuel truck should also be grounded to the aircraft and the ground.

Carburetion is the process by which the air entering the engine is measured and the correct amount of fuel is metered into it. The fuel is vaporized and evenly distributed to all cylinders. Aircraft reciprocating engines may be equipped with float-type carburetors, pressure carburetors, or fuel-injection systems. Float-type carburetors are used on most of the smaller engines because of their simplicity. Their operation is based on the pressure drop caused by the high velocity of the air flowing into the engine through the venturi. The pressure drop is proportional to the volume of air being pulled into the cylinders, and the amount of fuel metered into this air is determined by the pressure drop.

A float-type carburetor is an efficient refrigerator. Both the expansion of the air leaving the venturi and the vaporization of the fuel drop the temperature of the air flowing into the engine. This temperature drop causes moisture to condense out of the air and freeze, blocking the flow of air into the engine. The formation of **carburetor ice** does not require ambient air temperature to be below freezing, but it is most likely to form when the air temperature is between 20°F and 70°F, and there is visible moisture present or the humidity is high. The first indication of carburetor ice on an airplane equipped with a fixed-pitch propeller is a drop in RPM. On an airplane with a constant-speed propeller, this first indication is a drop in manifold pressure. The presence of carburetor ice can be verified on an airplane equipped with a fixed-pitch propeller by noting the RPM after carburetor heat has been applied. If the RPM decreases at first, then gradually increases, carburetor ice was present.

Two of the main disadvantages of a float-type carburetor, uneven mixture distribution and carburetor icing, are overcome by the **fuel injection system**. The air entering the engine is measured, and the correct amount of fuel for this air is metered and distributed to the intake valve, then mixed with the air as it enters the engine cylinder. This method of fuel-air mixing, inside the warm intake valve chamber, prevents the temperature drop which can occur in carburetor systems.

AIR, RTC, LTA, WSC, PPC, LSA

6644. If the grade of fuel used in an aircraft engine is lower than that specified, it may cause

A— detonation.
B— lower cylinder head temperatures.
C— a decrease in power which could overstress internal engine components.

If a lower grade is used than that specified for the engine, detonation can occur and the engine will most likely be damaged. (PLT250) — FAA-H-8083-25

Answer (B) is incorrect because a lower grade of fuel will cause higher cylinder head temperatures. Answer (C) is incorrect because this is the result of detonation.

AIR, RTC, LTA, WSC, PPC, LSA

6643. To properly purge water from the fuel system of an aircraft equipped with fuel tank sumps and a fuel strainer quick drain, it is necessary to drain fuel from the

A— fuel strainer drain.
B— lowest point in the fuel system.
C— fuel strainer drain and the fuel tank sumps.

Many aircraft are equipped with fuel strainers located at the lowest point in the fuel lines and sump drains installed at the lowest point in each fuel tank. In order to completely purge all of the liquid water from the fuel system, the fuel strainer drain and the sumps in all of the tanks must be drained. (PLT253) — FAA-H-8083-25

AIR, RTC, LTA, WSC, PPC, LSA

6706. The amount of water absorbed in aviation fuels will

A— remain the same regardless of temperature changes.
B— increase as the temperature of the fuel increases.
C— increase as the temperature of the fuel decreases.

All fuels absorb moisture from the air and contain water in both dissolved form and as a liquid. Auto gas can absorb more water than Avgas because of the alcohol content. The amount of dissolved water a fuel can hold is determined by the fuel temperature. Warm fuel can hold more dissolved water than cold fuel. When the temperature of the fuel is decreased, some of the dissolved water precipitates out and falls to the bottom of the tank as a liquid. (PLT251) — FAA-H-8083-25

AIR, RTC, LTA, WSC, PPC, LSA

6645. What is the main reason fuel tank vents must be open? To allow

A— proper air pressure within the tanks for maintaining a steady fuel flow.
B— excess fuel to drain overboard when heat expands the volume of fuel within the tanks.
C— fuel fumes to escape from the tanks, thus eliminating the possibility of the tanks exploding.

Fuel tanks must be vented to the atmosphere to allow for proper air pressure above the fuel at all times. If a tank vent becomes plugged, the flow of fuel to the engine can be restricted or stopped entirely. (PLT253) — FAA-H-8083-25

Answers (B) and (C) are incorrect because while some vents do allow excess fuel to drain and fumes to escape, their primary purpose is to allow proper air pressure to maintain a steady fuel flow.

AIR, RTC, LTA, WSC, PPC, LSA

6663. Running a fuel tank dry before switching tanks is not a good practice because

A— any foreign matter in the tank will be pumped into the fuel system.
B— the engine-driven fuel pump is lubricated by fuel and operating on a dry tank may cause pump failure.
C— the engine-driven fuel pump or electric fuel boost pump draw air into the fuel system and cause vapor lock.

It is an unwise practice to run a fuel tank completely dry before switching tanks because the engine-driven fuel pump or electric boost pump may draw air into the fuel lines and cause a vapor lock that prevents fuel reaching the carburetor or fuel injection system. (PLT153) — FAA-H-8083-25

Answer (A) is incorrect because any foreign matter will be filtered out by the fuel filter. Answer (B) is incorrect because engine failure will result before any damage can be done to the fuel pump.

Answers

| 6644 | [A] | 6643 | [C] | 6706 | [B] | 6645 | [A] | 6663 | [C] |

AIR, RTC, LTA, WSC, PPC, LSA

6647. When refueling aircraft, which precaution would be adequate for eliminating the potential hazard of static electricity?

A— Ensure that battery and ignition switches are off.
B— Connect a ground wire from the fuel truck to ground.
C— Connect a ground wire between the aircraft, fuel truck, fuel nozzle, and ground.

Static electricity, formed by the friction of air passing over the surfaces of an aircraft in flight and by the flow of fuel through the hose and nozzle, creates a fire hazard during refueling. To guard against the possibility of a spark igniting the fuel fumes, a ground wire should be attached to the aircraft before the cap is removed from the tank. The refueling nozzle should be grounded to the aircraft before refueling is begun and throughout the refueling process. The fuel truck should also be grounded to the aircraft and the ground. (PLT250) — FAA-H-8083-25

Answer (A) is incorrect because eliminating electrical flow in the aircraft will not prevent static electricity from developing during fueling. Answer (B) is incorrect because the aircraft and fuel nozzle also need to be grounded.

AIR, RTC, LTA, WSC, PPC, LSA

6656. The operating principle of float-type carburetors is based on the

A— measurement of the fuel flow into the induction system.
B— difference in air pressure at the venturi throat and the throttle valve.
C— increase in air velocity in the throat of a venturi causing a decrease in air pressure.

Fuel is drawn from a float-type carburetor by the pressure differential between the air at the discharge nozzle in the venturi and the air above the fuel in the float chamber. An increase in air velocity through the carburetor venturi drops the pressure at the discharge nozzle, and more fuel is sprayed into the air entering the engine. (PLT191) — FAA-H-8083-25

Answer (A) is incorrect because measurement of the fuel flow into the induction system is controlled by the mixture control. Answer (B) is incorrect because the difference in air pressure is between the venturi throat and the air inlet.

AIR, RTC, LTA, WSC, PPC, LSA

6657. One advantage of fuel injection systems over carburetor systems is

A— easier hot-engine starting.
B— better fuel distribution to the cylinders.
C— less difficulty with hot weather vapor locks during ground operations.

Fuel injection systems are superior to carburetor systems because of the better distribution of the fuel-air mixture to the cylinders. The fuel-air mixture in a carburetor system flows from the carburetor to the cylinders through the intake pipes, some of which are longer than others. In a fuel-injected engine, the fuel is discharged directly into the cylinder heads. Only air flows through the intake pipes. (PLT191) — FAA-H-8083-25

Answer (A) is incorrect because fuel injection systems are susceptible to vapor lock during hot-engine starting. Answer (C) is incorrect because fuel injection systems have more difficulty with hot weather vapor lock.

AIR, RTC, LTA, WSC, PPC, LSA

6655. Fuel injection systems, compared to carburetor systems, are generally considered to be

A— just as susceptible to impact icing.
B— more susceptible to evaporative icing.
C— less susceptible to icing unless visible moisture is present.

The fuel injection system is generally considered to be less susceptible to icing than the carburetor system. Impact icing of the air intake, however, is a possibility in either system. (PLT253) — FAA-H-8083-25

Answers

6647   [C]   6656   [C]   6657   [B]   6655   [A]

AIR, RTC, LTA, WSC, PPC, LSA

6658. The presence of carburetor ice in an aircraft equipped with a fixed-pitch propeller can be verified by applying carburetor heat and noting

A— a decrease in RPM and then a constant RPM indication.

B— a decrease in RPM and then a gradual increase in RPM.

C— an increase in RPM and then a gradual decrease in RPM.

You can verify the presence of carburetor ice by applying carburetor heat and watching the tachometer. If there is carburetor ice, the RPM will momentarily decrease because the warm air enriches the mixture. Then, as the ice melts, the airflow into the cylinders increases and the RPM gradually increases. If there is no carburetor ice, pulling on the carburetor heat will cause the RPM to decrease, but there will be no increase in RPM until carburetor heat is removed. (PLT190) — FAA-H-8083-25

AIR, RTC, LTA, WSC, PPC, LSA

7244. Generally speaking, the use of carburetor heat tends to

A— decrease engine performance.

B— increase engine performance.

C— have no effect on engine performance.

The use of carburetor heat causes a decrease in engine power, sometimes up to 15 percent, because the heated air is less dense than the outside air that had been entering the engine. (PLT190) — FAA-H-8083-25

AIR, RTC, WSC, PPC, LSA

7290. Leaving the carburetor heat on during takeoff

A— leans the mixture for more power on takeoff.

B— will decrease the takeoff distance.

C— will increase the ground roll.

Use of carburetor heat enriches the mixture, which tends to reduce the output of the engine and also increases the operating temperature. Therefore, the heat should not be used when full power is required (such as during takeoff) or during normal engine operations, except to check for the presence of, or removal of carburetor ice. A decrease in engine output will increase the distance required to reach lift-off speed. Therefore, it will increase ground roll. (PLT189) — FAA-H-8083-25

AIR, RTC, LTA, WSC, PPC, LSA

6659. The first indication of carburetor icing in an aircraft equipped with a constant-speed propeller would most likely be a

A— decrease in RPM.

B— decrease in manifold pressure.

C— rough running engine followed by loss of RPM.

The first indication of carburetor ice in an engine equipped with a constant-speed propeller is a decrease in manifold pressure. (PLT190) — FAA-H-8083-25

AIR, RTC, LTA, WSC, PPC, LSA

6660. The first indication of carburetor ice in an aircraft with a fixed-pitch propeller is

A— a decrease in RPM.

B— a decrease in manifold pressure.

C— an increase in manifold pressure.

The first indication of carburetor ice in an engine equipped with a fixed-pitch propeller is a decrease in RPM. Carburetor ice decreases the efficiency of the engine, causing the RPM to drop off. (PLT190) — FAA-H-8083-25

AIR, RTC, WSC, PPC, LSA

7291. Which condition is most favorable to the development of carburetor icing?

A— Any temperature below freezing and a relative humidity of less than 50 percent.

B— Temperature between 32 and 50°F and low humidity.

C— Temperature between 20 and 70°F and high humidity.

If the temperature is between -7°C (20°F) and 21°C (70°F) with visible moisture or high humidity, the pilot should be constantly on the alert for carburetor ice. (PLT190) — FAA-H-8083-25

Answers (A) and (B) are incorrect because carburetor icing is more likely with high humidity.

Answers

6658 [B]	7244 [A]	7290 [C]	6659 [B]	6660 [A]	7291 [C]

AIR, RTC, WSC, PPC, LSA

7292. In an aircraft equipped with a fixed-pitch propeller and a float-type carburetor, the first indication of carburetor ice would most likely be

A— a drop in oil temperature and cylinder head temperature.
B— engine roughness.
C— loss of RPM.

For airplanes with a fixed-pitch propeller, the first indication of carburetor ice is loss of RPM. (PLT190) — FAA-H-8083-25

Answers (A) and (B) are incorrect because these symptoms may develop, but only after a loss of RPM.

AIR, RTC, LTA, WSC, PPC, LSA

6661. The low temperature that causes carburetor ice in an engine equipped with a float-type carburetor is normally the result of the

A— compression of air at the carburetor venturi.
B— freezing temperature of the air entering the carburetor.
C— vaporization of fuel and expansion of air in the carburetor.

The low temperature that causes ice to form in the induction system of an aircraft engine equipped with a float carburetor normally comes from two sources:

1. The vaporization of the fuel at the discharge nozzle.

2. The expansion of the air after it passes through the venturi in the carburetor.

(PLT190) — FAA-H-8083-25

AIR, RTC, LTA, WSC, PPC, LSA

6662. Concerning carburetor icing, which statement is true?

A— The first indication of carburetor icing, in an aircraft equipped with a fixed-pitch propeller, is a decrease in manifold pressure.
B— Carburetor icing will form in a carburetor whenever the ambient temperature is below freezing with a reduced or closed throttle setting.
C— Carburetor icing would most likely form when the air temperature is between -7°C and 21°C and visible moisture or high humidity is present.

If the temperature is between -7°C (20°F) and 21°C (70°F), with visible moisture or high humidity, the pilot should constantly be on the alert for carburetor ice. (PLT190) — FAA-H-8083-25

Answer (A) is incorrect because the first indication of carburetor icing will be a drop in RPM in airplanes equipped with fixed-pitch propellers. Answer (B) is incorrect because during low or closed throttle setting, an engine is particularly susceptible to carburetor icing.

Answers

7292   [C]   6661   [C]   6662   [C]

Fuel-Air Mixture Control

For an aircraft engine to develop its power, it must be supplied with the correct mixture of aviation gasoline and air. The ratio of the mixture must be maintained within close limits, and the pilot must be able to vary it to allow the engine to operate most efficiently. Some modern light-sport 4-stroke engines have automatic mixture controls, while 2-stroke carbureted engines need to have the jets changed for operations at higher altitude airports.

The **fuel-air mixture** ratio is the ratio of the weight of the fuel to the weight of the air entering the cylinders. This ratio is set so that it is correct for full-power operation in normal density conditions (such as on the ground) when the mixture control is in the FULL RICH position. When the aircraft climbs to altitude, the air is less dense and fewer pounds of air are taken into the engine, but the fuel metered into this less-dense air remains constant. The mixture becomes excessively rich and the engine loses power. To maintain efficient engine operation at altitude, the pilot must use the mixture control to lean the mixture. This reduces the amount of fuel entering the combustion chamber and keeps the fuel-air mixture ratio in the efficient operating range.

Without the proper mixture ratio, three conditions can develop in the engine: If the mixture is too rich, the spark plugs will be fouled, and if it is too lean, the engine is likely to detonate and overheat. **Detonation** is the condition in the engine cylinder in which excessive heat and pressure cause the fuel-air mixture to explode (burn instantaneously) rather than burning evenly as it should. **Preignition** could also occur, which is the uncontrolled combustion of the fuel/air mixture in advance of the normal ignition.

It is possible for the pilot to monitor the fuel-air mixture being delivered to the cylinders by observing the **Exhaust Gas Temperature** (EGT) indicator. The temperature of the gases leaving the cylinders is an indicator of the fuel-air mixture being burned. The highest temperature is produced by the mixture of 15 parts of air to one part of fuel. But burning this mixture can be harmful to the engine. The engine manufacturer recommends the mixture ratio desirable for full power and for cruise.

The normal leaning procedure using an EGT consists of setting the engine up for cruise power, then leaning the mixture until the EGT peaks, then enriching the mixture until the EGT drops a specified number of degrees. This puts the mixture on the rich side of peak EGT.

For a 2-stroke engine, the jets should be installed for the proper mixture at the lowest altitude airports. Climbing to altitude will cause the engine to run rich, which is better than running too lean. This could create too high an EGT and stop the engine.

AIR, RTC, LTA, WSC, PPC, LSA

6652. Fuel/air ratio is the ratio between the

A— volume of fuel and volume of air entering the cylinder.
B— weight of fuel and weight of air entering the cylinder.
C— weight of fuel and weight of air entering the carburetor.

The fuel-air mixture ratio used in aircraft engines is the ratio of the weight of the fuel to the weight of the air in the mixture entering the cylinders. (PLT249) — FAA-H-8083-25

AIR, RTC, LTA, WSC, PPC, LSA

6648. As flight altitude increases, what will occur if no leaning is made with the mixture control?

A— The volume of air entering the carburetor decreases and the amount of fuel decreases.
B— The density of air entering the carburetor decreases and the amount of fuel increases.
C— The density of air entering the carburetor decreases and the amount of fuel remains constant.

Answers

6652   [B]   6648   [C]

As an aircraft goes up in altitude, the air taken into the engine becomes less dense; it weighs less per unit volume. A carburetor meters the fuel to the engine according to the volume of air that enters the cylinders, but the engine burns the fuel on the basis of the weight of the air. Since the weight of the air entering the carburetor decreases while the weight of fuel remains the same, the fuel-air mixture becomes excessively rich, and the engine will lose power if the mixture is not leaned. (PLT253) — FAA-H-8083-25

AIR, RTC, WSC, PPC, LSA

7294. The best power mixture is that fuel/air ratio at which

A— cylinder head temperatures are the coolest.
B— the most power can be obtained for any given throttle setting.
C— a given power can be obtained with the highest manifold pressure or throttle setting.

The throttle setting determines the amount of air flowing into the engine. The mixture control is then adjusted to get the best fuel/air ratio, resulting in the best power the engine can develop at this particular throttle setting. (PLT253) — FAA-H-8083-25

Answer (A) is incorrect because the cylinder heads will be the coolest when mixture is richest. Answer (C) is incorrect because this describes the highest power setting.

AIR, RTC, WSC, PPC, LSA

7302. Unless adjusted, the fuel/air mixture becomes richer with an increase in altitude because the amount of fuel

A— decreases while the volume of air decreases.
B— remains constant while the volume of air decreases.
C— remains constant while the density of air decreases.

Fuel flow remains constant if no adjustments are made. The same volume of air goes into the carburetor, but the weight and density of the air is less, causing an excessively rich mixture, which causes spark plug fouling and decreased power. (PLT249) — FAA-H-8083-25

AIR, RTC, WSC, PPC, LSA

7303. The basic purpose of adjusting the fuel/air mixture control at altitude is to

A— decrease the fuel flow to compensate for decreased air density.
B— decrease the amount of fuel in the mixture to compensate for increased air density.
C— increase the amount of fuel in the mixture to compensate for the decrease in pressure and density of the air.

Fuel flow remains constant if no adjustments are made. The same volume of air goes into the carburetor, but the weight and density of the air is less, causing an excessively rich mixture, which causes spark plug fouling and decreased power. (PLT249) — FAA-H-8083-25

AIR, RTC, WSC, PPC, LSA

7304. The pilot controls the air/fuel ratio with the

A— throttle.
B— manifold pressure.
C— mixture control.

The fuel/air ratio of the combustible mixture delivered to the engine is controlled by the mixture control. (PLT249) — FAA-H-8083-25

Answer (A) is incorrect because the throttle regulates the total volume of fuel and air entering the combustion chamber. Answer (B) is incorrect because the manifold pressure indicates the engine's power output.

AIR, RTC, WSC, PPC, LSA

7305. At high altitudes, an excessively rich mixture will cause the

A— engine to overheat.
B— fouling of spark plugs.
C— engine to operate smoother even though fuel consumption is increased.

Fuel flow remains constant if no adjustments are made. The same volume of air goes into the carburetor, but the weight and density of the air is less, causing an excessively rich mixture, which causes spark plug fouling and decreased power. (PLT253) — FAA-H-8083-25

Answer (A) is incorrect because a lean mixture will cause the engine to overheat. Answer (C) is incorrect because an engine runs smoother when the mixture is adjusted for the altitude.

Answers

7294 [B]	7302 [C]	7303 [A]	7304 [C]	7305 [B]

AIR, RTC, LTA, WSC, PPC, LSA

6649. When the pilot leans the mixture control, what is being accomplished?

A— The volume of air entering the carburetor is being reduced.
B— The volume of air entering the carburetor is being increased.
C— The amount of fuel entering the combustion chamber is being reduced.

When a pilot leans the fuel-air mixture, the amount of fuel entering the combustion chamber is reduced. As the altitude is increased, the air density decreases. The carburetor meters fuel according to the volume of air that flows through it, and the engine burns the fuel-air mixture according to the weight of the air. (PLT253) — FAA-H-8083-25

AIR, RTC, LTA, WSC, PPC, LSA

6650. The main purpose of the mixture control is to

A— increase the air supplied to the engine.
B— adjust the fuel flow to obtain the proper air/fuel ratio.
C— decrease the fuel supplied to the engine as the aircraft descends.

Aircraft engines are equipped with mixture controls to adjust the fuel flow to obtain the proper fuel-air mixture ratio. (PLT249) — FAA-H-8083-25

Answer (A) is incorrect because the fuel flow to the engine is affected by the mixture control knob. Answer (C) is incorrect because the fuel supplied to the engine should be increased in a descent.

AIR, RTC, LTA, WSC, PPC, LSA

6651. Proper mixture control and better economy in the operation of a fuel injected engine can be achieved best by use of

A— a fuel-flow gauge.
B— an exhaust gas temperature indicator.
C— the recommended manifold and RPM setting for a particular altitude.

An exhaust gas temperature (EGT) indicator is used to show when the engine is receiving the correct fuel-air mixture for the existing operating conditions. The temperature of the exhaust gas gives an indication of the fuel-air mixture being used. (PLT253) — FAA-H-8083-25

Answer (A) is incorrect because the fuel-flow gauge indicates how much fuel is flowing to the engine (not how much should be flowing). Answer (C) is incorrect because manifold pressure and RPM setting do not affect mixture control.

AIR, RTC, LTA, WSC, PPC, LSA

7242. The uncontrolled firing of the fuel/air charge in advance of normal spark ignition is known as

A— instantaneous combustion.
B— detonation.
C— pre-ignition.

Preignition is the uncontrolled combustion of the fuel/air mixture in advance of the normal ignition. (PLT478) — FAA-H-8083-25

Answers (A) and (B) are incorrect because detonation is an instantaneous combustion of the fuel/air mixture within the cylinder's combustion chamber.

AIR, RTC, LTA, WSC, PPC, LSA

7243. The uncontrolled firing of the fuel/air charge in advance of normal spark ignition is known as

A— combustion.
B— pre-ignition.
C— detonation.

Preignition is the uncontrolled combustion of the fuel/air mixture in advance of the normal ignition. (PLT478) — FAA-H-8083-25

Answer (A) is incorrect because combustion is the controlled firing of the fuel/air charge. Answer (C) is incorrect because detonation is an instantaneous combustion of the fuel/air mixture within the cylinder's combustion chamber.

Answers

| 6649 | [C] | 6650 | [B] | 6651 | [B] | 7242 | [C] | 7243 | [B] |

Induction Systems

An aircraft engine develops its power by converting a given weight of fuel and air into heat. As the aircraft goes up in altitude, the density and thus, the weight of the air, decrease and the engine is no longer able to develop the power it produced at sea level.

Manifold pressure is an indirect indicator of the amount of power an engine is developing. When the engine is not operating, the manifold pressure is the same as the existing atmospheric pressure. This is 29.92 inches of mercury, absolute (29" Hg). When the engine is started and idling, the manifold pressure is low, and when the engine is developing full power, the manifold pressure approaches the pressure of the ambient air. The manifold pressure of a nonsupercharged engine can never be more than slightly greater than the ambient air pressure. However, both an internal supercharger or a turbocharger can increase the engine manifold pressure above that of the surrounding air.

To increase the power available at altitude, airplane engines may be fitted with **turbochargers**. These are air compressors driven by a turbine in the exhaust system. A turbocharger does cause a loss in power because of the back pressure it produces which restricts the flow of exhaust gases from the engine. But it produces more power than is lost by increasing the density of the air before it enters the engine cylinders.

The **critical altitude** of an aircraft engine is the maximum altitude, under standard atmospheric conditions, at which the engine will develop its rated horsepower.

When climbing in an aircraft equipped with a turbocharged engine, the manifold pressure will remain approximately constant until the critical altitude of the engine is reached. From this point on, the power will decrease as altitude is increased.

AIR, WSC, PPC, LSA, RTC

6686. During climbing flight using a turbocharged airplane, the manifold pressure will remain approximately constant until the

A— engine's critical altitude is reached.
B— airplane's service ceiling is reached.
C— waste gate is fully open and the turbine is operating at minimum speed.

A turbocharger is an exhaust-driven air compressor that compresses the air before it enters the engine through the carburetor or fuel injection system. An automatic turbocharger regulator controls the speed of the turbocharger to maintain a relatively constant manifold pressure until the aircraft engine reaches its critical altitude, which is the highest altitude at which an engine can develop its rated horsepower. (PLT499) — FAA-H-8083-25

AIR, RTC, LTA, WSC, PPC, LSA

6683. Prior to starting the engine, the manifold pressure gauge usually indicates approximately 29" Hg. This is because the

A— pointer on the gauge is stuck at the full-power indication.
B— throttle is closed, trapping high air pressure in the manifold.
C— pressure within the manifold is the same as atmospheric pressure.

The manifold pressure gauge is a type of barometer that measures the absolute air pressure inside the engine induction system. When the engine is not operating, it indicates the existing atmospheric pressure, which is normally in the neighborhood of 29 to 30 inches of mercury. (PLT278) — FAA-H-8083-25

Answers

6686   [A]   6683   [C]

AIR, RTC, LTA, WSC, PPC
6684. What energy source is used to drive the turbine of a turbocharged airplane?

A— Ignition system.
B— Engine compressor.
C— Engine exhaust gases.

The compressor for a turbocharger used on a reciprocating aircraft engine is driven by a turbine through which engine exhaust gasses pass. (PLT499) — FAA-H-8083-25

Detonation

Detonation is an instantaneous burning of the fuel-air mixture inside an engine cylinder that occurs when the fuel-air mixture reaches its critical pressure and temperature. Detonation is actually an explosion that can damage the engine.

Operating the engine with too lean a mixture, induction air that is too hot, cylinder head temperature that is too high, manifold pressure that is too high, or a fuel of too low a grade can cause the fuel-air mixture to detonate.

AIR, RTC, LTA, WSC, PPC, LSA
6653. Detonation in an aircraft engine is most likely to occur whenever the

A— fuel/air ratio is such that the mixture burns extremely slow.
B— engine is operated under conditions which cause the fuel mixture to burn instantaneously.
C— fuel being used is of a higher grade than recommended by the engine manufacturer.

Detonation is an instantaneous burning of the fuel-air mixture inside an engine cylinder that occurs when the fuel-air mixture reaches its critical pressure and temperature. Detonation is actually an explosion that produces damaging pressures inside the engine. (PLT115) — FAA-H-8083-25

Answer (A) is incorrect because detonation occurs when the fuel-air mixture burns instantaneously. Answer (C) is incorrect because detonation occurs when the fuel is a lower grade than recommended.

AIR, RTC, LTA, WSC, PPC, LSA
6654. Detonation occurs at high power settings when the

A— fuel mixture explodes instead of burning progressively and evenly.
B— fuel mixture is ignited too early by red-hot carbon deposits in the cylinder.
C— intake valve opens before the previous charge of fuel has finished burning in the cylinder.

Detonation is an instantaneous burning of the fuel-air mixture inside an engine cylinder that occurs when the fuel-air mixture reaches its critical pressure and temperature. Detonation is actually an explosion that produces damaging pressures inside the engine. (PLT115) — FAA-H-8083-25

AIR, RTC, WSC, PPC, LSA
7295. Detonation occurs in a reciprocating aircraft engine when

A— the spark plugs are fouled or shorted out or the wiring is defective.
B— hot spots in the combustion chamber ignite the fuel/air mixture in advance of normal ignition.
C— the unburned charge in the cylinders explodes instead of burning normally.

Detonation is a sudden explosion, or instantaneous combustion, of the fuel/air mixture in the cylinders, producing extreme heat and severe structural stresses on the engine. (PLT115) — FAA-H-8083-25

Answer (A) is incorrect because detonation does not have anything to do with the wiring. Answer (B) is incorrect because this describes preignition, not detonation.

Answers

6684 [C]   6653 [B]   6654 [A]   7295 [C]

AIR, RTC, WSC, PPC, LSA

7296. If a pilot suspects that the engine (with a fixed-pitch propeller) is detonating during climb-out after takeoff, the initial corrective action to take would be to

A— lean the mixture.
B— lower the nose slightly to increase airspeed.
C— apply carburetor heat.

To prevent detonation, the pilot should use the correct grade of fuel, maintain a sufficiently-rich mixture, open the throttle smoothly, and keep the temperature of the engine within recommended operating limits. Some aircraft have an automatically-enriched mixture for enhanced cooling in takeoff and climb-out at full throttle. Lowering the nose will allow the aircraft to gain airspeed, which eventually lowers the engine temperature. (PLT115) — FAA-H-8083-25

Answer (A) is incorrect because leaning the mixture increases engine temperatures; detonation results from excessively-high engine temperatures. Answer (C) is incorrect because although a richer fuel mixture results from applying carburetor heat, the heat may offset the cooling effect of the mixture change. The most efficient initial action would be to increase airspeed.

AIR, RTC, WSC, PPC, LSA

7298. Detonation can be caused by

A— a short ground operation.
B— a "rich" mixture.
C— using a lower grade of fuel than recommended.

Detonation is a sudden explosion or shock to a small area of the piston top, rather than the normal smooth burn in the combustion chamber. It can be caused by low-grade fuel or a lean mixture. (PLT115) — FAA-H-8083-25

AIR, RTC, WSC, PPC, LSA

7301. Detonation occurs in a reciprocating aircraft engine when

A— there is an explosive increase of fuel caused by too rich a fuel/air mixture.
B— the spark plugs receive an electrical jolt caused by a short in the wiring.
C— the unburned fuel/air charge in the cylinders is subjected to instantaneous combustion.

Detonation is a sudden explosion, or instantaneous combustion, of the fuel/air mixture in the cylinders, producing extreme heat and severe structural stresses on the engine. (PLT115) — FAA-H-8083-25

Answer (A) is incorrect because detonation is caused by too lean a mixture. Answer (B) is incorrect because detonation does not have anything to do with the wiring.

Propeller Design

A propeller is a rotating airfoil that produces thrust by an aerodynamic action. A low pressure is produced over the back of the propeller blade (from the perspective of outside the cockpit, looking at the front of the airplane), the portion that corresponds to the curved top of a wing, and a high pressure is produced at the flat face of the propeller that corresponds to the bottom of a wing. This pressure difference pulls air through the propeller, and this in turn pulls the airplane forward.

The efficiency of a propeller is a measure of the ratio of the thrust horsepower produced by the engine-propeller combination to the brake horsepower of the engine. **Propeller efficiency** varies between 50% and 87%, depending on how much the propeller slips.

The blade angle of a propeller is the angle between the chord line of the blade and the plane of propeller rotation. This angle is high near the blade root, because the radius of rotation is small and the speed is low. Near the tip, the blade speed is high and the blade angle is low. This change in blade angle, or geometric pitch, is called twist, and permits a relatively constant angle of attack along the length of the blade when the propeller is in cruising flight.

The geometric pitch of a propeller is the distance the propeller would advance in one revolution if it were turning in a solid. The effective pitch of a propeller is the distance the propeller actually advances in the air. Slip is the difference between the geometric and the effective pitch.

Answers

7296 [B]   7298 [C]   7301 [C]

AIR, WSC, LSA, PPC

6664. Which statement is true regarding propeller efficiency? Propeller efficiency is the

A— ratio of thrust horsepower to brake horsepower.
B— actual distance a propeller advances in one revolution.
C— difference between the geometric pitch of the propeller and its effective pitch.

Propeller efficiency is the ratio of thrust horsepower (the amount of power actually available to push or pull the aircraft through the air) to brake horsepower (the power delivered by the engine to the propeller shaft). (PLT351) — FAA-H-8083-25

AIR, WSC, LSA, PPC

6590. Blade angle of a propeller is defined as the angle between the

A— angle of attack and chord line.
B— chord line and plane of rotation.
C— angle of attack and line of thrust.

The blade angle of a propeller is the acute angle between the chord line of a blade and the plane of rotation. (PLT351) — FAA-H-8083-25

AIR, WSC, LSA, PPC

6588. Propeller slip is the difference between the

A— geometric pitch and blade angle of the propeller.
B— geometric pitch and the effective pitch of the propeller.
C— plane of rotation of the propeller and forward velocity of the aircraft.

Propeller slip is the difference between geometric pitch (the distance the propeller would move through the air if the air were solid) and effective pitch of the propeller (the distance the propeller actually moves through the air). (PLT351) — FAA-H-8083-25

AIR, WSC, LSA, PPC

6589. The distance a propeller actually advances in one revolution is

A— twisting.
B— effective pitch.
C— geometric pitch.

The effective pitch of a propeller is the distance it actually advances in one revolution. (PLT351) — FAA-H-8083-25

Answer (A) is incorrect because twisting is the change in blade angle from the hub to the tip. Answer (C) is incorrect because geometric pitch is the distance the propeller would move through the air if the air were solid.

AIR, WSC, LSA, PPC

6592. The reason for variations in geometric pitch (twisting) along a propeller blade is that it

A— prevents the portion of the blade near the hub to stall during cruising flight.
B— permits a relatively constant angle of attack along its length when in cruising flight.
C— permits a relatively constant angle of incidence along its length when in cruising flight.

The pitch angle of a propeller blade decreases toward the tip. The reason is that the angle of attack is a function of both pitch angle and speed, and the speed of a propeller blade increases from the hub to the tip. In order to keep a relatively constant angle of attack along the blade, the blade angle must decrease from root to tip. (PLT351) — FAA-H-8083-25

Answers

6664 [A]   6590 [B]   6588 [B]   6589 [B]   6592 [B]

Propeller Forces

A rotating propeller has a characteristic known as **gyroscopic precession**. This causes a force applied to the blade at one point to be felt not at the point of application, but at a point 90° ahead, in the direction of rotation. If the tail of a tail-wheel-type airplane is suddenly raised for takeoff, a forward force is applied to the top of the propeller disk, and this force is felt on the right side of the disk. This forces the airplane, now balanced on its two main wheels and moving at a speed when the rudder is not very effective, to yaw to the left. In flight, gyroscopic precession on the propeller will cause any sudden yawing about the vertical axis to produce a pitching moment. *See* Figure 3-4.

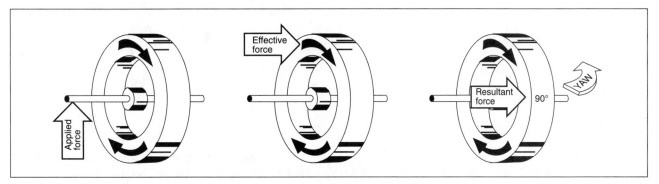

Figure 3-4. Gyroscopic precession

The propellers on most single-engine airplanes built in the United States rotate in a clockwise direction as viewed from the cockpit. This rotation causes the air moved backward by the propeller to spiral around the fuselage and strike the bottom of the left horizontal stabilizer and the left side of the vertical fin. The **spiraling slipstream** increases the angle of attack and lift of the left horizontal stabilizer, which tends to rotate the airplane to the right about its longitudinal axis. It also increases the angle of attack of the vertical fin so that it causes the airplane to rotate to the left about its vertical axis. *See* Figure 3-5.

The **P-factor** causes the propeller of an airplane flying at a high angle of attack to produce a force which causes the airplane to yaw to the left about its vertical axis. When flying at a low angle of attack, the propeller blade moving upward and the one moving downward have the same angle of attack and their thrust is symmetrical. But when the airplane's angle of attack is high, the angle of attack of the rising propeller blade on the left side of the airplane is decreased, and the angle of attack of the descending blade on the right side is increased. This difference in the angle of attack of the propeller blades on the opposite sides of the airplane produces an asymmetrical thrust, which tends to yaw the airplane to the left about its vertical axis. *See* Figure 3-6.

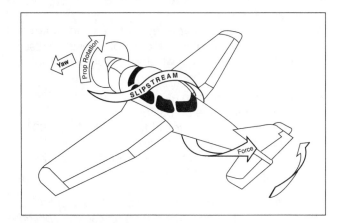

Figure 3-5. Spiraling slipstream

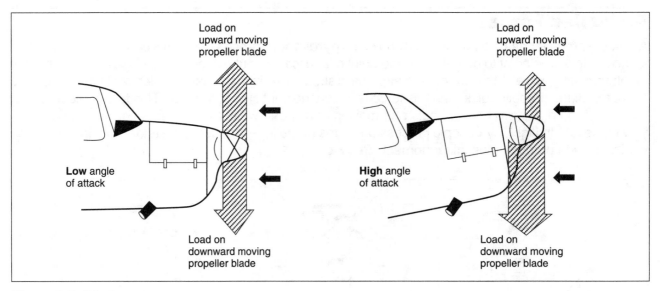

Figure 3-6. P-factor

AIR, WSC, LSA, PPC

6587. As a result of gyroscopic precession, it can be said that any

A— pitching around the lateral axis results in a rolling moment.
B— yawing around the vertical axis results in a pitching moment.
C— pitching around the longitudinal axis results in a yawing moment.

A spinning propeller acts as a gyroscope, and any time a propeller-driven airplane yaws about its vertical axis, gyroscopic precession of the propeller produces a pitching moment about its lateral axis. An airplane will also yaw when it is pitched about its lateral axis. (PLT118) — FAA-H-8083-25

AIR, WSC, LSA, PPC

6593. With regard to gyroscopic precession, when a force is applied at a point on the rim of a spinning disc, the resultant force acts in which direction and at what point?

A— In the same direction as the applied force, 90° ahead in the plane of rotation.
B— In the opposite direction of the applied force, 90° ahead in the plane of rotation.
C— In the opposite direction of the applied force, at the point of the applied force.

Gyroscopic precession is a characteristic of a spinning wheel (the propeller acts as such) that causes an applied force to be felt not at the point of application, but at a point 90° from the point of application, in the direction of rotation (ahead of the force). The resultant force acts in the same direction as the applied force. An upward force applied to the shaft will produce an effective force on the top of the wheel. This, in turn, produces a resultant force 90° away in the direction of rotation that causes the wheel to yaw to the left. (PLT118) — FAA-H-8083-25

AIR, LSA

6591. A propeller rotating clockwise, as seen from the rear, creates a spiraling slipstream that tends to rotate the aircraft to the

A— right around the vertical axis, and to the left around the longitudinal axis.
B— left around the vertical axis, and to the right around the longitudinal axis.
C— left around the vertical axis, and to the left around the longitudinal axis.

A propeller rotating in a clockwise direction produces a corkscrewing slipstream that strikes the left side of the vertical fin creating an angle of attack that causes it to produce lift toward the right. This horizontal lift pulls the tail to the right and the nose to the left, rotating the airplane to the left about its vertical axis. The same corkscrewing action increases the angle of attack of the left horizontal stabilizer and produces a rolling action to the right about the longitudinal axis. (PLT095) — FAA-H-8083-25

Answers

6587   [B]   6593   [A]   6591   [B]

Critical Engine of a Multi-Engine Airplane

When an airplane is flying at a high angle of attack, the descending propeller blade has a higher angle of attack than the ascending blade. The descending blade, the one normally on the right side of the engine, produces more thrust than the blade on the left side, and as a result, at high angles of attack, the asymmetrical thrust tends to pull the airplane to the left.

The critical engine of a light multi-engine airplane on which both engines rotate clockwise is the left engine. Both engines produce more thrust on their right side and try to rotate the airplane to the left.

The center of thrust of the right propeller is a greater distance from the vertical axis of the airplane, and it produces a greater left-yawing force than the left propeller.

If the left engine quits during a climbout, the longer moment arm of the right propeller thrust can create a potentially dangerous yawing action. *See* Figure 3-7.

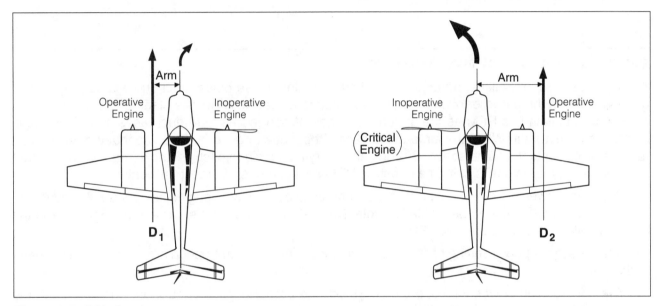

Figure 3-7. Critical engine

AIR

6594. The critical engine on most light multiengine airplanes with clockwise rotating propellers is the

A— left engine, because of the P-factor of the left propeller.
B— right engine, because of the P-factor of the left propeller.
C— left engine, because of the P-factor of the right propeller.

When both engines of a conventional twin-engine airplane rotate in the same direction (clockwise as viewed from the rear), the P-factor causes the center of thrust of the right engine to be outboard of the engine while the center of thrust of the left engine is inboard of the engine. In this configuration, the left engine is the critical engine. (PLT347) — FAA-H-8083-3

AIR

6595. On a multiengine airplane with engines which rotate clockwise, the critical engine is the

A— left engine, because the right engine center of thrust is closer to the centerline of the fuselage.
B— right engine, because the left engine center of thrust is closer to the centerline of the fuselage.
C— left engine, because the right engine center of thrust is farther away from the centerline of the fuselage.

The critical engine of a light multi-engine airplane on which both engines rotate clockwise is the left engine. P-factor causes both engines to produce a center of thrust on the right side of the engine that tries to rotate the airplane to the left. (PLT347) — FAA-H-8083-3

Answers

6594　[C]　　　　6595　[C]

AIR

6596. On a multiengine airplane, where the propellers rotate in the same direction, why is the loss of power on one engine more critical than the loss of power on the other engine?

A— The corkscrew pattern of airflow from one propeller is less effective against the airflow from the critical engine.

B— The torque reaction from operation of the critical engine is more severe around the vertical axis as well as the longitudinal axis.

C— The asymmetric propeller thrust or P-factor results in the center of thrust from one engine being farther from the airplane centerline than the center of thrust from the other engine.

The critical engine of a light multi-engine airplane on which both engines rotate clockwise is the left engine. The asymmetrical thrust of both engines tries to rotate the airplane to the left. The center of thrust of the right propeller is farther from the vertical axis of the airplane, and it will produce a greater left-yawing force than the left propeller. (PLT347) — FAA-H-8083-3

Constant-Speed Propellers

A constant-speed propeller is an adjustable-pitch propeller whose blade pitch angle is controlled by a governor. When the propeller pitch control is adjusted to a specific RPM, the blade angle automatically adjusts to maintain this RPM as the air load changes. When the air load decreases, the blade angle increases to restore it. When the air load increases, the blade angle decreases so that the engine can turn the propeller at the same speed. By constantly varying the blade pitch setting to maintain a constant propeller load, the engine is held at a constant RPM so it can operate most efficiently.

Maximum power and maximum thrust can be produced by an aircraft engine equipped with a constant-speed propeller when the propeller blade angle is adjusted to produce a small angle of attack, and the engine is allowed to develop high RPM.

Changes to the power setting of an engine equipped with a constant-speed propeller should be made in this way:

• When increasing power, increase the RPM with the propeller pitch control and then increase the manifold pressure with the throttle.

• When decreasing power, decrease manifold pressure with the throttle, then decrease RPM with the propeller pitch control.

AIR

6685. What is the primary advantage of a constant-speed propeller?

A— To maintain a specific engine speed.

B— To obtain a pitch setting that is suitable for each flight situation and power setting.

C— To obtain and maintain a selected pitch angle of the blades regardless of the flight situation or power setting.

A constant-speed propeller permits the pilot to select the blade angle that will result in the most efficient performance for a particular flight condition. (PLT350) — FAA-H-8083-25

Answer (A) is incorrect because engine speed will vary with different phases of flight. Answer (C) is incorrect because the advantage of a constant-speed propeller is that it maintains a selected angle of attack.

Answers

6596   [C]   6685   [B]

AIR

6665. When operating an aircraft with a constant-speed propeller, which procedure places the least stress on cylinder components?

A— When power settings are being increased, increase manifold pressure before RPM.

B— When power settings are being decreased, reduce manifold pressure before RPM.

C— Whether power settings are being increased or decreased, RPM is adjusted before manifold pressure.

In order to put the least stress on the engine when reducing power on an engine equipped with a constant-speed propeller, first reduce the manifold pressure with the throttle, and then reduce the RPM with the propeller pitch control. (PLT351) — FAA-H-8083-25

AIR

6666. To absorb maximum engine power and to develop maximum thrust, a constant-speed propeller should be adjusted to a blade angle which will produce a

A— large angle of attack and low RPM.

B— large angle of attack and high RPM.

C— small angle of attack and high RPM.

The power developed by a reciprocating engine depends upon, among other things, the engine speed, or RPM. For an engine to develop its maximum power for takeoff, a constant-speed propeller should be set to a blade angle that will produce a small angle of attack so the engine can develop a high RPM. (PLT351) — FAA-H-8083-25

Rotorcraft Systems

The **pitch angle** of a helicopter rotor blade is the acute angle between the chord line of the blade and the plane of rotor rotation.

In a semirigid rotor system, the rotor blades are rigidly interconnected to the hub, but the hub is free to tilt and rock with respect to the rotor shaft. In this system in which only two-bladed rotors are used, the blades flap as a unit; that is, as one blade flaps up, the other blade flaps down an equal amount. The hinge which permits the flapping or seesaw effect is called a **teetering hinge**.

A **rocking hinge**, perpendicular to the teetering hinge and parallel to the rotor blades, allows the head to rock in response to tilting of the swash plate by the cyclic pitch control. This changes the pitch angle an equal amount on each blade — decreasing it on one blade and increasing it on the other.

In a **fully articulated rotor system**, each blade is attached to the hub by three hinges, oriented at approximately right angles to each other. A horizontal hinge, called the flapping hinge allows the blades to move up and down independently. A vertical hinge, called a drag, or lag hinge, allows each blade to move back and forth in the plane of the rotor disk. This movement is called dragging, or hunting. The blades can also rotate about their spanwise axis to change their individual blade pitch angle, or feather.

Fully articulated helicopter rotor systems generally use three or more blades, and each blade can flap, drag, and feather independently of the other blades.

The freewheeling unit in a helicopter rotor system allows the engine to automatically disengage from the rotor when the engine stops or slows below the corresponding rotor RPM. This makes autorotation possible.

Because a helicopter rotor system weighs so much more than a propeller, a helicopter must have some way to disconnect the engine from the rotor to relieve the starter load. For this reason, it is necessary to have a clutch between the engine and the rotor. The clutch in a helicopter rotor system allows the engine to be started without the load, and when the engine is running properly, the rotor load can be gradually applied.

Continued

Answers

6665   [B]   6666   [C]

High-frequency vibrations are associated with the engine in most helicopters and are impossible to count, because of their high frequency. A high-frequency vibration that suddenly occurs during flight could be an indication of a transmission bearing failure. Such a failure will result in vibrations whose frequencies are directly related to the engine speed. Abnormal low-frequency vibrations in a helicopter are always associated with the main rotor.

RTC

6598. The rotor blade pitch angle is the acute angle between the blade chord line and the

A— angle of attack.
B— rotor plane of rotation.
C— direction of the relative wind.

The pitch angle of a helicopter rotor blade is the acute angle between the chord line of the blade and the plane of rotor rotation. (PLT470) — FAA-H-8083-21

RTC

6695. Which statement is true concerning rotor systems?

A— The main rotor blades of a semirigid rotor system can flap and feather as a unit.
B— The horizontal flapping hinge on a fully articulated rotor system enables the main rotor blades to hunt.
C— Dampers are normally incorporated in a fully articulated rotor system to prevent excessive motion about the spanwise axis of each rotor blade.

In a semirigid rotor system, the blades are rigidly interconnected to the hub, but the hub is free to tilt and rock with respect to the rotor shaft. The blades flap and feather as a unit. (PLT470) — FAA-H-8083-21

RTC

6696. The main rotor blades of a fully-articulated rotor system can

A— flap and feather collectively.
B— flap, drag, and feather independently.
C— flap and drag independently, but can feather collectively only.

In a fully-articulated rotor system, each blade is attached to the hub by a horizontal, or flapping hinge, a vertical, or drag hinge, and are free to rotate about their spanwise axis. Each blade can flap, drag, and feather independently. (PLT470) — FAA-H-8083-21

RTC

6697. What is the primary purpose of the freewheeling unit?

A— It allows the engine to be started without driving the main rotor system.
B— It provides disengagement of the engine from the rotor system for autorotation purposes.
C— It provides speed reduction between the engine, main rotor system, and tail rotor system.

The freewheeling unit provides for autorotative capabilities by automatically disconnecting the rotor system from the engine when the engine stops or slows below the corresponding rotor RPM. This allows the engine to be disengaged from the rotor for autorotation. (PLT471) — FAA-H-8083-21

RTC

6698. What is the primary purpose of the clutch?

A— It allows the engine to be started without driving the main rotor system.
B— It provides disengagement of the engine from the rotor system for autorotation.
C— It transmits engine power to the main rotor, tail rotor, generator/alternator, and other accessories.

The clutch allows the engine to be started without driving the main rotor system. When the engine is running properly, the rotor load can be gradually applied. (PLT471) — FAA-H-8083-21

RTC

6701. In most helicopters, what is one cause of in-flight medium frequency vibrations?

A— Control system out of rig.
B— Improper rigging of tail rotor.
C— Defective bearings in main transmission.

Medium frequency vibrations are a result of trouble with the tail rotor such as improper rigging. (PLT472) — FAA-H-8083-21

Answers

| 6598 | [B] | 6695 | [A] | 6696 | [B] | 6697 | [B] | 6698 | [A] | 6701 | [B] |

RTC
6702. A high-frequency vibration that suddenly occurs during flight could be an indication of a defective

A— transmission.
B— ignition system.
C— freewheeling unit.

High-frequency vibrations in a helicopter are normally associated with the engine. A high-frequency vibration, directly related to the speed of the engine, that suddenly occurs in flight could be an indication of a failure of a bearing in the transmission. (PLT472) — FAA-H-8083-21

RTC
6703. A high-frequency vibration in flight would most likely indicate potential trouble with

A— the balance of the main rotor blades.
B— worn parts in the main rotor system.
C— a piston engine malfunction.

Piston engines usually produce a normal amount of high-frequency vibration, which is aggravated by engine malfunctions such as spark plug fouling, incorrect magneto timing, carburetor icing and/or incorrect fuel/air mixture. (PLT472) — FAA-H-8083-21

RTC
6700-1. Low-frequency vibrations are normally associated with the

A— engine.
B— main rotor.
C— tail rotor.

Abnormal low-frequency vibrations in a helicopter are normally associated with the main rotor. (PLT472) — FAA-H-8083-21

RTC
7061. Ground resonance is most likely to occur when

A— there is a sudden change in velocity of the plane of rotation.
B— a series of shocks cause the rotor system to become out of balance.
C— initial ground contact is made with a combination of high gross weight and low RPM.

Ground resonance may develop when a series of shocks cause the rotor head to become unbalanced. (PLT259) — FAA-H-8083-21

Glider Instrumentation

Variometers used in sailplanes are so sensitive that they indicate climbs and descents as a result of changes in airspeed. A total energy compensator for a variometer reduces the climb and dive errors that are caused by airspeed changes and cancels out errors caused by "stick thermals" and changes in airspeed. The variometer shows only when the sailplane is climbing in rising air currents.

GLI
6716. The advantage of total energy compensators is that this system

A— adds the effect of stick thermals to the total energy produced by thermals.
B— reduces climb and dive errors on variometer indications caused by airspeed changes.
C— compensates for air pressure changes while climbing or descending.

Variometers used in sailplanes are so sensitive that they indicate climbs and descents as a result of changes in airspeed. A total energy compensator for a variometer reduces the climb and dive errors that are caused by airspeed changes. (PLT216) — FAA-H-8083-13

GLI
6717. Which is true concerning total energy compensators?

A— The instrument responds only to up and down air currents.
B— The instrument indicates the average rate of climb in a thermal.
C— The instrument reacts to climbs and descents like a conventional rate-of-climb indicator.

A total energy compensator for a variometer cancels out errors caused by changes in airspeed, and shows only when the sailplane is climbing in rising air currents. (PLT216) — FAA-H-8083-13

Answers

6702 [A]	6703 [C]	6700-1 [B]	7061 [B]	6716 [B]	6717 [A]

Balloon Fuel Systems

LTA
6721. The best way to determine burner BTU availability is the

A— burner sound.
B— tank quantity.
C— fuel pressure gauge.

BTUs (British Thermal Units) are a measure of heat per a given time. The greater the pressure, the greater the volume of fuel and therefore, heat. (PLT253) — Balloon Digest

LTA
6722. The valve located on each tank that indicates the tank is filled to 80 percent capacity is the

A— main tank valve.
B— vapor-bleed valve.
C— fuel pressure valve.

Vapor-bleed valve or spit tube, located on each tank, indicates when the tank is filled to 80% capacity. (PLT254) — Balloon Digest

LTA
6723. Why should propane lines be bled after each use?

A— Fire may result from spontaneous combustion.
B— Heat may expand the propane and rupture the lines.
C— If the temperature is below freezing, the propane may freeze.

The fuel in the lines is in a liquid state. Any heating would cause the fuel to expand and possibly rupture the line. (PLT253) — Balloon Digest

LTA
6724. How should a balloon fuel system be checked for leaks prior to flight?

A— Look, listen, and smell.
B— Check for unusual discoloration on burner coils.
C— Cover all fittings and hoses with soapy water and look for small bubbles.

Propane under pressure will cause a hissing sound when leaking and it has an artificial odor added to aid in detection. (PLT253) — Balloon Digest

LTA
6725. The purpose of the preheating coil used in hot air balloons is to

A— prevent ice from forming in the fuel lines.
B— warm the fuel tanks for more efficient fuel flow.
C— vaporize the fuel for more efficient burner operation.

Hot air balloon burners perform the following three functions:

1. *Vaporize the liquid propane supplied to them;*

2. *Mix the propane vapor with air to form a combustible mixture; and*

3. *Burn the resulting mixture to form an essentially directional flow of very hot gases.*

All burners commonly in use on hot air balloons have preheat coils surrounding the base of the flame. The liquid propane flows through these coils on its way through the burner. Since the coils are heated directly by the flame, they are not hot enough to vaporize the liquid propane flowing through them. If the propane is not vaporized, it does not mix well with the air, and burns in a long, yellow flame which radiates a great amount of heat. Properly vaporized propane burns with a mostly blue flame. (PLT253) — Balloon Ground School

LTA
6726. Why is nylon line best for tethering a balloon?

A— It does not stretch under tension.
B— It is not flexible and therefore can withstand tension without breaking.
C— It stretches under tension, but recovers to normal size when tension is removed, giving it excellent shock-absorbing qualities.

Nylon has great elasticity and as such, is a good shock absorber. (PLT184) — Balloon Ground School

LTA
6727. Propane is used in a balloon fuel system because it

A— is slow to vaporize.
B— provides natural pressure for fuel movement.
C— contains methanol for clean burning and improved performance.

Propane is used because it has a lower boiling point and higher vapor pressure. (PLT251) — Balloon Ground School

Answers

6721 [C]	6722 [B]	6723 [B]	6724 [A]	6725 [C]	6726 [C]
6727 [B]					

LTA
6728. Why should methanol be added to propane fuel?

A— Helps detect leaks in the fuel system.
B— Helps prevent moisture from forming in the fuel system.
C— Increases pressure and boiling temperature for operations in colder climates.

Methanol mixes with water and acts as an antifreeze. (PLT253) — Balloon Ground School

LTA
6729. While in flight, ice begins forming on the outside of the fuel tank in use. This could indicate

A— water in the fuel.
B— a broken dip tube.
C— a leak in the fuel line.

Vaporized fuel being drawn off reduces the tank pressure, allowing liquid fuel in the tank to boil off, reducing the temperature of the tank. (PLT253) — Balloon Ground School

LTA
6730. Why should special precautions be taken when filling propane bottles?

A— Propane is very cold and may cause freeze burns.
B— During transfer, propane reaches a high temperature and can cause severe burns.
C— Propane is under high pressure when transferred from storage tanks to propane bottles.

Gloves should be worn when refueling or changing tanks to prevent freeze burns. (PLT253) — Balloon Ground School

LTA
6847. What is the weight of propane?

A— 4.2 pounds per gallon.
B— 6.0 pounds per gallon.
C— 7.5 pounds per gallon.

Propane weighs 4.2 pounds per gallon. (PLT251) — Balloon Digest

LTA
6848. What effect, if any, does ambient temperature have on propane tank pressure?

A— It has no effect.
B— As temperature decreases, propane tank pressure decreases.
C— As temperature decreases, propane tank pressure increases.

Propane boils at -40°F. The colder the ambient air, the colder the tank and the less pressure the tank will have. The greater the pressure, the greater the volume of fuel to the burner. (PLT253) — Balloon Digest

LTA
6849. Propane is preferred over butane for fuel in hot air balloons because

A— it develops higher pressure.
B— it has a higher boiling point.
C— butane is very explosive under pressure.

Propane is preferred over butane and other hydrocarbons in balloon design because propane has a lower boiling point. Propane = -44°F, butane = 32°F. Therefore, propane has a consistently higher vapor pressure for a given temperature. (PLT251) — Balloon Digest

LTA
7196. Prior to balloon flight on a cold, winter day, it may be necessary to preheat propane tanks because

A— ice may have formed in the lines to the burners.
B— the temperature of liquid propane controls burner pressure during combustion.
C— propane needs to be at a temperature which will allow it to go from a liquid to a gaseous state.

Temperature of the liquid propane controls the burning pressure during combustion and therefore the lifting capability of the balloon. (PLT254) — Balloon Digest

Answers

6728 [B]	6729 [C]	6730 [A]	6847 [A]	6848 [B]	6849 [A]
7196 [B]					

LTA

7196-1. The purpose of the heat exchange coil as used in hot air balloons is to

A— prevent ice from forming in the fuel lines.
B— warm the fuel tanks for more efficient fuel flow.
C— vaporize the fuel for more efficient burner operation.

The main liquid tank valve controls the flow of liquid propane to the burner, while the blast valve controls fuel flow at the heater. With the liquid tank valve open, opening the burner blast permits liquid propane to enter the heat exchange coil where it is either completely or partially vaporized. After exiting the heat exchange coil through the orifices in the lower portion of the coil, the propane is ignited by the pilot light. (PLT253) — FAA-H-8083-11

Light-Sport Aircraft Systems
Including Powered Parachute and Weight-Shift Control

PPC, WSC, LSA

7248. The formation of ice in a carburetor's throat is indicated by

A— rough engine operation, followed by a decrease in oil pressure.
B— a rapid increase in RPM, followed by rough engine operation.
C— a drop in RPM, followed by rough engine operation.

Carb ice restricts the airflow into the engine reducing its power and resultant RPM, which also results in rough engine operation. (PLT190) — FAA-H-8083-29

Answers (A) and (B) are incorrect because oil pressure is not significantly affected by carb ice, and carb ice will not increase RPM.

PPC, WSC, LSA

7249. The purpose of the fuel tank vent system is to

A— remove dangerous vapors from the aircraft and prevent an explosion.
B— allow air to enter the tank as fuel is consumed.
C— ensure a proper fuel to air ratio.

Fuel tanks are not normally sealed systems; they need air venting because the fuel level is falling, therefore no vacuum builds up in the fuel tank. (PLT253) — FAA-H-8083-29

Answer (A) is incorrect because fuel tanks are isolated and fuel vapors are prevalent within the fuel tank confined area. Answer (C) relates to 2-stroke engines only. It is incorrect because fuel and oil are mixed either before the mixture is poured into the fuel tank (premix), or after when oil is injected into the air/fuel mixture oil before it goes into the combustion chamber.

PPC, WSC, LSA

7250. A standby source of fuel to an engine in a powered parachute is typically

A— from an electrically powered pump.
B— through gravity feed.
C— from a pressurized fuel tank.

Some engines use an electric boost pump similar to an airplane to supply a back-up pump in case the engine-driven fuel pump fails when low to the ground. (PLT253) — FAA-H-8083-29

Answer (B) is incorrect because if a gravity feed system was used, then this would supply fuel and no standby pump would be needed. Answer (C) is incorrect because pressurized fuel tanks are not normally used for light-sport aircraft.

PPC, WSC, LSA

7251. The fuel vents on many powered parachutes and weight shift control aircraft are located

A— in the fuel cap.
B— adjacent to the crankcase breather.
C— in the fuel tank pressure relief valve.

The fuel vent in many but not all fuel tanks is in the fuel cap. (PLT253) — FAA-H-8083-29

Answer (B) is incorrect because the crankcase breather is used on a 4-stroke engine and has nothing to do with the fuel supply system on a 2-stroke engine. Answer (C) is incorrect because most PPCs do not have pressurized fuel tanks nor a fuel tank pressure relief valve.

Answers

7196-1   [C]   7248   [C]   7249   [B]   7250   [A]   7251   [A]

PPC, WSC, LSA

7252. Combusted fuel is expelled from a 2-cycle engine through an

A— exhaust valve and exhaust port.
B— exhaust valve.
C— exhaust port.

All 2-stroke engines expel exhaust through a passage called the exhaust port. (PLT343) — FAA-H-8083-29

Answers (A) and (B) are incorrect because only some higher power engines use an exhaust valve, while all have an exhaust port.

PPC, WSC, LSA

7253. Fuel enters a two-cycle engine through an

A— intake port and intake valve.
B— intake port and reed valve.
C— intake valve and reed valve.

The air/fuel/oil mixture enters the crankcase through an intake port that some types of valve systems use to close off the crankcase and pressurize the air/fuel/oil mixture, before it is ported up to the top of the piston. Many engines use the positioning of the piston as the intake valve system, others use a rotary valve, while still others use a one-way flow "reed" or "poppet" valve. (PLT343) — FAA-H-8083-29

Answer (B) is incorrect because not all two-stroke engines use a reed valve. Answer (C) is incorrect because you must have an intake port.

PPC, WSC, LSA

7254. The first indication of carburetor ice in an aircraft with a four-cycle engine and fixed-pitch propeller is

A— an increase in RPM.
B— a decrease in RPM.
C— a decrease in oil pressure.

The first symptom of carb ice in a 4-stroke engine is a reduction in engine RPM. (PLT190) — FAA-H-8083-29

Answer (A) is incorrect because carb ice reduces RPM. Answer (C) is incorrect because carb ice has no noticeable effect on oil pressure.

PPC, WSC, LSA

7255. Air cooled engines dissipate heat

A— through cooling fins on the cylinder and head.
B— by air flowing through the radiator fins.
C— through the cylinder head temperature probe.

Air cooled engines use fins on the cylinder and head, forcing air past them as the primary means to dissipate heat. (PLT343) — FAA-H-8083-29

Answer (B) is incorrect because air cooled engines do not have separate radiators; only water and oil coolers need a radiator. Answer (C) is incorrect because the probe is not used to dissipate heat.

PPC, WSC, LSA

7256. Coolant in a liquid cooled engine is normally circulated by

A— capillary attraction.
B— an electric pump.
C— an engine driven pump.

Most liquid-cooled systems are driven from some mechanical source or pump on the engine. (PLT342) — FAA-H-8083-29

Answer (A) is incorrect because capillary attraction is not normally used for engine cooling. Answer (B) is incorrect because electric pumps are usually used as coolant pumps.

PPC, WSC, LSA

6482. High EGT on a 2-cycle engine could be caused by

A— high oil temperature and low oil pressure.
B— pre-ignition, detonation or an air intake leak.
C— improper engine operation.

Some exhaust systems have an exhaust gas temperature (EGT) probe which provides the temperature of the gases at the exhaust manifold. This temperature varies with power and with the ratio of fuel to air entering the cylinders (mixture). When there is a problem with carburetion, the EGT gauge will normally be the first notification for a pilot. (PLT278) — FAA-H-8083-29

Answers

7252 [C]	7253 [A]	7254 [B]	7255 [A]	7256 [C]	6482 [C]

PPC, WSC, LSA

7257. In order to improve engine efficiency, two-cycle engine exhaust systems are tuned to

A— close the exhaust valve to stop the fuel mixture from exiting the cylinder.

B— stop the fuel mixture from exiting the cylinder before combustion.

C— use a reed valve to stop the fuel mixture from exiting the cylinder.

If there is not an exhaust valve, tuned exhaust systems are designed to provide back pressure pulses at the exhaust port. The tuned exhaust bounces pressure back at the appropriate time, so the fuel mixture stays in the combustion chamber while both intake and exhaust ports are open. (PLT343) — FAA-H-8083-29

Answer (A) is incorrect because if the exhaust port has a valve, it is not as critical to have a tuned exhaust to provide back pressure at the exhaust port. There are not usually exhaust valves in a 2-stroke engine; however, some 2-stroke engines do have them. An example of this is the RAVE exhaust valve on the ROTAX 618. Answer (C) is incorrect because the reed valve is typically used for the intake air/ fuel mixture.

PPC, WSC, LSA

7258. 2-cycle engine thrust and fuel efficiency can be greatly compromised when

A— exhaust systems are installed that are not specifically tuned for an engine.

B— carbon deposits build up on exhaust valves.

C— intake valve lifters fail to pressurize and provide adequate fuel to the combustion chamber.

The exhaust systems should be tuned to the engine for maximum efficiency. (PLT343) — FAA-H-8083-29

Answer (B) is incorrect because most 2-stroke engines do not have exhaust valves. Answer (C) is incorrect because not all 2-stroke engines have intake valve lifters.

PPC, WSC, LSA

7259. The purpose of a kill switch is to

A— shut off the fuel to the carburetor.

B— ground the lead wire to the ignition coil shutting down the powerplant.

C— ground the battery eliminating current for the ignition system.

The kill switch shuts down the engine. (PLT207) — FAA-H-8083-29

Answer (A) is incorrect because a fuel valve shuts off fuel. Answer (C) is incorrect because the battery should already be grounded.

PPC, WSC, LSA

7260. A typical two-cycle engine ignition coil is powered by

A— a battery.

B— a battery or an alternator.

C— a magneto.

The magneto is an engine-driven generator that powers the ignition system and also supplies extra power to aircraft electrical system. (PLT478) — FAA-H-8083-29

Answers (A) and (B) are incorrect because the battery is further down the line, and is also powered by the magneto.

PPC, WSC, LSA

7261. Many 4-cycle engines utilize what type of lubrication system?

A— Forced.

B— Gravity.

C— Fuel/oil mixture.

Most 4-stroke engines have an oil pump that forces the oil through the system. (PLT324) — FAA-H-8083-29

Answer (B) is incorrect because gravity systems are not a typical oil supply system. Answer (C) is incorrect because a fuel/oil mixture system is on 2-stroke engines only.

PPC, WSC, LSA

7262. Adding more oil to the fuel than specified by the manufacturer of a 2-cycle engine will result in

A— increased engine performance.

B— increased carbon buildup and engine fouling.

C— increased engine lubrication and optimal performance.

Extra oil in the fuel would cause inefficient burning and more carbon buildup as a result. (PLT251) — FAA-H-8083-29

Answers (A) and (C) are incorrect because oil does not increase performance.

Answers

7257 [B]	7258 [A]	7259 [B]	7260 [C]	7261 [A]	7262 [B]

PPC, WSC, LSA

7263. Pilots should refrain from revving an engine with a reduction drive because

A— the crankshaft counterbalances may be dislodged and cause extreme engine vibration.
B— the propeller blade tips may exceed their RPM limits.
C— the torque exerted on the gears during excessive acceleration and deceleration can cause the gear box to self-destruct.

Revving the engine causes more stress than not revving it; it is good practice to not rev it unnecessarily. (PLT343) — FAA-H-8083-29

Answer (A) is incorrect because not all engines have counterbalances. Answer (B) is incorrect because the propeller is designed to not exceed its maximum RPM at full power.

PPC, WSC, LSA

7271. During preflight, the fuel vent system should always be checked

A— to ensure the vent is closed.
B— to ensure the vent is open.
C— to ensure the vent system pressure is in the green range.

The fuel vent needs to be open for flight for the air to fill the fuel tank as the fuel is consumed. (PLT253) — FAA-H-8083-29

Answer (A) is incorrect because a closed fuel vent would cause a power loss in flight when air is unable to fill the tank as fuel is used. Answer (C) is incorrect because there is no pressure in the fuel tank since it is vented.

PPC, WSC, LSA

7280. Carburetor ice can form

A— only at temperatures near freezing and the humidity near the saturation point.
B— when the outside air temperature is as high as 100 degrees F and the humidity is as low as 50%.
C— at any temperature or humidity level.

Carburetor ice can form when the outside air temperature is as high as 100°F and the humidity is as low as 50%. This is not the optimum conditions for the ice to form, but it can form under these conditions. (PLT190) — FAA-H-8083-29

Answer (A) is incorrect because carb ice can form when it is as high at 100°F. Answer (C) is incorrect because some moisture is needed to form the ice.

Answers

7263 [C]   7271 [B]   7280 [B]

Chapter 4
Aircraft Performance

Altitude

Density altitude is the altitude in standard air where the density is the same as the existing density. It is affected by the pressure, temperature, and moisture content of the air. A decrease in pressure and an increase in temperature both decrease the density of the air and increase the density altitude. Since water vapor is less dense than dry air, an increase in the humidity of the air will also increase the density altitude. Density altitude is used for computing aircraft performance, and it may be found on charts or by the use of flight computers.

Problem:

Find the density altitude at an airport elevation of 5,515 feet, an outside air temperature (OAT) of 30°C, and an altimeter setting of 29.40 inches of mercury, using FAA Figure 24.

Solution:

1. Find the pressure altitude of the airport by applying the Pressure Altitude Correction Factor (found to the right of the chart) to the airport elevation. PA Conversion Factor for an altimeter setting of 29.40 is 485 feet. Pressure altitude of the airport is: 5,515 + 485 = 6,000 feet.

   In an actual flight situation, pressure altitude is found by setting the barometric scale of the altimeter to 29.92" Hg, and reading the altimeter.

2. Follow the vertical line for 30°C upward until it intersects the diagonal line for 6,000 feet pressure altitude. From this intersection, project a line to the left until it intersects the density altitude scale. This scale is intersected at 9,100 feet.

   Density altitude can also be found quickly and accurately by using the CX-2 Pathfinder electronic flight computer:

1. Enter the Press Alt program.
2. Enter the field elevation of 5,515 feet at the PAlt prompt.

   In an actual flight situation, you find the pressure altitude by setting your altimeter barometric scale to 29.92 inches of mercury and reading the altimeter.

3. Enter 29.40 at the Hg prompt. Enter the Density Alt program.
4. Enter 30 at the OAT prompt.
5. The density altitude is 9,009 feet. The difference between the answer found using the chart, and the answer found using the computer is due to the greater accuracy of the electronic computer.

Effect of Density Altitude on Aircraft Performance

An increase in density altitude produces a two-fold effect on takeoff performance:

1. A greater takeoff true airspeed is required to provide the needed lift.
2. The engine and propeller efficiencies are both reduced and the acceleration rate is slower than at a low density altitude.

   Since water vapor is less dense than dry air, an increase in humidity, with atmospheric pressure and temperature remaining the same, will increase the density altitude and require a longer takeoff distance for an airplane.

ALL

6741. (Refer to Figure 24.) Determine the density altitude.

Airport elevation...5,515 ft
OAT ....30°C
Altimeter setting.. 29.40" Hg

A— 6,000 feet.
B— 8,450 feet.
C— 9,100 feet.

1. Find the pressure altitude of the airport by applying the Pressure Altitude Correction Factor, found to the right of the chart, to the airport elevation. PA Conversion Factor for an altimeter setting of 29.40 is 485 feet. Pressure altitude of the airport is: 5,515 + 485 = 6,000 feet.

2. Follow the vertical line for 30°C upward until it intersects the diagonal line for 6,000 feet pressure altitude. From this intersection, project a line to the left until it intersects the density altitude scale. This scale is intersected at 9,100 feet.

(PLT005) — FAA-H-8083-25

ALL

6742. (Refer to Figure 24.) Determine the density altitude.

Airport elevation...3,795 ft
OAT ....24°C
Altimeter setting.. 29.70" Hg

A— 5,700 feet.
B— 5,900 feet.
C— 4,000 feet.

1. Find the pressure altitude of the airport by applying the Pressure Altitude Correction Factor, found to the right of the chart, to the airport elevation. PA Conversion Factor for an altimeter setting of 29.70 is 205 feet. Pressure altitude of the airport is: 3,795 + 205 = 4,000 feet.

2. Follow the vertical line for 24°C upward until it intersects the diagonal line for 4,000 feet pressure altitude. From this intersection, project a line to the left until it intersects the density altitude scale. This scale is intersected at 5,900 feet.

(PLT005) — FAA-H-8083-25

ALL

6743. (Refer to Figure 24.) Determine the density altitude.

Airport elevation...3,450 ft
OAT ....35°C
Altimeter setting.. 30.40" Hg

A— 3,400 feet.
B— 6,650 feet.
C— 5,950 feet.

1. Find the pressure altitude of the airport by applying the Pressure Altitude Correction Factor, found to the right of the chart, to the airport elevation. PA Conversion Factor for an altimeter setting of 30.40 is -440 feet. Pressure altitude of the airport is: 3,450 – 440 = 3,010 feet.

2. Follow the vertical line for 35°C upward until it intersects the diagonal line for 3,010 feet pressure altitude. From this intersection, project a line to the left until it intersects the density altitude scale. This scale is intersected at 5,950 feet.

(PLT005) — FAA-H-8083-25

ALL

7310. (Refer to Figure 24.) What is the effect of a temperature increase from 30 to 50°F on the density altitude if the pressure altitude remains at 3,000 feet MSL?

A— 900-foot increase.
B— 1,100-foot decrease.
C— 1,300-foot increase.

Referencing FAA Figure 24, use the following steps:

1. Enter the density altitude chart at 30°F. Proceed upward to the 3,000-foot pressure altitude line. From the point of intersection, move left to the edge of the chart and read a density altitude of 1,650 feet.

2. Enter the density altitude chart at 50°F. Proceed upward to the 3,000-foot pressure altitude line. From the point of intersection, move left to the edge of the chart and read a density altitude of 2,950 feet.

3. Find the difference between the two values:

   2,950 – 1,650 = 1,300 foot (increase).

(PLT005) — FAA-H-8083-25

Answers

6741 [C]   6742 [B]   6743 [C]   7310 [C]

ALL

7286. (Refer to figure 24.) Determine the pressure altitude at an airport that is 3,563 feet MSL with an altimeter setting of 29.96.

A— 3,527 feet MSL.
B— 3,556 feet MSL.
C— 3,639 feet MSL.

Referencing FAA Figure 24, use the following steps:

1. *Since the altimeter setting that is given is not shown in FAA Figure 24, interpolation is necessary. Locate the settings immediately above and below the given value of 29.96" Hg:*

Altimeter Setting	Conversion Factor
29.92	0 feet
30.00	-73 feet

2. *Determine the difference between the two conversion factors:*

   0 – 73 = -73 feet

   The setting 29.96 is halfway between the two values, so:

   -73 ÷ 2 = -36.5 feet

3. *Determine the amount of difference to be subtracted from the 30.00" Hg conversion factor.*

4. *Subtract the correction factor from the airport elevation to find pressure altitude:*

   3,563.0 – 36.5 = 3,526.5 feet MSL (pressure altitude)

(PLT019) — FAA-H-8083-25

ALL

7308. What effect does high density altitude, as compared to low density altitude, have on propeller efficiency and why?

A— Efficiency is increased due to less friction on the propeller blades.
B— Efficiency is reduced because the propeller exerts less force at high density altitudes than at low density.
C— Efficiency is reduced due to the increased force of the propeller in the thinner air.

The propeller produces thrust in proportion to the mass of air being accelerated through the rotating blades. If the air is less dense, propeller efficiency is decreased. (PLT351) — FAA-H-8083-25

ALL

7308-1. What effect does high density altitude have on aircraft performance?

A— It increases engine performance.
B— It reduces climb performance.
C— It increases takeoff performance.

High density altitude reduces all aircraft performance parameters. To the pilot, this means that the normal horsepower output is reduced, propeller efficiency is reduced and a higher true airspeed is required to sustain the aircraft throughout its operating parameters. It means an increase in runway length requirements for takeoff and landings, and decreased rate of climb. (PLT127) — AIM ¶7-5-6

ALL, RTC

6744. Density altitude increases with

A— an increase in temperature only.
B— increases in pressure, temperature, and moisture content of the air.
C— increases in temperature and moisture content of the air, and a decrease in pressure.

Density altitude is the altitude in standard air where the density is the same as the existing density. It is affected by the pressure, temperature, and moisture content of the air. Both a decrease in pressure and an increase in temperature decrease the density of the air and increase the density altitude. Since water vapor is less dense than dry air, an increase in the moisture content of the air will also increase the density altitude. (PLT127) — FAA-H-8083-25

ALL

6745. What would increase the density altitude at a given airport?

A— An increase in air temperature.
B— A decrease in relative humidity.
C— An increase in atmospheric pressure.

An increase in air temperature will decrease the density of the air and increase the density altitude of a given airport. (PLT127) — FAA-H-8083-25

Answers (B) and (C) are incorrect because a decrease in relative humidity and an increase in atmospheric pressure would decrease the density altitude.

Answers

7286 [A]	7308 [B]	7308-1 [B]	6744 [C]	6745 [A]

ALL

6746. Which statement is true regarding takeoff performance with high density altitude conditions?

A— The acceleration rate will increase since the lighter air creates less drag.

B— The acceleration rate is slower because the engine and propeller efficiency is reduced.

C— A higher-than-normal indicated airspeed is required to produce sufficient lift since the air is less dense.

An increase in density altitude produces a two-fold effect on takeoff performance:

1. *A greater takeoff true airspeed is required to provide the needed lift.*

2. *The engine and propeller efficiencies are both reduced, and the acceleration rate is slower than at a low density altitude.*

(PLT127) — FAA-H-8083-25

ALL

6746-1. When density altitude is beyond capability as indicated on the performance chart,

A— interpolate the data and attempt takeoff.

B— extrapolate the data and attempt takeoff.

C— do not attempt takeoff until conditions permit calculations to provide the data to determine a safe takeoff and climb out.

Pilots should not commence flight operations until preflight planning calculations show safe and viable conditions exist. (PLT373) — FAA-H-8083-2

ALL

6747. If the atmospheric pressure and temperature remain the same, how would an increase in humidity affect takeoff performance?

A— Longer takeoff distance; the air is more dense.

B— Longer takeoff distance; the air is less dense.

C— Shorter takeoff distance; the air is more dense.

Density altitude is the altitude in standard air where the density is the same as the existing density. It is determined by the pressure, temperature, and moisture content of the air. Since water vapor is less dense than dry air, an increase in humidity, with atmospheric pressure and temperature remaining the same, will increase the density altitude and require a longer takeoff distance for an airplane. (PLT127) — FAA-H-8083-25

ALL

6747-1. What is pressure altitude?

A— The indicated altitude corrected for position and installation error.

B— The altitude indicated when the barometric pressure scale is set to 29.92.

C— The indicated altitude corrected for nonstandard temperature and pressure.

The pressure altitude can be determined by either of two methods:

1. *Setting the barometric scale of the altimeter to 29.92 and reading the indicated altitude, or*

2. *Applying a correction factor to the elevation (true altitude) according to the reported "altimeter setting."*

(PLT023) — FAA-H-8083-25

Answers

6746   [B]   6746-1   [C]   6747   [B]   6747-1   [B]

Takeoff Performance

The upslope or downslope of a runway (**runway gradient**) is important when runway length and takeoff distance are critical. An uphill slope of a runway produces a retarding force which decreases acceleration and results in a longer ground run needed for takeoff.

The takeoff ground roll and distance needed to clear a 50-foot obstacle can be computed by using the Takeoff Data Chart in FAA Figure 26. Charts of this type are furnished in the POH, and their use requires a great deal of interpolation.

Problem:

Find the takeoff run required for this airplane at a pressure altitude of 2,500 feet, temperature of 24°C, weight of 2,400 pounds, and a 25-knot headwind, refer to FAA Figure 26.

Solution:

1. Find the ground roll required for a 25-knot headwind at 2,200 pounds.
   a. Find the ground roll for 2,500 feet, 15-knot headwind at 2,200 pounds: 245 feet.
   b. Find the ground roll for 2,500 feet, 30-knot headwind at 2,200 pounds: 120 feet.
   c. The difference for a 15-knot headwind increase is 125 feet.
   d. Every 5-knots of headwind decreases the ground roll by 125 ÷ 3 = 41.7 feet
   e. The ground roll required for a 25-knot headwind at 2,200 pounds is: 245 − (2 x 41.7) = 161.6 feet.
2. Find the ground roll required for a 25-knot headwind at 2,600 pounds.
   a. Find the ground roll for 2,500 feet, 15-knot headwind at 2,600 pounds: 370 feet.
   b. Find the ground roll for 2,500 feet, 30-knot headwind at 2,600 pounds: 200 feet.
   c. The difference for a 15-knot headwind increase is 170 feet.
   d. Every 5-knots of headwind decreases the ground roll by 170 ÷ 3 = 56.7 feet
   e. The ground roll required for a 25-knot headwind at 2,600 pounds is: 370 − (2 x 56.7) = 256.6 feet.
3. Find the required ground roll required for 2,400 pounds.
   a. Ground roll for 2,200 pounds = 161.6 feet.
   b. Ground roll for 2,600 pounds = 256.6 feet.
   c. Difference = 95 feet
   d. The ground roll increases 95 ÷ 4 = 23.75 feet for each 100-pound increase in weight.
   e. The ground roll required for 2,400 pounds is: 161.6 + (2 x 23.75) = 209.1 feet
4. Apply correction for nonstandard temperature. The average change in temperature used by this chart is 2°C for each thousand feet.
   a. Standard temperature at 2,500 feet is 10°C.
   b. Existing temperature is 24°C. This is 24 − 10 = 14°C above standard
   c. The ground roll increases 10% for each 14°C above standard temperature.
   d. The ground roll is 209.1 + 10% = 230.01 feet.

Continued

Another type of takeoff performance chart is shown in the Maximum Performance Takeoff Distance chart in FAA Figure 28.

Problem:

Determine the approximate total distance required to clear a 50-foot obstacle.

Temperature .... 20°C

Pressure altitude.. 1,000 feet

Surface .... sod

Weight .... 5,300 pounds

Wind .... 15 knots headwind

Solution:

1. Find the maximum performance takeoff distance required to takeoff and clear a 50-foot obstacle at 1,000 feet pressure altitude and a gross weight of 5,300 pounds, with an outside air temperature of 20°C.

    a. Find the distance required to clear a 50-foot obstacle for 5,500 pounds at 1,000 feet PA and an OAT of 20°C: 1,950 feet.

    b. Find the distance required to clear a 50-foot obstacle for 5,100 pounds at 1,000 feet PA and an OAT of 20°C: 1,620 feet.

    c. The difference in distance for a 400-pound increase in weight is 330 feet.

    d. Each 100-pound increase in weight increases the distance required to clear a 50-foot obstacle by 82.5 feet.

    e. The distance required to clear a 50-foot obstacle at 5,300-pound weight is: 1620 + (2 x 82.5) = 1,785 feet.

2. Since the takeoff is made from a sod surface, this distance must be increased by 8%:

    1,785 + 8% = 1,927.8 feet.

3. The takeoff is made with a 15-knot headwind, and the takeoff run is reduced by 7% for each 10 knots of headwind:

    1,927.8 – 10.5% = 1,725.4 feet

AIR, WSC, PPC, LSA

6749. What effect does an uphill runway slope have upon takeoff performance?

A— Decreases takeoff speed.
B— Increases takeoff distance.
C— Decreases takeoff distance.

An uphill slope of a runway produces a retarding force which decreases acceleration and results in a longer ground run needed for takeoff. (PLT129) — FAA-H-8083-25

Answer (A) is incorrect because indicated speed will be the same at a given density altitude. Answer (C) is incorrect because a downhill slope will decrease the takeoff distance.

AIR, WSC, PPC, LSA

6753. (Refer to Figure 26.) Determine the ground run required for takeoff.

Temperature .... 24°C
Pressure altitude... 2,500 ft
Weight .... 2,400 lb
Headwind... 25 kts

A— 256 feet.
B— 370 feet.
C— 230 feet.

Answers

6749   [B]   6753   [C]

1. Find the ground roll required for a 25-knot headwind at 2,200 pounds.

   a. Find the ground roll for 2,500 feet, 15-knot headwind at 2,200 pounds: 245 feet.

   b. Find the ground roll for 2,500 feet, 30-knot headwind at 2,200 pounds: 120 feet.

   c. The difference for a 15-knot headwind increase is 125 feet.

   d. Every 5-knots of headwind decreases the ground roll by 125 ÷ 3 = 41.7 feet.

   e. The ground roll required for a 25-knot headwind at 2,200 pounds is: 245 – (2 x 41.7) = 161.6 feet.

2. Find the ground roll required for a 25-knot headwind at 2,600 pounds.

   a. Find the ground roll for 2,500 feet, 15-knot headwind at 2,600 pounds: 370 feet.

   b. Find the ground roll for 2,500 feet, 30-knot headwind at 2,600 pounds: 200 feet.

   c. The difference for a 15-knot headwind increase is 170 feet.

   d. Every 5-knots of headwind decreases the ground roll by 170 ÷ 3 = 56.7 feet.

   e. The ground roll required for a 25-knot headwind at 2,600 pounds is: 370 – (2 x 56.7) = 256.6 feet.

3. Find the required ground roll required for 2,400 pounds.

   a. Ground roll for 2,200 pounds = 161.6 feet.

   b. Ground roll for 2,600 pounds = 256.6 feet.

   c. Difference = 95 feet

   d. The ground roll increases 95 ÷ 4 = 23.75 feet for each 100-pound increase in weight.

   e. The ground roll required for 2,400 pounds is:

   161.6 + (2 x 23.75) = 209.1 feet

4. Apply correction for nonstandard temperature. The average change in temperature used by this chart is 2°C for each thousand feet.

   a. Standard temperature at 2,500 feet is 10°C.

   b. Existing temperature is 24°C.

   This is 24 – 10 = 14°C above standard.

   c. The ground roll increases 10% for each 14°C above standard temperature.

   d. The ground roll is 209.1 + 10% = 230.01 feet.

(PLT011) — FAA-H-8083-25

AIR, WSC, PPC, LSA

6754. (Refer to Figure 26.) Determine the ground roll required for takeoff.

Temperature .... 25°C
Pressure altitude... 2,000 ft
Weight .... 2,200 lb
Headwind... 15 kts

A— 205 feet.
B— 261 feet.
C— 237 feet.

1. Find the ground roll required for a 15-knot head-wind at sea level for 2,200 lbs.: 205 feet.

2. Find the ground roll required for a 15-knot head-wind at 2,500 feet at 2,200 lbs: 245 feet.

3. Find the ground roll required for 2,000 feet PA.

   a. Ground roll for 2,500 feet PA = 245 feet

   b. Ground roll for sea level = 205 feet

   c. Difference = 40 feet

   d. The ground roll increases 40 ÷ 5 = 8 feet for each 500-foot increase in pressure altitude.

   e. The ground roll required for 2,000 feet PS is: 205 + (4 x 8) = 237 feet.

4. Apply correction for nonstandard temperature. The average change in temperature used by this chart is 2°C for each thousand feet.

   a. Standard temperature at 2,000 feet is:

   10° + 1° = 11°.

   b. Existing temperature is 25°C. This is:

   25° – 11° = 14° above standard.

   c. The ground roll increases 10% for each 14° above standard temperature.

   d. The ground roll is 237 + 10% = 260.7 feet.

(PLT011) — FAA-H-8083-25

Answers

6754 [B]

AIR, WSC, PPC, LSA

6755. (Refer to Figure 26.) Determine the takeoff distance required to clear a 50-foot obstacle.

Temperature ....23°C
Pressure altitude...3,000 ft
Weight ....2,400 lb
Headwind...15 kts

A— 754 feet.
B— 718 feet.
C— 653 feet.

1. Find the takeoff distance required for a 15-knot headwind at 2,500 feet.

   a. Find the takeoff distance for 2,500 feet, 15-knot headwind at 2,200 pounds: 525 feet.

   b. Find the takeoff distance for 2,500 feet, 15-knot headwind at 2,600 pounds: 735 feet.

   c. The difference for a 400 pound increase is 210 feet.

   d. Every 100 pounds increases the takeoff distance by 210 ÷ 4 = 52.5 feet.

   e. The takeoff distance required for a 15-knot headwind at 2,400 pounds is 525 + (2 x 52.5) = 630 feet.

2. Find the takeoff distance required for a 15-knot headwind at 5,000 feet.

   a. Find the takeoff distance for 5,000 feet, 15-knot headwind at 2,200 pounds: 615 feet.

   b. Find the takeoff distance for 5,000 feet, 15-knot headwind at 2,600 pounds: 870 feet.

   c. The difference for a 400 pound increase is 255 feet.

   d. Every 100 pounds increases the takeoff distance by 255 ÷ 4 = 63.75 feet.

   e. The takeoff distance required for a 15-knot headwind at 2,400 pounds is 615 + (2 x 63.75) = 742.5 feet.

3. Find the takeoff distance required for 3,000 feet PA.

   a. Takeoff distance for 5,000 feet PA = 742.5 feet

   b. Takeoff distance for 2,500 feet PA = 630 feet

   c. Difference = 112.5 feet.

   d. The takeoff distance increases 112.5 ÷ 25 = 4.5 feet for each 100-foot increase in PA.

   e. The takeoff distance required for 3,000 feet PA is 630 + (5 x 4.5) = 652.5 feet

4. Apply correction for nonstandard temperature. The average change in temperature used by this chart is 2°C for each thousand feet.

   a. Standard temperature at 3,000 feet is:

      10 – 1 = 9°C.

   b. Existing temperature is 23°C. This is 23 – 9 = 14°C above standard temperature.

   c. The takeoff distance increases 10% for each 14°C above standard temperature.

   d. The takeoff distance is 652.5 + 10% = 717.75 feet.

(PLT012) — FAA-H-8083-25

AIR, WSC, PPC, LSA

6756. (Refer to Figure 26.) Determine the takeoff distance required to clear a 50-foot obstacle.

Temperature ....3°C
Pressure altitude.. 6,000 ft
Weight .... 3,000 lb
Headwind...15 kts

A— 1,464 feet.
B— 1,215 feet.
C— 1,331 feet.

1. The takeoff distance required for a 15-knot headwind at 5,000 feet, 3,000 pounds is 1,215 feet.

2. The takeoff distance required for a 15-knot headwind at 7,500 feet, 3,000 pounds is 1,505 feet.

3. Find the takeoff distance required for 6,000 feet PA.

   a. Takeoff distance for 7,500 feet PA = 1,505 feet.

   b. Takeoff distance for 5,000 feet PA = 1,215 feet.

   c. Difference = 290 feet

   d. The takeoff distance increases 290 ÷ 25 = 11.6 feet for each 100-foot increase in pressure altitude.

   e. The takeoff distance required for 6,000 feet PA is: 1,215 + (10 x 11.6) = 1,331 feet.

4. Apply correction for nonstandard temperature. The average change in temperature used by this chart is 2°C for each thousand feet.

   a. Standard temperature at 6,000 feet is:

      5°C – 2 = 3°C

   b. Existing temperature is 3°C, so it is not necessary to correct for nonstandard temperature.

(PLT012) — FAA-H-8083-25

Answers

6755   [B]   6756   [C]

AIR, WSC, PPC, LSA
6761. (Refer to Figure 28.) Determine the approximate total distance required to clear a 50-foot obstacle.

Temperature ....20°C
Pressure altitude.. 1,000 ft
Surface .... sod
Weight .... 5,300 lb
Wind .... 15 kts headwind

A— 1,724 feet.
B— 1,816 feet.
C— 2,061 feet.

1. *Find the maximum performance takeoff distance required to takeoff and clear a 50-foot obstacle at 1,000 feet pressure altitude and a gross weight of 5,300 pounds, with an outside air temperature of 20°C.*

   a. *Find the distance required to clear a 50-foot obstacle for 5,500 pounds at 1,000 feet PA and an OAT of 20°C: 1,950 feet.*

   b. *Find the distance required to clear a 50-foot obstacle for 5,100 pounds at 1,000 feet PA and an OAT of 20°C: 1,620 feet.*

   c. *The difference in distance for a 400-pound increase in weight is 330 feet.*

   d. *Each 100-pound increase in weight increases the distance required to clear a 50-foot obstacle by 82.5 feet.*

   e. *The distance required to clear a 50-foot obstacle at 5,300-pound weight is: 1620 + (2 x 82.5) = 1,785 feet.*

2. *Since the takeoff is made from a sod surface, this distance must be increased by 8%: 1,785 + 8% = 1,927.8 feet.*

3. *The takeoff is made with a 15-knot headwind, and the takeoff run is reduced by 7% for each 10 knots of headwind: 1,927.8 – 10.5% = 1,725.4 feet*

(PLT011) — FAA-H-8083-25

AIR, WSC, PPC, LSA
6762. (Refer to Figure 28.) Determine the approximate total distance required to clear a 50-foot obstacle.

Temperature ....25°C
Pressure altitude.. 2,500 ft
Surface ....asphalt
Weight .... 5,500 lb
Wind ....2 kts tailwind

A— 2,228 feet.
B— 2,294 feet.
C— 2,462 feet.

1. *Find the maximum performance takeoff distance required to takeoff and clear a 50-foot obstacle at 2,000 feet pressure altitude and a gross weight of 5,500 pounds, with an outside air temperature of 25°C.*

   a. *Find the distance required to clear a 50-foot obstacle for 5,500 pounds at 2,000 feet PA and an OAT of 30°C: 2,300 feet.*

   b. *Find the distance required to clear a 50-foot obstacle for 5,500 pounds at 2,000 feet PA and an OAT of 20°C: 2,150 feet.*

   c. *The difference in distance for a 10° increase in temperature is 150 feet.*

   d. *Each 1° increase in temperature increases the distance required to clear a 50-foot obstacle by 15 feet.*

   e. *The distance required to clear a 50-foot obstacle at 25°C is: 2,150 + (5 x 15) = 2,225 feet.*

2. *Find the maximum performance takeoff distance required to takeoff and clear a 50-foot obstacle at 3,000 feet pressure altitude and a gross weight of 5,500 pounds, with an outside air temperature of 25°C.*

   a. *Find the distance required to clear a 50-foot obstacle for 5,500 pounds at 3,000 feet PA and an OAT of 30°C: 2,550 feet.*

   b. *Find the distance required to clear a 50-foot obstacle for 5,500 pounds at 2,000 feet PA and an OAT of 20°C: 2,380 feet.*

   c. *The difference in distance for a 10° increase in temperature is 170 feet.*

   d. *Each 1° increase in temperature increases the distance required to clear a 50-foot obstacle by 17 feet.*

   e. *The distance required to clear a 50-foot obstacle at 25° is: 2,380 + (5 x 17) = 2,465 feet.*

Continued

Answers

6761　[A]　　　　6762　[C]

3. Find the takeoff distance required for 2,500 feet PA.

   a. Takeoff distance for 2,000 feet PA = 2,225 feet

   b. Takeoff distance for 3,000 feet PA = 2,465 feet

   c. Difference = 240 feet

   d. The takeoff distance increases 240 ÷ 10 = 24 feet for each 100-foot increase in pressure altitude.

   e. The takeoff distance required for 2,500 feet PA is: 2,225 + (5 x 24) = 2,345 feet.

4. The takeoff is increased by 5% for the 2-knot tailwind: 2,345 + 5% = 2,462.25 feet.

(PLT011) — FAA-H-8083-25

AIR, WSC, PPC, LSA

6763. (Refer to Figure 28.) Determine the approximate total distance required to clear a 50-foot obstacle.

Temperature .... 35°C
Pressure altitude .... 3,000 ft
Surface .... sod
Weight .... 5,100 lb
Wind .... 20 kts headwind

A— 1,969 feet.
B— 2,023 feet.
C— 2,289 feet.

1. Find the maximum performance takeoff distance required to takeoff and clear a 50-foot obstacle at 3,000 feet pressure altitude and a gross weight of 5,100 pounds, with an outside air temperature of 35°C.

   a. Find the distance required to clear a 50-foot obstacle for 5,100 pounds at 3,000 feet PA and an OAT of 30°C: 2,100 feet.

   b. Find the distance required to clear a 50-foot obstacle for 5,100 pounds at 3,000 feet PA and an OAT of 40°C: 2,260 feet.

   c. The difference in distance for a 10° increase in temperature is 160 feet.

   d. Each 1° increase in temperature increases the distance required to clear a 50-foot obstacle by 16 feet.

   e. The distance required to clear a 50-foot obstacle at 35° is: 2,100 + (5 x 16) = 2,180 feet.

2. Since the takeoff is made from a sod surface, this distance must be increased by 8%: 2,180 + 8% = 2,354.4 feet.

3. The takeoff is made with a 20-knot headwind, and the takeoff run is reduced by 7% for each 10 knots of headwind: 2,354.4 – 14% = 2,024.78 feet.

(PLT011) — FAA-H-8083-25

Climb Performance

An airplane's climb performance can be calculated by using a chart such as the one in FAA Figure 27, which is included in many POHs.

Problem:

Find the indicated airspeed that will give the greatest gain in altitude in a unit of time at 3,200 feet.

Solution:

Follow the line that represents 3,200-foot altitude to the right until it intersects the line for the best rate of climb. From this intersection, follow a line down until it intersects the indicated airspeed scale. An indicated airspeed of 113 KIAS will give the greatest gain in altitude in a unit of time at 3,200 feet.

Answers

6763 [B]

AIR, WSC, LSA

6757. (Refer to Figure 27.) The indicated airspeed that would give the greatest gain in altitude in a unit of time at 3,200 feet is determined to be

A— 93 KIAS.
B— 94 KIAS.
C— 112 KIAS.

Follow the line that represents 3,200-foot altitude to the right until it intersects the line for the best rate of climb. From this intersection, follow a line down until it intersects the indicated airspeed scale. An indicated airspeed of 113 KIAS will give the greatest gain in altitude in a unit of time at 3,200 feet. (PLT011) — FAA-H-8083-25

AIR, WSC, LSA

6758. (Refer to Figure 27.) What indicated airspeed at 3,000 feet would result in the greatest increase in altitude for a given distance?

A— 94 KIAS.
B— 113 KIAS.
C— 115 KIAS.

Follow the line that represents 3,000-foot altitude to the right until it intersects the line for the best angle of climb. From this intersection, follow a line down until it intersects the indicated airspeed scale. An indicated airspeed of 94 knots will give the greatest gain in altitude for a given distance at 3,000 feet. (PLT004) — FAA-H-8083-25

AIR, WSC, LSA

6759. (Refer to Figure 27.) To maintain the best rate of climb, the indicated speed should be

A— maintained at a constant value during the climb.
B— adjusted to maintain the specified rate of climb.
C— reduced approximately .8 knots per 1,000 feet of altitude.

Indicated airspeed decreases from 115 knots at sea level to 107 knots at 10,000 feet to maintain best rate of climb. 8 knots divided by 10,000 feet equals .8 knots per 1,000 feet. (PLT004) — FAA-H-8083-25

Answer (A) is incorrect because the indicated airspeed decreases with altitude. Answer (B) is incorrect because the rate of climb decreases with altitude.

Range Performance

The maximum range of a propeller-driven airplane occurs when the airplane is operating at the angle of attack that produces the maximum lift over drag (L/D) ratio, **L/D$_{MAX}$**. At the angle of attack that produces L/D$_{MAX}$, the induced drag and the parasite drag are equal, and the total drag is minimum.

AIR, WSC, PPC, LSA, MCI

6760. In a propeller-driven airplane, maximum range occurs at

A— minimum drag required.
B— minimum power required.
C— maximum lift/drag ratio.

The maximum range of a propeller-driven airplane occurs when the airplane is operating at the angle of attack that produces the maximum lift over drag (L/D) ratio, L/D$_{MAX}$. At the angle of attack that produces L/D$_{MAX}$, the induced drag and the parasite drag are equal and the total drag is minimum. (PLT242) — FAA-H-8083-3

Answer (A) is incorrect because minimum drag does not guarantee maximum lift/drag ratio. Answer (B) is incorrect because maximum endurance occurs at minimum power required.

Answers

6757 [C]	6758 [A]	6759 [C]	6760 [C]

Glide Distance

Glide distance can be found by using a chart such as FAA Figure 29.

Problem:

Find the distance you can glide from 5,500 feet above the terrain with a 10-knot tailwind.

Solution:

1. Follow a line to the right from the height above terrain of 5,500 feet until it intersects the slanted line.

2. From this intersection, draw a line downward until it intersects the glide distance. This intersection is at 12 statute miles.

3. According to Note 1, increase this distance by 10% for each 10-knot tailwind: 10% x 12 = 1.2 miles.

4. The airplane for which this curve was prepared will glide 12 + 1.2 = 13.2 miles from a height of 5,500 feet above the terrain with the help of a 10-knot tailwind.

AIR, WSC, PPC, LSA

6764. (Refer to Figure 29.) What is the approximate glide distance?

Height above terrain .... 5,500 ft
Tailwind .... 10 kts

A— 11 miles.
B— 12 miles.
C— 13 miles.

1. Follow a line to the right from the height above terrain of 5,500 feet until it intersects the slanted line.

2. From this intersection, draw a line downward until it intersects the glide distance. This intersection is at 12 statute miles.

3. According to Note 1, increase this distance by 10% for each 10-knot tailwind: 10% x 12 = 1.2 miles.

4. The airplane for which this curve was prepared will glide 12 + 1.2 = 13.2 miles from a height of 5,500 feet above the terrain with the help of a 10-knot tailwind.

(PLT006) — FAA-H-8083-25

AIR, WSC, PPC, LSA

6765. (Refer to Figure 29.) What is the approximate glide distance?

Height above terrain .... 10,500 ft
Tailwind .... 20 kts

A— 24 miles.
B— 26 miles.
C— 28 miles.

1. Follow a line to the right from the height above terrain of 10,500 feet until it intersects the slanted line.

2. From this intersection, draw a line downward until it intersects the glide distance. This intersection is at 23 statute miles.

3. According to Note 1, increase this distance by 10% for each 10-knot tailwind: 20% x 23 = 4.6 miles.

4. The airplane for which this curve was prepared will glide 23 + 4.6 = 27.6 miles from a height of 10,500 feet above the terrain with the help of a 20-knot tailwind.

(PLT006) — FAA-H-8083-25

AIR, WSC, PPC, LSA

6766. (Refer to Figure 29.) What is the approximate glide distance?

Height above terrain .... 7,500 ft
Headwind .... 30 kts

A— 11.5 miles.
B— 16.5 miles.
C— 21.5 miles.

1. Follow a line to the right from the height above terrain of 7,500 feet until it intersects the slanted line.

2. From this intersection, draw a line downward until it intersects the glide distance. This intersection is at 16.5 statute miles.

3. According to Note 2, decrease this distance by 10% for each 10-knot headwind: 30% x 16.5 = 4.95 miles.

4. The airplane for which this curve was prepared will glide 16.5 – 4.95 = 11.55 miles from a height of 7,500 feet above the terrain despite the 30-knot headwind.

(PLT006) — FAA-H-8083-25

Answers

6764   [C]   6765   [C]   6766   [A]

Stall Speed Performance

The stall speed of an airplane under the various configurations of flaps and gear, and angles of bank can be found by referring to a Stall Speed Chart such as the one in FAA Figure 25.

Problem:

Find the indicated stall speed for this airplane with the gear down and the flaps at 15° and the bank angle at 30°, referring to FAA Figure 25.

Solution:

1. Find the calibrated airspeed for stall at 20° bank angle with gear down and flaps at 15°: 83 KCAS.
2. Find the calibrated airspeed for stall at 40° bank angle with gear down and flaps at 15°: 92 KCAS.
3. Interpolate to find calibrated airspeed for stall at 30° bank angle with gear down and flaps at 15°:

    92-83 = 9. 9 ÷ 2 = 4.5. 83 + 4.5 = 87.5 KCAS

4. Use the Airspeed Calibration table, in the flaps 15° columns to convert 87.5 KCAS to KIAS:

    94 – 86 = 8. 87.5 is 1.5/8 of the way (that is, 1.5 ÷ 8) between these two speeds;

    18.75% of the way between 80 and 90 is:

    80 + (10 x .1875) = 81.875 KIAS.

5. 87.5 KCAS is equivalent to 81.875 KIAS.

AIR, WSC, PPC, LSA

6750. (Refer to Figure 25.) What would be the indicated stall speed in a 30° banked turn with the gear down and flaps set at 15°?

A— 77 KIAS.
B— 82 KIAS.
C— 88 KIAS.

1. *Find the calibrated airspeed for stall at 20° bank angle with gear down and flaps at 15°: 83 KCAS.*

2. *Find the calibrated airspeed for stall at 40° bank angle with gear down and flaps at 15°: 92 KCAS.*

3. *Interpolate to find calibrated airspeed for stall at 30° bank angle with gear down and flaps at 15°:*

    92 – 83 = 9. 9 ÷ 2 = 4.5. 83 + 4.5 = 87.5 KCAS

4. *Use the Airspeed Calibration table, in the flaps 15° columns to convert 87.5 KCAS to KIAS: 94 – 86 = 8. 87.5 is 1.5/8 of the way between these two speeds; 18.75% of the way between 80 and 90 is:*

    80 + (10 x .1875) = 81.875 KIAS

5. *87.5 KCAS is equivalent to 81.875 KIAS.*

(PLT018) — FAA-H-8083-25

AIR, WSC, PPC, LSA

6751. (Refer to Figure 25.) What would be the indicated stall speed in a 60° banked turn with the gear and flaps up?

A— 110 KIAS.
B— 117 KIAS.
C— 121 KIAS.

1. *Find the calibrated airspeed for stall at 60° bank angle with gear down and flaps up: 119 KCAS.*

2. *Go to the Airspeed Correction Table. In the Flaps 0° columns and convert 119 KCAS to KIAS. This requires interpolation: 122 – 102 = 20 knots, 119 knots is 17/20 of the way between these two speeds; 85% of the way between 120 and 100 knots is: 100 + (20 x .85) = 117 knots. 119 KCAS is equivalent to an IAS of 117 knots.*

(PLT018) — FAA-H-8083-25

Answers

6750   [B]   6751   [B]

AIR, WSC, PPC, LSA

6752. (Refer to Figure 25.) What would be the indicated stall speed during a 40° banked turn with the gear down and flaps set at 45°?

A— 81 KIAS.

B— 83 KIAS.

C— 89 KIAS.

1. *Find the calibrated airspeed for stall at 40° bank angle with gear down and flaps at 45°: 87 knots.*

2. *Go to the Airspeed Correction Table. In the Flaps 45° columns and convert 87 KCAS to KIAS. This requires interpolation: 93 – 84 = 9 knots, 87 knots is 3/9 of the way between these two speeds; 33% of the way between 90 and 80 knots is: 80 + (10 x .33) = 83.3 knots. 87 KCAS is equivalent to an IAS of 83.3 knots.*

(PLT018) — FAA-H-8083-25

Landing Performance

The landing ground roll and landing distance needed over a 50-foot obstacle can be computed by using the Normal Landing Chart in FAA Figure 31. Charts of this type are furnished in the POH.

Problem:

Find the total landing distance required for this airplane over a 50-foot obstacle at a pressure altitude of 4,000 feet, temperature of 15°C, weight of 3,000 pounds and a 22-knot headwind.

Solution:

1. Follow the 4,000-foot pressure altitude curve to the right until it intersects the vertical line for 15°C. From this intersection, draw a line to the right until it intersects the left reference line.

2. From this point, draw a line diagonally upward to the right, parallel to the lines that are already there. Follow this line up until it intersects the vertical line for 3,000-pound weight.

3. Draw a line to the right until it intersects the right reference line.

4. From this point, draw a line downward to the right paralleling the existing lines.

5. Draw a line upward from the 22-knot headwind index until it intersects the diagonal line you have just drawn.

6. From this point, draw a line to the right until it intersects the index for the total landing distance over a 50-foot obstacle. This is at 1,175 feet.

Answers

6752 [B]

ALL
7141. What can a pilot expect when landing at an airport located in the mountains?

A— Higher true airspeed and longer landing distance.
B— Higher indicated airspeed and shorter landing distance.
C— Lower true airspeed and longer landing distance.

When landing at a high-altitude airport, the same indicated airspeed should be used as at low-elevation fields. Due to the less dense air at altitude, the same indicated airspeed actually results in higher true airspeed, a faster landing speed, and more importantly, a longer landing distance. (PLT127) — AIM ¶7-5-6

Answer (B) is incorrect because the indicated airspeed should remain the same and the landing distance will be longer. Answer (C) is incorrect because true airspeed will be higher in the mountains.

AIR, WSC, PPC, LSA
6773. (Refer to Figure 31.) What is the total landing distance over a 50-foot obstacle?

Temperature .... 15°C
Pressure altitude.. 4,000 ft
Weight .... 3,000 lb
Headwind...22 kts

A— 1,250 feet.
B— 1,175 feet.
C— 1,050 feet.

1. *Follow the 4,000-foot pressure altitude curve to the right until it intersects the vertical line for 15°C. From this intersection, draw a line to the right until it intersects the left reference line.*

2. *From this point, draw a line diagonally upward to the right, parallel to the lines that are already there. Follow this line up until it intersects the vertical line for 3,000-pound weight.*

3. *Draw a line to the right until it intersects the right reference line.*

4. *From this point, draw a line downward to the right paralleling the existing lines.*

5. *Draw a line upward from the 22-knot headwind index until it intersects the diagonal line you have just drawn.*

6. *From this point, draw a line to the right until it intersects the index for the total landing distance over a 50-foot obstacle. This is at 1,175 feet.*

(PLT008) — FAA-H-8083-25

AIR, WSC, PPC, LSA
6774. (Refer to Figure 31.) Determine the approximate ground roll.

Temperature .... 33°C
Pressure altitude... 6,000 ft
Weight .... 2,800 lb
Headwind...14 kts

A— 742 feet.
B— 1,280 feet.
C— 1,480 feet.

1. *Follow the 6,000-foot pressure altitude curve to the right until it intersects the vertical line for 33°C. From this intersection, draw a line to the right until it intersects the left reference line.*

2. *From this point, draw a line diagonally upward to the right, parallel to the lines that are already there. Follow this line up until it intersects the vertical line for 2,800-pound weight.*

3. *Draw a line to the right until it intersects the right reference line.*

4. *From this point, draw a line downward to the right paralleling the existing lines.*

5. *Draw a line upward from the 14-knot headwind index until it intersects the diagonal line you have just drawn.*

6. *From this point, draw a line to the right until it intersects the index for the landing distance. This is at 1,400 feet.*

7. *The Note says the ground roll is approximately 53% of total landing distance over a 50-foot obstacle: 1,400 x .53 = 742 feet.*

(PLT008) — FAA-H-8083-25

Answers

7141   [A]   6773   [B]   6774   [A]

AIR, WSC, PPC, LSA

6775. (Refer to Figure 31.) What is the total landing distance over a 50-foot obstacle?

Temperature ....35°C
Pressure altitude... 2,000 ft
Weight .... 3,400 lb
Headwind...10 kts

A— 1,650 feet.
B— 1,575 feet.
C— 1,475 feet.

1. Follow the 2,000-foot pressure altitude curve to the right until it intersects the vertical line for 35°C. From this intersection, draw a line to the right until it intersects the left reference line.

2. From this point, draw a line diagonally upward to the right, parallel to the lines that are already there. Follow this line up until it intersects the vertical line for 3,400-pound weight.

3. Draw a line to the right until it intersects the right reference line.

4. From this point, draw a line downward to the right paralleling the existing lines.

5. Draw a line upward from the 10-knot headwind index until it intersects the diagonal line you have just drawn.

6. From this point, draw a line to the right until it intersects the index for the total landing distance over a 50-foot obstacle. This is at 1,475 feet.

(PLT008) — FAA-H-8083-25

Multi-Engine Performance

The single-engine service ceiling of a twin-engine airplane is the maximum density altitude at which the **single-engine best rate-of-climb speed** (V_{YSE}) will produce a 50-foot-per-minute rate of climb.

When one engine fails on a conventional, light, twin-engine airplane, performance is not halved, but is actually reduced by 80% or more. When one engine fails, the airplane not only loses power, but the drag increases considerably because of the asymmetric thrust produced as one engine carries all of the load.

The airplane should be capable of allowing a pilot to maintain heading when flying at minimum control speed with the critical engine inoperative (V_{MC}), but it may not allow altitude to be gained, or even held. Since the power of an unsupercharged engine decreases with altitude, V_{MC} decreases as altitude is increased. This makes it possible to maintain directional control at a lower airspeed at altitude than at sea level. The thrust moment of the operating engine becomes less at altitude, decreasing the need for the rudder's yawing force. Since V_{MC} is a function of engine power, it is possible for the airplane at altitude to reach its stalling speed prior to losing directional control.

When one engine fails on a light, conventional twin-engine airplane, and full power is applied to the operative engine, the airplane will try to roll as well as yaw into the inoperative engine as the airspeed drops below V_{MC}. This tendency becomes greater as the airspeed is further reduced. Banking toward the inoperative engine increases V_{MC} at the rate of about 3 knots per degree of bank, while banking toward the operative engine reduces V_{MC}.

V_{MC} is highest when the center of gravity is at the rear-most allowable position. The airplane rotates about its center of gravity, and the moments, when considering V_{MC}, are measured using the CG as the reference. A rearward CG shortens the arm between the CG and the center of the rudder's horizontal lift. This means that a higher force (higher airspeed) is needed to counteract the engine-out yaw when the CG is aft, than when it is further forward.

Answers

6775   [C]

AIR

6809. What is the significance of the blue radial line on the airspeed indicator of a light multiengine airplane and when is it to be used? It indicates the

A— minimum speed at which the airplane is controllable when the critical engine is suddenly made inoperative and should be used at all altitudes when an engine is inoperative.

B— speed which will provide the maximum altitude gain in a given time when one engine is inoperative and should be used for climb and final approach during engine-out operations.

C— speed which will provide the greatest height for a given distance of forward travel when one engine is inoperative and should be used for all climbs during engine-out operations.

The blue radial line on the airspeed indicator installed in a light multi-engine airplane indicates the best rate-of-climb airspeed with one engine inoperative (V_{YSE}). This is the airspeed which will provide the maximum altitude gain in a given time when one engine is inoperative. V_{YSE} should be used when climbing on one engine and when making the final approach during engine-out operations. (PLT132) — FAA-H-8083-3

Answer (A) is incorrect because V_{MC} is indicated by the red radial line. Answer (C) is incorrect because V_{XSE} is not marked on the airspeed indicator.

AIR

6807. In a twin-engine airplane, the single-engine service ceiling is the maximum density altitude at which V_{YSE} will produce

A— 50 feet per minute rate of climb.
B— 100 feet per minute rate of climb.
C— 500 feet per minute rate of climb.

The single-engine service ceiling of a twin-engine airplane is the maximum density altitude at which the single-engine best rate-of-climb speed (V_{YSE}) will produce a 50-foot-per-minute rate of climb. (PLT132) — FAA-H-8083-3

AIR

6808. When one engine fails on a twin-engine airplane, the resulting performance loss

A— may reduce the rate of climb by 80 percent or more.

B— reduces cruise indicated airspeed by 50 percent or more.

C— is approximately 50 percent since 50 percent of the normally available thrust is lost.

When one engine fails on a light, conventional, twin-engine airplane, performance is not halved, but it is actually reduced by 80% or more. When one engine fails, the airplane not only loses power, but the drag increases considerably because of the asymmetric thrust produced as one engine carries all of the load. (PLT223) — FAA-H-8083-3

AIR

6810. When operating a light multiengine airplane at V_{MC}, the pilot should expect performance to be sufficient to maintain

A— heading.
B— heading and altitude.
C— heading, altitude, and be able to climb at 50 feet per minute.

V_{MC} is the minimum airspeed at which an airplane is controllable when the critical engine is suddenly made inoperative. The airplane should be capable of allowing a pilot to maintain heading when flying at V_{MC}, but it may not allow altitude to be gained, or even held. (PLT223) — FAA-H-8083-3

AIR

6811. For an airplane with reciprocating, non-turbocharged engines, V_{MC}

A— decreases with altitude.
B— increases with altitude.
C— is not affected by altitude.

Since the power of an unsupercharged engine decreases with altitude, the minimum controllable airspeed, V_{MC}, decreases as altitude is increased. As the power decreases, the thrust moment of the operating engine becomes less, decreasing the need for the rudder's yawing force. (PLT132) — FAA-H-8083-3

Answers

6809 [B]   6807 [A]   6808 [A]   6810 [A]   6811 [A]

AIR
6812. Which is true regarding the operation of a multi-engine airplane with one engine inoperative?

A— Banking toward the operating engine increases V_{MC}.

B— Banking toward the inoperative engine increases V_{MC}.

C— V_{MC} is a designed performance factor which must be proven during type certification and will not change as long as the ball is centered with appropriate rudder pressure.

When one engine is out on a light, conventional twin-engine airplane and full power is applied to the operative engine, the airplane will try to roll as well as yaw into the inoperative engine as the airspeed drops below V_{MC}. This tendency becomes greater as the airspeed is further reduced. Banking toward the inoperative engine increases V_{MC} at the rate of about 3 knots per degree of bank. (PLT223) — FAA-H-8083-3

Answer (A) is incorrect because banking toward the operative engine reduces V_{MC}. Answer (C) is incorrect because if the ball is centered, the airplane will sideslip toward the inoperative engine, which increases drag and increases V_{MC}.

AIR
6813. Which condition causes V_{MC} to be the highest?

A— CG is at the most forward allowable position.

B— CG is at the most rearward allowable position.

C— Gross weight is at the maximum allowable value.

V_{MC} is the highest when the center of gravity is at the rearmost allowable position. The airplane rotates about its center of gravity, and the moments, when considering V_{MC}, are measured using the CG as the reference. A rearward CG shortens the arm between the CG and the center of the rudder's horizontal lift. This means that a higher force (higher airspeed) is needed to counteract the engine-out yaw when the CG is aft, than when it is further forward. (PLT223) — FAA-H-8083-3

Answers (A) and (C) are incorrect because a forward CG and increased weight reduces V_{MC}.

Wind Components

We can find the crosswind, headwind, or tail wind component for flight or for takeoff or landing by using a Wind Component Chart, such as that in FAA Figure 30, or by using an electronic flight computer. Charts such as that in FAA Figure 30 are printed on the card of some E6-B flight computers.

Problem:

Find the crosswind component a pilot would have when landing on runway 30 with a wind from 020° at 15 knots.

Solution:

1. The wind angle is the difference between the aircraft heading and the direction from which the wind is blowing. The wind is blowing from 020°, and the aircraft is landing on runway 30. Therefore, the wind angle is (360° − 300°) + 20 = 80°.

2. Follow the arc for 15 knots until it intersects the 80° radial for the wind angle.

3. From the intersection of the 15-knot arc and the radial for the 80° wind angle, draw a line downward until it intersects the crosswind component: 15 knots.

4. An aircraft landing on runway 30 with a wind from 020° at 15 knots will have a 15-knot crosswind.

This same problem can be quickly and accurately worked on the CX-2 Pathfinder electronic flight computer:

1. Select the X/H-Wind program.

Answers

6812   [B]   6813   [B]

2. Enter the wind direction of 020°. (W Dir)

3. Enter the wind speed of 15 knots. (W Spd)

4. Enter the Runway number 30. (Rwy)

5. Read the crosswind component (X-Wind) of 15 knots, and the headwind component (H-Wind) of -3 knots.

ALL

6767. (Refer to Figure 30.) Determine the approximate crosswind component.

Landing Rwy... 30
Wind .... 020° at 15 kts

A— 4 knots.
B— 15 knots.
C— 22 knots.

1. *The wind angle is the difference between the aircraft heading and the direction from which the wind is blowing. The wind is blowing from 020°, and the aircraft is landing on runway 30. Therefore, the wind angle is (360° – 300°) + 20 = 80°.*

2. *Follow the arc for 15 knots until it intersects the 80° radial for the wind angle.*

3. *From the intersection of the 15-knot arc and the radial for the 80° wind angle, draw a line down-ward until it intersects the crosswind component: 15 knots.*

4. *An aircraft landing on runway 30 with a wind from 020° at 15 knots will have a 15-knot crosswind.*

(PLT013) — FAA-H-8083-25

ALL

6768. (Refer to Figure 30.) Determine the approximate crosswind component.

Landing Rwy... 03
Wind .... 060° at 35 kts

A— 12 knots.
B— 18 knots.
C— 22 knots.

1. *The wind angle is the difference between the aircraft heading and the direction from which the wind is blowing. The wind is blowing from 060°, and the aircraft is landing on runway 03. Therefore, the wind angle is 60° – 30° = 30°.*

2. *Follow the arc for 35 knots until it intersects the 30° radial for the wind angle.*

3. *From the intersection of the 35-knot arc and the radial for the 30° wind angle, draw a line down-ward until it intersects the crosswind component: 18 knots.*

4. *An aircraft landing on runway 03 with a wind from 060° at 35 knots will have a 18-knot crosswind.*

(PLT013) — FAA-H-8083-25

Answers

6767 [B]   6768 [B]

ALL

6769. (Refer to Figure 30.) Determine the approximate crosswind component.

Landing Rwy..22
Wind ....260° at 23 kts

A— 10 knots.
B— 15 knots.
C— 17 knots.

1. *The wind angle is the difference between the aircraft heading and the direction from which the wind is blowing. The wind is blowing from 260°, and the aircraft is landing on runway 22. Therefore, the wind angle is 260° – 220° = 040°.*

2. *Follow the arc for 23 knots until it intersects the 40° radial for the wind angle.*

3. *From the intersection of the 23-knot arc and the radial for the 40° wind angle, draw a line down-ward until it intersects the crosswind component: 15 knots.*

4. *An aircraft landing on runway 22 with a wind from 260° at 23 knots will have a 15-knot crosswind.*

(PLT013) — FAA-H-8083-25

ALL

6769-1. (Refer to Figure 30.) What is the crosswind component for a landing on Runway 18 if the tower reports the wind as 220° at 30 knots?

A— 19 knots.
B— 23 knots.
C— 30 knots.

1. *The wind angle is the difference between the aircraft heading and the direction from which the wind is blowing. The wind is blowing from 220°, and the aircraft is landing on runway 18. Therefore, the wind angle is 220° – 180° = 040°.*

2. *Follow the arc for 30 knots until it intersects the 40° radial for the wind angle.*

3. *From the intersection of the 30-knot arc and the radial for the 40° wind angle, draw a line downward until it intersects the crosswind component: 19 knots.*

4. *An aircraft landing on runway 18 with a wind from 220° at 30 knots will have a 19-knot crosswind.*

(PLT013) — FAA-H-8083-25

AIR, WSC, PPC, LSA

6770. (Refer to Figure 30.) Using a maximum demonstrated crosswind component equal to 0.2 V_{S0}, what is a pilot able to determine?

V_{S0} ....70 kts
Landing Rwy..35
Wind ....300° at 20 kts

A— Headwind component is excessive.
B— Headwind component exceeds the crosswind component.
C— Maximum demonstrated crosswind component is exceeded.

1. *The wind angle is the difference between the aircraft heading and the direction from which the wind is blowing. The wind is blowing from 300°, and the aircraft is landing on runway 35. Therefore, the wind angle is 300° – 350° = -50° + 360° = 310°.*

2. *Follow the arc for 20 knots until it intersects the 310° radial for the wind angle.*

3. *From the intersection of the 20-knot arc and the radial for the 310° wind angle, draw a line down-ward until it intersects the crosswind component: 15.25 knots.*

4. *Calculate the maximum demonstrated crosswind component: 70 x .2 = 14 knots.*

5. *Therefore, the maximum demonstrated crosswind component is exceeded.*

(PLT013) — FAA-H-8083-25

Answers (A) and (B) are incorrect because headwind component is not a crucial factor for landing considerations.

Answers

6769   [B]   6769-1   [A]   6770   [C]

AIR, WSC, PPC, LSA

6771. (Refer to Figure 30.) Using a maximum demonstrated crosswind component equal to 0.2 V_{S0}, what is a pilot able to determine?

V_{S0} ....60 kts
Landing Rwy.. 12
Wind .... 150° at 20 kts

A— Headwind component is excessive.
B— Crosswind component is within safe limits.
C— Maximum demonstrated crosswind component is exceeded.

1. The wind angle is the difference between the aircraft heading and the direction from which the wind is blowing. The wind is blowing from 150°, and the aircraft is landing on runway 12. Therefore, the wind angle is 150° – 120° = 30°.

2. Follow the arc for 20 knots until it intersects the 30° radial for the wind angle.

3. From the intersection of the 20-knot arc and the radial for the 30° wind angle, draw a line down-ward until it intersects the crosswind component: 10 knots.

4. Calculate the maximum demonstrated crosswind component: 60 x .2 = 12 knots.

5. Therefore, the maximum crosswind component is within safe limits.

(PLT013) — FAA-H-8083-25

AIR, WSC, PPC, LSA

6772. (Refer to Figure 30.) Using a maximum demonstrated crosswind component equal to 0.2 V_{S0}, what is a pilot able to determine?

V_{S0} ....65 kts
Landing Rwy.. 17
Wind .... 200° at 30 kts

A— Crosswind component is within safe limits.
B— Crosswind component exceeds the headwind component.
C— Maximum demonstrated crosswind component is exceeded.

1. The wind angle is the difference between the aircraft heading and the direction from which the wind is blowing. The wind is blowing from 200°, and the aircraft is landing on runway 17. Therefore, the wind angle is 200° – 170° = 30°.

2. Follow the arc for 30 knots until it intersects the 30° radial for the wind angle.

3. From the intersection of the 30-knot arc and the radial for the 30° wind angle, draw a line down-ward until it intersects the crosswind component: 15 knots.

4. Calculate the maximum demonstrated crosswind component: 65 x .2 = 13 knots.

5. Therefore, the maximum demonstrated crosswind component is exceeded.

(PLT013) — FAA-H-8083-25

Answers

6771   [B]   6772   [C]

Helicopter Performance

The most favorable conditions for rotorcraft performance are the combination of low density altitude, light gross weight, and moderate to strong wind. Low density altitude increases both the performance of the engine and the lift produced by the rotors. The low gross weight allows the helicopter to operate with less than maximum performance, and a moderate to strong wind allows the helicopter to obtain translational lift with a minimum ground speed.

Water vapor is only about 5/8 as heavy as dry air, and when the relative humidity is high, the air is less dense than standard air. Because of this less dense air, the engine develops less power and the rotors produce less lift than they would in standard conditions. If all other factors remain the same, an increase in relative humidity will lower the hover ceiling of a helicopter.

RTC

6619. The V_{NE} of a helicopter is limited by

A— centrifugal twisting moment of the rotor blades.
B— lateral controllability or retreating blade stall.
C— available horsepower of the engine which may be converted to torque.

The stall of a rotor blade limits the high airspeed potential of a helicopter. The airflow over the retreating blade of the helicopter slows down as forward airspeed of the helicopter increases; the airflow over the advancing blade speeds up as forward speed increases. (PLT470) — FAA-H-8083-21

RTC

6830. The most favorable combination of conditions for rotorcraft performance is

A— low density altitude, low gross weight, and moderate to strong wind.
B— low density altitude, high gross weight, and calm to light wind.
C— high density altitude, low gross weight, and moderate to strong wind.

The most favorable conditions for rotorcraft performance are the combination of low density altitude, light gross weight, and moderate to strong wind. Low density altitude increases both the performance of the engine and the lift produced by the rotors. The low gross weight allows the helicopter to operate with less than maximum performance, and a moderate to strong wind allows the helicopter to obtain translational lift with a minimum ground speed. (PLT124) — FAA-H-8083-21

RTC

6704. When operating a gyroplane in conditions favorable to carburetor icing, the carburetor heat control should be

A— adjusted so the carburetor air temperature gauge indicates in the green arc.
B— ON when practicing power-off maneuvers such as autorotations but OFF at all other times.
C— OFF during takeoffs, approaches, and landings; other times, adjusted to keep carburetor air temperature in the green arc.

When there are indications of carburetor icing, full carburetor heat should be applied until the manifold pressure returns to normal and the engine is running smoothly. The carburetor heat should be adjusted so that the carburetor air temperature gauge indicates a safe operating range. (PLT190) — FAA-H-8083-21

RTC

6831-1. If all other factors remain the same, an increase in relative humidity will

A— decrease the hovering ceiling because the air is less dense.
B— increase the hovering ceiling because the air is more dense.
C— decrease the hovering ceiling because the air is more dense.

Water vapor is only about 5/8 as heavy as dry air, and when the relative humidity is high, the air is less dense than standard air. Because of this less dense air, the engine develops less power and the rotors produce less lift than they would in standard conditions. If all other factors remain the same, an increase in relative humidity will lower the hover ceiling of a helicopter. (PLT124) — FAA-H-8083-21

Answers

6619   [B]   6830   [A]   6704   [A]   6831-1   [A]

RTC

6831-2. Performance of a helicopter can be determined by

A— the highest altitude that can be maintained in a hover following liftoff.
B— knowing the density altitude, gross weight, and surface wind.
C— the formula pi times the rotor diameter divided by the blade area.

There are three major factors limiting helicopter performance at high altitudes: gross weight, density altitude, and wind. (PLT124) — FAA-H-8083-21

RTC

6832. As altitude increases, the V_{NE} of most helicopters

A— increases.
B— decreases.
C— remains the same.

As altitude increase, the V_{NE} decreases for most helicopters. (PLT035) — FAA-H-8083-21

RTC

6834. Which technique is recommended during hot weather operations in a helicopter?

A— Descend rapidly during approaches.
B— During takeoff, accelerate slowly into forward flight.
C— During takeoff, accelerate quickly into forward flight.

Flight technique in hot weather:

1. *Make full use of wind and translational lift.*
2. *Hover as low as possible and no longer than necessary.*
3. *Maintain maximum allowable engine RPM.*
4. *Accelerate very slowly into forward flight.*
5. *Employ running takeoffs and landings when necessary.*
6. *Use caution in maximum performance takeoff and steep approaches.*

(PLT219) — FAA-H-8083-21

Balloon Performance

LTA

6841. What constitutes the payload of a balloon?

A— Total gross weight.
B— Total weight of passengers, cargo and baggage.
C— Difference between empty weight and maximum certified gross weight.

Payload is the weight of occupants, cargo and baggage. (PLT121) — FAA-H-8083-11

LTA

6842. (Refer to Figure 39.) Determine the maximum payload for a balloon flying at 1,500 feet at an ambient temperature of 87°F.

A— 515 pounds.
B— 565 pounds.
C— 585 pounds.

Enter graph from ambient temperature line. The maximum payload for a balloon flying at 1,500 feet at an ambient temperature of 87°F is 565 pounds. (PLT057) — Balloon Ground School

LTA

6843. (Refer to Figure 39.) What is the maximum altitude for a balloon if the gross weight is 1,060 pounds and standard temperature exists at all altitudes?

A— 4,000 feet.
B— 5,000 feet.
C— 7,000 feet.

1. *Find the 1,060 pounds on the gross weight scale.*
2. *Follow that line to the standard temperature line.*
3. *This intersection indicates 7,000 feet.*

(PLT057) — Balloon Ground School

Answers

6831-2 [B]	6832 [B]	6834 [B]	6841 [B]	6842 [B]	6843 [C]

LTA

6844. (Refer to Figure 39.) What is the maximum altitude for a balloon if the gross weight is 960 pounds and the ambient temperature is 76°F?

A— 2,000 feet.
B— 2,500 feet.
C— 4,000 feet.

1. *Find 960 pounds on the gross weight scale.*

2. *Follow that line to 76°F.*

3. *This intersection indicates 2,000 feet.*

(PLT057) — Balloon Ground School

LTA

6845. (Refer to Figure 39.) Determine the maximum weight allowable for a pilot and passengers for a balloon flight at approximately 1,000 feet with a temperature of 68°F. Launch with 20 gallons of propane.

A— 601 pounds.
B— 620 pounds.
C— 705 pounds.

The standard weight of propane is 4.23 pounds per gallon.

1. *Enter the chart at the 68°F ambient temperature value. Move upward to a point about 1/5 of the distance between the sea level and 5,000 foot pressure altitude curves.*

2. *From that point draw a line to the left and read the gross weight as 1,040 pounds.*

3. *Calculate the weight of 20 gallons of propane:*

   20 x 4.23 = 85 pounds

4. *Compute the available lift:*

Item	*Weight*
Gross weight	*1,040 lbs*
Empty weight	*335 lbs*
Fuel weight	*– 85 lbs*
Pilot and passengers	*620 lbs*

(PLT057) — Balloon Ground School

LTA

6846. (Refer to Figure 39.) Determine the maximum weight allowable for a pilot and passengers for a balloon flight at approximately 2,000 feet with a standard temperature. Launch with 20 gallons of propane.

A— 631 pounds.
B— 641 pounds.
C— 701 pounds.

1. *Empty weight = 335 pounds. (Include 20 gallons of propane or 20 x 4.2 pounds per gallon or 84 pounds.)*

2. *Weight of balloon and fuel = 419 pounds.*

3. *Along the standard temperature line find 2,000 feet. Follow this line to the gross weight scale = 1,120 pounds.*

4. *Subtract balloon/fuel weight (419 pounds) from gross weight (1,120), 1,120 – 419 = 701 pounds.*

(PLT057) — Balloon Ground School

Answers

6844 [A]   6845   [B]   6846   [C]

Principles of Weight and Balance

It is important, when loading an airplane for a flight, that the maximum allowable gross weight is not exceeded and that the center of gravity is within the allowable limits. In calculating weight and balance problems, these factors are important:

- The **center of gravity** of an airplane is measured along its longitudinal axis in inches from a reference called the **datum**.
- The **arm** of a weight is the distance in inches from the datum. If the weight is ahead of, or to the left of the datum, the arm is negative, and if it is behind, or to the right of the datum, the arm is positive.
- A **moment** is a force that tends to cause rotation about a point, and is measured in pound-inches. A moment is the product of the weight of the item, in pounds, and the distance from the datum in inches.
- The center of gravity of an airplane is found by **dividing the total moment by the total weight**.

Excessive weight reduces the flight performance of an aircraft by:

1. Requiring a higher takeoff speed.
2. Requiring a longer takeoff.
3. Reducing the rate and angle of climb.
4. Lowering the maximum altitude.
5. Giving the aircraft a shorter range.
6. Reducing the cruising speed.
7. Reducing maneuverability.
8. Giving the aircraft a higher stalling speed.
9. Requiring a higher landing speed.
10. Requiring a longer landing roll.
11. Putting an excessive weight on the nosewheel.

With excessive weight, the aircraft will accelerate more slowly with the same power output and a higher airspeed is needed to generate enough lift for takeoff.

Loading an aircraft so its CG is behind the aft limit causes the aircraft to become less **longitudinally stable** and less controllable. When the CG is at or near its aft limit, the tail surfaces exert less down-load and there is less stabilizing down-pitching moment. This can reduce the aircraft's ability to recover from stalls and spins. If the CG is too far aft, the elevator may not have enough power to get the nose down to bring the aircraft out of its stalled condition. The aircraft will enter a **spin**, and the aft CG will cause the spin to flatten out, making recovery very difficult or impossible.

When an aircraft is loaded with its CG at its aft limit, the horizontal tail surfaces will be required to exert the least amount of down-load. This relieves the wing of part of its load and allows it to maintain altitude with a lower angle of attack. The drag is less, and the aircraft has a faster cruising speed.

The disadvantage of having the CG at its aft limit is the decrease in longitudinal stability. A neutral load on the tail surfaces in cruising flight produces the most efficient overall performance and fastest cruising speed, but it also results in longitudinal instability. The problem caused by this instability is overcome by sophisticated automatic flight control systems in many of the modern high-performance aircraft.

When an aircraft is loaded at its most forward CG location, **nose-up trim** is needed to maintain level cruising flight. Nose-up trim causes the tail surfaces to produce a greater down-load on the aft portion of the fuselage, and this adds to the wing loading and increases the total lift the wing must produce to maintain altitude. When the wing flies at a higher angle of attack to produce the extra lift, it produces more induced drag.

The indicated airspeed produced by a constant power at a constant altitude will be lower when the CG is at the forward limits than it is when the CG is further aft.

Moving the CG from the aft limit to beyond the forward limit will cause the aircraft to **stall** at a higher speed. The additional downward force produced by the horizontal stabilizer to overcome the nose-down pitching tendency increases the wing loading and requires a higher speed before reaching its stalling angle of attack. The aircraft will also cruise slower because the additional downward tail load increases the wing loading and requires a higher angle of attack.

One advantage of a forward CG location is that an aircraft becomes more longitudinally stable as the CG is moved forward. The forward CG increases the tendency for the nose to drop as the airspeed decreases.

Forward CG is most critical during landing. If it is too far forward, the elevators may not have enough power to get the tail down enough for a proper approach and flare.

A high gross weight and a forward CG will increase the stall speed of an aircraft. Both the forward CG and the high gross weight require the aircraft to be flown at a higher speed before it reaches its stalling angle of attack.

ALL
6804. The center of gravity of an aircraft is computed along the

A— lateral axis.
B— vertical axis.
C— longitudinal axis.

The CG of an aircraft is computed along its longitudinal axis. The location of the CG is normally given in inches from the datum or in percent of the mean aerodynamic chord (% MAC). (PLT314) — FAA-H-8083-1

ALL
6805. The center of gravity of an aircraft can be determined by

A— dividing total arm by total moment.
B— dividing total moment by total weight.
C— multiplying total arm by total weight.

The CG of an aircraft is found by dividing the total moment (in pound-inches) by the total weight (in pounds). (PLT021) — FAA-H-8083-1

ALL
7309. With respect to using the weight information given in a typical aircraft owner's manual for computing gross weight, it is important to know that if items have been installed in the aircraft in addition to the original equipment, the

A— allowable useful load is decreased.
B— allowable useful load remains unchanged.
C— maximum allowable gross weight is increased.

The empty weight and moment given in most manufacturers' handbooks are for the basic aircraft prior to the installation of additional optional equipment. When the owner later adds items such as radio navigation equipment, autopilot, deicers, etc., the empty weight and the moment are changed. These changes must be recorded in the aircraft's weight and balance data and used in all computations. (PLT328) — FAA-H-8083-25

Answers

| 6804 | [C] | 6805 | [B] | 7309 | [A] |

AIR, WSC, MCI

6802. If the nosewheel of an airplane moves aft during gear retraction, how would this aft movement affect the CG location of that airplane? It would

A— cause the CG location to move aft.
B— have no effect on the CG location.
C— cause the CG location to move forward.

When the nosewheel of an aircraft moves aft during retraction, it causes the CG location of the airplane to move aft. (PLT021) — FAA-H-8083-1

AIR, WSC, MCI

6803. If the landing gear on an airplane moves forward during retraction, the total moment will

A— increase.
B— decrease.
C— remain the same.

Moments used in weight and balance are the product of the weight of an object and its arm, or distance from the datum. Assuming the datum is ahead of the landing gear, moving the landing gear forward during retraction decreases its arm; therefore, the total moments will decrease. (PLT021) — FAA-H-8083-1

AIR, WSC, LSA, PPC, MCI

6815. How does increased weight affect the takeoff distance of an airplane?

A— The airplane will accelerate more slowly with the same power output, but the same airspeed is required to generate necessary lift for takeoff.
B— The airplane will accelerate more slowly with the same power output, and a higher airspeed is required to generate necessary lift for takeoff.
C— Every airplane has the same acceleration factor with the same power output, but a higher airspeed is needed to overcome the increased ground effect.

Excessive weight reduces the flight performance of an airplane by requiring a higher takeoff speed and a longer takeoff run. (PLT134) — FAA-H-8083-25

Answer (A) is incorrect because a higher takeoff speed is needed to generate enough lift for takeoff. Answer (C) is incorrect because the airplane will accelerate more slowly with the same power output.

AIR, LSA, MCI

6823. To maintain level flight in an airplane which is loaded with the CG at the forward limit, an additional download must be imposed on the horizontal stabilizer. This in turn produces

A— an additional load which the wing must support.
B— a lesser load that must be supported by the wing.
C— a decrease in drag and results in a faster airspeed.

When an airplane is loaded at its most forward CG location, nose-up trim is required to maintain level cruising flight. Nose-up trim increases the down-load produced by the horizontal tail surfaces. This down-load is an aerodynamic load, but it must be supported by the wing in the same way as any other weight. (PLT240) — FAA-H-8083-1

Answer (B) is incorrect because a forward CG produces a higher wing loading. Answer (C) is incorrect because a forward CG products increased drag and a slower cruising speed.

AIR, GLI, LSA, MCI

6816. An aircraft is loaded with the CG aft of the aft limit. What effect will this have on controllability?

A— Stall and spin recovery may be difficult or impossible.
B— A stall will occur at a lower airspeed, but recovery will be easier because of reduced wing loading.
C— A stall will occur at a higher indicated airspeed due to the greater downloading on the elevator.

Loading an aircraft so its CG is aft of the aft limit will have a serious effect upon longitudinal stability and can reduce the aircraft's capability to recover from stalls and spins. The elevator may not have enough power in a spin to get the nose down so the aircraft can be brought out of its stalled condition. (PLT240) — FAA-H-8083-25

Answer (B) is incorrect because a stall will occur at a lower airspeed, but recovery will be more difficult because of high load factors. Answer (C) is incorrect because a stall will occur at a higher indicated airspeed due to the greater down-loading on the elevator caused by a forward CG location.

Answers

6802 [A]	6803 [B]	6815 [B]	6823 [A]	6816 [A]

AIR, GLI, LSA, MCI

6818. An aircraft is loaded with the CG at the aft limit. What are the performance characteristics compared with the CG at the forward limit?

A— The aft CG provides the highest stall speed and cruising speed.

B— The aft CG provides the lowest stalling speed, the highest cruising speed, and least stability.

C— Cruising speed is lower because of more induced drag created by the elevator or stabilizer being required to provide more lift with an aft CG.

When an aircraft is loaded with its CG at its aft limit, the horizontal tail surfaces will be required to exert the least amount of down-load. This relieves the wing of part of its load and allows it to maintain altitude with a lower angle of attack, decreasing the stall speed. The drag is less, and the aircraft has a faster cruising speed. The disadvantage of having the CG at its aft limit is the decrease in longitudinal stability. (PLT240) — FAA-H-8083-25

Answer (A) is incorrect because an aft CG provides the lowest stall speed. Answer (C) is incorrect because cruise speed is higher with aft CG because of decreased wing loading resulting in decreased drag.

AIR, GLI, LSA, MCI

6821. As the CG moves aft, an aircraft becomes

A— less stable and less controllable.

B— less stable, yet easier to control.

C— more stable and controllable as long as the aft CG is not exceeded.

An aircraft becomes less stable and less controllable as the CG is moved aft. When the CG is at or near its aft limit, the tail surfaces exert less down-load because there is less stabilizing down-pitching moment. (PLT240) — FAA-H-8083-25

AIR, GLI, LSA, MCI

6825. As the CG location is changed, recovery from a stall becomes progressively

A— less difficult as the CG moves rearward.

B— more difficult as the CG moves rearward.

C— more difficult as the CG moves either forward or rearward.

The recovery from a stall in any aircraft becomes progressively more difficult as its center of gravity moves rearward. In order to lower the nose to recover from a stall, an aerodynamic force must be produced by the elevators to raise the tail and lower the nose. If the CG is too far aft, the elevators may not have enough power with the low airspeed to get the nose down. (PLT240) — FAA-H-8083-25

AIR, GLI, LSA, MCI

6826. What is the effect of center of gravity on the spin characteristics of a fixed-wing aircraft? If the CG is too far

A— aft, a flat spin may develop.

B— forward, spin entry will be difficult.

C— aft, spins can become high-speed spirals.

The recovery from a stall in any aircraft becomes progressively more difficult as its center of gravity moves aft. This is particularly important in spin recovery, as there is a point in rearward loading of any aircraft at which a flat spin will develop. (PLT245) — FAA-H-8083-25

Answer (B) is incorrect because stall speed is higher with a forward CG, making spin entry easier. Answer (C) is incorrect because the wings are not stalled in a high-speed spiral.

AIR, GLI, LSA, MCI

6817. The stalling speed of an aircraft will be highest when the aircraft is loaded with a

A— high gross weight and aft CG.

B— low gross weight and forward CG.

C— high gross weight and forward CG.

A high gross weight and a forward CG will increase the stall speed of an aircraft. The additional downward force produced by the stabilizer to overcome the nose-down pitching tendency increases the wing loading, causing the stalling angle of attack to be reached at a higher speed. (PLT312) — FAA-H-8083-25

Answer (A) is incorrect because a forward CG increases the stalling speed. Answer (B) is incorrect because high gross weight increases the stalling speed.

Answers

| 6818 | [B] | 6821 | [A] | 6825 | [B] | 6826 | [A] | 6817 | [C] |

AIR, GLI, LSA, MCI

6819. If the CG of an aircraft is moved from the aft limit to beyond the forward limit, how will it affect the cruising and stalling speed?

A— Increase both the cruising speed and stalling speed.

B— Decrease both the cruising speed and stalling speed.

C— Decrease the cruising speed and increase the stalling speed.

Moving the CG from the aft limit to beyond the forward limit will cause the aircraft to stall at a higher speed, and the aircraft will cruise at a slower airspeed. The additional downward force produced by the stabilizer to overcome the nose-down pitching tendency increases the wing loading, causing the stalling angle of attack to be reached at a higher speed. The aircraft will cruise slower because the additional downward tail load increases the wing loading, requiring a higher angle of attack which increases induced drag. (PLT240) — FAA-H-8083-25

Answers (A) and (B) are incorrect because cruise speed is decreased, and stall speed is increased, with a forward CG.

AIR, GLI, LSA, MCI

6820. When an aircraft's forward CG limit is exceeded, it will affect the flight characteristics of the aircraft by producing

A— improved performance since it reduces the induced drag.

B— higher stalling speeds and more longitudinal stability.

C— very light elevator control forces which make it easy to inadvertently overstress the aircraft.

A CG location ahead of the forward limit will cause the aircraft to stall at a higher speed, because the additional downward force produced by the stabilizer to overcome the nose-down pitching tendency increases the wing loading, causing the stalling angle of attack to be reached at a higher speed. One advantage of a forward CG location is that an aircraft becomes more longitudinally stable as the CG is moved forward. The forward CG increases the tendency for the nose to drop as the airspeed decreases. (PLT240) — FAA-H-8083-25

AIR, GLI, LSA, MCI

6822. What is characteristic of the indicated airspeed if the CG is at the most forward allowable position and constant power and altitude are maintained?

A— There is no relationship between CG location and indicated airspeed.

B— Indicated airspeed will be less than it would be with the CG in the most rearward allowable position.

C— Indicated airspeed will be greater than it would be with the CG in the most rearward allowable position.

When an aircraft is loaded at its most forward CG location, nose-up trim is needed to maintain level cruising flight. Nose-up trim causes the tail surfaces to produce a greater down-load on the aft portion of the fuselage, and this adds to the wing loading and increases the total lift the wing must produce in order to maintain altitude. When the wing flies at a higher angle of attack to produce the extra lift, it produces more induced drag. The indicated airspeed for a constant power and altitude will be lower if the CG is at the forward limits than it would be if the CG were further aft. (PLT240) — FAA-H-8083-25

Answer (A) is incorrect because CG location affects indicated airspeed. Answer (C) is incorrect because the airspeed will be less with a forward CG.

AIR, GLI, WSC, LSA, MCI

6824. Under which condition is a forward CG most critical?

A— On takeoff.

B— On landing.

C— When in an unusual attitude.

Forward CG is most critical during landing. If it is too far forward, the elevators may not have enough power to get the tail down for a proper approach and flare. (PLT240) — FAA-H-8083-25

Answers

6819 [C]   6820 [B]   6822 [B]   6824 [B]

The Law of the Lever

Weight and balance problems are based on the physical law of the lever. This law states that a lever is balanced when the weight on one side of the fulcrum multiplied by its arm is equal to the weight on the opposite side multiplied by its arm. In other words, the lever is balanced when the algebraic sum of the moments about the fulcrum is zero. This is the condition in which the positive moments (those that try to rotate the lever clockwise) are equal to the negative moments (those that try to rotate it counter-clockwise).

Weight A × Arm A = Weight B × Arm B

Problem:

Item	Weight (lbs)	Arm (in)	Moment (lb-in)
Weight A	90	-50	-4,500
Weight B	?	-25	+4,500
			0

Solution:

Weight B × 25 = 4,500

4,500 ÷ 25 = Weight B

Weight B = 180 lbs

A common weight and balance problem involves shifting the CG by moving around passengers or cargo. This can be solved by a simple math equation:

$$\text{Distance Weight is Shifted} = \frac{\text{Total Weight} \times \text{Change in CG}}{\text{Weight Shifted}}$$

ALL

6776. (Refer to Figure 32.) What weight must be placed at B to balance the lever if A = 40?

A— 20 lbs
B— 40 lbs
C— 80 lbs

Law of the Lever: Weight A × Arm A = Weight B × Arm B

Tip: For the purpose of solving the problem, disregard the negative and refer to both arms as positive.

1. *Find the moment with the given information, Weight A = 40 lbs, Arm A = 50*

   40 × 50 = 2,000 in-lb

2. *Solve for Weight B:*

   2,000 = Weight B × 25

   2,000 ÷ 25 = Weight B

   Weight B = 80 lbs

Check your math to verify: to simplify Steps 1 and 2, we removed the notation of negative and referred to both arms as positive, understanding that the end solution will include both a negative moment and positive moment. The lever is balanced when the algebraic sum of both moments is equal to zero, – (Side A) and + (Side B).

   40 lbs × -50 in-lbs = -2,000 (Side A)
   80 lbs × 25 in-lbs = 2,000 (Side B)
   -2,000 + 2,000 = 0 (The fulcrum is balanced.)

(PLT021) — FAA-H-8083-1

Answers

6776   [C]

ALL
6777. (Refer to Figure 32.) What weight must be placed at A to balance the lever if B = 150?

A— 75 lbs
B— 300 lbs
C— 80 lbs

Law of the Lever: Weight A × Arm A = Weight B × Arm B

Tip: For the purpose of solving the problem, disregard the negative and refer to both arms as positive.

1. Find the moment with the given information, Weight B = 150 lbs, Arm B = 25

    150 × 25 = 3,750 in-lb

2. Next solve for Weight A:

    3,750 = Weight A × 50

    3,750 ÷ 50 = Weight A

    Weight A = 75 lbs

Check your math to verify: to simplify Steps 1 and 2, we removed the notation of negative and referred to both arms as positive, understanding that the end solution will include both a negative moment and positive moment. The lever is balanced when the algebraic sum of both moments is equal to zero, – (Side A) and + (Side B).

    75 lbs × -50 in-lb = -3,750 (Side A)
    150 lbs × 25 in-lb = 3,750 (Side B)
    -3,750 + 3,750 = 0 (The fulcrum is balanced.)

(PLT021) — FAA-H-8083-1

ALL
6778. (Refer to Figure 33.) GIVEN: A = 100, B = 200, C = 200. To obtain a new CG of 50, Weight B must be shifted

A— 55 inches right.
B— 22 inches left.
C— 55 inches left.

Distance Weight B is shifted = (Total Weight × Change in CG) ÷ Weight Shifted

1. Determine how much the CG is being moved: 72 to 50 = -22 inches left; this is the change in CG.

2. Distance Weight B is shifted = (500 × -22) ÷ 200

3. Distance Weight B is shifted = -55, or 55 inches to the left.

(PLT021) — FAA-H-8083-1

Answer (A) is incorrect because moving weight B to the right results in a positive increase in CG. Answer (B) is incorrect because 22 inches left is the change in CG from old to new.

ALL
6779. (Refer to Figure 33.) GIVEN: A = 100, B = 200, C = 200. Shifting the CG to 80 requires moving weight B

A— 20 inches right.
B— 20 inches left.
C— to a datum of 120 inches.

Distance Weight B is shifted = (Total Weight × Change in CG) ÷ Weight Shifted

1. Determine how much the CG is being moved: 72 to 80 = 8 inches right; this is the change in CG.

2. Distance Weight B is shifted = (500 × 8) ÷ 200

3. Distance Weight B is shifted = 20, or 20 inches to the right.

Because both weights B and C weigh the same, either weight may be moved 20 inches to the right to shift the CG from 72 to 80. (PLT021) — FAA-H-8083-1

Answer (B) is incorrect because moving weight B 20 inches left results in a CG less than 72. Answer (C) is incorrect because moving weight C (not B) to a new datum of 120 inches would result in the CG becoming 80.

ALL
6780. (Refer to Figure 34.) GIVEN: A = 500, B = 200, C = 400. To balance the board about its center, weight B needs to be moved

A— 25 inches right.
B— 50 inches right.
C— to an arm of 50.

Remember, the board is balanced when the sum of all moments equals 0 (Left = Right).

Item	Weight (lbs)	Arm (in)	Moment (lb-in)
Weight A	500	-50	-25,000
Weight B	200	?	?
Weight C	400	50	+20,000

1. Determine the moment for the given Weights A and C.

2. The right side of the board will require an additional 5,000 lbs-in moment to equal the left.

3. Determine the arm for Weight B by dividing the required moment by weight (5,000 ÷ 200 = 25).

To balance the board Weight B will need to be moved +50 inches right from -25 to +25. (PLT021) — FAA-H-8083-1

Answer (A) is incorrect because moving weight B 25 inches right results in an arm of 0. Answer (C) is incorrect because moving weight B to an arm of 50 results in a sum of all moments of 5,000.

Answers

6777 [A]   6778 [C]   6779 [A]   6780 [B]

ALL

6781. (Refer to Figure 34.) GIVEN: A = 300, B = 375, C = 600. To balance the board about its center, Weight B needs to be moved

A— 15 inches right.
B— to an arm of 40.
C— 15 inches left.

Remember, the board is balanced when the sum of all moments equals 0 (Left = Right).

Item	Weight (lbs)	Arm (in)	Moment (lb-in)
Weight A	300	-50	-15,000
Weight B	375	?	?
Weight C	600	50	+30,000

1. Determine the moment for the given Weights A and C.

2. The left side of the board will require an additional -15,000 lbs-in moment to equal the right.

3. Determine the arm for weight B by dividing the required moment by weight (-15,000 ÷ 375 = -40).

To balance the board weight B will need to be moved -15 inches left from -25 to -40. (PLT021) — FAA-H-8083-1

Answer (A) is incorrect because moving weight B 15 inches right results in an arm of -10. Answer (B) is incorrect because an arm of 40 would increase the moment on the right side.

ALL

6782. (Refer to Figure 35.) If 50 pounds of weight is located at point X and 100 pounds at point Z, how much weight must be located at point Y to balance the plank?

A— 30 pounds.
B— 50 pounds.
C— 300 pounds.

Find the moments left and right of the fulcrum, and set them equal to one another:

left = right
50(50) + Y(25) = 100(100)
2,500 + 25Y = 10,000
25Y = 7,500
Y = 300 pounds

(PLT021) — FAA-H-8083-25

ALL

6783. (Refer to Figure 35.) If 50 pounds of weight is located at point X and 100 pounds at point Y, how much weight must be located at point Z to balance the plank?

A— 150 pounds.
B— 100 pounds.
C— 50 pounds.

Find the moments left and right of the fulcrum, and set them equal to one another:

left = right
50(50) + 100(25) = Z(100)
5,000 = 100Z
Z = 50 pounds

(PLT021) — FAA-H-8083-25

ALL

6784. (Refer to Figure 35.) If 50-pound weights are located at points X, Y, and Z, how would point Z have to be shifted to balance the plank?

A— 25 inches to the left.
B— 2.5 inches to the left.
C— 2.5 inches to the right.

1. Find the moments left and right of the fulcrum, and set them equal to one another:

    left = right
    50(50) + 50(25) = 50(Z)
    3,750 = 50Z
    Z = 75 inches

2. The 50-pound weight must be 75 inches from the fulcrum to be in balance. It is currently located at 100 inches, therefore the weight should be shifted 25 inches to the left.

(PLT021) — FAA-H-8083-25

Answers

6781 [C]	6782 [C]	6783 [C]	6784 [A]

Finding the Center of Gravity

The **datum** is a location specified by the manufacturer of an aircraft from which all measurements are made to determine the weight and balance of an aircraft. The datum may be located anywhere. Commonly used datum locations are:

- Leading edge of the wing
- Center line of the main spar
- A given distance ahead of the nose of the aircraft

Locating the datum ahead of the nose of the aircraft makes all moments positive and prevents many arithmetic errors.

In weight and balance problems, weight is specified in pounds, and the arm is specified in inches. The **moment** is the product of the distance between the item and the datum multiplied by the weight of the item. It is expressed in **pound-inches**. The arm of each item is its distance from the datum in inches. Find the total weight and the total moment and divide the total moment by the total weight to find the distance from the datum to the center of gravity.

Problem:

Find the center of gravity when this information is known.

Weight A	120 lbs	at 15" aft of datum
Weight B	200 lbs	at 117" aft of datum
Weight C	75 lbs	at 195" aft of datum

Solution:

Make a table:

Item	Weight	Arm	Moment
Weight A	120	15	1,800
Weight B	200	117	23,400
Weight C	+75	195	+14,625
Totals	395		39,825

CG = Total Moment ÷ Total Weight

39,825 ÷ 395 = 100.8 inches from the datum

This problem can also be quickly and accurately worked on the CX-2 Pathfinder electronic flight computer:

1. Define problem to have 3 items and a reduction factor of 1.
2. Enter the WT/Arm program.
3. Enter the Weight A of 120 pounds.
4. Enter the Arm of 15.
5. Enter Weight B of 200 pounds.
6. Enter the Arm of B, which is 117.
7. Enter Weight C of 75 pounds.
8. Enter the Arm of C, which is 195.

Continued

9. The total weight of 395 pounds and the CG of 100.8 appear on the display. The CG is located 100.8 inches aft of the datum.

To find the CG of an airplane using the charts of FAA Figure 36, compile the same "Weight x Arm = Moment" chart previously used. To find the moments not given in the charts, multiply the weight by the arms that are given and divide by 100:

Item	Weight		Moment
Airplane	2,110		1,652
Pilot & front seat	375	x 85/100	319
Rear passengers (aft)	245	x 136/100	333
Baggage	65	x 150/100	98
Fuel (70 gal.)	+420		+315
Totals	3,215		2,717

The allowable gross weight of the airplane as shown in the **Gross Weight Moment Limits** Chart is 3,400 pounds. The airplane, as loaded, weighs 3,215 pounds, which is 185 pounds under the allowable gross weight.

In the Gross Weight Moment Limits Chart, follow a line representing 3,215 pounds to the left until it intersects the diagonal line representing the 2,717 inch-pound moment/100. This intersection is within the envelope, which means that the CG is located within the allowable limits.

To work this type of problem on the CX-2 Pathfinder electronic flight computer:

1. Multiply the empty weight moment of 1,652 by the reduction factor of 100 to get the moment of 165,200. Divide this by the empty weight of 2,110 to get the **empty weight center of gravity** (EWCG) of 78.29 inches.

2. Enter the WT/Arm program. Enter the airplane weight empty of 2,110 pounds.

3. Enter the airplane EWCG of 78.29.

4. We are using the default reduction factor of 1; enter the weight of the pilot and front seat passenger of 375 pounds.

5. Enter the arm of the front seats, which is 85.

6. Enter the weight of the rear seat occupants of 245.

7. Enter the arm of the rear seat in the aft position, which is 136.

8. Enter the weight of the baggage, which is 65 pounds.

9. Enter the arm of the baggage, which is 150.

10. Enter the weight of the fuel (70 x 6 = 420).

11. Enter the arm of the fuel, which is 75.

12. Read the gross weight of 3,215 pounds. The allowable gross weight is 3,400, so the airplane is 185 pounds under the allowable gross weight.

13. The CG of 84.5 appears on the display. In the Gross Weight Moment Limits Chart, follow the dashed line, parallel to the existing lines, upward from the 84.5 inch CG, until it crosses a horizontal line for 3,215 pounds. This intersection is inside the heavy lines, indicating that the CG at this weight is within allowable limits.

AIR, LSA, MCI

6785. Based on this information, the CG would be located how far aft of datum?

Weight A .... 120 lb at 15" aft of datum
Weight B .... 200 lb at 117" aft of datum
Weight C .... 75 lb at 195" aft of datum

A— 100.8 inches.
B— 109.0 inches.
C— 121.7 inches.

1. Multiply weight x arm to find the moments, and find the total weight and moment:

Item	Weight	Arm	Moment
Weight A	120	15	1,800
Weight B	200	117	23,400
Weight C	+75	195	+14,625
Totals	395		39,825

2. Divide the total moment by the total weight to find the CG:
> CG = Total Moment ÷ Total Weight
> 39,825 ÷ 395 = 100.8 inches

(PLT021) — FAA-H-8083-25

AIR, LSA, MCI

6786. Based on this information, the CG would be located how far aft of datum?

Weight D .... 160 lb at 45" aft of datum
Weight E .... 170 lb at 145" aft of datum
Weight F .... 105 lb at 185" aft of datum

A— 86.0 inches.
B— 117.8 inches.
C— 125.0 inches.

1. Multiply weight x arm to find the moments, and find the total weight and moment:

Item	Weight	Arm	Moment
Weight D	160	45	7,200
Weight E	170	145	24,650
Weight F	+105	185	+19,425
Totals	435		51,275

2. Divide the total moment by the total weight to find the CG:
> CG = Total Moment ÷ Total Weight
> 51,275 ÷ 435 = 117.9 inches

(PLT021) — FAA-H-8083-25

AIR, LSA, MCI

6787. Based on this information, the CG would be located how far aft of datum?

Weight X .... 130 lb at 17" aft of datum
Weight Y .... 110 lb at 110" aft of datum
Weight Z .... 75 lb at 210" aft of datum

A— 89.1 inches.
B— 95.4 inches.
C— 106.9 inches.

1. Multiply weight x arm to find the moments, and find the total weight and moment:

Item	Weight	Arm	Moment
Weight A	130	17	2,210
Weight B	110	110	12,100
Weight C	+75	210	+15,750
Totals	315		30,060

2. Divide the total moment by the total weight to find the CG:
> CG = Total Moment ÷ Total Weight
> 30,060 ÷ 315 = 95.4 inches

(PLT021) — FAA-H-8083-25

AIR, LSA, MCI

6799. (Refer to Figure 36.) Determine the condition of the airplane:

Pilot and copilot .... 375 lb
Passengers – aft position .... 245 lb
Baggage .... 65 lb
Fuel .... 70 gal

A— 185 pounds under allowable gross weight; CG is located within limits.
B— 162 pounds under allowable gross weight; CG is located within limits.
C— 162 pounds under allowable gross weight; CG is located aft of the aft limit.

1. Calculate the total weight and moment. To find the moments not given in the charts, multiply the weight by the arms that are given and divide by 100:

Item	Weight	Arm	Moment
Airplane	2,110		1,652
Pilot & front seat	375	x 85/100	319
Passengers (aft)	245	x 136/100	333
Baggage	65	x 150/100	98
Fuel (70 gal.)	+420		+315
Totals	3,215		2,717

Continued

---

2. The allowable gross weight of the airplane as shown in the Gross Weight Moment Limits Chart is 3,400 pounds. The airplane, as loaded, weighs 3,215 pounds, which is 185 pounds under the allowable gross weight.

3. In the Gross Weight Moment Limits Chart, follow a line representing 3,215 pounds to the left until it intersects the diagonal line representing the 2,717 inch-pound moment/100. This intersection is within the envelope, which means that the CG is located within the allowable limits.

(PLT021) — FAA-H-8083-25

AIR, LSA, MCI
6800. (Refer to Figure 36.) Determine the condition of the airplane:

Pilot and copilot .... 400 lb
Passengers – aft position .... 240 lb
Baggage .... 20 lb
Fuel... 75 gal

A— 157 pounds under allowable gross weight; CG is located within limits.

B— 180 pounds under allowable gross weight; CG is located within limits.

C— 180 pounds under allowable gross weight, but CG is located aft of the aft limit.

1. Calculate the total weight and moment. To find the moments that are not given in the charts, multiply the weight by the arms that are given and divide by 100:

Item	Weight	Arm	Moment
Airplane	2,110		1,652
Pilot & copilot	400		340
Passengers (aft)	240	x 136.0/100	326
Baggage	20		30
Fuel (75 gal.)	+450		+338
Totals	3,220		2,686

2. The maximum allowable gross weight of the aircraft as shown in the Gross Weight Moment Limits Chart is 3,400 pounds. The airplane, as loaded, weighs 3,220 pounds, which is 180 pounds under the allowable gross weight.

3. In the Gross Weight Moment Limits Chart, follow a line representing 3,220 pounds over to the left until it intersects the diagonal line representing the 2,686 inch-pound moment/100. This intersection is within the envelope, which means that the CG is located within limits.

(PLT021) — FAA-H-8083-25

AIR, LSA, MCI
6801. (Refer to Figure 36.) Determine the condition of the airplane:

Pilot and copilot .... 316 lb
Passengers (rear)
   Fwd... 130 lb
   Aft .... 147 lb
Baggage .... 50 lb
Fuel... 75 gal

A— 163 pounds under allowable gross weight; CG 82 inches aft of datum.

B— 197 pounds under allowable gross weight; CG 83.6 inches aft of datum.

C— 197 pounds under allowable gross weight; CG 84.6 inches aft of datum.

1. Calculate the total weight and moment. To find the moments that are not given in the charts, multiply the weight by the arms that are given and divide by 100:

Item	Weight	Arm	Moment
Airplane	2,110		1,652
Pilot & copilot	316	x 85.0/100	268.6
Rear passenger (fwd)	130	x 111.0/100	144.3
Rear passenger (aft)	147	x 136.0/100	199.92
Baggage	50		75
Fuel (75 gal.)	+450		+338
Totals	3,203		2,677.82

2. The maximum allowable gross weight of the aircraft as shown in the Gross Weight Moment Limits Chart is 3,400 pounds. The airplane, as loaded, weighs 3,203 pounds, which is 198 pounds under the allowable gross weight.

3. In the Gross Weight Moment Limits Chart, follow a line representing 3,203 pounds over to the left until it intersects the diagonal line representing the 2,690 inch-pound moment/100. The CG under these loading conditions is 84.0 inches aft of the datum.

4. Double-check the graph using the formula:

$$\frac{M}{W} = CG \qquad \frac{2,677.82}{3,203} \times 100 = 83.6$$

(PLT021) — FAA-H-8083-25

Answers

6800   **[B]**   6801   **[B]**

AIR, LSA, MCI

6801-1. (Refer to Figure 36.) What effect does a 35-gallon fuel burn (main tanks) have on the weight and balance if the airplane weighed 2,890 pounds and the MOM/100 was 2,452 at takeoff?

A— Weight is reduced by 210 pounds and the CG is aft of limits.

B— Weight is reduced by 210 pounds and the CG is unaffected.

C— Weight is reduced to 2,680 pounds and the CG moves forward.

The original CG is 2,452 / 2,890 = 85. Figure 36 includes a table summarizing fuel weights and moments. Burning 35 gallons of fuel will result in a 210 pound reduction, making the new airplane weigh 2,680 pounds (2,890 – 210). The moment is reduced by 158, making the new MOM/100 = 2,294. The new CG is 2,294 / 2,680 = 86, which moves the CG aft of limits. (PLT021) — FAA-H-8083-25

Weight to be Added or Removed

The amount of weight needed to be added or removed at a particular station to move the CG to a specific location can be found by using these steps.

Problem:

The aircraft weighs 2,900 pounds. CG location is at station 115.0. Aft CG limit is at station 116.0. What is the maximum weight which can be added at station 130.0 without exceeding the aft CG limit?

Solution:

The formula to use for this problem is:

$$\frac{\text{Weight to be added or removed}}{\text{Old total weight}} = \frac{\text{Change in CG}}{\text{Distance from weight to new CG}}$$

Rearrange the formula:

$$\text{Weight to be added or removed} = \frac{\text{Old total weight x change in CG}}{\text{Distance from weight to new CG}}$$

$$\frac{2,900 \times (116.0 - 115.0)}{(130.0 - 116.0)}$$

$$\frac{2,900}{14} = 207 \text{ pounds}$$

Problem:

Find the new location of the CG after a given weight is added or removed:

1. Find the new location of the CG after 90 pounds are removed from Station 140.

2. Aircraft weight is 6,230 pounds.

3. CG location is Station 79.

Continued

Answers

6801-1   [A]

Solution:

1. Make a chart similar to this:

Item	Weight	Arm	Moment
Airplane	6,230	79.0	492,170
Weight	−90	140.0	−12,600
New Totals	6,140		479,570

2. To find the new CG, divide the new total moment by the new total weight:

CG = Moment ÷ Weight

479,570 ÷ 6,140 = 78.1

The CG after the removal of the weight is located at station 78.1.

This problem can be worked quickly and accurately on the CX-2 Pathfinder electronic flight computer:

1. Define the problem to have 2 items and a reduction factor of 1.
2. Enter the WT/Arm program.
3. Enter the aircraft weight of 6,230 pounds.
4. Enter the CG location of Station 79.
5. Enter weight to be removed of -90 pounds.
6. Enter the station from which the weight was removed, Station 140.
7. The new aircraft weight of 6,140 pounds and the new CG of 78.1 appear on the display. The CG is now located at Station 78.1.

AIR, LSA, MCI

6788. What is the maximum weight that could be added at Station 130.0 without exceeding the aft CG limit?

Total weight... 2,900 lb
CG location... Station 115.0
Aft CG limit .... Station 116.0

A— 14 pounds.
B— 140 pounds.
C— 207 pounds.

$$\frac{\text{Weight to be added or removed}}{\text{Old total weight}} = \frac{\text{Change in CG}}{\text{Distance from weight to new CG}}$$

Rearrange the formula:

$$\text{Weight to be added or removed} = \frac{\text{Old total weight} \times \text{change in CG}}{\text{Distance from weight to new CG}}$$

$$\frac{2{,}900 \times (116.0 - 115.0)}{(130.0 - 116.0)}$$

$$\frac{2{,}900}{14} = 207 \text{ pounds}$$

(PLT021) — FAA-H-8083-25

AIR, LSA, MCI

6790. How much weight could be added at Station 160 without exceeding the aft CG limit?

Aircraft weight.. 8,300 lb
CG location.. Station 90.0
Aft CG limit .... Station 90.5

A— 59.7 pounds.
B— 16.5 pounds.
C— 13.9 pounds.

$$\frac{\text{Weight to be added}}{\text{Old total weight}} = \frac{\text{Change in CG}}{\substack{\text{Distance from weight} \\ \text{to new CG}}}$$

Rearrange the formula:

$$\text{Weight to be added or removed} = \frac{\text{Old total weight} \times \text{change in CG}}{\substack{\text{Distance from weight} \\ \text{to new CG}}}$$

$$\frac{8,300 \times (90.5 - 90.0)}{(160 - 90.5)}$$

$$\frac{4,150}{69.5} = 59.7 \text{ pounds}$$

(PLT021) — FAA-H-8083-25

AIR, LSA, MCI

6791. How much weight could be added at Station 120 without exceeding the aft CG limit?

Aircraft weight.. 9,500 lb
CG location.. Station 90.0
Aft CG limit .... Station 90.5

A— 61.0 pounds.
B— 110.5 pounds.
C— 161.0 pounds.

$$\frac{\text{Weight to be added or removed}}{\text{Old total weight}} = \frac{\text{Change in CG}}{\substack{\text{Distance from weight} \\ \text{to new CG}}}$$

Rearrange the formula:

$$\text{Weight to be added or removed} = \frac{\text{Old total weight} \times \text{change in CG}}{\substack{\text{Distance from weight} \\ \text{to new CG}}}$$

$$\frac{9,500 \times (90.5 - 90.0)}{(120 - 90.5)}$$

$$\frac{4,750}{29.5} = 161.0 \text{ pounds}$$

(PLT021) — FAA-H-8083-25

AIR, LSA, MCI

6792. What is the maximum weight that could be added at Station 150.0 without exceeding the aft CG limit?

Aircraft weight.. 5,000 lb
CG location.. Station 80.0
Aft CG limit .... Station 80.5

A— 70.0 pounds.
B— 69.5 pounds.
C— 35.9 pounds.

$$\frac{\text{Weight to be added or removed}}{\text{Old total weight}} = \frac{\text{Change in CG}}{\substack{\text{Distance from weight} \\ \text{to new CG}}}$$

Rearrange the formula:

$$\text{Weight to be added or removed} = \frac{\text{Old total weight} \times \text{change in CG}}{\substack{\text{Distance from weight} \\ \text{to new CG}}}$$

$$\frac{5,000 \times (80.5 - 80.0)}{(150 - 80.5)}$$

$$\frac{2,500}{69.5} = 35.9 \text{ pounds}$$

(PLT021) — FAA-H-8083-25

Answers

6790 [A]   6791 [C]   6792 [C]

AIR, LSA, MCI

6793. What is the location of the CG if 90 pounds are removed from Station 140?

Aircraft weight.. 6,230 lb
CG location... Station 79

A— 79.9.
B— 78.1.
C— 77.9.

1. Calculate the new weight and moment:

Item	Weight	Arm	Moment
Airplane	6,230	79.0	492,170
Weight	−90	140.0	−12,600
New Totals	6,140		479,570

2. To find the new CG, divide the new total moment by the new total weight:
   CG = Moment ÷ Weight
   479,570 ÷ 6,140 = 78.1

(PLT021) — FAA-H-8083-25

AIR, LSA, MCI

6794. What is the location of the CG if 146 pounds are removed from Station 150?

Aircraft weight.. 7,152 lb
CG location... Station 82

A— 83.4.
B— 81.3.
C— 80.6.

1. Calculate the new weight and moment:

Item	Weight	Arm	Moment
Airplane	7,152	82.0	586,464
Weight	−146	150.0	−21,900
New Totals	7,006		564,564

2. To find the new CG, divide the new total moment by the new total weight:
   CG = Moment ÷ Weight
   564,564 ÷ 7,006 = 80.6

(PLT021) — FAA-H-8083-25

AIR, LSA, MCI

6789. What would be the new CG location if 135 pounds of weight were added at Station 109.0?

Total weight... 2,340 lb
CG location... Station 103.0

A— Station 103.3.
B— Station 104.2.
C— Station 109.3.

1. Calculate the new weight and moment:

Item	Weight	Arm	Moment
Airplane	2,340	103.0	241,020
Weight	+135	109.0	+14,715
New Totals	2,475		255,735

2. To find the new CG, divide the new total moment by the new total weight:
   CG = Moment ÷ Weight
   255,735 ÷ 2,475 = 103.33

(PLT021) — FAA-H-8083-25

AIR, LSA, MCI

6795. What is the location of the CG if 60 pounds are removed from Station 70?

Aircraft weight.. 8,420 lb
CG location... Station 85

A— 85.1.
B— 84.9.
C— 84.1.

1. Calculate the new weight and moment:

Item	Weight	Arm	Moment
Airplane	8,420	85.0	715,700
Weight	−60	70.0	−4,200
New Totals	8,360		711,500

2. To find the new CG, divide the new total moment by the new total weight:
   CG = Moment ÷ Weight
   711,500 ÷ 8,360 = 85.1

(PLT021) — FAA-H-8083-25

Answers

6793 [B]   6789 [A]   6794 [C]   6795 [A]

Weight to be Shifted

The amount of weight that must be shifted to move the CG to a desired location may be found by using this formula:

$$\frac{\text{Weight to be shifted}}{\text{Old total weight}} = \frac{\text{Change in CG}}{\text{Distance weight is shifted}}$$

Rearrange the formula:

$$\text{Weight to be shifted} = \frac{\text{Total weight x change in CG}}{\text{Distance weight is shifted}}$$

$$\frac{7{,}500 \times (80.5 - 79.5)}{(150.0 - 30.0)}$$

$$\frac{7{,}500}{120.0} = 62.5 \text{ pounds}$$

This formula can also be arranged to find the new CG after a weight is shifted by rearranging it as:

$$\text{Change in CG} = \frac{\text{Weight to be shifted x Distance weight is shifted}}{\text{Total Weight}}$$

$$= \frac{100 \times 100}{2800}$$

$$= 3.57 \text{ inches}$$

To work this type of problem on the CX-2 Pathfinder electronic flight computer:

1. Define the problem to have 3 items and a reduction factor of 1.
2. Enter the WT/Arm program.
3. Enter the aircraft weight of 2,800 pounds.
4. Enter the CG location of Station 120.0.
5. Enter weight to be shifted by first removing it from its old location and adding it to the new location. Enter the removed weight of -100 pounds.
6. Enter the station from which the weight was removed, Station 130.0.
7. Enter the weight of +100 pounds.
8. Enter the station to which the weight is being moved, which is 30.0.
9. The new CG of 116.4 appears on the display. The CG is now located at Station 116.4, which is ahead of the allowable forward CG limit of 117.0.

6796. How much weight must be shifted from Station 150.0 to Station 30.0 to move the CG to exactly the aft CG limit?

Total weight.. 7,500 lb
CG location...Station 80.5
Aft CG limit ....Station 79.5

A— 68.9 pounds.
B— 65.8 pounds.
C— 62.5 pounds.

$$\text{Weight to be shifted} = \frac{\text{Total weight} \times \text{change in CG}}{\text{Distance weight is shifted}}$$

$$\frac{7,500 \times (80.5 - 79.5)}{(150.0 - 30.0)}$$

$$\frac{7,500}{120.0} = 62.5 \text{ pounds}$$

(PLT021) — FAA-H-8083-25

6797. Could 100 pounds of weight be shifted from Station 130.0 to Station 30.0 without exceeding the forward CG limit?

Total weight.. 2,800 lb
CG location...Station 120.0
Forward CG limit...................................Station 117.0

A— No; the new CG would be located at Station 116.89.
B— No; the new CG would be located at Station 116.42.
C— Yes; the new CG would be located at Station 117.89.

This formula can also be arranged to find the new CG after a weight is shifted by rearranging it as:

$$\text{Change in CG} = \frac{\text{Weight to be shifted} \times \text{Distance weight is shifted}}{\text{Total Weight}}$$

$$= \frac{100 \times 100}{2,800}$$

$$= 3.57 \text{ inches}$$

The CG is shifted forward 3.57 inches, which moves it to 116.43 inches aft of the datum. This is ahead of the allowable forward limit of 117.0 inches. (PLT021) — FAA-H-8083-25

6798. Could 100 pounds of weight be shifted from Station 30.0 to Station 120.0 without exceeding the aft CG limit?

Total weight.. 4,750 lb
CG location...Station 115.8
Aft CG limit ....Station 118.0

A— Yes; the CG would remain at Station 115.8.
B— No; the new CG would be located at Station 118.15.
C— Yes; the new CG would be located at Station 117.69.

This formula can also be arranged to find the new CG after a weight is shifted by rearranging it as:

$$\text{Change in CG} = \frac{\text{Weight to be shifted} \times \text{Distance weight is shifted}}{\text{Total Weight}}$$

$$= \frac{100 \times 90}{4,750}$$

$$= 1.89 \text{ inches}$$

The CG is shifted aft 1.89 inches which moves it to 117.69 inches aft of the datum, which is ahead of the allowable aft limit of 118.0 inches. (PLT021) — FAA-H-8083-25

Answers

6796   [C]   6797   [B]   6798   [C]

Helicopter Weight and Balance

If a helicopter is loaded with its CG aft of the allowable limits, it will have a tail-low attitude, and will require an excessive forward displacement of the cyclic stick to maintain the desired position over the ground while hovering in a no-wind condition. It may even be impossible to hover. This situation will be aggravated if the fuel tanks are located forward of the CG, because, as fuel is used from these tanks, the CG will shift further aft.

With the CG aft of the limit, it may not be possible to fly in the upper allowable airspeed range, because there is not enough forward cyclic displacement to maintain the necessary nose-low attitude. The helicopter will be dangerous to fly in gusty or rough air. If it should pitch up because of gusty winds during high-speed flight, the nose will start to rise, and full forward cyclic stick may not be sufficient to hold it down, or to lower it once it rises.

RTC

6827-1. If the CG is located aft of allowable limits, the pilot may find it impossible to

A— raise the nose, if necessary, during flight in gusty wind conditions.

B— recognize this out-of-balance condition when hovering in strong headwinds.

C— fly in the upper allowable airspeed range due to insufficient forward cyclic control.

If a helicopter is loaded with its CG aft of the allowable limits, it will have a tail-low attitude, and it will require an excessive forward displacement of the cyclic stick to maintain a hover in a no-wind condition. It may even be impossible to hover. It may not be possible to fly in the upper allowable airspeed range, because there is not enough forward cyclic displacement to maintain the necessary nose-low attitude. (PLT240) — FAA-H-8083-21

RTC

6827-3. Aft center of gravity in a helicopter limits the

A— ability to stop, flare, or recover from a steep descent.

B— center of pressure travel along the blades.

C— upper allowable airspeed range.

If flight is continued with an aft CG condition, the pilot may find it impossible to fly in the upper allowable airspeed range due to insufficient forward cyclic displacement to maintain a nose-low attitude. (PLT240) — FAA-H-8083-21

RTC

6827-4. Too much forward cyclic during flight is probably due to

A— tendency of the nose to pitch up due to transverse flow effect.

B— excessive forward speed at maximum gross weight.

C— critical aft CG.

A critical aft CG will cause too much forward cyclic stick during flight. (PLT240) — FAA-H-8083-21

RTC

6828. While hovering immediately after lift-off, an excessive amount of forward cyclic is required to maintain the desired position over the ground. If flight is continued, this situation will be

A— aggravated if the fuel tanks are located aft of the CG.

B— unimproved regardless of the location of the fuel tanks.

C— aggravated if the fuel tanks are located forward of the CG.

If a helicopter has an aft CG, the pilot will have to use an excessive amount of forward cyclic stick to maintain the desired position over the ground. This situation will be aggravated if the fuel tanks are located forward of the CG, because, as fuel is used from these tanks, the CG will shift further aft. (PLT240) — FAA-H-8083-21

Answers

6827-1   [C]   6827-3   [C]   6827-4   [C]   6828   [C]

RTC

6829. A helicopter is loaded in such a manner that the CG is located aft of the aft allowable CG limit. Which statement is true about this hazardous situation?

A— In case of an autorotation, sufficient aft cyclic control may not be available to flare properly.

B— This out-of-balance situation would be easily recognized when hovering in a strong headwind.

C— Should the helicopter pitch up due to gusty winds during high-speed flight, there may not be sufficient forward cyclic control available to lower the nose.

When a helicopter is loaded with its CG aft of the allowable limit, it is dangerous to fly in gusty or rough air. If the helicopter should pitch up because of gusty winds during high-speed flight, the nose will start to rise, and full forward cyclic stick may not be sufficient to hold it down or to lower it once it rises. (PLT240) — FAA-H-8083-21

Answers

6829   [C]

Chapter 5
Weather and Weather Services

The Earth's Atmosphere

The earth's atmosphere is a mixture of gases made up primarily of nitrogen and oxygen. The atmosphere is in layers, with each layer having its own characteristics:

Troposphere — This is the layer nearest the surface. It extends upward for about 7 miles, and it has all of our weather because it contains water vapor. Temperature decreases steadily with altitude in the troposphere.

Tropopause — This is the boundary between the troposphere and the stratosphere. The tropopause slopes from about 20,000 feet over the poles to about 65,000 feet over the equator, and it is higher in summer than in winter.

Stratosphere — This is the layer above the troposphere in which there is relatively little change of temperature with altitude, except for a warming trend near the top.

Energy received from the sun is the primary driving force of the weather on the earth. The earth receives energy from the sun in the form of solar radiation. The earth and its atmosphere reflect about 55% of the radiation and absorb the remaining 45%, converting it to heat. The earth in turn radiates energy, and this outgoing radiation is called "terrestrial radiation."

The standard temperature of the atmosphere at mean sea level is 15°C and 59°F. The standard pressure at mean sea level is 29.92 inches of mercury, 1013.2 millibars, and 14.69 pounds per square inch.

ALL
6161. In what part of the atmosphere does most weather occur?

A— Tropopause.
B— Troposphere.
C— Stratosphere.

Most of the weather occurs in the lower layer of our atmosphere, which is called the troposphere. (PLT203) — AC 00-6

ALL
6162. Which is the primary driving force of weather on the Earth?

A— The Sun.
B— Coriolis.
C— Rotation of the Earth.

Energy received from the sun is the primary driving force of the weather on the earth. (PLT492) — AC 00-6

ALL
6173. What are the standard temperature and pressure values for mean sea level?

A— 15°F and 29.92" Hg.
B— 59°C and 29.92 mb.
C— 59°F and 1013.2 mb.

The standard sea level temperature is 15°C (59°F), and the standard sea level atmospheric pressure is 29.92 inches of mercury, or 1013.2 millibars. (PLT206) — AC 00-6

Answers

6161   [B]   6162   [A]   6173   [C]

Temperature, Pressure and Density

Almost all weather is caused by heat transferred to the earth by the sun, through solar radiation. Much of this energy is reradiated, but that which is retained is converted into heat.

The temperature of the air in the troposphere decreases with altitude at a rate of 2°C per 1,000 feet. This is called the **average lapse rate**. There are two other lapse rates that are of interest to pilots: dry adiabatic lapse rate and moist adiabatic lapse rate. The dry adiabatic lapse rate is the change in temperature with altitude for unsaturated air; it is 3°C per 1,000 feet. Moist adiabatic lapse rate is the change in temperature with altitude for saturated air. Because of the condensation of moisture from this air, the moist adiabatic lapse rate is less than the dry adiabatic lapse rate. The actual rate depends upon the dew point of the air. When we know the temperature at any given level and the lapse rate, we can find the freezing level:

1. Find the difference between the existing temperature and freezing temperature (0°C).

2. Divide this difference in temperature by 2 to find the number of thousand feet above the existing level at which the temperature will be 0°C.

A **temperature inversion** is a change in temperature in which the air gets warmer as the altitude increases. A surface inversion occurs when terrestrial radiation on a clear night cools the surface of the land and lowers the temperature of the air immediately above the surface. The air temperature increases with altitude for a few hundred feet. An inversion aloft occurs when a current of warm air aloft overruns cold air near the surface. A low-level temperature inversion with high relative humidity will trap fog, smoke, low clouds, and other restrictions to visibility. The air will normally be smooth in an inversion.

Pressure altitude is the altitude measured above the standard pressure level at sea level of 29.92" of mercury (Hg), or 1013.2 millibars (mb). In the lower levels of the troposphere, the atmospheric pressure decreases approximately 1" Hg for each 1,000-foot increase in altitude. We can find the pressure altitude by setting the barometric scale of the altimeter to 29.92" Hg, or 1013.2 mb, and reading the altimeter indication. We can also compute the approximate pressure altitude by using this standard lapse rate of 1" Hg per 1,000 feet. If the altimeter indicates 1,850 feet when the barometric scale is set to 30.18 inches of mercury, it would indicate 260 feet lower if it were set to the standard sea level pressure of 29.92" Hg.

The density of the air is affected by its temperature, pressure, and moisture content. It is the density of the air that determines the performance of an aircraft engine and the aerodynamic forces that are produced by an airfoil. **Density altitude** is the altitude in standard air where the density is the same as that of the existing air. It is found by correcting pressure altitude for nonstandard temperature. As the density of the air decreases because of an increase in temperature or water vapor, or a decrease in pressure, the density altitude increases. An airspeed indicator is a differential pressure indicator which measures the dynamic pressure of the air. When the density of the air decreases, the static pressure will decrease and the true airspeed will increase.

ALL
6163. The average lapse rate in the troposphere is

A— 2.0°C per 1,000 feet.
B— 3.0°C per 1,000 feet.
C— 5.4°C per 1,000 feet.

The average lapse rate (change in temperature with altitude) is 2°C per 1,000 feet. (PLT203) — AC 00-6

ALL

6166. If the air temperature is +6°C at an elevation of 700 feet and a standard (average) temperature lapse rate exists, what will be the approximate freezing level?

A— 6,700 feet MSL.
B— 3,700 feet MSL.
C— 2,700 feet MSL.

The air temperature is +6°C at an elevation of 700 feet, and the air cools 2°C each thousand feet. For the moisture to freeze, the air must cool to a temperature of 0°C. Its temperature must drop 6°, which will require 3,000 feet. The freezing level will be 3,000 + 700 feet, or 3,700 feet MSL. (PLT492) — AC 00-6

ALL

6167. If the air temperature is +12°C at an elevation of 1,250 feet and a standard (average) temperature lapse rate exists, what will be the approximate freezing level?

A— 7,250 feet MSL.
B— 5,250 feet MSL.
C— 4,250 feet MSL.

The air temperature is +12°C at an elevation of 1,250 feet, and the air cools 2°C each thousand feet. For the moisture to freeze, the air must cool to a temperature of 0°C. This will be 12 ÷ 2 = 6,000 feet above the surface of 1,250 feet (6,000 + 1,250). Therefore, the freezing level is 7,250 feet MSL. (PLT492) — AC 00-6

ALL

6167-1. An increase in temperature with an increase in altitude

A— is indication of an inversion.
B— denotes the beginning of the stratosphere.
C— means a cold front passage.

An increase in temperature with altitude is defined as an inversion; i.e., the lapse rate is inverted. (PLT512) — AC 00-6

ALL

6167-2. A surface inversion can

A— indicate the chance of gusty winds.
B— produce poor visibility.
C— mean an unstable air mass.

A surface inversion can place a strong "lid" above smoke and haze. The result is poor visibility in the lower levels of the atmosphere, especially near industrial areas. (PLT512) — AC00-6

ALL

6164. The most frequent type of ground- or surface-based temperature inversion is that produced by

A— terrestrial radiation on a clear, relatively still night.
B— warm air being lifted rapidly aloft in the vicinity of mountainous terrain.
C— the movement of colder air under warm air or the movement of warm air over cold air.

Terrestrial radiation on a clear night cools the surface of the land and lowers the temperature of the air immediately above the surface. This causes a surface inversion in which the air temperature increases with altitude for a few hundred feet. (PLT301) — AC 00-6

Answer (B) is incorrect because this describes how upslope fog is produced. Answer (C) is incorrect because this describes temperature inversions aloft.

ALL

6165. Which weather conditions should be expected beneath a low-level temperature inversion layer when the relative humidity is high?

A— Light wind shear and poor visibility due to light rain.
B— Smooth air and poor visibility due to fog, haze, or low clouds.
C— Turbulent air and poor visibility due to fog, low stratus type clouds, and showery precipitation.

A low-level temperature inversion with high relative humidity will trap fog, smoke, low clouds, and other restrictions to visibility. The air will normally be smooth in an inversion. (PLT301) — AC 00-6

ALL

6168. An altimeter indicates 1,850 feet MSL when set to 30.18. What is the approximate pressure altitude?

A— 1,590 feet.
B— 1,824 feet.
C— 2,110 feet.

In the lower levels of the troposphere, the atmospheric pressure decreases approximately 1" Hg for each 1,000-foot increase in altitude, and pressure altitude is based on a sea level pressure of 29.92" Hg. If the altimeter indicates 1,850 feet MSL when it is set to 30.18" Hg, it will indicate 260 feet lower when it is set to 29.92" Hg (30.18 – 29.92 = .26). Therefore, the pressure altitude is 1,590 feet (1,850 – 260 = 1,590). (PLT041) — AC 00-6

Answers

6166 [B]	6167 [A]	6167-1 [A]	6167-2 [B]	6164 [A]	6165 [B]
6168 [A]					

ALL

6169. An aircraft is flying at a constant power setting and constant indicated altitude. If the outside air temperature (OAT) increases, true airspeed will

A— increase and true altitude will decrease.
B— increase and true altitude will increase.
C— decrease and true altitude will increase.

True airspeed and true altitude are based on the existing outside air temperature, which affects the density of the air. While flying at a constant power setting and a constant indicated altitude, an increase in OAT will cause the air to become less dense. Both the true airspeed and the true altitude will increase. (PLT127) — AC 00-6

ALL

6170. An aircraft is flying at a constant power setting and constant indicated altitude. If the outside air temperature (OAT) decreases, true airspeed will

A— decrease, and true altitude will decrease.
B— increase, and true altitude will increase.
C— increase, and true altitude will decrease.

True airspeed and true altitude are based on the existing outside air temperature, which affects the density of the air. While flying at a constant power setting and a constant indicated altitude, a decrease in OAT will cause the air to become more dense, and the true airspeed will decrease and the true altitude will be lower than indicated altitude. (PLT206) — AC 00-6

ALL

6171. As density altitude increases, which will occur if a constant indicated airspeed is maintained in a no-wind condition?

A— True airspeed increases; groundspeed decreases.
B— True airspeed decreases; groundspeed decreases.
C— True airspeed increases; groundspeed increases.

True airspeed is based on the density of the air, which is affected by pressure, temperature, and humidity which together determine air density. While flying at a constant indicated airspeed, an increase in density altitude will indicate that the air has become less dense, and the true airspeed as well as ground speed will increase. (PLT127) — AC 00-6

ALL

6172. Density altitude may be determined by correcting

A— true altitude for nonstandard temperature.
B— pressure altitude for nonstandard temperature.
C— indicated altitude for temperature variations.

Density altitude is the altitude in the standard atmosphere where the air density is the same as where you are. Density altitude is found by correcting pressure altitude for nonstandard temperature. (PLT127) — AC 00-6

Wind

Differences in temperature create differences in pressure, and these pressure differences cause winds to blow. We can tell a lot about the wind by studying weather maps that show lines of equal barometric pressure, called **isobars**. When isobars are close together on a surface weather map, the pressure gradient is steep. There is a large amount of pressure change in a small distance, and the wind velocities are strong. Wind blows from an area of high pressure into an area of low pressure, but it does not cross the isobars at right angles.

The **Coriolis Force**, caused by the rotation of the earth, acts at right angles to the wind, and in the Northern Hemisphere it deflects the wind to the right until it blows parallel to the isobars.

There is a third force that acts on the wind to change its direction. This is **friction** between the wind and the surface over which it is blowing. Friction slows the wind. The rougher the terrain and the stronger the wind speed, the greater the frictional effect. As the frictional force slows the windspeed, the Coriolis Force decreases but friction does not affect the pressure gradient force, and the pressure gradient and Coriolis Forces are no longer in balance. The stronger pressure gradient force turns the wind at an angle across the isobars toward the low pressure area.

Answers

6169   [B]   6170   [A]   6171   [C]   6172   [B]

The winds at altitude pretty much follow the isobars, but because of friction, surface winds flow at an angle across the isobars. In the Northern Hemisphere, the wind flows around a low pressure area in a counterclockwise direction. This is called **cyclonic flow**. When planning a long east to west flight, you can get an advantage from the winds by flying to the north of a low pressure area and to the south of a high pressure area. *See* Figure 5-1. The wind circulation in the Northern Hemisphere is clockwise out of a high and counterclockwise into a low. When flying from a high-pressure area into a low-pressure area, the wind will blow from the left.

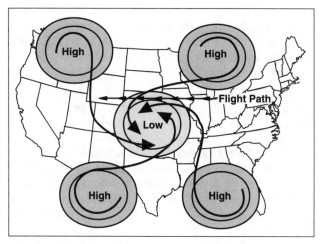

Figure 5-1. Wind circulation in the Northern Hemisphere

The wind velocities are generally greater in a low-pressure area than in a high-pressure area, so when flying from a high pressure into a low, the wind velocities will be increasing. Air flowing counterclockwise into a low-pressure area cannot flow outward against the pressure gradient, nor can it go downward into the ground; it must go upward. Therefore, a low pressure area, or **trough**, is an area of rising air. Air moving out of a high, or **ridge**, flows in a clockwise direction and depletes the quantity of air. Highs and ridges, therefore, are areas of descending air.

Convective circulation patterns associated with sea breezes occur because land surfaces warm and cool more rapidly than do water surfaces. The land is warmer than the sea during the day and wind blows from the cool water to warm land. At night the wind reverses and blows from the cool land to warmer water.

ALL
6174. What causes wind?

A— Coriolis force.
B— Pressure differences.
C— The rotation of the Earth.

Wind, which is the movement of air, is caused by pressure differences in the atmosphere. (PLT516) — AC 00-6

ALL
6175. The windflow around a low pressure is

A— cyclonic.
B— adiabatic.
C— anticyclonic.

Because of the Coriolis Force, the wind flow around a low-pressure area in the Northern Hemisphere is counterclockwise. This direction of flow is called cyclonic flow. (PLT516) — AC 00-6

Answer (B) is incorrect because adiabatic refers to the cooling of air as it rises. Answer (C) is incorrect because anticyclonic refers to a high-pressure system.

ALL
6176. Winds at 5,000 feet AGL on a particular flight are southwesterly while most of the surface winds are southerly. This difference in direction is primarily due to

A— local terrain effects on pressure.
B— stronger Coriolis force at the surface.
C— friction between the wind and the surface.

Friction between the wind and the surface of the earth slows the wind and decreases the effect of the Coriolis Force. Since friction does not decrease the pressure gradient, the Coriolis Force and pressure gradient are not in balance near the surface, and the force of the pressure gradient turns the wind at an angle across the isobars toward the lower pressure. This action explains the shift of wind from southerly near the surface to southwesterly at 5,000 feet. (PLT516) — AC 00-6

Answers

6174 [B]   6175 [A]   6176 [C]

ALL

6177. In the Northern Hemisphere, a pilot making a long distance flight from east to west would most likely find favorable winds associated with high- and low-pressure systems by flying to the

A— north of a high and a low.
B— north of a high and to the south of a low.
C— south of a high and to the north of a low.

In the Northern Hemisphere, the wind blows counterclockwise around a low and clockwise around a high. For this reason, a pilot making a long distance flight from east to west would likely find the best tail winds by flying to the south of a high and north of a low. (PLT517) — AC 00-6

ALL

6178. When flying from a high- to a low-pressure area in the Northern Hemisphere, the wind direction and velocity will be from the

A— left and increasing.
B— left and decreasing.
C— right and increasing.

The wind circulation in the Northern Hemisphere is clockwise out of a high and counterclockwise into a low. When flying from a high-pressure area into a low-pressure area, the wind will blow from the left. The wind velocities are generally higher in a low-pressure area than in a high-pressure area, so on this flight the wind velocities will be increasing. (PLT517) — AC 00-6

ALL

6179. The general circulation of air associated with a high-pressure area in the Northern Hemisphere is

A— inward, upward, and clockwise.
B— outward, downward, and clockwise.
C— outward, upward, and counterclockwise.

In the Northern Hemisphere, the air circulating out of a high-pressure area flows outward in a clockwise direction, and as it leaves, it descends. (PLT517) — AC 00-6

ALL

6180. Which statement is true regarding high- or low-pressure systems?

A— A high-pressure area or ridge is an area of rising air.
B— A low-pressure area or trough is an area of rising air.
C— A high-pressure area is a trough of descending air.

Air flowing counterclockwise into a low-pressure area cannot flow outward against the pressure gradient, nor can it go downward into the ground; it must go upward. Therefore, a low-pressure area, or trough, is an area of rising air. (PLT510) — AC 00-6

Moisture and Precipitation

Relative humidity is the ratio of the amount of water vapor in the air to the amount the air can hold at its present temperature. **Dew point** is the temperature at which a mass of air can no longer hold water in its vapor state. It is the temperature to which the air must be cooled for it to become saturated. The difference between the temperature and the dew point, (the spread), decreases as the relative humidity of the air increases.

Precipitation is a term that includes all types of atmospheric particles that grow in size and weight until they can no longer remain suspended, and they fall. Some rain evaporates before it reaches the ground. This is called virga, which appears as dark streamers hanging below the cloud.

When cold air moves over a warm lake, the warm water adds heat and water vapor to the air. This additional water in the air condenses out as the air is cooled on the lee side of the lake and causes showers. If the air is warmer than the water in the lake, the air may become saturated by evaporation from the water while also becoming cooler in the low levels by contact with the cool water. This causes fog which often becomes extensive and dense to the lee of a lake.

Answers

6177   [C]   6178   [A]   6179   [B]   6180   [B]

Rain falling through colder air may become supercooled, freezing on impact as freezing rain; or it may freeze during its descent, falling as ice pellets. Ice pellets always indicate freezing rain at a higher altitude.

Sublimation is the process in which ice forms on a surface directly from water vapor on a cold, clear night. The water does not pass through the liquid state as it changes from water vapor into ice.

ALL
6181. Which is an operational consideration regarding actual air temperature and dewpoint temperature spread?

A— The temperature spread decreases as the relative humidity decreases.

B— The temperature spread decreases as the relative humidity increases.

C— The temperature spread increases as the relative humidity increases.

The difference between the temperature and the dew point, the spread, decreases as the relative humidity of the air (the ratio of the amount of moisture in the air to the amount the air can hold at its present temperature) increases. (PLT492) — AC 00-6

ALL
6182. The ratio of the existing water vapor in the air, as compared to the maximum amount that could exist at a given temperature, is called

A— the dewpoint.

B— saturation point.

C— relative humidity.

Relative humidity is the ratio of the existing water vapor in the air, as compared to the maximum amount that could exist at a given temperature. (PLT512) — AC 00-6

Answer (A) is incorrect because dew point is the temperature which air must be cooled to become saturated. Answer (B) is incorrect because saturation point is when the water vapor present is the maximum possible at the existing temperature.

ALL
6185. When warm air moves over a cold lake, what weather phenomenon is likely to occur on the leeward side of the lake?

A— Fog.

B— Showers.

C— Cloudiness.

When warm air blows across a cold lake, the air will become saturated by evaporation from the water while also becoming cooler in the low levels by contact with the cool water. Fog often becomes extensive and dense to the lee of the lake. (PLT226) — AC 00-6

Answer (B) is incorrect because showers are produced on the leeward side of a lake when cold air moves over a warm lake. Answer (C) is incorrect because clouds are produced when there is convective development.

ALL
6186. Streamers of precipitation trailing beneath clouds but evaporating before reaching the ground are known as

A— virga.

B— sublimation.

C— condensation trails.

Rain that evaporates before it reaches the ground is called virga. Virga appears as streamers trailing beneath clouds. (PLT512) — AC 00-6

Answer (B) is incorrect because sublimation is the process of ice changing directly to water vapor, or vice versa, without passing through the liquid stage. Answer (C) is incorrect because condensation trails are cloud-like streamers which frequently are generated in the wake of aircraft flying in clear, cold, humid air.

ALL
6183. What is the process by which ice can form on a surface directly from water vapor on a cold, clear night?

A— Sublimation.

B— Condensation.

C— Supersaturation.

Sublimation is the process in which ice forms on a surface directly from water vapor on a cold, clear night. The water does not become a liquid as it passes from water vapor to ice. (PLT344) — AC 00-6

Answer (B) is incorrect because condensation is when gas changes into a liquid. Answer (C) is incorrect because supersaturation is when excess water exists in the air.

Answers

6181 [B]	6182 [C]	6185 [A]	6186 [A]	6183 [A]

ALL

6184. Which precipitation type usually indicates freezing rain at higher altitudes?

A— Snow.
B— Hail.
C— Ice pellets.

Rain falling through colder air may become super-cooled, freezing on impact as freezing rain; or it may freeze during its descent, falling as ice pellets. Ice pellets usually indicate freezing rain at a higher altitude. (PLT344) — AC 00-6

Stable and Unstable Air

Stable air resists any upward or downward displacement. Unstable air allows an upward or downward disturbance to grow into a vertical or convective current. Atmospheric stability can be determined by the ambient, or existing lapse rate, which is the actual decrease in temperature with altitude.

Unsaturated air moving upward cools at about 3.0°C (5.4°F) per 1,000 feet. Moving downward, it warms at the same rate. If a body of unsaturated air has a lapse rate greater than that of the air surrounding it, it is colder than the surrounding air and is stable, causing it to sink. But if its lapse rate is lower than that of the surrounding air, it is unstable. It is warmer than the surrounding air, and it accelerates upward, causing a convective current.

Unstable air is characterized by cumuliform clouds, showery precipitation, rough air (turbulence), and good visibility except in blowing obstructions. Stable air, on the other hand, is characterized by restricted visibility, usually caused by haze and smoke.

ALL

6187. From which measurement of the atmosphere can stability be determined?

A— Ambient lapse rate.
B— Atmospheric pressure.
C— Difference between standard temperature and surface temperature.

Atmospheric stability can be determined by the ambient (existing) lapse rate. The lapse rate is the decrease in temperature with altitude. (PLT173) — AC 00-6

ALL

6188. The formation of either predominantly stratiform or predominantly cumuliform clouds is dependent upon the

A— source of lift.
B— stability of the air being lifted.
C— percent of moisture content of the air being lifted.

The cloud types that form in an air mass are normally determined by the stability of the air that is being lifted. Stratiform clouds normally form in stable air, and cumuliform clouds normally form in unstable air. (PLT192) — AC 00-6

Answers (A) and (C) are incorrect because stratiform clouds can form without a source of lift.

ALL

6195. The weather condition normally associated with unstable air is

A— stratiform clouds.
B— fair to poor visibility.
C— good visibility, except in blowing sand or snow.

Unstable air is characterized by cumuliform clouds, showery precipitation, rough air (turbulence), and good visibility except in blowing obstructions. (PLT511) — AC 00-6

Answers (A) and (B) are incorrect because stratiform clouds and fair to poor visibility are characteristic of stable air.

ALL

6199. What is a characteristic of stable air?

A— Excellent visibility.
B— Restricted visibility.
C— Showery-type precipitation.

Restricted visibility, usually caused by haze and smoke, is a characteristic of stable air. (PLT511) — AC 00-6

Answers (A) and (C) are incorrect because excellent visibility and showery-type precipitation are characteristics of unstable air.

Answers

6184 [C]	6187 [A]	6188 [B]	6195 [C]	6199 [B]

Clouds

Clouds may be divided into four distinct families:

1. **High clouds** — These clouds are made almost entirely of ice crystals and their bases range from 16,500 feet to 45,000 feet. Cirrus, cirrostratus, and cirrocumulus are high clouds.

2. **Middle clouds** — The bases of these clouds range from 6,500 feet to 23,000 feet. Altostratus, altocumulus, and nimbostratus are middle clouds. The altocumulus castellanus cloud is a middle cloud with a high base and a billowing top. These clouds indicate mid-level instability, turbulence, and icing. Nimbostratus is a gray or dark massive cloud layer, diffused by more or less continuous rain, snow, or ice pellets. Nimbostratus is classified as a middle cloud, although it may merge into very low stratus or stratocumulus. Very little turbulence is present, but these clouds can pose a serious icing problem if temperatures are near or below freezing.

3. **Low clouds** — The bases of these clouds range from near the surface up to 6,500 feet. Stratus, stratocumulus, and cumulus are low clouds

4. **Clouds with extensive vertical development** — The bases of these clouds range from 1,000 feet or less to more than 10,000 feet. Towering cumulus and cumulonimbus are vertical development clouds.

When a body of unsaturated air is lifted, it cools until it reaches its dewpoint temperature. At this temperature, the water vapor becomes water droplets and clouds form. Clouds formed in stable air are predominantly stratiform, or layer-like clouds, while clouds formed in unstable air are cumuliform, or billowing clouds. Cumulonimbus clouds, or thunderstorms, are formed when moist unstable air is lifted. The base of cumuliform clouds form at the altitude where the temperature and dew point become the same. Dew point decreases at approximately 1°F (0.5°C) per 1,000 feet, and unsaturated air in a convective current cools at 5.4°F (3°C) per 1,000 feet. The temperature and dew point come together at a rate of 4.4°F (2.5°C) per 1,000 feet. To find the height of the base of a convective cloud, in thousands of feet, divide this rate into the temperature/dew point spread.

ALL

6189. At approximately what altitude above the surface would you expect the base of cumuliform clouds if the surface air temperature is 77°F and the dewpoint is 53°F?

A— 9,600 feet AGL.
B— 8,000 feet AGL.
C— 5,500 feet AGL.

To find the height of the base of a convective cloud, in thousands of feet, divide the spread in °F by 4.4. The spread between the surface temperature and dew point is 24°F (77° − 53°). 24 ÷ 4.4 = 5.45. The base of the cloud will be approximately 5,500 feet above the ground (AGL). (PLT192) — AC 00-6

ALL

6190. At approximately what altitude above the surface would you expect the base of cumuliform clouds if the surface air temperature is 33°C and the dewpoint is 15°C?

A— 4,100 feet AGL.
B— 6,000 feet AGL.
C— 7,200 feet AGL.

To find the height of the base of a convective cloud, in thousands of feet, divide the spread in °C by 2.5. The spread between the surface temperature and dew point is 18°C (33° − 15°). 18 ÷ 2.5 = 7.2. The base of the cloud will be 7,200 feet above the ground (AGL). (PLT192) — AC 00-6

Answers

6189   [C]   6190   [C]

ALL

6191. If clouds form as a result of very stable, moist air being forced to ascend a mountain slope, the clouds will be

A— cirrus type with no vertical development or turbulence.
B— cumulonimbus with considerable vertical development and heavy rains.
C— stratus type with little vertical development and little or no turbulence.

The cloud types that form in an air mass are normally determined by the stability of the air that is being lifted. When very stable, moist air is forced to ascend a mountain slope, the clouds will be stratus type with little vertical development and little or no turbulence. (PLT192) — AC 00-6

Answer (A) is incorrect because cirrus clouds are high clouds. Answer (B) is incorrect because cumulonimbus clouds with vertical development are a result of unstable air.

ALL

6193. Which middle level clouds are characterized by rain, snow, or ice pellets posing a serious icing problem if temperatures are near or below freezing?

A— Nimbostratus.
B— Altostratus lenticular.
C— Altocumulus castellanus.

Nimbostratus is a gray or dark massive cloud layer, diffused by more or less continuous rain, snow, or ice pellets. Nimbostratus clouds can pose a serious icing problem if temperatures are near or below freezing. (PLT192) — AC 00-6

ALL

6242. (Refer to Figure 2.) Over what area would you expect to find ceilings consisting of possible terrain obstructions and IFR conditions?

A— H.
B— F.
C— G.

A pilot flying in the vicinity of area G should expect to encounter IFR weather with possible terrain obscuration as denoted by the shading. (PLT192) — AC 00-45

Answer (A) is incorrect, area H is shaded to show ceilings of less than 1,000 feet. Answer (B) is incorrect, area F is shaded to show ceilings 1,000 feet or greater.

ALL

6245. (Refer to Figure 2A.) For overall flight planning purposes, which route would you expect to have primarily VFR conditions?

A— O to L.
B— O to C.
C— O to M.

For a flight from area O to area C you should expect VFR conditions with ceilings 1,000 feet or greater. (PLT192) — AC 00-45

Answer (A) is incorrect because at the midpoint in this route the pilot should expect to encounter IFR conditions with possible terrain obscurations. Answer (C) is incorrect, there is significant IFR weather and possible terrain obscurations along this route of flight and at arrival point.

Answers

6191 [C]	6193 [A]	6242 [C]	6245 [B]

Air Masses and Fronts

When a cold, moist air mass moves over a warm surface, the air is warmed from below and has an unstable lapse rate. The air is turbulent with strong updrafts and there are cumuliform clouds and good visibility. Often cumulonimbus clouds form, and any precipitation is showery in nature. If the surface temperature is high, strong updrafts and cumulonimbus clouds can be expected.

If warm, moist air moves over a cold surface, the air is cooled and has a stable lapse rate. The air is smooth, and there are stratiform clouds and fog and poor visibility. Any precipitation is steady or continuous.

Fronts are the zones between two different air masses. Across this zone the temperature, humidity, and wind direction and velocity change, often changing rapidly over a short distance. There are three basic types of fronts:

1. **Cold front** — A cold air mass is overtaking and replacing warmer air. The front moves at about the speed of the wind component perpendicular to the front, just above the frictional layer.

2. **Warm front** — A warm air mass is overtaking and replacing colder air. The cold, dense air hugs the surface and the warm air slides up and over it. Warm fronts move much more slowly than cold fronts. In a warm front caused by moist, stable air overrunning cold air, clouds are stratiform and widespread over the shallow front. Precipitation is continuous and induces widespread stratus in the cold air. Smooth air is associated with a stable-air warm front. If the warm front is caused by moist unstable air, cumuliform clouds will form. Precipitation from cumuliform clouds is of a showery type and the air in the clouds is turbulent.

3. **Stationary front** — When neither air mass is replacing the other, the front is stationary, and it shows no movement. The wind blows parallel to the frontal zone.

Frontal waves and cyclones (areas of low pressure) usually form on slow-moving cold fronts or stationary fronts. A wave forms along the front, and as it increases in size, cyclonic (counterclockwise) circulation develops. One section begins to move as a warm front while the section next to it moves as a cold front. When the cold front catches up with the warm front, the two close together, or occlude, and form an **occluded front**. When a wave forms on a stationary front running east and west across the United States, the cold air circulates counterclockwise and forms a cold front to the west of the wave and a warm front to the east.

In a cold-front occlusion, a mass of cold air forces its way under a mass of warm air, and the coldest air is under the cold front. When the cold front overtakes the warm front, it lifts the warm front aloft, and the air ahead of the warm front is warmer than the air behind the overtaking cold front.

ALL

6194. Consider the following air mass characteristics:

1. Cumuliform clouds.
2. Stable lapse rate.
3. Unstable lapse rate.
4. Stratiform clouds and fog.
5. Smooth air (above the friction level) and poor visibility.
6. Turbulence up to about 10,000 feet and good visibility except in areas of precipitation.

A moist air mass, which is colder than the surface over which it passes, frequently has which of the above characteristics?

A— 1, 3, and 6.
B— 3, 4, and 5.
C— 2, 4, and 5.

When a moist air mass is colder than the surface over which it passes, it will be warmed from below and the air will become unstable. Air with an unstable lapse rate will cause cumuliform clouds to form, and there will be turbulence up to about 10,000 feet, with good visibility except in areas of precipitation. (PLT511) — AC 00-6

Answer (B) is incorrect because these are characteristic of stable air. Answer (C) is incorrect because these are characteristic of a moist air mass which is warmer than the surface under it.

ALL

6196. A moist, unstable air mass is characterized by

A— poor visibility and smooth air.
B— cumuliform clouds and showery precipitation.
C— stratiform clouds and continuous precipitation.

Cumuliform clouds and showery precipitation are characteristics of a moist, unstable air mass. (PLT511) — AC 00-6

Answers (A) and (C) are incorrect because these are all characteristics of stable air.

ALL

6197. What type weather is associated with an advancing warm front that has moist, unstable air?

A— Stratiform clouds, lightning, steady precipitation.
B— Cumuliform clouds, smooth air, steady precipitation.
C— Cumuliform clouds, turbulent air, showery-type precipitation.

An advancing warm front which has moist, unstable air will cause cumuliform clouds to form. Precipitation from cumuliform clouds is of a shower type, and the air within the clouds is turbulent. (PLT511) — AC 00-6

ALL

6198. A moist, cold air mass that is being warmed from below is characterized, in part, by

A— fog and drizzle.
B— showers and thunderstorms.
C— continuous heavy precipitation.

When a moist, cold air mass is warmed from below, it becomes unstable. Unstable air is characterized in part by showers and thunderstorms. (PLT511) — AC 00-6

Answers (A) and (C) are incorrect because fog, drizzle, and continuous precipitation is characteristic of stable air.

ALL

6200. What type weather can one expect from moist, unstable air and very warm surface temperature?

A— Fog and low stratus clouds.
B— Continuous heavy precipitation.
C— Strong updrafts and cumulonimbus clouds.

Strong updrafts and cumulonimbus clouds can be expected from moist, unstable air and a very warm surface temperature. (PLT192) — AC 00-6

Answers (A) and (B) are incorrect because these are all characteristics of stable air.

ALL

6201. What is a typical characteristic of a stable air mass?

A— Cumuliform clouds.
B— Showery precipitation.
C— Continuous precipitation.

Continuous precipitation is a characteristic typical of a stable air mass. (PLT511) — AC 00-6

Answers (A) and (B) are incorrect because cumuliform clouds and showery precipitation is characteristic of unstable air.

Answers

| 6194 [A] | 6196 [B] | 6197 [C] | 6198 [B] | 6200 [C] | 6201 [C] |

ALL

6202. A moist, warm air mass that is being cooled from below is characterized, in part, by

A— smooth air.
B— cumuliform clouds.
C— showers and thunderstorms.

Smooth air is normally found in a moist, warm air mass that is being cooled from below. When the air is cooled from below, it is stable. (PLT511) — AC 00-6

Answers (B) and (C) are incorrect because cumuliform clouds, showers, and thunderstorms are characteristics of unstable air.

ALL

6203. Frontal waves normally form on

A— stationary or occluded fronts.
B— slow-moving warm fronts or occluded fronts.
C— slow-moving cold fronts or stationary fronts.

Frontal waves and cyclones (areas of low pressure) usually form on slow-moving cold fronts or on stationary fronts. (PLT511) — AC 00-6

ALL

6204. Cool air moving over a warm surface is generally characterized by

A— instability and showers.
B— stability, fog, and drizzle.
C— instability and continuous precipitation.

A moist, cold air mass that is being warmed from below is unstable, and it is characterized in part by instability and showers. (PLT511) — AC 00-6

ALL

6205. If a wave were to form on a stationary front running east and west across the United States, that portion east of the wave would normally

A— remain stationary with that portion west of the wave becoming a cold front.
B— become a warm front and that portion west of the wave would become a cold front.
C— become a cold front and that portion west of the wave would become a warm front.

When a wave forms on a stationary front running east and west across the United States, the cold air circulates counterclockwise and forms a cold front to the west of the wave and a warm front to the east. (PLT511) — AC 00-6

ALL

6206. Which statement is true regarding a cold front occlusion?

A— The air ahead of the warm front is warmer than the air behind the overtaking cold front.
B— The air ahead of the warm front has the same temperature as the air behind the overtaking cold front.
C— The air between the warm front and cold front is colder than either the air ahead of the warm front or the air behind the overtaking cold front.

In a cold-front occlusion, a mass of cold air forces its way under a mass of warm air, and the coldest air is under the cold front. When the cold front overtakes the warm front, it lifts the warm front aloft, and the air ahead of the warm front is warmer than the air behind the overtaking cold front. (PLT511) — AC 00-6

Answers

6202 [A]   6203 [C]   6204 [A]   6205 [B]   6206 [A]

Turbulence

Convective currents are one cause of turbulence at low altitudes. These currents are localized and have vertical ascending and descending air in the same general area. For every rising current, there is a corresponding descending current. Convective currents in moist air are easily identified by the presence of towering cumulus clouds. These clouds form when moist air is lifted until its temperature and dew point are the same.

When stable air crosses a mountain barrier, the air flowing up the windward side is relatively smooth, and the wind crossing the barrier tends to flow in layers. The air dips sharply downward immediately to the lee side of a ridge before rising and falling in a wave motion for a considerable distance downstream. The waves remain nearly stationary while the wind blows rapidly through them. Wave crests extend well above the highest mountains, sometimes into the lower stratosphere.

Under each wave crest is a rotary circulation, or **rotor**, which forms below the elevation of the mountain peaks. Turbulence can be violent in the rotor, and it is most severe in and below the standing rotors just beneath the wave crests at or below mountain-top levels. If the air is humid and the wave is of large amplitude, crests of the standing waves may be marked by stationary lens-shaped clouds called standing lenticular clouds. Flight over the mountains may be hazardous in high wind conditions because of the violent downdrafts in these waves on the lee side, especially when flying into the wind.

Wind shear is a serious type of turbulence associated with either a wind shift or a wind speed gradient that occurs within a very short distance, and can occur at any level of the atmosphere. There are three basic types of wind shear that are of interest:

1. Wind shear associated with a low-level temperature inversion.

2. Wind shear in a frontal zone.

3. Clear air turbulence at high levels associated with a jet stream.

A **temperature inversion** can form near the surface on a clear night with calm or light surface wind. If the wind above the inversion is relatively strong, a wind shear zone may develop between the calm and the stronger winds above.

Eddies in the shear zone cause airspeed fluctuations as an aircraft climbs or descends through the inversion. When passing through the inversion, an aircraft is most likely either climbing from takeoff or approaching to land; therefore, airspeed is slow — only a few knots above the stall speed. The fluctuation in airspeed can induce a stall precariously close to the ground.

Microbursts are small-scale intense downdrafts which, upon reaching the surface, spread outward in all directions from the downdraft center. This causes the presence of both vertical and horizontal wind shears that can be extremely hazardous to all types and categories of aircraft, especially at low altitudes. Due to their small size, short life-span, and the fact that they can occur over areas without surface precipitation, microbursts are not easily detectable using conventional weather radar or wind shear alert systems.

An individual microburst will seldom last longer than 15 minutes from the time it strikes the ground until dissipation. The horizontal winds continue to increase during the first 5 minutes, with the maximum intensity winds lasting 2 to 4 minutes. The downdrafts in a microburst can be as strong as 6,000 feet per minute. Horizontal winds near the surface can be as strong as 45 knots resulting in a 90-knot shear (head wind to tail wind change for a traversing aircraft) across the microburst. These strong horizontal winds occur within a few hundred feet of the ground.

ALL

6207. Consider the following statements about mountain waves:

1. Mountain waves always develop in a series on the upwind (windward) side of mountain ridges.

2. In a mountain wave, the air dips sharply downward immediately to the lee side of a ridge, before rising and falling in a wave motion for a considerable distance downstream.

3. If the air is humid and the wave is of large amplitude, lenticular (lens-shaped) clouds mark the wave's crest.

4. In a typical wave, the greatest amplitude is seldom more than 1,000 feet above the ridge crest elevation.

From the statements above, select those which are true.

A— 2 and 3.
B— 1, 2, and 3.
C— 1, 3, and 4.

With regard to mountain waves, statements 2 and 3 are both true. In a mountain wave, the air dips sharply downward immediately to the lee side of a ridge, before rising and falling in a wave motion for a considerable distance downstream. If the air is humid and the wave is large in amplitude, lenticular (lens-shaped) clouds mark the wave's crest. (PLT511) — AC 00-6

Answer (B) is incorrect because mountain waves develop on the downwind side of mountain ridges. Answer (C) is incorrect because mountain waves develop on the downwind side of mountains, and the wave crest may extend into the lower stratosphere.

ALL

6208. When flying low over hilly terrain, ridges, or mountain ranges, the greatest potential danger from turbulent air currents will usually be encountered on the

A— leeward side when flying with the wind.
B— leeward side when flying into the wind.
C— windward side when flying into the wind.

The greatest potential danger from turbulent air currents while flying low over hilly terrain, ridges, or mountain ranges is normally found on the leeward side when flying into the wind. (PLT501) — AC 00-6

ALL

6209. Low-level wind shear, which results in a sudden change of wind direction, may occur

A— after a warm front has passed.
B— when surface winds are light and variable.
C— when there is a low-level temperature inversion with strong winds above the inversion.

A temperature inversion can form near the surface on a clear night when there is a light surface wind. If the wind above the inversion is relatively strong, a low-level wind shear zone may develop which causes a sudden change in wind direction. (PLT518) — AC 00-6

Answer (A) is incorrect because low-level wind shear is usually associated with cold fronts. Answer (B) is incorrect because the temperature inversion must have strong winds above it.

ALL

6210. Which condition could be expected if a strong temperature inversion exists near the surface?

A— Strong, steady downdrafts and an increase in OAT.
B— A wind shear with the possibility of a sudden loss of airspeed.
C— An OAT increase or decrease with a constant wind condition.

A temperature inversion can form near the surface on a clear night when there is a light surface wind. If the wind above the inversion is relatively strong, a low-level wind shear zone may develop between the calm and the stronger winds above it. Eddies in the shear zone cause airspeed fluctuations as an aircraft climbs or descends through the inversion. (PLT518) — AC 00-6

Answer (A) is incorrect because temperature inversions do not have downdrafts or updrafts. Answer (C) is incorrect because the OAT increases and the wind may differ on both sides of the inversion.

Answers

6207 [A]   6208 [B]   6209 [C]   6210 [B]

ALL

6313. What is the expected duration of an individual microburst?

A— One microburst may continue for as long as an hour.

B— Five minutes with maximum winds lasting approximately 2 to 4 minutes.

C— Seldom longer than 15 minutes from the time the burst strikes the ground until dissipation.

An individual microburst will seldom last longer than 15 minutes from the time it strikes the ground until dissipation. (PLT317) — AIM ¶7-1-25

Answer (A) is incorrect because microbursts seldom last longer than 15 minutes. Answer (B) is incorrect because the horizontal winds continue to increase during the first 5 minutes with the maximum intensity winds lasting 2 to 4 minutes, and they are only a portion of the microburst.

ALL

6314. Maximum downdrafts in a microburst encounter may be as strong as

A— 6,000 feet per minute.

B— 4,500 feet per minute.

C— 1,500 feet per minute.

The downdrafts in a microburst can be as strong as 6,000 feet per minute. (PLT317) — AIM ¶7-1-25

ALL

6315. How long do the maximum intensity winds last in an individual microburst?

A— 2 to 4 minutes.

B— 5 to 10 minutes.

C— 15 minutes.

An individual microburst will seldom last longer than 15 minutes from the time it strikes the ground until dissipation. The horizontal winds continue to increase during the first 5 minutes, with the maximum intensity winds lasting 2 to 4 minutes. (PLT518) — AIM ¶7-1-25

ALL

6244. (Refer to Figure 13A.) In what region would you expect to encounter the greatest turbulence intensities?

A— Central region of the U.S.

B— Southeast U.S.

C— Northwest U.S.

The Central region of the U.S. is indicating the greatest intensities of turbulence with large areas of moderate or greater, including two PIREPs reporting light and moderate turbulence. (PLT518) — AC 00-45

Answer (B) is incorrect because the Southeast region of the U.S. is shaded with areas of white and green indicating none to light turbulence. Answer (C) is incorrect because you should expect to encounter some areas of light turbulence with a few small pockets of moderate or greater over Idaho.

Icing

Two conditions are necessary for the formation of structural ice on an aircraft in flight:

1. The aircraft must be flying through visible moisture.

2. The temperature at the point where the moisture strikes the airplane must be 0°C or colder.

Aerodynamic cooling can lower the temperature of an airfoil to 0°C, even though the ambient temperature is a few degrees warmer. The most rapid accumulation of clear ice on an aircraft may occur when flying through cumuliform clouds when the temperature is between 0°C and -15°C. Freezing rain is most generally caused by rain falling from air which has a temperature of more than 0°C into air having a temperature of 0°C or less.

Answers

6313   [C]   6314   [A]   6315   [A]   6244   [A]

ALL

6211. Which situation would most likely result in freezing rain?

A— Rain falling from air which has a temperature of more than 0°C into air having a temperature of 0°C or less.

B— Rain falling from air which has a temperature of 0°C or less into air having a temperature of more than 0°C.

C— Rain which has a supercooled temperature of 0°C or less falling into air having a temperature of more than 0°C.

Freezing rain is most generally caused by rain falling from air which has a temperature of more than 0°C into air having a temperature of 0°C or less. (PLT263) — AC 00-6

ALL

6212. The most rapid accumulation of clear ice on an aircraft in flight may occur with temperatures between 0°C to -15°C in

A— cumuliform clouds.

B— stratiform clouds.

C— any clouds or dry snow.

The most rapid accumulation of clear ice on an aircraft may occur when flying through cumuliform clouds when the temperature is between 0°C and -15°C. (PLT493) — AC 00-6

Answer (B) is incorrect because stratiform clouds are normally associated with rime ice. Answer (C) is incorrect because dry snow will not accumulate as ice.

ALL

7240. During an IFR cross-country flight you picked up rime icing which you estimate is 1/2" thick on the leading edge of the wings. You are now below the clouds at 2000 feet AGL and are approaching your destination airport under VFR. Visibility under the clouds is more than 10 miles, winds at the destination airport are 8 knots right down the runway, and the surface temperature is 3 degrees Celsius. You decide to:

A— use a faster than normal approach and landing speed.

B— approach and land at your normal speed since the ice is not thick enough to have any noticeable effect.

C— fly your approach slower than normal to lessen the "wind chill" effect and break up the ice.

Ice will accumulate unevenly on the airplane. It will add weight and drag, and decrease thrust and lift. With ice accumulations, landing approaches should be made with a minimum wing flap setting and with an added margin of airspeed. Sudden and large configuration and airspeed changes should be avoided. (PLT493) — FAA-H-8083-3

Answer (B) is incorrect because ice having a thickness similar to sandpaper on the leading edge and upper surface of a wing can reduce wing lift by as much as 30% and increase drag by 40%. Answer (C) is incorrect because ice will increase drag, requiring additional lift (airspeed); "wind chill" effect cannot be relied upon to melt/remove the ice that has already accumulated; flying slower than normal increases the possibility of a stall due to the decreased lift.

ALL

6213. Which is an operational consideration regarding aircraft structural icing?

A— It is unnecessary for an aircraft to fly through rain or cloud droplets for structural ice to form.

B— Clear ice is most likely to form on an airplane when flying through stratified clouds or light drizzle.

C— In order for structural ice to form, the temperature at the point where moisture strikes the aircraft must be 0°C (32°F) or colder.

Two conditions are necessary for the formation of structural icing in flight:

1. The aircraft must be flying through visible water, such as rain or cloud droplets.

2. The temperature at the point where the moisture strikes the aircraft must be 0°C or colder.

Aerodynamic cooling can lower the temperature of an airfoil to 0°C, even though the ambient temperature is a few degrees warmer. (PLT263) — AC 00-6

ALL

6243. (Refer to Figure 13.) PIREPs along the west coast of the United States are indicating

A— several SLD threats.

B— light to heavy icing.

C— light icing.

There are two PIREP symbols shown along the west coast of the United States, both in the region of California reporting light icing as indicated by the U with single short vertical line. (PLT518) — AC 00-45

Answer (A) is incorrect because although several SLD threats are shown this is not considered a PIREP. Answer (B) is incorrect because even though the figure is shaded along the west coast with trace to heavy icing indicating current and forecast conditions for those regions, the question specifically ask for PIREP information.

Answers

6211 [A]	6212 [A]	7240 [A]	6213 [C]	6243 [C]

Thunderstorms

A thunderstorm is a violent, localized storm produced by a cumulonimbus cloud. For a thunderstorm to form these conditions must be met:

1. There must be sufficient water vapor.

2. There must be an unstable lapse rate.

3. There must be some form of upward boost to start the storm process in motion.

The life cycle of a thunderstorm consists of three stages:

1. The **cumulus stage**. All of the air movement is upward, and the raindrops are growing in size.

2. The **mature stage**. Precipitation begins to fall from the cloud base, and downdrafts as well as updrafts exist. This is the stage of development in which all of the hazards reach their greatest intensity.

3. The **dissipating stage**. All air movement is downward; the storm dies rapidly.

A **squall line** is a nonfrontal, narrow band of active thunderstorms. Often it develops ahead of a cold front in moist, unstable air, but it may develop in unstable air far removed from any front. Squall lines often contain severe steady-state thunderstorms and present the most intense weather hazards to aircraft, which include destructive winds, heavy hail, and tornadoes. They usually form rapidly, generally reaching their maximum intensity during the late afternoon and the first few hours of darkness.

Hail is possible in any thunderstorm, especially beneath the anvil of a large cumulonimbus. It forms in the mature stage, when supercooled drops of water begin to freeze. Once a drop freezes, other drops latch on and freeze so that the hailstone grows as it is carried up and down inside the cloud by the vertical wind currents. Hail falls out of the bottom of the cloud, and some is thrown from the top into clear air several miles ahead of the cloud movement. Large hail is most commonly found in thunderstorms which have strong updrafts and large liquid water content. It is produced during the mature stage of a cumulonimbus cloud, or thunderstorm, in which there are strong updrafts and a large amount of liquid water. Water is carried above the freezing level where it freezes. It escapes from the updraft and drops down where it collects more water and is again carried upward and freezes. Hailstones can grow to the size of golf balls and cause serious damage to persons and property on the ground. Hailstones may be thrown outward from a storm cloud and have been observed in clear air several miles from the parent thunderstorm.

ALL

6214. What are the minimum requirements for the formation of a thunderstorm?

A— Sufficient moisture and a lifting action.
B— Sufficient moisture, an unstable lapse rate, and lifting action.
C— Towering cumulus clouds, sufficient moisture, and a frontal zone.

For a thunderstorm to form, the air must have:
1. Sufficient moisture.
2. An unstable lapse rate.
3. An initial upward boost (lifting) to start the storm process in motion.

(PLT495) — AC 00-6

ALL

6215. Select the true statement pertaining to the life cycle of a thunderstorm.

A— The initial stage of a thunderstorm is always indicated by the development of a nimbus cloud.
B— The beginning of rain at the Earth's surface indicates the mature stage of the thunderstorm.
C— The beginning of rain at the Earth's surface indicates the dissipating stage of the thunderstorm.

Precipitation beginning to fall from the cloud base signals that a downdraft has developed and the thunderstorm cell has entered its mature stage. (PLT495) — AC 00-6

Answer (A) is incorrect because the initial stage is the cumulus stage, which is when the storm builds with updrafts, generally without rain. Answer (C) is incorrect because the dissipating stage of the thunderstorm is the final stage of the storm.

Answers

6214 **[B]**   6215 **[B]**

ALL

6216. Tornadoes are most likely to occur with which type of thunderstorms?

A— Tropical thunderstorms during the mature stage.
B— Squall line thunderstorms that form ahead of warm fronts.
C— Steady-state thunderstorms associated with cold fronts or squall lines.

Tornadoes are most likely to occur in steady-state thunderstorms associated with cold fronts or squall lines. (PLT495) — AC 00-6

Answer (A) is incorrect because tropical thunderstorms do not usually reach the steady-state situation required for tornadoes to form. Answer (B) is incorrect because squall lines form ahead of cold fronts.

ALL

6217. What feature is associated with the cumulus stage of a thunderstorm?

A— Frequent lightning.
B— Continuous updrafts.
C— Beginning of rain at the surface.

The key feature of the cumulus stage of a thunderstorm is the continuous updrafts. The updrafts vary in strength and extend from very near the surface to the cloud top. (PLT495) — AC 00-6

Answer (A) is incorrect because lightning generally occurs after the downdrafts have developed. Answer (C) is incorrect because the beginning of rain at the surface represents the mature stage.

ALL

6218. Which type of cloud is associated with violent turbulence and a tendency toward the production of funnel clouds?

A— Cumulonimbus mamma.
B— Standing lenticular.
C— Altocumulus castellanus.

Frequently cumulonimbus mamma clouds occur in connection with violent thunderstorms and tornadoes. The cloud displays rounded irregular pockets or festoons from its base and is a signpost of violent turbulence. (PLT192) — AC 00-6

Answer (B) is incorrect because standing lenticular clouds indicate mountain waves. Answer (C) is incorrect because altocumulus castellanus are middle clouds which indicate instability and turbulence, but do not produce tornadoes.

ALL

6219. A squall line is usually associated with a

A— stationary front.
B— fast-moving cold front.
C— fast-moving warm front.

A squall line is a nonfrontal, narrow band of active thunderstorms that often develops ahead of a fast-moving cold front in moist, unstable air. (PLT475) — AC 00-6

ALL

6220. Consider the following statements regarding hail as an in-flight hazard and select those which are correct.

1. There is a correlation between the visual appearance of thunderstorms and the amount of hail within them.

2. Large hail is most commonly found in thunderstorms which have strong updrafts and large liquid water content.

3. Hail may be found at any level within a thunderstorm but not in the clear air outside of the storm cloud.

4. Hail is usually produced during the mature stage of the thunderstorm's lifespan.

5. Hailstones may be thrown upward and outward from a storm cloud for several miles.

The true statements are:

A— 2, 4, and 5.
B— 1, 2, and 3.
C— 1, 2, 4, and 5.

Statements 2, 4, and 5 are true regarding hail as an in-flight hazard to aircraft. Large hail is most commonly found in thunderstorms which have strong updrafts and large liquid water content. Hail is usually produced during the mature stage of the thunderstorm's life span. Hailstones may be thrown upward and outward from a storm cloud for several miles. (PLT495) — AC 00-6

Answers (B) and (C) are incorrect because there is not a correlation between the visual appearance of thunderstorms and the amount of hail within them, and hail may be thrown out of the storm for several miles.

Answers

6216 [C]	6217 [B]	6218 [A]	6219 [B]	6220 [A]

ALL

6221. Which statement is true concerning the in-flight hazard of hail?

A— Hail is usually produced by altocumulus clouds.
B— Rain at the surface indicates the absence of hail aloft.
C— Hailstones may be thrown outward from a storm cloud for several miles.

Hailstones may be thrown outward from a storm cloud for several miles. Hail has been observed in clear air several miles from the parent thunderstorm. (PLT261) — AC 00-6

Answer (A) is incorrect because hail is usually produced by cumulonimbus clouds. Answer (B) is incorrect because hail can be present aloft regardless of the precipitation at the surface.

ALL

6222. Hail, an in-flight hazard, is most likely to be associated with

A— cumulus clouds.
B— stratocumulus clouds.
C— cumulonimbus clouds.

The in-flight hazard of hail is most likely to be associated with cumulonimbus clouds. (PLT261) — AC 00-6A, Chapter 11

ALL

6223. Hail will most likely be encountered

A— beneath the anvil cloud of a large cumulonimbus.
B— during the dissipating stage of the cumulonimbus.
C— above the cumulonimbus cloud well above the freezing level.

Hail is most likely encountered beneath the anvil cloud of a large cumulonimbus. (PLT261) — AC 00-6

Fog

Fog is a surface-based cloud composed of either water droplets or ice crystals. Fog forms when the temperature/dew point spread is small and the relative humidity is high. It may be formed by cooling the air to its dew point, or by adding moisture to air near the ground. Some of the most common types of fog are:

Radiation fog — forms near the surface when terrestrial radiation cools the ground, and the ground in turn cools the adjacent air. When the air is cooled to its dew point, fog forms. Radiation fog is most likely to occur when there is high humidity during the early evening, on a cool cloudless night with light winds and favorable topography. Radiation fog is restricted to land because water surfaces cool little from nighttime radiation.

Advection fog — forms when moist air moves over colder ground or water. Advection fog deepens as wind speed increases up to about 15 knots. Wind much stronger than 15 knots lifts the fog into a layer of low stratus or stratocumulus. Advection fog is usually more extensive and much more persistent than radiation fog, and it can move in rapidly regardless of the time of day or night.

Upslope fog — forms as a result of moist, stable air being cooled adiabatically as it moves up sloping terrain. Once the upslope wind ceases, the fog dissipates.

Precipitation-induced fog — forms when relatively warm rain or drizzle falls through cool air, as happens in a warm front. Evaporation from the precipitation saturates the cool air and forms fog.

Ice fog — occurs in cold weather when the temperature is much below freezing and water vapor sublimates directly as ice crystals.

If a high-pressure air mass stagnates over an industrial area, it will concentrate smoke and haze and cause poor surface visibility with little chance of improvement.

Answers

6221   [C]   6222   [C]   6223   [A]

ALL

6224. One condition necessary for the formation of fog is

A— calm air.
B— visible moisture.
C— high relative humidity.

High relative humidity, causing a small temperature/dew point spread, is necessary for fog to form. (PLT226) — AC 00-6

ALL

6225. Radiation fog is most likely to occur under what conditions?

A— Warm, moist air being forced upslope by light winds resulting in the air being cooled and condensed.
B— High humidity during the early evening, cool cloudless night with light winds, and favorable topography.
C— Low temperature/dewpoint spread, calm wind conditions, the presence of hydroscopic nuclei, low overcast, and favorable topography.

Radiation fog is most likely to occur when there is high humidity during the early evening, cool cloudless night with light winds and favorable topography. (PLT226) — AC 00-6

Answer (A) is incorrect because this describes the conditions necessary for upslope fog to form. Answer (C) is incorrect because a low overcast would prevent the ground from cooling enough.

ALL

6226. Advection fog is formed as a result of

A— moist air moving over a colder surface.
B— the addition of moisture to a mass of cold air as it moves over a body of water.
C— the ground cooling adjacent air to the dewpoint temperature on clear, calm nights.

Advection fog forms when moist air moves over a colder surface. (PLT226) — AC 00-6

Answer (B) is incorrect because advection fog forms when moist air moves over a colder surface. Answer (C) is incorrect because this describes the conditions for radiation fog to form.

ALL

6227. With respect to advection fog, which statement is true?

A— It forms almost exclusively at night or near daybreak.
B— It forms when unstable air is cooled adiabatically.
C— It can appear suddenly during day or night, and it is more persistent than radiation fog.

Advection fog is usually more extensive and much more persistent than radiation fog. Advection fog can move in rapidly, regardless of the time of day or night. (PLT226) — AC 00-6

Answer (A) is incorrect because radiation fog forms almost exclusively at night or near daybreak. Answer (B) is incorrect because upslope fog forms when stable air is cooled adiabatically.

ALL

6228. Which in-flight hazard is most commonly associated with warm fronts?

A— Ground fog.
B— Advection fog.
C— Precipitation-induced fog.

When relatively warm rain or drizzle falls through cool air, as happens in a warm front, evaporation from the precipitation saturates the cool air and forms fog. Precipitation-induced fog can become quite dense and continue for an extended period of time. (PLT263) — AC 00-6

Answer (A) is incorrect because ground fog is a type of radiation fog, and occurs on cool, still, cloudless nights. Answer (B) is incorrect because advection fog forms when warm, humid air passes over a colder surface.

ALL

7311. You may anticipate fog when the temperature-dew point spread is

A— 15°F or less and decreasing.
B— 15°F or more and increasing.
C— 5°F or less and decreasing.

Small temperature/dewpoint spread (high relative humidity) is essential for fog to form. Anticipate fog when the temperature/dewpoint spread is 5°F or less and decreasing. (PLT344) — AC 00-6

Answers

| 6224 [C] | 6225 [B] | 6226 [A] | 6227 [C] | 6228 [C] | 7311 [C] |

ALL

6229. Fog associated with a warm front is a result of saturation due to

A— nocturnal cooling.
B— evaporation of precipitation.
C— evaporation of surface moisture.

When relatively warm rain or drizzle falls through cool air, evaporation from the precipitation saturates the cool air and forms fog. Precipitation-induced fog can become quite dense and continue for an extended period of time. Precipitation-induced fog is most commonly associated with warm fronts, but can occur with slow moving cold fronts and with stationary fronts. (PLT226) — AC 00-6

Answer (A) is incorrect because nocturnal cooling produces radiation fog. Answer (C) is incorrect because evaporation of surface moisture is associated with radiation fog.

High-Altitude Weather

Clear air turbulence (CAT) is most likely to be encountered in areas where vertical wind shear exceeds six knots per 1,000 feet or horizontal wind shear exceeds 40 knots per 150 miles.

ALL

6230. In reference to clear air turbulence (CAT), areas to be avoided are those where horizontal wind shear exceeds

A— 40 knots per 150 miles.
B— 10 knots per 50 miles.
C— 6 knots per 1,000 feet.

Clear air turbulence is most likely to be encountered in areas where vertical wind shear exceeds 6 knots per 1,000 feet, or horizontal wind shear exceeds 40 knots per 150 miles. (PLT518) — AC 00-6

Soaring Weather

Convective circulation patterns associated with sea breezes are caused by the land absorbing and radiating heat faster than the water. The land is heated on warm, sunny days, and sea breezes usually begin during the early forenoon, reach a maximum during the afternoon, and subside around dusk after the land has cooled. The leading edge of the cool sea breeze forces the warmer air inland to rise. Rising air from over the land returns seaward at a higher altitude to complete the convective cell.

Cool air must sink to force the warm air upward in **thermals**. Therefore, in small-scale convection, thermals and downdrafts coexist side by side. The net upward displacement of the air must equal the net downward displacement. Fast rising thermals generally cover a small percentage of a convective area, while slower downdrafts predominate over the remaining greater portion.

Thermals are strongest under smooth cumulus clouds that have concave bases and sharp upper outlines. The most favorable type of thermals for cross-country soaring are found along "thermal streets," which are generally parallel to the wind. A pilot can soar under a cloud street maintaining generally continuous flight and seldom, if ever, have to circle. In the central and eastern United States, the most favorable weather for cross-country soaring occurs behind a cold front. Most thermal cross-country flying in these areas is done after a cold front passes and ahead of the following high-pressure center.

The movement of surface dust and smoke can be used as an indication of a thermal. The rising air in a thermal will cause the streamers of dust or smoke to converge in the low-pressure area caused by the rising air. You must be careful when soaring in a dust devil to avoid the eye of the vortex. A wall of turbulence surrounds the core, or the eye.

Answers

6229   [B]   6230   [A]

A **thermal index (TI)** is a forecast value based on the temperature difference between sinking and rising air at a given altitude. The greater the temperature difference, the stronger the thermals. A TI of -10 predicts very good lift and a long soaring day. A TI of -5 indicates good lift, and a TI of +5 shows no hope of thermals at the reported altitude. For thermals to exist, the existing lapse rate must be equal to or greater than the dry adiabatic rate of cooling.

Soaring under stable-air conditions can be done in the lift that is found on the upwind side of hills or ridges when moderate winds are blowing. A **mountain wave**, in a manner similar to that in a thermal, means turbulence to powered aircraft; but to a slowly moving sailcraft, it produces lift and sink above the level of the mountain crest.

As air spills over the crest like a waterfall, it causes strong downdrafts. The violent overturning forms a series of "rotors" in the wind shadow of the mountain, which are hazardous even to a sailplane. Clouds resembling long bands of stratocumulus sometimes mark the area of overturning air. These "rotor clouds" appear to remain stationary, parallel to the range, and stand a few miles leeward of the mountains. Turbulence is most frequent and most severe in the standing rotors just beneath the wave crests at or below mountain-top levels. The greatest potential danger from vertical and rotor-type currents in the vicinity of mountain ranges is usually encountered beneath the wave crests on the leeward side at or below mountain-top levels. This turbulence will generally be encountered as you are flying into the wind, attempting to climb over the area of lift. A strong mountain wave requires:

1. Marked stability in the airstream disturbed by the mountains. Rapidly building cumulus over the mountains visually marks the air as unstable; convection evidenced by the cumulus tends to deter wave formation.

2. Wind speed at the level of the summit should exceed a minimum which varies from 15 to 25 knots, depending on the height of the range. Upper winds should increase or at least remain constant with height up to the tropopause.

3. Wind direction should be within 30° of normal to the range. Lift diminishes as winds more nearly parallel the range.

GLI

6239. Convective circulation patterns associated with sea breezes are caused by

A— land absorbing and radiating heat faster than the water.
B— warm and less dense air moving inland from over the water, causing it to rise.
C— cool and less dense air moving inland from over the water, causing it to rise.

Convective circulation patterns associated with sea breezes are caused by the land absorbing and radiating heat faster than the water. The land is heated on warm, sunny days, and sea breezes usually begin during the early forenoon, reach a maximum during the afternoon, and subside around dusk after the land has cooled. (PLT510) — AC 00-6

GLI

6234. Select the true statement concerning thermals.

A— Strong thermals have proportionately increased sink in the air between them.
B— Thermals will not develop unless the Sun's rays strike the Earth at a vertical angle.
C— A thermal invariably remains directly above the surface area from which it developed.

Cool air must sink to force the warm air upward in thermals. Therefore, in small-scale convection, thermals and downdrafts coexist side by side. The net upward displacement of the air must equal the net downward displacement. Strong thermals have proportionately increased sink in the air between them. (PLT494) — AC 00-6

Answer (B) is incorrect because thermals develop whenever the sun's rays warm the earth unevenly. Answer (C) is incorrect because thermals will move with wind.

Answers
6239 [A]   6234 [A]

GLI

6238. One of the best visual indications of a thermal is a

A— smooth cumulus cloud with a concave base.
B— broken to overcast sky with cumulus clouds.
C— fragmented cumulus cloud with a concave base.

Thermals are strongest under smooth cumulus clouds that have concave bases and sharp upper outlines. (PLT494) — AC 00-6

GLI

6240. Which is true regarding the development of convective circulation?

A— Cool air must sink to force the warm air upward.
B— Warm air is less dense and rises on its own accord.
C— Cool air surrounding convective circulation sinks at a greater rate than the warmer air rises (within the thermal), thus forcing the warmer air upward.

Cool air must sink to force the warm air upward in thermals. Therefore, in small-scale convection, thermals and downdrafts coexist side by side. The net upward displacement of air must equal the net downward displacement. (PLT510) — AC 00-6

GLI

6231. Which statement is true regarding the effect of fronts on soaring conditions?

A— A slow-moving front provides the strongest lift.
B— Excellent soaring conditions usually exist in the cold air ahead of a warm front.
C— Frequently the air behind a cold front provides excellent soaring for several days.

In the central and eastern United States, the most favorable weather for cross-country soaring occurs behind a cold front. Most thermal cross-country flying in these areas is done after a cold front passes and ahead of the following high-pressure center. (PLT511) — AC 00-6

GLI

6237. An important precaution when soaring in a dust devil is to

A— avoid the eye of the vortex because of extreme turbulence.
B— avoid steep turns on the upwind side to prevent being blown into the vortex.
C— avoid the clear area at the outside edge of the dust because of severe downdrafts.

When soaring in a dust devil, you should avoid the eye of the vortex, because of a wall of turbulence which surrounds the core, or the eye. (PLT494) — AC 00-6

GLI

6236. Which thermal indices would predict the best probability of good soaring conditions?

A— +5.
B— -5.
C— -10.

A thermal index is a forecast value based on the temperature difference between sinking and rising air at a given altitude. The greater the temperature difference, the stronger the thermals. A TI of -10 predicts very good lift and a long soaring day. (PLT494) — AC 00-6

Answer (A) is incorrect because a TI of +5 shows no hope of thermals at the reported altitude. Answer (B) is incorrect because a TI of -5 indicates good lift, but not as good as -10.

GLI

6232. The conditions most favorable to wave formation over mountainous areas are a layer of

A— unstable air at mountaintop altitude and a wind of at least 15 to 25 knots blowing across the ridge.
B— stable air at mountaintop altitude and a wind of at least 15 to 25 knots blowing across the ridge.
C— moist, unstable air at mountaintop altitude and a wind of less than 5 knots blowing across the ridge.

A strong mountain wave requires stability in the airstream disturbed by the mountains, wind speed at the level of the summit of at least 15 to 25 knots, and the wind blowing within 30° perpendicular to the range. Lift diminishes as winds more nearly parallel the range. (PLT474) — AC 00-6

Answers

6238 [A]	6240 [A]	6231 [C]	6237 [A]	6236 [C]	6232 [B]

GLI

6233. When soaring in the vicinity of mountain ranges, the greatest potential danger from vertical and rotor-type currents will usually be encountered on the

A— leeward side when flying with the wind.
B— leeward side when flying into the wind.
C— windward side when flying into the wind.

The greatest potential danger from vertical and rotor-type currents in the vicinity of mountain ranges is usually encountered beneath the wave crests on the leeward side at or below mountain-top levels. This turbulence will generally be encountered as you are flying into the wind, attempting to climb over the area of lift. (PLT501) — AC 00-6

GLI

6235. One of the most dangerous features of mountain waves is the turbulent areas in and

A— below rotor clouds.
B— above rotor clouds.
C— below lenticular clouds.

A mountain wave means turbulence as it produces lift and sink above the level of the mountain crest. As air spills over the crest like a waterfall, it causes strong downdrafts. The violent overturning forms a series of "rotors" in the wind shadow of the mountain. Clouds resembling long bands of stratocumulus sometimes mark the area of overturning air. These "rotor clouds" appear to remain stationary, parallel to the range, and stand a few miles leeward of the mountains. Turbulence is most frequent and most severe in the standing rotors just beneath the wave crests at or below mountain-top levels. (PLT501) — AC 00-6

GLI

6241. Under what condition can enough lift be found for soaring under stable weather conditions?

A— Over steep escarpments or cliffs.
B— In mountain waves that form on the upwind side of the mountains.
C— On the upwind side of hills or ridges with moderate winds present.

Soaring under stable-air conditions can be done in the lift that is found on the upwind side of hills or ridges when moderate winds are blowing. (PLT494) — AC 00-6

Answers

6233   [B]   6235   [A]   6241   [C]

Aviation Routine Weather Report (METAR)

An international weather reporting code is used for weather reports (METAR) and forecasts (TAFs) worldwide. The reports follow the format shown in Figure 5-2.

For aviation purposes, the ceiling is the lowest broken or overcast layer, or vertical visibility into an obscuration.

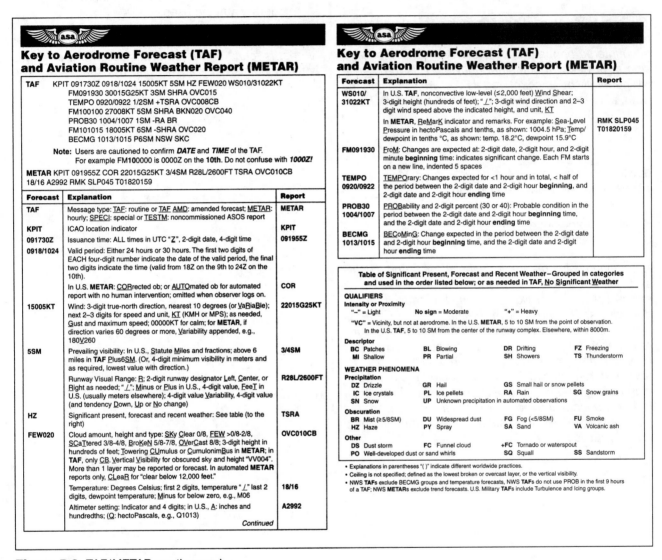

Figure 5-2. TAF/METAR weather card

ALL

6247. (Refer to Figure 3.) Which station is reporting the wind as calm?

A— KDAL.
B— KFTW.
C— KTYR.

The only station reporting calm wind conditions in the surface weather report is KDAL, indicated by ØØØØØKT. (PLT059) — AC 00-45

Answer (B) is incorrect because KFTW is indicating winds 090° at 4 knots (09004KT). Answer (C) is incorrect because KTYR is indicating winds 080° at 4 knots (08004KT).

ALL

6248. (Refer to Figure 3.) What is the reported duration of the rain at the time of the observation at KAUS?

A— 25 minutes.
B— 26 minutes
C— 36 minutes.

The duration of the rain at KAUS has been 26 minutes. The report was made 51 minutes past the hour (301651Z). From the remarks (RMK), we know that the rain began at 25 minutes past the hour (RAB25). Therefore, 25 minutes subtracted from 51 minutes indicates that it has been raining for 26 minutes. (PLT059) — AC 00-45

ALL

6248-1. (Refer to Figure 3.) What is the reported duration of the rain at the time of the observation at KBRO?

A— 25 minutes.
B— 6 minutes.
C— 19 minutes.

The duration of the rain at KBRO has been 6 minutes. From the remarks (RMK), we know that the rain began at 19 minutes past the hour (RAB19) and ended 25 minutes past the hour (RAE25). Therefore, 19 minutes subtracted from 25 minutes indicates that it has been raining for 6 minutes. (PLT059) — AC 00-45

ALL

6249. Consider the following statements regarding an Aviation Routine Weather Report (METAR).

1. A vertical visibility entry does not constitute a ceiling.

2. Fog (FG) can be reported only if the visibility is less than 5/8 mile.

3. The ceiling layer will be designated by a "C".

4. Mist (BR) can be reported only if the visibility is 5/8 mile up to six miles.

5. Temperatures reported below zero will be prefixed with a "-".

6. There is no provision to report partial obscurations.

Select the true statements.

A— 2, 4, and 6.
B— 2, 3, and 5.
C— 1, 2, 5, and 6.

A ceiling layer is not designated in the METAR code. For aviation purposes, the ceiling is the lowest broken or overcast layer, or vertical visibility into an obscuration. Also, there is no provision for reporting thin layers in the METAR code. Temperature and dew point are reported in a two-digit form in degrees Celsius. Temperatures below zero are prefixed with an "M". (PLT059) — AC 00-45

Answers (B) and (C) are incorrect because vertical visibility can constitute a ceiling, ceiling layer is not designated, and below zero temperatures are prefixed "M".

ALL

6250. (Refer to Figure 3.) Which station is reporting the lowest ceiling?

A— KAMA.
B— KFTW.
C— KDAL.

KAMA is reporting a 700-foot overcast ceiling (OVC007). KFTW is reporting 600 feet vertical visibility (VV006). KDAL is reporting a 900-foot overcast ceiling (OVC009). (PLT059) — AC 00-45

Answers

6247 [A]   6248 [B]   6248-1 [B]   6249 [A]   6250 [B]

ALL

6251. (Refer to Figure 3.) The temperature/dewpoint spread at KAUS is

A— 4°C.
B— 4°F.
C— 7°C.

Temperatures and dew point are reported in a two-digit form in degrees Celsius. Temperatures below zero are prefixed with an "M." Austin airport (KAUS) is reporting a temperature of 21°, and dew point of 17° (21/17). (PLT059) — AC 00-45

ALL

6252. (Refer to Figure 3.) In the report for KBRO, what is the reported ceiling?

A— 2,000 feet.
B— 13,000 feet.
C— 25,000 feet.

An overcast layer is reported at 25,000 feet (OVC250). (PLT059) — AC 00-45

Answers (A) and (B) are incorrect because there are scattered clouds at 2,000 and 13,000, but scattered clouds do not constitute a ceiling.

ALL

6253. GIVEN:

KOUN 151355Z AUTO 22010KT 10SM CLR BLO 120 13/10 A2993 RMK A02 $.

The ASOS report indicates that the location is

A— reporting a temperature of 45°F.
B— possibly in need of maintenance.
C— augmented with a weather observer.

The dollar sign ($) indicates that the site may be in need of maintenance. (PLT059) — AC 00-45

Answer (A) is incorrect because the location is reporting a temperature of 13°C, which is 55.4°F. Answer (C) is incorrect because "A02" indicates this location operates completely without human intervention.

ALL

6254. GIVEN:

KPNC 131215 AUTO 33025KT 1/2SM OVC005 00/M03 A2990 RMK A02 SLPNO.

This ASOS report indicates that the

A— temperature is missing.
B— station reports every 15 minutes.
C— sea level pressure is not available.

This ASOS report indicates that the sea level pressure is not available (SLPNO). (PLT059) — AIM ¶7-1-11

Answer (A) is incorrect because "00M03" indicates the temperature is zero, and the dew point is negative 3°C. Answer (B) is incorrect because the ASOS will provide continuous minute-by-minute observations.

ALL

6255. Which statement is true concerning ASOS/AWOS weather reporting systems?

A— Each AWOS station is part of a nationwide network of weather reporting stations.
B— ASOS locations perform weather observing functions necessary to generate METAR reports.
C— Both ASOS and AWOS have the capability of reporting density altitude, as long as it exceeds the airport elevation by more than 1,000 feet.

ASOS is designed to support aviation operations and weather forecast activities. The ASOS will provide continuous minute-by-minute observations and perform the basic observing functions necessary to generate an aviation routine weather report (METAR) and other aviation weather information. (PLT059) — AIM ¶7-1-11

Answer (A) is incorrect because selected individual systems may be incorporated into nationwide data collection and dissemination networks in the future. Answer (C) is incorrect because only the AWOS has the capability of reporting density altitude.

Answers

6251 [A]	6252 [C]	6253 [B]	6254 [C]	6255 [B]

Pilot Reports (UA)

Aircraft in flight are the only means of directly observing cloud tops, icing, and turbulence; therefore, no observation is more timely than one made from the cockpit. While the FAA encourages pilots to report inflight weather, a report of any unforecast weather is required by regulation. A **PIREP (UA)** is usually transmitted in a prescribed format. *See* Figure 5-3.

Pilots seeking weather avoidance assistance should keep in mind that ATC radar limitations and frequency congestion may limit the controller's capability to provide this service.

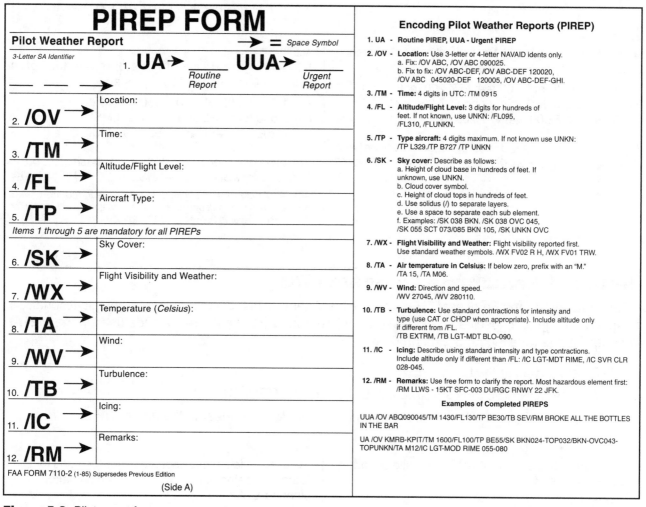

Figure 5-3. Pilot report form

ALL

6258. (Refer to Figure 4.) The wind and temperature at 12,000 feet MSL as reported by a pilot are

A— 090° at 21 knots and -9°.
B— 090° at 21 MPH and -9°F.
C— 080° at 21 knots and -7°C.

The temperature is reported as -7°C (TA M7), and the wind at 12,000 feet MSL is reported as 080° at 21 knots (WV 08021). (PLT061) — AC 00-45

ALL

6259. (Refer to Figure 4.) The intensity of the turbulence reported at a specific altitude is

A— moderate from 5,500 feet to 7,200 feet.
B— moderate at 5,500 feet and at 7,200 feet.
C— light from 5,500 feet to 7,200 feet.

Light turbulence was reported between 5,500 feet and 7,200 feet MSL (TB LGT 055-072). (PLT061) — AC 00-45

ALL

6260. (Refer to Figure 4.) If the terrain elevation is 1,295 feet MSL, what is the height above ground level of the base of the ceiling?

A— 505 feet AGL.
B— 6,586 feet AGL.
C— 1,295 feet AGL.

The base of the ceiling is reported as broken at 1,800 feet (SK BKN 018). This means the base of the ceiling is 505 feet AGL (1800–1295). (PLT061) — AC 00-45

ALL

6261. (Refer to Figure 4.) The base and tops of the overcast layer reported by a pilot are

A— 1,800 feet MSL and 5,500 feet MSL.
B— 5,500 feet AGL and 7,200 feet MSL.
C— 7,200 feet MSL and 8,900 feet MSL.

The overcast layer is reported with the base at 7,200 feet MSL and tops at 8,900 feet MSL. (PLT061) — AC 00-45

Answer (A) is incorrect because this is the reported broken layer. Answer (B) is incorrect because pilot reports are issued in MSL and the overcast layer is between 7,200 and 8,900 feet.

Terminal Aerodrome Forecast (TAF)

A Terminal Aerodrome Forecast (TAF) is a concise statement of the expected meteorological conditions at an airport during a specified period (usually 24 hours). TAFs use the same code used in the METAR weather reports (*see* Figure 5-2, page 5-28).

TAFs are issued in the following format:

TYPE / LOCATION / ISSUANCE TIME / VALID TIME / FORECAST

Note: the "/" above are for separation purposes and do not appear in the actual TAFs.

ALL

6262. (Refer to Figure 5.) What is the valid period for the TAF for KMEM?

A— 1800Z to 1800Z.
B— 1200Z to 1800Z.
C— 1200Z to 1200Z.

The valid period of the forecast is a two-digit date followed by the two-digit beginning and two-digit ending hours in UTC. The valid period for the KMEM TAF is 1800Z to 1800Z (121818). (PLT081) — AC 00-45

ALL

6262-1. Which primary source should be used to obtain forecast weather information at your destination for the planned ETA?

A— Winds Aloft Chart.
B— Weather Depiction Charts.
C— Terminal Aerodrome Forecast (TAF).

A TAF is a concise statement of the expected meteorological conditions at an airport during a specified period (usually 24 hours). (PLT288) — AC 00-45

Answer (A) is incorrect because the winds aloft forecast does not provide information beyond the wind direction and speed for specified locations and altitudes. Answer (B) is incorrect because weather depiction charts show current weather, not forecasts.

Answers

| 6258 [C] | 6259 [C] | 6260 [A] | 6261 [C] | 6262 [A] | 6262-1 [C] |

ALL
6263. (Refer to Figure 5.) In the TAF for KMEM, what does "SHRA" stand for?

A— Rain showers.
B— A shift in wind direction is expected.
C— A significant change in precipitation is possible.

The second line of the KMEM TAF ends with SHRA, which means rain showers. (PLT081) — AC 00-45

ALL
6264. (Refer to Figure 5.) In between 1000Z and 1200Z the visibility at KMEM is forecast to be

A— 6 statute miles.
B— 1/2 statute mile.
C— 3 statute miles.

The 4th line of the KMEM TAF provides information on the forecast between 1000 and 1200Z (BECMG 1012). The visibility is forecast to be 3 statute miles (3SM). (PLT072) — AC 00-45

Answer (A) is incorrect because visibility is forecast to be greater than 6 SM (P6SM) between 2200 and 0000Z. Answer (B) is incorrect because 1/2-mile visibility is a temporary condition forecast between 1200 and 1400Z.

ALL
6265. Vertical visibility is shown on Terminal Aerodrome Forecasts (TAF) reports when the sky is

A— overcast.
B— obscured.
C— partially obscured.

When the sky is totally obscured, vertical visibility into the obscuration is forecast in the format "VVhhh" where VV denotes vertical visibility and hhh is the expected vertical visibility in hundreds of feet. There is no provision in the TAF code to forecast partial obscurations. (PLT072) — AC 00-45

ALL
7327. When the visibility is greater than 6 SM on a TAF, it is expressed as

A— 6PSM.
B— P6SM.
C— 6SMP.

Expected visibilities greater than 6 miles are forecast as a "plus 6SM" (P6SM). (PLT288) — AC 00-45

ALL
7328. What is the wind shear forecast in the following TAF?
TAF KCVG 231051Z 231212 12012KT 4SM -RA BR OVC008 WS005/27050KT TEMPO 1719 1/2SM -RA FG FM1930 09012KT 1SM -DZ BR VV003 BECMG 2021 5SM HZ=

A— 5 feet AGL from 270° at 50 KT.
B— 50 feet AGL from 270° at 50 KT.
C— 500 feet AGL from 270° at 50 KT.

WS005/27050KT—low level wind shear at 500 feet, wind 270° at 50 knots. (PLT288) — AC 00-45

ALL
6266. (Refer to Figure 5.) In the TAF from KOKC, the clear sky becomes

A— overcast at 200 feet with the probability of becoming 400 feet overcast during the forecast period between 2200Z and 2400Z.
B— overcast at 2,000 feet during the forecast period between 2200Z and 2400Z.
C— overcast at 200 feet with a 40% probability of becoming overcast at 600 feet during the forecast period between 2200Z and 2400Z.

The sky is expected to change from clear (SKC) to overcast at 2,000 feet (OVC020) between 2200 and 2400Z (2224). (PLT072) — AC 00-45

ALL
6267. To determine the freezing level and areas of probable icing aloft, you should refer to

A— a TAF.
B— an AIRMET or SIGMET.
C— a METAR.

Hazardous weather, i.e., IFR, icing, and turbulence conditions), are included in the In-Flight Aviation Weather Advisories (convective SIGMET, SIGMET, and AIRMET). (PLT290) — AC 00-45

Answers

6263 [A]	6264 [C]	6265 [B]	7327 [B]	7328 [C]	6266 [B]
6267 [B]					

Graphical Forecasts for Aviation (GFA)

The GFA at the Aviation Weather Center (AWC) website is an interactive web-based display providing continuously updated observed and forecast weather information over the continental United States (CONUS). It is intended to give users a complete picture of weather critical to aviation safety. The GFA display shows user-selected weather categories, each containing multiple fields of interest at altitudes from the surface up to FL480. Depending on the field of interest chosen, weather information is available from -6 in the past (observed) to +15 hours in the future (forecast).

The GFA is not considered a weather product but an aggregate of several existing weather products. The information and data from the various weather products are overlaid on a high-resolution basemap of the United States: **www.aviationweather.gov/gfa**. The user selects flight levels and current time period for either observed or forecast weather information. Mouse-clicking or hovering over the map provides additional information in textual format, such as current METAR or TAF for a selected airport. The GFA replaces the textual area forecast (FA) for the CONUS and Hawaii with a more modern digital solution for obtaining weather information.

ALL
6268. To best determine general forecast weather conditions covering a flight information region, the pilot should refer to

A— Graphical Forecasts for Aviation (GFA).
B— Terminal Area Forecasts (TAF).
C— Satellite Maps.

The Graphical Forecasts for Aviation (GFA) are intended to provide the necessary aviation weather information to give users a complete picture of the weather that may impact flight in the continental U.S. (CONUS). (PLT290) — AC 00-45

Winds and Temperatures Aloft Forecast (FB)

The winds and temperatures aloft forecast is displayed in a 6-digit format (DDffTT). It shows wind direction (DD), wind velocity (ff), and the temperature (TT) that is forecast to exist at specified levels. For example, "234502" decodes as: winds from 230 degrees true north, at 45 knots, temperatures 02°C.

When the wind speed (ff) is between 100 and 199 knots, the wind direction (DD) portion of the code will be greater than 50. In cases such as this, you will need to subtract 50 from the coded wind direction, and add 100 to the coded wind speed in order to decipher the code. For example, "734502" decodes as: winds from 230 degrees true north at 145 knots, temperature 02°C.

Temperatures with a negative symbol in front of them (DDff-37) are negative. For flight levels above 24,000, temperatures are always negative and will not have a negative symbol. Light and variable winds or wind speeds below 5 knots are indicated by 9900, followed by the forecast temperature. For example, the coded winds aloft forecast for flight level FL270 (flight level 27,000) is "990017" and decodes as: winds are light and variable, temperature negative 17.

The observed winds aloft chart shows temperature, wind direction, and speed at selected stations. Arrows with pennants and barbs indicate wind direction and speed. Each pennant is 50 knots, each barb is 10 knots, and each half barb is 5 knots. Wind direction is shown by an arrow drawn to the nearest 10 degrees, with the second digit of the coded direction entered at the outer end of the arrow. Thus, a wind in the northwest quadrant with the digit 3 indicates 330 degrees, and a wind in the southwest quadrant with the digit 3 indicates 230 degrees.

Answers

6268 [B]

ALL

6278. (Refer to Figure 7.) What wind is forecast for STL at 9,000 feet?

A— 230° true at 32 knots.
B— 230° magnetic at 25 knots.
C— 230° true at 25 knots.

The entry 2332+02 indicates the winds are forecast to be 230° true at 32 knots for STL at 9,000 feet. (PLT076) — AC 00-45

Answers (B) and (C) are incorrect because winds aloft forecasts provide wind direction in tens of degrees with reference to true north; 25 knots is the forecast for STL at 6,000 feet.

ALL

6279. (Refer to Figure 7.) Determine the wind and temperature aloft forecast for DEN at 9,000 feet.

A— 230° true at 53 knots, temperature -47°C.
B— 230° magnetic at 53 knots, temperature 47°C.
C— 230° true at 21 knots, temperature -4°C.

The entry 2321-04 indicates the wind and temperature aloft forecast to be 230° true at 21 knots, -4°C for DEN at 9,000 feet. (PLT076) — AC 00-45

Answer (A) is incorrect because this is the wind velocity and temperature at 30,000 feet. Answer (B) is incorrect because the winds aloft forecast is provided with reference to true north and these represent the numbers for the forecast at 30,000 feet.

ALL

6280. (Refer to Figure 7.) Determine the wind and temperature aloft forecast for MKC at 6,000 feet.

A— 050° true at 7 knots, temperature missing.
B— 200° true at 6 knots, temperature +3°C.
C— 200° magnetic at 6 knots, temperature +3°C.

The entry 2006+03 indicates the wind and temperature aloft forecast to be 200° true at 6 knots, 3°C for MKC at 6,000 feet. (PLT076) — AC 00-45

Answer (A) is incorrect because this is the forecast for MKC at 3,000 feet. Answer (C) is incorrect because the winds aloft forecast references true north.

In-Flight Weather Advisories (WA, WS, WST)

In-Flight Weather Advisories advise pilots en route of the possibility of encountering hazardous flying conditions that may not have been forecast at the time of the preflight weather briefing.

AIRMETs (WA) contain information on weather that may be hazardous to single engine, other light aircraft, and VFR pilots. The items covered are moderate icing or turbulence, sustained winds of 30 knots or more at the surface, widespread areas of IFR conditions, and extensive mountain obscurement.

SIGMETs (WS) advise of weather potentially hazardous to all aircraft. The items covered are severe icing, severe or extreme turbulence, and widespread sandstorms, dust storms or volcanic ash lowering visibility to less than 3 miles.

SIGMETs and AIRMETs are broadcast upon receipt and at 30-minute intervals (H + 15 and H + 45) during the first hour. If the advisory is still in effect after the first hour, an alert notice will be broadcast. Pilots may contact the nearest FSS to ascertain whether the advisory is pertinent to their flight.

Convective SIGMETs (WST) cover weather developments such as tornadoes, lines of thunderstorms, and embedded thunderstorms, hail greater than or equal to 3/4-inch diameter, and they also imply severe or greater turbulence, severe icing, and low-level wind shear. Convective SIGMET Bulletins are issued hourly at H + 55. Unscheduled Convective SIGMETs are broadcast upon receipt and at 15-minute intervals at the first hour (H + 15, H + 30, H + 45).

Answers

6278   [A]   6279   [C]   6280   [B]

ALL

6276. Which in-flight advisory would contain information on severe icing?

A— PIREP.
B— SIGMET.
C— CONVECTIVE SIGMET.

A SIGMET is an advisory for weather potentially hazardous to all aircraft. SIGMETs cover:

1. Severe icing

2. Severe or extreme turbulence

3. Dust storms, sandstorms, or volcanic ash lowering visibilities to less than 3 miles.

(PLT290) — AC 00-45

ALL

6277. What information is contained in a CONVECTIVE SIGMET in the conterminous United States?

A— Moderate thunderstorms and surface winds greater than 40 knots.
B— Tornadoes, embedded thunderstorms, and hail 3/4 inch or greater in diameter.
C— Severe icing, severe turbulence, or widespread dust storms lowering visibility to less than 3 miles.

Convective SIGMETs issued in the conterminous United States include:

1. Tornadoes

2. Lines of thunderstorms

3. Embedded thunderstorms

4. Hail greater than or equal to 3/4-inch diameter

(PLT290) — AC 00-45

ALL

6277-1. Convective SIGMETs are issued for which weather conditions?

A— Any thunderstorm with a severity level of VIP 2 or more.
B— Cumulonimbus clouds with tops above the tropopause and thunderstorms with 1/2-inch hail or funnel clouds.
C— Embedded thunderstorms, lines of thunderstorms, and thunderstorms with 3/4-inch hail or tornadoes.

Convective SIGMETs are issued in the conterminous U.S. for any of the following:

1. Severe thunderstorms due to surface winds greater than or equal to 50 knots or hail at the surface greater than or equal to 3/4 inches in diameter or tornadoes;

2. Embedded thunderstorms;

3. Lines of thunderstorms; or

4. Thunderstorms greater than or equal to VIP level four affecting 40% or more of an area at least 3,000 square miles.

(PLT290) — AC 00-45

ALL

6275. What information would be covered in an AIRMET?

A— Severe turbulence.
B— Extensive mountain obscurement.
C— Hail of 3/4 inch or greater diameter.

An AIRMET is an advisory for weather that may be hazardous to single-engine and other light aircraft and VFR pilots. AIRMETs include information on extensive mountain obscurement. (PLT290) — AC 00-45

Answer (A) is incorrect because severe turbulence would be included in a SIGMET. Answer (C) is incorrect because hail 3/4 inch or greater in diameter would be included in a CONVECTIVE SIGMET.

Surface Analysis Chart

The Surface Analysis Chart, or Surface Weather chart, is a computer-prepared chart covering the contiguous 48 states and the adjacent areas. These charts are transmitted every 3 hours. The date-time group shows the valid time in GMT, and the chart shows the conditions that were existing at the time the observations were made. Isobars are solid lines that depict the sea level pressure pattern. They are usually spaced at 4-millibar (mb) intervals, and are identified with a two-digit number for the last two digits in the millibar pressure. For example, the isobar identified as 32 is the 1032.0 mb isobar. The isobar marked 92 is the 992.0 mb isobar. The closeness of the isobars shows the pressure gradient.

Answers

6276 [B]   6277 [B]   6277-1 [C]   6275 [B]

The closer together the isobars, the steeper the pressure gradient, or the change in pressure, for a given horizontal distance.

Fronts are identified by the coded lines shown in Figure 5-4. The shape of the pips identifies the type of front, and which side of the line they are on shows which direction the front is moving. A stationary front has the warm-front pips on one side and the cold-front pips on the opposite side. A **frontogenesis** is a front that is building up, and a **frontolysis** is one that is dissipating.

A three-digit code marked along the front identifies the type of front, intensity, and characteristic. The weather existing at each station is shown by a station model such as the one in Figure 5-5.

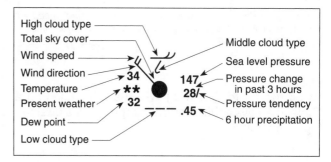

Figure 5-5. Station model for Surface Analysis Charts

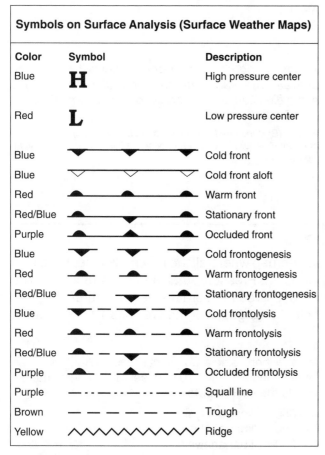

Figure 5-4. Surface Analysis Chart symbols

Color	Symbol	Description
Blue	**H**	High pressure center
Red	**L**	Low pressure center
Blue		Cold front
Blue		Cold front aloft
Red		Warm front
Red/Blue		Stationary front
Purple		Occluded front
Blue		Cold frontogenesis
Red		Warm frontogenesis
Red/Blue		Stationary frontogenesis
Blue		Cold frontolysis
Red		Warm frontolysis
Red/Blue		Stationary frontolysis
Purple		Occluded frontolysis
Purple		Squall line
Brown		Trough
Yellow		Ridge

(**Symbols on Surface Analysis (Surface Weather Maps)**)

6281. On a Surface Analysis Weather Chart, isobars are usually spaced at intervals of

A— 2 millibars.
B— 4 millibars.
C— 6 millibars.

Isobars are solid lines depicting the sea-level pressure pattern and are usually spaced at intervals of 4 millibars. (PLT287) — AC 00-45

6282. The position of fronts and pressure systems (as of chart time) is best determined by referring to a

A— Surface Analysis Chart.
B— Radar Summary Chart.
C— Weather Depiction Chart.

The position of fronts and pressure systems is shown on a Surface Analysis Weather Chart by the use of broken lines to represent the fronts. A space between the warm or cold pips indicates frontogenesis—the front is building up. A dash between the warm or cold pips indicates frontolysis—the front is dissipating. (PLT071) — AC 00-45

6283. (Refer to Figure 8.) What does symbol 12 mean on a Surface Analysis Weather Chart?

A— Squall line.
B— Occluded front.
C— High-pressure ridge.

A line on a Surface Analysis Weather Chart made up of dashes separated by two dots indicates the location of a squall line. (PLT287) — AC 00-45

Answer (B) is incorrect because an occluded front is indicated by a line with alternating semicircles and triangles. Answer (C) is incorrect because a high-pressure ridge is indicated by a zigzagging line.

Answers

6281 **[B]**   6282 **[A]**   6283 **[A]**

ALL

6283-1. (Refer to Figure 8.) What does symbol 9 mean on a Surface Analysis Weather Chart?

A— Tropical wave.
B— Ridge.
C— Trough.

A segmented brown line on a Surface Analysis Chart represents a trough, an area of relatively low pressure. (PLT287) — AC 00-45

Answer (A) is incorrect because a tropical wave is indicated by a solid brown line. Answer (B) is incorrect because a ridge is indicated by a yellow zigzagging line.

ALL

6284. (Refer to Figure 9.) Which symbol used on a Surface Analysis Weather Chart represents a dissipating warm front?

A— 1.
B— 2.
C— 3.

A dissipating warm front (warm frontolysis) is shown by the dash between the warm front pips. (PLT287) — AC 00-45

Answer (A) is incorrect because this illustrates a warm front. Answer (C) is incorrect because this illustrates the formation of a warm front.

ALL

6284-1. (Refer to Figure 9.) Which symbol used on a Surface Analysis Weather Chart represents a dissipating occluded front?

A— 4.
B— 3.
C— 2.

A dissipating occluded front is shown by the dash between the warm and cold front pips facing in the same direction, the symbol is colored purple. (PLT287) — AC 00-45

Answer (B) is incorrect because this illustrates a dissipating stationary front. Answer (C) is incorrect because this illustrates a dissipating warm front.

Constant Pressure Analysis Charts

A Constant Pressure Analysis Chart is an upper air weather map where all the information depicted is at the specified pressure-level of the chart. Each of the Constant Pressure Analysis charts (850 MB, 700 MB, 500 MB, 300 MB, 250 MB, and 200 MB) can provide observed temperature, temperature/dew point spread, wind, height of the pressure surface, and the height changes over the previous 12-hour period.

ALL

6311. From which of the following can the observed temperature, wind, and temperature/dewpoint spread be determined at specified flight levels?

A— Stability Charts.
B— Winds Aloft Forecasts.
C— Constant Pressure Charts.

Constant Pressure Charts are used to show a pilot the observed temperature, wind, and temperature/dew point spread at specified flight levels. (PLT283) — AC 00-45

Answer (A) is incorrect because Stability Charts are used to forecast the type of clouds and precipitation that is expected to form. Answer (B) is incorrect because Winds Aloft Forecasts include the forecast wind and temperature.

ALL

6312. When using a Constant Pressure Analysis Chart for planning a flight at 10,000 feet MSL, which analysis should the pilot refer to?

A— 850-millibar analysis.
B— 700-millibar analysis.
C— 500-millibar analysis.

The 700-millibar Constant Pressure Chart shows the conditions that exist at a pressure altitude of 10,000 feet. This is the chart that should be used for planning a flight at this altitude. (PLT283) — AC 00-45

Answer (A) is incorrect because the 850-millibar chart is used to about 5,000 feet. Answer (C) is incorrect because the 500-millibar chart is used to about 18,000 feet.

Answers

6283-1   [C]   6284   [B]   6284-1   [A]   6311   [C]   6312   [B]

Convective Outlook Chart

The Convective Outlook Chart (previously called Severe Weather Outlook Chart) is used primarily for advance planning. It provides an outlook for general and severe thunderstorms, tornadoes, and tornado-watch areas. Single-hatched areas will be annotated to indicate either slight, moderate, or high risk of possible severe thunderstorms. Crosshatched areas indicate a forecast risk of tornadoes.

An area labeled **APCHG** on a Convective Outlook Chart indicates probable general thunderstorm activity may approach severe intensity, which means winds greater than or equal to 35 knots, but less than 50 knots, and/or hail greater than or equal to 1/2 inch in diameter, but less than 3/4 inch in diameter (surface conditions).

Tornado watches are plotted only if a tornado watch is in effect at chart time. The watch area is cross-hatched, and no coverage is specified.

ALL

6304. (Refer to Figure 15.) What percent coverage of severe thunderstorms is forecast to occur in the area of moderate risk in the north-central United States?

A— 6 to 10.
B— 10 to 50.
C— 50 to 90.

The area of moderate risk has a 6% to 10% coverage. This means that 11 to 21 radar grid boxes contain severe thunderstorms per 100,000 square miles. (PLT066) — AC 00-45

ALL

6305. Regarding Convective Outlook Charts, when well-organized severe thunderstorms are expected, but in small numbers and/or low coverage, the risk is referred to as

A— POSSIBLE.
B— MDT.
C— SLGT.

Slight (SLGT) risk implies well-organized severe thunderstorms are expected but in small numbers and/or low coverage. (PLT051) — AC 00-45

Answer (A) is incorrect because POSSIBLE is not used as a risk area in convective outlook charts. Answer (B) is incorrect because moderate (MDT) risks imply a greater concentration of severe thunderstorms, and in most situations, greater magnitude of severe weather.

ALL

6306. (Refer to Figure 16.) The echo tops over Northern Indiana on the convective weather forecast are

A— 50,000 feet.
B— 35,000 feet.
C— 45,000 feet.

The cell over Northern Indiana is depicted to be moving at 35 knots with echo tops at 50,000 denoted by 35/500. (PLT051) — AC 00-45

ALL

6306-1. (Refer to Figure 16.) The cell over Central Indiana is forecast to be moving in what direction?

A— Northwest at 35 knots.
B— Southeast at 32 knots.
C— Stationary.

The solid blue line over central Indiana depicts the movement of the cell to be southeast at 32 knots. (PLT051) — AC 00-45

ALL

7318. How will an area of thunderstorm activity that may grow to severe intensity be indicated on the Severe Weather Outlook Chart?

A— SLGT within cross-hatched areas.
B— APCHG within any area.
C— SVR within any area.

On a Severe Weather Outlook Chart, an area labeled "APCHG" indicates that probable general thunderstorm activity may approach severe intensity. (PLT051) — AC 00-45

Answer (A) is incorrect because a cross-hatched area identifies a tornado watch area. Answer (C) is incorrect because the term SVR is not used on the Severe Weather Outlook Chart.

Answers

6304 [A]	6305 [C]	6306 [A]	6306-1 [B]	7318 [B]

Chapter 6
Enroute Flight and Navigation

Enroute Flight

When it becomes necessary to divert to an alternate airport, select the most suitable alternate, estimate the magnetic course to the alternate, and turn to the approximate heading to establish this course immediately. After becoming established on the new course, apply the new wind correction and compute the actual distance, estimated time, and fuel required.

Aeronautical charts are drawn using the geographic north pole as the north reference. However, a magnetic compass points to the magnetic north pole, which is not located at the geographic pole. The compass error caused by the angular difference between true north and magnetic north is called **magnetic variation**. Variation changes with the location on the earth, but it is the same on all headings within the location.

Aeronautical charts show the variation error with **isogonic lines** that run diagonally and irregularly across the charts. Each line is labeled with the variation error that runs along it, and the pilot must apply the correction for this error to relate the magnetic course to the true course. Westerly variation must be added to the true course or true heading to get the magnetic course or heading. Easterly variation must be subtracted from the true course or true heading to get magnetic course or magnetic heading.

To determine the true heading required to fly a desired true course, crab the airplane into the wind. If the wind is from the left, subtract the wind correction angle. If the wind is from the right, add the correction. *See* Figure 6-1.

The most widely used charts for VFR navigation of small, slow airplanes are Sectional Charts. These charts are drawn to a scale of 1:500,000 (1 inch = 6.89 nautical miles), and are revised every six months, except for some Alaskan charts which are revised every 12 months. Sectional Charts are drawn on a grid in which the meridians of longitude are non-parallel straight lines that encircle the earth from pole to pole and cross the equator at right angles. When planning a long distance flight, measure the true course from the mid-meridian to get an average true course.

Course				Heading
True	±	WCA	=	True
±				±
Variation				Variation
=				=
Magnetic	±	WCA	=	Magnetic
±				±
Deviation				Deviation
=				=
Compass	±	WCA	=	Compass

Figure 6-1. Course/heading formula

ALL

6905. When diverting to an alternate airport because of an emergency, pilots should

A— rely upon radio as the primary method of navigation.

B— complete all plotting, measuring, and computations involved before diverting.

C— apply rule-of-thumb computations, estimates, and other appropriate shortcuts to divert to the new course as soon as possible.

In diverting to an alternate airport, select the most suitable alternate, determine the magnetic course to the alternate, and turn to the approximate heading to establish this course immediately. After becoming established on the new course, apply the new wind correction and compute the actual distance, estimated time, and fuel required. (PLT319) — FAA-H-8083-25

Answer (A) is incorrect because the pilot may use any means of navigation. Answer (B) is incorrect because, in an emergency, the pilot should divert to an alternate airport as soon as possible.

Answers

6905 [C]

ALL

6882. When converting from true course to magnetic heading, a pilot should

A— subtract easterly variation and right wind correction angle.
B— add westerly variation and subtract left wind correction angle.
C— subtract westerly variation and add right wind correction angle.

When converting a true course to a true heading, subtract a left wind correction angle or add a right wind correction angle. When converting from a true heading to a magnetic heading, add westerly variation or subtract easterly variation. (PLT198) — FAA-H-8083-25

Answer (A) is incorrect because right wind correction is added. Answer (C) is incorrect because westerly variation is added.

ALL

6883. When converting from magnetic course to true course, a pilot should

A— add easterly variation regardless of heading.
B— add westerly variation regardless of heading.
C— subtract easterly variation when on a heading of 360°.

When converting from a magnetic course to a true course, add easterly variation or subtract westerly variation. (PLT198) — FAA-H-8083-25

Answer (B) is incorrect because westerly variation is subtracted. Answer (C) is incorrect because heading is not a factor in course conversion.

ALL

6884. When converting from true heading to true course, a pilot should

A— add right wind correction angle.
B— add left deviation correction angle.
C— subtract right wind correction angle.

When converting from a true heading to a true course, subtract a right wind correction angle or add a left wind correction angle. (PLT198) — FAA-H-8083-25

Answer (A) is incorrect because right wind correction angle is added when converting from true course to true heading. Answer (B) is incorrect because deviation is used to compute compass heading.

ALL

6885. The angular difference between true north and magnetic north is

A— magnetic deviation.
B— magnetic variation.
C— compass acceleration error.

The compass error caused by the angular difference between true north and magnetic north is called magnetic variation. (PLT320) — FAA-H-8083-25

Answer (A) is incorrect because deviation is due to magnetic influences within the aircraft. Answer (C) is incorrect because compass acceleration error occurs when the aircraft speeds up.

ALL

6877. Which statement about longitude and latitude is true?

A— Lines of longitude are parallel to the Equator.
B— Lines of longitude cross the Equator at right angles.
C— The 0° line of latitude passes through Greenwich, England.

Meridians of longitude encircle the earth from pole to pole, and all meridians cross the equator at right angles. (PLT101) — FAA-H-8083-25

Answer (A) is incorrect because lines of latitude are parallel to the equator. Answer (C) is incorrect because the 0° line of longitude passes through Greenwich, England.

ALL

6878. When planning a distance flight, true course measurements on a Sectional Aeronautical Chart should be made at a meridian near the midpoint of the course because the

A— values of isogonic lines change from point to point.
B— angles formed by lines of longitude and the course line vary from point to point.
C— angles formed by isogonic lines and lines of latitude vary from point to point.

Sectional Aeronautical Charts are made on grid in which the meridians of longitude are nonparallel straight lines that all meet at the earth's poles. When planning a long distance flight, measure the true course from the mid-meridian to get an average true course. (PLT101) — FAA-H-8083-25

Answers

| 6882 [B] | 6883 [A] | 6884 [C] | 6885 [B] | 6877 [B] | 6878 [B] |

ALL

6933. (Refer to Figure 44.) Where does the floor of controlled airspace begin over Ft. Worth Alliance (AFW) Airport (area 1)?

A— Surface.
B— 700 feet AGL.
C— 4,000 feet MSL.

Ft. Worth Alliance (AFW) Airport is in the middle of the far left of the chart. Ft. Worth Alliance (AFW) Airport lies within the dashed blue line which indicates Class D airspace. Therefore the floor of the controlled airspace over Ft. Worth Alliance (AFW) Airport is at the surface. (PLT064) — AIM ¶3-2-1

ALL

6934. (Refer to Figure 44.) The airspace overlying Addison Airport (area 4) is classified as

A— Class D below 3,000 feet.
B— Class B from the surface to 10,000 feet.
C— Class D from the surface up to and including 3,000 feet.

Area 4 is in the lower of the top-right quadrant. Addison Airport is within the blue dashed line, indicating Class D airspace. The Class B airspace over Addison extends from 3,000 feet MSL to 11,000 feet MSL, indicated by the 110 over 30. The upper limit's negative sign indicates up to, but not including, 3,000. (PLT064) — AIM ¶3-2-1

Answer (B) is incorrect because Class B airspace begins at 3,000 feet MSL and extends to 11,000 feet MSL. Answer (C) is incorrect because Class D airspace extends from the surface up to, but not including, 3,000 feet.

ALL

6935. (Refer to Figure 44.) What altitude should be selected to avoid operating in Class B airspace on a flight from Northwest Airport (area 2) to McKinney Airport (area 5)?

A— 2,500 feet MSL.
B— 3,000 feet MSL.
C— 3,500 feet MSL.

Areas 2 and 5 are in the top half of the chart. The Class B airspace base is 3,000 feet MSL on a direct course between Northwest Airport and McKinney Airport. Transitioning at 2,500 feet would avoid the Class B airspace. (PLT064) — AIM ¶3-2-1

ALL

6935-1. (Refer to Figure 44.) An aircraft takes off from Hicks Airport (area 1) and flies northeast towards Northwest Airport (area 2). What maximum altitude could be flown to remain under the class B airspace?

A— 4,000 feet MSL.
B— 2,500 feet MSL.
C— 3,200 feet MSL.

Areas 2 and 5 are in the top half of the chart. The Class B airspace base is 3,000 feet MSL near Northwest Airport. Transitioning at 2,500 feet would avoid the Class B airspace. (PLT064) — AIM ¶3-2-1

ALL

6936. (Refer to Figure 44.) What minimum avionics equipment is necessary to operate in the airspace up to 3,000 feet MSL over Northwest Airport (area 2)?

A— None required.
B— Transponder and encoding altimeter.
C— Two-way radio communications equipment, transponder, and encoding altimeter.

Area 2 is in the upper-left quadrant of the chart. Northwest Airport in Class G airspace from the surface to 700 feet AGL, Class E from 700 feet AGL to below 3,000 feet MSL, and Class B airspace from 3,000 feet MSL to 11,000 feet MSL. Aircraft operating within 30 NM of the primary airport of a Class B airspace must be equipped with a transponder with altitude encoding capability. (PLT064) — 14 CFR §91.131

Answer (A) is incorrect because a transponder and encoding altimeter are required within 30 NM of the primary Class B airspace. Answer (C) is incorrect because two-way radio communications equipment is not required in Class G or E airspace.

ALL

6937. (Refer to Figure 44.) When, if ever, are two-way radio communications required while enroute from Lancaster Airport (area 3) direct to McKinney Airport (area 5) at 2,700 feet MSL?

A— None required.
B— Before entering the Class B airspace.
C— Immediately after takeoff since the airport is located within Class B airspace.

Areas 3 and 5 are on the right side of the chart. Class B airspace over Lancaster Airport extends from 4,000 feet MSL to 11,000 feet MSL. However, a direct flight between Lancaster and McKinney would enter a segment of Class B airspace extending from 2,500 feet MSL to 11,000.

Continued

Answers

6933   [A]   6934   [A]   6935   [A]   6935-1   [B]   6936   [B]   6937   [B]

Unless otherwise authorized by ATC, aircraft must be equipped with an operable two-way radio capable of communicating with ATC on appropriate frequencies for that Class B airspace. (PLT064) — AIM ¶3-2-3

Answer (A) is incorrect because two-way radio communications are required for the portion of the flight in the Class B airspace. Answer (C) is incorrect because the Class B airspace over Lancaster Airport begins at 4,000 feet MSL.

ALL
6938. (Refer to Figure 44.) Select the correct statement concerning special VFR operations at Addison Airport (area 4).

A— Special VFR operations are not permitted.
B— These operations are permitted at all times.
C— Airplanes are prohibited from conducting special VFR operations.

Area 4 is in the lower left corner of the upper-right quadrant. Special VFR operations are permitted unless "NO SVFR" appears above the airport identifier. There is no restriction shown for the Addison Airport. (PLT064) — AIM ¶4-4-6

Answers (A) and (C) are incorrect because the "NO SVFR" is for the Dallas Love field.

ALL
6939. (Refer to Figure 44.) Select the correct statement concerning the Maverick VOR (area 6).

A— The VOR has Transcribed Weather Broadcast (TWEB) capability.
B— Hazardous In-Flight Weather Advisory Service (HIWAS) is not available over the VOR.
C— A pilot may receive transmissions from Fort Worth Flight Service Station over the VOR frequency.

The VOR box would need to show a black circle with a reversed-out "H" in the corner of the box. (PLT064) — Sectional Chart Legend

Answer (A) is incorrect because the VOR box would need a "T" inside a circle to indicate TWEB capability. Answer (C) is incorrect because the frequency (113.1) is underlined, indicating no voice capability.

ALL
6940. (Refer to Figure 44.) Select the correct statement concerning the obstruction 7 SM west of McKinney Airport (area 5).

A— The obstruction is unlighted.
B— The obstruction has high-intensity lights.
C— The elevation of the top of the obstruction is 729 feet AGL.

Area 5 is in the upper-right quadrant. The obstruction 7 SM west of McKinney Airport has high-intensity lights, as indicated by the lighting marks radiating from the top of the obstruction. (PLT064) — Sectional Chart Legend

Answer (A) is incorrect because the obstruction has high-intensity lights. Answer (C) is incorrect because the height of the obstruction is 819 feet AGL, indicated by the number in parenthesis.

ALL
6941. (Refer to Figure 44.) An aircraft takes off from Hicks Airport (area 1) and flies northeast towards Northwest Airport (area 2). What maximum elevation figure would assure obstruction clearance during the flight?

A— 3,200 feet MSL.
B— 1,700 feet MSL.
C— 1,900 feet MSL.

Areas 1 and 2 are in the upper-left quadrant. The boldface blue numbers shown in quadrangle bounded by ticked lines of latitude and longitude are the maximum elevation figures (MEF). The 3^2 MEF figure (which indicates 3,200 feet MSL) northwest of Northwest Airport would ensure clearance. (PLT064) — Sectional Chart Legend

---

ALL
6942. (Refer to Figure 45.) Where does the floor of controlled airspace begin over McCampbell Airport (area 1)?

A— Surface.
B— 718 feet AGL.
C— 700 feet MSL.

Area 1 is in the upper-right quadrant of the chart. McCampbell Airport is within the magenta shaded area, which indicates that Class E airspace extends from 700 feet AGL to the base of the overlying airspace (in this case, Class A airspace, beginning at 18,000 feet MSL). The elevation of the airport is 18 feet MSL, so the floor of the controlled airspace is 718 feet MSL. (PLT064) — AIM ¶3-2-1

Answer (A) is incorrect because the magenta shaded area indicates that Class E airspace begins at 700 feet AGL. Answer (C) is incorrect because 700 feet MSL would be below the lateral limits of Class E airspace.

ALL
6943. (Refer to Figure 45.) The controlled airspace located at the Corpus Christi VORTAC (area 5) begins at

A— the surface.
B— 700 feet AGL.
C— 1,200 feet MSL.

Area 5 is in the upper-right quadrant of the chart. The Corpus Christi VORTAC is just inside the magenta sec-

---

Answers

6938 [B]	6939 [B]	6940 [B]	6941 [A]	6942 [C]	6943 [B]

tion indicating Class E airspace starting at 700 feet AGL proceeding up to the base of Class C airspace of 1,200 feet MSL. (PLT064) — AIM ¶3-2-1

Answer (A) is incorrect because magenta shading indicates Class E airspace begins at 700 feet AGL. Answer (C) is incorrect because 1,200 feet is the beginning of Class C airspace, but the control begins with the Class E airspace at 700 feet AGL.

ALL

6944. (Refer to Figure 45.) When are two-way radio communications required on a flight from Bishop Airport (area 4) to McCampbell Airport (area 1) at an altitude of 2,000 feet MSL?

A— Entering the Corpus Christi Class C airspace.
B— Leaving and entering the alert areas and entering Corpus Christi Class C airspace.
C— Leaving and entering the alert areas, entering the Corpus Christi Class C airspace, and passing through the Cabaniss Field Class D airspace.

Area 4 is in the center of the chart, and area 1 is in the upper-right quadrant of the chart. On a flight from Bishop Airport to McCampbell Airport at 2,000 feet MSL, two-way radio communications are required when entering the Corpus Christi Class C airspace. (PLT064) — 14 CFR §91.130

Answer (B) is incorrect because two-way communications are not required in alert areas. Answer (C) is incorrect because two-way communications are not required in alert areas, and a direct flight will not pass through the Cabaniss Field Class D airspace.

ALL

6945. (Refer to Figure 45.) Assuming owner permission, what minimum avionics equipment is required for operation into Cuddihy Airport (area 8)?

A— Two-way radio communications equipment.
B— None, if altitude remains at or below 1,200 feet MSL.
C— Two-way radio communications equipment and transponder with encoding altimeter.

Area 8 is in the center of the chart. Two-way radio communications and transponder with encoding altimeter are required for operation into Cuddihy Airport because it is located within the Corpus Christi Class C airspace, indicated by the solid magenta lines. (PLT064) — 14 CFR §91.130

Answer (A) is incorrect because the airport is in the Class C airspace from the surface to 4,000 feet, which requires two-way communications, a transponder, and encoding altimeter. Answer (B) is incorrect because the Class C airspace extends from the surface to 4,000 feet.

ALL

6946. (Refer to Figure 45.) The airspace beginning at the surface overlying NAS Kingsville (area 2) is

A— an Alert Area.
B— Class D airspace.
C— a military operations area (MOA).

Area 2 is in the lower-left quadrant of the chart. The blue dashed circle surrounding NAS Kingsville indicates Class D airspace extending from the surface to the base of the overlying Class E Airspace (which begins at 2,500 feet MSL). (PLT064) — AIM ¶3-2-1

Answers (A) and (C) are incorrect because the vertical limits of the alert area and Kingsville 2 MOA are not indicated, but the airport is definitely lying within Class D airspace, which begins at the surface.

ALL

6947. (Refer to Figure 45.) What are the requirements for operating in the alert area (area 6) just west of Corpus Christi International Airport (area 3)?

A— Contact with approach control on frequency 120.9 is required.
B— Prior permission must be obtained from the controlling agency.
C— There are no requirements, but pilots should be extremely cautious due to extensive student training.

Areas 6 and 3 are in the center of the chart. U.S. alert areas, such as the one just west of Corpus Christi International Airport, contain a high volume of pilot training or unusual type of aerial activity. Pilots should be particularly alert when flying in these areas. (PLT064) — AIM ¶3-2-1

Answers (A) and (B) are incorrect because contacting approach control and prior permission is not necessary to enter alert areas.

ALL

6948. (Refer to Figure 45.) While on a flight from Alice Airport (area 7) to McCampbell Airport (area 1) at 5,500 feet MSL, when, if ever, is a transponder required?

A— Transponder is not required.
B— Required when overflying the Corpus Christi Class C airspace.
C— Required when leaving and entering the alert areas and overflying the Corpus Christi Class C airspace.

Continued

Answers

6944 [A]   6945 [C]   6946 [B]   6947 [C]   6948 [B]

Area 1 is on the right side of the chart, and area 7 is the center of the left side of the chart. The flight will overfly the Corpus Christi Class C airspace, which requires a transponder. (PLT064) — AIM ¶4-1-20, 14 CFR §91.215

Answer (A) is incorrect because a transponder with encoding altimeter is required for operations in or over Class C airspace. Answer (C) is incorrect because a transponder is not required in alert areas.

ALL

6949. (Refer to Figure 45.) What is the elevation of the top of the obstruction located approximately 3 NM northwest of McCampbell Airport (area 1)?

A— 280 feet AGL.
B— 353 feet MSL.
C— 315 feet MSL.

Area 1 is in the upper-right quadrant of the chart. The elevation of the obstruction located 3 NM northwest of McCampbell Airport is 315 feet MSL. (PLT064) — Sectional Chart Legend

ALL

6949-1. (Refer to Figure 45.) What is the elevation of the Thomas (T69) Airport (area 5)?

A— 122 feet MSL.
B— 43 feet MSL.
C— 48 feet MSL.

The "48" below the airport name is the airport elevation in feet MSL. (PLT064) — Sectional Chart Legend

Answer (A) is incorrect because this is the CTAF frequency. Answer (B) is incorrect because this is the length of the longest runway.

ALL

6950. (Refer to Figure 46.) Where does the floor of controlled airspace begin over Half Moon Bay Airport (area 1)?

A— Surface.
B— 700 feet AGL.
C— 5,000 feet MSL.

Area 1 is in the lower-left quadrant of the chart. Half Moon Bay Airport is in a magenta-shaded area, which indicates the Class E airspace begins at 700 feet AGL and extends to the overlying airspace (in this case, Class B airspace at 5,000 feet MSL). (PLT064) — AIM ¶3-2-1

ALL

6951. (Refer to Figure 46.) When are two-way radio communications required on a flight from Gnoss Airport (area 4) to Livermore Airport (area 5) at an altitude of 3,500 feet AGL? When entering

A— the Class B airspace.
B— the Livermore Airport Class D airspace.
C— both the Class B airspace and the Livermore Airport Class D airspace.

Area 4 is in the upper-left corner of the chart, and area 5 is in the center of the right side of the chart. A direct flight from Gnoss Airport to Livermore Airport at an altitude of 3,500 feet AGL will pass below the San Francisco Class B airspace. The blue dashed lines around Livermore Airport indicate Class D airspace extending from the surface to a specified altitude (2,900 feet MSL, in this case). Two-way radio communications are required to enter Class D airspace. (PLT064) — AIM ¶3-2-1

Answers (A) and (C) are incorrect because the flight will pass beneath the Class B airspace.

ALL

6952. (Refer to Figure 46.) What is the height of the Class D airspace over Livermore Airport (area 5)?

A— 2,900 feet MSL.
B— 3,000 feet AGL.
C— Base of the overlying Class B airspace.

Area 5 is in the middle of the right side of the chart. The height of the Class D airspace over Livermore Airport is 2,900 feet MSL, indicated by the [29]. (PLT064) — Sectional Chart Legend

Answer (B) is incorrect because the Class D airspace extends from the surface to 2,900 feet MSL. Answer (C) is incorrect because the airport lies within the 30-NM Mode-C veil, but there is no overlying Class B airspace.

ALL

6953. (Refer to Figure 46.) While on a flight from Livermore Airport (area 5) to Gnoss Airport (area 4), you contact San Francisco Approach Control and request clearance through the Class B airspace. The controller states "Radar contact, standby." What are you authorized to do?

A— You may enter the airspace since the controller advised you "Radar contact."
B— You may enter the airspace since you have established two-way radio communications.
C— You may not enter the airspace until you have received authorization from ATC.

Answers

6949　[C]　　　6949-1　[C]　　　6950　[B]　　　6951　[B]　　　6952　[A]　　　6953　[C]

Area 5 is in the middle of the right side of the chart, and area 4 is in the upper left-hand corner. A flight from Livermore Airport to Gnoss Airport passes through Class B airspace. You are not to enter the Class B airspace until you have received authorization from ATC. "Radar contact, standby" simply means the controller has you on the radar screen, it does not give you permission to enter the airspace. (PLT044) — AIM ¶3-2-1

ALL
6954. (Refer to Figure 46.) At what altitude does the Class B airspace begin over Hayward Airport (area 3)?

A— Surface.
B— 1,500 feet MSL.
C— 3,000 feet MSL.

Area 3 is in the middle of the chart. Class B airspace begins at 3,000 feet MSL over Hayward Airport, indicated by the 80/30. (PLT064) — AIM ¶3-2-3

Answer (A) is incorrect because the Class C airspace over Hayward Airport extends from 1,500 feet MSL. Answer (B) is incorrect because the Class B airspace west of the Hayward Airport extends from 2,100 feet MSL.

ALL
6954-1. (Refer to Figure 46.) At what altitude does the Class D airspace terminate over Hayward Airport (area 3)?

A— Surface.
B— 1,500 feet MSL.
C— 3,000 feet MSL.

The dashed blue line around Hayward Airport depicts Class D airspace. The blue [15] defines the ceiling of the Class D airspace in hundreds of feet. (PLT064) — AIM ¶3-2-5

ALL
6955. (Refer to Figure 46.) What is the ceiling of the Class C airspace surrounding San Jose International Airport (area 2)?

A— 2,500 feet AGL.
B— 4,000 feet MSL.
C— 6,000 feet MSL.

Area 2 is in the lower right quadrant of the chart. The ceiling of the Class C airspace surrounding San Jose International Airport is 4,000 feet MSL, indicated by the 40/SFC in magenta inside the inner circle. (PLT064) — AIM ¶3-2-4

Answer (A) is incorrect because Class B, C, and D airspace altitudes are given in MSL. Answer (C) is incorrect because the Class B airspace extends from 6,000 feet to 8,000 feet MSL.

ALL
6956. (Refer to Figure 46.) The minimum avionics equipment necessary to operate in the airspace above 10,000 feet MSL over San Francisco International Airport (area 6) is

A— transponder and encoding altimeter.
B— two-way radio communications equipment.
C— two-way radio communications equipment, transponder, and encoding altimeter.

Area 6 is in the center of the left side of the chart. The solid blue lines surrounding the airport and the 100/SFC indicate that the Class B airspace extends from the surface to 10,000 feet. The airspace above Class B airspace requires the use of transponder and encoding altimeter. (PLT064) — 14 CFR §91.131

ALL
6957. (Refer to Figure 46.) What does the figure 2^4 (area 3) indicate?

A— Maximum elevation figure for that quadrangle.
B— Minimum safe altitude when approaching San Francisco.
C— Height above ground of the tallest obstruction for that quadrangle.

Area 3 is in the center of the left side of the chart. The figure 2^4 is the maximum elevation figure (MEF) for the chart. This indicates the maximum elevation in this grid of the chart. The highest elevation in the section of the chart bounded by the ticked longitude and latitude lines is 2,400 feet above mean sea level, and include both terrain and obstruction features. (PLT064) — Sectional Chart Legend

Answer (B) is incorrect because minimum safe altitudes are depicted on IFR approach plates. Answer (C) is incorrect because MEFs are given in MSL and are based on both terrain and obstructions.

Answers

6954 [C]	6954-1 [B]	6955 [B]	6956 [A]	6957 [A]

ALL

6958. (Refer to Figure 46.) An aircraft takes off from Gnoss Airport (area 4) and flies eastward to Rio Vista Airport (area 7). What maximum elevation figure would assure obstruction clearance during the flight?

A— 2,200 feet MSL.
B— 4,200 feet MSL.
C— 3,200 feet MSL.

Area 4 is in the top left of the chart, and area 7 is in the upper right corner of the chart. The maximum elevation to ensure obstacle clearance during the flight would be 3,200 feet MSL, indicated by the 3^2 in area 4. (PLT064) — Sectional Chart Legend

ALL

7096. (Refer to Figure 46.) The area south of GNOSS (Area 4) is a

A— free flight zone.
B— parachute drop area.
C— closed airport.

The crossed-out hollow circle north of NOVATO depicts an abandoned airport. (PLT064) — Sectional Chart legend

The Wind Triangle

True course is determined by measuring the course on an aeronautical chart. **True airspeed** is known by applying the appropriate correction to the indication of the airspeed indicator. The wind direction and velocity are known from reports or forecasts from the Flight Service Stations.

The true heading and the ground speed can be found by drawing a wind triangle of vectors. One side of the triangle is the wind direction and velocity, one side is the true heading and true airspeed, the final side is the track, or true course, and the ground speed. Each side of a wind triangle is the vector sum of the other two sides.

ALL

6879. (Refer to Figure 40.) The line from point A to point B of the wind triangle represents

A— true heading and airspeed.
B— true course and groundspeed.
C— groundspeed and true heading.

The line A to B of the wind triangle represents true heading and the true airspeed. It is the vector sum of the lines C to B (the true course and ground speed) and C to A (the wind direction and speed). (PLT012) — FAA-H-8083-25

Answer (B) is incorrect because this is represented by the line from point C to B. Answer (C) is incorrect because these are the values found by using the wind triangle.

ALL

6880. (Refer to Figure 40.) The line from point C to point B of the wind triangle represents

A— airspeed and heading.
B— groundspeed and true course.
C— true heading and groundspeed.

The line from point C to B of the wind triangle represents the ground speed and true course. (PLT012) — FAA-H-8083-25

Answer (A) is incorrect because this is represented by the line from point A to B. Answer (C) is incorrect because these are the values found by using the wind triangle.

ALL

6881. (Refer to Figure 40.) The line from point C to point A of the wind triangle represents

A— wind direction and velocity.
B— true course and groundspeed.
C— true heading and groundspeed.

The line from point C to A of the wind triangle represents the wind direction and speed (velocity). (PLT012) — FAA-H-8083-25

Answer (B) is incorrect because this is represented by the line from point C to B. Answer (C) is incorrect because these are the values found by using the wind triangle.

Answers

6958   [C]   7096   [C]   6879   [A]   6880   [B]   6881   [A]

The Flight Computer
Finding Time, Distance, Ground Speed

ASA's CX-2 Pathfinder is an electronic flight computer and can be used in place of the E6-B. This aviation computer can solve all flight planning problems, as well as perform standard mathematical calculations.

Problem:

Calculate the distance and time upon reaching 8,500 feet MSL. Given:

Departure path.. straight out

Takeoff time .... 1030 DST

Winds during climb .... 180° at 30 knots

True course during climb .... 160°

Airport elevation.. 1,500 feet

True airspeed .... 125 knots

Rate of climb.. 500 fpm

Solution:

1. Find the ground speed and heading (use Hdg/GS on CX-2 menu):

   Wind direction (W Dir) .... 180°

   Wind speed (W Spd) .... 30 knots

   Course (Crs) .... 160°

   True airspeed (TAS) .... 125 knots

   Ground speed (GS) .... 96.4 knots

   Heading (Hdg) .... 165°

2. Find the total distance required to climb to get to 8,500 feet:

   8,500 (destination) – 1,500 (airport elevation) = 7,000 feet

3. Calculate the time to climb 7,000 feet:

   7,000 (total climb) ÷ 500 (rate of climb) = 14 minutes

4. Find the distance flown (use Dist Flown on CX-2 menu):

   Time (Time)... 14 minutes

   Ground speed (GS) .... 96.4 knots

   Distance (Dist) .... 22.5 NM

5. Find the time arrived at 8,500 feet (add takeoff time to time flown to get ETA):

   Takeoff time .... 1030 DST

   Time flown .... 14 minutes

   ETA... 1044 DST

Therefore, the takeoff and climb to altitude will require 22.5 NM, and you will arrive at 1044 DST.

AIR, RTC, LSA, WSC, PPC
6856. GIVEN:

Departure path	straight out
Takeoff time	1030 DST
Winds during climb	180° at 30 kts
True course during climb	160°
Airport elevation	1,500 ft
True airspeed	125 kts
Rate of climb	500 ft/min

What would be the distance and time upon reaching 8,500 feet MSL?

A— 20 NM and 1047 DST.
B— 23 NM and 1044 DST.
C— 25 NM and 1047 DST.

1. Find the ground speed and heading (Hdg/GS):

Wind direction	180°
Wind speed	30 knots
Course	160°
True airspeed	125 knots
Ground speed	96.4 knots
Heading	165°

2. Find the total distance required to climb to get to 8,500 feet:

8,500 (destination) – 1,500 (airport elevation)
= 7,000 feet

3. Calculate the time to climb 7,000 feet:

7,000 (total climb) ÷ 500 (rate of climb)
= 14 minutes

4. Find the distance flown:

Time	14 minutes
Ground speed	96.4 knots
Distance	22.5 NM

5. Find the time arrived at 8,500 feet:

Takeoff time	1030 DST
Time flown	14 minutes
ETA	1044 DST

(PLT012) — FAA-H-8083-25

AIR, RTC, LSA, WSC, PPC
6857. GIVEN:

Departure path	straight out
Takeoff time	1435Z
Winds during climb	175° at 25 kts
True course during climb	155°
Airport elevation	2,000 ft
True airspeed	130 kts
Rate of climb	500 ft/min

What would be the distance and time upon reaching 8,000 feet MSL?

A— 27 NM and 1455Z.
B— 24 NM and 1452Z.
C— 21 NM and 1447Z.

1. Find the ground speed and heading (Hdg/GS):

Wind direction	175°
Wind speed	25 knots
Course	155°
True airspeed	130 knots
Ground speed	106.2 knots
Heading	159°

2. Find the total distance required to climb to get to 8,000 feet:

8,000 (destination) – 2,000 (airport elevation)
= 6,000 feet

3. Calculate the time to climb 6,000 feet:

6,000 (total climb) ÷ 500 (rate of climb)
= 12 minutes

4. Find the distance flown (Dist Flown):

Time	12 minutes
Ground speed	106.2 knots
Distance	21.2 NM

5. Find the time arrived at 8,000 feet:

Takeoff time	1435 DST
Time flown	12 minutes
ETA	1447 DST

(PLT012) — FAA-H-8083-25

Answers

6856   [B]   6857   [C]

ALL

6857-1. On a cross-country flight, point X is crossed at 1015 local. What is your expected arrival time at point Y? Use the following information to determine your ETA.

Distance between X and Y ....32 NM
True course ....100°
Forecast wind .... 240° at 25 kts
Pressure altitude.. 5,500 ft
Ambient temperature...................................... +05°C
Indicated airspeed ....110 knots

A— 1033 local.
B— 1031 local.
C— 1029 local.

Using your CX-2 Flight Computer:

1. *Determine your plan TAS using the given, CAS (expressed as IAS) 110 knots, OAT +05°C, and pressure altitude 5,500 feet. TAS = 119.5 knots.*

2. *Next determine your ground speed based on the following conditions, true course 100°, TAS 119.5 knots, wind direction 240°, and wind speed 25 knots. GS = 137.6 knots (round up to 138 knots).*

3. *From here you can find the duration to fly from point X to point Y 32 NM at 138 knot GS = 14 minutes.*

4. *1015 + 0014 = ETA 1029 local.*

(PLT012) — FAA-H-8083-25

AIR, RTC, LSA, WSC, PPC

6858. GIVEN:

Distance..300 NM
True course ....260°
Wind .... 245° at 45 kts
True airspeed ....119 kts
Rate of fuel consumption........................... 12.7 gal/hr

What would be the approximate groundspeed and amount of fuel consumed?

A— 75 knots; 49.1 gallons.
B— 84 knots; 46.1 gallons.
C— 75 knots; 50.8 gallons.

1. *Find the ground speed and heading (Hdg/GS):*

   Wind direction... 245°
   Wind speed... 45 kts
   Course... 260°
   True airspeed... 119 kts
   Ground speed... 75.0 kts
   Heading... 254°

2. *Calculate the time flown (LegTime):*

   Distance.. 300 NM
   Ground speed... 75.0 kts
   Time flown..04:00:00

3. *Calculate the fuel burn:*

   Time flown..04:00:00
   Fuel burn rate...................................... 12.7 gal/hr
   Fuel consumed.................................. 50.8 gallons

(PLT012) — FAA-H-8083-25

AIR, RTC, LSA, WSC, PPC

6859. GIVEN:

Distance...200 NM
True course ....320°
Wind .... 215° at 25 kts
True airspeed ....116 kts
Rate of fuel consumption............................ 19 gal/hr

What would be the approximate groundspeed and amount of fuel consumed?

A— 132 knots; 28.9 gallons.
B— 120 knots; 31.7 gallons.
C— 115 knots; 33.1 gallons.

1. *Find the ground speed and heading (Hdg/GS):*

   Wind direction... 215°
   Wind speed... 25 kts
   Course... 320°
   True airspeed... 116 kts
   Ground speed... 119.9 kts
   Heading... 308°

2. *Calculate the time flown (LegTime):*

   Distance.. 200 NM
   Ground speed... 119.9 kts
   Time flown..01:40:04

3. *Calculate the fuel burn:*

   Time flown..01:40:04
   Fuel burn rate... 19 gal/hr
   Fuel consumed.................................. 31.7 gallons

(PLT012) — FAA-H-8083-25

Answers

6857-1 [C]   6858   [C]   6859   [B]

Finding Magnetic Heading and Ground Speed

Problem:

Find the ground speed and magnetic heading given the following conditions:

True course	258°
Variation...	10° East
Indicated airspeed	142 knots
Ambient temperature...	+05°C
Pressure altitude..	6,500 feet
Forecast wind	350° at 30 knots

Solution:

1. Find true airspeed (Plan TAS on CX-2 menu):

Pressure altitude (P Alt).......................................	6,500 feet
Temperature (T°C)..	+5°C
Calibrated airspeed (CAS)...................................	142 knots (use indicated airspeed)
True airspeed (TAS)	157.1

2. Find ground speed (Hdg/GS on CX-2 menu):

Wind direction (W Dir)	350°
Wind speed (W Spd)	30 knots
Course (Crs)	258°
True airspeed (TAS)	157.1 knots
Ground speed (GS)	155.3 knots
True heading (Hdg)..	269°

3. Find magnetic heading:

    269 − 10 = 259°

AIR, RTC, LSA, WSC, PPC

6886. GIVEN:

True course ....258°	
Variation... 10° E	
Indicated airspeed ....142 kts	
Ambient temperature...+05°C	
Pressure altitude.. 6,500 ft	
Forecast wind .... 350° at 30 kts	

Under these conditions, the magnetic heading and groundspeed would be approximately

A— 260° and 155 knots.
B— 270° and 157 knots.
C— 280° and 155 knots.

1. *Find true airspeed (Plan TAS on CX-2 menu):*

Pressure altitude....................................6,500 feet	
Temperature ....+5°C	
Calibrated airspeed .... 142 knots	
(use indicated airspeed)	
True airspeed...157.1	

2. *Find ground speed (Hdg/GS on CX-2 menu):*

Wind direction.. 350°	
Wind speed.. 30 knots	
Course... 258°	
True airspeed...................................... 157.1 knots	
Ground speed.................................... 155.3 knots	
True heading... 269°	

3. *Find magnetic heading:*

    269 − 10 = 259°

(PLT012) — FAA-H-8083-25

AIR, RTC, LSA, WSC, PPC
6887. GIVEN:

True course ....330°
Variation.................................... 15° E
Indicated airspeed ....160 kts
Ambient temperature ....-10°C
Pressure altitude............................ 4,500 ft
Forecast wind ....090° at 25 kts

Under these conditions, the magnetic heading and groundspeed would be approximately

A— 323° and 177 knots.
B— 332° and 166 knots.
C— 340° and 177 knots.

1. *Find true airspeed (Plan TAS on CX-2 menu):*

   Pressure altitude....................................4,500 feet
   Temperature ....-10°C
   Calibrated airspeed .... 160 knots
   (use indicated airspeed)
   True airspeed..................................165.9

2. *Find ground speed (Hdg/GS on CX-2 menu):*

   Wind direction.................................. 090°
   Wind speed.................................. 25 knots
   Course.................................. 330°
   True airspeed.................................. 165.9 knots
   Ground speed.................................. 176.9 knots
   True heading.................................. 338°

3. *Find magnetic heading:*

   338 – 15 = 323°

(PLT012) — FAA-H-8083-25

AIR, RTC, LSA, WSC, PPC
6888. GIVEN:

True course ....238°
Variation... 3° W
Indicated airspeed ....160 kts
Ambient temperature ....-15°C
Pressure altitude............................... 8,500 ft
Forecast wind .... 160° at 25 kts

Under these conditions, the magnetic heading and groundspeed would be approximately

A— 224° and 171 knots.
B— 233° and 171 knots.
C— 241° and 178 knots.

1. *Find true airspeed (Plan TAS on CX-2 menu):*

   Pressure altitude....................................8,500 feet
   Temperature ....-15°C
   Calibrated airspeed .... 160 knots
   (use indicated airspeed)
   True airspeed..................................176.9

2. *Find ground speed (Hdg/GS on CX-2 menu):*

   Wind direction.................................. 160°
   Wind speed.................................. 25 knots
   Course.................................. 238°
   True airspeed.................................. 176.9 knots
   Ground speed.................................. 170.0 knots
   True heading.................................. 230°

3. *Find magnetic heading:*

   230 + 3 = 233°

(PLT012) — FAA-H-8083-25

Answers

6887   [A]   6888   [B]

Finding Wind Direction and Velocity

When the true heading, true airspeed, the ground track and ground speed are known, the wind direction and velocity can be found.

Problem:

Determine the wind direction and speed given the following conditions (use Unknown Wind on CX-2 menu):

True heading (Hdg) .... 135°

Ground speed (GS) .... 140 knots

True airspeed (TAS) .... 135 knots

Ground track (Crs).. 130°

Solution:

Wind direction (W Dir) .... 246°

Wind speed (W Spd) .... 13 knots

AIR, RTC, LSA, WSC, PPC

6874. If a true heading of 135° results in a ground track of 130° and a true airspeed of 135 knots results in a groundspeed of 140 knots, the wind would be from

A— 019° and 12 knots.
B— 200° and 13 knots.
C— 246° and 13 knots.

Use Unknown Wind on CX-2 menu:

True heading... 135°
Ground speed... 140 knots
True airspeed.. 135 knots
Ground track... 130°
Wind direction... 246°
Wind speed... 13 knots

(PLT012) — FAA-H-8083-25

AIR, RTC, LSA, WSC, PPC

6875. If a true heading of 350° results in a ground track of 335° and a true airspeed of 140 knots results in a groundspeed of 115 knots, the wind would be from

A— 015° and 30 knots.
B— 035° and 40 knots.
C— 290° and 40 knots.

Use Unknown Wind on CX-2 menu:

True heading... 350°
Ground speed... 115 knots
True airspeed.. 140 knots
Ground track.. 335°
Wind direction... 036°
Wind speed... 41 knots

(PLT012) — FAA-H-8083-25

AIR, RTC, LSA, WSC, PPC

6876. If a true heading of 230° results in a ground track of 250° and a true airspeed of 160 knots results in a groundspeed of 175 knots, the wind would be from

A— 135° and 59 knots.
B— 165° and 60 knots.
C— 343° and 60 knots.

Use Unknown Wind on CX-2 menu:

True heading... 230°
Ground speed... 175 knots
True airspeed.. 160 knots
Ground track.. 250°
Wind direction... 136°
Wind speed... 60 knots

(PLT012) — FAA-H-8083-25

Answers

6874 [C]   6875 [B]   6876 [A]

Finding Distance Traveled

When the ground speed and lapsed time are known, the distance traveled can be found (use Dist Flown on CX-2 menu):

Lapsed time (Time).. 2-1/2 minutes

Ground speed (GS) .... 98 knots

Distance flown (Dist)... 4.1 NM

AIR, RTC, LSA, WSC, PPC

6869. How far will an aircraft travel in 2-1/2 minutes with a groundspeed of 98 knots?

A— 2.45 NM.
B— 3.35 NM.
C— 4.08 NM.

Use Dist Flown on CX-2 menu:

Lapsed time...2-1/2 minutes
Ground speed.. 98 knots
Distance flown .... 4.1 NM

(PLT012) — FAA-H-8083-25

AIR, RTC, LSA, WSC, PPC

6870. How far will an aircraft travel in 3-1/2 minutes if its groundspeed is 165 knots?

A— 5.8 NM.
B— 9.6 NM.
C— 12.8 NM.

Use Dist Flown on CX-2 menu:

Lapsed time...3-1/2 minutes
Ground speed... 165 knots
Distance flown .... 9.6 NM

(PLT012) — FAA-H-8083-25

Finding Fuel Required

When the fuel consumption and the ground speed are known, the amount of fuel required to fly a given distance can be found.

Problem:

Find the fuel required given the following conditions:

Fuel consumption .... 15.3 GPH

Ground speed.. 167 knots

Distance to travel.. 620 NM

Solution:

1. Find the leg time (use Leg Time on CX-2 menu):

   Distance (Dist) .... 620 NM

   Ground speed (GS) .... 167 knots

   Time flown 03:42:45

2. Find the fuel consumption (use Fuel Burn on CX-2 menu):

   Time flown (Time) 03:42:45

   Fuel burn rate (FPH).. 15.3 GPH

   Fuel burned (Fuel) .... 56.8 gallons

Answers

6869   [C]   6870   [B]

AIR, RTC, LSA, WSC, PPC

6864. If fuel consumption is 15.3 gallons per hour and groundspeed is 167 knots, how much fuel is required for an aircraft to travel 620 NM?

A— 63 gallons.
B— 60 gallons.
C— 57 gallons.

1. Find the leg time (use Leg Time on CX-2 menu):

   Distance.. 620 NM
   Ground speed... 167 knots
   Time flown 03:42:45

2. Find the fuel consumption:

   Time flown 03:42:45
   Fuel burn rate .... 15.3 GPH
   Fuel burned .... 56.8 gallons

(PLT015) — FAA-H-8083-25

AIR, RTC, LSA, WSC, PPC

6865. If an aircraft is consuming 91 pounds of fuel per hour and groundspeed is 168 knots, how much fuel is required to travel 457 NM?

A— 291 pounds.
B— 265 pounds.
C— 248 pounds.

1. Find the leg time (use Leg Time on CX-2 menu):

   Distance.. 457 NM
   Ground speed... 168 knots
   Time flown 02:43:13

2. Find the fuel consumption:

   Time flown 02:43:13
   Fuel burn rate ....91 pounds/hour
   Fuel burned ....247.5 pounds

(PLT012) — FAA-H-8083-25

Finding Range Available

The range available in an aircraft can be found when the fuel on board, the fuel consumption rate, the ground speed, the flight time since takeoff, and the required reserve are known. 14 CFR §91.151 requires that for VFR flight, an airplane start off with enough fuel to fly to the point of intended destination, and after that for 30 minutes in the daytime and 45 minutes at night.

Problem:

How much farther can the airplane can fly, under day VFR conditions, according to 14 CFR Part 91? Given:

Usable fuel at takeoff... 36 gallons

Fuel consumption rate... 12.4 GPH

Constant ground speed .... 140 knots

Flight time since takeoff... 48 minutes

Solution:

1. Find the total amount of flight time provided by the usable fuel at takeoff (use Endurance on CX-2 menu):

   Usable fuel at takeoff.. 36 gallons

   Fuel burn rate .... 12.4 GPH

   Time available.. 02:54:12

2. Find the total time available, accounting for regulations and time already flown:

   02:54:12 – 00:30:00 – 00:48:00 = 01:36:12

3. Calculate the distance available to fly (use Dist Flown on CX-2 menu):

   Time available.. 01:36:12

   Ground speed... 140 knots

   Distance... 224.5 NM

Answers

6864   [C]   6865   [C]

AIR, RTC, LSA, WSC, PPC,
6860. GIVEN:

Usable fuel at takeoff.. 36 gal
Fuel consumption rate............................... 12.4 gal/hr
Constant groundspeed ....140 kts
Flight time since takeoff.................................. 48 min

According to Part 91, how much farther can an airplane be flown under day VFR?

A— 294 NM.
B— 224 NM.
C— 189 NM.

1. Find the total amount of flight time provided by the usable fuel at takeoff:

    Usable fuel at takeoff............................. 36 gallons
    Fuel burn rate .... 12.4 GPH
    Time available..02:54:12

2. Find the total time available, accounting for regulations and time already flown:

    02:54:12 – 00:30:00 – 00:48:00 = 01:36:12

3. Calculate the distance available to fly:

    Time available...01:36:12
    Ground speed.. 140 knots
    Distance.. 224.5 NM

(PLT012) — FAA-H-8083-25

AIR, RTC, LSA, WSC, PPC
6861. GIVEN:

Usable fuel at takeoff.. 36 gal
Fuel consumption rate............................... 12.4 gal/hr
Constant groundspeed ....140 kts
Flight time since takeoff.................................. 48 min

According to FAR Part 91, how much farther can an airplane be flown under night VFR?

A— 189 NM.
B— 224 NM.
C— 294 NM.

1. Find the total amount of flight time provided by the usable fuel at takeoff (Endurance on CX-2 menu):

    Usable fuel at takeoff............................. 36 gallons
    Fuel burn rate .... 12.4 GPH
    Time available..02:54:12

2. Find the total time available, accounting for regulations and time already flown:

    02:54:12 – 00:45:00 – 00:48:00 = 01:21:12

3. Calculate the distance available to fly (Dist Flown):

    Time available...01:21:12
    Ground speed.. 140 knots
    Distance.. 189.5 NM

(PLT012) — FAA-H-8083-25

AIR, RTC, LSA, WSC, PPC
6862. GIVEN:

Usable fuel at takeoff.. 40 gal
Fuel consumption rate............................... 12.2 gal/hr
Constant groundspeed ....120 kts
Flight time since takeoff............................. 1 hr 30 min

According to Part 91, how much farther can an airplane be flown under night VFR?

A— 216 NM.
B— 156 NM.
C— 121 NM.

1. Find the total amount of flight time provided by the usable fuel at takeoff (Endurance on CX-2 menu):

    Usable fuel at takeoff............................. 40 gallons
    Fuel burn rate .... 12.2 GPH
    Time available..03:16:43

2. Find the total time available, accounting for regulations and time already flown:

    03:16:43 – 00:45:00 – 01:30:00 = 01:01:43

3. Calculate the distance available to fly (Dist Flown):

    Time available...01:01:43
    Ground speed.. 120 knots
    Distance.. 123.4 NM

(PLT012) — FAA-H-8083-25

Answers

6860   [B]   6861   [A]   6862   [C]

Finding the Required Airspeed

The required airspeed can be found, when a specific point needs to be reached at a certain time.

Problem:

Find the required airspeed given the following conditions:

Distance between points A and B .... 70 NM

Time between points A and B .... 30 minutes

Forecast wind .... 310° at 15 knots

Pressure altitude.. 8,000 feet

Ambient temperature... -10°C

True course .... 270°

Solution:

1. Find the ground speed that must be made between points A and B (GS on CX-2 menu):

    Distance (Dist) .... 70 NM

    Time to travel (Time).. 30 minutes

    Ground speed (GS) .... 140 knots

2. Find the true airspeed (Hdg/TAS on CX-2 menu):

    Wind direction (W Dir) .... 310°

    Wind speed (W Spd) .... 15 knots

    Course (Crs) .... 270°

    Ground speed (GS) .... 140 knots

    True airspeed (TAS) .... 151.8 knots

    True heading (Hdg)... 274°

3. Find the required indicated airspeed (or calibrated airspeed) (ReqCAS on CX-2 menu):

    Pressure altitude (P Alt) .... 8,000 feet

    Temperature (T°C) .... -10°C

    True airspeed (TAS) .... 151.8 knots

    Indicated airspeed (CAS) .... 137.1 knots (same as calibrated)

AIR, RTC, LSA, WSC

6866. On a cross-country flight, point A is crossed at 1500 hours and the plan is to reach point B at 1530 hours. Use the following information to determine the indicated airspeed required to reach point B on schedule.

Distance between A and B..............................70 NM
Forecast wind .... 310° at 15 kts
Pressure altitude.. 8,000 ft
Ambient temperature ....-10°C
True course ....270°

The required indicated airspeed would be approximately

A— 126 knots.
B— 137 knots.
C— 152 knots.

1. Find the ground speed that must be made between points A and B (GS on CX-2 menu):

   Distance... 70 NM
   Time to travel...................................... 30 minutes
   Ground speed.. 140 knots

2. Find the true airspeed (Hdg/TAS):

   Wind direction.. 310°
   Wind speed.. 15 knots
   Course... 270°
   Ground speed.. 140 knots
   True airspeed...................................... 151.8 knots
   True heading.. 274°

3. Find the required indicated airspeed (or calibrated airspeed) (ReqCAS):

   Pressure altitude...................................8,000 feet
   Temperature ....-10°C
   True airspeed...................................... 151.8 knots
   Indicated airspeed.............................. 137.1 knots
   (same as calibrated)

(PLT012) — FAA-H-8083-25

AIR, RTC, LSA, WSC

6867. On a cross-country flight, point X is crossed at 1015 and arrival at point Y is expected at 1025. Use the following information to determine the indicated airspeed required to reach point Y on schedule.

Distance between X and Y ....27 NM
Forecast wind .... 240° at 30 kts
Pressure altitude..5,500 ft
Ambient temperature ....+05°C
True course ....100°

The required indicated airspeed would be approximately

A— 162 knots.
B— 140 knots.
C— 128 knots.

1. Find the ground speed that must be made between points A and B (GS on CX-2 menu):

   Distance... 27 NM
   Time to travel...................................... 10 minutes
   Ground speed.. 162 knots

2. Find the true airspeed (Hdg/TAS):

   Wind direction.. 240°
   Wind speed.. 30 knots
   Course... 100°
   Ground speed.. 162 knots
   True airspeed...................................... 140.3 knots
   True heading.. 108°

3. Find the required indicated airspeed (or calibrated airspeed) (ReqCAS):

   Pressure altitude...................................5,500 feet
   Temperature ....+5°C
   True airspeed...................................... 140.3 knots
   Indicated airspeed.............................. 129.2 knots
   (same as calibrated)

(PLT012) — FAA-H-8083-25

Answers

6866　[B]　　　　6867　[C]

AIR, RTC, LSA, WSC

6868. On a cross-country flight, point X is crossed at 1550 and the plan is to reach point Y at 1620. Use the following information to determine the indicated airspeed required to reach point Y on schedule.

Distance between X and Y ....70 NM
Forecast wind .... 115° at 25 kts
Pressure altitude.. 9,000 ft
Ambient temperature...-05°C
True course ....088°

The required indicated airspeed would be approximately

A— 138 knots.
B— 143 knots.
C— 162 knots.

1. Find the ground speed that must be made between points A and B (GS on CX-2 menu):

Distance... 70 NM
Time to travel... 30 minutes
Ground speed... 140 knots

2. Find the true airspeed (Hdg/TAS):

Wind direction... 115°
Wind speed... 25 knots
Course.. 088°
Ground speed.. 140 knots
True airspeed....................................... 162.7 knots
True heading..092°

3. Find the required indicated airspeed (or calibrated airspeed) (ReqCAS):

Pressure altitude.....................................9,000 feet
Temperature ....-5°C
True airspeed....................................... 162.7 knots
Indicated airspeed .... 142.9 knots
(same as calibrated)

(PLT012) — FAA-H-8083-25

Off-Course Correction

After flying for a given distance, you find yourself a known distance off course. You can find the correction angle needed to return the airplane to the desired course in a specific distance by using this simple relationship:

$$\frac{\text{Miles off course}}{\text{Miles flown or to fly}} = \frac{\text{Degrees to parallel or converge}}{60}$$

Problem:

After 141 miles are flown from the departure point, the aircraft's position is located 11 miles off course. If 71 miles remain to be flown, what approximate total correction should be made to converge on the destination?

Solution:

1. Find the change in heading needed to parallel the original course with the formula:

$$\text{Degrees to parallel} = \frac{\text{miles off course x 60}}{\text{miles flown}}$$

$$\frac{11 \times 60}{141} = 4.68°$$

2. Find the change in heading needed to converge on the destination in 71 miles with the formula:

$$\text{Degrees to converge} = \frac{\text{miles off course x 60}}{\text{miles to fly}}$$

$$\frac{11 \times 60}{71} = 9.29°$$

3. Add these two corrections to find the total correction required to converge on the destination:

4.68 + 9.29 = 13.97°

AIR, RTC, GLI, LTA

6871. After 141 miles are flown from the departure point, the aircraft's position is located 11 miles off course. If 71 miles remain to be flown, what approximate total correction should be made to converge on the destination?

A— 8°.
B— 11°.
C— 14°.

1. *Find the change in heading needed to parallel the original course with the formula:*

$$\text{Degrees to parallel} = \frac{\text{miles off course x 60}}{\text{miles flown}}$$

$$\frac{11 \times 60}{141} = 4.68°$$

2. *Find the change in heading needed to converge on the destination in 71 miles with the formula:*

$$\text{Degrees to converge} = \frac{\text{miles off course x 60}}{\text{miles to fly}}$$

$$\frac{11 \times 60}{71} = 9.29°$$

3. *Add these two corrections to find the total correction required to converge on the destination:*

4.68 + 9.29 = 13.97°

(PLT012) — FAA-H-8083-25

AIR, RTC, GLI, LTA

6872. After 150 miles are flown from the departure point, the aircraft's position is located 8 miles off course. If 160 miles remain to be flown, what approximate total correction should be made to converge on the destination?

A— 6°.
B— 9°.
C— 12°.

1. *Find the change in heading needed to parallel the original course with the formula:*

$$\text{Degrees to parallel} = \frac{\text{miles off course x 60}}{\text{miles flown}}$$

$$\frac{8 \times 60}{150} = 3.2°$$

2. *Find the change in heading needed to converge on the destination in 160 miles with the formula:*

$$\text{Degrees to converge} = \frac{\text{miles off course x 60}}{\text{miles to fly}}$$

$$\frac{8 \times 60}{160} = 3°$$

3. *Add these two corrections to find the total correction required to converge on the destination:*

3.2 + 3 = 6.2°

(PLT012) — FAA-H-8083-25

Answers

6871 [C]   6872 [A]

AIR, RTC, GLI, LTA
6873. After 240 miles are flown from the departure point, the aircraft's position is located 25 miles off course. If 100 miles remain to be flown, what approximate total correction should be made to converge on the destination?

A— 15°.
B— 21°.
C— 30°.

1. Find the change in heading needed to parallel the original course with the formula:

$$\text{Degrees to parallel} = \frac{\text{miles off course} \times 60}{\text{miles flown}}$$

$$\frac{25 \times 60}{240} = 6.25°$$

2. Find the change in heading needed to converge on the destination in 100 miles with the formula:

$$\text{Degrees to converge} = \frac{\text{miles off course} \times 60}{\text{miles to fly}}$$

$$\frac{25 \times 60}{100} = 15°$$

3. Add these two corrections to find the total correction required to converge on the destination:

$$6.25 + 15 = 21.25°$$

(PLT012) — FAA-H-8083-25

Very High Frequency Omni-Directional Range (VOR)

Radio signals in the very high frequency (VHF) band are nominally in the frequency range of 30 to 300 megahertz (MHz). They operate according to the line-of-sight principle, following the same rules as light, and do not bend to conform to the surface of the earth. VHF reception distance varies in proportion to the altitude of the receiving equipment. The higher the aircraft, the greater the reception distance.

VHF Omni-Directional Range stations (VORs) operate within the 108.0 to 117.95 MHz frequency band and have a power output necessary to provide coverage within their assigned operational service volume. They are subject to line-of-sight restrictions and their range varies with the altitude of the receiving equipment. There are three classes of VOR:

- HVOR Range below 18,000 feet is 40 miles, range between 18,000 feet and FL450 is 130 miles, range above FL450 is 100 miles.
- LVOR Range below 18,000 feet is 40 miles.
- TVOR Range below 12,000 feet is 25 miles.

To orient where the aircraft is in relation to the VOR, first determine which radial is selected (look at the OBS setting). Next, determine whether the aircraft is flying to or away from the station (look at the TO/FROM indicator), to find which hemisphere the aircraft is in. Last, determine how far off course the aircraft is from the selected course (look at the CDI needle deflection) to find which quadrant the aircraft is in. Remember that aircraft heading does not affect orientation to the VOR. If the station is directly abeam of the aircraft, the TO/FROM Indicator will show a neutral flag.

AIR, RTC
6900. (Refer to Figure 42.) At which aircraft position(s) would you receive OMNI indication V?

A— 2 only.
B— 6 only.
C— 5 and 8.

A FROM indication, with a 180° course selection, means the aircraft is in the southern hemisphere. A left CDI needle means the aircraft is in the left quadrant. Airplane 2 fits this description. Remember that the VOR works without regard to the aircraft heading. (PLT276) — FAA-H-8083-25

Answer (B) is incorrect because aircraft 6 would have a TO indication with a right CDI deflection. Answer (C) is incorrect because aircrafts 5 and 8 would have right CDI deflections.

Answers
6873   [B]   6900   [A]

AIR, RTC

6901. (Refer to Figure 42.) At which aircraft position(s) would you receive OMNI indication X?

A— 1 and 3.
B— 3 and 7.
C— 7 only.

A neutral flag indication, with a 180° course selection, means the aircraft is in the middle. A left CDI needle means the aircraft is in the left quadrant. Airplanes 1 and 3 fit this description. Remember that the VOR works without regard to the aircraft heading. (PLT276) — FAA-H-8083-25

Answers (B) and (C) are incorrect because aircraft 7 would have a right CDI deflection.

AIR, RTC

6902. (Refer to Figure 42.) At which aircraft position(s) would you receive OMNI indication U?

A— 1 and 2.
B— 2 only.
C— 6 only.

A TO indication, with a 180° course selection, means the aircraft is in the northern hemisphere. A right CDI needle means the aircraft is in the right quadrant. Airplane 6 fits this description. Remember that the VOR works without regard to the aircraft heading. (PLT276) — FAA-H-8083-25

Answers (A) and (B) are incorrect because aircraft 1 would have a neutral flag and a left CDI deflection, and aircraft 2 would have a FROM indication, with a left CDI deflection.

AIR, RTC

6903. (Refer to Figure 42.) Which OMNI indication would you receive for aircraft 8?

A— T.
B— V.
C— W.

Airplane 8 is in the southern hemisphere with a 180° OBS setting (which requires a FROM indication), and is in the right quadrant (which requires a right CDI deflection). This description fits VOR indicator W. (PLT276) — FAA-H-8083-25

AIR, RTC

6904. (Refer to Figure 42.) Which OMNI indications would you receive for aircraft 5 and 7?

A— T and X.
B— V and X.
C— W and Z.

Airplane 5 is in the southern hemisphere with a 180° OBS setting (which requires a FROM indication), and is in the right quadrant (which requires a right CDI deflection). This description fits VOR indicator W. Airplane 7 is in the middle hemisphere with a 180° OBS setting (which requires a neutral flag), and is in the right quadrant (which requires a right CDI deflection). This description fits VOR indicator Z. (PLT276) — FAA-H-8083-25

Time and Distance to the Station Using VOR

The time to the station is found by the formula:

$$\text{Time to station} = \frac{60 \times \text{minutes between bearing changes}}{\text{degree of bearing change}}$$

The distance to the station is found by the formula:

$$\text{Distance to station} = \frac{\text{TAS} \times \text{minutes between bearing changes}}{\text{degree of bearing change}}$$

Problem:

While maintaining a magnetic heading of 060° and a true airspeed of 130 knots, the 150° radial of a VOR is crossed at 1137 and the 140° radial at 1145. What is the approximate time to the station?

Continued

Answers

6901   [A]   6902   [C]   6903   [C]   6904   [C]

Solution:

$$\text{Time to station} = \frac{60 \text{ x minutes between bearing changes}}{\text{degree of bearing change}}$$

$$= \frac{60 \text{ x } 8}{10}$$

$$= 48 \text{ minutes}$$

Problem:

Given these conditions, find the distance to the station.

Solution:

$$\text{Distance to station} = \frac{\text{TAS x minutes between bearing changes}}{\text{degree of bearing change}}$$

$$= \frac{130 \text{ x } 8}{10}$$

$$= 104 \text{ NM}$$

Therefore, the station is 104 nautical miles away.

AIR, RTC

6919. While maintaining a magnetic heading of 060° and a true airspeed of 130 knots, the 150° radial of a VOR is crossed at 1137 and the 140° radial at 1145. The approximate time and distance to the station would be

A— 38 minutes and 82 NM.
B— 42 minutes and 91 NM.
C— 48 minutes and 104 NM.

$$\text{Time to Station} = \frac{60 \text{ x minutes between bearing changes}}{\text{degree of bearing change}}$$

$$\frac{60 \text{ x } 8}{10} = 48 \text{ minutes}$$

$$\text{Distance to Station} = \frac{\text{TAS x minutes between bearing changes}}{\text{degree of bearing change}}$$

$$\frac{130 \text{ x } 8}{10} = 104 \text{ NM}$$

(PLT014) — FAA-H-8083-15

AIR, RTC

6920. While maintaining a magnetic heading of 180° and a true airspeed of 130 knots, the 270° radial of a VOR is crossed at 1037 and the 260° radial at 1042. The approximate time and distance to the station would be

A— 30 minutes and 65 NM.
B— 42 minutes and 104 NM.
C— 44 minutes and 96 NM.

$$\text{Time to Station} = \frac{60 \text{ x minutes between bearing changes}}{\text{degree of bearing change}}$$

$$\frac{60 \text{ x } 5}{10} = 30 \text{ minutes}$$

$$\text{Distance to Station} = \frac{\text{TAS x minutes between bearing changes}}{\text{degree of bearing change}}$$

$$\frac{130 \text{ x } 5}{10} = 65 \text{ NM}$$

(PLT014) — FAA-H-8083-15

Answers

6919   [C]   6920   [A]

VOR Test (VOT)

To use the VOT service, tune in the VOT frequency on your VOR receiver. With the Course Deviation Indicator (CDI) centered, the Omni-Bearing Selector (OBS) should read 0° (or 360°) with the TO-FROM indicator showing FROM, or the Omni-Bearing Selector should read 180° with the TO/FROM indicator showing TO. Should the VOR receiver operate an RMI, it will indicate 180° TO on any OBS setting.

AIR, RTC

6922. When using a VOT to check the accuracy of a VOR receiver with an RMI, what should the RMI indicate if no error exists?

A— 180° FROM.
B— 180° TO.
C— 360° TO.

To use the VOT service, tune in the VOT frequency on your VOR receiver. If the VOR receiver operates an RMI, it will indicate 180° TO on any OBS setting. (PLT300) — AIM ¶1-1-4

AIR, RTC

6923. When using a VOT to check the accuracy of a VOR receiver, with the CDI centered, what should the OBS indicate if no error exists?

A— 360° TO, 270° FROM.
B— 180° FROM, 360° TO.
C— 180° TO, 360° FROM.

To use the VOT service, tune in the VOT frequency on your VOR receiver. With the CDI centered, the OBS should read 0° (360°) with a FROM indication, or 180° with a TO indication. (PLT300) — AIM ¶1-1-4

VORTAC

Note: Sport Pilot Instructors can disregard this section.

A VORTAC station is a VOR station collocated with a military TACAN station. Civilian airplanes use the VOR for direction to or from the station, and the DME portion of the TACAN for distance information to the station. When a VORTAC station is undergoing routine maintenance, the identification code is removed. The VORTAC provides three individual services:

1. VHF VOR azimuth

2. UHF TACAN azimuth

3. UHF TACAN distance information (DME)

AIR, RTC

6924. A particular VORTAC station is undergoing routine maintenance. This is evidenced by

A— removal of the identification feature.
B— removal of the voice feature of the TACAN.
C— transmitting a series of dashes after each identification signal.

When a VORTAC station is undergoing routine maintenance, the identification code is removed. (PLT300) — AIM ¶1-1-6

AIR, RTC

6925. The three individual navigation services provided by a VORTAC facility are

A— UHF VOR azimuth, VHF TACAN azimuth, and VHF TACAN distance information.
B— VHF VOR azimuth, UHF TACAN azimuth, and UHF TACAN distance information.
C— VHF VOR azimuth, VHF TACAN azimuth, and UHF TACAN distance information.

A VORTAC is a facility consisting of two components, VOR and TACAN, which provide three individual services:

1. VHF VOR azimuth

2. UHF TACAN azimuth

3. UHF TACAN distance information (DME)

(PLT322) — AIM ¶1-1-6

Answers

6922 [B]	6923 [C]	6924 [A]	6925 [B]

Distance Measuring Equipment (DME)

The mileage readout of **DME** is the direct distance in nautical miles between the aircraft and the DME ground facility. This is commonly referred to as the slant-range, or slant-line, distance. The slant-range error is greatest when the aircraft is directly above the facility at a high altitude. An aircraft flying at 6,000 feet AGL directly above the facility would indicate a DME distance of 1 nautical mile.

DME furnishes distance information with a high degree of accuracy. Reliable signals may be received at distances of up to 199 nautical miles at line-of-sight altitude, with an accuracy of better than 1/2 mile or 3% of the distance, whichever is greater.

The DME or TACAN coded identification is transmitted 1 time for each 3 or 4 times that the VOR or localizer coded identification is transmitted. When either the VOR or DME is inoperative, it is important to recognize which identifier is retained for the operative facility. A single coded identification with a repetition interval of approximately 30 seconds indicates that the DME is operative.

When in the VOR mode, lateral deflection of the needle in the CDI represents degrees the aircraft is off course. A full needle deflection indicates that the airplane is 10° or more off course.

AIR, RTC

6911. Which distance is commonly displayed by a DME indicator?

A— Slant-range distance in statute miles.
B— Slant-range distance in nautical miles.
C— The distance from the aircraft to a point at the same altitude directly above the VORTAC.

The mileage readout of a DME is the direct distance in nautical miles between the aircraft and the DME ground facility. This is commonly referred to as the slant-range, or slant-line, distance. (PLT202) — FAA-H-8083-15

AIR, RTC

6912. Which DME indication should you receive when you are directly over a VORTAC site at approximately 6,000 feet AGL?

A— 0.
B— 1.
C— 1.3.

Since the mileage readout of a DME is the direct distance in nautical miles between the aircraft and the DME ground facility, an aircraft flying at 6,000 feet AGL directly above the facility would indicate a DME distance of 1 nautical mile. (PLT202) — FAA-H-8083-15

AIR, RTC

6926. Which statement is true concerning the operation of DME?

A— DME operates in the VHF frequency band.
B— Distance information received from DME is the actual horizontal distance from the station.
C— DME coded identification is transmitted once for each three or four times that the VOR coded identification is transmitted.

The DME or TACAN coded identification is transmitted 1 time for each 3 or 4 times that the VOR or localizer coded identification is transmitted. (PLT202) — AIM ¶1-1-7

Answer (A) is incorrect because DME operates in the UHF frequency band. Answer (B) is incorrect because DME measures slant distance.

Answers

6911   [B]   6912   [B]   6926   [C]

Chapter 7
Procedures and Airport Operations

Airspace

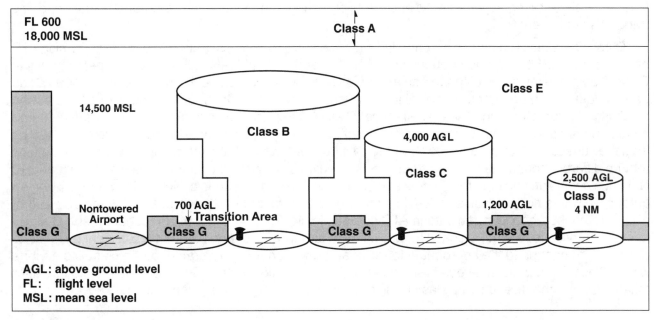

Figure 7-1. Airspace

Controlled airspace, that is, airspace within which some or all aircraft may be subject to air traffic control, consists of those areas designated as Class A, Class B, Class C, Class D, and Class E airspace.

Much of the controlled airspace begins at either 700 feet or 1,200 feet above the ground. The lateral limits and floors of Class E airspace of 700 feet are defined by a magenta vignette; while the lateral limits and floors of 1,200 feet are defined by a blue vignette if it abuts uncontrolled airspace. Floors other than 700 feet or 1,200 feet are indicated by a number indicating the floor.

Class A — Class A airspace extends from 18,000 feet MSL up to and including FL600 and is not depicted on VFR sectional charts. No flight under visual flight rules (VFR), including VFR-On-Top, is authorized in Class A airspace. Except as provided in 14 CFR Part 91.135, no person may operate an aircraft within Class A airspace unless it is operated under IFR at a specific flight level assigned by ATC.

Class B — Class B airspace consists of controlled airspace extending upward from the surface or higher, to specified altitudes. Each Class B airspace sector, outlined in blue on the sectional aeronautical chart, is labeled with its delimiting altitudes. On the Terminal Area Chart, each Class B airspace sector is outlined in blue and is labeled with its delimiting arcs, radials, and altitudes. Each Class B airspace location will contain at least one primary airport. An ATC clearance is required prior to operating within Class B airspace. A pilot landing or taking off from one of a group of 12 specific, busy airports must hold at least a Private Pilot Certificate. At other airports, a student pilot may not operate an aircraft on a solo flight within Class B airspace, or to, from, or at an airport located within Class B airspace, unless both ground and flight instruction has been received from an authorized instructor to operate within that Class B airspace or at that airport, and the flight and ground instruction has been received within that Class B airspace or at the specific airport for which the solo flight is authorized. The student's logbook must be endorsed within the preceding 90 days by the instructor who gave the flight training and the endorsement must specify that the student has been found competent to conduct solo flight operations in that Class B airspace or at that specific airport. Each airplane operating within Class B airspace must

Continued

be equipped with a two-way radio with appropriate ATC frequencies, and a 4096 code transponder with Mode C automatic altitude-reporting capability. No person may operate an aircraft in Class B airspace unless the aircraft is equipped with the applicable operating transponder and automatic altitude reporting (Mode C) equipment.

Class C — Class C airspace is controlled airspace surrounding designated airports within which ATC provides radar vectoring and sequencing for all IFR and VFR aircraft. Each airplane operating within Class C airspace must be equipped with a two-way radio with appropriate frequencies, and a 4096 Code transponder with Mode C automatic altitude-reporting capability. Communications with ATC must be established prior to entering Class C airspace. Class C airspace consists of two circles, both centered on the primary airport. The surface area has a radius of 5 NM. The airspace of the surface area extends from the surface of Class C airspace airport up to 4,000 feet above that airport, normally. Some situations require different boundaries. The shelf area has a radius of 10 NM. The airspace between the 5 and 10 NM rings begins at a height of 1,200 feet and extends to the same altitude ceiling as the surface area. An outer area with a normal radius of 20 NM surrounds the surface and shelf areas. Within the outer area, pilots are encouraged to participate in ATC communications, but it is not a VFR requirement. Class C airspace service for aircraft proceeding to a satellite airport will be terminated at a sufficient distance to allow time to change to the appropriate tower or advisory frequency. Aircraft departing satellite airports within Class C airspace shall establish two-way communication with ATC as soon as practicable after takeoff. On aeronautical charts, Class C airspace is depicted by solid magenta lines.

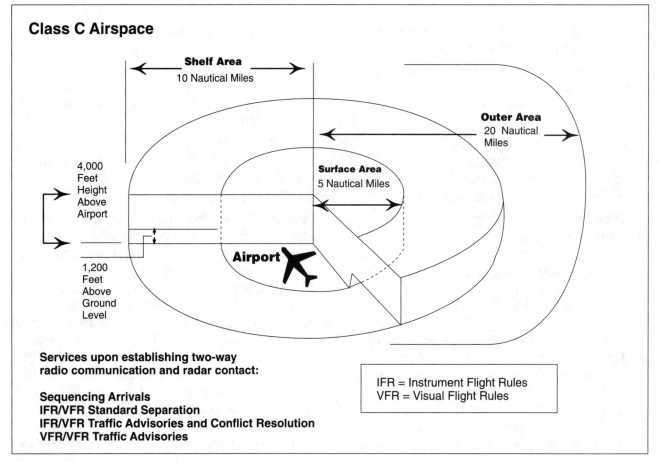

Figure 7-2. Class C airspace

No person may operate an aircraft in Class C airspace unless two-way radio communication is established with the ATC facility having jurisdiction over the Class C airspace prior to entering that area, and is thereafter maintained with ATC while within that area. A coded transponder is required for all aircraft in Class C airspace and in all airspace above the ceiling and within the lateral boundaries of Class C airspace upward to 10,000 feet MSL.

Class D — Class D airspace extends upward from the surface to approximately 2,500 feet AGL (the actual height is as needed). Class D airspace may include one or more airports and is normally 4 nautical miles in radius. The actual size and shape is depicted by a blue dashed line and numbers showing the top. When the ceiling of Class D airspace is less than 1,000 feet and/or the visibility is less than 3 statute miles, pilots wishing to takeoff or land must hold an instrument rating, must have filed an instrument flight plan, and must have received an appropriate clearance from ATC. In addition, the aircraft must be equipped for instrument flight. At some locations, a pilot who does not hold an instrument rating may be authorized to takeoff or land when the weather is less than that required for visual flight rules. When special VFR flight is prohibited, it will be depicted by "No SVFR" above the airport information on the chart. A turbine-powered airplane or a large airplane shall, unless otherwise required by the applicable distance from cloud criteria, enter the Class D airspace at an altitude of at least 1,500 feet above the surface of the airport and maintain at least 1,500 feet within the airport traffic area, including the traffic pattern, until further descent is required for a safe landing.

Class E — Magenta shading identifies Class E airspace starting at 700 feet AGL, and no shading (or blue if next to Class G airspace) identifies Class E airspace starting at 1,200 feet AGL. It may also start at other altitudes. All airspace from 14,500 feet to 17,999 feet is Class E airspace. It also includes the surface area of some airports with an instrument approach, but no control tower.

Class G — Class G airspace is airspace within which Air Traffic Control (ATC) has neither the authority nor responsibility to exercise any control over air traffic.

Aircraft are required to maintain specified cloud clearances and visibilities while in certain airspace. *See* Figure 7-3.

Altitude	Flight Visibility	Distance from Clouds
1,200 feet or less above the surface— Within controlled airspace	3 statute miles	500 feet below 1,000 feet above 2,000 feet horizontal
Outside controlled airspace: **Day** [except as provided in section 91.155(b)]	1 statute mile*	Clear of clouds
Night [except as provided in section 91.155(b)]	3 statute miles	500 feet below 1,000 feet above 2,000 feet horizontal
More than 1,200 feet above the surface but less than 10,000 feet MSL— Within controlled airspace	3 statute miles	500 feet below 1,000 feet above 2,000 feet horizontal
Outside controlled airspace: **Day**	1 statute mile*	500 feet below 1,000 feet above 2,000 feet horizontal
Night	3 statute miles	500 feet below 1,000 feet above 2,000 feet horizontal
More than 1,200 feet above the surface and at or above 10,000 feet MSL—	5 statute miles	1,000 feet below 1,000 feet above 1 mile horizontal

Figure 7-3. Cloud clearance and visibility requirements in Class E and G airspace

*3 statute miles for Sport Pilots

Prohibited Areas are blocks of airspace within which the flight of aircraft is prohibited.

Restricted Areas denote the presence of unusual, often invisible, hazards to aircraft such as artillery firing, aerial gunnery, or guided missiles. Penetration of Restricted Areas without authorization from the using or controlling agency may be extremely hazardous to the aircraft and its occupants.

Warning Areas contain the same hazardous activities as those found in Restricted Areas, but are located in international airspace.

Military Operations Areas (MOAs) consist of airspace established for the purpose of separating certain military training activities from instrument flight rules (IFR) traffic. Pilots operating under VFR should exercise extreme caution while flying within an active MOA. Any Flight Service Station (FSS) within 100 miles of the area will provide information concerning MOA hours of operation. Prior to entering an active MOA, pilots should contact the controlling agency for traffic advisories.

Alert Areas may contain a high volume of pilot training activities or an unusual type of aerial activity, neither of which is hazardous to aircraft. Pilots of participating aircraft, as well as pilots transiting the area, are equally responsible for collision avoidance.

Military Training Routes (MTRs) have been developed for use by the military for the purpose of conducting low-altitude, high-speed training. Generally, MTRs are established below 10,000 feet MSL for operations at speeds in excess of 250 knots.

ALL
6928. Within the contiguous United States, the floor of Class A airspace is

A— 14,500 feet MSL.
B— 18,000 feet MSL.
C— 18,000 feet AGL.

Class A airspace includes specified airspace within the contiguous U.S. from 18,000 feet MSL to and including FL600. (PLT161) — AIM ¶3-2-2

ALL
6440. In which type of airspace are VFR flights prohibited?

A— Class A.
B— Class B.
C— Class C.

Except as provided in 14 CFR Part 91.135, no person may operate an aircraft within Class A airspace, unless it is operated under IFR at a specific flight level assigned by ATC. (PLT161) — 14 CFR §91.135

ALL
6445. When operating VFR in Class B airspace, what are the visibility and cloud clearance requirements?

A— 3 SM visibility and clear of clouds.
B— 3 SM visibility, 500 feet below, 1,000 feet above, and 2,000 feet horizontal distance from clouds.
C— 1 SM visibility, 500 feet below, 1,000 feet above, and 2,000 feet horizontal distance from clouds.

Class B airspace requires 3 SM flight visibility and clear of clouds. (PLT163) — 14 CFR §91.155

ALL
6438. Which is true regarding VFR operations in Class B airspace?

A— An operating VOR is required.
B— A Private Pilot Certificate is required for all flight within this airspace.
C— Solo student pilots are authorized to fly in Class B airspace if they meet certain requirements.

A solo student pilot may be authorized to operate an aircraft according to VFR in Class B airspace if he/she meets the requirements of 14 CFR §61.95. (PLT161) — 14 CFR §91.131

Answers

6928 [B]	6440 [A]	6445 [A]	6438 [C]

ALL

6439. Which equipment is required when operating an aircraft within Class B airspace?

A— A VOR or TACAN receiver.
B— Two-way radio communications.
C— Two-way radio communications and transponder with encoding altimeter.

No person may operate an aircraft in Class B airspace unless the aircraft is equipped with a 4096 code transponder with altitude reporting capability. (PLT161) — 14 CFR §91.131

ALL

6960. (Refer to Figure 47.) What is the radius of the surface area (circle C)?

A— 5 miles.
B— 10 miles.
C— 15 miles.

The surface area of Class C airspace has a normal radius of 5 nautical miles from the center of the primary airport. (PLT161) — AIM ¶3-2-4

ALL

6965. To operate an aircraft within Class C airspace from a satellite airport without an operating control tower, a pilot must

A— monitor ATC until clear of the Class C airspace.
B— contact ATC as soon as practicable after takeoff.
C— secure prior approval from ATC before takeoff at the airport.

Aircraft departing satellite airports/heliports within the Class C airspace shall establish two-way radio communication with ATC as soon as possible. (PLT161) — AIM ¶3-2-4

ALL

6961. (Refer to Figure 47.) What is the radius of the shelf area (circle A)?

A— 5 miles.
B— 10 miles.
C— 15 miles.

The shelf area of Class C airspace has a normal radius of 10 nautical miles from the center of the primary airport. (PLT040) — AIM ¶3-2-4

ALL

6962. (Refer to Figure 47.) Which altitude (box 2) is applicable to the base of the shelf area?

A— 700 feet AGL.
B— 1,200 feet MSL.
C— 1,200 feet AGL.

The base of the shelf area of Class C airspace is 1,200 feet AGL. (PLT040) — AIM ¶3-2-4

ALL

6963. (Refer to Figure 47.) Which altitude (box 1) is applicable to the vertical extent of the surface and shelf areas of this Class C airspace?

A— 3,000 feet AGL.
B— 3,000 feet above airport.
C— 4,000 feet above airport.

Both the surface and shelf areas of Class C airspace extend upward to an altitude of 4,000 feet above the surface of the primary airport. (PLT040) — AIM ¶3-2-4

ALL

6959. (Refer to Figure 47.) What is the normal radius of the outer area (area B)?

A— 10 NM.
B— 20 NM.
C— 25 NM.

The outer area of Class C airspace normally has a radius of 20 nautical miles, with some variations based on specific site requirements. (PLT161) — AIM ¶3-2-4

ALL

6964. What minimum avionics equipment is required for operation within Class C airspace?

A— Two-way communications.
B— Two-way communications and transponder with automatic altitude reporting capability.
C— Two-way communications, transponder with automatic altitude reporting capability, and VOR.

The minimum equipment required for operation in Class C airspace is an operating two-way communications radio and a transponder with automatic altitude reporting capability. (PLT161) — AIM ¶3-2-4

Answers

6439 [C]	6960 [A]	6965 [B]	6961 [B]	6962 [C]	6963 [C]
6959 [B]	6964 [B]				

ALL

6966. All operations within Class C airspace must be

A— in accordance with instrument flight rules.
B— on a flight plan filed prior to arrival or departure.
C— in an aircraft equipped with a transponder with automatic altitude reporting capability and in communication with the responsible ATC facility.

No person may operate an aircraft in Class C airspace unless there is an operating Mode C transponder and two-way radio communication is established with ATC, prior to entering Class C airspace and thereafter maintained with ATC while within that area. (PLT161) — AIM ¶3-2-4

Answer (A) is incorrect because visual flight rules are also used within Class C airspace. Answer (B) is incorrect because flight plans are not required in Class C airspace.

ALL

6480. What are the requirements, if any, to overfly Class C airspace?

A— None, provided the flight remains above the airspace ceiling.
B— Transponder with automatic altitude reporting capability is required above the airspace ceiling and upward to 10,000 feet MSL.
C— Two-way radio communications must be established with ATC and transponder must be operating at all times.

No person may operate an aircraft in Class C airspace unless two-way radio communication is established with the ATC facility having jurisdiction over the Class C airspace prior to entering that area and is thereafter maintained with ATC while within that area. A coded transponder is required for all aircraft in Class C airspace and in all airspace above the ceiling and within the lateral boundaries of Class C airspace upward to 10,000 feet MSL. (PLT161) — 14 CFR §91.130 and §91.215

ALL

6436. An airport without a control tower lies within the controlled airspace of an airport with an operating tower. According to regulations, two-way radio communications with ATC are required for landing clearance at

A— both airports, as well as to fly through the area.
B— the tower-controlled airport only, as well as to fly through the area.
C— the tower-controlled airport only, but not required to fly through the area.

For arrival and through flights in Class D airspace, each person must establish two-way radio communications with the ATC facility providing air traffic services prior to entering that airspace and thereafter maintain that communication while within that airspace. (PLT161) — 14 CFR §91.129

Answer (A) is incorrect because an ATC clearance is not required to land at a non-controlled airport. Answer (C) is incorrect because radio communications with ATC is required to fly through Class D airspace.

ALL

6448. Normally, the vertical limits of Class D airspace extend up to and including how many feet above the surface?

A— 2,500 feet.
B— 3,000 feet.
C— 4,000 feet.

Unless otherwise specifically designated (by 14 CFR Part 93), Class D airspace consists of the airspace within a horizontal radius of 4 nautical miles from the geographic center of any airport at which a control tower is operating, extending from the surface up to 2,500 feet above the elevation of the airport. Actual dimensions will be shown on appropriate charts. (PLT161) — AIM ¶3-2-5

ALL

6930. When a control tower, located on an airport within Class D airspace ceases operation for the day, what happens to the airspace designation?

A— The airspace designation normally will not change.
B— The airspace remains Class D airspace as long as a weather observer or automated weather system is available.
C— The airspace reverts to Class E or a combination of Class E and G airspace during the hours the tower is not in operation.

Class D airspace requires an operational control tower. When that tower ceases to operate, it reverts to Class E airspace. Without weather reporting capability, Class E airspace reverts to Class G airspace. (PLT162) — AIM ¶3-2-5

Answers

6966 [C]	6480 [B]	6436 [B]	6448 [A]	6930 [C]

ALL

6931. The vertical limit of Class D airspace will normally be designated at

A— the base of the Class E airspace.
B— up to, and including, 2,500 feet AGL.
C— up to, but not including, 3,000 feet AGL.

Class D airspace will normally be designated at up to and including 2,500 feet above the surface of the airport. (PLT161) — AIM ¶3-2-5

ALL

6435. A turbine-powered or large airplane is required to enter an airport traffic pattern at an altitude of at least

A— 1,000 feet AGL.
B— 1,500 feet AGL.
C— 2,000 feet AGL.

A turbine-powered airplane or a large airplane shall, unless otherwise required by the applicable distance from cloud criteria, enter Class D airspace at an altitude of at least 1,500 feet above the surface of the airport and maintain at least 1,500 feet within Class D airspace, including the traffic pattern, until further descent is required for a safe landing. (PLT146) — 14 CFR §91.129

ALL

6446. The minimum visibility for VFR flight in Class E airspace increases from 3 to 5 SM beginning at an altitude of

A— 10,000 feet MSL.
B— 14,500 feet MSL.
C— 1,200 feet AGL and at or above 10,000 feet MSL.

Visibility for VFR in Class E airspace increases from 3 to 5 miles, at or above 10,000 feet. (PLT163) — 14 CFR §91.155

ALL

6929. With certain exceptions, Class E airspace extends upward from either 700 feet or 1,200 feet AGL to, but does not include,

A— 10,000 feet MSL.
B— 14,500 feet MSL.
C— 18,000 feet MSL.

Class E airspace extends upward to (but not including) 18,000 feet MSL. (PLT161) — 14 CFR §71.71

ALL

6932. Class E airspace within the contiguous United States extends upward from either 700 feet or 1,200 feet AGL to, but not including

A— 3,000 feet MSL.
B— 14,500 feet MSL.
C— the base of the overlying controlled airspace.

Class E airspace extends upward until it reaches the overlying controlled airspace. (PLT161) — 14 CFR §71.71

ALL

6449. During operations within controlled airspace at altitudes of more than 1,200 feet AGL, but less than 10,000 feet MSL, the minimum horizontal distance from clouds requirement for VFR flight is

A— 1 mile.
B— 2,000 feet.
C— 1,000 feet.

While operating VFR within controlled airspace at altitudes of more than 1,200 feet AGL, but less than 10,000 feet MSL, the minimum horizontal distance that must be maintained from clouds is 2,000 feet. (PLT163) — 14 CFR §91.155

ALL

6451. While in Class E airspace in VFR conditions, what in-flight visibility is required when flying more than 1,200 feet AGL and at or above 10,000 feet MSL?

A— 5 SM.
B— 3 SM.
C— 1 SM.

While operating VFR in either Class E or Class G airspace at an altitude of more than 1,200 feet AGL, and more than 10,000 feet MSL, the minimum in-flight visibility allowed is 5 statute miles. (PLT161) — 14 CFR §91.155

Answers

| 6931 | [B] | 6435 | [B] | 6446 | [A] | 6929 | [C] | 6932 | [C] | 6449 | [B] |
| 6451 | [A] | | | | | | | | | | |

ALL

6450. While in Class G airspace in VFR conditions, what minimum distance from clouds should be maintained when flying more than 1,200 feet AGL, and at or above 10,000 feet MSL?

A— 500 feet below; 1,000 feet above; 1 mile horizontal.

B— 1,000 feet below; 1,000 feet above; 1 mile horizontal.

C— 500 feet below; 1,000 feet above; 2,000 feet horizontal.

While operating VFR in either Class G or Class E airspace at altitudes of more than 1,200 feet AGL, and above 10,000 feet MSL, the minimum clearance from clouds is 1,000 feet below, 1,000 feet above, and 1 mile horizontal. (PLT163) — 14 CFR §91.155

ALL

6971. A military operations area (MOA) is airspace of defined vertical and lateral limits established for the purpose of

A— separating certain military training activities from IFR traffic.

B— military services conducting VFR low altitude navigation, tactical training, and flight testing.

C— denoting the existence of unusual hazards to aircraft, such as artillery firing, aerial gunnery, or guided missiles.

Military Operation Areas (MOAs) consist of airspace of defined vertical and lateral limits, established for the purpose of separating certain military training activities from IFR traffic. (PLT393) — AIM ¶3-4-5

ALL

6972. When operating VFR in a military operations area (MOA), a pilot

A— must operate only when military activity is not being conducted.

B— should exercise extreme caution when military activity is being conducted.

C— must obtain a clearance from the controlling agency prior to entering the MOA.

Pilots operating under VFR should exercise extreme caution while flying within an MOA when military activity is being conducted. The activity status (active/inactive) of MOAs may change frequently. Therefore, pilots should contact any FSS within 100 miles of the area to obtain

accurate real-time information concerning the MOA hours of operation. Prior to entering an active MOA, pilots should contact the controlling agency for traffic advisories. (PLT393) — AIM ¶3-4-5

Answer (A) is incorrect because there is no restriction for VFR activity within these areas. Answer (C) is incorrect because a clearance is not required to enter an MOA.

ALL

6975. If a military training route has flights operating at or below 1,500 feet AGL, it will be designated by

A— VR and a three digit number only.

B— IR or VR and a four digit number.

C— IR or VR and a three digit number.

Military Training Routes (MTRs) in which flights are conducted at or below 1,500 feet AGL are designated by the letters IR or VR and a four-digit number. (PLT393) — AIM ¶3-5-2

ALL

6969. Flight through a restricted area should not be accomplished unless the pilot has

A— filed an IFR flight plan.

B— received prior authorization from the controlling agency.

C— received prior permission from the commanding officer of the nearest military base.

Restricted Areas denote the existence of unusual, often invisible, hazards to aircraft, such as artillery firing, aerial gunnery, or guided missiles. Authorization must be received prior to entering any Restricted Areas. (PLT393) — AIM ¶3-4-3

ALL

6970. A warning area is airspace of defined dimensions established

A— for training purposes in the vicinity of military bases.

B— from three nautical miles outward from the coast of the U.S.

C— over either domestic or international waters for the purpose of separating military from civilian aircraft.

A Warning Area is airspace of defined dimensions, extending from three nautical miles outward from the coast of the United States, that contains activity that may be hazardous to nonparticipating aircraft. (PLT393) — AIM ¶3-4-4

Answers

6450 [B]	6971 [A]	6972 [B]	6975 [B]	6969 [B]	6970 [B]

ALL
6973. Flight through a military operations area (MOA) is

A— never permitted.
B— permitted anytime, but caution should be exercised because of military activity.
C— permitted at certain times, but only with prior permission from the appropriate authority.

Pilots operating under VFR should exercise extreme caution while flying within an MOA when military activity is being conducted. The activity status (active/inactive) of MOAs may change frequently. Therefore, pilots should contact any FSS within 100 miles of the area to obtain hours of operation. (PLT393) — AIM ¶3-4-5

ALL
6973-1. Public figures are protected by

A— special use airspace.
B— prohibited areas.
C— temporary flight restriction.

Temporary flight restrictions are imposed in order to:

1. *Protect persons and property in the air or on the surface from an existing or imminent flight-associated hazard;*

2. *Provide a safe environment for the operation of disaster relief aircraft;*

3. *Prevent an unsafe congestion of sightseeing aircraft above an incident;*

4. *Protect the President, Vice President, or other public figures; and,*

5. *Provide a safe environment for space agency operations.*

Pilots are expected to check appropriate NOTAMs during flight planning when conducting flight in an area where a temporary flight restriction (TFR) is in effect. (PLT376) — AIM ¶3-5-3

AIR
6455. When operating an airplane within Class D airspace under special VFR, the flight visibility is required to be at least

A— 3 SM.
B— 2 SM.
C— 1 SM.

No person may operate an aircraft (other than a helicopter) within the lateral boundaries of Class B, C, D, or E airspace designated for an airport under Special VFR unless flight visibility is at least 1 statute mile. (PLT163) — 14 CFR §91.157

AIR
6456. No person may operate an airplane within Class D and E airspace between sunset and sunrise under special VFR unless the

A— flight visibility is at least 3 miles.
B— airplane is equipped for instrument flight.
C— flight can be conducted 500 feet below the clouds.

No person may operate an aircraft (other than a helicopter) within the lateral boundaries of Class B, C, D, or E airspace designated for an airport under the special weather minimums of this section between sunset and sunrise, unless that person meets the applicable requirements for instrument flight, and the aircraft is equipped for IFR flight. (PLT162) — 14 CFR §91.157

AIR
6457. Regulations stipulate that, at an airport located within Class E airspace and at which ground visibility is not reported, takeoffs and landings of airplanes under special VFR are

A— not authorized.
B— authorized if the flight visibility is at least 1 SM.
C— authorized only if another airport in that designated airspace reports a ground visibility of 1 SM.

No person may operate an aircraft within the lateral boundaries of Class B, C, D, or E airspace designated for an airport under the Special VFR weather minimums where ground visibility is not reported, unless flight visibility during landing and takeoff is at least 1 statute mile. (PLT162) — 14 CFR §91.157

Answers

6973 [B]   6973-1 [C]   6455 [C]   6456 [B]   6457 [B]

AIR, RTC, GLI, LTA

6453. (Refer to Figure 45.) What are the visibility and cloud clearance requirements in an airplane at night when conducting takeoffs and landings at McCampbell Airport (area 1)?

A— 3 SM visibility and clear of clouds.
B— 3 SM, cloud clearances 500 feet below, 1,000 feet above, 2,000 feet horizontal.
C— Remain clear of clouds and operate at a speed that allows adequate opportunity to see other traffic and obstructions in time to avoid a collision.

McCampbell Airport lies within a magenta shaded area. This indicates that Class E airspace extends from 700 feet AGL. In Class E airspace, the night requirements are 3 statute miles, cloud clearances 500 feet below, 1,000 feet above, 2,000 feet horizontal. (PLT163) — 14 CFR §91.155

AIR, RTC, GLI, LTA

6454. While in Class G airspace under day VFR conditions, what in-flight visibility is required when flying more than 1,200 feet AGL and less than 10,000 feet MSL?

A— 5 SM.
B— 3 SM.
C— 1 SM.

While operating VFR in Class G airspace at an altitude of more than 1,200 feet AGL and less than 10,000 feet MSL, the minimum in-flight visibility allowed is 1 statute mile during the day. (PLT163) — 14 CFR §91.155

AIR, RTC, GLI, LTA

6447. An airplane may be operated in uncontrolled airspace at night below 1,200 feet above the surface under the following conditions:

A— Clear of clouds and 1 mile visibility.
B— Clear of clouds and 3 miles visibility.
C— Less than 3 miles but more than 1 mile visibility in an airport traffic pattern and within one-half mile of the runway.

An airplane may be operated under VFR in Class G airspace when the visibility is less than 3 miles but not less than 1 mile during night hours, if it is operated clear of clouds and operated in an airport traffic pattern within 1/2 mile of the runway. (PLT163) — 14 CFR §91.155

ALL

6317. (Refer to Figure 47.) Class C airspace usually extends up to

A— 3,000 feet MSL.
B— 3,000 feet above airport.
C— 4,000 feet above airport.

The airspace of the surface area extends from the surface of Class C airspace up to 4,000 feet above that airport, normally. (PLT040) — AIM ¶3-2-4

Answers

| 6453 | [B] | 6454 | [C] | 6447 | [C] | 6317 | [C] |

Chart Supplements U.S. (previously A/FD)

The Chart Supplements U.S. (previously Airport/Facility Directory or A/FD) is a publication designed primarily as a pilot's operational manual containing all airports, seaplane bases, and heliports open to the public including communications data, navigational facilities, and certain special notices and procedures. Directories are re-issued in their entirety every 56 days.

Runway Gradient

The gradient (upslope or downslope) of a runway is important in determining both the takeoff and landing distance of an airplane. This information is furnished in the Chart Supplements U.S. if it is greater than 0.3% (approximately 15 feet in a mile). If no gradient is listed at the end of the line, the gradient is less than 0.3%.

Control Tower Operating Hours

The hours of operation of the control tower are shown in the Chart Supplements U.S. under the "Airport Remarks" section. The Z indicates that these times are given in UTC, or Universal Coordinated Time (GMT, or Zulu time). To convert UTC time into local time, use the conversion factor found in the first line about the airport. The symbol ‡ means that when daylight savings time is in effect, the effective times will be one (1) hour earlier.

Information relating to parachute jump areas is contained in 14 CFR Part 105. Tabulations of parachute jump sites in the U.S. are contained in the Chart Supplements U.S.

ALL
7152. (Refer to Figure 55.) What is the elevation of the Cowboy VORTAC?

A— 287 feet MSL.
B— 450 feet MSL.
C— 660 feet MSL.

The information about the Cowboy VORTAC is shown in the Radio Aids to Navigation Section. 450/6E means that the VORTAC elevation is 450 feet MSL and the variation at the VORTAC is 6° east. (PLT078) — Chart Supplements U.S.

ALL
7153. (Refer to Figure 55.) On what frequency can a pilot activate the approach lights at Dallas Executive when the control tower is not in operation?

A— 120.15.
B— 127.25.
C— 122.95.

When the control tower at Dallas Executive is closed, a pilot can activate the Sequenced Flashing Lead-In lights (LDIN) on runway 31, and the VASI on runway 13 by keying the mic on 127.25. (PLT078) — Chart Supplements U.S.

ALL
7154. (Refer to Figure 55.) Select the correct state-ment concerning Dallas Love Field.

A— Right traffic is in effect for all runways.
B— The runway gradient for Rwy 18 is less than .3 percent.
C— The touchdown zone elevation for Rwy 13R is 53 feet.

There is no runway gradient shown for Runway 18 at Dallas Love field. When the runway gradient is missing, the gradient is less than 0.3%. (PLT078) — Chart Supplements U.S.

Answer (A) is incorrect because Runway 31L and 13L use left traffic. Answer (C) is incorrect because the threshold crossing height (TCH) (not the touchdown zone elevation) for Runway 13R is 53 feet.

Answers

7152   [B]   7153   [B]   7154   [B]

ALL
7155. (Refer to Figure 55.) At what time of day does the tower shut down at Dallas Executive?

A— 0330Z.
B— 1400Z.
C— 2100 local.

The control tower on Dallas Executive field operates from (1400-0300Z). In the airport location line, the notation UTC-6(-5DT) tells us that to find the local standard time, subtract 6 hours from the time given. Therefore, the tower operates from 0800 (1400–6) to 2100 local standard time (0300–6). (PLT078) — Chart Supplements U.S.

ALL
7151. Information concerning parachute jumping sites may be found in the

A— NOTAMs.
B— Chart Supplements U.S.
C— Graphic Notices and Supplemental Data.

Information relating to parachute jump areas is contained in 14 CFR Part 105, and tabulations of parachute jump sites in the U.S. are contained in the Chart Supplements U.S. (PLT078) — Chart Supplements U.S.

Notices to Airmen (NOTAM)

Notices to Airmen (NOTAMs) provide the most current information available. They provide time-critical information on airports and changes that affect the national airspace system and are of concern to instrument flight rule (IFR) operations. NOTAM information is classified into four categories: NOTAM (D) or distant, Flight Data Center (FDC) NOTAMs, pointer NOTAMs, and military NOTAMs.

NOTAM-Ds are attached to hourly weather reports and are available at flight service stations (AFSS/FSS). FDC NOTAMs are issued by the National Flight Data Center and contain regulatory information, such as temporary flight restrictions or an amendment to instrument approach procedures.

Pointer NOTAMs highlight or point out another NOTAM, such as an FDC or NOTAM (D). This type of NOTAM will assist pilots in cross-referencing important information that may not be found under an airport or NAVAID identifier. Military NOTAMs pertain to U.S. Air Force, Army, Marine, and Navy NAVAIDs/airports that are part of the NAS.

NOTAM-Ds and FDC NOTAMs are contained in the Notices to Airmen publication, which is issued every 28 days. Prior to any flight, pilots should check for any NOTAMs that could affect their intended flight.

ALL
7129. When information is disseminated for a navigational facility, it will be located in

A— FDC NOTAMs.
B— NOTAM (L) distribution.
C— NOTAM (D) distribution.

NOTAM (D) information is disseminated for all navigational facilities that are part of the National Airspace System (NAS), for all IFR airports with approved IAPs, and for those VFR airports annotated with the NOTAM Service Symbol (§) in the Chart Supplements U.S. (PLT323) — AIM ¶5-1-3

Answer (A) is incorrect because FDC NOTAMs are regulatory in nature. Answer (B) is incorrect because NOTAM (L) is distributed locally, advises of taxiway closures, airport beacon outage, and equipment near runways.

ALL
7130. When information is disseminated about a taxiway closure, it will be located in

A— FDC NOTAMs.
B— Pointer NOTAMs.
C— NOTAM (D) distribution.

NOTAM (D) information includes such data as taxiway closures, personnel and equipment near or crossing runways, airport rotating beacon outages, and airport lighting aids that do not affect instrument approach criteria, such as VASI. (PLT323) — AIM ¶5-1-3

Answer (A) is incorrect because FDC NOTAMs are regulatory in nature. Answer (B) is incorrect because pointer NOTAMs are used to highlight or point out another NOTAM.

Answers

7155 [C]	7151 [B]	7129 [C]	7130 [C]

Communications

ATIS (Automatic Terminal Information Service) is the continuous broadcast of recorded non-control information in selected high-activity terminal areas. ATIS information includes the time of the latest weather sequence, ceiling and visibility (if the weather is less than a ceiling of 5,000 feet and a visibility is 5 miles or less), obstructions to visibility, temperature, dew point, wind direction and velocity, altimeter setting, instrument approach and runways in use, and other pertinent remarks. The frequency on which ATIS is transmitted is shown in the information box for the airport on sectional charts, and in the communications section of the Chart Supplements U.S. ATIS broadcasts are updated upon the receipt of any official weather, regardless of content changes and reported values. A new recording will also be made when there is a change in other pertinent data, such as runway change, instrument approach in use, etc.

Traffic information will give the location of a target which may constitute traffic for an aircraft that is radar identified. The location is given in azimuth from the aircraft in terms of the 12-hour clock. Traffic at 3 o'clock is off the right wing tip, traffic at 12 o'clock is off the nose, and traffic at 9 o'clock is off the left wing tip. Traffic at 11 o'clock would be between the left wing tip and the nose of the aircraft. Azimuth information given by an Air Traffic Controller is based on the ground track of the aircraft as it is observed. The pilot will have to apply a correction to the reported azimuth if a drift-correction angle is being used to maintain the track.

Under no circumstances should a pilot of a civil aircraft operate the transponder on code 7777. This code is reserved for military interceptor operations. When a pilot is involved in a hijack operation, he/she should set code 7500 on the transponder to alert ATC.

The **UNICOM** frequency for an airport with an operating control tower is 122.95 MHz. All inbound traffic should monitor and communicate as appropriate on the designated **Common Traffic Advisory Frequency (CTAF)** from 10 miles to landing. Departing aircraft should monitor/communicate on the appropriate frequency from start-up, during taxi, and until 10 miles from the airport, unless the Federal Aviation Regulations or local procedures require otherwise. "Self-announce" is a procedure whereby pilots broadcast their position, intended flight activity, or ground operations on the designated Common Traffic Advisory Frequency (CTAF). This procedure is used primarily at airports which do not have an FSS on the airport. The self-announcement procedure should also be used if a pilot is unable to communicate with the FSS on the designated CTAF. When there is no tower, FSS, or UNICOM station on the airport, use MULTICOM frequency 122.9 MHz for self-announce procedures. Such airports will be identified in appropriate aeronautical information publications.

If a pilot intends to land at a controlled airport and the radio fails, he/she should remain outside or above the airport traffic area until the direction and flow of traffic have been determined, then join the airport traffic pattern. If only the transmitter is inoperative, a pilot should monitor the primary local control frequency as depicted on sectional charts for landing or traffic information, and look for a light signal which may be addressed to his/her aircraft. During hours of daylight, pilots should acknowledge tower transmissions or light signals by rocking the wings, and at night, by blinking the landing or navigation lights.

ALL
7120. Absence of the sky condition and visibility on an ATIS broadcast indicates that

A— weather conditions are at or above VFR minimums.
B— the sky condition is clear and visibility is unrestricted.
C— the ceiling is at least 5,000 feet and visibility is 5 miles or more.

The absence of a sky condition or ceiling and/or visibility on ATIS indicates a ceiling of 5,000 feet or above and visibility of five miles or more. (PLT196) — AIM ¶4-1-13

Answers

7120   [C]

ALL

7121. When are ATIS broadcasts updated?

A— Only when the ceiling and/or visibility changes by a reportable value.

B— Every 30 minutes if weather conditions are below basic VFR; otherwise, hourly.

C— Upon receipt of any official weather, regardless of content change or reported values.

ATIS broadcasts are updated upon the receipt of any official weather, regardless of content changes and reported values. A new recording will also be made when there is a change in other pertinent data, such as runway change, instrument approach in use, etc. (PLT196) — AIM ¶4-1-13

ALL

7122. When an air traffic controller issues radar traffic information in relation to the 12-hour clock, the reference the controller uses is the aircraft's

A— true course.

B— ground track.

C— magnetic heading.

Azimuth information given by an air traffic controller is based on the ground track of the aircraft as it is observed. The pilot will have to apply a correction to the reported azimuth using a drift-correction angle to maintain the track. (PLT370) — AIM ¶4-1-15

ALL

7123. Which transponder code should the pilot of a civilian aircraft never use?

A— 7500.

B— 7600.

C— 7777.

Under no circumstances should a pilot of a civil aircraft operate the transponder on code 7777. This code is reserved for military interceptor operations. (PLT497) — AIM ¶4-1-20

ALL

7123-1. When making routine transponder code changes, pilots should avoid inadvent selection of which codes?

A— 0700, 1700, 7000.

B— 1200, 1500, 7000.

C— 7500, 7600, 7700.

When making routine code changes, pilots should avoid selecting codes 7500, 7600 or 7700, thereby preventing false alarms at automated ground facilities. (PLT497) — AIM ¶4-1-20

ALL

7117. The UNICOM frequency at airports with a control tower is

A— 123.0.

B— 122.95.

C— 122.8.

The UNICOM frequency for an airport with an operating control tower is 122.95 MHz. (PLT435) — AIM ¶4-1-11

Answers (A) and (C) are incorrect because 123.0 and 122.8 are UNICOM frequencies for airports without a control tower.

ALL

7118. As standard operating practice, all inbound traffic to an airport without a control tower should continuously monitor the appropriate facility from a distance of

A— 25 miles.

B— 20 miles.

C— 10 miles.

All inbound traffic should monitor and communicate as appropriate on the designated Common Traffic Advisory Frequency (CTAF) from 10 miles to landing. (PLT435) — AIM ¶4-1-9

ALL

7119. When landing at an airport that does not have a tower, FSS, or UNICOM, you should broadcast your intentions on

A— 122.9 MHz.

B— 123.0 MHz.

C— 123.6 MHz.

When there is no tower, FSS, or UNICOM station on the airport, use MULTICOM frequency 122.9 MHz for self-announce procedures. Such airports will be identified in appropriate aeronautical information publications. (PLT435) — AIM ¶4-1-9

Answers

| 7121 | [C] | 7122 | [B] | 7123 | [C] | 7123-1 | [C] | 7117 | [B] | 7118 | [C] |
| 7119 | [A] | | | | | | | | | | |

ALL
7124. If the aircraft's radio fails, what is the recommended procedure when landing at a controlled airport?

A— Select 7700 on your transponder, fly a normal traffic pattern, and land.
B— Flash your landing lights and make shallow banks in opposite directions while circling the airport.
C— Observe the traffic flow, enter the pattern, and look for a light signal from the tower.

If intending to land at a controlled airport and the radio fails, remain outside or above the airport traffic area until the direction and flow of traffic have been determined, then join the airport traffic pattern. Monitor the primary local control frequency as depicted on sectional charts for landing or traffic information, and look for a light signal which may be addressed to your aircraft. (PLT502) — AIM ¶4-2-13

Airport Lighting

The **Visual Approach Slope Indicator (VASI)** is a system of lights so arranged to provide visual descent guidance information during the approach to a runway. These lights are visible from 3 to 5 miles during the day and up to 20 miles or more at night. The visual glide path of the VASI provides safe obstruction clearance within ±10° of the extended runway center line and up to 4 nautical miles from the runway threshold. In a 2-bar VASI, the light will be white when you are overshooting the runway and red when you are undershooting it. In order to touch down at the proper position on the runway, you should overshoot the near light and undershoot the far light. When you are on the glide slope, you will see a red light over a white light. As you depart to the high side of the glide slope, the far bars will change from red to pink to white. The lower glide path of a 3-bar VASI is provided by the near and middle bars, and is normally set at 3°. The upper glide path, provided by the middle and far bars, is normally 1/4° higher. The upper glide path is intended for use only by high cockpit aircraft, to provide a sufficient threshold crossing height. When you are on the upper glide path, the near and middle bars are white, and the far bar (upper bar) is red.

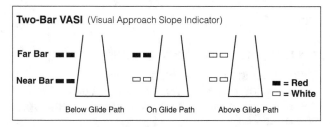

Figure 7-4. Two-bar VASI

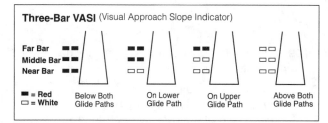

Figure 7-5. Three-bar VASI

The **Precision Approach Path Indicator (PAPI)** uses light units similar to the VASI, but they are installed in a single row of either 2 or 4 light units. PAPI has an effective visual range of about 5 miles during the day and up to 20 miles at night. When the aircraft is more than 3.5° high, all the lights will be white; when slightly high, 3 white and one red, on glide path, 2 white and 2 red. When slightly below (2.8°), 1 white and 3 red, and when more than 2.5° low, the pilot will see 4 red lights.

Runway edge lights are white, except on instrument runways where amber replaces white on the last 2,000 feet or half of the runway length (whichever is less) to form a caution zone for landings. Runway center line lighting systems in the final 3,000 feet, as viewed from the takeoff or approach position, are used as runway-remaining lights. Alternate red and white lights are seen from the 3,000-foot points to the 1,000-foot points, and all red lights are seen for the last 1,000 feet of the runway.

Answers

7124   [C]

Military airport beacons flash alternately white and green, but are differentiated from civil bea-cons by a dual peaked (two quick) white flashes between the green flashes. A rotating beacon that flashes white only is installed on an unlighted land airport. In Class B, C, D, or E airspace, operation of the airport beacon during the hours of daylight often indicates that the weather conditions are below basic VFR minimums. The ground visibility is less than 3 miles, and/or the ceiling is less than 1,000 feet.

Radio control of lighting is available at selected airports, to provide airborne control of lights by keying the aircraft's microphone. When the microphone is keyed 7 times within 5 seconds, the lights are turned on to their highest intensity available (HIRL). When it is keyed 5 times within 5 seconds, the lights will be turned on to medium or lower intensity (MIRL). When it is keyed 3 times within 5 seconds, the lights will be turned on the lowest intensity available (LIRL).

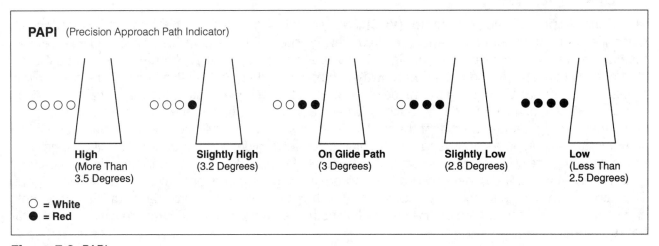

Figure 7-6. PAPI

ALL

7109. A series of continuous red lights in the runway centerline lighting indicates

A— 3,000 feet of runway remaining.
B— 1,000 feet of runway remaining.
C— the beginning of the runway overrun area.

Runway center line lighting systems in the final 3,000 feet, as viewed from the takeoff or approach position, are used as runway-remaining lights. Alternate red and white lights are seen from the 3,000-foot points to the 1,000-foot points, and all red lights are seen for the last 1,000 feet of the runway. (PLT141) — AIM ¶2-1-5

ALL

7111. A military airfield can be identified by

A— a white and red rotating beacon.
B— white flashing sequence lights (strobes).
C— a green and dual-peaked white rotating beacon.

Military airport beacons flash alternately white and green, with dual peaked (two quick) white flashes between the green flashes. (PLT141) —AIM ¶2-1-9

Answers
7109   [B]   7111   [C]

AIR, RTC, LSA, WSC, PPC

7103. The visual glidepath of a 2-bar VASI provides safe obstruction clearance within plus or minus 10° of the extended runway centerline and to a distance of how many miles from the runway threshold?

A— 4 NM.
B— 6 NM.
C— 10 NM.

The visual glide path of the VASI provides safe obstruction clearance within ±10° of the extended runway center line and up to 4 nautical miles from the runway threshold. (PLT147) — AIM ¶2-1-2

AIR, RTC, LSA, WSC, PPC

7104. Which indications would a pilot see while approaching to land on a runway served by a 2-bar VASI?

A— If below the glidepath, the near bars will be red and the far bars white.
B— If on the glidepath, the near bars will appear red and the far bars will appear white.
C— If departing to the high side of the glidepath, the far bars will change from red to pink to white.

In a 2-bar VASI, the light will be white when you are overshooting the runway and red when you are undershooting it. When you are on the glide slope, you will see a red light over a white light. As you depart to the high side of the glide slope, the far bars will change from red to pink to white. (PLT147) — AIM ¶2-1-2

AIR, RTC, LSA, WSC, PPC

7104-1. A slightly below glidepath indication on a 2-bar VASI glidepath is indicated by

A— two red lights over two white lights.
B— two white lights over two red lights.
C— two red lights over two more red lights.

The below-glideslope indication from a two-bar VASI is red over red lights. (PLT147) — AIM ¶2-1-2

AIR, RTC, LSA, WSC, PPC

7105. When on the upper glidepath of a 3-bar VASI what would be the colors of the lights?

A— All three sets of lights would be white.
B— The near bar is white and the middle and far bars are red.
C— The near and middle bars are white and the upper bar is red.

When you are on the upper glide path, the near and middle bars are white, and the far bar (upper bar) is red. (PLT147) — AIM ¶2-1-2

AIR, RTC

7108. A slightly low indication on a PAPI glidepath is indicated by

A— four red lights.
B— one red light and three white lights.
C— one white light and three red lights.

When slightly low on a PAPI glide path (2.8°), you will see one white light and three red lights. (PLT147) — AIM ¶2-1-2

AIR, RTC, LSA, WSC, PPC

7110. An airport has pilot controlled lighting but runways without approach lights. How many times should you key your microphone to turn on the MIRL at medium intensity?

A— 5 clicks.
B— 3 clicks.
C— None, the MIRL is left on all night.

When the microphone is keyed 5 times within 5 seconds, the lights will be turned on to medium or lower intensity (MIRL). (PLT145) — AIM ¶2-1-8

Answer (B) is incorrect because 3 clicks will turn the lights on the lowest intensity. Answer (C) is incorrect because the pilot-controlled lights are usually off until activated by the pilot.

Answers

| 7103 [A] | 7104 [C] | 7104-1 [C] | 7105 [C] | 7108 [C] | 7110 [A] |

Airport Marking Aids and Signs

Runway numbers and letters are determined from the approach direction. The runway number is the whole number nearest one-tenth of the magnetic azimuth of the center line of the runway, measured clockwise from magnetic north. Runway 8 has a magnetic direction of 080°, and the other end of this runway is runway 26, which has a magnetic direction of 260°.

A series of arrows painted along the center line of the approach end of a runway signifies that this portion of the runway is not suitable for landing. These arrows terminate at the displaced threshold marker. This portion of the runway can be used for taxing, for the landing rollout, and for takeoff. *See* Figure 7-7.

In Figure 7-8, point B on runway 12 is the displaced threshold of the runway. This is the beginning of the portion of the runway that is usable for landing. The portion of runway 12 on which the arrows are painted can be used for taxing and for beginning the takeoff run.

Area A on runway 12 is usable for taxi and takeoff, but it cannot be used for landing. Area E on runway 30 is a stopway area that appears usable, but which is actually unusable due to the nature of its structure. It can be used only as an overrun.

Taxiway holding lines consist of two continuous and two dashed lines, spaced six inches between lines, perpendicular to the taxiway center line. More recently, hold lines also consist of one or more signs at the edge of the taxiway, with white characters on a red sign face.

When instructed by ATC to "hold short of a runway," the pilot should stop so that no part of the aircraft extends beyond the holding line. When approaching the holding line from the side with the continuous lines, a pilot should not cross the holding line without ATC clearance at a controlled airport or, at uncontrolled airports, without making sure of adequate separation from other aircraft. An aircraft exiting the runway is not clear until all parts of the aircraft have crossed the holding line. *See* Figure 7-9.

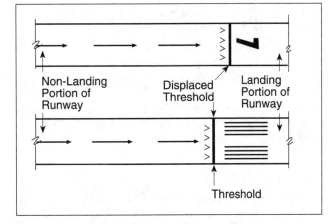

Figure 7-7. Displaced threshold

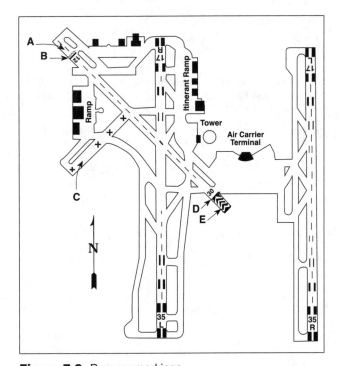

Figure 7-8. Runway markings

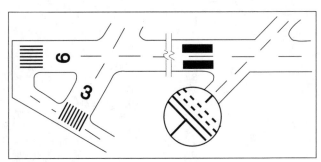

Figure 7-9. Holding line

ALL, AIR, RTC, GLI

7113. The numbers 8 and 26 on the approach ends of the runway indicate that the runway is orientated approximately

A— 008° and 026° true.
B— 080° and 260° true.
C— 080° and 260° magnetic.

The runway number is the whole number nearest one-tenth of the magnetic azimuth of the center line of the runway, measured clockwise from magnetic north. Runway 8 has a magnetic direction of 080°, and the other end of this runway is runway 26, which has a magnetic direction of 260°. (PLT141) — AIM ¶2-3-3

ALL, AIR, RTC, GLI

7114. What does a series of arrows painted on the approach end of a runway signify?

A— That area is restricted solely to taxi operations.
B— That portion of the runway is not suitable for landing.
C— That portion of the runway is the designated touchdown zone.

A series of arrows painted along the center line of the approach end of a runway signifies that this portion of the runway is not suitable for landing. (PLT141) — AIM ¶2-3-3

Answer (A) is incorrect because this area may be used for taxiing, the landing rollout, and takeoff. Answer (C) is incorrect because the designated touchdown zone is identified by a series of six lines parallel to the runway direction.

ALL, AIR, RTC, GLI

7115. When approaching taxiway holding lines from the side with the continuous lines, the pilot

A— may continue taxiing.
B— should not cross the lines without ATC clearance.
C— should continue taxiing until all parts of the aircraft have crossed the lines.

When approaching the holding line from the side with the continuous lines, a pilot should not cross the holding line without ATC clearance at a controlled airport, or without making sure of adequate separation from other aircraft at uncontrolled airports. (PLT141) — AIM ¶2-3-5

Answers (A) and (C) are incorrect because no part of the aircraft may cross the hold line without ATC clearance.

ALL, AIR, RTC, GLI

7231. What is the purpose of the runway hold position sign?

A— Denotes entrance to runway from a taxiway.
B— Denotes area protected for an aircraft approaching or departing a runway.
C— Denotes taxiway location.

Mandatory instruction signs are used to denote an entrance to a runway or critical area and areas where an aircraft is prohibited from entering. (PLT141) — AIM ¶2-3-8

ALL, AIR, RTC, GLI

7232. What is the purpose for the runway hold position markings on the taxiway?

A— Identifies area where aircraft are prohibited.
B— Allows an aircraft permission onto the runway.
C— Holds aircraft short of the runway.

Runway holding position markings indicate where an aircraft is supposed to stop. When used on a taxiway, these markings identify the locations where an aircraft is supposed to stop when it does not have clearance to proceed onto the runway. (PLT141) — AIM ¶2-3-5

ALL, AIR, RTC, GLI

7233. What does a destination sign identify?

A— Entrance to the runway from a taxiway.
B— Runway on which an aircraft is located.
C— Direction to takeoff runways.

Outbound destination signs define directions to takeoff runways. (PLT141) — AIM ¶2-3-11

Answer (A) is incorrect because this is a runway marking. Answer (B) is incorrect because this is a runway location sign.

ALL, AIR, RTC, GLI

7234. What is the purpose of the taxiway ending marker sign?

A— Identifies area where aircraft are prohibited.
B— Indicates taxiway does not continue beyond intersection.
C— Provides general taxiing direction to named taxiway.

Taxiway ending marker is an airport sign indicating the taxiway does not continue. (PLT141) — FAA-H-8083-25

Answer (A) is incorrect because this is the purpose of a no entry sign. Answer (C) is incorrect because this is the purpose of direction signs.

Answers

7113	[C]	7114	[B]	7115	[B]	7231	[A]	7232	[C]	7233	[C]
7234	[B]

ALL, AIR, RTC, GLI

7235. The "No Entry" sign identifies

A— paved area where aircraft entry is prohibited.
B— area that does not continue beyond intersection.
C— the exit boundary for the runway protected area.

The "no entry" sign prohibits an aircraft from entering an area. Typically, this sign would be located on a taxiway intended to be used in only one direction or at the intersection of vehicle roadways with runways, taxiways or aprons where the roadway may be mistaken as a taxiway or other aircraft movement surface. (PLT141) — AIM ¶2-3-8

Answer (B) is incorrect because this is the purpose of a hold position sign. Answer (C) is incorrect because this is the purpose of the runway boundary sign.

ALL, AIR, RTC, GLI

7235-1. The "ILS critical area boundary sign" identifies

A— the exit boundary for the runway protected area.
B— the edge of the ILS critical area.
C— the area where an aircraft is prohibited from entering.

The ILS critical area sign is located adjacent to the ILS holding position marking on the pavement and can be seen by pilots leaving the critical area. The sign is intended to provide pilots with another visual cue which they can use as a guide in deciding when they are clear of the ILS critical area. (PLT141) — AIM ¶2-3-9

ALL, AIR, RTC, GLI

7236. What is the purpose of the yellow demarcation bar marking?

A— Delineates entrance to runway from a taxiway.
B— Delineates beginning of runway available for landing when pavement is aligned with runway on approach side.
C— Delineates runway with a displaced threshold from a blast pad, stopway or taxiway that precedes the runway.

A demarcation bar delineates a runway with a displaced threshold from a blast pad, stopway or taxiway that precedes the runway. A demarcation bar is 3 feet (1 m) wide and yellow, since it is not located on the runway. (PLT141) — AIM ¶2-3-3

ALL, AIR, RTC, GLI

7237. When turning onto a taxiway from another taxiway, what is the purpose of the taxiway directional sign?

A— Indicates direction to take-off runway.
B— Indicates designation and direction of exit taxiway from runway.
C— Indicates designation and direction of taxiway leading out of an intersection.

The taxiway directional sign identifies the designation(s) of the intersecting taxiway(s) leading out of the intersection that a pilot would normally be expected to turn onto or hold short of. (PLT141) — AIM ¶2-3-10

Answer (A) is incorrect because this is the purpose of the runway location sign. Answer (B) is incorrect because this is the purpose of the destination sign.

ALL, AIR, RTC, GLI

7238. What purpose does the taxiway location sign serve?

A— Provides general taxiing direction to named runway.
B— Denotes entrance to runway from a taxiway.
C— Identifies taxiway on which an aircraft is located.

The taxiway location signs are used to identify the taxiway on which the aircraft is located. (PLT141) — AIM ¶2-3-9

Answer (A) is incorrect because this is the purpose of destination signs. Answer (B) is incorrect because this is the purpose of runway hold position signs.

ALL, AIR, RTC, GLI

7239. When exiting the runway, what is the purpose of the runway exit sign?

A— Indicates designation and direction of exit taxiway from runway.
B— Indicates designation and direction of taxiway leading out of an intersection.
C— Indicates direction to take-off runway.

Runway exit signs provide direction to turn to exit runway onto named taxiway. (PLT141) — FAA-H-8083-25

Answer (B) is incorrect because this is the purpose of the taxiway directional sign. Answer (C) is incorrect because this is the purpose of the direction sign.

Answers

| 7235 [A] | 7235-1 [B] | 7236 [C] | 7237 [C] | 7238 [C] | 7239 [A] |

ALL, AIR, RTC, GLI

7241. (Refer to Runway Incursion Figure.) You have requested taxi instructions for takeoff using Runway 16. The controller issues the following taxi instructions: "N123, Taxi to runway 16." Where are you required to stop in order to be in compliancewith the controller's instructions?

A— 5 (Five).
B— 6 (Six).
C— 9 (Nine).

When ATC clears an aircraft to "taxi to" an assigned takeoff runway, the absence of holding instructions does not authorize the aircraft to "cross" all runways which the taxi route intersects except the assigned takeoff runway. A clearance must be obtained prior to crossing any runway. It does not include authorization to "taxi onto" or "cross" the assigned takeoff runway at any point. You should taxi and hold short of runway 16, which is position 5. (PLT141) — AIM ¶4-3-18

Answer (B) is incorrect because "taxi to" does not authorize the aircraft to "taxi onto" the assigned takeoff runway. Answer (C) is incorrect because the airplane should taxi the most direct route to the assigned runway unless instructed otherwise; position 9 would not be encountered for the airplane at the west ramp to taxi to runway 16.

RTC

7116. (Refer to Figure 53.) If you were making an approach to a helicopter landing area that was marked for public use, which diagram would you most likely see?

A— 1.
B— 2.
C— 3.

The "H" inside the box identifies the landing and takeoff area at a public use heliport. (PLT141) — AIM ¶2-3-6

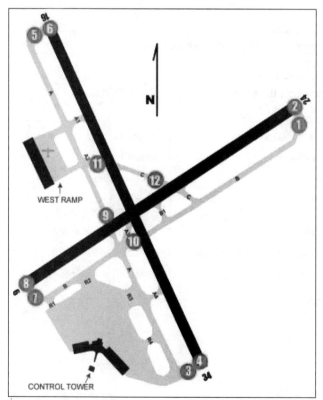

Runway Incursion

Answers

7241   [A]   7116   [A]

Airport Operation

The recommended entry position for an airport traffic pattern is 45° to the midpoint of the downwind leg at traffic pattern altitude. The segmented circle around the wind cone in Figure 7-10 indicates that when landing on runway 35 you should use a left-hand traffic pattern, when landing on runway 17, you should use a right-hand pattern, and when landing on runway 27, you should use a right-hand pattern.

Vehicles on the surface of an airport on which a control tower is operating will be controlled by radio or light signals, using the same signals as are used for aircraft on the ground. *See* Figure 7-11.

Pilots are encouraged to turn on their landing and position lights any time:

- the engine(s) are running day or night
- when operating on airport surfaces during perods of reduced visibility and when snow- or ice-control vehicles are or may be operating
- during takeoff; i.e., either after takeoff clearance has been received or when beginning the takeoff roll
- when operating below 10,000 feet, day or night, especially when operating within 10 miles of any airport or in conditions of reduced visibility and in areas where flocks of birds may be expected

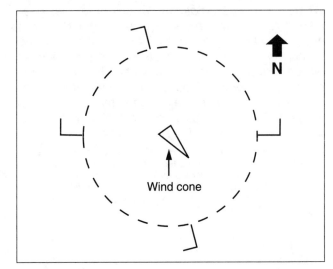

Figure 7-10. Segmented circle and wind cone

Color and type of signal	Movement of vehicles, equipment and personnel	Aircraft on the ground	Aircraft in flight
Steady green	Cleared to cross, proceed or go	Cleared for takeoff	Cleared to land
Flashing green	Not applicable	Cleared for taxi	Return for landing (to be followed by steady green at the proper time)
Steady red	STOP	STOP	Give way to other aircraft and continue circling
Flashing red	Clear the taxiway/runway	Taxi clear of the runway in use	Airport unsafe, do not land
Flashing white	Return to starting point on airport	Return to starting point on airport	Not applicable
Alternating red and green	Exercise extreme caution	Exercise extreme caution	Exercise extreme caution

Figure 7-11. Light signals

ALL

7125. The recommended entry position to an airport traffic pattern is

A— 45° to the base leg just below traffic pattern altitude.

B— to enter 45° at the midpoint of the downwind leg at traffic pattern altitude.

C— to cross directly over the airport at traffic pattern altitude and join the downwind leg.

The recommended entry position for an airport traffic pattern is 45° to the midpoint of the downwind leg at traffic pattern altitude. (PLT150) — AIM ¶4-3-3

ALL

7126. (Refer to Figure 54.) The segmented circle indicates that the airport traffic pattern is

A— left-hand for Rwy 17 and right-hand for Rwy 35.

B— right-hand for Rwy 35 and right-hand for Rwy 9.

C— left-hand for Rwy 35 and right-hand for Rwy 17.

The segmented circle around the wind cone indicates that when landing on runway 35 you should use a left-hand traffic pattern, and when landing on runway 17, you should use a right-hand pattern. (PLT146) — AIM ¶4-3-3

ALL

7127. (Refer to Figure 54.) Which runway and traffic pattern should be used as indicated by the wind cone in the segmented circle?

A— Right-hand traffic on Rwy 17.

B— Left-hand traffic on Rwy 27 or Rwy 35.

C— Left-hand traffic on Rwy 35 or right-hand traffic on Rwy 27.

The wind cone indicates the wind is from the northwest, so the pilot could use runways 35 or 27. The segmented circle around the wind cone indicates that when landing on runway 35, you should use a left-hand pattern, and when landing on runway 27, you should use a right-hand pattern. (PLT150) — AIM ¶4-3-3

ALL

7128. Pilots are encouraged to turn on their landing lights when operating below 10,000 feet, day or night, and when operating within

A— Class B airspace.

B— 10 miles of any airport.

C— 5 miles of a controlled airport.

Pilots are encouraged to turn on their landing lights when operating below 10,000 feet, day or night, especially when operating within 10 miles of any airport or in conditions of reduced visibility and in areas where flocks of birds may be expected. (PLT119) — AIM ¶4-3-23

Answers

7125 [B]   7126 [C]   7127 [C]   7128 [B]

Wake Turbulence

Lift is generated by the creation of a pressure differential over the wing surface. The lowest pressure occurs over the upper wing surface and the highest pressure under the wing. This pressure differential triggers the roll-up of the airflow aft of the wing, resulting in swirling air masses trailing downstream of the wing tips. After the roll-up is completed, the wake consists of two counter-rotating cylindrical vortices. The vortex circulation is outward, upward, and around the wing tips when viewed from either ahead or behind the aircraft.

Since trailing vortices are a by-product of wing lift, **wing-tip vortices** are generated from the moment an aircraft leaves the ground. Prior to takeoff or touchdown, pilots should note the rotation or touchdown point of the preceding large aircraft. When departing behind a large aircraft, note the large aircraft's rotation point. Rotate prior to the large aircraft's rotation point, and continue to climb above and stay upwind of the large aircraft's climb path until you are able to turn clear of its wake. When landing behind a large aircraft on the same runway, stay at or above the large aircraft's final approach flight path, note his touchdown point, and land beyond it.

Flight tests have shown that the vortices from large aircraft sink at a rate of about 400 to 500 feet per minute, and they tend to level off at a distance of about 900 feet below the flight path of the generating aircraft. Vortex strength diminishes with time and distance behind the generating aircraft.

A crosswind will decrease the lateral movement of the upwind vortex and increase the movement of the downwind vortex. Thus a light wind of 3 to 7 knots would result in the upwind vortex remaining in the touchdown zone for a period of time and hasten the drift of the downwind vortex toward another runway. The conditions are the same for an airplane taking off.

ALL

7135. How does the wake turbulence vortex circulate around each wingtip?

A— Inward, upward, and around each tip.
B— Inward, upward, and counterclockwise.
C— Outward, upward, and around each tip.

The vortex circulation is outward, upward, and around the wing tips when viewed from either ahead or behind the aircraft. (PLT509) — AIM ¶7-3-4

ALL

7136. What effect would a crosswind of 5 knots or less have on the wingtip vortices generated by a large aircraft that had just taken off?

A— A light crosswind would rapidly dissipate the strength of both vortices.
B— The upwind vortex would tend to remain on the runway longer than the downwind vortex.
C— Both vortices would move downwind at a greater rate than if the surface wind was directly down the landing runway.

A crosswind will decrease the lateral movement of the upwind vortex and increase the movement of the downwind vortex. Thus a light wind of 3 to 7 knots would result in the upwind vortex remaining in the touchdown zone for a period of time and hasten the drift of the downwind vortex toward another runway. (PLT509) — AIM ¶7-3-4

Answers

7135 [C]   7136 [B]

ALL

7137. During a takeoff made behind a departing large jet airplane, the pilot can minimize the hazard of wingtip vortices by

A— remaining below the jet's flightpath until able to turn clear of its wake.
B— extending the takeoff roll and not rotating until well beyond the jet's rotation point.
C— being airborne prior to reaching the jet's flightpath until able to turn clear of its wake.

When departing behind a large aircraft, note the large aircraft's rotation point. Rotate prior to the large aircraft's rotation point, and continue to climb above and stay upwind of the large aircraft's climb path until you are able to turn clear of the wake. (PLT509) — AIM ¶7-3-6

ALL

7138. When landing behind a large jet aircraft, at which point on the runway should you plan to land?

A— Beyond the jet's touchdown point.
B— At least 1,000 feet beyond the jet's touchdown point.
C— If any crosswind, land on the windward side of the runway and prior to the jet's touchdown point.

When landing behind a large aircraft on the same runway, stay at or above the large aircraft's final approach flight path, note the touchdown point, and land beyond it. (PLT509) — AIM ¶7-3-6

ALL

7139. Which statement is true regarding wingtip vortices?

A— Helicopter rotors generate downwash turbulence only, not vortices.
B— Vortices generated by helicopters in forward flight are similar to those generated by fixed wing aircraft.
C— Vortices tend to remain level for a period of time before sinking below the generating aircraft's flightpath.

In forward flight, departing or landing helicopters produce a pair of high velocity trailing vortices similar to wing-tip vortices of large fixed wing aircraft. Pilots of small aircraft should use caution when operating behind or crossing behind landing and departing helicopters. (PLT509) — AIM ¶7-3-7

ALL

7140. Due to the effects of wake turbulence, what minimum separation does ATC provide for a small aircraft landing behind a heavy jet?

A— 4 miles.
B— 5 miles.
C— 6 miles.

In order to avoid the effects of wake turbulence, ATC provides a minimum separation of 6 miles between a small aircraft landing behind a heavy jet. (PLT509) — AIM ¶7-3-9

Answers

| 7137 | [C] | 7138 | [A] | 7139 | [B] | 7140 | [C] |

Flight Plans

Pilots are encouraged to give their departure times directly to the FSS serving the departure airport, or as otherwise indicated by the FSS when the flight plan is filed. This will ensure more efficient flight plan service and permit the FSS to advise you of significant changes in aeronautical facilities or meteorological conditions. When a **VFR flight plan** is filed, it will be held by the FSS until 1 hour after the proposed departure time, unless an actual departure time or a revised proposed departure time is received.

A pilot is responsible for ensuring that the VFR or DVFR flight plan is canceled. You should close your flight plan with the nearest FSS, or if one is not available, you may request any ATC facility to relay your cancellation to the FSS. Control towers do not automatically close VFR or DVFR flight plans, since they do not know if a particular VFR aircraft is on a flight plan. If you fail to report or cancel your flight plan within one-half hour after your ETA, search and rescue procedures are started.

ALL
7131. How long will a Flight Service Station hold a VFR flight plan past the proposed departure time?

A— 30 minutes.
B— 1 hour.
C— 2 hours.

When a VFR flight plan is filed, it will be held by the FSS until 1 hour after the proposed departure time, unless an actual departure time or a revised proposed departure time is received. (PLT225) — AIM ¶5-1-4

ALL
7134. How much time do you have to close a VFR flight plan before search and rescue procedures are initiated?

A— One hour after your ATA.
B— One-half hour after landing.
C— One-half hour after your ETA.

If you fail to report or cancel your flight plan within one-half hour after your ETA, search and rescue proce-dures are started. (PLT225) — AIM ¶5-1-13

Answers

7131   [B]   7134   [C]

Chapter 8
Regulations

Continued

Definitions and Abbreviations

Although "FAR" is used as the acronym for "Federal Aviation Regulations," and found throughout the regulations themselves and hundreds of other publications, the FAA is now actively discouraging its use. "FAR" also means "Federal Acquisition Regulations." To eliminate any possible confusion, the FAA cites the federal aviation regulations with reference to Title 14 of the Code of Federal Regulations. For example, "FAR Part 91.3" is referenced as "14 CFR Part 91 Section 3."

A crewmember is a person assigned to duty in the aircraft during flight. This includes pilots, flight engineers, navigators, flight attendants or anyone else assigned to duty in the airplane.

Operational control with respect to a flight, means the exercise of authority over initiating, conducting, or terminating a flight.

Stopway is an area designated for use in decelerating an aborted takeoff. It cannot be used as part of the takeoff distance but can be considered as part of the accelerate-stop distance.

V_2 (Takeoff Safety Speed) ensures that the airplane can maintain an acceptable climb gradient with the critical engine inoperative.

ALL

6316-2. Which is a definition of the term "crewmember"?

A— Any person assigned to duty in an aircraft during flight except a pilot or flight engineer.

B— A person assigned to perform duty in an aircraft during flight time.

C— Only a pilot, flight engineer, or flight navigator assigned to duty in an aircraft during flight time.

"Crewmember" means a person assigned to perform duty in an aircraft during flight time. (PLT395) — 14 CFR §1.1

Answer (A) is incorrect because "crewmember" also includes the pilot and flight engineer. Answer (C) is incorrect because "crewmember" pertains to anyone assigned duty in the aircraft during flight.

ALL

6316-3. Regulations concerning the operational control of a flight refer to

A— the specific duties of any required crewmember.

B— exercising authority over initiating, conducting, or terminating a flight.

C— exercising the privileges of pilot in command of an aircraft.

"Operational control," with respect to flight, means the exercise of authority over initiating, conducting or terminating a flight. (PLT432) — 14 CFR §1.1

Answer (A) is incorrect because "crewmember" refers to any person assigned to perform duty in an aircraft during flight time, which includes cabin crew as well as cockpit crew. Answer (C) is incorrect because "pilot-in-command" refers to the pilot responsible for the operation and safety of an aircraft during flight time, which does not include the initiation of a flight.

ALL

6316-4. A "stopway" can be defined as an area

A— designated for use in decelerating the airplane during an aborted takeoff.

B— at least the same width as the runway capable of supporting an airplane during a normal takeoff.

C— not as wide as the runway but capable of supporting an airplane during a normal takeoff.

"Stopway" means an area beyond the takeoff runway, able to support the airplane, for use in decelerating the airplane during an aborted takeoff. (PLT034) — 14 CFR §1.1

Answer (B) is incorrect because it describes the nonlanding portion of a runway behind a displaced threshold, which may be suitable for taxiing, landing rollout, and takeoff of aircraft. Answer (C) is incorrect because it describes an area that exists before a displaced threshold.

AIR

6316-5. What is V_2 speed?

A— Minimum takeoff speed.

B— Takeoff safety speed.

C— Takeoff decision speed.

V_2 means takeoff safety speed. (PLT132) — 14 CFR §1.2

Answer (A) is incorrect because minimum takeoff speed doesn't describe a defined V-speed. Answer (C) is incorrect because V_1 is takeoff decision speed.

Answers

6316-2 [B]   6316-3 [B]   6316-4 [A]   6316-5 [B]

AIR

6316-6. What is the abbreviation for minimum controllable airspeed?

A— V_S.
B— V_{MC}.
C— V_A.

V_S means the stalling speed or the minimum steady flight speed at which the airplane is controllable. (PLT132) — 14 CFR §1.2

Answer (B) is incorrect because V_{MC} means minimum control speed with the critical engine inoperative. Answer (C) is incorrect V_A is the design maneuvering speed.

Accident Reports

The operator of an aircraft shall immediately, and by the most expeditious means available, notify the nearest National Transportation Safety Board (NTSB) field office when an aircraft accident occurs. The operator of the involved aircraft shall file a report within 10 days after an accident. An aircraft **accident** is defined as an occurrence associated with the operation of an aircraft which takes place between the time any person boards the aircraft with the intention of flight and all such persons have disembarked, and in which any person suffers death or serious injury, or in which the aircraft receives substantial damage. **Substantial damage** is defined as damage or failure which adversely affects the structural strength, performance, or flight characteristics of the aircraft, and which would normally require major repair or replacement of the affected component.

A serious injury, according to the NTSB, means any injury which:

1. Requires hospitalization for more than 48 hours, commencing within 7 days from the date of the injury;
2. Results in a fracture of any bone (except simple fractures of fingers, toes, or nose);
3. Causes severe hemorrhages, nerve, muscle, or tendon damage;
4. Involves any internal organ; or
5. Involves second- or third-degree burns affecting more than 5% of the body surface.

A report on an **incident** for which notification is required by NTSB §830.5(a) shall be filed only as requested by an authorized representative of the board. An immediate notification is also required for any incident involving:

1. Flight control system malfunction or failure;
2. Inability of any required flight crewmember to perform normal flight duties as a result of injury or illness;
3. Failure of structural components of a turbine engine excluding compressor and turbine blades and vanes;
4. Inflight fire;
5. Aircraft inflight collision;
6. Damage to property, other than the aircraft, estimated to exceed $25,000 for repair or fair market value in the event of total loss.

Answers

6316-6   [A]

ALL

6495. The NTSB defines a serious injury as any injury which

A— causes severe tendon damage.
B— results in a simple fracture of the nose.
C— involves first degree burns over 5 percent of the body.

A "serious injury" means, among other things, any injury which causes severe hemorrhages, nerve, muscle, or tendon damage. (PLT395) — NTSB §830.2

Answer (B) is incorrect because a simple fracture of the nose does not qualify as a serious injury. Answer (C) is incorrect because any burns over more than 5% of the body, or any second or third degree burns, qualify as a serious injury.

ALL

6496. Notification to the NTSB is required when there has been substantial damage which

A— adversely affects aircraft performance.
B— causes small punctured holes in the skin or fabric.
C— results in more than $25,000 for repairs to the aircraft.

The operator of an aircraft shall immediately, and by the most expeditious means available, notify the nearest National Transportation Safety Board field office when an aircraft accident occurs. An aircraft accident is defined as an occurrence associated with the operation of an aircraft which takes place between the time any person boards the aircraft with the intention of flight and all such persons have disembarked, and in which any person suffers death or serious injury, or in which the aircraft receives substantial damage. Substantial damage is defined as damage or failure which adversely affects the structural strength, performance, or flight characteristics of the aircraft. (PLT366) — NTSB §§830.5, 830.2

Answer (B) is incorrect because small punctured holes do not qualify as substantial damage. Answer (C) is incorrect because notification is required if more than $25,000 damage is done to property other than the aircraft.

ALL

6497. NTSB Part 830 requires an immediate notification as a result of which incident?

A— Aircraft collide on the ground.
B— Flight control system malfunction.
C— Damage to property, other than the aircraft, estimated to exceed $10,000.

The operator of an aircraft shall immediately, and by the most expeditious means available, notify the nearest National Transportation Safety Board field office when an aircraft accident or an incident involving flight control system malfunction or failure occurs. (PLT366) — NTSB §830.5

Answer (A) is incorrect because only an in-flight collision would require immediate notification. Answer (C) is incorrect because only damage to property other than the aircraft estimated to exceed $25,000 would require immediate notification.

ALL

6498. If an aircraft is involved in an accident which results in substantial damage to the aircraft, the nearest NTSB field office shall be notified

A— immediately.
B— within 7 days.
C— within 10 days.

The operator of an aircraft shall immediately, and by the most expeditious means available, notify the nearest National Transportation Safety Board field office when an aircraft accident which results in substantial damage to the aircraft occurs. (PLT366) — NTSB §830.5

ALL

6499. The operator of an aircraft that has been involved in an accident is required to file a report within how many days?

A— 3.
B— 7.
C— 10.

The operator of an aircraft shall file a report within 10 days after an accident. (PLT366) — NTSB §830.15

ALL

6500. The operator of an aircraft that has been involved in an incident is required to submit a report to the nearest field office of the NTSB

A— within 7 days.
B— within 10 days.
C— only if requested to do so.

A report on an incident for which notification is required shall be filed only as requested by an authorized representative of the board. (PLT366) — NTSB §830.15

Required Documents

No person may act as pilot-in-command or in any other capacity as a required pilot flight crewmember of a civil aircraft of United States registry unless a current pilot certificate is in his/her possession, or readily accessible in the aircraft.

Except for balloon pilots piloting balloons and glider pilots piloting gliders, no person may act as pilot-in-command or in any other capacity as a required pilot flight crewmember of an aircraft unless an appropriate current medical certificate is in his/her possession, or readily accessible in the aircraft.

Except as provided in 14 CFR §91.715, no person may operate a civil aircraft unless it has within it the following:

1. An appropriate and current **airworthiness certificate**

2. A copy of the applicable **operations specifications** (operating limitations)

3. A **registration certificate** issued to its owner

No person may operate a U.S.-registered civil aircraft for which an Airplane or Rotorcraft Flight manual is required by 14 CFR §21.5 unless there is available in the aircraft a current approved Airplane or Rotorcraft Flight Manual, approved manual material, markings, and placards or any combination thereof.

Each certificate holder's manual must contain enroute flight, navigation, and communication procedures for the dispatch, release or continuance of flight if any item of equipment required for the particular type of operation becomes inoperative or unserviceable en route.

When a cockpit voice recorder is required on an airplane, it must be operated continuously from the start of the use of the checklist (before starting engines for the purpose of flight), to completion of the final checklist at the termination of flight. Information recorded more than 30 minutes earlier may be erased or otherwise obliterated.

ALL

6410. An aircraft's operating limitations may be found in the

A— FAA-approved aircraft flight manual.
B— owner's handbook published by the aircraft manufacturer.
C— aircraft flight manual, approved manual material, markings, and placards, or any combination thereof.

No person may operate a U.S.-registered civil aircraft for which an Aircraft Flight manual is required by 14 CFR §21.5 unless there is available in the aircraft a current approved Flight Manual, approved manual material, markings, and placards or any combination thereof. (PLT373) — 14 CFR §91.9

ALL

6462. Regarding certificates and documents, no person may operate an aircraft unless it has within it an

A— Airworthiness Certificate and minimum equipment list (MEL).
B— Airworthiness Certificate, aircraft and engine logbooks, and owner's handbook.
C— Airworthiness Certificate, Registration Certificate, and approved flight manual.

Except as provided in 14 CFR §91.715, no person may operate a civil aircraft unless it has within it the following:

1. An appropriate and current Airworthiness Certificate

2. A copy of the applicable operations specifications issued under 14 CFR §21.197(c) (operating limitations)

3. A registration certificate issued to its owner

(PLT377) — 14 CFR §§91.9, 91.203

Answers

6410   [C]   6462   [C]

ALL

6484. Who is primarily responsible for maintaining an aircraft in an airworthy condition?

A— Mechanic.
B— Pilot in command.
C— Owner or operator of the aircraft.

The owner or operator of an aircraft is primarily responsible for maintaining that aircraft in an airworthy condition. (PLT374) — 14 CFR §91.403

ALL

6493. Aircraft maintenance records must include the current status of

A— all appropriate Airworthiness Certificates.
B— life-limited parts of only engine and airframe.
C— life-limited parts of each airframe, engine, propeller, rotor, and appliance.

Each registered owner or operator shall keep records containing the following information: the current status of life-limited parts of each airframe, engine, propeller, rotor, and appliance. (PLT425) — 14 CFR §91.417

ALL

6494-1. A new maintenance record being used for an aircraft engine rebuilt by the manufacturer must include the previous

A— operating hours of the engine.
B— annual inspections performed on the engine.
C— changes required by airworthiness directives.

Each manufacturer or agency that grants zero time to an engine rebuilt by it shall enter, in the new record, each change made as required by Airworthiness Directives. (PLT425) — 14 CFR §91.421

AIR, RTC, MCI

6494-2. If an instrument on a multiengine airplane is inoperative, which document dictates whether the flight may continue en route?

A— Certificate holder's manual.
B— Amended flight/dispatch release.
C— Original dispatch release.

Each certificate holder's manual must contain enroute flight, navigation, and communication procedures for the dispatch, release or continuance of flight if any item of equipment required for the particular type of operation becomes inoperative or unserviceable en route. (PLT282) — 14 CFR §121.135

AIR, RTC, MCI

6494-3. Information recorded during normal operation by a required cockpit voice recorder in a passenger-carrying airplane

A— may all be erased except the last 30 minutes.
B— may be erased only once each flight.
C— must be retained for 30 minutes after landing.

When a cockpit voice recorder is required on an airplane, it must be operated continuously from the start of the use of the checklist (before starting engines for the purpose of flight), to completion of the final checklist at the termination of flight. Information recorded more than 30 minutes earlier may be erased or otherwise obliterated. (PLT388) — 14 CFR §121.359

AIR, RTC, LTA, MCI

6318. What document(s) must you have with you while operating as pilot in command of an aircraft?

A— An appropriate pilot certificate and a current medical certificate.
B— A certificate showing accomplishment of a checkout in the aircraft and a current flight review.
C— A pilot logbook with endorsements showing accomplishment of a current flight review and recency of experience.

No person may act as pilot-in-command or in any other capacity as a required pilot flight crewmember of a civil aircraft of United States registry unless a current pilot certificate is in his/her possession or readily accessible in the aircraft. Except for balloon pilots piloting balloons and glider pilots piloting gliders, no person may act as pilot-in-command or in any other capacity as a required pilot flight crewmember of an aircraft unless an appropriate current medical certificate is in his/her personal possession, or readily accessible in the aircraft. (PLT443) — 14 CFR §61.3

Answers

| 6484 | [C] | 6493 | [C] | 6494-1 | [C] | 6494-2 | [A] | 6494-3 | [A] | 6318 | [A] |

Medical Certificates

Student pilot, recreational pilot, and private pilot operations, other than glider and balloon pilots, require a third-class medical certificate or compliance with BasicMed—which is detailed in 14 CFR Part 68.

The **BasicMed** privileges apply to persons exercising student, recreational, and private pilot privileges when acting as pilot in command (PIC). It also applies to persons exercising flight instructor privileges when acting as PIC. You cannot use BasicMed privileges to fly as a safety pilot, except when that pilot is acting as PIC. Pilots operating under BasicMed must hold a current and valid U.S. driver's license and comply with all medical requirements or restrictions associated with that license. Applicants operating under BasicMed regulations must also complete the comprehensive medical examination checklist (CMEC) in collaboration with a physical examination by a state-licensed physician. You physical must be completed within the last 48 months and the CMEC completed within the last 24 months. When operating under BasicMed, pilots are limited to:

1. Fly with no more than five passengers.

2. Fly an aircraft with a maximum certificated takeoff weight of no more than 6,000 lbs.

3. Fly an aircraft that is authorized to carry no more than 6 occupants.

4. Flights within the United States, at an indicated airspeed of 250 knots or less, and at an altitude at or below 18,000 feet mean sea level (MSL).

5. You may not fly for compensation or hire.

If operating beyond these limitations, pilots must obtain an FAA Medical Certificate. A **third-class medical certificate** expires at the end of:

1. The 60th month after the month of the date of the examination shown on the certificate if the person has not reached his or her 40th birthday on or before the date of examination; or

2. The 24th month after the month of the date of examination shown on the certificate if the person has reached his or her 40th birthday on or before the date of the examination.

The holder of a **second-class medical certificate** may exercise commercial privileges during the first 12 calendar months, but the certificate is valid only for private pilot privileges during the following (12 or 48) calendar months, depending on the applicant's age.

The holder of a **first-class medical certificate** may exercise Airline Transport Pilot privileges during the first (6 or 12) calendar months, commercial privileges during the following (6 or 0) calendar months, and private pilot privileges during the following (12 or 48) calendar months, depending on the applicant's age. To state another way, a medical certificate may last 6 months to a year with first-class privileges, 12 months (from the date of the examination) with second-class privileges, and 2 or 5 years with third-class privileges — depending on whether the applicant is above or below 40 years of age.

Each type of medical certificate is valid through the last day of the month (of the month it expires), regardless of the day the physical examination was given.

AIR, MCI

6336. An applicant who holds a Commercial Pilot Certificate with ASEL ratings is seeking a MEL rating at the commercial level. On August 1, 2007, the applicant shows you a second class medical dated January 2, 2006. May the applicant take the practical test?

A— No.
B— Yes.
C— Yes, but at the private pilot skill level.

To be eligible for a flight test, the applicant must hold at least a current third-class medical certificate. (PLT407) — 14 CFR §61.39

Answers (A) and (C) are incorrect because although a second-class medical certificate is required for commercial privileges, only a third-class medical is required when adding a rating to an existing certificate.

AIR, RTC, LTA, MCI

6323. If a Second-Class Medical Certificate was issued to a commercial pilot 13 months ago, during the next 11 months this pilot may

A— not act as pilot in command or carry passengers or property.
B— act as pilot in command and carry passengers or property, but not for compensation or hire.
C— act as pilot in command for compensation or hire, but may not carry passengers or property for compensation or hire.

For operations requiring only a private or student pilot certificate, a second-class medical certificate expires at the end of the last day of the 24th or 36th month (depending on the applicant's age) after the month of the date of examination shown on the certificate. This does not allow a commercial pilot to carry passengers or property for compensation or hire after the last day of the 12th month after the date of the examination. (PLT447) — 14 CFR §61.23

Answers (A) and (C) are incorrect because the pilot may not exercise commercial privileges for the last 11 months.

AIR, RTC, LTA, MCI

6324. A Third-Class Medical Certificate was issued on May 3 to a person over 40 years of age. To exercise the privileges of a Private Pilot Certificate, the medical certificate will be valid through

A— May 3, 24 months later.
B— May 31, 24 months later.
C— May 31, 36 months later.

A third-class medical certificate expires at the end of the last day of the 24th month after the month of the date of the examination shown on the certificate if the person has reached his or her 40th birthday on or before the date of examination, for operations requiring a private pilot certificate. (PLT447) — 14 CFR §61.23

AIR, RTC, LTA, MCI

7312. Can a 43-year old student pilot fly solo with a first-class medical certificate that was issued 15 months ago?

A— No; 1st class medical certificates are not issued to student pilots.
B— No; student pilots must hold a 3rd class medical certificate.
C— Yes; the pilot may exercise student pilot privileges.

Student pilots are required to hold a third-class medical certificate. A medical certificate may last 6 months with first-class (ATP) privileges, 12 months with second-class (Commercial) privileges, and 2 years with third-class privileges for a pilot above 40 years of age. (PLT447) — 14 CFR §61.23

AIR, RTC, LTA, MCI

6325. A Second-Class Medical Certificate issued January 18 of this year will expire

A— January 18 of next year for private pilot privileges.
B— January 31 of next year for commercial pilot privileges.
C— January 31, 2 years later for commercial pilot privileges.

A second-class medical certificate expires at the end of the last day of the 12th month after the month of the date of examination shown on the certificate, for operations requiring a commercial pilot certificate. It expires at the end of the last day of the 24th or 60th month (depending on the applicant's age) after the month of the date of examination shown on the certificate, for operations requiring only a private or student pilot certificate. A certificate issued on January 18 of this year will expire on January 31 of the next year for commercial pilot privileges, but it may be used for private pilot privileges until January 31, two (or five, depending on the applicant's age) years later. (PLT447) — 14 CFR §61.23

Answer (A) is incorrect because medical certificates expire on the last day of the month. Answer (C) is incorrect because a second-class medical certificate expires at the end of the 12th month for commercial privileges.

Answers

| 6336 | [B] | 6323 | [B] | 6324 | [B] | 7312 | [C] | 6325 | [B] |

Student Pilot Certification

A student pilot certificate issued after April 1st 2016 is done so with no expiration date and remains valid indefinitely unless suspended, surrendered, or revoked. To be eligible for a student pilot certificate limited to airplanes, powered parachutes, and weight-shift control, an applicant must be at least 16 years of age, 14 for the operation of a glider or balloon.

A student pilot may not operate an aircraft in solo flight unless the student pilot's logbook has been endorsed for the specific make and model aircraft to be flown, and unless within the preceding 90 days his/her pilot logbook has been endorsed by an authorized flight instructor who has provided instruction in the make and model of aircraft in which the solo flight is made, and who finds that the applicant is competent to make a safe solo flight in that aircraft.

Prior to being authorized to conduct a solo flight, a student pilot must have received and logged instruction in the applicable maneuvers and procedures for the make and model of aircraft to be flown in solo flight, and must have demonstrated proficiency to an acceptable performance level as judged by the instructor who endorses the student's pilot certificate. As appropriate to the aircraft to be flown in solo flight, the student pilot must have received presolo flight training in:

1. Flight preparation procedures, including preflight inspections, powerplant operation, and aircraft systems

2. Taxiing or surface operations, including runups

3. Takeoffs and landings, including normal and crosswind

4. Straight-and-level flight and turns in both directions

5. Climbs and climbing turns

6. Airport traffic patterns, including entry and departure procedure, and collision, wind shear, and wake turbulence avoidance

7. Descents with and without turns, using high and low drag configurations

8. Flight at various airspeeds from cruise to slow flight

9. Stall entries from various flight attitudes and power combinations with recovery initiated at the first indication of a stall, and recovery from a full stall

10. Emergency procedures and equipment malfunctions

11. Ground reference maneuvers

12. Approaches to a landing area with simulated engine malfunctions

13. Slips to a landing

14. Go-arounds

A student pilot may not operate an aircraft in a solo cross-country flight, nor may he/she, except in an emergency, make a solo flight landing at any point other than the airport of takeoff, until he/she meets the requirements prescribed in Part 61. However, an authorized flight instructor may allow a student to practice solo takeoffs and landings at another airport within 25 NM from the airport at which the student receives instruction, if the instructor finds the student competent to make those landings and takeoffs, and the flight training specific to the destination airport (including the route to and from, takeoffs and landings, and traffic pattern entry and exit) has taken place. Also, the instructor must have flown with that student prior to authorizing those takeoffs and landings, and endorsed the student pilot's logbook accordingly.

The term *cross-country flight* means a flight beyond a radius of 25 nautical miles from the point of takeoff. A flight instructor must endorse a student pilot's logbook for solo cross-country flights. There are three types of these endorsements:

1. An endorsement in the student pilot's logbook that the instructor has reviewed the preflight planning and preparation for each solo cross-country flight, and the pilot is prepared to make the flight safely under the known circumstances and the conditions listed by the instructor in the logbook.

2. The instructor may also endorse the logbook for repeated solo cross-country flights under stipulated conditions over a course of not more than 50 nautical miles from the point of departure if he/she has given the student flight instruction in both directions over the route, including takeoffs and landings at the airports to be used.

3. The student pilot certificate must be endorsed for cross-country operations.

ALL
6321. What is the duration of a student pilot certificate?

A— Indefinite.
B— 12 calendar months from the month in which it was issued.
C— 24 calendar months from the month in which it was issued.

Student pilot certificates issued after April 1st 2016 will have no expiration date. The certificate will remain valid unless it is surrendered, suspended, or revoked. (PLT457) — 14 CFR §61.19

ALL
6363. Which is a required endorsement by an authorized flight instructor for a student pilot to operate an aircraft in solo flight?

A— An endorsement that instruction was given in the make and model of aircraft to be soloed within the preceding 6 months.
B— An endorsement within the preceding 90 days stating that instruction was given in the make and model aircraft to be flown and the student is competent to make a safe solo flight.
C— An endorsement made within the preceding 180 days that instruction was given in the make of aircraft to be soloed and that the instructor found the applicant competent to make a safe flight in that aircraft.

A student pilot may not operate an aircraft in solo flight unless within the preceding 90 days his/her pilot logbook has been endorsed by an authorized flight instructor who has given him/her instruction in the make and model of aircraft in which the solo flight is made, and who finds that he/she has met the requirements of this section and finds that he/she is competent to make a safe solo flight in that aircraft. (PLT407) — 14 CFR §61.87

Answers (A) and (C) are incorrect because the endorsement must have been within the preceding 90 days, and it must state the student is competent to make safe solo flight.

ALL
6371. Are students authorized to make repeated solo cross-country flights without each flight being logbook endorsed?

A— No; each solo cross-country flight requires a logbook endorsement.
B— Yes; provided the flights take place under stipulated conditions.
C— Yes; but only if the flights remain within 25 NM of the point of departure.

An instructor may endorse a student pilot's logbook for repeated solo cross-country flights under stipulated conditions over a course of not more than 50 nautical miles from the point of departure if he/she has given the student flight instruction in both directions over the route, including takeoffs and landings at the airports to be used. (PLT457) — 14 CFR §61.93

Answer (A) is incorrect because an endorsement can be issued for repeated specific cross-country flight within 50 NM. Answer (C) is incorrect because the flight must remain within 50 NM of the point of departure.

Answers

| 6321 | [A] | 6363 | [B] | 6371 | [B] |

ALL

6372. One requirement for a student pilot to be authorized to make a solo cross-country flight is an endorsement

A— in the student's logbook that the instructor has given the student cross-country instruction in the model of aircraft to be used.

B— in the student's logbook that the preflight planning and preparation has been reviewed and the student is prepared to make the flight safely.

C— on the student pilot certificate stating the student is competent to make cross-country flights in the category, class, and type of aircraft involved.

A student pilot must have the following endorsements from an authorized flight instructor: an endorsement in the pilot logbook that the instructor has reviewed the preflight planning and preparation for each solo cross-country flight, and the pilot is prepared to make the flight safely under the known circumstances and the conditions listed by the instructor in the logbook. (PLT457) — 14 CFR §61.93

Answer (A) is incorrect because the instruction only needs to be in the category of aircraft to be used. Answer (C) is incorrect because the student pilot certificate is endorsed for the category of aircraft to be flown.

ALL

6373. May repeated solo cross-country flights over the same route be made by a student without receiving an endorsement from a flight instructor for each flight?

A— No; an endorsement is required for each solo cross-country flight.

B— Yes; if the route is no more than 50 NM from the point of departure and instruction was given in both directions over the route.

C— Yes; if the total route is no more than 25 NM from the point of departure and the student has received at least 3 hours of cross-country instruction and logged at least 5 hours of solo cross country flight.

An instructor may endorse a student pilot's logbook for repeated solo cross-country flights under stipulated conditions over a course of not more than 50 nautical miles from the point of departure if he/she has given the student flight instruction in both directions over the route, including takeoffs and landings at the airports to be used. (PLT457) — 14 CFR §61.93

Answer (A) is incorrect because an endorsement can be issued for repeated specific cross-country flights within 50 NM of the departure point. Answer (C) is incorrect because the flight must remain within 50 NM of the departure point.

ALL

6375. Who is authorized to endorse a student pilot logbook authorizing flight in Class B airspace?

A— Any flight instructor.

B— Only the flight instructor who conducted the training.

C— Any flight instructor who has personal knowledge of the flight training received.

A student pilot may not operate an aircraft on a solo flight in Class B airspace unless the logbook of that student pilot has been endorsed within the preceding 90 days for conducting solo flight in that specific Class B airspace by the instructor who gave the flight training. (PLT457) — 14 CFR §61.95

ALL, AIR, RTC

6368. Prior to solo flight, a student must have received flight instruction in

A— ground reference maneuvers.

B— unusual attitude recoveries.

C— basic radio navigation procedures.

Prior to being authorized to conduct a solo flight, a student pilot must have received and logged instruction in at least the applicable maneuvers and procedures listed in paragraphs (d) through (j) of 14 CFR §61.87 for the make and model of aircraft to be flown in solo flight, and must have demonstrated proficiency to an acceptable performance level as judged by the instructor who endorses the student's pilot certificate. This list includes ground reference maneuvers. (PLT407) — 14 CFR §61.87

Answer (B) is incorrect because unusual attitude recovery practice is not necessary until prior to the private pilot practical test. Answer (C) is incorrect because basic radio navigation procedures are required prior to solo cross-country flight.

AIR, WSC, PPC, MCI

6360. To be eligible for a student pilot certificate limited to airplanes, an applicant is required to be at least how old?

A— 14 years.

B— 16 years.

C— 17 years.

To be eligible for a student pilot certificate limited to airplanes, an applicant must be at least 16 years of age. (PLT457) — 14 CFR §61.83

Answer (A) is incorrect because 14 years is the minimum age for a student pilot certificate limited to glider or balloon operations. Answer (C) is incorrect because 17 years is the minimum age for a private pilot certificate.

Answers

6372	[B]	6373	[B]	6375	[B]	6368	[A]	6360	[B]

ALL

7313. An application for a student pilot certificate must be submitted in person to any of the following

A— Flight standards district office, flight instructor, designated pilot examiner.

B— Aviation medical examiner, designated pilot examiner, flight instructor.

C— Aviation medical examiner, FAA inspector, designated pilot examiner.

Applications for student pilot certificates must be submitted in person by the applicant to a flight standards district office, designated pilot examiner, flight instructor, or an airman certification representative associated with a pilot school. (PLT407) — 14 CFR §61.85

Recreational Pilot Certification

The recreational pilot certificate fits between the student and private pilot certificates. Recreational pilot limitations include: may not carry more than one passenger, pay less than the pro rata share of the operating expenses of a flight with a passenger (provided the expenses involve only fuel, oil, airport expenses, or aircraft rental fees), fly an aircraft with more than 4 seats or with more than 180 HP nor with retractable landing gear, demonstrate an aircraft to a prospective buyer, fly between sunset and sunrise, or fly in airspace in which communication with air traffic control is required. Recreational pilots may fly beyond 50 NM from the departure airport with training and endorsements from an authorized instructor.

To be eligible for a recreational pilot certificate, a person must be at least 17 years of age and must hold at least a current third-class medical certificate.

A recreational pilot who has logged fewer than 400 flight hours and who has not logged pilot-in-command time in an aircraft within the preceding 180 days may not act as pilot-in-command of an aircraft until he/she has received flight instruction from an authorized flight instructor who certifies in the pilot's logbook that the pilot is competent to act as pilot-in-command of the aircraft.

AIR, RTC, GLI, LTA, MCI

6376. A recreational pilot certificate may be issued for

A— airships, gliders, and balloons.

B— airplanes, gyroplanes, and helicopters.

C— airplanes, gliders, helicopters, and gyroplanes.

A recreational pilot may not act as pilot-in-command of an aircraft that is classified as a glider, airship, or balloon. (PLT448) — 14 CFR §61.101

AIR, RTC, MCI

6346-1. When is a recreational pilot required to carry a logbook with the required endorsement?

A— When flying during the hours between sunrise to sunset.

B— On all flights when serving as pilot in command.

C— Any flight up to 50 miles from the airport at which instruction was received.

A person who holds a recreational pilot certificate may act as pilot-in-command of an aircraft on a flight within 50 NM from the departure airport, provided that person has received ground and flight training from an authorized instructor, been found proficient to operate the aircraft at the departure airport and the area within 50 NM from that airport, and received an endorsement, which is carried on the person's possession in the aircraft. (PLT457) — 14 §61.101

Answers

7313   [A]   6376   [B]   6346-1   [B]

AIR, RTC, MCI

6377. A recreational pilot with less than 400 hours' flight time may not act as pilot in command unless the pilot has

A— logged pilot-in-command time in the last 90 days.
B— logged pilot-in-command time in the last 180 days.
C— received flight instruction from an instructor who certifies the pilot is competent to conduct flights beyond 50 miles.

A recreational pilot who has logged fewer than 400 flight hours and who has not logged pilot-in-command time in an aircraft within the preceding 180 days may not act as pilot-in-command of an aircraft until the pilot has received flight instruction from an authorized flight instructor who certifies in the pilot's logbook that the pilot is competent to act as pilot-in-command of the aircraft. (PLT448) — 14 CFR §61.101

Answer (A) is incorrect because the pilot must have logged PIC time in the last 180 days. Answer (C) is incorrect because if the pilot has not logged PIC time in the last 180 days, then he/she must receive flight instruction from a CFI who certifies he/she is competent to act as PIC.

Private Pilot Certification

To be eligible for a private pilot certificate with an airplane, weight-shift control, or powered parachute rating, a person must be at least 17 years of age, and hold at least a current third-class medical certificate. An applicant for a private pilot certificate with an airplane or weight-shift control rating must have had at least a total of 40 hours of flight instruction. A powered parachute requires 25 hours of flight time with 10 hours of instruction. Solo flight time, which must include the following:

Airplanes:

1. 3 hours of night instruction, including 10 takeoffs and landings and one cross-country flight over 100 NM

2. 3 hours of cross-country instruction, and 3 hours of instrument instruction from an authorized flight instructor and 5 hours of solo cross-country flight, each flight with a landing at a point more than 50 NM from the original departure point. One flight must be at least 150 NM, with landings at a minimum of 3 points, one of which is at least 50 NM from the original departure point.

An applicant for Private Pilot—Airplane who operates in Alaska flying gyroplane, weight-shift control and powered parachute is not required to have night training; instead, a "night flying prohibited" restriction may be placed on the private pilot certificate.

AIR, MCI, RTC

6378. Your student is not interested in flying at night. May he/she take the practical test for a private pilot certificate without any night flight training?

A— No, your student must have logged some night flight training in order to be eligible.
B— No, your student must have logged at least 3 hours of night flight training in order to be issued a certificate.
C— Yes, but after satisfactory completion of the practical test, the certificate will be issued with the limitation "Night Flying Prohibited."

A private pilot airplane candidate is required to log instruction in a number of maneuvers, including night flying, with takeoffs, landings, and VFR navigation, in order to qualify for the private pilot certificate. (PLT451) — 14 CFR §61.109

Answer (A) is incorrect because the student must log 3 hours of dual night flight, to include 10 takeoffs and landings and one cross-country flight of over 100 nautical miles total distance. Answer (C) is incorrect because the student must have night instruction, even if he/she is not interested in flying at night (with the exception of pilots in Alaska seeking the "night flying prohibited" certificate endorsement).

Answers

6377   [B]   6378   [B]

AIR, MCI

6379. Your student, who is preparing for a private pilot practical test in a single-engine airplane, received 3.5 hours of cross-country flight training including flights of 1.9 hours, 1.0 hours, and .6 hours. Is your student eligible to take the practical test?

A— No.
B— Yes.
C— Yes but, if test is satisfactory, certificate will have an ICAO limitation on it.

The student meets the requirements of three hours of cross-country with an authorized flight instructor. (PLT405) — 14 CFR §61.109

Answer (A) is incorrect because the student meets the 3 hours of flight training (dual) cross-country requirements. Answer (C) is incorrect because the ICAO limitation applies to pilots based on small islands who do not have 3 hours of solo cross-country time.

AIR, MCI

6380. What night flight training is required for an unrestricted private pilot certificate with an airplane rating?

A— 3 hours to include 10 takeoffs and 10 landings and one cross-country flight of over 100 nautical miles.
B— 3 hours to include five takeoffs and five landings (each landing from a traffic pattern).
C— 1 hour to include three takeoffs and three landings.

An applicant for a private pilot certificate with an airplane rating must have 3 hours of night flight training that includes one cross-country flight of over 100 NM, and 10 takeoffs and 10 landings to a full stop (with each landing involving a flight in the traffic pattern) at an airport. (PLT407) — 14 CFR §61.109

AIR, MCI

6382. Your student has received 3.0 hours of night flight training including five takeoffs and landings. Is your student eligible to take the private pilot practical test?

A— No.
B— Yes, but the pilot certificate would bear the limitation "Night Flying Prohibited."
C— Yes but the pilot certificate would bear the restriction, "Holder does not meet ICAO requirements."

Applicants for a private pilot certificate with an airplane rating must have at least 3 hours of flight instruction at night, including 10 takeoffs and landings and one cross-country flight of over 100 NM. (PLT451) — 14 CFR §61.109

Answer (B) is incorrect because the night-flying requirements exception applies only to students who receive flight training in, and reside in, the state of Alaska. Answer (C) is incorrect because the ICAO restriction refers to pilots based on small islands who do not have 3 hours of solo cross-country time.

AIR, MCI

6381. With respect to day cross-country experience requirements, a private pilot-airplane applicant must have a minimum of

A— 3 hours' dual and 5 hours' solo.
B— 3 hours' dual and 10 hours' solo.
C— 5 hours' dual and 10 hours' solo.

An applicant for a private pilot certificate with an airplane rating must have had at least a total of 40 hours of flight instruction and solo flight time, which must include 3 hours of cross-country instruction from an authorized flight instructor and 5 hours of solo cross-country flight, each flight with a landing at a point more than 50 NM from the original departure point. One flight must be at least 150 NM, with landings at a minimum of 3 points, one of which is at least 50 NM from the original departure point. (PLT451) — 14 CFR §61.109

Answer (B) is incorrect because the private pilot applicant only needs 5 hours of solo cross-country time. Answer (C) is incorrect because the private pilot applicant needs only 3 hours of dual cross-country time.

AIR, RTC, MCI

7314. Can any of a private pilot's airplane flight training apply to meet requirements for adding a helicopter rating?

A— Yes; all the dual airplane time applies to the helicopter experience requirements.
B— No; all the dual experience requirements must be accomplished in the helicopter.
C— Some of the airplane training will apply to the helicopter experience requirements.

To add a helicopter rating to a private pilot certificate, the applicant must have 20 hours of flight training from an authorized instructor. This 20 hours includes 3 hours of cross-country, 3 hours of night flying, and 3 hours in preparation for the practical exam all "in a helicopter." The remaining 11 hours does not specify what aircraft must be used for the flight training; the airplane experience can apply here. (PLT451) — 14 CFR §61.109

Answers

| 6379 | [B] | 6380 | [A] | 6382 | [A] | 6381 | [A] | 7314 | [C] |

AIR, RTC, MCI

7314-1. Your student holds a private pilot certificate with an airplane rating and wishes to obtain a rotorcraft category rating. You inform the student that

A— none of the training/flight experience obtained toward the airplane rating can be used for the rotorcraft rating.

B— he/she must complete the rotorcraft practical test in its entirety as per the private pilot rotorcraft practical test standards.

C— some of the training/flight experience acquired toward the airplane rating can be used to meet the requirements for a rotorcraft category rating.

Some of the airplane experience can count towards the rotorcraft rating requirements. The Practical Test Standards includes an additional rating task table which details which tasks are required components to the practical exam for someone adding a helicopter rating to an existing private pilot certificate. (PLT451) — 14 CFR §61.109, 8081-15

AIR, RTC, MCI

7315. A student has a private pilot certificate with an airplane rating. Does he need to fulfill all the experience requirements for an initial private pilot certificate with a helicopter rating to add a helicopter rating to his existing pilot certificate?

A— Yes; all aeronautical experience requirements must be accomplished in a helicopter.

B— No; some of the dual and solo airplane flight training experience will apply towards the helicopter requirements.

C— No; some of the dual flight training experience will apply towards the helicopter requirements.

To add a helicopter rating to a private pilot certificate, the applicant must have 20 hours of flight training from an authorized instructor. This 20 hours includes 3 hours of cross-country, 3 hours of night flying, and 3 hours in preparation for the practical exam all "in a helicopter." The remaining 11 hours does not specify what aircraft must be used for the flight training; the airplane experience can apply here. Adding a helicopter rating to an existing pilot certificate also requires 10 hours of solo flying in a helicopter. (PLT451) — 14 CFR §61.109

AIR, RTC, MCI

7315-1. A foreign national received flight training and completed solo flights outside the U.S. and comes to you to complete flight training and obtain a private pilot certificate. As a CFI, you know that

A— you can continue with the student, endorsing the 14 CFR part 61 requirements once they have been met.

B— the student will need to complete all required flight training in the U.S. with an authorized flight instructor.

C— you can endorse the student for the practical exam upon completion of flight training and the student will have a limitation on the certificate indicating it was issued based on training provided by a non-FAA CFI.

Authorized instructors may provide the endorsements necessary to qualify a student for a practical exam. (PLT451) — 14 CFR §§61.1, 61.39, 61.195

Answer (B) is incorrect because there is no requirement that all flight training requirements be accomplished in the U.S. Answer (C) is incorrect because there is no such limitation available for an FAA certificate.

Commercial Pilot Certification

To be eligible for a commercial pilot certificate, a person must be at least 18 years of age, and must hold at least a valid third-class medical certificate. A second-class medical certificate is required to exercise commercial pilot privileges. An applicant for a commercial pilot certificate with an airplane rating must have a total of at least 250 hours of flight time as a pilot. This must include a total of at least 50 hours as pilot-in-command of cross-country flights.

A commercial airplane pilot must hold an instrument rating (airplane), or the commercial pilot certificate is endorsed with a limitation prohibiting the carriage of passengers for hire in airplanes on cross-country flights of more than 50 nautical miles or at night.

Answers

7314-1   [C]   7315   [C]   7315-1   [A]

AIR, RTC, GLI, LTA, MCI

6385. What is the minimum age required to be eligible for a commercial pilot certificate?

A— 17.
B— 18.
C— 21.

To be eligible for a commercial pilot certificate, a person must be at least 18 years of age. (PLT448) — 14 CFR §61.123

AIR, RTC, GLI, LTA, MCI

6386. To be eligible for a commercial pilot certificate, one of the requirements is for the applicant to hold at least a valid

A— First-Class Medical Certificate.
B— Second-Class Medical Certificate.
C— Third-Class Medical Certificate.

A third-class medical certificate is required prior to taking a checkride in an aircraft for a certificate or rating at the recreational, private, commercial, or ATP certificate level. (PLT448) — 14 CFR §61.23

AIR, MCI

6388. As pilot, what is the minimum flight time in an aircraft an applicant must have for a commercial pilot certificate with an airplane rating?

A— 250 hours.
B— 200 hours.
C— 150 hours.

An applicant for a commercial pilot certificate with an airplane rating must have a total of at least 250 hours of flight time as pilot, which may include not more than 50 hours of instruction by an authorized instructor in a ground trainer acceptable to the Administrator. (PLT451) — 14 CFR §61.129

Answer (A) is incorrect because although 250 hours total time is required, up to 50 hours may be instruction in a simulator. Answer (C) is incorrect because 200 hours is required in an aircraft.

AIR, MCI

6389. An applicant for a commercial pilot certificate with ASEL ratings presents a logbook with 254 hours total time. Of that, 20 hours are logged as SIC in single-engine airplanes certificated for single pilot operations. You determine this time was accumulated as safety pilot with another pilot who was flying "under the hood." Does the applicant have enough total time to be eligible for the practical test?

A— Yes.
B— No, because SIC time does not count towards hours for certification requirements.
C— No, only one-half of the SIC time can be counted towards certification requirements.

An applicant for a commercial pilot certificate with an airplane rating must have a total of 250 hours of flight time, including 100 hours in a powered aircraft, 50 hours of flight instruction, and 100 hours of PIC time. The hour requirements are met if the 20 hours are logged as safety pilot. (PLT451) — 14 CFR §61.129

Answer (B) is incorrect because SIC time counts toward the total time. Answer (C) is incorrect because all of the SIC time counts toward the total time.

AIR, MCI

6390. Under FAR Part 61, a commercial pilot-airplane applicant is required to have a minimum of how much cross-country experience?

A— 30 hours.
B— 40 hours.
C— 50 hours.

An applicant for a commercial pilot certificate with an airplane rating must have a total of at least 50 hours of cross-country flights as pilot-in-command. (PLT407) — 14 CFR §61.129

Answers

6385 [B]	6386 [C]	6388 [B]	6389 [A]	6390 [C]

AIR, MCI

6391. What limitation is imposed on a newly certificated commercial airplane pilot if that person does not hold an instrument pilot rating?

A— The carrying of passengers for hire on cross-country flights of more than 50 NM or at night is prohibited.

B— The carrying of passengers for hire on cross-country flights is limited to 50 NM for night flights, but not limited for day flights.

C— The carrying of passengers or property for hire on cross-country flights is limited to 50 NM and the carrying of passengers for hire at night is prohibited.

A newly certificated commercial airplane pilot must hold an instrument rating (airplane), or the commercial pilot certificate is endorsed with a limitation prohibiting the carriage of passengers for hire in airplanes on cross-country flights of more than 50 nautical miles or at night. (PLT443) — 14 CFR §61.133

Answer (B) is incorrect because a commercial pilot without an instrument rating may not carry passengers for hire at night. Answer (C) is incorrect because the commercial pilot may carry property for hire.

AIR, RTC, MCI

7316. Your student has a commercial certificate with an airplane rating. In order for him to be certificated to fly the Sikorsky-61 as a commercial pilot, as an instructor you know that he will need to

A— take a practical test in a helicopter and have a commercial helicopter certificate with an instrument rating.

B— take a knowledge exam, pass a practical test, and have 10 hours in a Sikorsky-61.

C— have 10 hours in the Sikorsky-61 and take a practical test.

The student must have 10 hours in the Sikorsky-61 and take a practical test to add a helicopter rating to the existing commercial pilot certificate. (PLT407) — 14 CFR §61.129

Answer (A) is incorrect because an instrument rating is not required to operate a helicopter with commercial privileges. Answer (B) is incorrect because a knowledge exam is not required to add a helicopter rating to an existing commercial pilot certificate.

Ground and Flight Instructor Certification

General aviation flight instructor certificates are issued under 14 CFR Part 61 Subpart H. **Sport** Instructor certificates are issued under 14 CFR Part 61 Subpart K.

A **flight instructor certificate** expires at the end of the 24th month after the month in which it was last issued or renewed. An applicant for a flight instructor certificate must have received flight instruction from a flight instructor who has held a flight instructor certificate during the 24 months immediately preceding the date the instruction is given, who meets the general requirements for a flight instructor certificate, and who has given at least 200 hours of flight instruction. A person whose flight instructor certificate is suspended may not apply for any rating to be added to that certificate during the period of suspension.

Each certificated flight instructor must sign the logbook for each person to whom he/she has given flight or ground instruction and specify in that book the amount of time and the date on which it was given. In addition, he/she shall maintain a record in his/her flight instructor logbook or in a separate document containing the following (the record required by this section shall be retained by the flight instructor separately or in his/her logbook for at least 3 years):

1. The name of each person whose logbook or student pilot certificate he/she has endorsed for solo flight privileges. The record must include the type and date of each endorsement.

2. The name of each person for whom he/she has signed a certification for a written, flight, or practical test, including the kind of test, date of his/her certification, and the result of the test.

The holder of a flight instructor certificate who applies for an additional rating on that certificate must have had at least 15 hours as pilot-in-command in the category and class of aircraft appropriate to the rating sought.

Answers

6391　[A]　　　7316　[C]

The holder of a flight instructor certificate may not conduct more than 8 hours of flight instruction in any period of 24 consecutive hours. An ATP may not instruct for more than 8 hours in one day nor more than 36 hours in a 7-day period.

The holder of a flight instructor certificate may not endorse a student pilot certificate for solo cross-country flight privileges unless he/she has given that student pilot flight instruction required by this part for the endorsement and considers that the student is prepared to conduct the flight safely with the aircraft involved. Neither may he/she endorse a student pilot's logbook for local solo flight unless he/she has given that student pilot flight instruction and found that student pilot prepared for solo flight in the type of aircraft involved.

The holder of a flight instructor certificate may not authorize a student to make a solo flight unless he/she possesses a valid student pilot certificate endorsed for solo in the make and model aircraft to be flown.

The holder of a flight instructor certificate may not give flight instruction required for the issuance of a certificate or a category, or class rating in a multi-engine airplane or a helicopter unless he/she has had at least 5 hours of experience as pilot-in-command in the make and model of that airplane or helicopter, as the case may be.

The holder of a flight instructor certificate may have his/her certificate renewed for an additional period of 24 months if he/she passes the practical test for a flight instructor certificate and the rating involved, or those portions of that test that the Administrator considers necessary to determine his/her competency as a flight instructor.

The flight instructor certificate may be renewed without taking the practical test if the record of instruction shows that he/she is a competent flight instructor or he/she completes an instructor refresher course within 3 months of the application for renewal.

The holder of an expired flight instructor certificate may exchange that certificate for a new certificate by passing the practical test prescribed in 14 CFR §61.187. He/she may not renew it by any other means.

A person who holds a **basic ground instructor** rating is authorized to provide ground training in the aeronautical knowledge areas required for the issuance of a recreational or private pilot certificate, ground training required for a recreational and private pilot flight review, and a recommendation for a knowledge test required for the issuance of a recreational or private pilot certificate.

A person who holds an **advanced ground instructor** rating is authorized to provide ground training in the aeronautical knowledge areas required for the issuance of any certificate or rating (except the instrument rating), ground training for any flight review, and a recommendation for a knowledge test required for the issuance of any certificate.

A person who holds an **instrument ground instructor** rating is authorized to provide ground training in the aeronautical knowledge areas required for an instrument rating, ground training required for an instrument proficiency check, and a recommendation for a knowledge test required for an instrument rating.

The holder of a ground instructor certificate may not perform the duties of a ground instructor unless, within the preceding 12 months, the person has served as a ground instructor or flight instructor, completed a Flight Instructor Refresher Clinic (FIRC), or the person has received an endorsement from an authorized ground or flight instructor certifying that the person has demonstrated satisfactory proficiency in the subject areas required for a ground instructor.

Flight Instructors with a Sport Pilot Rating

Flight instructors who let their medical expire can operate under Part 61 Subpart K as sport pilot flight instructors, instructing in light-sport aircraft.

ALL
6319. A person whose Flight Instructor Certificate has been suspended may not

A— give flight training, but may apply for a rating to be added to that certificate.
B— apply for any rating to be added to that certificate during the period of suspension.
C— apply for any Flight Instructor Certificate for a period of 1 year after the date of the suspension.

A person whose flight instructor certificate is suspended may not apply for any rating to be added to that certificate during the period of suspension. (PLT405) — 14 CFR §61.13

Answer (A) is incorrect because flight instruction cannot be given without a current flight instructor certificate. Answer (C) is incorrect because the suspension period is specified, but not necessarily 1 year.

ALL
6322. What is the duration of a Flight Instructor Certificate?

A— Indefinite, unless suspended or revoked.
B— 24 months after the month in which it was issued or renewed.
C— Indefinite, as long as the holder has a current pilot and medical certificate appropriate to the pilot privileges being exercised.

A flight instructor certificate expires at the end of the 24th month after the month in which it was last issued or renewed. (PLT411) — 14 CFR §61.19

ALL
6397. The type and date of each student pilot endorsement given shall be maintained by each flight instructor. For what period of time is this record required to be retained?

A— 1 year.
B— 2 years.
C— 3 years.

Each certificated flight instructor shall sign the logbook for each person to whom he/she has given flight or ground instruction and specify in that book the amount of time and the date on which it was given. In addition, he/she shall maintain a record in his/her flight instructor logbook or in a separate document. The record shall be retained by the flight instructor separately or in his/her logbook for at least 3 years. (PLT457) — 14 CFR §§61.189, 61.423

ALL
6399. During any 24 consecutive hours, an instructor is limited to how many hours of flight training?

A— 8.
B— 10.
C— 12.

The holder of a flight instructor certificate may not conduct more than 8 hours of flight instruction in any period of 24 consecutive hours. (PLT409) — 14 CFR §§61.195, 61.415

ALL
6400. To endorse a student pilot for solo cross-country privileges, an instructor is required, in part, to have

A— given that student the required cross-country flight training and checked the flight planning.
B— determined that the student's preparation, planning, and procedures are adequate for the proposed flight under the existing conditions.
C— assurance from another instructor that the student is prepared to conduct the flight safely under current conditions.

A flight instructor may not endorse a student pilot certificate and logbook for a solo cross-country flight, unless that flight instructor has determined the student's flight preparation, planning, equipment, and proposed procedures are adequate for the proposed flight under the existing conditions and within any limitations listed in the logbook that the instructor considers necessary for the safety of flight. (PLT457) — 14 CFR §§61.195, 61.415

ALL
6401. To endorse a student pilot's logbook for solo flight, an instructor is required, in part, to have

A— given that student cross-country flight training.
B— given that student flight training in the type of aircraft involved.
C— at least 5 hours of experience as pilot in command in the aircraft involved.

The holder of a flight instructor certificate may not endorse a student pilot's logbook for local solo flight unless he/she has given that student pilot flight instruction and found that student pilot prepared for solo flight in the type of aircraft involved. (PLT457) — 14 CFR §§61.195, 61.415

Answer (A) is incorrect because cross-country instruction is not required prior to solo flight. Answer (C) is incorrect because 5 hours of experience is required only to give instruction in a multi-engine airplane.

Answers

6319 [B]	6322 [B]	6397 [C]	6399 [A]	6400 [B]	6401 [B]

ALL

6405-1. The holder of an expired Flight Instructor Certificate may exchange that certificate for a new one by

A— passing the appropriate practical test.
B— presenting a satisfactory record of training.
C— successfully completing a flight instructor refresher course.

The holder of an expired flight instructor certificate may exchange that certificate for a new certificate by passing the practical test prescribed in 14 CFR §61.187. (PLT418) — 14 CFR §§61.199, 61.405

Answers (B) and (C) are incorrect because a flight test is required after a flight instructor certificate has expired.

ALL

6404. A Flight Instructor Certificate may be renewed by

A— passing both a knowledge and a practical test.
B— providing a record of training showing evidence the applicant has given at least 80 hours of flight training in the last 24 months.
C— successfully completing a flight instructor refresher course within 3 calendar months prior to renewal.

The holder of a flight instructor certificate may renew his/her certificate for an additional period of 24 months if: (1) he/she passes the practical test for a flight instructor certificate and the rating involved, or those portions of that test the Administrator considers necessary to determine his/her competency as a flight instructor, (2) presents a record of training students that shows during the preceding 24 calendar months the instructor has endorsed at least five students for a practical test for a certificate or rating, and at least 80 percent of those students passed the test on the first attempt, or (3) presents a graduation certificate showing the person has successfully completed an approved flight instructor refresher course. (PLT386) — 14 CFR §61.197

Answer (A) is incorrect because a knowledge test is not required. Answer (B) is incorrect because the candidate must present a record showing a 80% success rate for at least five students signed off for a certificate or rating.

ALL, MCI

6404-1. A flight instructor's certificate, with multi-engine and instrument ratings, expires. As a CFI you know that

A— a checkride in a single-engine airplane will renew all ratings.
B— a checkride in a multi-engine airplane reinstates both single and multi-engine privileges, but not instrument.
C— the applicant must take an instrument checkride in a multiengine airplane to restore all ratings.

The holder of an expired flight instructor certificate may reinstate that flight instructor certificate and rating by completing a flight instructor certification practical test for one of the ratings held on the expired flight instructor certificate, or completing a flight instructor certification practical test for an additional rating. (PLT386) — 14 CFR §61.199

ALL

6405-2. The holder of a Ground Instructor Certificate with a basic rating is authorized to provide ground training required for

A— a flight instructor refresher course.
B— all aeronautical knowledge areas for a recreational or private pilot certificate.
C— any flight review or instrument proficiency check.

A person who holds a basic ground instructor rating is authorized to provide ground training in the aeronautical knowledge areas required for the issuance of a sport, recreational or private pilot certificate, ground training required for a sport, recreational and private pilot flight review, and a recommendation for a knowledge test required for the issuance of a sport, recreational or private pilot certificate. (PLT418) — 14 CFR §61.215

Answer (A) is incorrect because a flight instructor certificate is required to provide the ground training for a flight instructor refresher course. Answer (C) is incorrect because an advanced ground instructor certificate is required to provide the ground training for any flight review and an instrument ground instructor certificate is necessary for instrument proficiency checks.

Answers

6405-1 [A]   6404 [C]   6404-1 [A]   6405-2 [B]

ALL

6405-3. The holder of a Ground Instructor Certificate with an advanced rating is authorized to provide

A— ground training in aeronautical knowledge areas for any pilot certificate or rating (except the instrument rating).
B— a recommendation for an instrument rating knowledge test.
C— ground training for any flight review or instrument proficiency check.

A person who holds an advanced ground instructor rating is authorized to provide ground training in the aeronautical knowledge areas required for the issuance of any certificate or rating (except the instrument rating), ground training for any flight review, and a recommendation for a knowledge test required for the issuance of any certificate. (PLT418) — 14 CFR §61.215

Answers (B) and (C) are incorrect because an instrument ground instructor certificate is required to recommend a candidate for an instrument rating knowledge test or provide ground training for an instrument proficiency check.

ALL

6405-4. The holder of a Ground Instructor Certificate with an advanced rating is authorized to provide

A— a recommendation for a knowledge test required for the issuance of any certificate under 14 CFR Part 143.
B— ground training required for any flight review.
C— a recommendation for a knowledge test for the issuance of an instrument rating.

A person who holds an advanced ground instructor rating is authorized to provide ground training in the aeronautical knowledge areas required for the issuance of any certificate or rating (except the instrument rating), ground training for any flight review, and a recommendation for a knowledge test required for the issuance of any certificate. (PLT418) — 14 CFR §61.215

Answer (A) is incorrect because although 14 CFR Part 143 used to contain the regulations for ground instructors, this Part is currently reserved for future use. Answer (C) is incorrect because an instrument ground instructor certificate is required to recommend a candidate for a knowledge test for an instrument rating.

ALL

6405-5. The holder of a Ground Instructor Certificate may not exercise the privileges of that certificate unless that person has

A— successfully completed a refresher course within 3 months prior to expiration.
B— passed a practical test within the preceding 12 months.
C— served as a ground instructor within the preceding 12 months.

The holder of a ground instructor certificate may not perform the duties of a ground instructor unless, within the preceding 12 months, the person has served as a ground instructor, or the person has received an endorsement from an authorized ground or flight instructor certifying that the person has demonstrated satisfactory proficiency in the subject areas required for a ground instructor. (PLT418) — 14 CFR §61.217

AIR, RTC, MCI

6402. Certain flight training is required for the issuance of a certificate. If that instruction is in a helicopter or multi-engine airplane, the instructor is required, in part, to have

A— given at least 200 hours of flight training.
B— given at least 25 hours of flight training in the particular make and model aircraft.
C— at least 5 hours of experience as pilot in command in the make and model of aircraft involved.

The holder of a flight instructor certificate may not give flight training required for the issuance of a certificate or a category, or class rating in a multi-engine airplane or a helicopter unless he/she has had at least 5 hours of experience as pilot-in-command in the make and model of that airplane or helicopter, as the case may be. (PLT407) — 14 CFR §61.195

AIR, RTC, MCI

6403. The minimum pilot-in-command time requirement for a flight instructor with multiengine privileges to give training to a student for a multiengine rating is

A— 5 hours in the make and model of aircraft in which training is to be given.
B— 10 hours in the make of aircraft in which the training is to be given.
C— 15 hours in the make and model of aircraft in which training is to be given.

Answers

6405-3 [A]   6405-4 [B]   6405-5 [C]   6402 [C]   6403 [A]

The holder of a flight instructor certificate may not give flight training required for the issuance of a certificate or a category or class rating in a multi-engine airplane or a helicopter unless he/she has had at least 5 hours of experience as pilot-in-command in the make and model of that airplane or helicopter, as the case may be. (PLT411) — 14 CFR §61.195

AIR, MCI

6395. What requirement(s) must an authorized instructor meet in order to prepare an airplane applicant for an initial Flight Instructor Certificate?

A— Logged a minimum of 80 hours of flight training time.

B— Held a Flight Instructor Certificate for at least 12 months immediately preceding the date the training is given.

C— Held a Flight Instructor Certificate for at least 24 months and given a minimum of 200 hours of flight training.

An applicant for a flight instructor certificate under Subpart H must have received flight instruction from a flight instructor who has held a flight instructor certificate during the 24 months immediately preceding the date the training is given, who meets the general requirements for a flight instructor certificate, and who has given at least 200 hours of flight training. (PLT411) — 14 CFR §61.195

Answer (A) is incorrect because the flight instructor must have 200 hours of flight instruction experience. Answer (B) is incorrect because the flight instructor must have held his/her certificate for at least 24 months.

AIR, RTC, LTA, GLI, MCI

6398. A flight instructor who applies for an additional rating on that certificate must have a minimum of how many hours as pilot in command in the category and class of aircraft appropriate to the rating sought?

A— 15.

B— No minimum number of hours.

C— 5.

The holder of a flight instructor certificate under Subpart H who applies for an additional rating on that certificate must have had at least 15 hours as pilot-in-command in the category and class of aircraft appropriate to the rating sought. (PLT411) — 14 CFR §61.183

AIR, RTC, LTA, GLI, MCI

6394-2. What restriction is imposed regarding flight instruction of other pilots in air transportation service by an airline transport pilot?

A— 30 hours in any 7-day period.

B— 7 hours in any 1-day period.

C— 36 hours in any 7-day period.

An airline transport pilot may instruct other pilots in air transportation service in aircraft of the category, class and type for which he/she is rated. However, the ATP may not instruct for more than 8 hours in one day nor more than 36 hours in any 7-day period. (PLT409) — 14 CFR §61.167

Flight Instruction, Reviews and Records

All time logged as flight training, instrument flight training, pilot ground trainer training, or ground training time must be certified by an appropriately rated and certificated instructor from whom it was received.

No person may act as pilot-in-command of an aircraft unless, within the preceding 24 calendar months, that person has accomplished a **flight review**, in an aircraft for which he/she is rated, by an appropriately certificated instructor or other person designated by the Administrator, and has had his/her logbook endorsed by that person who gave him/her the review certifying that he/she has satisfactorily accomplished the flight review.

The flight review consists of a minimum of 1 hour of ground instruction and, for other than glider pilots, 1 hour of flight training.

The aeronautical training and experience used to meet the requirements for a certificate or rating, or the recent flight experience requirements, must be shown by a reliable record. The logging of other flight time is not required.

Answers

| 6395 | [C] | 6398 | [A] | 6394-2 | [C] |

ALL

6344. Which training time must be certified by the instructor from whom it was received?

A— Flight training.
B— Flight training and training in a flight training device.
C— All flight training, flight simulator training, and ground training.

All time logged as flight training, instrument flight training, pilot ground trainer instruction, or ground training time must be certified by an appropriately rated and certificated instructor from whom it was received. (PLT407) — 14 CFR §61.51

Answers (A) and (B) are incorrect because both flight and ground training must be certified by the instructor.

ALL

6347. A flight review is not required if a pilot has completed, within the time specified,

A— an industry-sponsored refresher clinic.
B— a pilot proficiency check conducted by the FAA.
C— an instrument proficiency check conducted by an instructor with the Armed Forces.

A person who has within the period specified, satisfactorily completed a pilot proficiency check (excluding proficiency checks for adding category/class under Subpart K) conducted by the FAA, need not accomplish the flight review. (PLT407) — 14 CFR §61.56

Answer (A) is incorrect because a refresher clinic cannot substitute for a flight review. Answer (C) is incorrect because an instrument proficiency check can only count as a flight review if arranged prior to the review, and include all the requirements for a flight review as well as the IPC.

ALL

6348. A flight review will consist of

A— a minimum of 1 hour ground training and 1 hour flight training.
B— at least 1 hour of flight time to include at least three takeoffs and landings.
C— three takeoffs and landings and a review of those maneuvers necessary for the pilot to demonstrate the appropriate pilot privileges.

The flight review required consists of a minimum of 1 hour of flight training and 1 hour of ground training. (PLT407) — 14 CFR §61.56

Answers (B) and (C) are incorrect because the review must consist of a minimum of 1 hour flight training and 1 hour of ground training, but the number of takeoffs and landings are at the discretion of the issuing flight instructor.

ALL

6349. A flight instructor who has not satisfactorily accomplished a flight review or passed a required proficiency check within the prescribed time is

A— not authorized to fly solo.
B— authorized to fly solo only.
C— not authorized to give instruction except to holders of Recreational Pilot Certificates.

No person may act as pilot-in-command of an aircraft unless, within the preceding 24 calendar months, that person has accomplished a flight review given to him/her, in an aircraft for which he/she is rated, by an appropriately certificated instructor or other person designated by the Administrator, and has had his/her logbook endorsed by that person who gave him/her the review certifying that he/she has satisfactorily accomplished the flight review. (PLT407) — 14 CFR §61.56

Answer (B) is incorrect because a flight instructor may not act as PIC until meeting the flight review requirements. Answer (C) is incorrect because a flight instructor may give instruction to a pilot appropriately rated in the aircraft being used as long as he/she is not acting as PIC.

ALL

6345. What flight time must be recorded by a pilot exercising the privileges of a commercial certificate?

A— All flight time.
B— Only the flight time necessary to meet the recent flight experience requirements.
C— All flight time flown for hire with passengers and/ or cargo aboard the aircraft.

The aeronautical training and experience used to meet the requirements for a certificate or rating, or the recent flight experience requirements, must be shown by a reliable record. The logging of other flight time is not required. (PLT409) — 14 CFR §61.51

Answers

| 6344 | [C] | 6347 | [B] | 6348 | [A] | 6349 | [A] | 6345 | [B] |

AIR, MCI

6351. What recent flight experience must be met before a commercial airplane pilot may fly solo in an airplane?

A— Three takeoffs and three landings within the preceding 90 days in an airplane.

B— Satisfactorily accomplished a flight review in any aircraft for which rated within the preceding 24 calendar months.

C— Satisfactorily accomplished a flight review within the preceding 24 calendar months, but this review must be in an airplane.

No person may act as pilot-in-command of an aircraft unless, within the preceding 24 calendar months, that person has accomplished a flight review given to him/her, in an aircraft for which he/she is rated, by an appropriately certificated instructor or other person designated by the Administrator, and has had his/her logbook endorsed by that person who gave him/her the review certifying that he/she has satisfactorily accomplished the flight review. (PLT443) — 14 CFR §61.56

Answer (A) is incorrect because three takeoffs and landings every 90 days are required to carry passengers. Answer (C) is incorrect because the flight review may be completed in any aircraft for which the pilot is rated.

Required Endorsements

A student pilot may not operate an aircraft on a solo flight in Class B airspace unless:

1. The student pilot has received both ground and flight instruction from an authorized instructor in Class B airspace and the flight instruction was received in the specific Class B airspace for which solo flight is authorized.

2. The logbook of that student pilot has been endorsed within the preceding 90 days for conducting solo flight in that specific Class B airspace by the instructor who gave the flight training; and

3. The logbook endorsement specifies that the student pilot has received the required ground and flight instruction and has been found competent to conduct solo flight in that specific Class B airspace.

A person holding a private or commercial pilot certificate may not act as pilot-in-command of an airplane that has more than 200 horsepower, or that has a retractable landing gear, flaps, and a controllable propeller, unless he/she has received ground and flight instruction from an authorized flight instructor who has certified in his/her logbook that he/she is competent to pilot an airplane that has more than 200 horsepower, or that has retractable landing gear, flaps, and a controllable propeller, as the case may be. However, this instruction is not required if he/she has logged flight time as pilot-in-command of a high-performance airplane before August 4, 1997.

No person may act as pilot-in-command of a pressurized airplane which operates above 25,000 feet MSL unless he/she has completed the training required by 14 CFR §61.31 and has his/her logbook so endorsed.

No person may act as pilot-in-command of a tail wheel airplane unless that pilot has received flight instruction from an authorized flight instructor in normal and crosswind takeoffs and landings, wheel landings, (unless the airplane manufacturer has recommended against such landings), and go-around procedures in a tail wheel airplane. The instructor then makes an endorsement in the pilot's logbook certifying the pilot is competent in the above mentioned maneuvers. This endorsement is not required if the pilot has logged flight time as pilot-in-command of a tail wheel airplane prior to April 15, 1991.

A person who acts as a pilot-in-command of any of the following aircraft must hold a type rating for that aircraft: large aircraft, defined as any aircraft of more than 12,500 pounds maximum certificated takeoff weight (except lighter-than-air), turbojet-powered airplanes, other aircraft specified by the Administrator through aircraft type certificate procedures.

Answers

6351　[B]

ALL

6374. To operate an aircraft on a solo flight within Class B airspace, a student must have a logbook endorsement showing that he/she has

A— received flight instruction from any authorized flight instructor on operating within Class B airspace.

B— received ground instruction on and flight instruction in that specific airspace for which solo flight is authorized.

C— within the preceding 90 days, been found to be competent by any flight instructor having knowledge of the student's experience in that specific airspace.

A student pilot may not operate an aircraft on a solo flight in Class B airspace unless he/she has received both ground and flight instruction from an authorized instructor in that Class B airspace and the flight instruction was received in the specific Class B airspace for which solo flight is authorized. (PLT457) — 14 CFR §61.95

ALL

6437. What minimum pilot certificate will permit a pilot to enter Class B airspace?

A— Private Pilot Certificate.

B— Commercial Pilot Certificate.

C— Student Pilot Certificate with an appropriate endorsement.

A solo student pilot may be authorized to operate an aircraft according to VFR in Class B airspace if he/she meets the requirements of 14 CFR §61.95, and has the appropriate endorsement. (PLT161) — 14 CFR §61.95

Answer (A) is incorrect because a private pilot certificate is only necessary when taking off or landing at the busiest primary airports of Class B airspace. Answer (B) is incorrect because a student pilot certificate with the appropriate endorsement is required to enter all Class B airspace.

ALL

6326-2. Which of the following normally requires the pilot in command to hold a type rating?

A— Any turbojet-powered aircraft.

B— Any airplane which has a gross weight of 6,000 pounds or more.

C— Any multiengine airplane which is operated under interstate commerce.

A person who acts as a pilot-in-command of any of the following aircraft must hold a type rating for that aircraft: large aircraft, defined as any aircraft of more than 12,500 pounds maximum certificated takeoff weight (except lighter-than-air), turbojet-powered airplanes, other aircraft specified by the Administrator through aircraft type certificate procedures. (PLT443) — 14 CFR §61.31

AIR, MCI

6326-1. To act as pilot in command of an airplane that has more than 200 horsepower, a person holding a Private or Commercial Pilot Certificate is required to

A— successfully complete a practical test in such an airplane.

B— receive ground and flight training in an airplane that has more than 200 horsepower.

C— make three takeoffs and landings with an authorized instructor in an airplane of the same make and model.

A person holding a private or commercial pilot certificate may not act as pilot-in-command of an airplane that has more than 200 horsepower, or that has a retractable landing gear, flaps, and a controllable propeller, unless he/she has received ground and flight instruction from an authorized flight instructor who has certified in his/her logbook that he/she is competent to pilot such an airplane. (PLT407) — 14 CFR §61.31

AIR, MCI

6327. To act as pilot in command of an airplane with retractable landing gear, flaps, and controllable propeller, a person holding a Private or Commercial Pilot Certificate is required to

A— complete a practical test in such an airplane.

B— have made at least three takeoffs and landings in such an airplane in the last 90 days.

C— receive ground and flight training in such an airplane, and obtain a logbook endorsement of proficiency.

A person holding a private or commercial pilot certificate may not act as pilot-in-command of an airplane that has more than 200 horsepower, or that has a retractable landing gear, flaps, and a controllable propeller, unless he/she has received flight instruction from an authorized flight instructor who has certified in his/her logbook that he/she is competent to pilot such an airplane. (PLT407) — 14 CFR §61.31

Answers

6374 [B]	6437 [C]	6326-2 [A]	6326-1 [B]	6327 [C]

AIR, MCI

6328. No person may act as pilot in command of a pressurized airplane with a service ceiling or maximum operating altitude, whichever is lower, above 25,000 feet unless that person has

A— completed a physiological training program conducted by the FAA or a military service.
B— received ground and flight training in high altitude operations and a logbook endorsement certifying this training.
C— completed a pilot proficiency check for a pilot or instructor pilot certificate or rating conducted by the FAA after April 15, 1991.

No person may act as pilot-in-command of a pressurized airplane with a service ceiling or maximum operating altitude, whichever is lower, above 25,000 feet unless that person has received ground and flight training record endorsement from an authorized instructor certifying satisfactory completion of the training. (PLT407) — 14 CFR §61.31

AIR, LSA, MCI

6329-1. Which is applicable to a private pilot with ASEL ratings who has never flown a tailwheel airplane? The pilot

A— may fly solo with no instruction required.
B— must have received instruction and have a logbook endorsement before acting as pilot in command.
C— must have received at least 1 hour of instruction and have a logbook endorsement before carrying passengers.

No person may act as pilot-in-command of a tail wheel airplane unless that pilot has received flight instruction from an authorized flight instructor who has found the pilot competent to operate a tail wheel airplane and made an endorsement in the pilot's logbook. (PLT407) — 14 CFR §61.31

Answer (A) is incorrect because the pilot must have received instruction before flying as PIC (solo). Answer (C) is incorrect because the pilot must have received instruction before flying as PIC, regardless of whether passengers are carried, but there is no minimum amount of instruction required.

Pilot Tests

An applicant for an FAA Knowledge Exam must have proper identification at the time of application that contains the applicant's photograph, signature, date of birth, and residential address. To be eligible for a flight test for a certificate or an aircraft or instrument rating issued under this part, the applicant must have passed any required knowledge test since the beginning of the 24th month before the month in which he/she takes the flight test. For the recreational certificate and up, the applicant must hold a current medical certificate appropriate to the certificate he/she seeks, or in the case of a rating to be added to his/her pilot certificate, at least a current third-class medical certificate. Sport pilots can use their driver's license. The applicant must have a written statement from an authorized instructor certifying that he/she has given the applicant flight instruction in preparation for the flight test within 60 days preceding the date of application, and finds him/her competent to pass the test and to have satisfactory knowledge of the subject areas in which he/she has shown to be deficient by his/her FAA knowledge test report.

An applicant for a knowledge or flight test who fails that test may apply for retesting upon presenting a written statement from an authorized instructor certifying that he/she has given flight or ground instruction as appropriate to the applicant and finds him/her competent to pass the test.

No person whom the Administrator finds to have committed an act prohibited by paragraph (a) of 14 CFR §61.37 is eligible for any airman or ground instructor certificate or rating or to take any test for a period of 1 year after the date of that act. In addition, the commission of that act is a basis for suspending or revoking any airman or ground instructor certificate or rating held by that person. Paragraph (a) includes:

1. Copying or intentionally removing a knowledge test
2. Giving to another, or receiving from another, any part or copy of that test

Continued

Answers

6328　[B]　　　6329-1　[B]

3. Giving help on that test to, or receiving help on that test from any person during the period that test is being given

4. Taking any part of that test in behalf of another person

5. Using any unauthorized material or aid during the test.

ALL
6330. What minimum documentation is required to take an FAA knowledge test for any flight instructor rating?

A— Proper identification.
B— Proof of satisfactory completion of the appropriate ground training or home study course.
C— Authorization from an FAA inspector who has verified and endorsed the applicant's training record.

An applicant for a knowledge test must have proper identification at the time of application that contains the applicant's photograph, signature, date of birth, and residential address. (PLT482) — 14 CFR §61.35

ALL
6334. A written statement from an authorized instructor certifying that an applicant has received the required training in preparation for a practical test must be dated within how many days preceding the date of application?

A— 60.
B— 90.
C— 120.

To be eligible for a flight test for a certificate or an aircraft or instrument rating, the applicant must have a written statement from an authorized instructor certifying that he/she has given the applicant flight training in preparation for the flight test within 60 days preceding the date of application, and finds him/her competent to pass the test and to have satisfactory knowledge of the subject areas in which he/she has shown to be deficient by his/her FAA knowledge test report. (PLT457) — 14 CFR §61.39

ALL
6335. To be eligible for a practical test under 14 CFR Part 61, an applicant must have passed the appropriate knowledge test (when required) within the preceding

A— 6 calendar months.
B— 12 calendar months.
C— 24 calendar months

To be eligible for a flight test for a certificate or an aircraft or instrument rating issued under this part, the applicant must have passed any required knowledge test since the beginning of the 24th month before the month in which he/she takes the flight test. (PLT482) — 14 CFR §61.39

ALL
6337. If all increments for a practical test for a certificate or rating are not completed on one date, all remaining increments must be satisfactorily completed no later than

A— 90 days from the date of the test.
B— 120 days from the date of the test.
C— 60 days from the date of the test.

If a practical test is discontinued, the applicant is entitled credit for those areas of operation that were passed, but only if the applicant passes the remainder of the practical test within the 60-day period after the date the practical test was discontinued. (PLT482) — 14 CFR §61.43

ALL
6338. What is one requirement for an aircraft furnished for a practical test?

A— All flight instruments must be fully functioning.
B— Must have no prescribed operating limitations that prohibit its use in any required area of operation.
C— Dual flight controls and engine power controls must be operable and easily reached by both pilots in a normal manner.

Aircraft furnished for a flight test must have no prescribed operating limitations that prohibit its use in any pilot operation required on the test. (PLT482) — 14 CFR §61.45

Answer (A) is incorrect because only the instruments required for the flight test must be fully functional. Answer (C) is incorrect because dual controls are not necessary if the examiner determines the flight test can be conducted safely without them.

Answers

6330 [A]	6334 [A]	6335 [C]	6337 [C]	6338 [B]

ALL, GLI

6340. Your student took a practical test for a pilot certificate on January 10 and failed to meet standards. After being retested on January 13 and failing to meet standards again, when is your student eligible to retest?

A— January 13.
B— February 12.
C— February 13.

An applicant for a knowledge or practical test who fails that test may reapply for the test only after the applicant has received the necessary training and endorsement from an authorized instructor who has determined that the applicant is proficient to pass the test. (PLT457) — 14 CFR §61.49

ALL

6341. An applicant who fails a pilot knowledge test for the first time may apply for retesting after

A— waiting for a period of 20 days.
B— receiving 5 hours of ground instruction from an authorized ground instructor.
C— presenting an endorsement from an authorized instructor certifying that additional training has been given and the applicant is competent to pass the test.

The applicant may apply for retesting upon presenting an endorsement from an authorized instructor certifying that he/she has given flight or ground instruction, as appropriate, to the applicant and finds him/her competent to pass the test. (PLT482) — 14 CFR §61.49

ALL

6339. An applicant has failed a knowledge test for the second time. With training and an endorsement from an authorized instructor, when may the applicant apply for a retest?

A— Immediately.
B— After 30 days.
C— After 5 days.

An applicant for a knowledge or practical test who fails that test may reapply for the test only after the applicant has received the necessary training and endorsement from an authorized instructor who has determined that the applicant is proficient to pass the test. (PLT418) — 14 CFR §61.49

ALL

6343. An applicant who fails a practical test for the second time may apply for retesting after

A— 30 days have passed.
B— receiving the necessary instruction and an endorsement from an authorized instructor who gave the training.
C— presenting a letter of competency to the examiner signed by an authorized flight instructor.

An applicant for a knowledge or practical test who fails that test may reapply for the test only after the applicant has received the necessary training and endorsement from an authorized instructor who has determined that the applicant is proficient to pass the test. (PLT482) — 14 CFR §61.49

ALL

6343-1. A student fails his practical exam on his first attempt. Then he fails the test on January 13. When is the earliest he can take the test again?

A— Immediately.
B— February 13.
C— February 12.

An applicant for a knowledge or practical test who fails that test may reapply for the test only after the applicant has received: (1) The necessary training from an authorized instructor who has determined that the applicant is proficient to pass the test; and (2) An endorsement from an authorized instructor who gave the applicant the additional training. There is no wait period for retaking a practical exam. (PLT482) — 14 CFR §61.49

ALL

6331. A person who the Administrator finds has cheated or committed any unauthorized act while taking a knowledge test may not take another knowledge test within

A— 90 days.
B— 1 year.
C— 2 years.

No person whom the Administrator finds to have committed an act prohibited by paragraph (a) of 14 CFR §61.37 is eligible for any airman or ground instructor certificate or rating or to take any test therefore, under this chapter for a period of 1 year after the date of that act. In addition, the commission of that act is a basis for suspending or revoking any airman or ground instructor certificate or rating held by that person. (PLT482) — 14 CFR §61.37

Answers

6340 [A]   6341 [C]   6339 [A]   6343 [B]   6343-1 [A]   6331 [B]

ALL
6332. What action may be taken against a person whom the Administrator finds has cheated on a knowledge test?

A— That person will be required to wait 24 months before taking another knowledge test.
B— Any certificate or rating held by the person may be suspended or revoked.
C— That person may be required to wait a maximum of 6 months before applying for any other certificate or rating.

No person whom the Administrator finds to have committed an act prohibited by paragraph (a) of 14 CFR §61.37 is eligible for any airman or ground instructor certificate or rating or to take any test therefore, for a period of 1 year after the date of that act. In addition, the commission of that act is a basis for suspending or revoking any airman or ground instructor certificate or rating held by that person. (PLT448) — 14 CFR §61.37

AIR, RTC, MCI
6333. What class medical certificate, if any, is required for a person adding a rating to a pilot certificate?

A— None.
B— Second-Class.
C— Third-Class.

To be eligible for a flight test to add a rating to a pilot certificate, the applicant must hold at least a third-class medical certificate issued since the beginning of the 24th month in which he/she takes the flight test. (PLT427) — 14 CFR §61.39

AIR, GLI, LSA, MCI
6342. A flight instructor applicant must demonstrate spins in an airplane or glider when

A— the practical test for initial certification is being given.
B— being retested for deficiencies in instructional proficiency on stall awareness or spins demonstrated during an initial test.
C— the airplane or glider to be used for the practical test is certificated for spins and the applicant is being given an initial practical test.

An applicant for flight instructor certificate with an airplane category rating, or for a flight instructor certificate with a glider category rating, who has failed the practical test due to deficiencies in instructional proficiency on stall awareness, spin entry, spins, or spin recovery techniques must, during the retest, satisfactorily demonstrate both knowledge and skill in these areas in an aircraft of the appropriate category that is certificated for spins. (PLT419) — 14 CFR §61.49

Presolo Requirements

Before being authorized to fly solo, a student pilot must satisfactorily complete a knowledge examination covering the appropriate portions of 14 CFR Parts 61 and 91 that are applicable to student pilots, and the flight characteristics and operational limitations for the make and model aircraft to be flown. This examination must be administered and graded by the instructor who endorses the student's pilot certificate for solo flight.

ALL
6366. Who is responsible for administering the required knowledge test to a student pilot prior to solo flight?

A— The student's authorized instructor.
B— Any certificated ground instructor.
C— Any certificated flight instructor.

A student pilot must demonstrate satisfactory aeronautical knowledge on a knowledge test of the appropriate sections of Parts 61 and 91, airspace rules and procedures for the airport at which the solo flight will be performed, and flight characteristics and operational limitations for the make and model of aircraft to be flown. The student's authorized instructor must administer the test, and at the conclusion of the test review all incorrect answers with the student before authorizing that student to conduct a solo flight. (PLT419) — 14 CFR §61.87

Answers

6332 [B]   6333 [C]   6342 [B]   6366 [A]

ALL
6367. What subjects must be covered on the presolo knowledge test?

A— Principles of flight, weather, and aircraft systems.
B— Applicable regulations, flight characteristics, and operational limitations of make and model aircraft to be flown.
C— Density altitude, operations from a controlled airport, and radio communications with appropriate air traffic control facilities.

Before being authorized to fly solo, a student pilot must satisfactorily complete a knowledge examination covering the appropriate portions of 14 CFR Parts 61 and 91 that are applicable to student pilots, and the flight characteristics and operational limitations for the make and model aircraft to be flown. (PLT482) — 14 CFR §61.87

Recency of Experience

No person may act as pilot-in-command of any aircraft carrying passengers during the period beginning 1 hour after sunset and ending 1 hour before sunrise (as published in the American Air Almanac) unless, within the preceding 90 days, he/she has made at least 3 takeoffs and 3 landings to a full stop during that period in the category, class, and type (if a type rating is required) of aircraft to be used.

No person may act as pilot-in-command of any aircraft carrying passengers, or of an aircraft certificated for more than one required pilot flight crewmember, unless, within the preceding 90 days, he/she has made at least 3 takeoffs and 3 landings as the sole manipulator of the flight controls in an aircraft of the same category and class, and if a type rating is required, of the same type. If the aircraft is a tail wheel airplane, the landings must have been made to a full stop in a tail wheel airplane.

A person may log instrument time only for that flight time when the person operates the aircraft solely by reference to instruments under actual or simulated instrument flight conditions.

ALL
6352. To meet the recent flight experience requirements for acting as pilot in command carrying passengers at night, a pilot must have made, within the preceding 90 days and from 1 hour after sunset to 1 hour before sunrise, three takeoffs and three landings to a full stop in

A— the same category of aircraft to be used.
B— the same category and class of aircraft to be used.
C— the same category, class, and (if a type rating is required) type of aircraft to be used.

No person may act as pilot-in-command of any aircraft carrying passengers during the period beginning 1 hour after sunset and ending 1 hour before sunrise (as published in the American Air Almanac) unless, within the preceding 90 days, he/she has made at least 3 takeoffs and 3 landings to a full stop during that period, in the category, class, and type (if a type rating is required) of aircraft to be used. (PLT407) — 14 CFR §61.57

ALL
6354. If recency of experience requirements for night flight are not met and official sunset is 1830, the latest time passengers may be carried is

A— 1829.
B— 1859.
C— 1929.

No person may act as pilot-in-command of any aircraft carrying passengers during the period beginning 1 hour after sunset and ending 1 hour before sunrise (as published in the American Air Almanac) unless, within the preceding 90 days, he/she has made at least 3 takeoffs and 3 landings to a full stop during that period in the category and class of aircraft to be used. If the official sunset is 1830, a pilot who has not met the recency of experience requirements for night flight must not carry passengers after 1929. (PLT442) — 14 CFR §61.57

Answers

6367 [B]   6352 [C]   6354 [C]

AIR, MCI

6353. A private pilot has completed three takeoffs and three landings to a full stop within the preceding 90 days in a tricycle-gear airplane, single-engine land, and decides to take a passenger for a flight in a tailwheel airplane, single-engine land. Since these aircraft are of the same category and class, the pilot is current in

A— both airplanes.
B— the tricycle-gear airplane.
C— the tailwheel airplane.

No person may act as pilot-in-command of any aircraft carrying passengers nor in any aircraft certificated for more than one required pilot flight crewmember, unless, within the preceding 90 days, he/she has made at least 3 takeoffs and 3 landings as the sole manipulator of the flight controls in an aircraft of the same category and class and, if a type rating is required, of the same type. If the aircraft is a tail wheel airplane, the landings must have been made to a full stop in a tail wheel airplane. (PLT407) — 14 CFR §61.57

AIR, RTC, MCI

6346-2. What instrument flight time may be logged by a second in command of an aircraft requiring two pilots?

A— One-half the time the aircraft is in actual instrument conditions.
B— All of the time the second in command is controlling the aircraft solely by reference to flight instruments.
C— One-half the time the flight is on an IFR flight plan.

A person may log instrument time only for that flight time when the person operates the aircraft solely by reference to instruments under actual or simulated instrument flight conditions. (PLT409) — 14 CFR §61.51

Change of Permanent Mailing Address

The holder of a pilot or flight instructor certificate who has made a change in his/her permanent mailing address may not, after 30 days from the date he/she moved, exercise the privileges of his/her certificate unless he/she has notified in writing the Department of Transportation, Federal Aviation Administration, Airman Certification Branch, Box 25082, Oklahoma City, OK 73125 of his/her new address.

ALL

6355. The holder of a pilot or instructor certificate who fails to notify the FAA Airmen Certification Branch in writing of a change in permanent mailing address may exercise the privileges of that certificate for how many days after date of change?

A— 30.
B— 60.
C— 90.

The holder of a pilot or flight instructor certificate who has made a change in his/her permanent mailing address may not, after 30 days from the date he/she moved, exercise the privileges of his/her certificate unless he/she has notified in writing the Department of Transportation, Federal Aviation Administration, Airman Certification Branch, Box 25082, Oklahoma City, OK 73125, of his/her new address. (PLT387) — 14 CFR §61.60

ALL

6356. When a permanent change of address occurs, pilot or instructor privileges may not be exercised unless the FAA Airmen Certification Branch is notified, in writing, within

A— 30 days.
B— 60 days.
C— 90 days.

The holder of a pilot or flight instructor certificate who has made a change in his/her permanent mailing address may not, after 30 days from the date he/she moved, exercise the privileges of his/her certificate unless he/she has notified in writing the Department of Transportation, Federal Aviation Administration, Airman Certification Branch, Box 25082, Oklahoma City, OK 73125, of his/her new address. (PLT387) — 14 CFR §61.60

Answers

6353   [B]   6346-2   [B]   6355   [A]   6356   [A]

Glider Towing

No pilot may act as pilot-in-command of an aircraft towing a glider unless that person:

1. Holds at least a private pilot certificate with a category rating for powered aircraft.

2. Has logged at least 100 hours PIC in the aircraft category/class/type being used in the tow.

3. Has a logbook endorsement certifying ground and flight training in gliders.

4. Has logged 3 flights as the sole manipulator of the controls under a qualified tow pilot's supervision.

AIR, GLI

6358. A private pilot with an airplane single-engine land rating may act as pilot in command of an airplane towing a glider if, within the preceding 24 months, this pilot has made

A— ten actual or simulated glider tows.
B— three flights as pilot in command of a glider towed by an aircraft.
C— at least six flights as pilot in command of an airplane towing a glider within the preceding 6 months.

No pilot may act as pilot-in-command of an aircraft towing a glider unless he/she meets the following requirements: Within the preceding 24 months he/she has made at least 3 flights as pilot-in-command of a glider towed by an aircraft. (PLT407) — 14 CFR §61.69

Answers (A) and (C) are incorrect because the pilot must have made three actual or simulated glider tows in the last 12 months.

GLI

6329-2. To act as pilot in command of a glider using aerotow procedures, a person must have

A— received 5 hours of ground and flight training on aerotow procedures and operations in a glider, and completed a practical test.
B— received ground and flight training on aerotow procedures and operations in a glider, and received an endorsement from an authorized instructor certifying proficiency.
C— made three solo takeoffs in a glider of the same make and model using aerotow procedures, and received an endorsement from an authorized instructor certifying proficiency in the procedures.

No person may act as pilot-in-command of a glider using aerotow procedures, unless that person has satisfactorily accomplished ground and flight training on aerotow procedures and operations, and has received an endorsement from an authorized instructor who certifies in that pilot's logbook that the pilot has been found proficient in aerotow procedures and operations. (PLT407) — 14 CFR §61.31

Emergency Deviation from Rules

In an emergency requiring immediate action, the pilot-in-command of an aircraft may deviate from the Federal Aviation Regulations to the extent required to meet that emergency.

Each pilot-in-command who is given priority by ATC in an emergency, shall, if requested by ATC, submit a detailed report of that emergency within 48 hours to the chief of that ATC facility.

ALL

6406. If an in-flight emergency requires immediate action, a pilot in command may

A— deviate from FARs to the extent required to meet that emergency.
B— not deviate from FARs unless permission is obtained from air traffic control.
C— deviate from FARs to the extent required to meet the emergency, but must submit a written report to the Administrator within 24 hours.

In an emergency requiring immediate action, the pilot-in-command of an aircraft may deviate from the Federal Aviation Regulations to the extent required to meet that emergency. (PLT444) — 14 CFR §91.3

Answer (B) is incorrect because the pilot may deviate from the regulations without approval in an emergency. Answer (C) is incorrect because a written report is only required upon request.

Answers

6358 [B]	6329-2 [B]	6406 [A]

ALL

6430. What action is appropriate if you deviate from an air traffic control instruction during an emergency and are given priority?

A— Submit a report to the nearest FAA regional office within 48 hours.

B— Submit a report to the manager of the air traffic control facility within 24 hours.

C— If requested, submit a detailed report within 48 hours to the manager of the air traffic control facility.

Each pilot-in-command who is given priority by ATC in an emergency, shall, if requested by ATC, submit a detailed report of that emergency within 48 hours to the chief of that ATC facility. (PLT403) — 14 CFR §91.123

Preflight Planning

Each pilot-in-command shall, before beginning a flight, become familiar with all available information concerning that flight. This includes, for a flight under IFR or a flight not in the vicinity of an airport, weather reports and forecasts, fuel requirements, alternatives available if the planned flight cannot be completed, and any known traffic delays of which he/she has been advised by ATC. For any flight, pilots should become familiar with runway lengths at airports of intended use, and the appropriate takeoff and landing distance information. Flotation gear must be readily accessible to each occupant in the aircraft if a flight is being conducted for hire over water and beyond power-off gliding distance from shore.

ALL

6412. Which preflight action is required for every flight?

A— Check weather reports and forecasts.

B— Determine runway length at airports of intended use.

C— Determine alternatives if the flight cannot be completed.

Each pilot-in-command shall, before beginning a flight, become familiar with all available information concerning that flight. This information must include runway lengths at airports of intended use. (PLT445) — 14 CFR §91.103

Answers (A) and (C) are incorrect because these are not necessary for local VFR flights, although they are a good idea.

ALL

6413. The preflight action required by regulations relative to alternatives available, if the planned flight cannot be completed, is applicable to

A— IFR flights only.

B— any flight not in the vicinity of an airport.

C— any flight conducted for hire or compensation.

Each pilot-in-command shall, before beginning a flight, become familiar with all available information concerning that flight. This includes, for a flight under IFR, or for a flight not in the vicinity of an airport, weather reports and forecasts, fuel requirements, alternatives available if the planned flight cannot be completed, and any known traffic delays of which he/she has been advised by ATC. (PLT445) — 14 CFR §91.103

ALL

6464. When an aircraft is being flown over water, under what circumstances must approved flotation gear be readily available to each occupant?

A— At night and beyond gliding distance from shore.

B— Anytime the aircraft is beyond power-off gliding distance from shore.

C— When operating for hire beyond power-off gliding distance from shore.

Approved flotation gear readily available to each occupant is required on each aircraft if it is being flown for hire over water beyond power-off gliding distance from shore. "Shore" is defined as the area of the land adjacent to the water that is above the high water mark, excluding land areas which are intermittently under water. (PLT437) — 14 CFR §91.205

Answers

6430 [C]	6412 [B]	6413 [B]	6464 [C]

Use of Seatbelts

During takeoff and landing, and while en route, each required flight crewmember shall be at his/her station unless his/her absence is necessary in the performance of duties in connection with the operation of the aircraft or in connection with physiological needs, and keep the seatbelt fastened while at his/her station.

No person may take off or land a U.S.-registered civil aircraft (except balloons that incorporate baskets or gondolas and airships) unless the pilot-in-command of that aircraft ensures that each person on board has been notified to fasten his/her safety belt and shoulder harness, if installed.

ALL
6414. Which statement is true regarding the use of seatbelts and shoulder harnesses?

A— Crewmembers must keep seatbelts and shoulder harnesses fastened at all times during movement on the surface.
B— The pilot-in-command must ensure that each person on board an aircraft is briefed on how to fasten and unfasten seatbelts.
C— Passengers must keep seatbelts fastened at all times during movement on the surface but use of shoulder harnesses is optional.

No person may takeoff or land a U.S.-registered civil aircraft (except balloons that incorporate baskets or gondolas and airships) unless the pilot-in-command of that aircraft ensures that each person on board is briefed on how to fasten and unfasten that person's safety belt. (PLT384) — 14 CFR §91.107

Answers (A) and (C) are incorrect because crewmembers are only required to keep seatbelts and shoulder harnesses fastened during takeoff, landing, and en route; passengers must keep seatbelts and shoulder harnesses fastened during taxi.

Alcohol and Drugs

Except in an emergency, no pilot of a civil aircraft may allow a person who appears to be intoxicated or who demonstrates by manner or physical indications that the individual is under the influence of drugs (except a medical patient under proper care) to be carried in that aircraft.

No person may act or attempt to act as a crewmember of a civil aircraft within 8 hours after the consumption of any alcoholic beverage or while having .04% by weight or more alcohol in the blood.

A conviction for the violation of any Federal or state statute relating to the growing, processing, manufacture, sale, disposition, possession, transportation, or importation of narcotic drugs, marijuana, or depressant or stimulant drugs or substances is grounds for: (1) denial of an application for any certificate or rating issued under 14 CFR Part 61 for a period of up to 1 year after the date of final conviction; or (2) suspension or revocation of any certificate or rating issued under 14 CFR Part 61.

ALL
6320. Conviction of an offense involving alcohol or drugs is grounds for

A— permanent revocation of all certificates and ratings.
B— suspension or revocation of any certificate or rating issued under FAR Part 61.
C— denial of an application for any certificate or rating issued under FAR Part 61 for a period of up to 24 months after date of conviction.

A conviction for the violation of any Federal or state statute relating to the growing, processing, manufacture, sale, disposition, possession, transportation, or importation of narcotic drugs, marijuana, or depressant or stimulant drugs or substances is grounds for: (1) denial of an application for any certificate or rating issued under 14 CFR Part 61 for a period of up to 1 year after the date of final conviction; or (2) suspension or revocation of any certificate or rating issued under 14 CFR Part 61. (PLT463) — 14 CFR §61.15

Answer (A) is incorrect because a permanent revocation of all certificates and ratings is not required by the regulations. Answer (C) is incorrect because the denial of application is for a period of up to 1 year after the date of conviction.

Answers

6414 [B]   6320 [B]

ALL

6407. Under what condition, if any, may a pilot allow a person who is obviously under the influence of intoxicating liquors or drugs to be carried aboard an aircraft?

A— Under no condition.
B— Only if a second pilot is aboard.
C— Only if the person is a medical patient under proper care or in an emergency.

Except in an emergency, no pilot of a civil aircraft may allow a person who appears to be intoxicated or who demonstrates by manner or physical indications that the individual is under the influence of drugs (except a medical patient under proper care) to be carried in that aircraft. (PLT463) — 14 CFR §91.17

ALL

6408. A person may not act as a crewmember of a civil aircraft if alcoholic beverages have been consumed by that person within the preceding

A— 8 hours.
B— 12 hours.
C— 24 hours.

No person may act or attempt to act as a crewmember of a civil aircraft within 8 hours after the consumption of any alcoholic beverage. (PLT463) — 14 CFR §91.17

ALL

6409. No person may act as a crewmember of a civil aircraft with a minimum blood alcohol level of

A— any detectable amount.
B— .04 percent or greater.
C— 0.2 percent or greater.

No person may act or attempt to act as a crewmember of a civil aircraft while having .04% by weight or more alcohol in the blood. (PLT463) — 14 CFR §91.17

Parachutes

Unless each occupant of the aircraft is wearing an approved parachute, no pilot of a civil aircraft, carrying any person (other than a crewmember), may execute any intentional maneuver that exceeds a bank of 60° relative to the horizon, or a nose-up or nose-down attitude of 30° relative to the horizon. This does not apply to spins and other maneuvers required for a certificate or rating if given by a certified flight instructor.

No pilot of a civil aircraft may allow a parachute that is available for emergency use to be carried in that aircraft unless it is an approved type and if a chair-type (canopy in back), it has been packed by a certificated and appropriately-rated parachute rigger within the preceding 120 days.

ALL

6483. When must each occupant of an aircraft wear an approved parachute?

A— When flying over water beyond gliding distance to the shore.
B— When practicing spins or other flight maneuvers for any certificate or rating.
C— When an intentional maneuver that exceeds 30° noseup or nosedown relative to the horizon is made.

Unless each occupant of the aircraft is wearing an approved parachute, no pilot of a civil aircraft carrying any person (other than a crewmember) may execute any intentional maneuver that exceeds a nose-up or nose-down attitude of 30° relative to the horizon. (PLT404) — 14 CFR §91.307

Answer (A) is incorrect because approved flotation devices are required when flying over water beyond gliding distance to the shore when flying for hire. Answer (B) is incorrect because spins and other flight maneuvers may be performed when given by a flight instructor without parachutes when done for a certificate or rating.

Answers

6407   [C]   6408   [A]   6409   [B]   6483   [C]

Safety Pilot Requirements

No person may operate a civil aircraft in simulated instrument flight unless that aircraft has fully functioning dual controls, and an appropriately-rated pilot occupies the other seat as safety pilot.

AIR

6415. A pilot in a multiengine land airplane is planning to practice IFR procedures under a hood in VMC conditions. The safety pilot must possess at least a

A— Recreational Pilot Certificate with an airplane rating.

B— Private Pilot Certificate with airplane multiengine land rating and a current medical certificate.

C— Private Pilot Certificate with airplane and instrument ratings, but a current medical certificate is not required.

No person may operate a civil aircraft in simulated instrument flight unless the other control seat is occupied by a safety pilot who possesses at least a Private Pilot Certificate with category and class ratings appropriate to the aircraft being flown. (PLT448) — 14 CFR §91.109

Fuel Reserve Requirements

No person may begin a flight in an airplane under VFR unless (considering wind and forecast weather conditions) there is enough fuel to fly to the first point of intended landing and, assuming normal cruising speed, during daylight, to fly after that for at least 30 minutes. At night, the required amount of reserve is enough to fly to the first point of intended landing and, assuming normal cruising speed, at night, to fly after that for at least 45 minutes.

AIR, LSA

6441. What is the minimum fuel requirement for flight under VFR at night in an airplane? Enough to fly to

A— the first point of intended landing and to fly after that for 20 minutes at normal cruise speed.

B— the first point of intended landing and to fly after that for 30 minutes at normal cruise speed.

C— the first point of intended landing and to fly after that for 45 minutes at normal cruise speed.

No person may begin a flight in an airplane under VFR unless (considering wind and forecast weather conditions) there is enough fuel to fly to the first point of intended landing and, assuming normal cruising speed, at night, to fly after that for at least 45 minutes. (PLT413) — 14 CFR §91.151

AIR, LSA

6442. What is the minimum fuel requirement for flight under VFR during daylight hours in an airplane? Enough to fly to

A— the first point of intended landing and to fly after that for 20 minutes at normal cruise speed.

B— the first point of intended landing and to fly after that for 30 minutes at normal cruise speed.

C— the first point of intended landing and to fly after that for 45 minutes at normal cruise speed.

No person may begin a flight in an airplane under VFR unless (considering wind and forecast weather conditions) there is enough fuel to fly to the first point of intended landing and, assuming normal cruising speed, during the day, to fly after that for at least 30 minutes. (PLT413) — 14 CFR §91.151

Answers

6415   [B]   6441   [C]   6442   [B]

Transponder Requirements

A coded transponder with altitude reporting capability is required for flight in all airspace of the 48 contiguous states and the District of Columbia at and above 10,000 feet MSL and below the floor of a Class A airspace, excluding the airspace at and below 2,500 feet AGL.

ATC may authorize deviations on a continuing basis, or for individual flights, for operations of aircraft without a transponder, in which case the request for a deviation must be submitted to the ATC facility having jurisdiction over the airspace concerned at least 1 hour before the proposed operation.

ALL
6477. How long before the proposed operation should a request be submitted to the controlling ATC facility to operate in Class C airspace without the required altitude reporting transponder?

A— 1 hour.
B— 8 hours.
C— 24 hours.

ATC may authorize deviation from the requirement for operation in a Class C airspace without the required altitude reporting transponder if the request for the deviation is submitted to the ATC facility having jurisdiction over the airspace concerned at least 1 hour before the proposed operation. (PLT172) — 14 CFR §91.215

ALL
6478. A coded transponder with altitude reporting capability is required for all controlled airspace

A— below 14,500 feet MSL.
B— above 12,500 feet MSL (excluding airspace at or below 2,500 feet AGL).
C— at and above 10,000 feet MSL (excluding airspace at or below 2,500 feet AGL).

A coded transponder with altitude reporting capability is required for flight in all airspace of the 48 contiguous states and the District of Columbia at and above 10,000 feet MSL and below the floor of a Class A airspace, excluding the airspace at and below 2,500 feet AGL. (PLT161) — 14 CFR §91.215

ALL
6479. An altitude reporting coded transponder is required for all airspace

A— from the surface to 10,000 feet MSL within a 10 NM radius of any airport traffic pattern.
B— at and above 10,000 feet MSL and below the floor of Class A airspace (excluding airspace at or below 2,500 feet AGL).
C— within 25 NM of a Class B primary airport from the surface upward to 10,000 feet MSL (excluding airspace below 1,200 feet AGL).

A coded transponder with altitude reporting capability is required for flight in all airspace of the 48 contiguous states and the District of Columbia at and above 10,000 feet MSL and below the floor of a Class A airspace, excluding the airspace at and below 2,500 feet AGL. (PLT161) — 14 CFR §91.215

Minimum Equipment Lists

An aircraft can be operated with inoperative instruments or equipment under the provisions of a Minimum Equipment List (MEL) if the aircraft has within it a letter of authorization, issued by the FAA Flight Standards District Office having jurisdiction over the area in which the operator is located, authorizing operation of the aircraft under the Minimum Equipment List. The MEL lists the equipment that can be inoperative and still not affect the airworthiness of the aircraft.

Answers

6477   [A]   6478   [C]   6479   [B]

AIR, RTC, GLI, LTA, LSA
6474. The primary purpose of a minimum equipment list (MEL) is to

A— provide a list of equipment that must be operational at all times on the aircraft.
B— list the equipment that can be inoperative and still not affect the airworthiness of an aircraft.
C— list the minimum equipment that must be installed in all aircraft as required by airworthiness directives.

An approved minimum equipment list (MEL) provides for the operation of the aircraft with certain instruments and equipment in an inoperable condition. The MEL lists the equipment that can be inoperative and still not affect the airworthiness of the aircraft. (PLT405) — 14 CFR §91.213

Answer (A) is incorrect because this information is covered by the regulations and the aircraft flight manual. Answer (C) is incorrect because this information is covered by the airworthiness directive.

AIR, RTC, GLI, LTA, LSA
6475. Authority for approval of a minimum equipment list (MEL) must be obtained from the

A— Administrator.
B— FAA district office.
C— aircraft manufacturer.

An aircraft can be operated with inoperative instruments or equipment under the provisions of a Minimum Equipment List (MEL) if the aircraft has within it a letter of authorization, issued by the FAA Flight Standards District Office having jurisdiction over the area in which the operator is located, authorizing operation of the aircraft under the Minimum Equipment List. (PLT428) — 14 CFR §91.213

AIR, RTC, GLI, LTA, LSA
6476. Which action is appropriate if an aircraft, operating under FAR Part 91 and for which a master minimum equipment list has not been developed, is determined to have an inoperative instrument or piece of equipment that does not constitute a hazard to the aircraft? The item should be

A— removed and repaired prior to the next flight.
B— placarded "inoperative" and repaired during the next inspection.
C— deactivated and placarded "inoperative" but repairs can be deferred indefinitely.

An airplane for which a Minimum Equipment List has not been developed may be flown with inoperative instruments and equipment provided the instruments and equipment are not part of the VFR-day type certification instruments and equipment, and the inoperative instruments and equipment are either removed from the aircraft or deactivated and placarded "inoperative." (PLT405) — 14 CFR §91.213

Supplemental Oxygen

No person may operate a civil aircraft of U.S. registry at cabin pressure altitudes above 15,000 feet MSL, unless each occupant of the aircraft is provided with supplemental oxygen. When operating above 12,500 feet MSL, up to and including 14,000 feet MSL, the flight crew must be provided with and use oxygen for that time that is more than 30 minutes duration.

AIR, RTC, GLI, LTA
6472. Unless each occupant is provided with supplemental oxygen, no person may operate a civil aircraft of U.S. registry above a cabin pressure altitude of

A— 12,500 feet MSL.
B— 14,000 feet MSL.
C— 15,000 feet MSL.

No person may operate a civil aircraft of U.S. registry at cabin pressure altitudes above 15,000 feet MSL, unless each occupant of the aircraft is provided with supplemental oxygen. (PLT438) — 14 CFR §91.211

Answers (A) and (B) are incorrect because only the minimum flight crew must use supplemental oxygen above 12,500 feet (after 30 minutes) and 14,000 feet MSL (at all times).

Answers

6474   [B]   6475   [B]   6476   [C]   6472   [C]

AIR, RTC, GLI, LTA

6473. Which cabin pressure altitude allows a pilot to operate an aircraft up to 30 minutes without supplemental oxygen?

A— 12,500 feet MSL.
B— 12,600 feet MSL.
C— 14,100 feet MSL.

No person may operate a civil aircraft of U.S. registry at cabin pressure altitudes above 12,500 feet (MSL) up to and including 14,000 feet (MSL) unless the required minimum flight crew is provided with and uses supplemental oxygen for that part of the flight that is of more than 30 minutes duration at those altitudes. (PLT438) — 14 CFR §91.211

Lighting Requirements

Aircraft operating under night VFR must have an approved aviation red or aviation white **anticollision light system**. No person may, during the period from sunset to sunrise, operate an aircraft unless it has lighted position lights. No person may, during the period from to sunset to sunrise, park or move an aircraft in a night-flight operation area of an airport unless the aircraft is clearly illuminated, has lighted position lights, or is in an area which is marked by obstruction lights.

Aircraft on the ground and in the air, and vehicles on the airport, can be controlled from the tower by light signals. The meaning of the various signals is shown in the table in Figure 8-1.

Color and type of signal	Movement of vehicles, equipment and personnel	Aircraft on the ground	Aircraft in flight
Steady green	Cleared to cross, proceed or go	Cleared for takeoff	Cleared to land
Flashing green	Not applicable	Cleared for taxi	Return for landing (to be followed by steady green at the proper time)
Steady red	STOP	STOP	Give way to other aircraft and continue circling
Flashing red	Clear the taxiway/runway	Taxi clear of the runway in use	Airport unsafe, do not land
Flashing white	Return to starting point on airport	Return to starting point on airport	Not applicable
Alternating red and green	Exercise extreme caution	Exercise extreme caution	Exercise extreme caution

Figure 8-1. Light signals from the tower

ALL

6470. An aircraft not equipped with the required position lights must terminate flight

A— at sunset.
B— 30 minutes after sunset.
C— 1 hour after sunset.

No person may, during the period from sunset to sunrise, operate an aircraft unless it has lighted position lights. (PLT461) — 14 CFR §91.209

ALL

6469. Position lights are required to be displayed on all aircraft in flight from

A— sunset to sunrise.
B— 1 hour before sunset to 1 hour after sunrise.
C— 30 minutes before sunrise to 30 minutes after sunset.

No person may, during the period from sunset to sunrise, operate an aircraft unless it has lighted position lights. (PLT461) — 14 CFR §91.209

Answers

6473   [B]   6470   [A]   6469   [A]

ALL

6468. From sunset to sunrise, no person may park or move an aircraft in a night-flight operations area of an airport unless the aircraft

A— is in an area marked by obstruction lights.
B— is equipped with an electric landing or taxi light.
C— has lighted aviation red or white anticollision lights.

No person may, during the period from sunset to sunrise, park or move an aircraft in a night-flight operation area of an airport unless the aircraft is clearly illuminated, has lighted position lights, or is in an area which is marked by obstruction lights. (PLT461) — 14 CFR §91.209

ALL

6431. While in flight, a steady red light directed at you from the control tower means

A— continue flight; airport unsafe, do not land.
B— give way to other aircraft; continue circling.
C— return for landing; expect steady green light at the appropriate time.

A steady red light signal directed at an aircraft in flight means that the pilot should give way to other aircraft and continue circling. (PLT502) — 14 CFR §91.125

Answer (A) is incorrect because this is signaled with a flashing red light. Answer (C) is incorrect because this is signaled with a flashing green light.

ALL

6432. While in flight, an alternating red and green light directed at you from the control tower means

A— exercise extreme caution.
B— give way to other aircraft; continue circling.
C— return for landing; expect steady green light at proper time.

An alternating red and green light signal directed at an aircraft in flight means that the pilot should exercise extreme caution. (PLT502) — 14 CFR §91.125

Answer (B) is incorrect because this is signaled with a steady red light. Answer (C) is incorrect because this is signaled with a flashing green light.

ALL

6433. You receive a flashing white light from the control tower during run-up prior to takeoff; what action should you take?

A— Taxi clear of the runway in use.
B— Return to your starting point on the airport.
C— None; this light signal is applicable only to aircraft in flight.

A flashing white light signal directed at an aircraft during run-up prior to takeoff means that the pilot should return to the starting point on the airport. (PLT502) — 14 CFR §91.125

Answer (A) is incorrect because this is signaled by a flashing red light. Answer (C) is incorrect because a flashing white light is applicable only to aircraft on the ground.

ALL

6471. If an aircraft is not equipped for night flight and official sunset is 1730 EST, the latest a pilot may operate that aircraft without violating regulations is

A— 1629 EST.
B— 1729 EST.
C— 1829 EST.

No person may, during the period from sunset to sunrise, park or move an aircraft in a night-flight operation area of an airport unless the aircraft is clearly illuminated, has lighted position lights, or is in area which is marked by obstruction lights. If the official sunset is 1730 EST, the latest a pilot may operate an aircraft and not violate regulation is 1729 EST. (PLT220) — 14 CFR §91.209

AIR, RTC, LTA, LSA

6463. Which is required equipment for powered aircraft during VFR night flights?

A— Magnetic compass.
B— Sensitive altimeter and landing light.
C— VHF radio communications equipment.

A standard category aircraft operating under night VFR must have a magnetic direction indicator. (PLT405) — 14 CFR §91.205

Answer (B) is incorrect because a landing light is only required if the aircraft is operated for hire at night. Answer (C) is incorrect because VHF radio communications equipment is required for flight operated under IFR.

Answers

6468 [A]	6431 [B]	6432 [A]	6433 [B]	6471 [B]	6463 [A]

Emergency Locator Transmitter

Aircraft, while engaged in training operations conducted entirely within a 50-mile radius of the airport from which local flight operation began, are not required to have an Emergency Locator Transmitter (ELT) installed.

Batteries used in the emergency locator transmitters must be replaced (or recharged, if the battery is rechargeable) when the transmitter has been in use for more than **1 cumulative hour**. The new expiration date for the replacement (or recharge) of the battery must be legibly marked on the outside of the emergency locator transmitter and entered in the aircraft maintenance record.

No person may operate the aircraft more than 90 days after the ELT is initially removed from the aircraft for maintenance. ELTs must be inspected within 12 calendar months after the last inspection for (1) proper installation, (2) battery corrosion, (3) operation of the controls and crash sensor, and (4) the presence of a sufficient signal radiated from its antenna.

ELTs are not required on weight-shift control and powered parachute aircraft.

ALL

6465. What is the maximum distance from an airport that an aircraft engaged in training operations may be operated without an emergency locator transmitter?

A— 25 NM.
B— 50 NM.
C— 100 NM.

Aircraft, while engaged in training operations conducted entirely within a 50-mile radius of the airport from which local flight operation began, are not required to have an emergency locator transmitter installed. (PLT405) — 14 CFR §91.207

ALL

6466. How long may an aircraft be operated after the emergency locator transmitter has been initially removed for maintenance?

A— 90 days.
B— 30 days.
C— 7 days.

No person may operate the aircraft more than 90 days after the ELT is initially removed from the aircraft. (PLT208) — 14 CFR §91.207

ALL

6467-1. When are emergency locator transmitter batteries required to be replaced or recharged?

A— Every 24 months.
B— After 1 cumulative hour of use.
C— After 75 percent of their useful life has expired.

Batteries used in the emergency locator transmitters must be replaced (or recharged, if the battery is rechargeable) when the transmitter has been in use for more than 1 cumulative hour, or when 50% of their useful life (or, for rechargeable batteries, 50% of their useful life of charge) has expired. (PLT405) — 14 CFR §91.207

ALL

6467-2. How often are emergency locator transmitters required to be inspected?

A— Every 12 months.
B— Every 24 months.
C— After every 100 hours of flight time.

Each emergency locator transmitter must be inspected within 12 calendar months after the last inspection. (PLT404) — 14 CFR §91.207

Answers

6465　[B]　　　　6466　[A]　　　　6467-1　[B]　　　　6467-2　[A]

Formation Flights and Right-of-Way

No person may operate an aircraft, carrying passengers for hire, in formation flight.

Aircraft, while on final approach to land, or while landing, have the right-of-way over other aircraft in flight or operating on the surface. When two or more aircraft are approaching an airport for the purpose of landing, the aircraft at the lower altitude has the right-of-way, but it shall not take advantage of this rule to cut in front of another which is on final approach to land, or to overtake that aircraft. When aircraft are approaching each other head-on, or nearly so, each pilot of each aircraft shall alter course to the right.

ALL
6417. If on a night flight, the pilot of aircraft A observes only the green wingtip light of aircraft B, and the airplanes are converging, which aircraft has the right-of-way?

A— Aircraft A; it is to the left of aircraft B.
B— Aircraft B; it is to the right of aircraft A.
C— Aircraft A; it is to the right of aircraft B.

The green wing-tip light is on the right wing of an airplane. When the green light on airplane B is the only light seen from airplane A, airplane A must be on the right of airplane B. Airplane A, therefore, has the right-of-way. (PLT220) — 14 CFR §91.113

ALL
6418. When two or more aircraft are approaching an airport for the purpose of landing, the right-of-way belongs to the aircraft

A— that is the least maneuverable.
B— that is either ahead of or to the other's right regardless of altitude.
C— at the lower altitude, but it shall not take advantage of this rule to cut in front of or to overtake another.

Aircraft, while on final approach to land, or while landing, have the right-of-way over other aircraft in flight or operating on the surface. When two or more aircraft are approaching an airport for the purpose of landing, the aircraft at the lower altitude has the right-of-way. (PLT414) — 14 CFR §91.113

ALL
6419. What action should be taken if a glider and an airplane approach each other at the same altitude and on a head-on collision course?

A— Both should give way to the right.
B— The airplane should give way because it is more maneuverable.
C— The airplane should give way because the glider has the right-of-way.

When aircraft are approaching each other head-on, or nearly so, each pilot of each aircraft shall alter course to the right. (PLT414) — 14 CFR §91.113

ALL
6420. An airplane and an airship are converging. If the airship is left of the airplane's position, which aircraft has the right of way?

A— The airship.
B— The airplane.
C— Each should alter course to the right.

An airship has the right-of-way over an airplane or rotorcraft. (PLT414) — 14 CFR §91.113

ALL
6421. An airship has the right of way over which aircraft?

A— Glider.
B— Gyroplane.
C— Aircraft towing another aircraft.

A glider has the right-of-way over an airship, airplane, or rotorcraft. An airship has the right-of-way over an airplane or rotorcraft. An aircraft towing or refueling other aircraft has the right-of-way over all other engine-driven aircraft. (PLT414) — 14 CFR §91.113

Answers

6417 [C]	6418 [C]	6419 [A]	6420 [A]	6421 [B]

Maximum Authorized Speeds

Unless otherwise authorized by the Administrator, no person may operate an aircraft below 10,000 feet MSL at an indicated airspeed of more than 250 knots (288 MPH). Unless otherwise authorized or required by ATC, no person may operate an aircraft within 4 NM of Class C or D airspace at an Indicated Airspeed (IAS) of more than 200 knots (230 MPH). No person may operate an aircraft in the airspace underlying a Class B airspace, or in a VFR corridor designated through a Class B airspace at an Indicated Airspeed of more than 200 knots (230 MPH).

AIR, RTC, GLI, LTA, MCI

6422. When flying beneath the lateral limits of Class B airspace, the maximum indicated airspeed authorized is

A— 156 knots.
B— 200 knots.
C— 250 knots.

No person may operate an aircraft in the airspace underlying Class B, or in a VFR corridor designated through Class B airspace, at an Indicated Airspeed (IAS) of more than 200 knots (230 MPH). (PLT161) — 14 CFR §91.117

AIR, RTC, GLI, LTA, MCI

6423. Unless otherwise authorized, what is the maximum indicated airspeed at which an aircraft may be flown in a satellite airport traffic pattern located within Class B airspace?

A— 200 MPH.
B— 200 knots.
C— 250 knots.

Unless otherwise authorized by the Administrator, no person may operate an aircraft within Class B airspace at an Indicated Airspeed (IAS) of more than 250 knots (288 MPH). (PLT161) — 14 CFR §91.117

AIR, RTC, GLI, LTA, MCI

6424. Unless otherwise authorized or required by air traffic control, what is the maximum indicated airspeed at which a person may operate an aircraft below 10,000 feet MSL?

A— 200 knots.
B— 250 MPH.
C— 250 knots.

Unless otherwise authorized by the Administrator, no person may operate an aircraft below 10,000 feet MSL at an Indicated Airspeed (IAS) of more than 250 knots (288 MPH). (PLT161) — 14 CFR §91.117

AIR, RTC, GLI, LTA, MCI

6425. The maximum indicated airspeed permitted when operating an aircraft within 4 NM of the primary airport in Class D airspace is

A— 200 MPH.
B— 200 knots.
C— 250 knots.

Unless otherwise authorized or required by ATC, no person may operate an aircraft within Class C and D airspace at an Indicated Airspeed (IAS) of more than 200 knots (230 MPH). (PLT161) — 14 CFR §91.117

Answers

6422   [B]   6423   [C]   6424   [C]   6425   [B]

Distance from Obstructions

No person shall operate an aircraft over a congested area below an altitude of 1,000 feet above the highest obstacle within a horizontal radius of 2,000 feet of the aircraft. No person shall operate an aircraft over a sparsely populated area any closer than 500 feet to any person, vessel, vehicle, or structure. Except when necessary for takeoff or landing, no person may operate an aircraft anywhere below an altitude allowing, if a power unit fails, an emergency landing without undue hazard to persons or property on the surface.

ALL
6426. To operate an aircraft over any congested area, a pilot should maintain an altitude of at least

A— 500 feet above the highest obstacle within a horizontal radius of 1,000 feet.
B— 1,000 feet above the highest obstacle within a horizontal radius of 2,000 feet.
C— 2,000 feet above the highest obstacle within a horizontal radius of 1,000 feet.

No person shall operate an aircraft over any congested area below an altitude of 1,000 feet above the highest obstacle within a horizontal radius of 2,000 feet of the aircraft. (PLT430) — 14 CFR §91.119

ALL
6428. Except when necessary for takeoff or landing, what is the minimum safe altitude for a pilot to operate an aircraft anywhere?

A— An altitude of 1,000 feet above the highest obstacle within a horizontal radius of 2,000 feet.
B— An altitude of 500 feet above the surface and no closer than 500 feet to any person, vessel, vehicle, or structure.
C— An altitude allowing, if a power unit fails, an emergency landing without undue hazard to persons or property on the surface.

Except when necessary for takeoff or landing, no person may operate an aircraft anywhere below an altitude allowing, if a power unit fails, an emergency landing without undue hazard to persons or property on the surface. (PLT430) — 14 CFR §91.119

ALL
6427. The minimum distance at which an airplane may be operated over a structure which is located in a sparsely populated area is

A— 500 feet above the ground.
B— 500 feet from the structure.
C— 1,000 feet from the structure.

No person shall operate an aircraft over a sparsely populated area any closer than 500 feet to any person, vessel, vehicle, or structure. (PLT430) — 14 CFR §91.119

Flight Plan Airspeed

The flight plan should include the cruising altitude (or flight level) and the true airspeed for that altitude.

ALL
6444. What type airspeed at the planned cruise altitude should be entered on a flight plan?

A— True airspeed.
B— Indicated airspeed.
C— Estimated groundspeed.

The flight plan should include the cruising altitude (or flight level) and the true airspeed for that altitude. (PLT225) — 14 CFR §91.153

Answers

6426	[B]	6428	[C]	6427	[B]	6444	[A]

Flight from Noncontrolled Airports

Any person departing an airport without an operating control tower shall comply with any FAA traffic pattern established for that airport.

ALL
6434. What is the correct departure procedure at a noncontrolled airport?

A— The FAA-approved departure procedure for that airport.

B— Make all left turns, except a 45° right turn on the first crosswind leg.

C— Departure in any direction consistent with safety, after crossing the airport boundary.

Any person departing an airport without an operating control tower shall comply with any FAA traffic pattern established for that airport. (PLT052) — 14 CFR §91.127

VFR Cruising Altitudes

Cruising altitudes to be used when operating VFR above 3,000 feet AGL are based on the magnetic course being flown. While operating VFR above 3,000 feet AGL, but below 18,000 feet MSL, an air-craft flying a magnetic course between 000° and 179° inclusive shall fly at odd thousands plus 500 feet. An aircraft flying a magnetic course between 180° and 359° inclusive shall fly at even thousands plus 500 feet.

ALL
6460. When operating under VFR at more than 3,000 feet AGL, cruising altitudes to be maintained are based upon the

A— true course being flown.

B— magnetic course being flown.

C— magnetic heading being flown.

Cruising altitudes to be used when operating VFR above 3,000 feet AGL are based on the magnetic course being flown. (PLT430) — 14 CFR §91.159

ALL
6461. Which courses and altitudes are appropriate for VFR aircraft operating more than 3,000 feet AGL, but below 18,000 feet MSL?

A— True course 0° to 179° inclusive, odd thousands plus 500 feet.

B— Magnetic course 0° to 179° inclusive, even thousands plus 500 feet.

C— Magnetic course 180° to 359° inclusive, even thousands plus 500 feet.

While operating VFR above 3,000 feet AGL, but below 18,000 feet MSL, an aircraft flying a magnetic course between 180° and 359° inclusive shall fly at even thousands plus 500 feet. (PLT430) — 14 CFR §91.159

Answer (A) is incorrect because VFR cruising altitudes are based on magnetic course. Answer (B) is incorrect because easterly magnetic courses use altitudes at odd thousands plus 500 feet.

Maintenance, Preventive Maintenance and Alterations

No person may operate an aircraft, unless, within the preceding 12 calendar months, it has had an **annual inspection** in accordance with Part 43 of the regulations and has been approved for return to service by a person authorized by §43.7 of the regulations.

No inspection performed may be substituted for an annual inspection unless it is performed by a person authorized to perform annual inspections and is entered as an "annual" inspection in the required maintenance records. If an annual inspection is performed on July 12, this year, the next annual will be due no later than July 31, next year.

Answers

6434	[A]	6460	[B]	6461	[C]

No person may operate an aircraft carrying any person (other than a crewmember) for hire, and no person may give flight instruction for hire in an aircraft which that person provides, unless within the preceding 100 hours of time in service it has received an annual or 100-hour inspection and has been approved for return to service in accordance with Part 43 of the regulations. The 100-hour limit may be exceeded by not more than 10 hours while en route to reach a place where the inspection can be done. The excess time used to reach a place where the inspection can be done must be included in computing the next 100 hours' time in service.

An **Airworthiness Directive** is a regulatory notice sent out by the Federal Aviation Administration to the registered owner of an aircraft informing him/her of the discovery of a condition that keeps his/her aircraft from continuing to meet its conditions for airworthiness. It is the responsibility of the owner or operator of an aircraft to maintain that aircraft in an airworthy condition, including compliance with all Airworthiness Directives within the required time limit. The fact of compliance, the date of compliance, and the method of compliance must be recorded in the aircraft maintenance records.

No person may carry any person (other than crewmembers) in an aircraft that has been maintained, rebuilt, or altered in a manner that may have appreciably changed its flight characteristics or substantially affected its operation in flight until an appropriately-rated pilot with at least a private pilot Certificate flies the aircraft, makes an operational check of the maintenance performed or alteration made, and logs the flight in the aircraft records.

No person may use an ATC transponder unless within the preceding 24 calendar months it has been tested and inspected and found to comply with Appendix F of Part 43 of the regulations.

ALL
6486. Completion of an annual inspection and the return of an aircraft to service should always be indicated by

A— conduct of a test flight and the appropriate logbook entry.
B— the appropriate entries in the aircraft maintenance records.
C— the relicensing date on the Registration Certificate.

No inspection performed may be substituted for any inspection unless it is performed by a person authorized to perform annual inspections and is entered as an "annual" inspection in the required maintenance records. (PLT372) — 14 CFR §91.409

ALL
6488. An aircraft's last annual inspection was performed on July 12, this year. The next annual inspection will be due no later than

A— July 13, next year.
B— July 31, next year.
C— 12 calendar months after the date shown on the Airworthiness Certificate.

No person may operate an aircraft, unless, within the preceding 12 calendar months, it has had an annual inspection in accordance with 14 CFR Part 43 and has been approved for return to service by a person authorized by §43.7 of the regulations. If an annual inspection is performed on July 12, this year, the next annual will be due no later than July 31, next year. (PLT372) — 14 CFR §91.409

ALL
6489. Which is prohibited if the aircraft being used has not had a 100-hour inspection or annual inspection within the preceding 100 hours of time in service?

A— Giving flight instruction for hire.
B— Conducting any commercial operation.
C— Carrying passengers, either for hire or not for hire.

No person may operate an aircraft carrying any person (other than a crewmember) for hire, and no person may give flight instruction for hire in an aircraft which that person provides, unless within the preceding 100 hours of time in service it has received an annual or 100-hour inspection and has been approved for return to service in accordance with Part 43 of the regulations. (PLT372) — 14 CFR §91.409

ALL

6490. An aircraft operated for hire with passengers aboard has a 100-hour inspection performed after 90 hours in service. The next 100-hour inspection would be due after

A— 90 hours' time in service.
B— 100 hours' time in service.
C— 110 hours' time in service.

No person may operate an aircraft carrying any person (other than a crewmember) for hire, and no person may give flight instruction for hire in an aircraft which that person provides, unless within the preceding 100 hours of time in service it has received an annual or 100-hour inspection and has been approved for return to service in accordance with Part 43 of the regulations. If the aircraft was inspected after 90 hours in service, the next 100-hour inspection will be due after 100 hours of time in service. (PLT372) — 14 CFR §91.409

ALL

6485. Assuring compliance with airworthiness directives is the responsibility of the

A— FAA certificated mechanic.
B— pilot in command of the aircraft.
C— owner or operator of the aircraft.

The owner or operator of an aircraft is primarily responsible for maintaining that aircraft in an airworthy condition, including compliance with Part 39 (Airworthiness Directives) of the regulations. (PLT374) — 14 CFR §91.403

ALL

6487. If an aircraft's operation in flight was substantially affected by an alteration or repair, the aircraft documents must show that it was test flown and approved for return to service by an appropriately rated pilot prior to being flown

A— with passengers aboard.
B— for compensation or hire.
C— by instructors and students.

No person may carry any person (other than crewmembers) in an aircraft that has been maintained, rebuilt, or altered in a manner that may have appreciably changed its flight characteristics or substantially affected its operation in flight until an appropriately rated pilot with at least a private pilot certificate flies the aircraft, makes an operational check of the maintenance performed or alteration made, and logs the flight in the aircraft records. (PLT425) — 14 CFR §91.407

ALL

6491. If an ATC transponder installed in an aircraft has not been tested, inspected, and found to comply with regulations within a specified period, what is the limitation on its use?

A— Its use is not permitted.
B— It may be used anywhere except in Class A and B airspace.
C— It may be used for VFR flight but not for IFR flight.

No person may use an ATC transponder unless within the preceding 24 calendar months it has been tested and inspected and found to comply with Appendix F of Part 43 of the regulations. (PLT508) — 14 CFR §91.413

ALL

6492. What is the maximum time period during which a person may use an ATC transponder after it has been tested and inspected?

A— 12 calendar months.
B— 24 calendar months.
C— 36 calendar months.

No person may use an ATC transponder unless within the preceding 24 calendar months it has been tested and inspected and found to comply with Appendix F of 14 CFR Part 43. (PLT508) — 14 CFR §91.413

Answers

6490　[B]　　　6485　[C]　　　6487　[A]　　　6491　[A]　　　6492　[B]

Rotorcraft Regulations

Helicopters may be operated at less than the minimums prescribed for other aircraft if the operation is conducted without hazard to persons or property on the surface. When the visibility is less than 1 mile during day hours or less than 3 miles during night hours, a helicopter may be operated clear of clouds if operated at a speed that allows the pilot adequate opportunity to see any air traffic or obstruction in time to avoid a collision. A helicopter may be operated within the lateral boundaries of the surface areas of class B, C, D or E airspace designated for an airport at night under special VFR if it remains clear of clouds. The restrictions that apply to the aircraft being equipped for IFR flight do not apply to helicopters.

No person may begin a flight in a rotorcraft under VFR unless (considering wind and forecast weather conditions) there is enough fuel to fly to the first point of intended landing and, assuming normal cruising speed, to fly after that for at least 20 minutes.

Problem:

According to 14 CFR Part 91, how much farther can a rotorcraft be flown under VFR?

Usable fuel at takeoff	36 gallons
Fuel consumption rate	12.4 gal/hr
Constant ground speed	140 knots
Flight time since takeoff	48 minutes

Solution:

1. Divide the usable fuel at takeoff by the fuel consumption rate to find the length of time the fuel will allow you to fly:

   $36 \div 12.4 = 2.9$ hours, or 2 hours and 54 minutes

2. You have already flown for 48 minutes, so you have enough fuel left for 2 hours and 6 minutes:

   $2:54 - 0:48 = 2:06$

3. Allowing for the required 20 minutes of reserve fuel, you have 1 hour and 46 minutes of usable fuel:

   $2:06 - 0:20 = 1:46$

4. In 1 hour and 46 minutes (1.77 hours), at a ground speed of 140 knots, this fuel will carry you for 247 nautical miles:

   $140 \times 1.77 = 247$ NM

This problem can be quickly and accurately worked on the CX-2 Pathfinder:

1. Find the total amount of flight time provided by the usable fuel at takeoff.

2. Enter the Endurance program.

3. Enter the 36 gallons of usable fuel at takeoff.

4. Enter the fuel consumption rate of 12.4 gallons per hour.

5. The total time provided by the 36 gallons of fuel appears on the display.

6. Enter this 02:54:12 to find the amount of time available.

7. Subtract the 48 minutes already flown. The total time remaining of 02:06:12 appears.

8. Subtract the 20 minutes that you must have for rotorcraft VFR operation under 14 CFR §91.151. 1 hour, 46 minutes, 12 seconds of fuel are available for use.

9. Enter the Dist Fln program and enter the time of 01:46:12.

Continued

10. Enter the ground speed of 140 knots.

11. 247.8 shows on the display. This is the additional distance in nautical miles that can be flown and still have the 20 minutes reserve as required by 14 CFR §91.151.

All aircraft operating in Class C airspace must have an operable two-way radio and a transponder with altitude reporting capability.

To be eligible for a student pilot certificate limited to helicopters, an applicant must be at least 16 years of age. An applicant for a private pilot certificate with a rotorcraft category and helicopter class rating must have at least the following aeronautical experience: A minimum of 40 hours of flight instruction and solo flight time in aircraft, 19 of which must be in helicopters. An applicant for a commercial pilot certificate with a rotorcraft category rating and a helicopter class rating must have at least 150 hours of flight time as a pilot, including at least 100 hours in powered aircraft, 50 hours of which must be in a helicopter.

RTC, MCI

6429. A helicopter may be operated at less than the minimum safe altitudes prescribed by regulations for other aircraft if

A— the operation is conducted without hazard to persons or property.

B— an altitude of at least 500 feet is maintained over other than congested areas.

C— at least 500 feet is maintained above the highest obstacle within a radius of 1,000 feet.

Helicopters may be operated at less than the minimums prescribed for other aircraft if the operation is conducted without hazard to persons or property. (PLT430) — 14 CFR §91.119

RTC, MCI

6458. Which is required to operate a helicopter within Class E airspace between sunset and sunrise under special VFR?

A— The pilot must possess an instrument rating and have satisfied currency requirements.

B— The helicopter must be equipped for instrument flight and the visibility must be at least 1 mile.

C— The helicopter must be operated at a speed that allows the pilot the opportunity to see and avoid other traffic or obstructions.

When the visibility is less than 1 mile during day hours or less than 3 miles during night hours, a helicopter may be operated clear of clouds if operated at a speed that allows the pilot adequate opportunity to see any air traffic or obstruction in time to avoid a collision. (PLT467) — 14 CFR §91.157

RTC, MCI

6459. May a helicopter operate in Class E airspace at night under special VFR?

A— Yes; regulations permit this.

B— No; this is permitted for airplanes only.

C— Yes; but the pilot must be instrument rated and the helicopter must be instrument equipped.

A helicopter may be operated within the lateral boundaries of the surface areas of Class B, C, D or E airspace designated for an airport at night under special VFR if it remains clear of clouds. The restrictions that apply to the aircraft being equipped for IFR flight do not apply to helicopters. (PLT162) — 14 CFR §91.157

RTC, MCI

6443. What is the minimum fuel requirement for flight under VFR in a rotorcraft? Enough to fly to

A— the first point of intended landing and to fly after that for 20 minutes at normal cruise speed.

B— the first point of intended landing and to fly after that for 30 minutes at normal cruise speed.

C— the first point of intended landing and to fly after that for 45 minutes at normal cruise speed.

No person may begin a flight in a rotorcraft under VFR unless (considering wind and forecast weather conditions) there is enough fuel to fly to the first point of intended landing and, assuming normal cruising speed, to fly after that for at least 20 minutes. (PLT413) — 14 CFR §91.151

Answers

6429 [A]   6458 [C]   6459 [A]   6443 [A]

RTC, MCI

6863. GIVEN:

Usable fuel at takeoff...40 gal
Fuel consumption rate...............................12.2 gal/hr
Constant groundspeed.....................................120 kts
Flight time since takeoff............................1 hr 30 min

According to FAR Part 91, how much farther can a rotorcraft be flown under day VFR?

A— 215 NM.
B— 176 NM.
C— 121 NM.

1. Divide the usable fuel at takeoff by the fuel consumption rate to find the length of time the fuel will allow you to fly:

   40 ÷12.2 = 3.3 hours, or 3 hours and 18 minutes.

2. You have already flown for 1 hour 30 minutes, so you have enough fuel left for 1 hour and 48 minutes:

   3:18 – 1:30 = 1:48

3. Allowing for the required 20 minutes of reserve fuel, you have 1 hour and 46 minutes of usable fuel:

   1:48 – 0:20 = 1:28

In 1 hour and 28 minutes (1.47 hours), at a ground speed of 120 knots, this fuel will carry you for 120 x 1.47 = 176 NM and still have the required 20 minutes reserve of fuel. (PLT012) — FAA-H-8083-25

RTC, MCI

6481. Which operable equipment is required for operating a helicopter in Class C airspace?

A— Two-way radio.
B— Two-way radio and transponder with automatic altitude reporting capability.
C— Two-way radio, VOR, and transponder with automatic altitude reporting capability.

All aircraft operating in Class C airspace must have an operable two-way radio and a transponder with altitude reporting capability. (PLT161) — AIM ¶3-2-4

RTC, MCI

6359. An applicant who is seeking a Student Pilot Certificate limited to helicopters is required to be at least how old?

A— 16 years.
B— 17 years.
C— 18 years.

An applicant must be at least 16 years of age to be eligible for a student pilot certificate limited to helicopters. (PLT407) — 14 CFR §61.83

RTC, MCI

6383. What flight time is required for a Private Pilot Certificate with a helicopter rating?

A— A minimum of 40 hours including at least 15 hours of flight training in helicopters.
B— A minimum of 40 hours in helicopters with at least 15 hours of solo time.
C— A minimum of 40 hours, 19 hours of which must be in helicopters.

An applicant for a private pilot certificate with a rotorcraft category and helicopter class rating must have a minimum of 40 hours of flight time that includes at least 20 hours of flight training from an authorized instructor and 10 hours of solo flight training. (PLT409) — 14 CFR §61.109

Answer (A) is incorrect because 19 of the 40 hours must be completed in a helicopter. Answer (B) is incorrect because only 10 hours of solo time is required.

RTC, MCI

6392. As pilot, how much helicopter flight time should an applicant have for a Commercial Pilot Certificate with a helicopter rating?

A— 50 hours.
B— 100 hours.
C— 150 hours.

An applicant for a commercial pilot certificate with a rotorcraft category rating and a helicopter class rating must have at least 150 hours of flight time as a pilot, including at least 100 hours in powered aircraft, 50 hours of which must be in a helicopter. (PLT451) — 14 CFR §61.129

Answers

6863   [B]   6481   [B]   6359   [A]   6383   [C]   6392   [A]

Gyroplane Regulations

To be eligible for a student pilot certificate limited to gyroplanes, an applicant must be at least 16 years of age. An applicant for a private pilot certificate with a rotorcraft category rating and a gyroplane class rating must have at least 40 hours of flight instruction and solo time in aircraft. He/she must have at least 10 hours of solo time, 10 hours of which must be in a gyroplane. An applicant for a commercial pilot certificate with a rotorcraft category rating and a gyroplane class rating must have at least 150 hours of flight time as a pilot, including at least 100 hours in powered aircraft, 25 hours of which must be in a gyroplane.

RTC, MCI

6361. What is the minimum age requirement for the applicant who is seeking a Student Pilot Certificate limited to gyroplane operations?

A— 14 years.
B— 16 years.
C— 18 years.

An applicant must be at least 16 years of age to be eligible for a student pilot certificate limited to gyroplanes. (PLT457) — 14 CFR §61.83

RTC, MCI

6384. How much solo time in a gyroplane is required to be eligible for a Private Pilot Certificate with a gyroplane rating?

A— 10 hours.
B— 15 hours.
C— 20 hours.

An applicant for a private pilot certificate with a rotorcraft category rating and a gyroplane class rating must have at least 40 hours of flight instruction and solo time in aircraft. He/she must have at least 10 hours of solo time, 10 hours of which must be in a gyroplane. (PLT451) — 14 CFR §61.109

RTC, MCI

6393. As pilot, how much gyroplane flight time should an applicant have for a Commercial Pilot Certificate with a gyroplane rating?

A— 150 hours.
B— 100 hours.
C— 25 hours.

An applicant for a commercial pilot certificate with a rotorcraft category rating and a gyroplane class rating must have at least 150 hours of flight time as a pilot, including at least 100 hours in powered aircraft, 25 hours of which must be in a gyroplane. (PLT451) — 14 CFR §61.129

Glider Regulations

The flight review required by 14 CFR Part 61 consists of a minimum of 3 instructional flights in a glider, each of which includes a flight to traffic pattern altitude, and 1 hour of ground instruction; or 1 hour of flight instruction in a glider and 1 hour of ground instruction.

To be eligible for a student pilot certificate limited to gliders, an applicant must be at least 14 years of age. An applicant for a category rating to be added on his/her pilot certificate must meet the requirements for the issuance of the pilot certificate appropriate to the privileges for which the category rating is sought. But, the holder of a category rating for powered aircraft is not required to take a knowledge test for the addition of a glider rating on his/her pilot certificate. An applicant for a commercial pilot certificate with a glider rating must have at least 25 hours as pilot in gliders and 100 glider flights as pilot in command.

An applicant for an initial glider flight instructor certificate must have received flight instruction from a flight instructor who has held a flight instructor certificate during the 24 months immediately preceding the date the instruction is given, who meets the general requirements for a flight instructor certificate, and who has given at least 80 hours of glider flight instruction.

Answers

6361   [B]   6384   [A]   6369   [C]

GLI

6350. A flight review for a glider pilot must consist of at least 1 hour of ground instruction and

A— three takeoffs and landings.
B— 1 hour of flight training to include three 360° turns.
C— 1 hour of flight training or three instructional flights, each of which includes a flight to traffic pattern altitude.

The flight review consists of a minimum of 3 instruction-al flights, each of which includes a flight to traffic pattern altitude, in lieu of the 1 hour of flight training required, or 1 hour of flight instruction in a glider and 1 hour of ground instruction. (PLT407) — 14 CFR §61.56

GLI

6452. What minimum flight visibility is required when flying a glider above 10,000 feet MSL and more than 1,200 feet AGL?

A— 3 SM.
B— 5 NM.
C— 5 SM.

Above 10,000 feet MSL, more than 1,200 feet AGL, all aircraft must have 5 statute miles visibility. (PLT163) — 14 CFR §91.155

GLI

6357. A person seeking a private pilot glider rating is exempt from taking the knowledge test if that person

A— holds a rating for powered aircraft.
B— holds a pilot certificate for any category.
C— has taken a knowledge test for any powered rating within the preceding 24 months.

The holder of a category rating for powered aircraft is not required to take an FAA knowledge test for the addition of a glider category rating on his/her pilot certificate. (PLT407) — 14 CFR §61.63

GLI

6362. The minimum age requirement for the applicant who is seeking a Student Pilot Certificate limited to glider operations is

A— 14 years.
B— 16 years.
C— 17 years.

To be eligible for a student pilot certificate limited to gliders, an applicant must be at least 14 years of age. (PLT457) — 14 CFR §61.83

GLI

6394-1. An applicant for a Commercial Pilot Certificate with a glider rating must have at least

A— 35 glider flights launched by ground tow or 20 launched by aerotow.
B— 25 hours as pilot in gliders and 100 glider flights as pilot in command.
C— 200 hours of pilot time in heavier-than-air aircraft, including at least 10 glider flights as pilot in command during which 360° turns were made.

An applicant for a commercial pilot certificate with a glider rating must have at least 25 hours as pilot in gliders and 100 glider flights as pilot-in-command. (PLT451) — 14 CFR §61.129

GLI

6396. What requirement(s) must an authorized in-structor meet in order to prepare a glider applicant for an initial Flight Instructor Certificate rating?

A— Held a Flight Instructor Certificate for 24 months or given 200 hours of flight training.
B— Held a Flight Instructor Certificate for 12 months and given a minimum of 80 hours of training.
C— Held a Flight Instructor Certificate for at least 24 months and given a minimum of 80 hours of glider training.

An applicant for an initial glider flight instructor certificate must have received flight instruction from a flight instruc-tor who has held a flight instructor certificate during the 24 months immediately preceding the date the instruction is given, who meets the general requirements for a flight instructor certificate, and who has given at least 80 hours of glider flight instruction. (PLT411) — 14 CFR §61.195

Answers

6350   [C]   6452   [C]   6357   [A]   6362   [A]   6394-1   [B]   6396   [C]

Balloon Regulations

LTA

6387. To exercise the privileges of a commercial pilot certificate with a lighter-than-air category, balloon class rating, the minimum medical requirement is:

A— have no known medical condition that would make you unable to operate the aircraft safely.
B— signed statement certifying you have no known medical deficiencies that would hinder you while flying the aircraft.
C— second class medical certificate when carrying passengers for hire.

A person is not required to hold a medical certificate when exercising the privileges of a pilot certificate with a balloon class rating. (PLT443) — 14 CFR §61.23

LTA

6369. A student pilot may not operate a balloon in initial solo flight unless that pilot has

A— received a minimum of 5 hours flight instruction in a balloon.
B— a valid Student Pilot Certificate and logbook endorsement by an authorized flight instructor.
C— made at least 10 balloon flights under the supervision of an authorized flight instructor.

A student pilot may not operate an aircraft in solo flight unless his/her student pilot certificate is endorsed, and unless within the preceding 90 days his/her pilot logbook has been endorsed, by an authorized flight instructor who has given him/her instruction in the make and model of aircraft in which the solo flight is made, and who finds that he/she has met the requirements of 14 CFR §61.87 and finds that he/she is competent to make a safe solo flight in that aircraft. (PLT448) — 14 CFR §61.87

Answers

6387　[A]　　　　6369　[B]

Chapter 9
Flight Instruction and Maneuvers

Taxiing

When taxiing a tricycle-gear airplane with a **strong quartering tail wind**, the elevator should be held in the neutral or down position, and the aileron on the side from which the wind is blowing should be down so the air flowing over it will force the wing down. When a tricycle-gear airplane is taxied in a **strong quartering head wind**, the elevator should be held in the neutral position, and the upwind aileron should be up.

Before starting the pretakeoff check, the airplane should be positioned out of the way of other aircraft. It is recommended that the airplane be as nearly as possible headed into the wind, to obtain more accurate operating indications and to minimize engine overheating during run-up.

AIR, LSA, MCI

6976. To help prevent overturning when taxiing light tricycle-gear airplanes (especially high-wing type) in strong quartering tailwinds, the

A— elevator should be placed in the up position.
B— elevator should be placed in the down position.
C— aileron on the downwind side should be placed in the down position.

When taxiing a tricycle-gear airplane with a strong quartering tail wind, the elevator should be held in the down or neutral position, and the upwind aileron down. (PLT112) — FAA-H-8083-3

AIR, LSA

6977. Which aileron position should you generally use when taxiing in strong quartering headwinds?

A— Neutral.
B— Aileron up on the side from which the wind is blowing.
C— Aileron down on the side from which the wind is blowing.

When taxiing an airplane with a strong quartering head wind, the elevator should be held in the neutral position, and the upwind aileron should be up. (PLT112) — FAA-H-8083-3

AIR, LSA

6978. When taxiing with strong quartering tailwinds, which aileron position should be used?

A— Neutral.
B— Aileron up on the side from which the wind is blowing.
C— Aileron down on the side from which the wind is blowing.

When taxiing in a strong quartering tail wind, the aileron on the side from which the wind is blowing should be down so the air flowing over it will force the wing down. (PLT112) — FAA-H-8083-3

AIR, LSA

6979. Why should an airplane be headed into the wind for the pretakeoff check?

A— To prevent the need for more brake pressure to keep the airplane from moving forward.
B— To obtain more accurate operating indications and to minimize engine overheating during run-up.
C— To prevent excessive load factors which could occur during run-up if a crosswind condition exists.

Before starting the pretakeoff check, the airplane should be headed as nearly as possible into the wind, to obtain more accurate operating indications and to minimize engine overheating while the engine is being run up. (PLT486) — FAA-H-8083-3

Answer (A) is incorrect because the wind will not prevent the airplane from moving, should the brake pressure be inadequate. Answer (C) is incorrect because gravity is the only load factor that exists on the ground.

Answers

6976	[B]	6977	[B]	6978	[C]	6979	[B]

Takeoffs

For a soft- or rough-field takeoff, the airplane is lifted off at as low an airspeed as is possible, and immediately after lift-off, the nose is lowered to pick up speed before leaving ground effect.

For a short-field takeoff, the pitch attitude for minimum drag is used. The airplane is allowed to accelerate as rapidly as possible until the best angle-of-climb speed, V_X, is reached; then the airplane is rotated. The lift-off speed for a short-field takeoff is greater than that used for a soft- or rough-field takeoff.

AIR, WSC, LSA

6989. When explaining the techniques used for making short- and soft-field takeoffs, it would be correct to state that

A— during soft-field takeoffs, lift-off should be made as soon as possible.

B— during soft-field takeoffs, lift-off should be made only when best angle-of-climb speed is attained.

C— during short-field takeoffs, lift-off should be attempted only after best rate-of-climb speed is attained.

Takeoffs and climbs from soft fields require the use of operational techniques for getting the airplane airborne as quickly as possible to eliminate the drag caused by such field conditions as tall grass, soft sand, mud, and snow. (PLT486) — FAA-H-8083-3

Answers (B) and (C) are incorrect because short-field takeoffs use best angle-of-climb (VX).

AIR, WSC, LSA

6990. The indicated lift-off airspeed for short-field takeoffs in a particular aircraft will normally be

A— the same as for soft- or rough-field takeoffs.

B— greater than for soft- or rough-field takeoffs.

C— greater under tailwind conditions than required under headwind conditions.

For a soft- or rough-field takeoff, the aircraft is lifted off at as low an airspeed as is possible, and immediately after lift-off, the nose is lowered to pick up speed before leaving ground effect. The lift-off speed for a short-field takeoff is greater than that used for a soft- or rough-field takeoff. (PLT486) — FAA-H-8083-3

Answer (A) is incorrect because soft-field takeoffs lift off as soon as possible, which is usually before VX. Answer (C) is incorrect because soft- or short-field takeoffs should not be attempted with a tailwind.

ALL

7003. Immediately after takeoff, a downwind turn close to the ground is not good practice because it

A— decreases the rate of climb significantly.

B— causes an increase in the speed at which rotor stall occurs.

C— increases the hazards involved should an emergency landing become necessary.

A downwind turn close to the ground made immediately after takeoff increases the hazards involved if an emergency landing should become necessary. (PLT222) — FAA-H-8083-3

Answers

6989   [A]   6990   [B]   7003   [C]

Turns

There are four flight fundamentals involved in maneuvering an airplane:

1. Straight-and-level flight
2. Turns
3. Climbs
4. Descents

In a **coordinated turn**, centrifugal force exactly balances the horizontal component of lift. Increasing the rate of turn without using rudder increases the **horizontal component of lift** without an opposing increase in centrifugal force, and the aircraft slips to the inside of the turn.

In a right descending turn, the torque is decreased, and a slight amount of left rudder pressure is used to keep the nose from yawing excessively. If too much left rudder is used, the horizontal component of the lift will be greater than the centrifugal force, and the aircraft will slip to the right.

The student pilot in a side-by-side aircraft is sitting to the left side of the longitudinal axis about which the aircraft rolls. This causes the nose to appear to rise when making a correct left turn and appear to descend in a correct right turn. The student will have a tendency to dive to compensate for the apparent rising nose in a left turn and to climb to compensate for the apparent descent during a right turn.

Adverse yaw, caused by the induced drag from the down aileron, causes the nose of an aircraft to initially move in the direction opposite the desired direction of the turn. This is a slipping-turn entry, and more rudder pressure should be applied for the amount of aileron pressure being used. If the rudder is applied too soon, it will cause the nose of the aircraft to move in the direction of the turn before the bank is started.

To recover from an unintentional nose-low attitude during a steep turn, the pilot should first reduce the angle of bank with coordinated aileron and rudder pressure. Then back elevator pressure should be used to raise the aircraft's nose to the desired pitch attitude. After accomplishing this, the desired angle of bank can be re-established. Attempting to raise the nose first by increasing back elevator pressure will usually cause a tight descending spiral and could lead to overstressing the aircraft.

The deflection of the turn needle is dependent upon the rate of yaw. If a constant angle of bank is maintained in a coordinated turn, the rate of yaw and therefore, the displacement of the turn needle, will increase as the airspeed decreases. If a constant 30° angle of bank is held in a coordinated turn, a reduction in airspeed will cause an increase in the rate of turn and a decrease in the radius of the turn.

Maintaining a constant load factor, or G, while increasing the airspeed in a coordinated turn will increase the radius of the turn.

ALL
6980. Select the four flight fundamentals involved in maneuvering an aircraft.

A— Aircraft power, pitch, bank, and trim.
B— Starting, taxiing, takeoff, and landing.
C— Straight-and-level flight, turns, climbs, and descents.

The four flight fundamentals involved in maneuvering an aircraft are:

1. Straight-and-level flight

2. Turns

3. Climbs

4. Descents

(PLT219) — FAA-H-8083-3

Answers

6980   [C]

AIR, LSA, GLI

7051. Which would likely result in a slipping turn?

A— Not holding bottom rudder in a turn.
B— Increasing the rate of turn without using rudder.
C— Increasing the rate of turn without increasing bank.

In a coordinated turn, the centrifugal force exactly balances the horizontal component of lift. Increasing the rate of turn without using rudder increases the horizontal component of lift without an opposing increase in centrifugal force, and the aircraft slips to the inside of the turn. (PLT086) — FAA-H-8083-3

AIR, LSA, GLI

6982. During the entry to a right turn, the nose of the aircraft swings slightly to the left before it swings along the horizon to the right. This is a

A— slipping entry, caused by excessive right rudder pressure.
B— skidding entry; more right rudder pressure and less right aileron pressure should have been applied.
C— slipping entry; more right rudder pressure should have been applied for the amount of aileron pressure being used.

Adverse yaw, caused by the induced drag from the down aileron, causes the nose of an aircraft to initially move in the direction opposite the desired direction of the turn. This is a slipping-turn entry, and more rudder pressure should have been applied for the amount of aileron pressure being used. (PLT219) — FAA-H-8083-3

Answer (A) is incorrect because a slipping entry is caused by insufficient right rudder pressure or not applying the rudder soon enough. Answer (B) is incorrect because this describes a slipping entry.

AIR, LSA, GLI

6983. What will cause the nose of an aircraft to move in the direction of the turn before the bank starts in a turn entry?

A— Rudder being applied too late.
B— Rudder being applied too soon.
C— Failure to apply back elevator pressure.

Rudder being applied too soon will cause the nose of the aircraft to move in the direction of the turn before the bank is started in a turn entry. (PLT219) — FAA-H-8083-3

AIR, LSA, GLI

7052. Choose the true statement pertaining to a slip or skid in an airplane.

A— A skid occurs when the rate of turn is too slow for the amount of bank being used.
B— In a left climbing turn, if insufficient right rudder is applied to compensate for the increased torque effect, a slip will result.
C— In a right descending turn, if excessive left rudder is applied to compensate for the decreased torque effect, a slip will result.

In a right descending turn, the torque is decreased, and a slight amount of left rudder pressure is used to keep the nose from yawing excessively. If too much left rudder is used, the horizontal component of the lift will be greater than the centrifugal force, and the airplane will slip to the right. (PLT086) — FAA-H-8083-3

Answer (A) is incorrect because a skid occurs when the rate of turn is too fast for the amount of bank being used. Answer (B) is incorrect because insufficient right rudder in a climbing left turn will result in a skid.

AIR, LSA

6981. During level turns in side-by-side airplanes, which is characteristic of student performance?

A— Diving during right turns because the nose appears to rise during entry into these turns.
B— Diving during left turns because the nose appears to rise during entry into these turns.
C— Climbing during left turns because the nose appears to descend during entry into these turns.

The student pilot in a side-by-side airplane is sitting to the left side of the longitudinal axis about which the airplane rolls. This causes the nose to appear to rise when making a correct left turn and the student will have a tendency to dive to compensate for the apparent rising nose. (PLT219) — FAA-H-8083-3

Answer (A) is incorrect because the nose appears to descend when entering right turns. Answer (C) is incorrect because the nose appears to rise during left turns, so students have a tendency to descend.

Answers

| 7051 | [B] | 6982 | [C] | 6983 | [B] | 7052 | [C] | 6981 | [B] |

AIR, GLI, LSA

6984. How should a student be taught to correct for a nose-low attitude during a steep turn?

A— Apply back elevator pressure to attain the desired pitch attitude.
B— Reduce the angle of bank, then apply back elevator pressure to attain the desired pitch attitude.
C— Apply back elevator pressure to attain the desired pitch attitude, then reduce the angle of bank.

To recover from an unintentional nose-low attitude during a steep turn, the pilot should first reduce the angle of bank with coordinated aileron and rudder pressure. Then back elevator pressure should be used to raise the airplane's nose to the desired pitch attitude. After accomplishing this, the desired angle of bank can be re-established. (PLT219) — FAA-H-8083-3

Answer (A) is incorrect because applying back elevator pressure first will usually result in a tight descending spiral. Answer (C) is incorrect because this is opposite of the correct procedure.

AIR, GLI, LSA

6985. While holding a constant angle of bank in a coordinated turn, the displacement of the turn needle will

A— increase as airspeed decreases.
B— increase as airspeed increases.
C— remain constant regardless of airspeed.

The deflection of the turn needle is dependent upon the rate of yaw. If a constant angle of bank is maintained in a coordinated turn, the rate of yaw and thus the displacement of the turn needle will increase as the airspeed decreases. (PLT219) — FAA-H-8083-3

AIR, GLI, LSA, WSC

6986. During a 30° banked turn, what effect would a reduction in airspeed have on the rate and radius of turn?

A— The rate would increase; the radius would decrease.
B— The rate would decrease; the radius would increase.
C— The rate would decrease; the radius would decrease.

If a constant 30° angle of bank is held in a coordinated turn, a reduction in airspeed will cause an increase in the rate of turn, and a decrease in the radius of the turn. (PLT248) — FAA-H-8083-3

AIR, GLI, LSA, WSC

6987. During a level turn, increasing the airspeed while maintaining a constant load factor would result in

A— a decrease in radius of turn.
B— an increase in radius of turn.
C— an increase in centrifugal force.

Maintaining a constant load factor while increasing the airspeed in a coordinated turn will increase the radius of the turn. (PLT248) — FAA-H-8083-3

Answers

6984   [B]   6985   [A]   6986   [A]   6987   [B]

Turbulence and Wind Correction

When flying in severe turbulence, wing loading can be minimized by setting the power and trim to obtain an airspeed at or below the design maneuvering airspeed, maintaining a wings-level attitude, and accepting the variations in airspeed and altitude that will occur.

When flying straight-and-level and following a selected ground track, the preferred method of correcting for wind drift is to head (crab) the aircraft sufficiently into the wind to cause the aircraft to move forward into the wind at the same rate the wind is moving it sideways. This crab angle should be established by coordinated use of the controls.

AIR, WSC, LSA, MCI

6988. Which is the best technique for minimizing the wing-load factor when flying in severe turbulence?

A— Control airspeed with power, maintain wings level, and accept variations of altitude.

B— Control airspeed as closely as possible with elevator and power, and accept variations of bank and altitude.

C— Set power and trim to obtain an airspeed at or below maneuvering speed, maintain wings level, and accept variations of airspeed and altitude.

When flying in severe turbulence, wing loading can be minimized by setting the power and trim to obtain an airspeed at or below the design maneuvering airspeed, maintaining a wings-level attitude and accepting the variations in airspeed and altitude that will occur. (PLT312) — FAA-H-8083-25

AIR, GLI, WSC, LSA, MCI

7008. To properly compensate for a crosswind during straight-and-level cruising flight, the pilot should

A— hold rudder pressure toward the wind.

B— establish a proper heading into the wind by coordinated use of the controls.

C— hold aileron pressure toward the wind and hold opposite rudder pressure to prevent a turn.

When flying straight-and-level and following a selected ground track, the preferred method of correcting for wind drift is to head (crab) the aircraft sufficiently into the wind to cause the aircraft to move forward into the wind at the same rate the wind is moving it sideways. This crab angle should be established by coordinated use of the controls. (PLT112) — FAA-H-8083-3

Answers

6988 [C]   7008 [B]

Approaches and Landings

If the crab method of **drift correction** has been used throughout the final approach and round-out, the crab must be removed the instant before touchdown by applying rudder in order to align the aircraft's longitudinal axis with its direction of movement, and switching to the wing-low method of crosswind correction. The motion of the aircraft and its longitudinal axis should be parallel with the runway. A properly executed crosswind landing requires timely and accurate action. Failure to accomplish this results in severe side loads being imposed on the landing gear and imparts ground-looping, or swerving, tendencies.

The final approach for a short-field landing over obstacles is made at a steep approach angle and close to the aircraft's stalling speed. Initiation of the round-out, or flare, must be judged accurately to avoid flying into the ground, or stalling prematurely and sinking rapidly. If the approach speed is correct, there will be no floating during the flare, and there will be sufficient control to touch down properly.

When flying at speeds below **L/D$_{MAX}$**, thrust is inversely proportional to airspeed. As angle of attack is increased, airspeed decreases and more thrust is required to maintain a given airspeed. For these reasons, the throttle controls rate of climb or descent, and airspeed is controlled by the angle of attack.

A downwind landing, using the same airspeed as is used on a normal upwind landing, will result in a higher approach ground speed with the likelihood of overshooting the desired touchdown point. The ground speed at touchdown will be higher than normal, and the ground roll will be longer.

Specific information in the aircraft Flight Manual regarding the approach airspeed and the use of flaps always takes precedence over any rule of thumb. But if specific information is not known, a good rule of thumb for indicated airspeed during a turbulent-air approach is to use the normal approach speed plus one-half the wind-gust factor.

When the decision is made to discontinue an approach and perform a **go-around**, takeoff power should be applied immediately and the airplane's pitch attitude changed to slow or stop the descent. After the descent has been stopped, the flaps may be partially retracted or placed in the takeoff position, as recommended by the manufacturer. If the flaps are fully extended at low airspeed when using full power, the airplane is likely to have poor controllability. Although the need to discontinue a landing may occur at any point in the landing process, the most critical go-around will usually be one started at a point very close to the ground. Nevertheless, it is safer to make a go-around than it is to touch down while drifting or while in a crab, or than it is to make a hard drop-in landing from a high round-out, or a bounced landing.

Unless otherwise specified in the airplane's operating manual, it is generally recommended that the flaps be retracted, at least partially, before retracting the landing gear. There are two reasons for this: First, on most airplanes, full flaps produce more drag than the landing gear; and second, in case the airplane should inadvertently touch down as the go-around is initiated, it is most desirable to have the landing gear in the down-and-locked position.

If a pilot focuses on references that are too close, or if he/she looks directly downward, the references become blurred, and reactions will be either too abrupt or too late. In this case, the tendency is to overcontrol, round-out high, and make a full-stall "drop-in" landing. When the focus is too far ahead, accuracy in judging the closeness of the ground is lost, and the consequent reactions will be slow since there appears to be no necessity for any action. This is likely to result in a nose-first touchdown. Excessive airspeed on final approach usually results in the aircraft "floating." If the pilot misjudges the rate of sink during a landing and thinks the aircraft is descending faster than it should, there is a tendency to increase the pitch attitude and angle of attack too rapidly. This action not only stops the descent, but actually starts the aircraft climbing during the round-out in a condition known as **"ballooning."** To correct for slight ballooning, hold a constant landing attitude and allow the airplane to gradually decelerate and settle onto the runway. If the ballooning is severe, the throttle may be used to cushion the landing.

AIR, WSC, LSA

6993. During a power approach to a short-field landing, the correct airspeed may be verified by

A— the ability to land on a predetermined spot.
B— little or no floating during the landing flare.
C— the ability to maintain a constant angle of descent.

Because the final approach over obstacles is made at a steep approach angle and close to the airplane's stalling speed, the initiation of the round-out or flare must be judged accurately to avoid flying into the ground or stalling prematurely and sinking rapidly. A lack of floating during the flare, with sufficient control to touch down properly, is one verification that the approach speed is correct. (PLT170) — FAA-H-8083-3

AIR, LSA, WSC

6994. What is the correct procedure to follow if an aircraft is in the region of reverse command during a landing approach?

A— Increase angle of attack and power.
B— Decrease angle of attack and power.
C— Decrease angle of attack and increase power.

If an aircraft is in the region of reverse command during a landing approach, the pilot should decrease the angle of attack and increase power to increase airspeed. (PLT170) — FAA-H-8083-3

Answer (A) is incorrect because an increase in angle of attack would further decrease the airspeed. Answer (B) is incorrect because a decrease in power will further increase the sink rate.

AIR, LSA, WSC

6995. Which can result when operating in the region of reverse command?

A— It is not possible to climb.
B— Increased nose-up pitch does not affect rate of descent.
C— increased nose-up pitch causes increased rate of descent.

When operating in the region of reverse command, drag increases with a decrease in airspeed, which results in a further deficiency of power and an increased rate of descent. (PLT170) — FAA-H-8083-3

AIR, LSA

6998. If poor aircraft controllability is experienced during an emergency go-around with full flaps, the cause is most probably due to

A— excessive airspeed with full flaps extended.
B— the high-power, low-airspeed situation with the airplane trimmed for a full-flap configuration.
C— a reduction in the angle of attack with full flaps to the point where the aircraft control is greatly impaired.

When the decision is made to discontinue an approach and perform a go-around, takeoff power should be applied immediately and the airplane's pitch attitude changed to slow or stop the descent. After the descent has been stopped, the flaps may be partially retracted or placed in the takeoff position, as recommended by the manufacturer. When the flaps are fully extended at low airspeed and full power, the airplane is likely to have poor controllability. (PLT244) — FAA-H-8083-3

Answer (A) is incorrect because increased airspeed provides better control. Answer (C) is incorrect because the angle of attack increases with the addition of full power during a go-around with flaps down.

AIR, WSC, LSA, PPC

6999. A go-around from a poor landing approach should

A— not be attempted unless circumstances make it absolutely necessary.
B— generally be preferable to last minute attempts to prevent a bad landing.
C— not be attempted after the landing flare has been initiated regardless of airspeed.

It is safer to make a go-around than to touch down while drifting or while in a crab, or than it is to make a hard drop-in landing from a high round-out, or a bounced landing. (PLT170) — FAA-H-8083-3

Answer (A) is incorrect because a go-around should be executed whenever unfavorable conditions exist. Answer (C) is incorrect because the go-around can be started at any time in the landing process.

Answers

6993   [B]   6994   [C]   6995   [C]   6998   [B]   6999   [B]

AIR, LSA

7000. During go-arounds from a full-flap approach in conventional airplanes, which procedure should be used if the flight manual does not specify differently?

A— Start retracting the flaps first, then retract the gear.
B— Retract the gear first and adjust flaps only after reaching a safe altitude.
C— Retract the gear first since it has a far greater adverse effect on aircraft performance than do flaps.

Unless otherwise specified in the airplane's operating manual, it is generally recommended that the flaps be retracted (at least partially) before retracting the landing gear — for two reasons. First, on most airplanes, full flaps produce more drag than the landing gear; second, in case the airplane should inadvertently touch down as the go-around is initiated, it is most desirable to have the landing gear in the down-and-locked position. (PLT170) — FAA-H-8083-3

AIR, GLI, LSA

6991. To minimize the side loads placed on the landing gear during touchdown, the pilot should keep the

A— direction of motion of the aircraft parallel to the runway.
B— longitudinal axis of the aircraft parallel to the direction of its motion.
C— downwind wing lowered sufficiently to eliminate the tendency for the aircraft to drift.

If the crab method of drift correction has been used throughout the final approach and round-out, the crab must be removed the instant before touchdown by applying rudder in order to align the aircraft's longitudinal axis with its direction of movement, and switching to the wing-low method of crosswind correction. Failure to accomplish this results in severe side loads being imposed on the landing gear and imparts ground-looping (swerving) tendencies. (PLT314) — FAA-H-8083-3

Answer (A) is incorrect because the longitudinal axis of the aircraft needs to parallel the runway. Answer (C) is incorrect because the upwind wing needs to be lowered.

AIR, GLI, LSA

6992. Under normal conditions, a proper crosswind landing on a runway requires that, at the moment of touchdown, the

A— direction of motion of the aircraft and its longitudinal axis be parallel to the runway.
B— downwind wing be lowered sufficiently to eliminate the tendency for the aircraft to drift.
C— direction of motion of the aircraft and its lateral axis be perpendicular to the runway.

If the crab method of drift correction has been used throughout the final approach and round-out, the crab must be removed the instant before touchdown by applying rudder in order to align the aircraft's longitudinal axis with its direction of movement, and switching to the wing-low method of crosswind correction. The motion of the aircraft and its longitudinal axis should be parallel with the runway. (PLT170) — FAA-H-8083-3

Answer (B) is incorrect because the upwind wing must be lowered. Answer (C) is incorrect because, for this to be true, the direction of motion of the aircraft would have to be parallel to the runway.

AIR, GLI, WSC, LSA, PPC

6996. If an emergency situation requires a downwind landing, pilots should expect a faster

A— airspeed at touchdown, a longer ground roll, and better control throughout the landing roll.
B— groundspeed at touchdown, a longer ground roll, and the likelihood of overshooting the desired touchdown point.
C— groundspeed at touchdown, a shorter ground roll, and the likelihood of undershooting the desired touchdown point.

A downwind landing, using the same airspeed as is used on a normal upwind landing, will result in a higher approach ground speed, with the likelihood of overshooting the desired touchdown point. The ground speed at touchdown will be higher than normal, and the ground roll will be longer. (PLT208) — FAA-H-8083-3

Answer (A) is incorrect because the airspeed will be the same, and the control throughout the landing roll will be less due to the higher ground speed. Answer (C) is incorrect because the ground roll will be longer, and there will be a greater likelihood of overshooting the touchdown point.

Answers

7000   [A]   6991   [B]   6992   [A]   6996   [B]

AIR, GLI, WSC, LSA
6997. On final approach to landing, a faster-than-normal indicated airspeed should be used when

A— turbulent conditions exist.
B— ambient temperatures are above 90°F.
C— landing at airports above 5,000 feet MSL with above standard temperature conditions.

For an approach during turbulent conditions, a good rule of thumb for indicated airspeed is to use the normal approach speed plus one-half the wind-gust factor. (PLT170) — FAA-H-8083-3

Answer (B) is incorrect because indicated airspeed will be the same because it adjusts itself to temperature. Answer (C) is incorrect because the indicated airspeed will be the same regardless of the density altitude.

AIR, GLI, WSC, LSA, PPC
7001. One reason a student tends to round out high during landing is

A— changing focus gradually.
B— focusing on references too far ahead.
C— focusing on references that are too close or looking directly down.

If the pilot attempts to focus on references that are too close or if he/she looks directly down, the references become blurred, and reactions will be either too abrupt or too late. In this case, the pilot's tendency will be to overcontrol, round-out high, and make a full-stall "drop-in" landing. (PLT170) — FAA-H-8083-3

AIR, GLI, WSC, LSA, PPC
7002. What could be a result of a student focusing too far ahead during a landing approach?

A— Reactions will be either too abrupt or too late.
B— Rounding out too high and developing an excessive sink rate.
C— Difficulty in judging the closeness of the ground resulting in a nose-first touchdown.

When the pilot focuses too far ahead, accuracy in judging the closeness of the ground is lost, and the consequent reactions will be slow since there will appear to be no necessity for any action. This is likely to result in a nose-first touchdown. (PLT195) — FAA-H-8083-3

AIR, GLI, WSC, LSA
7005. What normally results from excessive airspeed on final approach?

A— Bouncing.
B— Floating.
C— Ballooning.

If the airspeed on final approach is excessive, it will usually result in the airplane floating. (PLT170) — FAA-H-8083-3

Answer (A) is incorrect because bouncing is the result of an improper attitude or an excessive sink rate. Answer (C) is incorrect because ballooning is the result of the pilot misjudging the sink rate.

AIR, GLI, WSC, LSA, PPC
7006. What normally results from misjudging the rate of sink during a landing?

A— Floating.
B— Ballooning.
C— Poor directional control.

If the pilot misjudges the rate of sink during a landing and thinks the aircraft is descending faster than it should, there is a tendency to increase the pitch attitude and angle of attack too rapidly. This action not only stops the descent, but actually starts the aircraft climbing. This climbing during the round-out is known as ballooning. (PLT170) — FAA-H-8083-3

Answer (A) is incorrect because floating results from excessive airspeed on final approach. Answer (C) is incorrect because poor directional control results from excessively slow approach speed, and poor coordination between aileron and rudder controls.

AIR, GLI, WSC, LSA
7007. What procedure should be used to correct for slight ballooning during landing?

A— Decrease power.
B— Decrease angle of attack.
C— Hold a constant landing attitude.

When ballooning is slight, a constant landing attitude should be held and the aircraft allowed to gradually decelerate and settle onto the runway. (PLT170) — FAA-H-8083-3

Answers

6997 [A]	7001 [C]	7002 [C]	7005 [B]	7006 [B]	7007 [C]

Rectangular Course

For best results when planning a **rectangular course**, the flight path should be positioned outside the field boundaries just far enough that they may be easily observed from either pilot seat by looking out the side of the aircraft. The closer the track of the aircraft is to the field boundaries, the steeper the bank necessary at the turning points. *See* Figure 9-1.

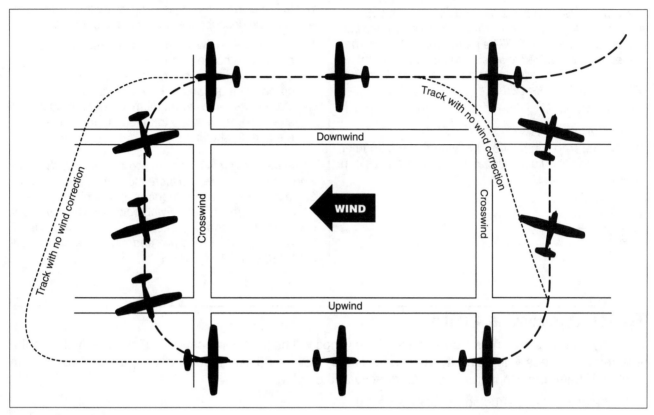

Figure 9-1. Rectangular Course

AIR, RTC, WSC, PPC, LSA, MCI

7009. When beginning a rectangular course, the determining factor in deciding the distance from the field boundary at which an aircraft should be flown is the

A— windspeed.
B— size of the rectangular area chosen.
C— steepness of the bank desired in the turns.

For best results when planning a rectangular course, the flight path should be positioned outside the field boundaries just far enough that they may be easily observed from either pilot seat by looking out the side of the aircraft. The closer the track of the aircraft is to the field boundaries, the steeper the bank necessary at the turning points. (PLT258) — FAA-H-8083-3

Answer (A) is incorrect because windspeed will determine the drift correction and the rate of turn. Answer (B) is incorrect because the size of the rectangular area chosen will not affect the distance from the field boundary.

AIR, RTC, WSC, PPC, LSA, MCI

7010. (Refer to Figure 48.) In flying the rectangular course, when would the aircraft be turned less than 90°?

A— Corners 1 and 4.
B— Corners 1 and 2.
C— Corners 2 and 4.

The aircraft will turn less than 90° at corners 1 and 4. At corner 1, the aircraft turns to a heading that is crabbed into the wind, which makes the turn less than 90°. At corner 4, the aircraft is crabbed into the wind when the turn is started, and the turn will be less than 90°. (PLT219) — FAA-H-8083-3

Answers

7009   [C]   7010   [A]

AIR, RTC, WSC, PPC, LSA

7011. (Refer to Figure 48.) In flying the rectangular course, when would the aircraft be turned more than 90°?

A— Corners 2 and 3.
B— Corners 1 and 3.
C— Corners 2 and 4.

The aircraft will turn more than 90° at corners 2 and 3. At corner 2, the aircraft starts the turn while crabbed into the wind, and the turn will be more than 90°. At corner 3, the aircraft is turned to a heading that will be crabbed into the wind. This will require a turn of more than 90°. (PLT219) — FAA-H-8083-3

AIR, RTC, WSC, PPC, LSA

7012. (Refer to Figure 48.) In flying the rectangular course, when should the aircraft bank vary from a steep bank to a medium bank?

A— Corner 1.
B— Corner 3.
C— Corners 2 and 3.

The bank will vary from steep to medium at corner 3. The turn is started when flying downwind, so the bank must be steep, and as the turn progresses, it is shallowed out to a medium bank. (PLT219) — FAA-H-8083-3

AIR, RTC, WSC, PPC, LSA

7013. (Refer to Figure 48.) In flying the rectangular course, which would describe the proper angle of bank?

A— Corner 1 shallow, corner 2 medium, corner 3 steep, and corner 4 shallow.
B— Corner 1 shallow, corner 2 medium to steep, corner 3 steep, and corner 4 medium to shallow.
C— Corner 1 shallow to medium, corner 2 medium to steep, corner 3 steep to medium, and corner 4 medium to shallow.

Since the aircraft is flying upwind at corner 1, the bank would begin shallow and increase to medium. At corner 2, the bank would begin medium and increase to steep. At corner 3, the aircraft is flying downwind and the bank will start steep and decrease to medium. At corner 4, the bank will start medium and decrease to shallow. (PLT219) — FAA-H-8083-3

Turns Around a Point

When flying **turns around a point**, the airplane wings will be in alignment with the pylon only during the time the airplane is flying directly upwind or directly downwind. At all other points, a **wind correction angle** will keep the wings from pointing directly at the pylon.

If the student is instructed to not exceed a 45° bank in a turn around a point maneuver, the best place to start is the point where the bank angle will be steepest, which is when flying downwind. Throughout the remainder of the maneuver, the bank will be shallowing out.

The ground speed will be equal where the airplane is flying with the same headwind component. The angle of bank will be the same only where the airplane is flying directly crosswind. *See* Figure 9-2.

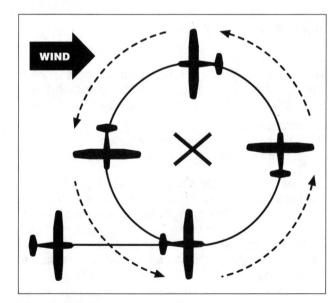

Figure 9-2. Turns around a point

AIR, WSC, PPC, LSA, MCI

7014. (Refer to Figure 49.) At which points will the wing (lateral axis) be in alignment with the pylon during turns around a point?

A— 1 and 5.
B— 3 and 7.
C— 1, 3, 5, and 7.

When flying a turn around a point, the wings will be in alignment with the pylon only during the time the aircraft is flying directly upwind or directly downwind. These two times are at points 3 and 7. At all other points, a wind correction angle will keep the wings from pointing directly at the pylon. (PLT219) — FAA-H-8083-3

Answers (A) and (C) are incorrect because points 1 and 5 will require a crab angle.

AIR, WSC, PPC, LSA

7015. (Refer to Figure 49.) If you instruct a student to practice turns around a point using a bank that is not to exceed 45° at its steepest point, it would be best to start at which of the positions shown?

A— 3.
B— 7.
C— 3 or 7.

To enter turns around a point, the aircraft should be flown on a downwind heading to one side of the selected point. This would be point 7. (PLT258) — FAA-H-8083-3

AIR, WSC, PPC, LSA

7016. During turns around a point, an imaginary line from the pilot's eye and parallel to the lateral axis should point to the pylon when the aircraft is abeam the point headed directly

A— crosswind.
B— downwind only.
C— upwind or downwind.

When flying a turn around a point, the wings will be in alignment with the pylon only during the time the aircraft is flying directly upwind or directly downwind. At other times the aircraft will be crabbed into the wind. (PLT258) — FAA-H-8083-3

AIR, WSC, PPC, LSA, MCI

7017. (Refer to Figure 49.) The groundspeed will be equal in which positions?

A— 1 and 5.
B— 1 and 5, 2 and 4, 6 and 8.
C— 1 and 5, 2 and 8, 4 and 6.

The ground speed will be equal only at points 1 and 5, 2 and 4, and 6 and 8 where the aircraft is flying with the same headwind component. (PLT258) — FAA-H-8083-3

AIR, WSC, PPC, LSA

7018. (Refer to Figure 49.) The angle of bank will be most nearly equal in which positions?

A— 3 and 7.
B— 1 and 5.
C— 4 and 6.

The angle of bank will be the same only at points 1 and 5, where the aircraft is flying directly crosswind. This will be midway between the steepest and shallowest angle. (PLT258) — FAA-H-8083-3

Answer (A) is incorrect because the bank is steepest at point 7, and shallowest at point 3. Answer (C) is incorrect because the bank is steeper at point 6 than at point 4.

AIR, WSC, PPC, LSA

7019. (Refer to Figure 49.) Which position will require the steepest bank?

A— 1.
B— 5.
C— 7.

The closer the aircraft is to a direct downwind heading where the ground speed is greatest, the steeper the angle of bank. This would be point 7. (PLT258) — FAA-H-8083-3

Answers (A) and (B) are incorrect because at points 1 and 5, the aircraft is headed crosswind.

Answers

| 7014 [B] | 7015 [B] | 7016 [C] | 7017 [B] | 7018 [B] | 7019 [C] |

S-Turns

In a steep turn, the ground speed will be the same when the aircraft has the same headwind component. The steepest angle of bank is required at the points where the aircraft is flying downwind. The aircraft will have to be crabbed into the wind the greatest amount where it is flying crosswind.

In the first half of an **S-turn**, the bank should begin shallow and increase in steepness as the aircraft turns crosswind, and become steepest where the turn is downwind. If the turn is started with too steep a bank angle, the bank will increase too rapidly and the upwind half of the "S" will be smaller than the downwind half. The turn will not be completed by the time the aircraft is over the reference line. *See Figure 9-3.*

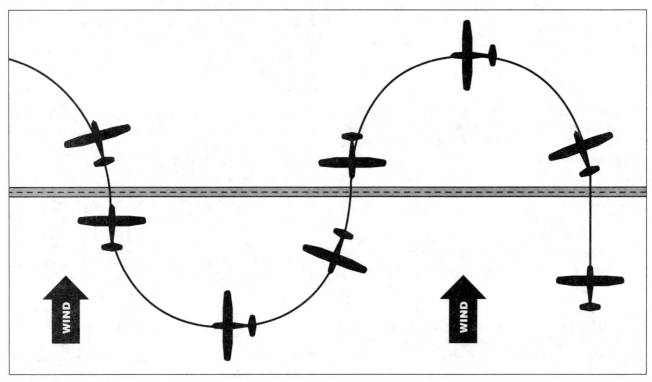

Figure 9-3. S-Turns

AIR, RTC, WSC, PPC, LSA

7020. (Refer to Figure 50.) In which positions will the groundspeeds be equal?

A— 2 and 5.
B— 1 and 6, 2 and 5.
C— 1 and 6, 2 and 5, 3 and 4.

The ground speed will be the same at points 1 and 6, 2 and 5, and 3 and 4. At these points the aircraft has the same headwind component. (PLT258) — FAA-H-8083-3

AIR, RTC, WSC, PPC, LSA

7021. (Refer to Figure 50.) During S-turn practice, which positions require the steeper angle of bank?

A— 4 and 5.
B— 3 and 4.
C— 2 and 5.

The steepest angle of bank is required at the points the aircraft is flying downwind, which are at points 3 and 4. (PLT219) — FAA-H-8083-3

Answers

7020   [C]   7021   [B]

AIR, RTC, WSC, PPC, LSA, MCI

7022. (Refer to Figure 50.) Proper execution of S-turns across a road requires that the aircraft be crabbed into the wind the greatest amounts at which points?

A— 3 and 4.
B— 2 and 5.
C— 1 and 6.

The aircraft will have to be crabbed into the wind the greatest amount at points 2 and 5 where it is flying crosswind. (PLT258) — FAA-H-8083-3

AIR, RTC, WSC, PPC, LSA

7023. (Refer to Figure 51.) While practicing S-turns, a consistently smaller half-circle is made on one side of the road than on the other, and this turn is not completed before crossing the road or reference line. This would most likely occur in turn

A— 1-2-3 because the bank is decreased too rapidly during the latter part of the turn.
B— 4-5-6 because the bank is increased too rapidly during the early part of the turn.
C— 4-5-6 because the bank is increased too slowly during the latter part of the turn.

In the half of an S-turn labeled 4-5-6, the bank should begin shallow and increase in steepness as the aircraft turns crosswind and become steepest at point 6 where the turn is downwind. If the turn at point 4 is started with too steep a bank angle, the bank will increase too rapidly, and the upwind half of the S will be smaller than the downwind half. The turn will not be completed by the time the aircraft is over the reference line. (PLT219) — FAA-H-8083-3

Eights-On-Pylons

When **eights-on-pylons** are conducted at the correct altitude, the reference line will always point directly at the pylon. If the reference point moves behind the pylon, the airplane is above its pivotal altitude. The pivotal altitude for eights-on-pylons depends primarily on the ground speed.

If the rudder is misused when attempting to hold the pylon during the performance of eights-on-pylons, the airplane will either slip or skid. The airplane is above the pivotal altitude when the bank angle is too steep for the rate of yaw and the airplane is slipping. The airplane is below the pivotal altitude when the rate of yaw is too great for the bank angle and the airplane is skidding. *See* Figure 9-4.

AIR

7024. In properly coordinated eights-on-pylons, if the reference point is behind the pylon, it means the

A— angle of bank is too shallow.
B— airplane is above the pivotal altitude.
C— airplane is below the pivotal altitude.

When eights-on-pylons are conducted at the correct altitude, the reference line will always point directly at the pylon. If the reference point moves behind the pylon, the airplane is above its pivotal altitude. (PLT219) — FAA-H-8083-3

AIR

7024-1. What is the primary control during eights-on pylons?

A— Aileron.
B— Rudder.
C— Elevator.

The instructor should emphasize that the elevators are the primary control for holding the pylons. Even a very slight variation in altitude effects a double correction, since in losing altitude, speed is gained, and even a slight climb reduces the airspeed. This variation in altitude, although important in holding the pylon, in most cases will be so slight as to be barely perceptible on a sensitive altimeter. (PLT219) — FAA-H-8083-3

Answers

7022 [B]   7023 [B]   7024 [B]   7024-1 [C]

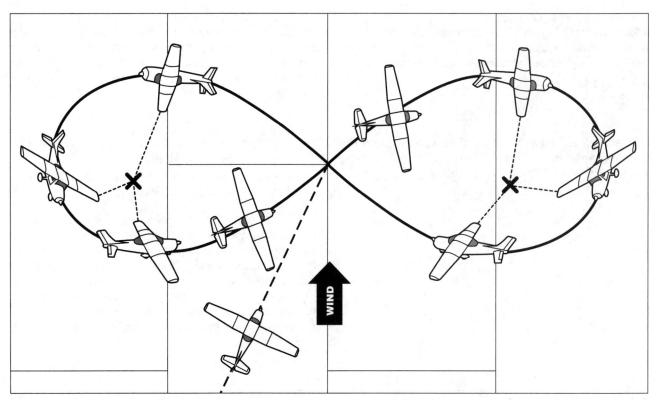

Figure 9-4. Eights-on-Pylons

AIR, MCI

7025. The pivotal altitude for eights-on-pylons is dependent primarily upon the

A— groundspeed.
B— true airspeed.
C— distance from the pylon.

The pivotal altitude for eights-on-pylons depends primarily on the ground speed. (PLT219) — FAA-H-8083-3

AIR

7026. If the wing moves behind the pylon during properly coordinated eights-on-pylons, the airplane is

A— flying too fast.
B— below pivotal altitude.
C— above pivotal altitude.

When eights-on-pylons are conducted at the correct altitude, the wing will always point directly at the pylon. If the wing moves behind the pylon, the airplane is above its pivotal altitude. (PLT219) — FAA-H-8083-3

AIR

7027. (Refer to Figure 52.) While performing eights-on-pylons, the turn-and-slip indicator appears as shown in "2." The pilot must

A— increase altitude to obtain the correct pivotal altitude, and correct the skidding turn.
B— decrease altitude to obtain the correct pivotal altitude, and correct the slipping turn.
C— decrease the bank to hold the reference point on the pylon without slipping, because the radius of turn is too small.

According to the turn-and-slip indicator 2, the airplane is skidding. The bank angle is too shallow for the rate of yaw being used, and the airplane is below its pivotal altitude. Increase the altitude to get back to the pivotal altitude, and correct the skidding turn. (PLT086) — FAA-H-8083-3

Answers

7025　[A]　　　　7026　[C]　　　　7027　[A]

AIR

7028. (Refer to Figure 52.) Misuse of rudder in attempting to hold the pylon during the performance of eights-on-pylons will result in which turn-and-slip indication?

A— "2" if above or below pivotal altitude.
B— "1" if below pivotal altitude; "2" if above pivotal altitude.
C— "1" if above pivotal altitude; "2" if below pivotal altitude.

If the rudder is misused when attempting to hold the pylon during the performance of eights-on-pylons, the airplane will either slip or skid. Turn-and-slip indicator 1 shows that the airplane is above the pivotal altitude. The bank angle is too steep for the rate of yaw, and the airplane is slipping. Turn-and-slip indicator 2 shows that the airplane is below the pivotal altitude. The rate of yaw is too great for the bank angle, and the airplane is skidding. (PLT086) — FAA-H-8083-3

Stalls and Slow Flight

The **crossed-control stall** is the type of stall most likely to occur during a poorly planned and executed turn from base to final during a landing approach. The objective of demonstrating a crossed-control stall is to show the effect of improper control technique and to emphasize the importance of using coordinated control pressures whenever making turns.

Maneuvers at slow flight are taught to develop the pilot's sense of feel and the ability to use the controls correctly. This type of flying improves proficiency for maneuvers in which very low airspeed is required, and allows the pilot to recognize how fast control effectiveness can be lost. In-flight practice at slow flight should cover two distinct flight situations:

1. Establishing and maintaining the airspeed appropriate for landing approaches and go-arounds in the aircraft being used; and

2. Turning flight at the slowest airspeed that the particular aircraft is able to continue controlled flight without stalling.

AIR, WSC, LSA

6316-1. Which is the correct symbol for the minimum steady flight speed at which an airplane is controllable?

A— V_S.
B— V_{S1}.
C— V_{S0}.

"V_S" refers to the stalling speed or the minimum steady flight speed at which the airplane is controllable. (PLT484) — 14 CFR §1.2

AIR, LSA, MCI

7036. Which is a correct spin recovery technique?

A— Apply forward elevator control followed by aileron opposite the spin.
B— Apply full forward elevator control followed by a coordinated rollout.
C— Reduce power to idle, apply opposite rudder and forward elevator control.

The first corrective action taken during any spin is to close the throttle. To recover from the spin, the pilot should apply opposite rudder and forward elevator control. (PLT219) — FAA-H-8083-3

AIR, LSA

7225. Which stall must be performed during a flight instructor – airplane practical test?

A— Power-on or power-off.
B— Accelerated.
C— Imminent.

The required stalls for the Flight Instructor – Airplane practical test are:

1. Power-on stalls (proficiency)

2. Power-off stalls (proficiency)

3. Crossed-control stalls (demonstration)

4. Elevator trim stalls (demonstration)

5. Secondary stalls (demonstration)

(PLT487) — FAA-S-ACS-6, FAA-S-8081-6

Answers

7028 [C]   6316-1 [A]   7036 [C]   7225 [A]

AIR, GLI, LSA

7029. The objective of a cross-control stall demonstration is to

A— emphasize the hazard of an excessive slip during a landing approach.

B— teach the proper recovery technique should this type of stall occur during final approach.

C— show the effect of improper control technique and emphasize the importance of coordinated control when making turns.

The objective of demonstrating a cross-control stall is to show the effect of improper control technique and to emphasize the importance of using coordinated control pressures whenever making turns. (PLT477) — FAA-H-8083-3

Answer (A) is incorrect because slips are not hazardous when adequate airspeed is maintained. Answer (B) is incorrect because recovery is not likely, should this type of stall occur during final approach. The objective is to teach students how to recognize the pending situation, so a cross-control stall can be avoided.

AIR, GLI, WSC, LSA

7030. Two distinct flight situations should be covered when teaching slow flight. These are the establishment and maintenance of

A— airspeeds appropriate for landing approaches, and flight at reduced airspeeds.

B— an airspeed which gives a stall warning indication, and an airspeed at which complete recovery can be made from stalls.

C— an airspeed at which the airplane is operating on the back side of the power curve, and an airspeed at which the elevator control can be held full-back with no further loss of control.

Practice in slow flight should cover two distinct flight situations:

1. Establishing and maintaining the airspeed appropriate for landing approaches and go-arounds in the aircraft used.

2. Turning flight at the slowest airspeed at which the particular aircraft is capable of continued controlled flight without stalling.

(PLT219) — FAA-H-8083-3

AIR, GLI, WSC, LSA

7031. The primary purpose of practicing operations at reduced airspeeds is to enable students to

A— safely fly airport traffic patterns at various airspeeds.

B— develop proficiency in anticipating the onset of power-on stalls.

C— develop proficiency in their sense of feel and their ability to use the controls properly at various speeds.

The objective of teaching maneuvering at slow flight is to develop the pilot's sense of feel and the ability to use the controls correctly. Maneuvering at this slow airspeed improves proficiency at performing maneuvers that require very low airspeed, and it allows the pilot to recognize the rapidity at which control effectiveness can be lost. (PLT219) — FAA-H-8083-3

AIR, GLI, LSA

7035. If inadequate right rudder is used during a climbing right turn, what may occur if the aircraft stalls?

A— A spin to the left.

B— A tendency to yaw to the right.

C— A tendency to roll to the right.

If inadequate right rudder is used during a climbing right turn, and the aircraft stalls, the left yawing movement created by torque, p-factor, and spiraling slipstream may cause a spin to the left. (PLT245) — FAA-H-8083-3

Answers

7029	[C]	7030	[A]	7031	[C]	7035	[A]

Steep Turns

An airplane will stall during a coordinated steep turn exactly as it does from straight flight, except that the pitching and rolling actions tend to be more sudden. The direction an airplane tends to roll during an accelerated stall is determined by whether the airplane is slipping or skidding, or is in a coordinated turn. If the airplane is slipping toward the inside of the turn at the time the stall occurs, it tends to roll rapidly toward the outside of the turn as the nose pitches down. The outside wing stalls before the inside wing. If the airplane is skidding toward the outside of the turn when it stalls, it will have a tendency to roll to the inside of the turn because the inside wing stalls first. If the airplane is in a coordinated turn at the time the stall occurs, the nose will pitch away from the pilot just as it does in a straight-flight stall, since both wings stall simultaneously.

In a **steep power turn**, the bank angle is steep enough that the airplane has an overbanking tendency, and the rudder is used to prevent excessive yawing.

If the airplane begins to gain altitude in a steep power turn, the bank should be increased by coordinated use of rudder and ailerons. If the airplane begins to lose altitude, the bank should be decreased by coordinated use of the rudder and ailerons. The rudder should never be used alone to control the altitude.

AIR, LSA

7033. If an accelerated stall occurs during a steep turn, in which direction would the aircraft tend to roll?

A— Toward the inside of the turn.
B— Toward the outside of the turn.
C— The direction of roll depends on whether the airplane is slipping, skidding, or in coordinated flight.

If the airplane is slipping toward the inside of the turn at the time the stall occurs, it tends to roll rapidly toward the outside of the turn. If the airplane is skidding toward the outside of the turn when the stall occurs, it will have a tendency to roll to the inside of the turn. If, however, the coordination of the turn at the time of the stall is accurate, the airplane's nose will pitch away from the pilot just as it does in a straight-flight stall. (PLT477) — FAA-H-8083-3

AIR, GLI, LSA, MCI

7032. If an accelerated stall occurs in a steep turn, how will the aircraft respond?

A— The inside wing stalls first because it is flying at a higher angle of attack.
B— The outside wing stalls first because it is flying at a higher angle of attack.
C— In a slip, the high wing stalls first; in a skid, the low wing stalls first; in coordinated flight, both wings stall at the same time.

An aircraft will stall during a coordinated steep turn exactly as it does from straight flight, except that the pitching and rolling actions tend to be more sudden. If the aircraft is slipping toward the inside of the turn at the time the stall occurs, it tends to roll rapidly toward the outside of the turn as the nose pitches down, because the outside wing stalls before the inside wing. If the aircraft is skidding toward the outside of the turn when it stalls, it will have a tendency to roll to the inside of the turn because the inside wing stalls first. If, however, the coordination of the turn at the time of the stall is accurate, the aircraft's nose will pitch away from the pilot just as it does in a straight-flight stall, since both wings stall simultaneously. (PLT245) — FAA-H-8083-3

Answers (A) and (B) are incorrect because the wing which stalls first is determined by the interference of airflow over the wing.

AIR, GLI, LSA

7034. Students should be taught that throughout a level, 720° steep turn to the right, the rudder is normally used to

A— prevent yawing.
B— control the rate of turn.
C— hold the aircraft in the turn once it is established.

In a steep power turn, the bank angle is steep enough that the aircraft has an overbanking tendency, and the rudder is used to prevent excessive yawing. (PLT219) — FAA-H-8083-3

Answers

7033   [C]   7032   [C]   7034   [A]

Chandelles

In the first 90° of a **chandelle**, the bank angle is held constant, and the pitch attitude is increased at a constant rate until it reaches its maximum at the 90°-point. During the second 90°, the pitch angle is held constant, and the bank angle is gradually reduced at a constant rate until the wings come level when the 180°-point is reached. At this point, the pitch attitude should be high and the airspeed about 5 knots above a stall.

If a chandelle is begun with a bank that is too steep, the airplane will turn too fast; not enough altitude will be gained and the pilot may pitch up abruptly to compensate. If it is begun with a bank that is too shallow, the pitch angle will increase excessively, and the airplane is likely to stall before it reaches the 180°-point. *See* Figure 9-5.

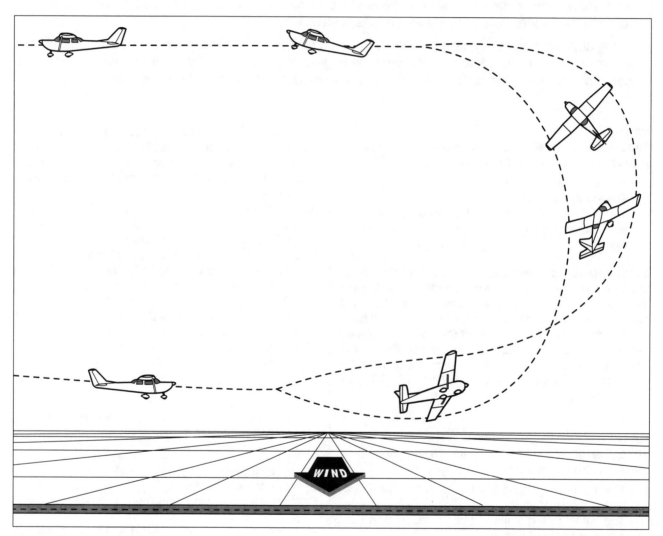

Figure 9-5. Chandelle

AIR

7037. Pilots who initiate a chandelle with a bank that is too steep will most likely

A— stall before completing the maneuver.
B— turn more than 180° before completing the rollout.
C— perform a comparatively level steep turn with a nose-high rollout at the 180° point.

If a chandelle is begun with a bank that is too steep, the airplane will make a comparatively level turn without enough airspeed loss. This would result in a tendency to raise the nose to reduce airspeed on rollout. (PLT219) — FAA-H-8083-3

Answer (A) is incorrect because the critical angle of attack is not likely to be reached. Answer (B) is incorrect because rollout is usually accomplished at 180°, regardless of the airspeed.

AIR

7038. What may occur if the initial bank is too shallow when performing a chandelle?

A— Completing the maneuver with excessive airspeed.
B— Stalling the aircraft before reaching the 180° point.
C— Completing the maneuver with too low a pitch attitude.

If a chandelle is begun with a bank that is too shallow, the pitch angle will increase excessively, and the airplane is likely to stall before it reaches the 180°-point. (PLT219) — FAA-H-8083-3

Answer (A) is incorrect because the maneuver will be completed with airspeed loss if the turn rate is too slow. Answer (C) is incorrect because the maneuver cannot be completed with the loss of airspeed.

AIR

7039. When performing a chandelle, where should maximum pitch occur?

A— 45° point.
B— 90° point.
C— 180° point.

In the first 90° of a chandelle, the bank angle is held constant, and the pitch attitude is increased at a constant rate until it reaches its maximum at the 90°-point. (PLT219) — FAA-H-8083-3

AIR, MCI

7040. Which best describes pitch and bank during the first 90° of a chandelle?

A— Changing pitch and bank.
B— Constant pitch and bank.
C— Constant bank and changing pitch.

In the first 90° of a chandelle, the bank angle is held constant, and the pitch attitude is increased at a constant rate until it reaches its maximum at the 90°-point. (PLT219) — FAA-H-8083-3

AIR

7041. Which best describes pitch and bank during the second 90° of a chandelle?

A— Changing pitch and bank.
B— Constant pitch and changing bank.
C— Constant bank and changing pitch.

During the second 90° of a chandelle, the pitch angle is held constant, and the bank angle is gradually reduced at a constant rate until the wings come level when the 180°-point is reached. (PLT219) — FAA-H-8083-3

Answers

7037 [C]	7038 [B]	7039 [B]	7040 [C]	7041 [B]

Lazy Eights

A **lazy eight** consists of two 180° turns, in opposite directions, while making a climb and a descent in a symmetrical pattern during each of the turns. The maximum pitch-up attitude should occur at the 45°-point. The minimum airspeed and steepest bank should be reached at the 90°-point where the altitude is maximum, and the pitch attitude is near level. The maximum pitch-down attitude should occur at the 135°-point. The altitude at the 180°-point should be the same as the entry altitude.

If a lazy eight is started with too rapid a roll rate, the 45°-point may be reached before the maximum pitch-up attitude is reached. If the climbing turn portions of a lazy eight are entered with banks that are too steep, the turn rate will be too fast for the rate of climb, and the 180° change of direction will be reached with an excess of airspeed. *See* Figure 9-6.

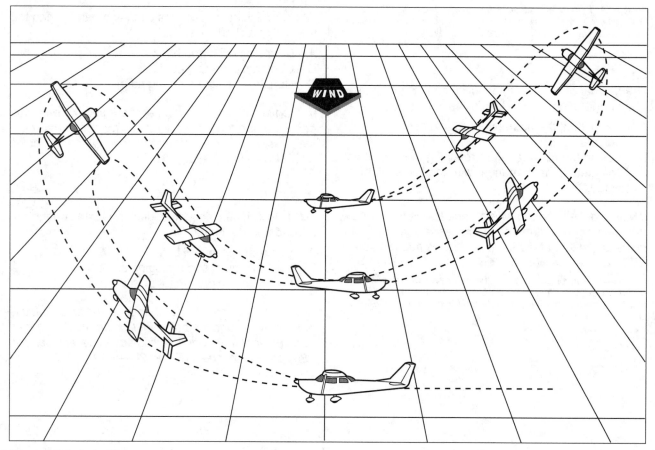

Figure 9-6. Lazy Eights

AIR
7042. When performing a lazy eight, where should the maximum pitchup attitude occur?

A— 45° point.
B— 90° point.
C— 180° point.

The maximum pitch-up attitude should occur at the 45°-point. (PLT219) — FAA-H-8083-3

Answers (B) and (C) are incorrect because the pitch attitude is level at the 90°- and 180°-points.

AIR

7043. When performing a lazy eight, when should the aircraft be at minimum airspeed?

A— 45° point.
B— 90° point.
C— 180° point.

The minimum airspeed should be reached at the 90°-point. (PLT219) — FAA-H-8083-3

Answer (A) is incorrect because the airspeed is decreasing at the 45°-point. Answer (C) is incorrect because the airspeed is at the maximum at the 180°-point.

AIR

7044. When performing a lazy eight, where should the maximum pitchdown attitude occur?

A— 90° point.
B— 135° point.
C— 180° point.

The maximum pitch-down attitude should occur at the 135°-point. (PLT219) — FAA-H-8083-3

Answers (A) and (C) are incorrect because the pitch attitude is level at the 90°- and 180°-points.

AIR

7045. When performing a lazy eight, when should the maximum altitude occur?

A— 45° point.
B— 90° point.
C— 180° point.

The maximum altitude should occur at the 90°-point. (PLT219) — FAA-H-8083-3

Answer (A) is incorrect because the maximum pitch occurs at the 45°-point. Answer (C) is incorrect because the minimum altitude occurs at the 180°-point.

AIR

7046. What should occur at the 90° point of a lazy eight?

A— Airspeed and altitude should be the same as at entry.
B— Maximum pitch attitude, minimum airspeed, and minimum bank.
C— Steepest bank, minimum airspeed, maximum altitude, and level pitch attitude.

At the 90°-point in a lazy eight, the bank is the steepest, the airspeed is minimum, the altitude is maximum, and the pitch attitude is level. (PLT219) — FAA-H-8083-3

AIR

7047. What would cause the 45° point to be reached before the maximum pitchup attitude during a lazy eight?

A— Beginning with too slow a rate of roll.
B— Beginning with too rapid a rate of roll.
C— Allowing the airspeed to remain too high causing the rate of turn to increase.

If the lazy eight is started with too rapid a roll rate, the 45°-point may be reached before the maximum pitch-up attitude is reached. (PLT219) — FAA-H-8083-3

Answer (A) is incorrect because beginning with too slow a rate of roll would result in arriving at the 45°-point too late. Answer (C) is incorrect because allowing the airspeed to remain too high would result in the rate of turn decreasing.

AIR, MCI

7048. Which is the most probable result if a pilot initiates the climbing turn portions of the lazy eight with banks that are too steep?

A— Completing each 180° change of direction with a net gain of altitude.
B— Attaining a pitch attitude that is too steep and stalling at the top of the climbing turn.
C— Turning at a rate too fast for the rate of climb and therefore, completing each 180° change of direction with excessive airspeed.

If the climbing turn portions of a lazy eight are entered with banks that are too steep, the turn rate will be too fast for the rate of climb. The 180° change of direction will be reached with excessive airspeed. (PLT219) — FAA-H-8083-3

AIR

7049. At what point in a lazy eight is it most likely necessary to exert opposing aileron and rudder pressures in order to maintain coordinated flight?

A— At the point of slowest speed.
B— At the point of fastest speed.
C— At the point of lowest pitch attitude.

It is possible at the point of lowest airspeed (the 90°-point) in a lazy eight for opposing aileron and rudder pressures to be required to maintain coordinated flight. This is because of the increased right rudder pressure needed to overcome torque as the airspeed decreases. (PLT219) — FAA-H-8083-3

Answers

| 7043 | [B] | 7044 | [B] | 7045 | [B] | 7046 | [C] | 7047 | [B] | 7048 | [C] |
| 7049 | [A] | | | | | | | | | | |

AIR
7050. (Refer to Figure 52.) During practice of lazy eights, the most probable cause of the uncoordinated situation at the completion of 90° of turn (indicated by the turn-and-slip indicator shown in "1") is the

A— use of too much right rudder pressure.
B— use of too much left rudder control pressure.
C— use of too little right rudder pressure.

A slip is shown in the turn-and-slip indicator "1," which is the result of too much right rudder pressure. (PLT086) — FAA-H-8083-3

Flight by Reference to Instruments

The **turn-and-slip indicator** and the **turn coordinator** have a inclinometer built into their display that shows the relationship between the centrifugal force and the horizontal component of lift that acts on the airplane in a turn.

In a coordinated turn, the horizontal component of lift and the centrifugal force are equal but operating in the opposite directions, and the ball stays in the center of the glass tube. When entering a turn, the horizontal component of lift should exactly balance the centrifugal force to keep the ball centered. If, while rolling into a right turn, the ball moves to the outside (to the left), the centrifugal force is greater than the horizontal component of lift, and the right rudder pressure should be slightly relaxed to allow the ball to return to the center. If, while rolling into a right turn, the ball moves to the inside (to the right), the horizontal component of lift is greater than the centrifugal force and more right rudder pressure is needed to center the ball.

The **pitch attitude** of an airplane is the angle between the longitudinal axis of the airplane and the actual horizon. In straight-and-level flight, the altimeter is the primary instrument for pitch control.

When entering a constant airspeed climb from straight-and-level flight, the attitude indicator is the primary pitch and supporting bank indicator. The heading indicator is the primary bank indicator and the turn coordinator is the supporting bank indicator. When establishing a level, standard-rate turn, the primary bank instrument for the beginning of the turn is the attitude indicator, and after the turn is established, the primary bank instrument is the turn coordinator.

In an unusual attitude, it is possible for the attitude indicator to exceed its limits and become unreliable. The airspeed indicator and altimeter can be relied upon to give pitch indication to initiate a recovery from an unusual flight attitude.

If the airspeed is increasing or is too high, reduce power to prevent excessive airspeed and loss of altitude. Correct the bank attitude with coordinated aileron and rudder pressure to straight flight by referring to the turn coordinator. Raise the nose to level flight attitude by smooth back elevator pressure. All components of control should be changed simultaneously for a smooth, proficient recovery.

During attitude instrument training, the pilot must develop three fundamental skills involved in all instrument flight maneuvers:

1. Instrument cross-check.

2. Instrument interpretation.

3. Aircraft control.

Answers

7050   [A]

When executing an ILS approach, the pilot must keep the aircraft on the electronic glide slope. This requires the ability to establish the proper rate of descent for the ground speed. As ground speed increases, the rate of descent required to maintain the glide slope must be increased; as ground speed decreases, the rate of descent required to maintain the glide slope also decreases. By first cross-checking the instruments and then interpreting them, the pilot is able to precisely control the aircraft to a successful landing.

ALL

7098. Which instrument provides the most pertinent information (primary) for pitch control in straight-and-level flight?

A— Altimeter.
B— Attitude indicator.
C— Airspeed indicator.

In straight-and-level flight, the altimeter is the primary instrument for pitch control. It will give a direct indication of a need for pitch control. (PLT336) — FAA-H-8083-15

AIR, RTC, GLI, LSA

7099. What instrument(s) is (are) supporting bank instrument(s) when entering a constant airspeed climb from straight-and-level flight?

A— Heading indicator.
B— Turn coordinator and heading indicator.
C— Attitude indicator and turn coordinator.

When entering a constant airspeed climb from straight-and-level flight, the attitude indicator is the primary pitch and supporting bank indicator. The heading indicator is the primary bank indicator and the turn coordinator is the supporting bank indicator. (PLT185) — FAA-H-8083-15

AIR, RTC, GLI, LSA

7100. Which instruments are considered primary and supporting for bank, respectively, when establishing a level standard rate turn?

A— Turn coordinator and heading indicator.
B— Attitude indicator and turn coordinator.
C— Turn coordinator and attitude indicator.

When establishing a level, standard-rate turn, the primary bank instrument for the beginning of the turn is the attitude indicator, and after the turn is established, the primary bank instrument is the turn coordinator. (PLT186) — FAA-H-8083-15

AIR, RTC, GLI, LSA, WSC

7102. Which is the correct sequence for recovery from a spiraling, nose-low, increasing airspeed, unusual flight attitude?

A— Increase pitch attitude, reduce power, and level wings.
B— Reduce power, correct bank attitude, and raise nose to a level attitude.
C— Reduce power, raise nose to a level attitude, and correct bank attitude.

If the airspeed is increasing or is too high, reduce power to prevent excessive airspeed and loss of altitude. Correct the bank attitude with coordinated aileron and rudder pressure to straight flight by referring to the turn coordinator. Raise the nose to level flight attitude by smooth back elevator pressure. All components of control should be changed simultaneously for a smooth, proficient recovery. (PLT208) — FAA-H-8083-15

AIR, LSA

7101. If an airplane is in an unusual flight attitude and the attitude indicator has exceeded its limits, which instruments should be relied upon to determine pitch attitude before recovery?

A— Airspeed indicator and altimeter.
B— Turn coordinator and vertical speed indicator.
C— Vertical speed indicator and airspeed indicator.

In an unusual attitude, it is possible for the attitude indicator to exceed its limits and become unreliable. The airspeed indicator and altimeter can be relied upon to give pitch indication to initiate a recovery from an unusual flight attitude. (PLT208) — FAA-H-8083-15

AIR, GLI, LSA

6584. (Refer to Figure 22.) While rolling into a right turn, if the inclinometer appears as illustrated in A, the HCL and CF vectors would be acting on the aircraft as illustrated in

A— 2, and more left pedal pressure is needed to center the ball.

B— 2, and more right pedal pressure is needed to center the ball.

C— 4, and more right pedal pressure is needed to center the ball.

If the ball moves to the inside of the turn, the horizontal component of lift is greater than the centrifugal force. This is shown in the force vectors 2. To correct this situation and center the ball, increase the rate of yaw with a little more right rudder pressure. (PLT346) — FAA-H-8083-3

AIR, GLI, LSA

6585. (Refer to Figure 22.) While rolling into a right turn, if the inclinometer appears as illustrated in C, the HCL and CF vectors would be acting on the aircraft as illustrated in

A— 3, and less right pedal pressure is needed to center the ball.

B— 5, and less right pedal pressure is needed to center the ball.

C— 5, and more right pedal pressure is needed to center the ball.

If the ball moves to the outside of the turn, the centrifugal force is greater than the horizontal component of lift. This is shown in the force vectors 5. To correct this situation and center the ball, decrease the rate of yaw with a little less right rudder pressure. (PLT346) — FAA-H-8083-3

AIR, GLI, LSA

6586. (Refer to Figure 22.) While rolling out of a left turn, if the inclinometer appears as illustrated in A, the HCL and CF vectors would be acting on the aircraft as illustrated in

A— 4, and more right pedal pressure is needed to center the ball.

B— 4, and more left pedal pressure is needed to center the ball.

C— 2, and more right pedal pressure is needed to center the ball.

If the ball moves to the outside of the turn, the centrifugal force is greater than the horizontal component of lift. This is shown in the force vectors 4. To correct this situation and center the ball, decrease the rate of yaw with a little more right rudder pressure. (PLT346) — FAA-H-8083-3

MCI

4832. The gyroscopic heading indicator is inoperative. What is the primary bank instrument in unaccelerated straight-and-level flight?

A— Magnetic compass.

B— Attitude indicator.

C— Miniature aircraft of turn coordinator.

The heading indicator provides the most pertinent banking information in unaccelerated straight-and-level flight, since banking means turning, and it is primary for bank. With gyroscopic heading indicator failure, the magnetic compass becomes the only heading indicator. (PLT215) — FAA-H-8083-15

Answer (B) is incorrect because the attitude indicator does not provide heading information needed to maintain straight flight. Answer (C) is incorrect because the miniature aircraft is the primary bank indicator in established standard rate turns (not in straight flight).

MCI

4836. What instruments are considered supporting bank instruments during a straight, stabilized climb at a constant rate?

A— Attitude indicator and turn coordinator.

B— Heading indicator and attitude indicator.

C— Heading indicator and turn coordinator.

The attitude indicator is primary only during transitions from one attitude to another. Once stabilized, the attitude indicator becomes a support instrument. The turn coordinator is a supporting instrument in straight flight. (PLT278) — FAA-H-8083-15

Answers (B) and (C) are incorrect because the heading indicator is used as the primary bank instrument in a straight climb.

Answers

| 6584 [B] | 6585 [B] | 6586 [A] | 4832 [A] | 4836 [A] |

MCI

4837. What instruments are primary for pitch, bank, and power, respectively, when transitioning into a constant airspeed climb from straight-and-level flight?

A— Attitude indicator, heading indicator, and manifold pressure gauge or tachometer.
B— Attitude indicator for both pitch and bank; airspeed indicator for power.
C— Vertical speed, attitude indicator, and manifold pressure or tachometer.

The attitude indicator is the primary pitch indicator during the transition, heading indicator for bank, and tachometer or manifold pressure for power. When the airspeed has stabilized, the airspeed indicator becomes primary for pitch. (PLT278) — FAA-H-8083-15

Answer (B) is incorrect because the heading indicator is a primary instrument for bank, and the manifold pressure gauge is primary for power. Answer (C) is incorrect because the attitude indicator is the primary instrument for pitch, and the heading indicator is primary for bank.

MCI

4838. What is the primary bank instrument once a standard rate turn is established?

A— Attitude indicator.
B— Turn coordinator.
C— Heading indicator.

The turn coordinator displays the movement of the aircraft on the roll axis that is proportional to the roll rate. Therefore, the turn coordinator is the primary bank instrument once a standard rate turn is established. (PLT187) — FAA-H-8083-15

Answer (A) is incorrect because the attitude indicator will be used as a primary bank instrument in establishing a standard rate turn, but not for maintaining the turn once it is established. Answer (C) is incorrect because the heading indicator is a primary bank instrument for straight flight.

MCI

4839. What does the miniature aircraft of the turn coordinator directly display?

A— Rate of roll and rate of turn.
B— Angle of bank and rate of turn.
C— Angle of bank.

The miniature aircraft of the turn coordinator displays rate of roll and rate of turn. (PLT187) — FAA-H-8083-15

Answers (B) and (C) are incorrect because the miniature aircraft of the turn coordinator does not directly display the bank angle of the aircraft.

MCI

4840. What is the correct sequence in which to use the three skills used in instrument flying?

A— Aircraft control, cross-check, and instrument interpretation.
B— Instrument interpretation, cross-check, and aircraft control.
C— Cross-check, instrument interpretation, and aircraft control.

During attitude instrument training, a pilot must develop three fundamental skills involved in all instrument flight maneuvers:

1. *instrument cross-check*

2. *instrument interpretation*

3. *aircraft control*

(PLT185) — FAA-H-8083-15

Answer (A) is incorrect because aircraft control is the third skill used in instrument flying. Answer (B) is incorrect because instrument interpretation is the second skill and cross-check is the first skill used in instrument flying.

MCI

4845-1. As power is increased to enter a 500 feet per minute rate of climb in straight flight, which instruments are primary for pitch, bank, and power respectively?

A— Attitude indicator, heading indicator, and manifold pressure gauge or tachometer.
B— VSI, attitude indicator, and airspeed indicator.
C— Airspeed indicator, attitude indicator, and manifold pressure gauge or tachometer.

As the power is increased to the approximate setting for the desired rate, simultaneously raise the miniature aircraft to the climbing attitude for the desired airspeed and rate of climb. As the power is increased, the AI is primary for pitch control until the vertical speed approaches the desired value. The heading indicator is primary for bank and the tachometer, or manifold pressure gauge, is primary for power. As the vertical speed needle stabilizes, it becomes primary for pitch. (PLT278) — FAA-H-8083-15

Answer (B) is incorrect because the vertical speed indicator becomes the primary instrument for pitch once a constant rate climb has been established. Answer (C) is incorrect because the heading indicator is primary for bank in straight flight.

Answers

4837 [A]	4838 [B]	4839 [A]	4840 [C]	4845-1 [A]

MCI

4845-2. As power is increased to enter a 500 feet per minute rate of climb in straight flight, which instruments are primary for pitch, bank, and power respectively?

A— Airspeed indicator, attitude indicator, and manifold pressure gauge or tachometer.
B— VSI, attitude indicator, and airspeed indicator.
C— Airspeed indicator, heading indicator, and manifold pressure gauge or tachometer.

To enter a constant-rate climb, increase power to the approximate setting for the desired rate. As power is applied, the airspeed indicator is primary for pitch until the vertical speed approaches the desired rate. (PLT278) — FAA-H-8083-15

MCI

4847. What indications are displayed by the miniature aircraft of a turn coordinator?

A— Rate of roll and rate of turn.
B— Direct indication of bank angle and pitch attitude.
C— Indirect indication of bank angle and pitch attitude.

The miniature aircraft of the turn coordinator displays only rate-of-roll and rate-of-turn. It does not directly display the bank angle of the aircraft. (PLT187) — FAA-H-8083-15

Answer (B) is incorrect because the turn coordinator is an indirect indication of bank angle and is not related to pitch attitude. Answer (C) is incorrect because the turn coordinator does not reflect pitch attitude.

MCI

4848. What is the primary pitch instrument during a stabilized climbing left turn at cruise climb airspeed?

A— Attitude indicator.
B— VSI.
C— Airspeed indicator.

For a constant airspeed climb (at cruising airspeed), once the airplane stabilizes at a constant airspeed and attitude, the airspeed indicator becomes the primary pitch instrument. (PLT278) — FAA-H-8083-15

Answers (A) and (B) are incorrect because the attitude indicator and vertical speed indicator are each used as supporting pitch instruments in a stabilized climb.

MCI

4849. What is the primary pitch instrument during a stabilized autorotation?

A— Altimeter.
B— Airspeed indicator.
C— VSI.

The airspeed indicator is the primary pitch instrument and should be adjusted to the recommended autorotation speed. (PLT175) — FAA-H-8083-15

MCI

4850-1. What is the primary pitch instrument when establishing a constant altitude standard rate turn?

A— Altimeter.
B— VSI.
C— Airspeed indicator.

The altimeter is the primary pitch instrument when establishing a level standard rate turn. (PLT166) — FAA-H-8083-15

Answer (B) is incorrect because the VSI is used as a supporting pitch instrument for establishing a level standard rate turn. Answer (C) is incorrect because the airspeed indicator is used as the primary power instrument when establishing a constant altitude standard rate turn.

MCI

4850-2. As a rule of thumb, altitude corrections of less than 100 feet should be corrected by using

A— two bar widths on the attitude indicator.
B— less than a full bar width on the attitude indicator.
C— less than half bar width on the attitude indicator.

As a rule of thumb, for errors of less than 100 feet, use a half-bar-width correction. (PLT185) — FAA-H-8083-15

MCI

4851. What is the initial primary bank instrument when establishing a level standard rate turn?

A— Turn coordinator.
B— Heading indicator.
C— Attitude indicator.

The attitude indicator is the initial primary bank instrument when establishing a level standard rate turn. (PLT185) — FAA-H-8083-15

Answer (A) is incorrect because after the turn has been established, the turn coordinator becomes the primary bank instrument. Answer (B) is incorrect because the heading indicator is used as the primary bank instrument for straight flight.

Answers

4845-2 [C]	4847 [A]	4848 [C]	4849 [B]	4850-1 [A]	4850-2 [B]
4851 [C]					

MCI
4853. What instrument(s) is(are) supporting bank instrument when entering a constant airspeed climb from straight-and-level flight?

A— Heading indicator.
B— Attitude indicator and turn coordinator.
C— Turn coordinator and heading indicator.

The attitude indicator and turn coordinator are the supporting bank instruments when entering a constant airspeed climb from straight-and-level flight. (PLT185) — FAA-H-8083-15

Answers (A) and (C) are incorrect because the heading indicator is used as the primary bank instrument for straight flight.

MCI
4855. What are the three fundamental skills involved in attitude instrument flying?

A— Instrument interpretation, trim application, and aircraft control.
B— Cross-check, instrument interpretation, and aircraft control.
C— Cross-check, emphasis, and aircraft control.

The three fundamental skills involved in all instrument flight maneuvers are:

1. instrument cross-check

2. instrument interpretation

3. aircraft control

(PLT186) — FAA-H-8083-15

Answer (A) is incorrect because application of trim is just one aspect of aircraft control. Answer (C) is incorrect because emphasis is a common error in instrument cross-checking.

MCI
4856. What indication is presented by the miniature aircraft of the turn coordinator?

A— Indirect indication of the bank attitude.
B— Direct indication of the bank attitude and the quality of the turn.
C— Quality of the turn.

The miniature aircraft of the turn coordinator displays only rate-of-roll and rate-of-turn. It only indirectly displays the bank angle of the aircraft. (PLT187) — FAA-H-8083-15

Answer (B) is incorrect because the turn coordinator does not provide a direct indication of bank. Answer (C) is incorrect because the ball in the turn coordinator displays the quality of the turn.

MCI
4858. What is the primary bank instrument while transitioning from straight-and-level flight to a standard rate turn to the left?

A— Attitude indicator.
B— Heading indicator.
C— Turn coordinator (miniature aircraft).

The attitude indicator is the initial primary bank instrument when establishing a level standard rate turn. (PLT185) — FAA-H-8083-15

Answer (B) is incorrect because the heading indicator is used as the primary bank instrument for straight flight. Answer (C) is incorrect because the turn coordinator is the primary bank instrument only after the turn has been established.

MCI
4859. What is the third fundamental skill in attitude instrument flying?

A— Instrument cross-check.
B— Power control.
C— Aircraft control.

The three fundamental skills involved in all instrument flight maneuvers are:

1. instrument cross-check

2. instrument interpretation

3. aircraft control

(PLT185) — FAA-H-8083-15

Answer (A) is incorrect because instrument cross-check is the first skill in instrument flying. Answer (B) is incorrect because the use of power control is only one aspect of aircraft control.

MCI
4862. What is the first fundamental skill in attitude instrument flying?

A— Aircraft control.
B— Instrument cross-check.
C— Instrument interpretation.

The three fundamental skills involved in all instrument flight maneuvers are:

1. instrument cross-check

2. instrument interpretation

3. aircraft control

(PLT185) — FAA-H-8083-15

Answer (A) is incorrect because aircraft control is the third fundamental skill in instrument flight. Answer (C) is incorrect because instrument interpretation is the second fundamental skill in instrument flight.

Answers

| 4853 [B] | 4855 [B] | 4856 [A] | 4858 [A] | 4859 [C] | 4862 [B] |

MCI

4863. As power is reduced to change airspeed from high to low cruise in level flight, which instruments are primary for pitch, bank, and power, respectively?

A— Attitude indicator, heading indicator, and manifold pressure gauge or tachometer.
B— Altimeter, attitude indicator, and airspeed indicator.
C— Altimeter, heading indicator, and manifold pressure gauge or tachometer.

As the power is reduced to change airspeed from high to low cruise in level flight the primary instruments are:

Pitch — Altimeter
Bank — Heading indicator
Power — Manifold pressure gauge (momentarily)

(PLT278) — FAA-H-8083-15

Answer (A) is incorrect because the altimeter is primary for pitch (not attitude indicator). Answer (B) is incorrect because the heading indicator is primary for bank (not attitude indicator), and manifold pressure gauge is momentarily the primary for power (not the airspeed indicator).

MCI

4865. Which instrument provides the most pertinent information (primary) for bank control in straight-and-level flight?

A— Turn-and-slip indicator.
B— Attitude indicator.
C— Heading indicator.

The primary instruments in straight-and-level flight are:

Primary Pitch—Altimeter
Primary Bank—Heading Indicator
Primary Power—Airspeed Indicator

See *the figure that follows. (PLT185) — FAA-H-8083-15*

Answer (A) is incorrect because the turn-and-slip indicator is a supporting bank instrument in straight-and-level flight. Answer (B) is incorrect because the attitude indicator is a supporting bank and pitch instrument in straight-and-level flight.

MCI

4866. Which instruments are considered primary and supporting for bank, respectively, when establishing a level standard rate turn?

A— Turn coordinator and attitude indicator.
B— Attitude indicator and turn coordinator.
C— Turn coordinator and heading indicator.

On the roll-in to a level standard rate turn, use the attitude indicator to establish the approximate angle of bank (primary), then check the miniature aircraft of the turn coordinator for a standard rate turn indication (secondary). (PLT186) — FAA-H-8083-15

Answer (A) is incorrect because the turn coordinator is the primary bank instrument, and the attitude instrument the supporting bank instrument, only after the standard rate turn has been established. Answer (C) is incorrect because the turn coordinator is the supporting bank instrument, and the heading indicator is neither a primary or supporting instrument, when establishing a standard rate turn.

MCI

4867. While recovering from an unusual flight attitude without the aid of the attitude indicator, approximate level pitch attitude is reached when the

A— airspeed and altimeter stop their movement and the VSI reverses its trend.
B— airspeed arrives at cruising speed, the altimeter reverses its trend, and the vertical speed stops its movement.
C— altimeter and vertical speed reverse their trend and the airspeed stops its movement.

When the rate of movement of altimeter and airspeed indicator needles decreases, and the vertical speed indicator reverses its trend, the aircraft is approaching level pitch attitude. (PLT297) — FAA-H-8083-15

Answer (B) is incorrect because the vertical speed indicator will lag and only show a decrease in vertical movement when it has stopped. Answer (C) is incorrect because the altimeter must stop (not just reverse its trend) in order to indicate a level pitch attitude.

MCI

4869. Which instruments, in addition to the attitude indicator, are pitch instruments?

A— Altimeter and airspeed only.
B— Altimeter and VSI only.
C— Altimeter, airspeed indicator, and vertical speed indicator.

In addition to the attitude indicator, the altimeter, airspeed indicator, and vertical speed indicator provide pitch information. (PLT186) — FAA-H-8083-15

Answer (A) is incorrect because the vertical speed indicator and airspeed indicator also provide pitch information. Answer (B) is incorrect because the airspeed indicator also provides pitch information.

Answers

| 4863 [C] | 4865 [C] | 4866 [B] | 4867 [A] | 4869 [C] |

MCI

4871. Which instrument provides the most pertinent information (primary) for pitch control in straight-and-level flight?

A— Attitude indicator.
B— Airspeed indicator.
C— Altimeter.

The primary instruments in straight-and-level flight are:

Primary Pitch — Altimeter
Primary Bank — Heading Indicator
Primary Power — Airspeed Indicator

(PLT336) — FAA-H-8083-15

Answer (A) is incorrect because the attitude indicator is the supporting pitch instrument in straight-and-level flight. Answer (B) is incorrect because the airspeed indicator is the primary power instrument in straight-and-level flight.

MCI

4872. Which instruments are considered to be supporting instruments for pitch during change of airspeed in a level turn?

A— Airspeed indicator and VSI.
B— Altimeter and attitude indicator.
C— Attitude indicator and VSI.

The attitude indicator and the vertical speed indicator are supporting instruments for pitch during change of airspeed in a level turn. See the figure that follows. (PLT186) — FAA-H-8083-15

Answer (A) is incorrect because the airspeed indicator is a supporting power instrument during a change of airspeed in a level turn. It then becomes the primary power instrument as the desired airspeed is obtained. Answer (B) is incorrect because the altimeter is the primary (not secondary) instrument for pitch in level flight.

MCI

4873-1. If an airplane is in an unusual flight attitude and the attitude indicator has exceeded its limits, which instruments should be relied on to determine pitch attitude before starting recovery?

A— Turn indicator and VSI.
B— Airspeed and altimeter.
C— VSI and airspeed to detect approaching V_{S1} or V_{MO}.

As soon as the unusual attitude is detected, the recovery should be initiated primarily by reference to the airspeed indicator (for pitch attitude), altimeter (for pitch attitude), vertical-speed indicator, and turn coordinator. (PLT297) — FAA-H-8083-15

Answer (A) is incorrect because the turn coordinator does not provide information about pitch attitude. Answer (C) is incorrect because the VSI is not as reliable as the altimeter in determining a climb or descent.

MCI

4873-2. If a helicopter is in an unusual flight attitude and the attitude indicator has exceeded its limits, which instruments should be relied on to determine pitch attitude before starting recovery?

A— Turn indicator and VSI.
B— Airspeed, VSI and altimeter.
C— VSI and airspeed to detect approaching V_{S1} or V_{MO}.

To recover from an unusual attitude, correct bank-and-pitch attitude, and adjust power as necessary. Pitch attitude should be corrected by reference to the altimeter, airspeed indicator, vertical speed indicator, and attitude indicator. (PLT297) — FAA-H-8083-15

MCI

4874. Which instrument is considered primary for power as the airspeed reaches the desired value during change of airspeed in a level turn?

A— Airspeed indicator.
B— Attitude indicator.
C— Altimeter.

The manifold pressure gauge (or tachometer) is primary for power control while the airspeed is changing in a level turn. As the airspeed approaches the new indication, the airspeed indicator becomes primary for power control. (PLT185) — FAA-H-8083-15

Answer (B) is incorrect because the attitude indicator is a supporting pitch and bank instrument in this scenario. Answer (C) is incorrect because the altimeter is a primary pitch instrument in this scenario.

Answers

| 4871 | [C] | 4872 | [C] | 4873-1 | [B] | 4873-2 | [B] | 4874 | [A] |

MCI

4875-1. Which is the correct sequence for recovery from a spiraling, nose-low, increasing airspeed, unusual flight attitude?

A— Increase pitch attitude, reduce power, and level wings.

B— Reduce power, correct the bank attitude, and raise the nose to a level attitude.

C— Reduce power, raise the nose to level attitude, and correct the bank attitude.

Reduce power to prevent excessive airspeed and loss of altitude, correct the bank attitude with coordinated aileron and rudder pressure to straight flight by referring to the turn coordinator. Raise the nose to level-flight attitude by smooth back-elevator pressure. (PLT297) — FAA-H-8083-15

Answer (A) is incorrect because power should be decreased first and then wings leveled. Answer (C) is incorrect because the wings should be level before the nose is pulled up, in order to minimize the effects of an excessive load factor.

MCI

4875-2. Which is the correct sequence for recovery from a spiraling, nose low, increasing airspeed, unusual flight attitude?

A— Increase pitch attitude, reduce power, and level wings.

B— Correct the bank attitude, raise the nose to a level attitude and reduce power.

C— Reduce power, raise the nose to level attitude, and correct the bank attitude.

To recover from an usual attitude, correct bank-and-pitch attitude, and adjust power as necessary. (PLT297) — FAA-H-8083-15

MCI

4876. Which instruments should be used to make a pitch correction when you have deviated from your assigned altitude?

A— Altimeter and VSI.

B— Manifold pressure gauge and VSI.

C— Attitude indicator, altimeter, and VSI.

The pitch instruments are the attitude indicator, the altimeter, the vertical-speed indicator and the airspeed indicator. When a pitch error is detected, corrective action should be taken promptly, but with light control pressures. (PLT186) — FAA-H-8083-15

Answer (A) is incorrect because an attitude indicator would also be used to make a pitch correction. Answer (B) is incorrect because the manifold pressure gauge is used as a power instrument (not pitch).

MCI

4878-2. During standard-rate turns, which instrument is considered "primary" for bank?

A— Heading indicator.

B— Turn and slip indicator or turn coordinator.

C— Attitude indicator.

On the roll-in, use the attitude indicator to establish the approximate angle of bank, then check the turn coordinator's miniature aircraft for a standard-rate turn indication. Maintain the bank for this rate of turn, using the turn coordinator's miniature aircraft as the primary bank reference and the attitude indicator as the supporting bank instrument. (PLT187) — FAA-H-8083-15

MCI

4882. Prior to starting an engine, you should check the turn-and-slip indicator to determine if the

A— needle indication properly corresponds to the angle of the wings or rotors with the horizon.

B— needle is approximately centered and the tube is full of fluid.

C— ball will move freely from one end of the tube to the other when the aircraft is rocked.

The following are items that should be checked before starting the engine(s):

1. *Check turn-and-slip indicator and magnetic compass for fluid level (should be full).*

2. *If instruments are electrical, turn on and listen for any unusual or irregular mechanical noise.*

3. *Check instruments for poor condition, mounting, marking, broken or loose knobs. Also check the power-off indications of the instrument pointers and warning flags.*

(PLT187) — FAA-H-8083-15

Answer (A) is incorrect because the needle is related to rate and direction of turn (not wings or rotors). Answer (C) is incorrect because the ball is checked during taxi and it is not necessary to rock the aircraft.

MCI

4883. What indications should you observe on the turn-and-slip indicator during taxi?

A— The ball moves freely opposite the turn, and the needle deflects in the direction of the turn.

B— The needle deflects in the direction of the turn, but the ball remains centered.

C— The ball deflects opposite the turn, but the needle remains centered.

Answers

| 4875-1 [B] | 4875-2 [B] | 4876 [C] | 4878-2 [B] | 4882 [B] | 4883 [A] |

You should observe the following on the turn-and-slip indicator during taxi:

1. Check and ensure the turn needle indicates proper direction of turn.

2. Check the ball for freedom of movement in the glass tube. Centrifugal force causes the ball to move to the outside of the turn.

(PLT187) — FAA-H-8083-15

Answer (B) is incorrect because the ball will move opposite to the direction of the turn. Answer (C) is incorrect because the needle moves in the direction of the turn.

MCI
4899. Conditions that determine the pitch attitude required to maintain level flight are

A— airspeed, air density, wing design, and angle of attack.
B— flightpath, wind velocity, and angle of attack.
C— relative wind, pressure altitude, and vertical lift component.

Factors that affect the attitude in maintaining level flight include airspeed, air density, wing design, and angle of attack. (PLT186) — FAA-H-8083-15

Answer (B) is incorrect because flight path and wind velocity do not determine pitch attitude. Answer (C) is incorrect because relative wind, pressure altitude, and vertical lift component do not determine the pitch attitude.

MCI
4900. Errors in both pitch and bank indication on an attitude indicator are usually at a maximum as the aircraft rolls out of a

A— 180° turn.
B— 270° turn.
C— 360° turn.

Errors in both pitch and bank indications occur during normal coordinated turns. These errors are caused by the movement of the pendulous vanes by centrifugal force, resulting in the precession of the gyro towards the inside of the turn. The error is greatest in a 180° steep turn. (PLT278) — FAA-H-8083-15

MCI
4904. If a standard rate turn is maintained, how much time would be required to turn to the left from a heading of 090° to a heading of 300°?

A— 30 seconds.
B— 40 seconds.
C— 50 seconds.

A standard rate turn is one during which the heading changes 3° per second. A turn to the left from 090° to 300° is a total turn of 150°. At a turn rate of 3° each second, this turn would require 150/3 or 50 seconds. (PLT187) — FAA-H-8083-15

MCI
4905. If a half-standard rate turn is maintained, how long would it take to turn 135°?

A— 1 minute.
B— 1 minute 20 seconds.
C— 1 minute 30 seconds.

A standard rate turn is one during which the heading changes 3° per second. In this case, the aircraft is turning one-half that rate, or 1.5° per second. Therefore, a turn of 135° would require 135/1.5 or 90 seconds (1 minute 30 seconds). (PLT187) — FAA-H-8083-15

MCI
4906. Approximately what percent of the indicated vertical speed should be used to determine the number of feet to lead the level-off from a climb to a specific altitude?

A— 10 percent.
B— 20 percent.
C— 25 percent.

The amount of lead varies with rate of climb and pilot technique. An effective practice is to lead the altitude by 10 percent of the vertical speed shown (500 fpm/50-foot lead—1,000 fpm/100-foot lead). (PLT185) — FAA-H-8083-15

Answers

| 4899 [A] | 4900 [A] | 4904 [C] | 4905 [C] | 4906 [A] |

MCI

4907. To level off from a descent to a specific altitude, the pilot should lead the level-off by approximately

A— 10 percent of the vertical speed.
B— 30 percent of the vertical speed.
C— 50 percent of the vertical speed.

The level-off from a descent at descent airspeed must be started before you reach the desired altitude. The amount of lead depends upon the rate of descent and control technique. With too little lead, you will tend to overshoot the selected altitude, unless your technique is rapid. An effective practice is to lead the altitude by 10 percent of the vertical speed shown. Assuming a 500-fpm rate of descent, lead the desired altitude by approximately 50 feet. (PLT185) — FAA-H-8083-15

MCI

4920. For maintaining level flight at constant thrust, which instrument would be the least appropriate for determining the need for a pitch change?

A— Altimeter.
B— VSI.
C— Attitude indicator.

The attitude indicator would be the least appropriate instrument for determining the need for a pitch change in level flight at constant thrust. Until level flight, as indicated by the attitude indicator, is identified and established by reference to the altimeter and VSI, there is no way of knowing if it is truly level flight. With constant thrust, any change in the altimeter or VSI indications shows a need for a pitch change. (PLT278) — FAA-H-8083-15

MCI

4921. The displacement of a turn coordinator during a coordinated turn will

A— indicate the angle of bank.
B— remain constant for a given bank regardless of airspeed.
C— increase as angle of bank increases.

The miniature aircraft of the turn coordinator displays only rate-of-roll and rate-of-turn. It does not directly display the bank angle of the aircraft. The displacement of a turn coordinator increases as angle of bank increases. (PLT187) — FAA-H-8083-15

Answer (A) is incorrect because the angle of bank is indirectly shown. Answer (B) is incorrect because the rate-of-turn varies with airspeed for any given bank angle, therefore the displacement of the turn coordinator will change with a change in airspeed.

MCI

4924. To enter a constant-airspeed descent from level-cruising flight, and maintain cruising airspeed, the pilot should

A— first adjust the pitch attitude to a descent using the attitude indicator as a reference, then adjust the power to maintain the cruising airspeed.
B— first reduce power, then adjust the pitch using the attitude indicator as a reference to establish a specific rate on the VSI.
C— simultaneously reduce power and adjust the pitch using the attitude indicator as a reference to maintain the cruising airspeed.

The following method for entering descents is effective either with or without an attitude indicator:

1. *Reduce airspeed to your selected descent airspeed while maintaining straight-and-level flight, then make a further reduction in power (to a predetermined setting); and*

2. *As the power is adjusted, simultaneously lower the nose to maintain constant airspeed, and trim off control pressures.*

(PLT125) — FAA-H-8083-15

Answer (A) is incorrect because adjusting the pitch attitude first will result in an increased airspeed. Answer (B) is incorrect because adjusting the power first will result in a decreased airspeed, and the airspeed indicator (not VSI) is used to maintain a constant airspeed.

MCI

4925. To level off at an airspeed higher than the descent speed, the addition of power should be made, assuming a 500 FPM rate of descent, at approximately

A— 50 to 100 feet above the desired altitude.
B— 100 to 150 feet above the desired altitude.
C— 150 to 200 feet above the desired altitude.

The level-off from a descent must be started before you reach the desired altitude. The amount of lead depends upon the rate of descent and control technique. Assuming a 500-fpm rate of descent, lead the altitude by 100–150 feet for level-off at an airspeed higher than descending speed. At the lead point, add power to the appropriate level flight cruise setting. (PLT125) — FAA-H-8083-15

Answers

| 4907 [A] | 4920 [C] | 4921 [C] | 4924 [C] | 4925 [B] |

MCI

4926. To level off from a descent maintaining the descending airspeed, the pilot should lead the desired altitude by approximately

A— 20 feet.
B— 50 feet.
C— 60 feet.

To level-off from a descent at descent airspeed, lead the desired altitude by approximately 50 feet, simultaneously adjusting the pitch attitude to level flight and adding power to a setting that will hold the airspeed constant. (PLT185) — FAA-H-8083-15

MCI

4927. During recoveries from unusual attitudes, level flight is attained the instant

A— the horizon bar on the attitude indicator is exactly overlapped with the miniature airplane.
B— a zero rate of climb is indicated on the VSI.
C— the altimeter and airspeed needles stop prior to reversing their direction of movement.

A level-pitch attitude is indicated by the reversal and stabilization of the airspeed indicator and altimeter needles. (PLT297) — FAA-H-8083-15

Answer (A) is incorrect because the precessing tendency of the attitude indicator makes it unreliable after recovery from an unusual attitude. Answer (B) is incorrect because the vertical speed indicator has a short lag time which does not allow it to show level flight at the instant it is achieved.

MCI

4604. What indication should be observed on a turn coordinator during a right turn while taxiing?

A— The miniature aircraft will show a turn to the left and the ball remains centered.
B— The miniature aircraft will show a turn to the right and the ball moves to the left.
C— Both the miniature aircraft and the ball will remain centered.

When an aircraft makes a taxiing right turn, the turn coordinator will show the same indications as a level, no-bank right turn in flight. Those indications are: The miniature airplane will show a right turn (the direction of turn and rate) while the ball will show an uncoordinated turn (a skid), by moving to the left. (PLT118) — FAA-H-8083-15

Answer (A) is incorrect because the ball would move to the outside of the turn due to centrifugal force. Answer (C) is incorrect because the miniature aircraft will show a turn to the right and the ball will move to the left.

MCI

7098-1. Which instrument provides the most pertinent information (primary) for pitch control in straight-and-level flight?

A— Altimeter.
B— Attitude indicator.
C— Airspeed indicator.

In straight-and-level flight, the altimeter is the primary instrument for pitch control. It will give a direct indication of a need for pitch control. (PLT336) — FAA-H-8083-15

MCI

7099-1. What instrument(s) is (are) supporting bank instrument(s) when entering a constant airspeed climb from straight-and-level flight?

A— Heading indicator.
B— Turn coordinator and heading indicator.
C— Attitude indicator and turn coordinator.

When entering a constant airspeed climb from straight-and-level flight, the attitude indicator is the primary pitch and supporting bank indicator. The heading indicator is the primary bank indicator and the turn coordinator is the supporting bank indicator. (PLT185) — FAA-H-8083-15

MCI

7100-1. Which instruments are considered primary and supporting for bank, respectively, when establishing a level standard rate turn?

A— Turn coordinator and heading indicator.
B— Attitude indicator and turn coordinator.
C— Turn coordinator and attitude indicator.

When establishing a level, standard-rate turn, the primary bank instrument for the beginning of the turn is the attitude indicator, and after the turn is established, the primary bank instrument is the turn coordinator. (PLT186) — FAA-H-8083-15

Answers

| 4926 | [B] | 4927 | [C] | 4604 | [B] | 7098-1 | [A] | 7099-1 | [C] | 7100-1 | [B] |

MCI

7102-1. Which is the correct sequence for recovery from a spiraling, nose-low increasing airspeed, unusual flight attitude?

A— Increase pitch attitude, reduce power, and level wings.

B— Reduce power, correct bank attitude, and raise nose to a level attitude.

C— Reduce power, raise nose to a level attitude, and correct bank attitude.

If the airspeed is increasing or is too high, reduce power to prevent excessive airspeed and loss of altitude. Correct the bank attitude with coordinated aileron and rudder pressure to straight flight by referring to the turn coordinator. Raise the nose to level flight attitude by smooth back elevator pressure. All components of control should be changed simultaneously for a smooth, proficient recovery. (PLT208) — FAA-H-8083-15

MCI

7101-1. If an airplane is in an unusual flight attitude and the attitude indicator has exceeded its limits, which instruments should be relied upon to determine pitch attitude before recovery?

A— Airspeed indicator and altimeter.

B— Turn indicator and vertical speed indicator.

C— Vertical speed indicator and airspeed indicator.

In an unusual attitude, it is possible for the attitude indicator to exceed its limits and become unreliable. The airspeed indicator and altimeter can be relied upon to give pitch indication to initiate a recovery from an unusual flight attitude. (PLT208) — FAA-H-8083-15

Helicopter Operation

Helicopter Controls

The **collective pitch control** simultaneously changes the pitch of all of the main rotor blades. It is connected through appropriate linkage to the throttle cam, so that the engine power is automatically increased as the collective pitch lever is raised and decreased as it is lowered. The collective pitch control should be used:

1. To correct for loss of lift during level turns at altitude.

2. To maintain desired engine power.

3. To correct a high rotor RPM during autorotations from altitude.

When taxiing a helicopter, the collective pitch controls starting, stopping, and the rate of taxi speed. The higher the collective pitch, the faster will be the taxi speed.

As collective pitch is increased to check the descent in a flare, autorotative descent, and landing, additional right pedal is required to maintain heading due to the reduction in rotor RPM and the resulting reduced effect of the tail rotor.

During a powered approach to a hover, the angle of descent is primarily controlled by collective pitch, the airspeed (and the ground speed) by the cyclic control, and heading on final approach is maintained with pedal control.

As you accelerate to effective **translational lift**, the helicopter will begin to climb, and the nose will tend to rise due to increased lift. At this point, adjust collective pitch to obtain normal climb power, and apply enough forward cyclic stick to overcome the tendency of the nose to rise.

During crosswind taxi, the cyclic stick should be held into the wind a sufficient amount to eliminate any drift.

Answers

7102-1 [B]   7101-1 [A]

If a helicopter experiences complete power failure during cruising flight, the collective pitch control should be lowered to reduce the pitch on all main rotor blades so that the proper rotor RPM can be maintained.

In a running takeoff in a crosswind, the ground track of the helicopter is maintained with cyclic control, and the heading is maintained with the antitorque pedals until a climb is established. **Antitorque pedals** are used to maintain heading during crosswind takeoffs and approaches, and right antitorque pedal is used when entering autorotation to maintain heading after the torque is lost.

If the antitorque system fails during hovering flight, quick action must be taken by the pilot. The throttle should be closed immediately without varying the collective pitch position to eliminate the turning effect. Simultaneously, the cyclic stick should be used to stop all sideward or rearward movements and place the helicopter in the landing attitude prior to touchdown. From this point, the procedure for a **hovering autorotation** should be followed. If the antitorque system fails during cruising flight, and a powered approach is commenced, the helicopter can be prevented from yawing to the right just prior to touchdown by decreasing the throttle to decrease the torque effect.

A slip occurs when a helicopter slides sideways toward the center of the turn. It is caused by an insufficient amount of pedal in the direction of turn (or too much in the direction opposite the turn) in relation to the amount of collective stick (power) used. In other words, if improper pedal pressure is held to keep the nose from following the turn, the helicopter will slip sideways toward the center of the turn. In a right descending turn, if insufficient right pedal is used to compensate for the decreased torque effect, a slip will result.

RTC

7054. During a climbing turn, the engine RPM is at the desired setting, but the manifold pressure is higher than desired. To maintain the desired engine RPM and correct the manifold pressure, what initial control action should be taken?

A— Decrease the collective pitch only.
B— Decrease the collective pitch and decrease the throttle.
C— Decrease the collective pitch and increase the throttle.

To reduce the manifold pressure and hold a constant RPM, decrease the collective pitch, which is the primary manifold pressure control. When the collective pitch is lowered, the drag on the rotor decreases and the RPM increases, which requires that you then decrease the throttle to bring the RPM back to the desired value. (PLT343) — FAA-H-8083-21

RTC

7055-1. The collective pitch control should be used to

1. correct for loss of lift during level turns at altitude.
2. maintain desired engine power.
3. correct a high rotor RPM during autorotations from altitude.

The correct statement(s) is(are)

A— 2.
B— 1 and 2.
C— 1, 2, and 3.

The collective pitch control simultaneously changes the pitch of all of the main rotor blades. It is connected through appropriate linkage to the throttle cam, so the engine power is automatically increased as the collective pitch lever is raised and decreased as it is lowered. The collective pitch control should be used:

1. To correct for loss of lift during level turns at altitude.

2. To maintain desired engine power.

3. To correct a high rotor RPM during autorotations from altitude.

(PLT470) — FAA-H-8083-21

Answers

7054   [B]   7055-1   [C]

RTC
7055-2. Large or unnecessary cyclic movements can, under certain conditions, cause a

A— flexing of the main rotor blades and possible damage to the tail rotor system.
B— change in the lift component and a partial loss of lift.
C— helicopter to be subjected to coriolis effect.

Avoid large or unnecessary movements of the cyclic control while at a hover. Such movements of the cyclic control can, under certain conditions, cause sufficient loss of lift to make the helicopter settle to the surface. (PLT470) — FAA-H-8083-21

RTC
7070. To taxi on the surface in a safe and efficient manner, helicopter pilots should use the

A— cyclic pitch to control starting, taxi speed, and stopping.
B— collective pitch to control starting, taxi speed, and stopping.
C— cyclic pitch to maintain heading during crosswind conditions.

When taxiing a helicopter on the surface, the collective pitch controls starting, stopping, and the rate of taxi speed. The higher the collective pitch, the faster will be the taxi speed. (PLT112) — FAA-H-8083-21

RTC
7075. After attaining effective translational lift during a normal takeoff, additional forward cyclic is required as the airspeed increases. Why is this action required?

A— To counteract gyroscopic precession.
B— To counteract the increase in lift which would result in the nose rising.
C— To counteract the dissymmetry of lift which causes the helicopter to roll to the left.

As you accelerate to effective translational lift, the helicopter will begin to climb, and the nose will tend to rise due to increased lift. At this point, adjust collective pitch to obtain normal climb power, and apply enough forward cyclic stick to overcome the tendency of the nose to rise. (PLT242) — FAA-H-8083-21

RTC
7076. During a normal approach to a hover, the cyclic pitch control is used primarily to

A— maintain heading.
B— control rate of closure.
C— control angle of descent.

During a normal approach to a hover, the angle of descent is primarily controlled by collective pitch. The airspeed (the rate of closure) is primarily controlled by the cyclic control, and heading on final approach is maintained with pedal control. (PLT112) — FAA-H-8083-21

RTC
7077. Which statement best describes the function of the controls during a powered approach to hover?

A— Collective pitch primarily controls angle of descent; cyclic pitch primarily controls groundspeed.
B— Cyclic pitch primarily controls angle of descent and groundspeed; collective pitch primarily controls rate of descent.
C— Collective pitch primarily controls angle of descent; rotor RPM primarily controls rate of descent; cyclic pitch primarily controls groundspeed.

During a powered approach to a hover, the angle of descent is primarily controlled by collective pitch, the airspeed (and the ground speed) is primarily controlled by the cyclic control, and heading on final approach is maintained with pedal control. (PLT112) — FAA-H-8083-21

RTC
7080. During a takeoff in a crosswind, which describes proper control technique?

A— Pedals control both heading and direction of movement.
B— Heading is maintained with cyclic; direction of movement (groundpath or track) is maintained with pedals.
C— Heading is maintained with pedals; direction of movement (groundpath or track) is maintained with cyclic.

In a crosswind takeoff, the ground track of the helicopter is maintained with cyclic control, and the heading is maintained with the antitorque pedals until a climb is established. (PLT486) — FAA-H-8083-21

Answers

7055-2 [B]	7070 [B]	7075 [B]	7076 [B]	7077 [A]	7080 [C]

RTC

7071. To taxi on the surface in a safe efficient manner, one should use the cyclic pitch to

A— control taxi speed.
B— maintain heading during crosswind conditions.
C— correct for drift during crosswind conditions.

During crosswind taxi, the cyclic stick should be held into the wind a sufficient amount to correct for drift. (PLT112) — FAA-H-8083-21

RTC

7056. The antitorque pedals should be used to

1. maintain heading during cruise flight.
2. correct for loss of torque during autorotations.
3. maintain heading during crosswind takeoffs and approaches.

The correct statements are

A— 2 and 3.
B— 1 and 3.
C— 1, 2, and 3.

The right antitorque pedal is used when entering autorotation to maintain heading after the torque is lost. Antitorque pedals are also used to maintain heading during crosswind takeoffs and approaches. (PLT346) — FAA-H-8083-21

RTC

7068-1. What action should be taken if the antitorque system fails during forward flight?

A— Immediately and smoothly apply aft cyclic.
B— Enter a normal autorotation by lowering the collective and rolling off the throttle.
C— Immediately apply additional throttle while slightly lowering the collective.

If the failure occurs in forward flight, enter a normal autorotation by lowering the collective and rolling off the throttle. (PLT208) — FAA-H-8083-21

RTC

7068-2. Cyclic control movement following anti-torque system failure in flight should be

A— rearward in order to control downward pitching of the nose.
B— to the left in order to counteract right yawing tendency.
C— kept to a minimum until pitching moment stops.

Cyclic control movements should be kept to a minimum until all pitching subsides. Avoid abrupt rearward movements of the cyclic stick. (PLT208) — FAA-H-8083-21

RTC

7069. What corrective action should be taken if the antitorque system should fail while at a hover?

A— Close the throttle and autorotate.
B— Apply left pedal as necessary to stop the torque-induced turn to the right.
C— Lower the collective pitch to reduce the load on the main rotor blades.

If the antitorque system fails while in a hover, the throttle should be closed immediately without varying the collective pitch position to eliminate the turning effect. Simultaneously, the cyclic stick should be used to stop all sideward or rearward movements and place the helicopter in the landing attitude. (PLT208) — FAA-H-8083-21

RTC

7074. Choose the most correct statement pertaining to slips and skids during helicopter flight.

A— A skid occurs when too much pedal is applied in the direction opposite the turn.
B— A skid occurs when the rate of turn is too slow for the amount of bank being used.
C— In a right descending turn, if insufficient right pedal is applied to compensate for the decreased torque effect, a slip will result.

A slip occurs when a helicopter slides sideways toward the center of the turn. If improper pedal pressure is used to keep the nose from following the turn, the helicopter will slip sideways toward the center of the turn. In a right descending turn, a slip will result if too little right pedal is applied to compensate for the decreased torque effect. (PLT112) — FAA-H-8083-21

Answers

7071　[C]	7056　[A]	7068-1　[B]	7068-2　[C]	7069　[A]	7074　[C]

Takeoffs and Hovering

A downwind turn close to the ground made immediately after takeoff increases the hazards involved, if an emergency landing should become necessary.

Tall grass tends to disperse or absorb the ground effect, and more power is required to hover over tall grass, especially in zero wind conditions. Takeoff from tall grass may be difficult.

RTC
7067. Which situation would require the highest power setting to hover?

A— Headed downwind in moderate windspeeds.
B— Headed crosswind in moderate windspeeds.
C— Over tall grass in zero wind conditions.

Tall grass tends to disperse or absorb the ground effect, and more power is needed to hover over tall grass, especially in zero wind conditions. Takeoff from tall grass may be difficult. (PLT268) — FAA-H-8083-21

Autorotation

The pilot's primary control of the rate of descent in **autorotation** is the airspeed. The rate of descent is high at zero airspeed and decreases to a minimum somewhere in the neighborhood of 50 to 60 miles per hour, depending upon the particular helicopter. If the glide is too flat, the airspeed is too high, and this can be corrected by increasing the rotor lift by applying aft cyclic pressure.

Forward speed during autorotative descent permits a pilot to incline the rotor disk rearward, thus causing a flare. The additional induced lift created by the greater volume of air flowing through the rotor momentarily checks forward speed as well as descent.

When a helicopter is flared during an autorotative landing, the rotor RPM momentarily increases because of the additional volume of air flowing upward through the rotor disc. This air increases the angle of attack of the blades and increases their lift. The horizontal component of this increased lift turns the rotor at a higher speed.

As the forward speed and descent rate near zero, the upward flow of air practically ceases, and the rotor RPM again decreases. The helicopter settles at a slightly increased rate, but with reduced forward speed. As the forward speed and descent rate decrease, the amount of air flowing upward through the rotor decreases, and the rotor RPM decreases.

The specific airspeed for autorotations is established for each type of helicopter on the basis of average weather and wind conditions and normal loading. When the helicopter is operated with excessive loads in high density altitude or strong gusty wind conditions, best performance is achieved from a slightly increased airspeed in the descent. By increasing the airspeed in these conditions, a pilot can achieve approximately the same glide angle in any set of circumstances and can estimate the touchdown point.

When making turns during an autorotative descent, generally use cyclic control only. Use of anti-torque pedals to assist or speed the turn causes loss of airspeed, downward pitching of the nose, and an increased sink rate.

RPM is most likely to increase above the maximum limit during a turn because of the increased back cyclic pressure, which induces a greater airflow through the rotor system. The use of excessive right pedal pressure will require additional back cyclic pressure, which will increase the rotor RPM.

Answers

7067   [C]

RTC

6617-1. Can the tail rotor produce thrust to the left?

A— No; only thrust to the right can be produced, causing tail movement to the left.

B— Yes; primarily so that hovering turns can be accomplished to the right.

C— Yes; primarily to counteract drag of the transmission during autorotation.

The capability for tail rotors to produce thrust to the left (negative pitch angle) is necessary because, during autorotation, the drag of the transmission tends to yaw the nose to the left. (PLT470) — FAA-H-8083-21

RTC

6617-2. Feathering of rotor blades means the angular change of the blades during a cycle of revolution in order to

A— equalize lift on the opposite (retreating and advancing blade) side of the disc.

B— equalize lift on upwind and downwind sides of the rotor disc.

C— counteract gyroscopic precession.

As the pitch angle of the rotor blades is changed, the angle of attack of each blade will also be changed. (PLT470) — FAA-H-8083-21

RTC

6617-3. During a cycle of revolution of the main rotor system, movement of the cyclic control in a helicopter changes the angle of

A— attack of the blades individually.

B— attack of the blades between the root end and the tip.

C— incidence of the blades individually.

When the cyclic stick is moved forward, the rotor disc tilts forward; when the cyclic is moved aft, the rotor disc tilts aft. Any increase in pitch angle increases the angle of attack; any decrease in pitch angle decreases the angle of attack. (PLT470) — FAA-H-8083-21

RTC

6617-4. The ability of a rotor blade to rotate about its spanwise axis is called

A— flapping.

B— feathering.

C— dragging or hunting.

The blades of a fully articulated rotor can also be feathered, that is, rotated about their spanwise axis. Feathering means the automatic and periodic changing of the pitch angle of the rotor blades. (PLT470) — FAA-H-8083-21

RTC

6621-1. The rotor RPM may momentarily increase during the flare portion of a flare-type autorotation. This increase in rotor RPM is due to

A— an increased downwash velocity.

B— a decrease in rotor drag brought about by a lack of forward motion.

C— the additional lift derived from the increased angle of attack of the main rotor disc.

When a helicopter is flared during an autorotative landing, the rotor RPM momentarily increases because of the additional volume of air flowing upward through the rotor disc. This air increases the angle of attack of the blades and increases their lift. (PLT470) — FAA-H-8083-21

RTC

7004. On a power-off final approach, a pilot establishes a glide attitude which is too flat. The proper recovery procedure for the subsequent high rate of descent is to

A— increase rotor lift by applying aft cyclic pressure.

B— increase power, and if altitude permits, lower the nose.

C— lower the nose immediately, but do not increase the power since this will again raise the nose.

The pilot's primary control of the rate of descent in autorotation is the airspeed. If the glide is too flat, the airspeed is too high, and this can be corrected by increasing the rotor lift by applying aft cyclic pressure. (PLT170) — FAA-H-8083-3

Answers

6617-1 [C]	6617-2 [A]	6617-3 [B]	6617-4 [B]	6621-1 [C]	7004 [A]

RTC
7088. Which is true about an autorotative descent?

A— Generally, only the cyclic control is used to make turns.
B— Collective pitch should be used to control rate of descent.
C— Rotor RPM will tend to decrease if a tight turn is made with a heavily loaded helicopter.

When making turns during an autorotative descent, generally use cyclic control only. Use of antitorque pedals to assist or speed the turn causes loss of airspeed and downward pitching of the nose, especially when the left pedal is used. When the autorotation is initiated, sufficient right pedal pressure should be used to maintain straight flight and prevent yawing to the left. The pressure should not be changed to assist the turn. (PLT470) — FAA-H-8083-21

RTC
7053. During the full-flare portion of a power-off landing, the rotor RPM tends to

A— increase initially.
B— decrease initially.
C— decrease during high density altitude days, and increase during low density altitude days.

Forward speed during autorotative descent permits a pilot to incline the rotor disk rearward, causing a flare. The additional induced lift created by the greater volume of air flowing through the rotor momentarily checks forward speed as well as descent. The greater volume of air flowing through the rotor disc initially increases the rotor RPM during the flare, but as the forward speed and descent rate near zero, the upward flow of air practically ceases, and the rotor RPM again decreases. (PLT170) — FAA-H-8083-21

RTC
7066. If complete power failure occurs while at cruising altitude, the collective pitch should be lowered, as necessary, to

A— uncouple the main rotor system from the engine.
B— engage the freewheeling unit so that proper rotor RPM can be maintained.
C— reduce the pitch on all main rotor blades so that proper rotor RPM can be maintained.

By immediately lowering collective pitch (which must be done in case of engine failure), lift and drag will be reduced and the helicopter will begin an immediate descent thus producing an upward flow of air through the rotor system. (PLT346) — FAA-H-8083-21

RTC
7078-1. When autorotating during high density altitude or strong gusty wind conditions, a slightly higher-than-normal airspeed is recommended because the

A— resulting slower rate of descent will allow more time for the pilot to estimate the touchdown point.
B— resulting glide angle will approximate that of a slightly reduced airspeed under conditions of light loads, low density altitude, or calm wind.
C— lower rotor speed will cause the rate of descent to approximate that of a slightly increased rotor speed under conditions of light loads, low density altitude, or calm wind.

When a helicopter is operated with excessive loads in high density altitude or strong gusty wind conditions, best performance is achieved from a slightly increased airspeed in the descent. By increasing the airspeed in these conditions, a pilot can achieve approximately the same glide angle used for a slightly reduced airspeed under conditions of light loads, low density altitude, or calm wind. This helps the pilot estimate the touchdown point. (PLT175) — FAA-H-8083-21

RTC
7078-2. Initially, collective pitch should be lowered in an autorotation in order to

A— maintain the desired angle of descent.
B— prevent an engine overspeed.
C— prevent loss of rotor RPM.

By immediately lowering collective pitch (which must be done in case of engine failure), lift and drag will be reduced, and the helicopter will begin an immediate descent, thus producing an upward flow of air through the rotor system. The impact of this upward flow of air on the rotor blades products a "ram" effect which provides sufficient thrust to maintain rotor RPM throughout the descent. (PLT175) — FAA-H-8083-21

Answers

7088 [A]   7053 [A]   7066 [C]   7078-1 [B]   7078-2 [C]

RTC
7089. When performing a touchdown autorotation, what action is most appropriate?

A— Anti-torque pedals should remain neutral after ground contact.
B— Skids should be in a longitudinally level attitude at touchdown.
C— Aft cyclic application after touchdown is desirable to decrease ground run.

As the helicopter approaches normal hovering altitude, maintain a landing attitude with cyclic control, maintain heading with pedals, apply sufficient collective pitch to cushion the touchdown, and be sure the helicopter is landing parallel to its direction of motion upon contact with the surface. (PLT470) — FAA-H-8083-21

RTC
7089-1. After coming to a complete stop following autorotation in a helicopter, what is the next step the pilot should take?

A— Raise the collective.
B— Lower the collective.
C— Apply aft cyclic.

Following autorotation, after touchdown and after the helicopter has come to a complete stop, lower the collective pitch to the full-down position. Do not try to stop the forward ground run with aft cyclic, as the main rotor blades can strike the tail boom. Rather, by lowering the collective slightly during the ground run, more weight is placed on the undercarriage, slowing the helicopter. (PLT470) — FAA-H-8083-21

RTC
7072. If excessive right pedal is applied during an autorotative turn to the right, the nose of the helicopter will tend to

A— pitch up and the rotor RPM will tend to increase.
B— pitch down and the rotor RPM will tend to increase.
C— pitch down and the rotor RPM will tend to decrease.

When making turns during an autorotative descent, generally use cyclic control only. Use of antitorque pedals to assist or speed the turn causes loss of airspeed and downward pitching of the nose. RPM will increase during a turn because the increased back cyclic pressure will cause a greater airflow through the rotor. The use of too much right pedal pressure will require additional back cyclic pressure, which will increase the rotor RPM. (PLT112) — FAA-H-8083-21

RTC
7073. Using right pedal to assist a right turn during an autorotative descent will probably result in what actions?

A— Pitchup of the nose, increase in rotor RPM, decrease in sink rate, and decrease in indicated airspeed.
B— Pitchdown of the nose, increase in the rotor RPM, increase in sink rate, and decrease in indicated airspeed.
C— Pitchdown of the nose, decrease in the rotor RPM, increase in sink rate, and increase in indicated airspeed.

When making turns during an autorotative descent, generally use cyclic control only. Use of antitorque pedals to assist or speed the turn causes loss of indicated airspeed, downward pitching of the nose, and an increased sink rate. RPM will increase during the turn because the increased back cyclic pressure causes more air to flow through the rotor. (PLT112) — FAA-H-8083-21

RTC
7079. During a flare autorotative descent and landing, additional right pedal is required to maintain heading after initial collective pitch is applied. This action is necessary because of

A— gyroscopic precession.
B— the reduction in rotor RPM.
C— translating tendency of helicopters during autorotation.

As collective pitch is increased to check the descent in a flare autorotative descent and landing, additional right pedal is required to maintain heading due to the reduction in rotor RPM and the resulting reduced effect of the tail rotor. (PLT125) — FAA-H-8083-21

Answers

| 7089 [B] | 7089-1 [B] | 7072 [B] | 7073 [B] | 7079 [B] |

Retreating Blade Stall

Retreating blade stall in a helicopter rotor is caused by an excessive angle of attack on the retreating blade. When vibrations from a blade stall are first felt, decrease the angle of attack. Do this by reducing the collective pitch, increasing the rotor RPM, and reducing the forward airspeed. A retreating blade stall is indicated by:

1. Abnormal 2-per-revolution vibration in a 2-blade rotor or 3-per-revolution in a 3-blade rotor.

2. Nose pitch up.

3. Tendency of the helicopter to roll.

RTC

6833-1. (Refer to Figure 37.) Blade tip stall is most likely to occur in what area?

A— 4 at low forward airspeed.
B— 2 at high forward airspeed.
C— 1 at high forward airspeed.

The airflow over the retreating blade slows down as forward airspeed of the helicopter increases. Blade stall occurs during powered flight at the tip of the retreating blade. (PLT477) — FAA-H-8083-21

RTC

7060. At the onset of retreating blade stall vibration, the pilot should

A— restrict use of all controls until vibration dissipates.
B— lower collective pitch, increase rotor RPM, reduce forward airspeed, and minimize maneuvering.
C— lower collective pitch, decrease rotor RPM, increase forward airspeed, and minimize maneuvering.

Retreating blade stall in a helicopter rotor is caused by an excessive angle of attack on the retreating blade. When vibrations from a blade stall are first felt, decrease the angle of attack by reducing the collective pitch, increasing the rotor RPM, reducing the forward airspeed, and minimize maneuvering. (PLT472) — FAA-H-8083-21

RTC

7057. What are the major indications of an incipient retreating blade stall situation, in order of occurrence?

A— Low-frequency vibration, pitchup of the nose, and a tendency for the aircraft to roll.
B— High-frequency vibration, pitchdown of the nose, and a tendency for the aircraft to roll.
C— Slow pitchup of the nose, high-frequency vibration, and a tendency for the aircraft to roll.

A retreating blade stall is indicated by:

1. *Abnormal 2-per-revolution vibration in a 2-blade rotor or 3-per-revolution in a 3-blade rotor*

2. *Nose pitch up*

3. *Tendency of the helicopter to roll*

(PLT470) — FAA-H-8083-21

RTC

7058. When operating at high forward airspeed, retreating blade stall is more likely to occur under conditions of

A— high gross weight, high RPM, and smooth air.
B— high gross weight, low RPM, and turbulent air.
C— low gross weight, high RPM, and high density altitude.

When operating at a high forward airspeed, a retreating blade stall is most likely to occur under conditions of:

1. *High gross weight*

2. *Low RPM*

3. *High density altitude*

4. *Steep or abrupt turns*

5. *Turbulent air*

(PLT470) — FAA-H-8083-21

Answers

6833-1   [C]   7060   [B]   7057   [A]   7058   [B]

RTC
7059. Which is true concerning retreating blade stall?

A— Aircraft will pitch up and roll to the right at the onset of the stall.

B— Nose of the aircraft will pitch down and may roll in either direction at the onset of the stall.

C— When operating at high forward airspeeds, turbulent air or steep and abrupt turns can cause a retreating blade stall.

The airflow over the retreating blade slows down as forward speed increases. The retreating blade must produce the same lift as the advancing blade. As airflow decreases, blade angle of attack must be increased to equalize lift causing the stall. (PLT470) — FAA-H-8083-21

Settling with Power

Settling with power is a helicopter operation in which the main rotor is operating in its own downwash. The flow of air through the center portion of the disk is upward, and the flow through the outer portion is downward.

A helicopter is most likely to enter a settling with power condition when the pilot is maintaining a forward airspeed of less than 10 MPH and a vertical or nearly vertical descent of at least 300 feet per minute. Recovery from settling with power can be accomplished by increasing the forward speed and/ or partially lowering the collective pitch.

RTC
7062. What action should be taken if ground resonance is encountered during a landing attempt?

A— Attempt to make a takeoff regardless of RPM situation.

B— Close throttle immediately and raise collective pitch to dampen vibrations.

C— Make an immediate takeoff if RPM is in proper range; otherwise, close throttle, and lower collective pitch.

Ground resonance occurs when the helicopter makes contact with the surface during landing. Corrective action would be to make an immediate takeoff if RPM is in proper range, otherwise close throttle and lower collective pitch. (PLT265) — FAA-H-8083-21

RTC
7063. The addition of power in a settling-with-power situation produces an

A— increase of airspeed.

B— even greater rate of descent.

C— increase in cyclic control effectiveness.

Addition of power will create an even greater rate of descent. This is described as settling in your downwash. (PLT264) — FAA-H-8083-21

RTC
7064. Recovery from settling with power should be initiated by

A— decreasing forward airspeed and/or partially raising the collective pitch.

B— increasing forward airspeed and/or partially lowering the collective pitch.

C— increasing forward airspeed and/or partially raising the collective pitch.

Recovery from settling with power can be accomplished by increasing the forward speed and/or partially lowering the collective pitch. (PLT264) — FAA-H-8083-21

RTC
7065. Under which situation is a helicopter most likely to enter the condition known as settling with power?

A— While maintaining altitude with a forward airspeed of less than 10 MPH.

B— While maintaining forward cruise airspeed with a rate of descent in excess of 300 feet per minute.

C— While maintaining a forward airspeed of less than 10 MPH with a rate of descent in excess of 300 feet per minute.

A helicopter is most likely to enter a settling with power condition when maintaining a forward airspeed of less than 10 MPH and a vertical or nearly vertical descent of at least 300 feet per minute. (PLT264) — FAA-H-8083-21

Answers

7059 [C]	7062 [C]	7063 [B]	7064 [B]	7065 [C]

Slope Operation

When making a slope landing with a helicopter, the **cyclic pitch control** should be used in the direction of the slope to hold the upwind skid against the slope, while the downslope skid is let down with collective pitch.

The steepness of the slope that can be used for a helicopter landing is determined by the amount of lateral cyclic stick travel available. Each make of helicopter generally has its own peculiar way of indicating to the pilot when lateral cyclic stick travel is about to run out, and a landing should not be attempted when the pilot is getting an indication that he/she is running out of lateral stick control.

As the upslope skid touches the ground during a slope landing, the cyclic stick should be applied in the direction of the slope to hold the skid against the slope. With the upslope skid against the slope, the downslope skid is lowered to the ground with the collective pitch.

RTC

7081. When making a slope landing, the cyclic pitch control should be used to

A— lower the downslope skid to the ground.
B— hold the upslope skid against the slope.
C— place the rotor disc parallel to the slope.

When making a slope landing with a helicopter, the cyclic pitch control should be used in the direction of the slope to hold the skid against the slope while the downslope skid is lowered with collective pitch. (PLT336) — FAA-H-8083-21

RTC

7082. The steepness of the slope on which a helicop-ter with skid-type landing gear can land is most dependent on

A— its gross weight.
B— the position of the CG.
C— the amount of lateral cyclic travel available.

The steepness of the slope that can be used for a helicopter landing is determined by the amount of lateral cyclic stick travel that is available. A landing should not be attempted when the pilot is getting an indication that he/she is running out of lateral stick control. (PLT336) — FAA-H-8083-21

RTC

7083. As the upslope skid touches the ground during a slope landing, the

A— cyclic pitch control should remain stationary to keep the aircraft from moving.
B— collective pitch control should be used to lower the downslope skid to the ground.
C— collective pitch should remain stationary and the cyclic pitch control should be used to lower the downslope skid to the ground.

As the upslope skid touches the ground during a slope landing, the cyclic stick should be applied in the direction of the slope to hold the skid against the slope, while the downslope skid is lowered to the ground with the collective pitch. (PLT336) — FAA-H-8083-21

Answers

7081   [B]   7082   [C]   7083   [B]

Rapid Decelerations

Although used primarily for coordination practice, decelerations can be used for a helicopter to make a quick stop in the air. The purpose of the maneuver is to maintain a constant altitude, heading, and RPM while slowing the helicopter to a desired ground speed. The rotor RPM will normally tend to increase during the entry and tend to decrease during the completion of the maneuver. Rapid decelerations should be practiced at an altitude high enough to permit a safe clearance between the tail rotor and the surface throughout the maneuver.

RTC

7085. Which statement pertaining to rapid decelerations is most accurate?

A— The primary purpose of this maneuver is to lose effective translational lift.
B— The rotor RPM will normally tend to increase during the entry and tend to decrease during the completion of the maneuver.
C— The nose of the helicopter will normally tend to yaw to the right during the entry and tend to yaw to the left during the completion of the maneuver.

The purpose of a rapid deceleration is to maintain a constant altitude, heading, and RPM while slowing the helicopter to a desired ground speed. The rotor RPM will normally tend to increase during the entry and tend to decrease during the completion of the maneuver. (PLT217) — FAA-H-8083-21

RTC

7086. If altitude is gained during a rapid deceleration, it is primarily because

A— the maneuver was initiated at too high an airspeed.
B— rotor RPM is allowed to increase too much as the collective pitch is lowered.
C— aft cyclic is increased too rapidly for the rate of decrease of the collective pitch.

A common error in a rapid deceleration is applying aft cyclic stick too rapidly initially, causing the helicopter to "balloon" (a sudden gain in altitude). (PLT217) — FAA-H-8083-21

RTC

7087. The proper action to initiate a rapid deceleration is to apply

A— forward cyclic while raising the collective and applying right pedal.
B— left cyclic while raising the collective and applying left pedal.
C— aft cyclic while lowering the collective and applying right pedal.

The deceleration is initiated by applying aft cyclic to reduce forward speed. Simultaneously, the collective pitch should be lowered as necessary to counteract any climbing tendency. As collective pitch is lowered, right pedal should be increased to maintain heading. (PLT217) — FAA-H-8083-21

Answers

7085   [B]   7086   [C]   7087   [C]

Pinnacle Approaches

During a pinnacle approach to a rooftop heliport under conditions of turbulence and high wind, the pilot should make a steeper-than-normal approach, maintaining the desired angle of descent with collective applications.

RTC
7090. When conducting a confined area operation, the primary purpose of the high reconnaissance is to determine

A— suitability of the area for landing.
B— height of obstructions surrounding the area.
C— if the area will be large enough to permit a safe takeoff after landing.

The primary purpose of the high reconnaissance is to determine the suitability of an area for a landing. In a high reconnaissance, the following items should be accomplished:

1. Determine wind direction and speed;

2. Select the most suitable flightpaths into and out of the area, with particular consideration being given to forced landing areas;

3. Plan the approach and select a point for touchdown and;

4. Locate and determine the size of barriers, if any, immediately around the area.

(PLT349) — FAA-H-8083-21

RTC
7091. During a pinnacle approach to a rooftop heliport under conditions of turbulence and high wind, the pilot should make a

A— shallow approach, maintaining a constant line of descent with cyclic applications.
B— normal approach, maintaining a slower-than-normal rate of descent with cyclic applications.
C— steeper-than-normal approach, maintaining the desired angle of descent with collective applications.

During a pinnacle approach to a rooftop heliport under conditions of turbulence and high wind, the pilot should make a steeper-than-normal approach, maintaining the desired angle of descent with collective applications. (PLT170) — FAA-H-8083-21

Running Landings

Adequate directional control is ensured while making a running landing in a helicopter by maintaining the normal operating RPM until the helicopter stops.

RTC
7084. Normal rotor RPM should be maintained during a running landing primarily to ensure

A— sufficient forward speed is available.
B— adequate directional control until the helicopter stops.
C— sufficient lift is available in case of an emergency.

To ensure directional control when making a running landing in a helicopter, the normal operating RPM should be maintained until the helicopter stops. (PLT336) — FAA-H-8083-21

Answers

7090   [A]   7091   [C]   7084   [B]

Gyroplane Flight Operation

The gyroplane **rotor blade spin-up lever** engages the engine to the rotor and at the same time decreases the pitch angle of the blades to minimize the engine load. For run-up, the pitch angle is 0°. During the transition from prerotation to flight, all rotor blades change pitch simultaneously, but to different angles of incidence.

The spinning rotor of a gyroplane acts as a large gyroscope, and abrupt control movement can cause damaging and excessive blade travel. When taxiing a gyroplane with the rotor blades turning, avoid abrupt control movements.

The normal landing for a gyroplane is a running, or roll-on, landing. On final approach, establish a crab angle into the wind to maintain a ground track that is aligned with the extended centerline of the runway. Just before touchdown, remove the crab angle and bank the gyroplane slightly into the wind to prevent drift. Maintain longitudinal alignment with the runway using the rudder.

RTC

6694. During the transition from prerotation to flight, all rotor blades change pitch

A— simultaneously to the same angle of incidence.
B— simultaneously but to different angles of incidence.
C— to the same degree at the same point in the cycle of rotation.

Compensation for dissymmetry of lift requires constant change in the blade angle of incidence, with one increasing as another simultaneously decreases. During the transition from prerotation to flight (or any time there is dissymmetry of lift) all rotor blades change pitch simultaneously, but to different angles of incidence. (PLT470) — FAA-H-8083-21

RTC

6835-1. Which is true concerning gyroplane operations?

A— Rotor RPM will decrease during a vertical descent regardless of weight or density altitude.
B— Minimum level flight speed is established when all available power is used to maintain constant altitude and airspeed.
C— A gyroplane can take off from any area in which it can safely land.

At the point where maximum power available is being used, no further reduction in airspeed is possible without initiating a descent. This speed is referred to as the minimum level flight speed. (PLT260) — FAA-H-8083-21

RTC

7092. Which is true concerning taxi procedures in a gyroplane?

A— In ideal conditions, taxi speed should be limited to no faster than a brisk walk.
B— Cyclic stick should be positioned slightly aft of neutral when taxiing.
C— Rotor blades should not be turning when taxiing over a rough surface.

A gyroplane should not be taxied in close proximity to people or obstructions while the rotor is turning. In addition, taxi speed should be limited to no faster than a brisk walk in ideal conditions, and adjusted appropriately according to the circumstances. (PLT149) — FAA-H-8083-21

Answer (B) is incorrect because the stick should be positioned forward. Answer (C) is incorrect because the pilot should taxi slowly over rough ground or for a long distance. It may be best to prerotate first.

RTC

7094. When landing a gyroplane in crosswind conditions, proper technique requires that the

A— longitudinal axis be parallel to the runway.
B— direction of motion and heading coincide with runway direction.
C— lateral axis of the gyroplane be parallel to the gyroplane's direction of motion.

On final approach, establish a crab angle into the wind to maintain a ground track that is aligned with the extended centerline of the runway. Just before touchdown, remove the crab angle and bank the gyroplane slightly into the wind to prevent drift. Maintain longitudinal alignment with the runway using the rudder. (PLT112) — FAA-H-8083-21

Answer (A) is incorrect because the longitudinal axis should align with the runway, not be next to it. Answer (C) is incorrect because the lateral axis should be perpendicular to the direction of motion.

Answers

6694 [B]	6835-1 [B]	7092 [A]	7094 [B]

Glider Flight Operation

Water ballast is used in some high-performance sailplanes to increase their cruising speed. The **L/D ratio** is a function of aerodynamic considerations and is independent of the sailplane weight. The added weight of the water ballast allows the sailplane to increase its lift by flying faster, rather than by increasing its angle of attack.

Rules of thumb for airspeeds to be used for various conditions are:

1. When passing through lift with no intention of working it, the airspeed that produces the minimum sink speed should be used.

2. To cover the greatest distance for each foot of descent when flying into a strong headwind, hold the airspeed at the best L/D speed plus 1/2 the estimated wind speed at the glider's flight altitude.

3. For the final approach speed, use 50% above the glider's stalling speed plus 1/2 the estimated wind speed.

If a steep wind gradient exists, a pilot not maintaining adequate speed control during the turn to base and final approach to landing will likely undershoot the desired landing spot, or the glider will stall. If there is an indication of a strong thermal on the final approach to landing, the pilot should close the spoilers and dive to increase his/her airspeed.

After attaining the proper climb speed, the pilot should smoothly increase the pitch attitude until reaching an altitude of at least 200 feet. A safe rule of thumb for pitch angle is to keep the pitch angle below 15° at 50 feet, 30° at 100 feet, and 45° at 200 feet.

When more than one glider is circling in a thermal, the turns should be made in the same direction as those made by the first glider to enter the thermal.

When slope soaring, make all reversing turns away from the ridge and into the wind. When making an off-field landing, it is nearly always best to land uphill, if possible, regardless of the wind direction. A safe off-field landing is normally ensured by maintaining an approach airspeed of at least 50% above the glider's stall speed, plus 1/2 the estimated wind speed.

GLI
7176. The reason for retaining water ballast while thermals are strong and dumping the water when thermals weaken is to

A— decrease forward speed.
B— increase forward speed.
C— decrease the rate of descent.

As the weight of the glider increases, the airspeed must be increased to maintain the same glide ratio. (PLT494) — FAA-H-8083-13

GLI
6713. For a winch tow, which is an advantage of the CG hook over the nose hook?

A— A shallower climb can be used during launch.
B— Glider is less likely to pitch up if the towline breaks.
C— Likelihood of applying too much back-stick pressure is reduced.

The center of gravity (CG) position requires less up elevator than the nose hook. (PLT021) — FAA-H-8083-13

GLI
6714. Which is true regarding glider tow hooks?

A— Use of a CG hook for aerotows would cause a glider to pitch up.
B— Use of a CG hook for winch tows would cause a glider to pitch up.
C— Use of a nose hitch for aerotows increases the climb attitude and release altitude.

The nose hook is primarily intended for the aero tow. (PLT304) — FAA-H-8083-13

Answers

7176 [B]   6713 [B]   6714 [A]

GLI
6719. What would be the approximate tensile strength of a rope with a 1,000 pound tensile strength if a knot develops in it?

A— 500 pounds.
B— 800 pounds.
C— 1,000 pounds.

Tensile strength is reduced by 50% if a knot develops. (PLT496) — FAA-H-8083-13

GLI
6720. What is the minimum allowable strength of a towline used for the aerotow of a glider having a certificated gross weight of 1,040 pounds?

A— 780 pounds.
B— 832 pounds.
C— 1,300 pounds.

The required breaking strength of the rope must be over 80% and less than 200% of the gross weight of the glider. (PLT496) — FAA-H-8083-13

GLI
7175. What consideration should be given in the choice of a towplane for use in aerotows?

A— Stall speed of the towplane.
B— Gross weight of the glider to be towed.
C— Towplane's low-wing loading and low-power loading.

Maximum tow speeds of some gliders may be low enough to cause a conflict with the stall speed of the towplane. (PLT401) — FAA-H-8083-13

GLI
7178. How can excessive towline slack that is allowed to develop during a glider tow be eliminated?

A— Increase pitch attitude until towline becomes taut.
B— Execute a shallow banked coordinated turn to either side.
C— Yaw the nose to one side with rudder while keeping the wings level with ailerons.

Yawing should be used to remove slack from the towline. (PLT304) — FAA-H-8083-13

GLI
7179. What could result if a glider pilot releases while in the low-tow position during an aerotow?

A— Nose of the glider would tend to pitch up after release.
B— Tow ring may strike and damage the glider after release.
C— Glider may be forced into the towplane's wake turbulence.

In the low-tow position, upon release, the tow ring may snap back and strike the glider, damaging it. (PLT304) — FAA-H-8083-13

GLI
7180. After signaling the tow pilot that the glider pilot cannot release, the tow pilot fishtails the airplane. The glider pilot should then plan to fly the final approach in

A— low-tow position and land before the towplane; but use no spoilers or brakes during the landing roll until after the towplane touches down.
B— high-tow position and extend the spoilers just prior to the towplane's touchdown.
C— the towplane's wake and extend the spoilers as needed for a normal landing.

Glider flies low tow, lands first, uses no brakes or skids to avoid stalling the tow plane. (PLT304) — FAA-H-8083-13

GLI
7177. When flying into a strong headwind on a long glide back to the airport, the recommended speed to use is the

A— best glide speed.
B— minimum sink speed.
C— best lift/drag speed plus half the estimated windspeed at the glider's flight altitude.

The proper airspeed to use when flying with a tailwind on a cross-country is the best L/D. This airspeed should be increased by one-half of the estimated wind velocity when flying into a headwind. (PLT257) — FAA-H-8083-13

Answers

6719 [A]	6720 [B]	7175 [A]	7178 [C]	7179 [B]	7180 [A]
7177 [C]					

GLI

7192. What is the suggested speed to fly when passing through lift with no intention to work the lift?

A— Best glide speed.
B— Minimum sink speed.
C— Best lift/drag speed.

If not stopping to work a thermal, the minimum sink speed should be used. (PLT474) — FAA-H-8083-13

GLI

7186. Unless adequate speed control is maintained during the turn to base and the final approach for a landing into the wind, which would most likely occur if a steep wind gradient existed?

A— The desired landing spot would be undershot or the glider would stall.
B— The airspeed on final approach would increase, causing the glider to overshoot the desired landing spot.
C— The wingtip on the outside of the turn would stall before the wingtip on the inside of the turn.

If a steep wind gradient exists, a pilot not maintaining adequate speed control during the turn to base and final approach to landing will likely undershoot the desired landing spot, or the glider will stall. (PLT170) — FAA-H-8083-13

GLI

7187. A rule of thumb for flying a final approach is to maintain a speed that is

A— 50 percent above the glider's stall speed, regardless of windspeed.
B— twice the glider's stall speed plus half the estimated windspeed.
C— 50 percent above the glider's stall speed plus half the estimated windspeed.

A good rule of thumb for the final approach speed is 50 percent above the glider's stalling speed plus half the estimated wind speed. (PLT170) — FAA-H-8083-13

GLI

7188. If swirling dust, leaves, or debris indicate a strong thermal on the final approach to a landing, it is recommended that the glider pilot

A— open the spoilers and reduce the airspeed.
B— close the spoilers and increase the airspeed.
C— open the spoilers and maintain a constant airspeed.

A pilot should close the spoilers and dive to increase the airspeed when an indication of a strong thermal on the final approach to landing is seen. (PLT494) — FAA-H-8083-13

GLI

6839. GIVEN:

Maximum auto winch tow speed .... 69 MPH
Surface wind.. 5 MPH
Wind gradient .... 5 MPH

What should the auto winch speed be when a glider reaches an altitude of 200 feet?

A— 44 MPH.
B— 49 MPH.
C— 59 MPH.

To determine auto winch speed, first subtract surface wind from placard speed, then subtract an additional 5 mph for safety. Subtract an additional 10 mph when glider reaches 200 feet and an additional 5 mph for wind gradient at 200 feet:

69 – 5 – 5 – 10 – 5 = 44 MPH

(PLT012) — FAA-H-8083-13

GLI

7181. During an autolaunch, the pitch angle of the glider should not exceed

A— 10° at 50 feet, 20° at 100 feet, and 45° at 200 feet.
B— 15° at 50 feet, 20° at 100 feet, and 40° at 200 feet.
C— 15° at 50 feet, 30° at 100 feet, and 45° at 200 feet.

After attaining the proper climb speed, the pilot should smoothly increase the pitch attitude until reaching an altitude of at least 200 feet. A safe rule of thumb for pitch angle is to keep the pitch angle below 15° at 50 feet, 30° at 100 feet, and 45° at 200 feet. (PLT304) — FAA-H-8083-13

Answers

7192 [B]	7186 [A]	7187 [C]	7188 [B]	6839 [A]	7181 [C]

GLI

7182. At what point during an autotow should the glider pilot establish the maximum pitch attitude for the climb?

A— 200 feet above the ground.
B— 100 feet above the ground.
C— Between 300 and 400 feet above the ground.

After attaining the proper climb speed, the pilot should smoothly increase the pitch attitude until reaching an altitude of at least 200 feet. A safe rule of thumb for pitch angle is to keep the pitch angle below 15° at 50 feet, 30° at 100 feet, and 45° at 200 feet. (PLT304) — FAA-H-8083-13

GLI

7183. When preparing for an autotow with a strong crosswind, where should the glider and towrope be positioned?

A— Obliquely to the line of takeoff on the upwind side of the tow vehicle.
B— Obliquely to the line of takeoff on the downwind side of the tow vehicle.
C— Directly behind the tow vehicle and crabbed into the wind with the wing runner holding the upwind wingtip.

The tow rope should be laid obliquely to the line of takeoff, so as to preclude the possibility of the glider over-running the rope during takeoff. (PLT304) — FAA-H-8083-13

GLI

7184. During a ground launch, how is the airspeed of a glider increased?

A— Raise the nose.
B— Lower the nose.
C— Increase speed of vehicle or winch.

A pilot is taught that raising the nose of his/her craft will slow it down. In ground launch, the opposite is true. The explanation is quite simple: in level flight the glider's speed is the same as the winch or tow car speed. When climbing, the horizontal speed is unchanged, but a vertical component of motion has been added. The resultant speed of the glider therefore increases in proportion to the steepness of the climb. (PLT304) — FAA-H-8083-13

GLI

7185. During a winch launch, which factor would most likely result in pitch oscillations?

A— Winching speed too fast.
B— Winching speed too slow.
C— Insufficient up-elevator control.

Porpoising or a rapid pitch oscillation may occur as the sailplane approaches the top of the climb. This phenomenon occurs as a result of the horizontal stabilizer stalling and unstalling in combination with the downward pull of the tow cable. (PLT304) — FAA-H-8083-13

GLI

7189. With regard to two or more gliders flying in the same thermal, which statement is true?

A— All turns should be to the right.
B— Turns should be in the same direction as the highest glider.
C— Turns should be made in the same direction as the first glider to enter the thermal.

When more than one glider is circling in a thermal, the turns should be made in the same direction as those made by the first glider to enter the thermal. (PLT474) — FAA-H-8083-13

GLI

7190. Which is true relating to the direction in which turns should be made during slope soaring?

A— All reversing turns should be made to the left.
B— All turns should be made downwind toward the slope.
C— All reversing turns should be made into the wind away from the slope.

When slope soaring, make all reversing turns away from the ridge and into the wind. (PLT474) — FAA-H-8083-13

Answers

7182 [A]	7183 [B]	7184 [A]	7185 [C]	7189 [C]	7190 [C]

GLI

7193. When making an off-field landing, it is recommended that the landing be accomplished

A— in pastures which are seldom cultivated.
B— uphill, if possible, regardless of the wind direction.
C— in cultivated fields where the crops have not yet been harvested.

When making an off-field landing, it is nearly always best to land uphill, if possible, regardless of the wind direction. (PLT170) — FAA-H-8083-13

GLI

7194. Which would most likely ensure a safe off-field landing?

A— Landing into the wind, regardless of the type or slope of the terrain.
B— Landing in a pasture or uncultivated field rather than one in cultivation and whose crops have been harvested.
C— Maintaining an approach airspeed of at least 50 percent above the glider's stall speed plus half the estimated windspeed.

A safe off-field landing is normally ensured by maintaining an approach airspeed of at least 50 percent above the glider's stall speed, plus half the estimated wind speed. (PLT474) — FAA-H-8083-13

Balloon Flight Operation

LTA

7195. What should a pilot do if a small hole is seen in the fabric of a balloon during inflation?

A— Continue the inflation and make a mental note of the location of the hole for later repair.
B— Instruct a ground crew member to inspect the hole and, if under 5 inches in length, continue the inflation.
C— Consult the flight manual to determine if the hole is within acceptable damage limits established for the balloon being flown.

Any hole in the fabric is dangerous because it is a weak point in the fabric and any stress on the fabric will allow the hole to tear bigger. "Preventive maintenance" in the form of mending rips and tears in the bag may be done by the owners, but any major repairs must be done by a certified airframe and powerplant mechanic, who also performs the annual checkup. Local unfamiliarity with the equipment often makes it advisable to contact the manufacturer for maintenance assistance. (PLT373) — FAA-H-8083-11

LTA

7197. The recommended size for a balloon launch site should be

A— 500 feet on the downwind side.
B— twice the height of the balloon.
C— 100 feet for every 1 knot of wind.

A balloon will move about 100 feet of travel for each knot of windspeed. (PLT184) — Balloon Ground School

LTA

7198. It may be possible to make changes in the direction of flight of a hot air balloon by

A— using the maneuvering vent.
B— operating at different flight altitudes.
C— flying a constant atmospheric pressure gradient.

The pilot might accomplish a change of direction in flight by changing altitude. (PLT183) — FAA-H-8083-11

LTA

7199. What action is most appropriate when an envelope over-temperature condition occurs?

A— Land as soon as practicable.
B— Descend and allow envelope to cool before landing.
C— Throw all unnecessary equipment overboard in order to lighten the load.

If the envelope temperature gauge has reached its maximum (redline), the pilot must land as soon as it is feasible to do so. (PLT208) — Balloon Ground School

Answers

| 7193 | [B] | 7194 | [C] | 7195 | [C] | 7197 | [C] | 7198 | [B] | 7199 | [A] |

LTA
7200. For a hot air balloon, the weigh-off procedure is helpful because the

A— pilot can adjust the altimeter to the correct setting.
B— ground crew can assure that downwind obstacles are clear.
C— pilot will learn what the equilibrium conditions are prior to being committed to fly.

A weigh-off is used to determine the static equilibrium of the balloon. (PLT267) — Powerline Excerpts

LTA
7203. The practice of allowing the ground crew to lift a balloon into the air is

A— a safe way to reduce stress on the envelope.
B— unsafe because it can lead to a sudden landing at an inopportune site just after lift-off.
C— considered to be good practice, particularly when obstacles must be cleared shortly after lift-off.

The practice of allowing ground crew to lift the balloon in an attempt to "shove" it up into the air is unsafe, for it can lead to a sudden landing at an inopportune site just after lift-off. (PLT180) — Powerline Excerpts

LTA
7204. How should a roundout from a moderate-rate ascent to level flight be made?

A— Vent at altitude and add heat upon settling back down to altitude.
B— Reduce the amount of heat gradually as the balloon approaches altitude.
C— Cool the envelope by venting and add heat just before arriving at the desired altitude.

The most efficient round-out is to reduce the frequency of blasts so that the envelope cools to a level flight temperature just as the balloon reaches the desired altitude. (PLT183) — Balloon Ground School

LTA
7205. All fuel tanks should be fired during preflight to determine

A— if there are any leaks in the tanks.
B— burner pressure and condition of the valves.
C— if the pilot light functions properly on each tank.

Burner output is dependent on fuel pressure. Proper valve operation is critical to safety and control. (PLT254) — Balloon Ground School

LTA
7206. In a balloon, best fuel economy in level flight can be accomplished by

A— evenly-spaced, short blasts of heat.
B— long blasts of heat, spaced as necessary.
C— noting the pyrometer and remaining at a constant temperature.

Obtaining the best fuel economy in level flight can be accomplished by using short blasts of heat. (PLT177) — Balloon Ground School

LTA
7207. If powerlines become a factor during a balloon flight, a pilot should know that

A— it is safer to contact the lines than chance ripping.
B— contact with powerlines creates no great hazard for a balloon.
C— it is better to chance ripping at 25 feet above the ground than contacting powerlines.

Powerlines are the single most hazardous obstacle to ballooning. (PLT208) — Balloon Ground School

LTA
7208. What is a potential hazard in a balloon during a climb that exceeds maximum rate?

A— Envelope may collapse.
B— Deflation port may be forced open.
C— Rapid flow of air may extinguish the burner and pilot light.

The positive pressure on the top of the envelope could force the deflation ports open. (PLT113) — Balloon Ground School

LTA
7209. What is the recommended ascent rate upon initial launch of a balloon?

A— Maximum ascent to altitude to avoid low-level thermals.
B— Shallow ascent to take maximum advantage of lighter winds.
C— A moderate rate of ascent to determine wind directions at different altitudes.

A moderate-rate ascent is recommended initially to accurately determine the wind direction at various altitudes. (PLT183) — Balloon Ground School

Answers

| 7200 [C] | 7203 [B] | 7204 [B] | 7205 [B] | 7206 [A] | 7207 [C] |
| 7208 [B] | 7209 [C] | | | | |

LTA

7210. What is one procedure for relighting the burner while in flight?

A— Open the blast valve full open and light the pilot light.

B— Open another tank valve, open the blast valve, and light the main jet using reduced flow.

C— Close the tank valves, vent the fuel lines, reopen the tank valves, and light the pilot light.

The pilot should open another tank valve, open the regular, or blast valve and light off the main jet with reduced flow. (PLT343) — Balloon Ground School

LTA

7211. If you are in a balloon over a heavily wooded area with no open fields in the vicinity and have only 10 minutes of fuel remaining, you should

A— stay low and keep flying in hopes you will find an open field.

B— climb as high as possible to see where the nearest landing field is.

C— land in the trees while you have sufficient fuel for a controlled landing.

A controlled landing is always best, to minimize damage and injury. (PLT184) — Balloon Ground School

LTA

7212. Prior to a high-wind landing in a balloon, occupants should be briefed to

A— kneel on the floor, face aft, and hang on to the basket.

B— crouch in basket, face direction of landing, hold on in two places, and stay in basket.

C— crouch on the floor in the center of the basket and jump out as soon as initial ground contact is made.

By facing forward with knees bent, the body is balanced and the legs act as springs absorbing the landing shock. It is important that everyone remain in the basket until the envelope cannot lift the balloon back into the air. (PLT184) — FAA-H-8083-11

LTA

7213. The windspeed is such that it is necessary to deflate the envelope as rapidly as possible during a landing. When should the deflation port be opened?

A— Just prior to ground contact.

B— The instant the basket contacts the surface.

C— As the balloon skips off the surface the first time and all ballast has been discharged.

In a high-wind landing, the envelope should be ripped just prior to ground contact. (PLT184) — Balloon Ground School

LTA

7214. What procedure is recommended when confronted with the necessity of having to land a balloon in turbulent conditions?

A— Land in the center of the largest available field.

B— Land in any available lake close to the upwind shore.

C— Land in trees to absorb shock forces and cushion the landing.

Turbulent air can and will suddenly change direction. Landing in a large field reduces the danger. (PLT184) — Balloon Ground School

Answers

| 7210 | [B] | 7211 | [C] | 7212 | [B] | 7213 | [A] | 7214 | [A] |

Chapter 10
Flight Physiology

Principles of Flight Instruction

"Integrated Flight Instruction" means that each flight maneuver should be performed by using both **outside visual references** and the **flight instruments**. When pilots use this technique, they develop proper habit patterns of instrument interpretation and aircraft control, which increases their overall piloting ability. This results in less difficulty in holding desired altitudes, controlling airspeed during takeoffs, climbs, descents, and landing approaches, and in maintaining headings in the traffic pattern, as well as on cross-country flights.

Distractions are used throughout the flight training process to help the student develop skill in maintaining control of the aircraft while his/her attention is diverted. Some appropriate distractions for flight training are:

- Simulated engine failure.
- Simulated radio tuning and communications.
- Identifying a field suitable for emergency landings.
- Identifying features or objects on the ground. This is appropriate for use when the student is practicing S-turns.

Aeronautical decision making (ADM) is a systematic approach to the mental process used by aircraft pilots to consistently determine the best course of action in response to a given set of circumstances.

Risk Management is the part of the decision making process which relies on situational awareness, problem recognition, and good judgment to reduce risks associated with each flight.

The ADM process addresses all aspects of decision making in the cockpit and identifies the steps involved in good decision making. Steps for good decision making are:

1. Identifying personal attitudes hazardous to safe flight.
2. Learning behavior modification techniques.
3. Learning how to recognize and cope with stress.
4. Developing risk assessment skills.
5. Using all resources in a multicrew situation.
6. Evaluating the effectiveness of one's ADM skills.

There are a number of classic behavioral traps into which pilots have been known to fall. Pilots, particularly those with considerable experience, as a rule always try to complete a flight as planned, please passengers, meet schedules, and generally demonstrate that they have the "right stuff." These tendencies ultimately may lead to practices that are dangerous and often illegal, and may lead to a mishap. All experienced pilots have fallen prey to, or have been tempted by, one or more of these tendencies in their flying careers. These dangerous tendencies or behavior patterns, which must be identified and eliminated, include:

Peer Pressure. Poor decision making based upon emotional response to peers rather than evaluating a situation objectively.

Mind Set. The inability to recognize and cope with changes in the situation different from those anticipated or planned.

Get-There-Itis. This tendency, common among pilots, clouds the vision and impairs judgment by causing a fixation on the original goal or destination combined with a total disregard for any alternative course of action.

Continued

Duck-Under Syndrome. The tendency to sneak a peek by descending below minimums during an approach. Based on a belief that there is always a built-in "fudge" factor that can be used or on an unwillingness to admit defeat and shoot a missed approach.

Scud Running. Pushing the capabilities of the pilot and the aircraft to the limits by trying to maintain visual contact with the terrain while trying to avoid physical contact with it. This attitude is characterized by the old pilot's joke: "If it's too bad to go IFR, we'll go VFR."

Continuing Visual Flight Rules (VFR) into instrument conditions often leads to spatial disorientation or collision with ground/obstacles. It is even more dangerous if the pilot is not instrument qualified or current.

Getting Behind the Aircraft. Allowing events or the situation to control your actions rather than the other way around. Characterized by a constant state of surprise at what happens next.

Loss of Positional or Situation Awareness. Another case of getting behind the aircraft which results in not knowing where you are, an inability to recognize deteriorating circumstances, and/or the misjudgment of the rate of deterioration.

Operating Without Adequate Fuel Reserves. Ignoring minimum fuel reserve requirements, either VFR or Instrument Flight Rules (IFR), is generally the result of overconfidence, lack of flight planning, or ignoring the regulations.

Descent Below the Minimum Enroute Altitude. The duck-under syndrome (mentioned above) manifesting itself during the enroute portion of an IFR flight.

Flying Outside the Envelope. Unjustified reliance on the (usually mistaken) belief that the aircraft's high performance capability meets the demands imposed by the pilot's (usually overestimated) flying skills.

Neglect of Flight Planning, Preflight Inspections, Checklists, etc. Unjustified reliance on the pilot's short and long term memory, regular flying skills, repetitive and familiar routes, etc.

Each ADM student should take the Self-Assessment Hazardous Attitude Inventory Test in order to gain a realistic perspective on his/her attitudes toward flying. The inventory test requires the pilot to provide a response which most accurately reflects the reasoning behind his/her decision. The pilot must choose one of the five given reasons for making that decision, even though the pilot may not consider any of the five choices acceptable. The inventory test presents extreme cases of incorrect pilot decision making in an effort to introduce the five types of hazardous attitudes.

ADM addresses the following five hazardous attitudes:

1. **Anti-authority** (don't tell me!). This attitude is found in people who do not like anyone telling them what to do. In a sense they are saying no one can tell me what to do. They may be resentful of having someone tell them what to do or may regard rules, regulations, and procedures as silly or unnecessary. However, it is always your prerogative to question authority if you feel it is in error. The antidote for this attitude is: Follow the rules. They are usually right.

2. **Impulsivity** (do something quickly!) is the attitude of people who frequently feel the need to do something — *anything* — immediately. They do not stop to think about what they are about to do, they do not select the best alternative, and they do the first thing that comes to mind. The antidote for this attitude is: Not so fast. Think first.

3. **Invulnerability** (it won't happen to me). Many people feel that accidents happen to others, but never to them. They know accidents can happen, and they know that anyone can be affected. They never really feel or believe that they will be personally involved. Pilots who think this way are more likely to take chances and increase risk. The antidote for this attitude is: It could happen to me.

4. **Macho** (I can do it). Pilots who are always trying to prove that they are better than anyone else are thinking "I can do it — I'll show them." Pilots with this type of attitude will try to prove themselves

by taking risks in order to impress others. While this pattern is thought to be a male characteristic, women are equally susceptible. The antidote for this attitude is: taking chances is foolish.

5. **Resignation** (what's the use?). Pilots who think "what's the use?" do not see themselves as being able to make a great deal of difference in what happens to them. When things go well, the pilot is apt to think that's good luck. When things go badly, the pilot may feel that "someone is out to get me," or attribute it to bad luck. The pilot will leave the action to others, for better or worse. Sometimes, such pilots will even go along with unreasonable requests just to be a "nice guy." The antidote for this attitude is: I'm not helpless. I can make a difference.

Hazardous attitudes which contribute to poor pilot judgment can be effectively counteracted by redirecting that hazardous attitude so that appropriate action can be taken. Recognition of hazardous thoughts is the first step in neutralizing them in the ADM process. Pilots should become familiar with a means of counteracting hazardous attitudes with an appropriate antidote thought. When a pilot recognizes a thought as hazardous, the pilot should label that thought as hazardous, then correct that thought by stating the corresponding antidote.

If you hope to succeed at reducing stress associated with crisis management in the air or with your job, it is essential to begin by making a personal assessment of stress in all areas of your life. Good **cockpit stress management** begins with good life stress management. Many of the stress coping techniques practiced for life stress management are not usually practical in flight. Rather, you must condition yourself to relax and think rationally when stress appears. The following checklist outlines some thoughts on cockpit stress management:

1. Avoid situations that distract you from flying the aircraft.

2. Reduce your workload to reduce stress levels. This will create a proper environment in which to make good decisions.

3. If an emergency does occur, be calm. Think for a moment, weigh the alternatives, then act.

4. Maintain proficiency in your aircraft; proficiency builds confidence. Familiarize yourself thoroughly with your aircraft, its systems, and emergency procedures.

5. Know and respect your own personal limits.

6. Do not let little mistakes bother you until they build into a big thing. Wait until after you land, then "debrief" and analyze past actions.

7. If flying is adding to your stress, either stop flying or seek professional help to manage your stress within acceptable limits.

The DECIDE Model, comprised of a six-step process, is intended to provide the pilot with a logical way of approaching decision making. The six elements of the DECIDE Model represent a continuous loop decision process which can be used to assist a pilot in the decision making process when he/she is faced with a change in a situation that requires a judgment. This DECIDE Model is primarily focused on the intellectual component, but can have an impact on the motivational component of judgment as well. If a pilot practices the DECIDE Model in all decision making, its use can become very natural and could result in better decisions being made under all types of situations.

1. **D**etect. The decisionmaker detects the fact that change has occurred.

2. **E**stimate. The decisionmaker estimates the need to counter or react to the change.

3. **C**hoose. The decisionmaker chooses a desirable outcome (in terms of success) for the flight.

4. **I**dentify. The decisionmaker identifies actions which could successfully control the change.

5. **D**o. The decisionmaker takes the necessary action.

6. **E**valuate. The decisionmaker evaluates the effect(s) of his/her action countering the change.

ALL

7168. During training flights, an instructor should interject realistic distractions to determine if a student can

A— learn despite stressful conditions.
B— maintain aircraft control while his/her attention is diverted.
C— perform maneuvers using the integrated method of flight instruction.

The purpose of distractions in flight training and evaluation is to determine if the student is able to maintain aircraft control while his/her attention is diverted. (PLT295) — AC 61-67

Answer (A) is incorrect because stressful conditions discourage learning. Answer (C) is incorrect because integrated flight instruction means that each flight maneuver should be performed by using both outside visual references and the flight instruments.

ALL

7168-1. How should an instructor introduce distractions?

A— Request that the student maintain a constant heading and altitude.
B— Ask the student to get something from the back seat.
C— Require the student to look for traffic.

Instructor responsibilities include teaching the student to divide his or her attention between the distracting task and maintaining control of the aircraft. Distractions should be realistic and divide the student attention away from normal operations. (PLT295) — FAA-H-8083-9A

Answers (A) and (C) are incorrect because these are normal pilot operations, not distractions.

ALL

7167-1. What are the four fundamental risk elements in the aeronautical decision making (ADM) process that comprise any given aviation situation?

A—Pilot, aircraft, environment, and mission.
B—Skill, stress, situational awareness, and aircraft.
C—Situational awareness, risk management, judgment, and skill.

Any aviation situation is comprised of one of these four elements: pilot, aircraft, environment, and mission. (PLT022) — FAA-H-8083-2

ALL

7167-2. When should a flight instructor begin teaching aeronautical decision making (ADM) to a student?

A— Beginning with the first lesson.
B— As soon as the student is able to control the aircraft during basic maneuvers.
C— After the student has completed the initial solo flight but before conducting cross country flights.

Students must be exposed to aeronautical decision making early in their pilot training, ideally during the first quarter of the student standard private pilot training course. (PLT481) — FAA-H-8083-2

ALL

7226-1. Aeronautical decision making (ADM) can be defined as a

A— mental process of analyzing all available information in a particular situation, making a timely decision on what action to take, and when to take the action.
B— decision making process which relies on good judgment to reduce risks associated with each flight.
C— systematic approach to the mental process used by pilots to consistently determine the best course of action in response to a given set of circumstances.

ADM is a systematic approach to the mental process used by aircraft pilots to consistently determine the best course of action in response to a given set of circumstances. (PLT022) — FAA-H-8083-2

ALL

7226-2. Risk management, as part of the aeronautical decision making (ADM) process, relies on which features to reduce the risks associated with each flight?

A— Application of stress management and risk element procedures.
B— The mental process of analyzing all information in a particular situation and making a timely decision on what action to take.
C— Situational awareness, problem recognition, and good judgment.

Risk Management is the part of the decision making process which relies on situational awareness, problem recognition, and good judgment to reduce risks associated with each flight. (PLT022) — FAA-H-8083-2

Answers

| 7168 [B] | 7168-1 [B] | 7167-1 [A] | 7167-2 [B] | 7226-1 [C] | 7226-2 [C] |

ALL

7226-3. The aeronautical decision making (ADM) process identifies several steps involved in good decision making. One of these steps is

A— making a rational evaluation of the required actions.
B— identifying personal attitudes hazardous to safe flight.
C— developing a "can do" attitude.

Steps for good decision making are: identifying personal attitudes hazardous to safe flight, learning behavior modification techniques, learning how to recognize and cope with stress, developing risk assessment skills, using all resources in a multicrew situation, and evaluating the effectiveness of one's ADM skills. (PLT103) — FAA-H-8083-2

ALL

7227-1. Examples of classic behavioral traps that experienced pilots may fall into are to

A— promote situational awareness and then necessary changes in behavior.
B— complete a flight as planned, please passengers, meet schedules, and "get the job done."
C— assume additional responsibilities and assert PIC authority.

There are a number of classic behavioral traps into which pilots have been known to fall. Pilots, particularly those with considerable experience, as a rule always try to complete a flight as planned, please passengers, meet schedules, and generally demonstrate that they have the "right stuff." (PLT270) — FAA-H-8083-2

Answers (A) and (C) are incorrect because promoting situation awareness and then necessary changes in behavior and asserting PIC authority are positive pilot behaviors.

ALL

7227-2. All experienced pilots have fallen prey to, or have been tempted by, one or more of these dangerous tendencies or behavior problems at some time in their career. Select the answer that best describes these tendencies.

A— Deficiencies in instrument skills and knowledge of aircraft systems or limitations.
B— Peer pressure, loss of situational awareness, and operating with inadequate fuel reserves.
C— Performance deficiencies due to stress from human factors such as fatigue, illness, or emotional problems.

There are a number of classic behavioral traps into which pilots have been known to fall. These dangerous tendencies or behavior patterns, which must be identified and eliminated, include: peer pressure, mind set, get-there-itis, duck-under syndrome, scud running, continuing visual flight rules into instrument conditions, getting behind the aircraft, loss of positional or situation awareness, operating without adequate fuel reserves, descent below the minimum enroute altitude, flying outside the envelope, neglect of flight planning, preflight inspections, checklists, etc. (PLT232) — FAA-H-8083-2

ALL

7227-3. In order to gain a realistic perspective on one's attitude toward flying, a pilot should

A— understand the need to complete the flight.
B— obtain both realistic and thorough flight instruction during training.
C— take a Self-Assessment Hazardous Attitude Inventory Test.

Each ADM student should take the Self-Assessment Hazardous Attitude Inventory Test in order to gain a realistic perspective on his/her attitudes toward flying. (PLT103) — FAA-H-8083-2

ALL

7228-1. Name some hazardous attitudes that can affect your judgment during the aeronautical decision making (ADM) process.

A— Impulsivity, antiestablishment, and reevaluation.
B— Antiauthority, impulsivity, and resignation.
C— Peer pressure and stress levels.

ADM addresses the following five hazardous attitudes: Antiauthority (don't tell me!), Impulsivity (do something quickly!), Invulnerability (it won't happen to me), Macho (I can do it), Resignation (what's the use?). (PLT103) — FAA-H-8083-2

ALL

7228-2. Hazardous attitudes which contribute to poor pilot judgment can be effectively counteracted by

A— an appropriate antidote.
B— taking meaningful steps to be more assertive with attitudes.
C— early recognition of these hazardous attitudes.

Pilots should become familiar with a means of counteracting hazardous attitudes with an appropriate antidote thought. (PLT103) — FAA-H-8083-2

Answers

7226-3 [B]   7227-1 [B]   7227-2 [B]   7227-3 [C]   7228-1 [B]   7228-2 [A]

ALL
7228-3. Hazardous attitudes occur to every pilot to some degree at some time. What are some of these hazardous attitudes?

A— Antiauthority, impulsivity, macho, resignation, and invulnerability.
B— Poor situational awareness, snap judgments, and lack of a decision making process.
C— Poor risk management and lack of stress management.

ADM addresses the following five hazardous attitudes: Antiauthority (don't tell me!), Impulsivity (do something quickly!), Invulnerability (it won't happen to me), Macho (I can do it), Resignation (what's the use?). (PLT103) — FAA-H-8083-2

ALL
7228-4. In the aeronautical decision making (ADM) process, what is the first step in neutralizing a hazardous attitude?

A— Recognizing hazardous thoughts.
B— Recognizing the invulnerability of the situation.
C— Making a rational judgement.

Hazardous attitudes which contribute to poor pilot judgment can be effectively counteracted by redirecting that hazardous attitude so that appropriate action can be taken. Recognition of hazardous thoughts is the first step in neutralizing them in the ADM process. (PLT022) — FAA-H-8083-2

ALL
7229-1. What should a pilot do when recognizing a thought as hazardous?

A— Correct this hazardous thought by making a thorough risk assessment.
B— Label the thought as hazardous and then correct that thought by stating the corresponding antidote.
C— Avoid allowing this hazardous thought to develop.

When a pilot recognizes a thought as hazardous, the pilot should label that thought as hazardous, then correct that thought by stating the corresponding antidote. (PLT103) — FAA-H-8083-2

ALL
7229-2. During a stall recovery, the instructor allows the student to exceed maneuvering speed. Which best illustrates an "antiauthority" reaction by the instructor?

A— The student should know how to recover from a stall by this time.
B— The aircraft can handle a lot more than the maneuvering speed.
C— There hasn't been a problem doing this in the past.

Antiauthority (don't tell me!). This attitude is found in people who do not like anyone telling them what to do. In a sense they are saying no one can tell me what to do. They may be resentful of having someone tell them what to do or may regard rules, regulations, and procedures as silly or unnecessary. (PLT103) — FAA-H-8083-2

ALL
7229-3. What is the antidote for a pilot with a "macho" attitude?

A— I'm not helpless. I can make a difference.
B— Follow the rules. They are usually right.
C— Taking chances is foolish.

Macho (I can do it). Pilots who are always trying to prove that they are better than anyone else are thinking "I can do it—I'll show them." Pilots with this type of attitude will try to prove themselves by taking risks in order to impress others. While this pattern is thought to be a male characteristic, women are equally susceptible. The antidote for this attitude is: taking chances is foolish. (PLT103) — FAA-H-8083-2

Answer (A) is incorrect because this is the antidote for a resignation attitude. Answer (B) is incorrect because this is the antidote for an antiauthority attitude.

ALL, FOI
7229-4. What is the antidote for an anti-authority hazardous attitude?

A— Do something quickly.
B— Not so fast. Think first.
C— Follow the rules.

The antiauthority (don't tell me!) attitude is found in people who do not like anyone telling them what to do. The antidote for this attitude is: follow the rules, they are usually right. (PLT103) — FAA-H-8083-2

Answers

7228-3   [A]   7228-4   [A]   7229-1   [B]   7229-2   [B]   7229-3   [C]   7229-4   [C]

ALL

7230-1. Success in reducing stress associated with a crisis in the cockpit begins with

A— eliminating the more serious life and cockpit stress issues.
B— knowing the exact cause of the stress.
C— assessing stress areas in one's personal life.

If you hope to succeed at reducing stress associated with crisis management in the air or with your job, it is essential to begin by making a personal assessment of stress in all areas of your life. (PLT272) — FAA-H-8083-2

ALL

7230-2. To help manage cockpit stress, a pilot should

A— think of life stress situations that are similar to those in flying.
B— try to relax and think rationally at the first sign of stress.
C— avoid situations that will degrade the ability to handle cockpit responsibilities.

Good cockpit stress management begins with good life stress management. Many of the stress coping techniques practiced for life stress management are not usually practical in flight. Rather, you must condition yourself to relax and think rationally when stress appears. (PLT272) — FAA-H-8083-2

ALL

7230-3. The DECIDE process consists of six elements to help provide a pilot a logical way of approaching aeronautical decision making. These elements are to

A— estimate, determine, choose, identify, detect, and evaluate.
B— determine, evaluate, choose, identify, do, and eliminate.
C— detect, estimate, choose, identify, do, and evaluate.

The DECIDE Model, comprised of a six step process, is intended to provide the pilot with a logical way of approaching decision making: Detect, Estimate, Choose, Identify, Do, and Evaluate. (PLT271) — FAA-H-8083-2

ALL, FOI

7321. What is the best way to teach students how to multi-task while flying?

A— Help students develop both types of multitasking abilities, including attention switching and simultaneous performance.
B— Help students develop attention switching skills.
C— Offer distractions while a student is learning a skill so they understand how to sequence the task.

Since doing several things at once is a natural part of aviation, instructors need to help students develop both types of multi-tasking abilities: attention switching and simultaneous performance. Before students are asked to perform several tasks at once, instructors should ensure that the student has devoted enough time to study and practice such that the individual tasks can be performed reasonably well in isolation. (PLT306) — FAA-H-8083-9

ALL

7325. Human behavior

A— rarely results in accidents unless deliberate actions are performed.
B— causes three out of four accidents.
C— is well understood, so behavioral induced accidents are exceedingly rare occurrences.

Three out of four accidents result from improper human performance. The human element is the most flexible, adaptable, and valuable part of the aviation system, but it is also the most vulnerable to influences that can adversely affect its performance. (PLT104) — FAA-H-8083-2

Answers

| 7230-1 | [C] | 7230-2 | [B] | 7230-3 | [C] | 7321 | [A] | 7325 | [B] |

Fitness for Flight

As little as one ounce of liquor, one bottle of beer, or four ounces of wine can impair flying skills. The alcohol consumed in these drinks is detectable in the breath and blood for at least three hours. Alcohol renders a pilot susceptible to disorientation and hypoxia. Even after the body completely destroys a moderate amount of alcohol, a pilot can be severely impaired for many hours by hangover. There is sim-ply no quick method for dissipating alcohol in the body or alleviating a hangover.

Pilots and passengers should allow sufficient time between scuba diving and flying, to rid the body of excess nitrogen absorbed during the dive. The recommended waiting time before flight to cabin pressure altitudes of 8,000 feet or less is at least 12 hours after diving which has not required controlled ascent (non-decompression diving), and at least 24 hours after diving which has required controlled ascent. The waiting time before flight to cabin pressure altitudes above 8,000 feet should be at least 24 hours after any scuba diving.

ALL

7142. Which statement is true regarding alcohol in the human system?

A— Alcohol renders a pilot more susceptible to hypoxia.

B— Small amounts of alcohol will not impair flying skills.

C— Coffee helps metabolize alcohol and alleviates a hangover.

Alcohol renders a pilot much more susceptible to disorientation and hypoxia. (PLT503) — AIM ¶8-1-1

Answer (B) is incorrect because as little as one ounce of liquor, one bottle of beer, or four ounces of wine can impair flying skills. Answer (C) is incorrect because there is simply no quick method to dissipate alcohol in the body or alleviate a hangover.

ALL

7143. If an individual has gone scuba diving which has not required a controlled ascent and will be flying to cabin pressure altitudes of 8,000 feet or less, the recommended waiting time is at least

A— 4 hours.

B— 12 hours.

C— 24 hours.

The recommended waiting time before flight to cabin pressure altitudes of 8,000 feet or less is at least 12 hours after diving which has not required controlled ascent (non-decompression diving). (PLT098) — AIM ¶8-1-2

Answer (A) is incorrect because 4 hours is not a recommended waiting period between scuba diving and flying. Answer (C) is incorrect because 24 hours is the recommended waiting period after diving which has required controlled ascent.

ALL

7144. If an individual has gone scuba diving which has required a controlled ascent and will be flying to cabin pressure altitudes of 8,000 feet or less, the recommended waiting time is at least

A— 8 hours.

B— 12 hours.

C— 24 hours.

The recommended waiting time before flight to cabin pressure altitudes of 8,000 feet or less is at least 24 hours after diving which has required controlled ascent. (PLT096) — AIM ¶8-1-2

Answer (A) is incorrect because 8 hours is not a recommended waiting period between scuba diving and flying. Answer (B) is incorrect because 12 hours is the recommended waiting period after diving which has not required controlled ascent (non-decompression diving).

Answers

7142 [A]   7143 [B]   7144 [C]

Supplemental Oxygen

The oxygen in the air causes approximately 21% of the total air pressure. At low altitudes, this partial pressure is sufficiently high to force oxygen into the blood through the lungs. As one goes up in altitude, the total air pressure becomes less, and above 28,000 feet, the pressure of the oxygen in the air is too low to force the oxygen into the blood. For the oxygen to enter the blood at high altitudes, the aircraft must be pressurized, or supplemental oxygen must be used.

Hypoxia is a state of oxygen deficiency in the body, sufficient to impair functions of the brain and other organs. Hypoxia from exposure to altitude is due only to the reduced barometric pressures encountered at altitude, for the concentration of oxygen in the atmosphere remains about 21% from the ground out to space. The most significant hazard of hypoxia at altitude is a crewmember engrossed in his/her flight duties may not notice the effects of hypoxia. These symptoms are typical of hypoxia:

1. An increased breathing rate, headache, fatigue
2. Light-headed or dizzy sensations, listlessness
3. Tingling or warm sensations, sweating
4. Poor coordination, impairment of judgment
5. Loss of vision or reduced vision, sleepiness
6. Cyanosis (blue coloring of skin, fingernails, and lips)
7. Behavior changes, feeling of well-being (euphoria)

Hyperventilation is a condition that can occur when there is a deficiency of carbon dioxide. This can be caused by an abnormal increase in the volume of air breathed in and out of the lungs and can occur subconsciously when a stressful situation is encountered in flight. It can also be caused by rapid or deep breathing while using oxygen. As hyperventilation blows off carbon dioxide that is needed by the body, a pilot can experience symptoms of light-headedness, suffocation, drowsiness, tingling in the extremities, and coolness, and react to them by breathing faster and deeper, causing even greater hyperventilation. The symptoms of hyperventilation subside within a few minutes after the rate and depth of breathing are consciously brought back under control. The buildup of carbon dioxide in the body can be hastened by controlled breathing, in and out, with a paper bag held over the nose and mouth.

ALL

7156. During a climb to 18,000 feet, the percentage of oxygen in the atmosphere

A— increases.
B— decreases.
C— remains the same.

Air contains about 20% oxygen, 79% nitrogen and 1% trace. Because the air is less dense at higher altitudes, it offers less actual oxygen per breath of air inhaled, even though oxygen and nitrogen are still mixed in the 20:79 ratio. (PLT096) — AIM ¶8-1-2

Answers (A) and (B) are incorrect because the atmospheric pressure changes, but the percentage of oxygen remains the same.

ALL

7157. Which statement concerning hypoxia is true?

A— Belligerence or a false sense of security may be symptoms of hypoxia.
B— Hypoxia is caused by nitrogen bubbles in the joints and bloodstream.
C— Forcing oneself to concentrate on the flight instruments will help to overcome the effects of hypoxia.

The most significant hazard characteristic of hypoxia at altitude is if a crewmember is engrossed in flight duties, he/she may not notice the effects of hypoxia. Individuals differ in their reaction to hypoxia, but tingling of the skin and a false sense of security are typical symptoms. (PLT330) — AIM ¶8-1-2

Answer (B) is incorrect because decompression sickness is caused by nitrogen bubbles in the joints and bloodstream. Answer (C) is incorrect because this is a technique which will help overcome the effects of spatial disorientation.

ALL

7159. What physical change would most likely occur to occupants of an unpressurized aircraft flying above 15,000 feet without supplemental oxygen?

A— Gases trapped in the body contract and prevent nitrogen from escaping the bloodstream.
B— The pressure in the middle ear becomes less than the atmospheric pressure in the cabin.
C— A blue coloration of the lips and fingernails develop along with tunnel vision.

At cabin pressure altitudes above 15,000 feet, the periphery of the visual field grays out to a point where only central vision remains (tunnel vision). A blue coloration (cyanosis) of the fingernails and lips develops. (PLT096) — AIM ¶8-1-2

ALL

7158. Hypoxia is the result of

A— excessive nitrogen in the bloodstream.
B— reduced barometric pressures at altitude.
C— decreasing amount of oxygen as your altitude increases.

Hypoxia is a state of oxygen deficiency in the body sufficient to impair functions of the brain and other organs. Hypoxia from exposure to altitude is due only to the reduced barometric pressures encountered at altitude, for the concentration of oxygen in the atmosphere remains about 21 percent from the ground out to space. (PLT330) — AIM ¶8-1-2

Answer (A) is incorrect because this describes decompression sickness, associated with scuba diving. Answer (C) is incorrect because the concentration of oxygen remains the same from the ground out to space; only the atmospheric pressure changes with altitude.

ALL

7163. How can smoking affect a pilot?

A— Can decrease night vision by up to 50 percent.
B— Reduces the oxygen-carrying capability of the blood.
C— Creates additional carbon dioxide gases in the body which often leads to hyperventilation.

Carbon monoxide inhaled in smoking can reduce the oxygen-carrying capacity of the blood to the degree that the amount of oxygen provided to body tissues will already be equivalent to the oxygen provided to the tissues when exposed to a cabin pressure altitude of several thousand feet. (PLT331) — FAA-H-8083-25

Answer (A) is incorrect because tobacco lowers the sensitivity of the eye and cuts night vision by approximately 20%. Answer (C) is incorrect because smoking deprives the body of oxygen because of the carbon monoxide content in smoke, which leads to hypoxia.

Answers

| 7156 | [C] | 7157 | [A] | 7159 | [C] | 7158 | [B] | 7163 | [B] |

ALL

7171. Anemic hypoxia has the same symptoms as hypoxic hypoxia but it is most often a result of

A— poor blood circulation.
B— a leaking exhaust manifold.
C— use of alcohol or drugs before flight.

Anemic (also known as hypemic) hypoxia is caused by contamination of blood with gases other than oxygen as a result of carbon monoxide poisoning (which could be caused by a leaking exhaust manifold), or excessive smoking. Hypoxic (altitude) hypoxia is caused by reduced oxygen pressure in the inhaled air at altitude. (PLT330) — AC 61-107

Answer (A) is incorrect because this describes stagnant hypoxia. Answer (C) is incorrect because this describes histotoxic hypoxia.

ALL

7160. Hyperventilation results in

A— a lack of carbon dioxide in the body.
B— a need to increase the flow of supplemental oxygen.
C— breathing too rapidly causing a lack of oxygen.

Hyperventilation, or an abnormal increase in the volume of air breathed in and out of the lungs, can occur subconsciously when a stressful situation is encountered in flight. Hyperventilation blows off carbon dioxide that is needed by the body. (PLT332) — AIM ¶8-1-3

Answer (B) is incorrect because the need for supplemental oxygen is due to hypoxia. Answer (C) is incorrect because breathing too rapidly causes a lack of carbon dioxide.

ALL

7161. Rapid or extra deep breathing while using oxygen can cause

A— cyanosis.
B— hyperventilation.
C— a build-up of carbon dioxide in the body.

The respiratory center of the brain reacts to the amount of carbon dioxide found in the blood stream. Hyperventilation is a condition that can occur when there is a deficiency of carbon dioxide, and this can be caused by rapid or extra deep breathing while using oxygen. (PLT332) — AIM ¶8-1-3

Answer (A) is incorrect because cyanosis is the blue coloration of the fingernails and lips, normally due to insufficient oxygen. Answer (C) is incorrect because rapid or extra deep breathing causes a reduction of carbon dioxide in the body.

ALL

7162. A person should be able to overcome the symptoms of hyperventilation by

A— increasing the breathing rate in order to increase lung ventilation.
B— slowing the breathing rate and increasing the amount of carbon dioxide in the body.
C— refraining from the use of alcohol and over-the-counter drugs such as antihistamines and tranquilizers.

The symptoms of hyperventilation subside within a few minutes after the rate and depth of breathing are consciously brought under control. The buildup of carbon dioxide in the body can be hastened by controlled breathing in and out of a paper bag held over the nose and mouth. (PLT332) — AIM ¶8-1-3

Answer (A) is incorrect because increasing the breathing rate would further aggravate hyperventilation. Answer (C) is incorrect because these things are not related to hyperventilation.

ALL

7170. The advantage of experiencing hypoxia in an altitude chamber is

A— it helps pilots learn to recognize their own symptoms in a controlled environment.
B— a person will be able to observe many hypoxic symptoms in several people at the same time.
C— when a person becomes hypoxic, air can quickly be readmitted to the chamber to revive that person.

Since symptoms of hypoxia do not vary in an individual, the ability to recognize hypoxia can be greatly improved by experiencing and witnessing the effects of hypoxia during an altitude chamber flight. (PLT330) — AC 61-107

Answer (B) is incorrect because the advantage is to identify the symptoms of hypoxia in oneself, not those of others. Answer (C) is incorrect because while this is true, it is not the main advantage.

Answers

7171 [B]   7160 [A]   7161 [B]   7162 [B]   7170 [A]

Spatial Disorientation, Vertigo, and Visual Illusions

Inside the ear are located three hollow, semicircular tubes arranged at approximately right angles to each other. In each tube is a sensory organ consisting of small hairs that project into a gelatinous substance. When the head turns, speeds up, slows down, or stops turning, the sensory hairs in the tube in the axis of turning are temporarily deflected, due to the motion of the fluid lagging behind the motion of the tube wall. When these hairs are deflected, the pilot may experience **spatial disorientation** or **vertigo**. Action can be taken to prevent spatial disorientation and its potentially disastrous consequences:

1. Always obtain preflight weather briefings.
2. Do not continue flight into adverse weather conditions or into dusk or darkness unless proficient in the use of flight instruments.
3. Ensure that when outside visual references are used, they are reliable, fixed points on the earth's surface.
4. Avoid sudden head movements, particularly during takeoffs, turns, and approaches to landing.
5. Remember that illness, medication, alcohol, fatigue, sleep loss, and mild hypoxia are likely to increase susceptibility to spatial disorientation.
6. Most importantly, become proficient in the use of flight instruments and rely upon them.

Rapid acceleration during takeoff can create the **illusion** of being in a nose-up attitude, and a disoriented pilot will push the aircraft into a nose-low, or dive attitude. Rapid deceleration caused by a quick reduction of the throttles can have the opposite effect, with the disoriented pilot pulling the aircraft into a nose-up, or stall attitude. An upsloping runway, upsloping terrain, or both, can create the illusion that the aircraft is at a higher altitude than it actually is. The pilot who does not recognize this illusion will fly a lower approach. A downsloping runway, downsloping approach terrain, or both can have the opposite effect.

Rain on the windscreen can create the illusion of greater height, and atmospheric haze causes the illusion of being a greater distance from the runway. The pilot who does not recognize these illusions will fly a lower approach.

In darkness, vision becomes more sensitive to light, a process called **dark adaptation**. Dark adaptation is impaired by exposure to cabin pressure altitudes above 5,000 feet, by carbon monoxide inhaled by smoking or from exhaust fumes, by deficiency in Vitamin A in the diet, and by prolonged exposure to bright sunlight.

ALL
7147. Which procedure is recommended to prevent or overcome spatial disorientation?

A— Avoid steep turns and rough control movements.
B— Rely entirely on the indications of the flight instruments.
C— Reduce head and eye movements to the greatest extent possible.

One of the most important steps to take in preventing and overcoming spatial disorientation is to develop the habit of relying on the indications of the flight instruments, unless the natural horizon or surface reference is clearly visible. (PLT334) — AIM ¶8-1-5

Answers (A) and (C) are incorrect because while these will help prevent spatial disorientation, they will not also help overcome it.

Answers
7147 [B]

ALL

7145. A rapid acceleration can create the illusion of being in a

A— left turn.
B— noseup attitude.
C— nosedown attitude.

A rapid acceleration during takeoff can create the illusion of being in a nose-up attitude, and a disoriented pilot will push the aircraft into a nose-low, or dive attitude. (PLT334) — AIM ¶8-1-5

Answer (A) is incorrect because the illusion of being in a left turn is the result of an abrupt correction of a banked attitude, or an abrupt head movement during a constant rate turn. Answer (C) is incorrect because this can happen with rapid deceleration.

ALL

7146. An illusion that the aircraft is at a higher altitude than it actually is, is produced by

A— atmospheric haze.
B— upsloping terrain.
C— downsloping terrain.

An upsloping runway, upsloping terrain, or both, can create the illusion that the aircraft is at a higher altitude than it actually is. The pilot who does not recognize this illusion will fly a lower approach. (PLT280) — AIM ¶8-1-5

Answer (A) is incorrect because atmospheric haze can create the illusion of being a greater distance from the runway than you actually are. Answer (C) is incorrect because downsloping terrain can create the illusion that the aircraft is lower than it actually is.

ALL

7148. What effect does haze have on the ability to see traffic or terrain features during flight?

A— Haze causes the eyes to focus at infinity.
B— The eyes tend to overwork in haze and do not detect relative movement easily.
C— All traffic or terrain features appear to be farther away than their actual distance.

Rain on the windscreen can create the illusion of greater height, and atmospheric haze causes the illusion of being a greater distance from the runway. The pilot who does not recognize these illusions will fly a lower approach. (PLT194) — AIM ¶8-1-5

Answer (A) is incorrect because haze causes the eyes to focus at a comfortable distance outside the cockpit, not at infinity. Answer (B) is incorrect because haze causes the eyes to relax and stare without really seeing.

ALL

7150. Dark adaptation is impaired by exposure to

A— carbon dioxide.
B— vitamin A in the diet.
C— cabin pressure altitudes above 5,000 feet.

In darkness, vision becomes more sensitive to light, a process called dark adaptation. Dark adaptation is impaired by exposure to cabin pressure altitudes above 5,000 feet, by carbon monoxide inhaled by smoking or from exhaust fumes, by deficiency in Vitamin A in the diet, and by prolonged exposure to bright sunlight. (PLT098) — AIM ¶8-1-6

Answer (A) is incorrect because it is carbon monoxide that can impair dark adaptation. Answer (B) is incorrect because Vitamin A will aid dark adaptation.

ALL

7169. Although not required, supplemental oxygen is recommended for use when flying at night above

A— 5,000 feet.
B— 10,000 feet.
C— 12,500 feet.

A deterioration in night vision occurs at a cabin pres-sure altitude as low as 5,000 feet. For optimum protection, pilots are encouraged to use supplemental oxygen above 10,000 feet during the day and above 5,000 feet at night. (PLT438) — AC 61-107

Answer (B) is incorrect because oxygen is recommended above 10,000 feet during the day. Answer (C) is incorrect because oxygen is required above 12,500 feet after 30 minutes, regardless of day or night operations.

Answers

| 7145 | [B] | 7146 | [B] | 7148 | [C] | 7150 | [C] | 7169 | [A] |

Motion Sickness

Motion sickness is caused by continued stimulation of the tiny portion of the inner ear which controls the pilot's sense of balance. Motion sickness, particularly among student pilots, is probably a result of combining anxiety, unfamiliarity, and the vibration or jogging received from the aircraft, and is usually overcome by experience. To overcome motion sickness, open up the air vents, loosen the clothing, use supplemental oxygen, and keep the eyes on a point outside the aircraft. Avoid unnecessary head movements, and cancel the flight and land as soon as possible.

ALL
7165. What suggestion could you make to students who are experiencing motion sickness?

A— Recommend taking medication to prevent motion sickness.
B— Have the students lower their head, shut their eyes, and take deep breaths.
C— Tell the students to avoid unnecessary head movement and to keep their eyes on a point outside the aircraft.

To overcome motion sickness, open up the air vents, loosen the clothing, use supplemental oxygen, and keep the eyes on a point outside the aircraft. Avoid unnecessary head movements, and cancel the flight and land as soon as possible. (PLT329) — FAA-H-8083-25

ALL
7166. Motion sickness is caused by

A— continued stimulation of the tiny portion of the inner ear which controls sense of balance.
B— an instability in the brain cells which affects balance and will generally be overcome with experience.
C— the movement of an aircraft causing the stomach to create an acid substance which causes the stomach lining to contract.

Motion sickness is caused by continued stimulation of the tiny hairs inside the channels of the inner ear which control one's sense of balance. (PLT329) — FAA-H-8083-25

Collision Avoidance

The eyes can focus only on a narrow viewing area, so effective **scanning** is accomplished with a series of short, regularly spaced eye movements that bring successive areas of the sky into the central visual field. Each movement should not exceed 10°, and each area should be observed for at least 1 second to enable detection.

An effective way of preventing a collision hazard in the traffic pattern is to enter the pattern at the correct position, midway of the downwind leg at an angle of 45°, at the correct traffic pattern altitude, and to continually scan the area for traffic.

The physical makeup of the eye is such that **off-center viewing** is most effective for night viewing. When you scan for other aircraft at night, do not look directly at the area you expect the aircraft to be flying, but rather scan slightly above or below the suspected area.

The FAA Near Mid-Air Collision Report indicates that 81% of the incidents occurred in clear skies and unrestricted visibility conditions, and 46% occurred over a VOR facility.

Answers

7165   [C]   7166   [A]

ALL

7149. Which technique should a student be taught to scan for traffic to the right and left during straight-and-level flight?

A— Continuous sweeping of the windshield from right to left.

B— Concentrate on relative movement detected in the peripheral vision area.

C— Systematically focus on different segments of the sky for short intervals.

Because the eyes can focus only on a narrow viewing area, effective scanning is accomplished with a series of short, regularly spaced eye movements that bring successive areas of the sky into the central visual field. Each movement should not exceed 10°, and each area should be observed for at least 1 second to enable detection. (PLT194) — AIM ¶8-1-6

ALL

7164. One aid in increasing night vision effectiveness would be to

A— look directly at objects.

B— force the eyes to view off center.

C— increase intensity of interior lighting.

The physical makeup of the eye is such that off-center viewing is most effective for night viewing. When you scan for other aircraft at night, do not look directly at the area you expect the aircraft to be flying, but force the eyes to look slightly off center. (PLT333) — FAA-H-8083-3

ALL

7172. What is an effective way to prevent a collision hazard in the traffic pattern?

A— Enter the pattern in a descent.

B— Maintain the proper traffic pattern altitude and continually scan the area.

C— Rely on radio reports from other aircraft who may be operating in the traffic pattern.

An effective way of preventing a collision hazard in the traffic pattern is to enter the pattern at the correct position, midway of the downwind leg at a 45° angle of the correct traffic pattern altitude, and to continually scan the area for traffic. (PLT194) — AC 90-48C

Answer (A) is incorrect because you should enter the pattern at traffic pattern altitude. Answer (C) is incorrect because not all aircraft may be using a radio, or on the same frequency as you.

ALL

7174. The most effective technique to use for detecting other aircraft at night is to

A— turn the head and sweep the eyes rapidly over the entire visible region.

B— avoid staring directly at the point where another aircraft is suspected to be flying.

C— avoid scanning the region below the horizon so as to avoid the effect of ground lights on the eyes.

The physical makeup of the eye is such that off-center viewing is most effective for night viewing. When you scan for other aircraft at night, do not look directly at the area you expect the aircraft to be flying, but rather scan slightly above or below the suspected area. (PLT194) — AC 90-48C

ALL

7173. Most midair collision accidents occur during

A— hazy days within the traffic pattern environment.

B— clear days in the vicinity of navigational aids.

C— night conditions during simulated instrument flight.

Most midair collision accidents and reported near midair collision incidents occur in good VFR weather conditions and during the hours of daylight. Most of these accident/incidents occur within 5 miles of an airport and/or near navigation aids. (PLT195) — FAA-H-8083-3

Answers

| 7149 | [C] | 7164 | [B] | 7172 | [B] | 7174 | [B] | 7173 | [B] |

Cross-Reference A
Question Number and Page Number

The following list of the numbered questions included in this ASA Test Prep is given in sequential order; however, as a result of our ongoing review of FAA test question databases, some question numbers may have been removed due to changes in the database. **All currently existing questions are accounted for in this list**. For more information about the questions included in ASA Test Preps, please read Pages ix–x in the front matter for this book.

Question Number	Page Number	Question Number	Page Number	Question Number	Page Number	Question Number	Page Number
4604	9–37	6002	1–6	6033-11	1–20	6051-1	1–25
4832	9–28	6002-1	1–6	6033-12	1–20	6052	1–26
4836	9–28	6003	1–6	6033-13	1–21	6053	1–26
4837	9–29	6004	1–9	6033-14	1–21	6054	1–26
4838	9–29	6005	1–10	6033-15	1–21	6054-1	1–26
4839	9–29	6005-1	1–10	6034	1–16	6055	1–26
4840	9–29	6006	1–10	6035	1–17	6055-1	1–27
4845-1	9–29	6007	1–11	6035-1	1–17	6056	1–27
4845-2	9–30	6008	1–10	6036	1–17	6057	1–28
4847	9–30	6009	1–10	6037	1–17	6058	1–28
4848	9–30	6010	1–10	6038	1–14	6059	1–28
4849	9–30	6011	1–7	6039-1	1–12	6060	1–28
4850-1	9–30	6012	1–8	6039-2	1–12	6061	1–29
4850-2	9–30	6013	1–9	6039-3	1–13	6062	1–29
4851	9–30	6014	1–6	6039-4	1–13	6063	1–29
4853	9–31	6015	1–6	6039-5	1–13	6064	1–29
4855	9–31	6016	1–7	6039-6	1–28	6065	1–30
4856	9–31	6017	1–8	6039-7	1–13	6066	1–36
4858	9–31	6018	1–9	6039-8	1–13	6067	1–30
4859	9–31	6019	1–8	6039-9	1–13	6068	1–33
4862	9–31	6020	1–9	6039-10	1–14	6069	1–30
4863	9–32	6020-1	1–9	6039-11	1–14	6070	1–30
4865	9–32	6021	1–7	6040-1	1–14	6071	1–38
4866	9–32	6022	1–7	6040-2	1–14	6072	1–38
4867	9–32	6023	1–7	6040-3	1–14	6073	1–38
4869	9–32	6024	1–7	6040-4	1–15	6074	1–38
4871	9–33	6025	1–8	6040-5	1–15	6075	1–39
4872	9–33	6026	1–8	6040-6	1–15	6076	1–33
4873-1	9–33	6027	1–11	6040-7	1–15	6077	1–35
4873-2	9–33	6027-1	1–11	6040-8	1–15	6077-1	1–35
4874	9–33	6027-2	1–11	6040-9	1–15	6078	1–35
4875-1	9–34	6027-3	1–11	6040-10	1–16	6079	1–33
4875-2	9–34	6027-4	1–11	6040-11	1–16	6080	1–33
4876	9–34	6027-5	1–12	6040-12	1–16	6081	1–34
4878-2	9–34	6028	1–12	6040-13	1–16	6082-1	1–34
4882	9–34	6029	1–12	6041	1–23	6082-2	1–34
4883	9–34	6030	1–8	6041-1	1–24	6082-3	1–34
4899	9–35	6031	1–17	6042	1–23	6082-4	1–34
4900	9–35	6032	1–17	6043	1–23	6082-5	1–34
4904	9–35	6033	1–18	6044	1–24	6083	1–36
4905	9–35	6033-1	1–18	6044-1	1–24	6084	1–35
4906	9–35	6033-2	1–18	6045	1–24	6085	1–36
4907	9–36	6033-3	1–18	6046	1–24	6086	1–36
4920	9–36	6033-4	1–18	6047	1–24	6087	1–36
4921	9–36	6033-5	1–19	6048	1–25	6088	1–35
4924	9–36	6033-6	1–19	6049	1–25	6089	1–38
4925	9–36	6033-7	1–19	6049-1	1–25	6090	1–36
4926	9–37	6033-8	1–19	6049-2	1–25	6091-1	1–37
4927	9–37	6033-9	1–20	6050	1–26	6091-2	1–37
6001	1–6	6033-10	1–20	6051	1–25	6091-3	1–37

Question Number	Page Number	Question Number	Page Number	Question Number	Page Number	Question Number	Page Number
6784	4–34	6839	9–54	6924	6–27	6987	9–7
6785	4–37	6840	2–44	6925	6–27	6988	9–8
6786	4–37	6841	4–25	6926	6–28	6989	9–4
6787	4–37	6842	4–25	6928	7–6	6990	9–4
6788	4–40	6843	4–25	6929	7–9	6991	9–11
6789	4–42	6844	4–26	6930	7–8	6992	9–11
6790	4–41	6845	4–26	6931	7–9	6993	9–10
6791	4–41	6846	4–26	6932	7–9	6994	9–10
6792	4–41	6847	3–39	6933	6–5	6995	9–10
6793	4–42	6848	3–39	6934	6–5	6996	9–11
6794	4–42	6849	3–39	6935	6–5	6997	9–12
6795	4–42	6850	2–46	6935-1	6–5	6998	9–10
6796	4–44	6851	2–48	6936	6–5	6999	9–10
6797	4–44	6852	2–48	6937	6–5	7000	9–11
6798	4–44	6853	2–48	6938	6–6	7001	9–12
6799	4–37	6854	2–46	6939	6–6	7002	9–12
6800	4–38	6855	2–46	6940	6–6	7003	9–4
6801	4–38	6856	6–12	6941	6–6	7004	9–43
6801-1	4–39	6857	6–12	6942	6–6	7005	9–12
6802	4–29	6857-1	6–13	6943	6–6	7006	9–12
6803	4–29	6858	6–13	6944	6–7	7007	9–12
6804	4–28	6859	6–13	6945	6–7	7008	9–8
6805	4–28	6860	6–19	6946	6–7	7009	9–13
6806	2–26	6861	6–19	6947	6–7	7010	9–13
6807	4–19	6862	6–19	6948	6–7	7011	9–14
6808	4–19	6863	8–51	6949	6–8	7012	9–14
6809	4–19	6864	6–18	6949-1	6–8	7013	9–14
6810	4–19	6865	6–18	6950	6–8	7014	9–15
6811	4–19	6866	6–21	6951	6–8	7015	9–15
6812	4–20	6867	6–21	6952	6–8	7016	9–15
6813	4–20	6868	6–22	6953	6–8	7017	9–15
6814	2–20	6869	6–17	6954	6–9	7018	9–15
6815	4–29	6870	6–17	6954-1	6–9	7019	9–15
6816	4–29	6871	6–23	6955	6–9	7020	9–16
6817	4–30	6872	6–23	6956	6–9	7021	9–16
6818	4–30	6873	6–24	6957	6–9	7022	9–17
6819	4–31	6874	6–16	6958	6–10	7023	9–17
6820	4–31	6875	6–16	6959	7–7	7024	9–17
6821	4–30	6876	6–16	6960	7–7	7024-1	9–17
6822	4–31	6877	6–4	6961	7–7	7025	9–18
6823	4–29	6878	6–4	6962	7–7	7026	9–18
6824	4–31	6879	6–10	6963	7–7	7027	9–18
6825	4–30	6880	6–10	6964	7–7	7028	9–19
6826	4–30	6881	6–10	6965	7–7	7029	9–20
6827-1	4–45	6882	6–4	6966	7–8	7030	9–20
6827-2	2–42	6883	6–4	6969	7–10	7031	9–20
6827-3	4–45	6884	6–4	6970	7–10	7032	9–21
6827-4	4–45	6885	6–4	6971	7–10	7033	9–21
6828	4–45	6886	6–14	6972	7–10	7034	9–21
6829	4–46	6887	6–15	6973	7–11	7035	9–20
6830	4–24	6888	6–15	6973-1	7–11	7036	9–19
6831-1	4–24	6900	6–24	6975	7–10	7037	9–23
6831-2	4–25	6901	6–25	6976	9–3	7038	9–23
6832	4–25	6902	6–25	6977	9–3	7039	9–23
6833-1	9–46	6903	6–25	6978	9–3	7040	9–23
6833-2	2–42	6904	6–25	6979	9–3	7041	9–23
6834	4–25	6905	6–3	6980	9–5	7042	9–24
6835-1	9–51	6911	6–28	6981	9–6	7043	9–25
6835-2	2–42	6912	6–28	6982	9–6	7044	9–25
6835-3	2–42	6919	6–26	6983	9–6	7045	9–25
6836	2–44	6920	6–26	6984	9–7	7046	9–25
6837	2–44	6922	6–27	6985	9–7	7047	9–25
6838	2–44	6923	6–27	6986	9–7	7048	9–25

Cross-Reference B
Learning Statement Code and Question Number

The expression "learning statement," as used in FAA airman testing, refers to measurable statements about the knowledge a student should be able to demonstrate following a certain segment of training. When you take the applicable airman knowledge test required for an airman pilot certificate or rating, you will receive an Airman Knowledge Test Report. The test report will list the learning statement codes for questions you have answered incorrectly. Match the codes given on your test report to the ones in the official FAA Learning Statement Codes (listed below in this cross-reference). Use Cross-Reference A in this book to find the page number for the question numbers listed below.

Your instructor is required to provide instruction on each of the areas of deficiency listed on your Airman Knowledge Test Report (as LSCs), and give you an endorsement for this instruction. The Airman Knowledge Test Report must be presented to the examiner conducting your practical test. During the oral portion of the practical test, the examiner is required to evaluate the noted areas of deficiency.

The FAA's learning statement codes are a hierarchical sequence of classification codes that places a knowledge item in a unique category, which can then be used for reference to source textbooks and study material. The LSCs are assigned to all FAA test questions in order to categorize them for placement on a given Knowledge Exam. This classification code system uses the following hierarchy (which is further detailed in the cross-reference table below):

- *Topic* — this is the overall subject matter topic code, the highest classification of overall subject matter a knowledge test item was developed to assess (for example, "Aerodynamics").

- *Content* — the secondary level subject matter code (for example, "Airspeed").

- *Specific* — the basic hierarchical classification code the subject matter for a knowledge test item (for example, "Thrust").

If you received a code on your Airman Test Report that is not listed in this cross-reference, email ASA at **cfi@asa2fly.com**. We will provide the definition so you can review that subject area.

The FAA appreciates testing experience feedback. You can contact the branch responsible for the FAA Knowledge Exams directly at:

Federal Aviation Administration
AFS-630, Airman Testing Standards Branch
PO Box 25082
Oklahoma City, OK 73125
Email: AFS630comments@faa.gov

Learning Statement Code	FAA Reference	Subject Description (or Topic ⟩ Content ⟩ Specific classification) Question Numbers
PLT004	FAA-H-8083-25	Aircraft Performance ⟩ Charts ⟩ Climb/Cruise Performance; Climb Performance Data; Maximum Climb Chart *6758, 6759*
PLT005	FAA-H-8083-25	Aircraft Performance ⟩ Computations ⟩ Determining Density Altitude *6741, 6742, 6743, 7310*
PLT006	FAA-H-8083-25	Aircraft Performance ⟩ Charts ⟩ Glide Distance Flight Operations ⟩ Emergency Procedures ⟩ Determining Glide Distance *6764, 6765, 6766*
PLT008	FAA-H-8083-25	Aircraft Performance ⟩ Computations ⟩ Determining Landing Distance Flight Operations ⟩ Landing ⟩ Slope Landing *6773, 6774, 6775*
PLT011	FAA-H-8083-25	Calculate aircraft performance — takeoff *6753, 6754, 6757, 6761, 6762, 6763*
PLT012	FAA-H-8083-13 FAA-H-8083-15 FAA-H-8083-25	Aircraft Performance ⟩ Computations ⟩ Basic Calculations; Computing Takeoff/Climb Distance; Cross-Country Soaring; Determining Landing Distance; Determining Takeoff Distance Aircraft Performance ⟩ Limitations ⟩ Basic Calculations Flight Operations ⟩ Launch Procedures ⟩ Computations Navigation ⟩ Dead Reckoning ⟩ Calculations Navigation ⟩ Pilotage ⟩ Calculations Navigation ⟩ Radio ⟩ ADF/NDB *6755, 6756, 6839, 6840, 6856, 6857, 6857-1, 6858, 6859, 6860, 6861, 6862, 6863, 6865, 6866, 6867, 6868, 6869, 6870, 6871, 6872, 6873, 6874, 6875, 6876, 6879, 6880, 6881, 6886, 6887, 6888*
PLT013	FAA-H-8083-3 FAA-H-8083-25	Aircraft Performance ⟩ Charts ⟩ Determining Crosswind Component Aircraft Performance ⟩ Limitations ⟩ Effects of Exceeding Flight Operations ⟩ Landing ⟩ Determining Crosswind Component *6767, 6768, 6769, 6769-1, 6770, 6771, 6772*
PLT014	FAA-H-8083-15	Navigation ⟩ Radio ⟩ ADF/NDB; VOR *6919, 6920*
PLT015	FAA-H-8083-25	Navigation ⟩ Dead Reckoning ⟩ Calculations *6864*
PLT018	FAA-H-8083-13 FAA-H-8083-25	Aerodynamics ⟩ Load Factor ⟩ Effect of Load Factor on Stalling Speed Aerodynamics ⟩ Principles of Flight ⟩ Load Factor; Pitch Attitude Aircraft Performance ⟩ Charts ⟩ Effect of Load Factor on Stalling Speed Aircraft Systems ⟩ Pitot/Static ⟩ Airspeed Indicator *6551, 6551-1, 6552, 6554, 6557, 6750, 6751, 6752*
PLT019	FAA-H-8083-25	Calculate pressure altitude *7286*
PLT021	FAA-H-8083-1 FAA-H-8083-13 FAA-H-8083-25	Weight and Balance ⟩ Aircraft Loading ⟩ Graphs; Limitations; Shifting Weight; Weight and Balance Charts; Weight and Balance Diagram Weight and Balance ⟩ Center of Gravity ⟩ Computations; Formulas; Shifting Weight; Winch Tow *6713, 6776, 6777, 6778, 6779, 6780, 6781, 6782, 6783, 6784, 6785, 6786, 6787, 6788, 6789, 6790, 6791, 6792, 6793, 6794, 6795, 6796, 6797, 6798, 6799, 6800, 6801, 6801-1, 6802, 6803, 6805*

Learning Statement Code	FAA Reference	Subject Description (or Topic ⟩ Content ⟩ Specific classification) Question Numbers
PLT022	AC 60-22 FAA-H-8083-9	Fundamentals of Instructing ⟩ Techniques-Flight Instruction ⟩ Aeronautical Decision Making Human Factors ⟩ ADM ⟩ Hazardous Attitude; Risk Elements; Risk Management *7167-1, 7226-1, 7226-2, 7228-4*
PLT023	AC 00-6	Weather ⟩ Meteorology ⟩ Density Altitude *6747-1, 7287, 7288*
PLT025	FAA-H-8083-25	Aerodynamics ⟩ Principles of Flight ⟩ Physics *6520*
PLT030	Goodyear Airship Op. Manual	Define false lift *6855*
PLT034	14 CFR 1	Regulations ⟩ 14 CFR Part 1 ⟩ Definition *6316-4*
PLT035	FAA-H-8083-21	Define V_{NE}/V_{NO} *6832*
PLT040	AIM	Airspace ⟩ Controlled ⟩ Class C *6317, 6961, 6962, 6963*
PLT041	AC 00-6	Weather ⟩ Meteorology ⟩ Pressure *6168*
PLT044	AIM	Airspace ⟩ Procedures ⟩ Communications *6953*
PLT046	FAA-H-8083-25	Aerodynamics ⟩ Principles of Flight ⟩ Drag *6555, 6556, 6559, 6560*
PLT051	AC 00-45	Weather ⟩ Aeronautical Weather Forecasts ⟩ Data Interpretation *6305, 6306, 6306-1, 7318*
PLT052	14 CFR 91	Regulations ⟩ Airspace Classes ⟩ Class E Airspace *6434*
PLT054	FAA-H-8083-13	Interpret information on a Glider Performance Graph *6837*
PLT057	Balloon Ground School	Interpret information on a Hot Air Balloon Performance Graph *6842, 6843, 6844, 6845, 6846*
PLT059	AC 00-45 AIM	Weather ⟩ Aeronautical Weather Reports ⟩ Aviation Routine Weather Reports (METAR) *6247, 6248, 6248-1, 6249, 6250, 6251, 6252, 6253, 6254, 6255*
PLT061	AC 00-45	Weather ⟩ Aeronautical Weather Reports ⟩ Pilot Reports *6258, 6259, 6260, 6261*
PLT064	14 CFR 91 AIM SAC	Airspace ⟩ Controlled ⟩ Class B; Class C; Class D; Class E; Equipment Required Airspace ⟩ Special Use ⟩ Procedures Navigation ⟩ Dead Reckoning ⟩ Aeronautical Charts Navigation ⟩ Pilotage ⟩ Aeronautical Charts Regulations ⟩ Airspace Classes ⟩ Visibility and Cloud Clearance *6933, 6934, 6935, 6935-1, 6936, 6937, 6938, 6939, 6940, 6941, 6942, 6943, 6944, 6945, 6946, 6947, 6948, 6949, 6949-1, 6950, 6951, 6952, 6954, 6954-1, 6955, 6956, 6957, 6958, 7096*

Learning Statement Code	FAA Reference	Subject Description (or Topic ⟩ Content ⟩ Specific classification) / Question Numbers
PLT066	AC 00-45	Weather ⟩ Charts/Maps ⟩ Severe Weather Outlook Charts *6304*
PLT071	AC 00-45	Weather ⟩ Charts/Maps ⟩ Surface Analysis Charts *6282*
PLT072	AC 00-45	Weather ⟩ Aeronautical Weather Forecasts ⟩ Data Interpretation Weather ⟩ Aeronautical Weather Reports ⟩ Aviation Routine Weather Reports (METAR) *6264, 6265, 6266*
PLT074	FAA-H-8083-25	Aerodynamics ⟩ Load Factor ⟩ Effect of Bank Angle on Stall Speed; Velocity/Load Factor Chart Aircraft Performance ⟩ Charts ⟩ Determining Load Factors Aircraft Performance ⟩ Limitations ⟩ Airspeeds *6544, 6545, 6546, 6546-1, 6547, 6548, 6549, 6550, 6553*
PLT076	AC 00-45	Weather ⟩ Aeronautical Weather Forecasts ⟩ Data Dissemination Weather ⟩ Charts/Maps ⟩ Winds/Temperatures Aloft *6278, 6279, 6280*
PLT078	Chart Supplements U.S.	Airport Operations ⟩ Runway Conditions ⟩ Pilotage ⟩ Chart Supplements U.S. *7151, 7152, 7153, 7154, 7155*
PLT081	AC 00-45	Weather ⟩ Aeronautical Weather Forecasts ⟩ Aviation Weather Forecasts; Data Dissemination *6262, 6263*
PLT086	FAA-H-8083-3 FAA-H-8083-21 FAA-H-8083-25	Aerodynamics ⟩ Principles of Flight ⟩ Forces Acting on Aircraft Flight Operations ⟩ Maneuvers ⟩ Advanced; Basic; Ground Reference *7027, 7028, 7050, 7051, 7052*
PLT088	FAA-8083-25	Interpret speed indicator readings *6737, 6738, 6739, 6740*
PLT095	FAA-H-8083-21 FAA-H-8083-25	Aircraft Systems ⟩ Propeller ⟩ Slipstream Aerodynamics ⟩ Stability/Control ⟩ Cyclic Control; Phugoid Oscillations *6569, 6591, 6618, 7283, 7284*
PLT096	AIM	Human Factors ⟩ Aeromedical Factors ⟩ Physiological *7144, 7156, 7159*
PLT098	AIM	Human Factors ⟩ Aeromedical Factors ⟩ Fitness for Flight *7143, 7150*
PLT101	FAA-H-8083-25	Navigation ⟩ Pilotage ⟩ Aeronautical Charts; Measurement of Direction *6877, 6878*
PLT103	AC 60-22 FAA-H-8083-2	Human Factors ⟩ ADM ⟩ Hazardous Attitude *7226-3, 7227-3, 7228-1, 7228-2, 7228-3, 7229-1, 7229-2, 7229-3, 7229-4*
PLT104	FAA-H-8083-2	Human Factors ⟩ ADM ⟩ Risk Management *7322, 7323, 7324, 7325*

Learning Statement Code	FAA Reference	Subject Description (or Topic ⟩ Content ⟩ Specific classification) / Question Numbers
PLT112	FAA-H-8083-3 FAA-H-8083-21	Aerodynamics ⟩ Stall/Spins ⟩ Spin Recovery Airport Operations ⟩ Taxiing ⟩ Collective Pitch; Control Positioning; Cyclic Pitch Flight Operations ⟩ Landing ⟩ Crosswind Landing Flight Operations ⟩ Maneuvers ⟩ Advanced; Basic *6976, 6977, 6978, 7008, 7070, 7071, 7072, 7073, 7074, 7076, 7077, 7094, 7097-5*
PLT113	14 CFR 1 14 CFR 61	Regulations ⟩ 14 CFR Part 1 ⟩ Certification Regulation Criteria Regulations ⟩ Knowledge/Practical Test ⟩ Required Aircraft/Equipment *7208*
PLT114	Goodyear Airship Op. Manual Powered Parachute Bible Trikes	Recall aircraft design — construction/function *6731, 7246, 7264, 7265, 7266, 7267, 7268, 7268-1, 7269, 7270, 7273, 7275, 7276, 7277, 7278, 7279*
PLT115	FAA-H-8083-25	Aircraft Systems ⟩ Powerplant ⟩ Mixture Control *6653, 6654, 7295, 7296, 7298, 7301*
PLT118	FAA-H-8083-25	Aircraft Systems ⟩ Flight Instruments ⟩ Heading Indicator Aircraft Systems ⟩ Propeller ⟩ Gyroscopic Action of the Propeller *6587, 6593, 6676*
PLT119	AIM	Flight Operations ⟩ Approach ⟩ Collision Avoidance *7128*
PLT120	FAA-H-8083-25	Aerodynamics ⟩ Load Factor ⟩ Maneuvering Speed *6541*
PLT121	FAA-H-8083-11	Aircraft Loading Calculations *6841*
PLT123	14 CFR 91	Regulations ⟩ VFR Flight Plan ⟩ Information Required *6736-2*
PLT124	AIM FAA-H-8083-21 FAA-H-8083-25	Aircraft Performance ⟩ Atmospheric Effects ⟩ Determining Density Altitude Aircraft Performance ⟩ Computations ⟩ Determining Density Altitude *6830, 6831-1, 6831-2*
PLT125	FAA-H-8083-3 FAA-H-8083-21	Flight Operations ⟩ Approach ⟩ Roundout (Flare) Flight Operations ⟩ Emergency Procedures ⟩ Autorotation *4924, 4925, 4926, 7079, 7221, 7245*
PLT126	AC 91-13	Aircraft Systems ⟩ Environmental ⟩ Cold Weather Operations *6710*
PLT127	AC 00-6 FAA-H-8083-3 FAA-H-8083-21	Weather ⟩ Meteorology ⟩ Density Altitude *6169, 6171, 6172, 6744, 6745, 6746, 6747, 6748, 7141, 7308-1*
PLT129	FAA-H-8083-21 FAA-H-8083-25	Aircraft Performance ⟩ Computations ⟩ Determining Takeoff Distance Flight Operations ⟩ Landing ⟩ Slope Operations *6749*
PLT131	FAA-H-8083-3	Aircraft Performance ⟩ Atmospheric Effects ⟩ Ground Effect *6537, 6538, 6539, 6540*

Learning Statement Code	FAA Reference	Subject Description (or *Topic*) *Content*) *Specific* classification) Question Numbers
PLT132	14 CFR 1 FAA-H-8083-3 FAA-H-8083-25	Aircraft Performance) Limitations) Airspeed; Effect of CG Location; Flight Instruments Regulations) 14 CFR Part 1) Means Minimum Takeoff Safety Speed *6316-5, 6316-6, 6807, 6809, 6811*
PLT134	FAA-H-8083-13	Flight Operations) Launch Procedures) Tow Plane Criteria *6815*
PLT141	AIM	Airport Operations) Lighting) Rotating Beacon; Runway Centerline Lighting Airport Operations) Marking/Signs) Direction to Takeoff Runway; Entrance to Runway; Entry Prohibited; Hold Position; Hold Position Markings; Hold Short; ILS; Runway; Runway with Displaced Threshold; Taxiway; Taxiway Directional Sign; Taxiway to Runway Marking *7109, 7111, 7113, 7114, 7115, 7116, 7231, 7232, 7233, 7234, 7235, 7235-1, 7236, 7237, 7238, 7239, 7241*
PLT145	AIM	Airport Operations) Lighting) Pilot Controlled Lighting *7110*
PLT146	AIM 14 CFR 91	Airport Operations) Traffic Patterns) Segmented Circle Regulations) Class D Airspace) Minimum Altitudes *6435, 7126*
PLT147	AIM	Airport Operations) Lighting) VASI *7103, 7104, 7104-1, 7105, 7108*
PLT149	FAA-H-8083-21	Airport Operations) Taxiing) Taxiing Procedures *7092*
PLT150	AIM	Airport Operations) Traffic Patterns) Traffic Pattern Entry *7125, 7127*
PLT153	Goodyear Airship Op. Manaul	Recall airship — flight operations *6633, 6634, 6635, 6636, 6638, 6640, 6663, 6733, 6735, 6853, 6854, 7218, 7220*
PLT154	Goodyear Airship Op. Manual	Recall airship — ground weigh-off / static / trim condition *7222*
PLT156	Goodyear Airship Op. Manual	Recall airship — maximum headway / flight at equilibrium *7216*
PLT157	Goodyear Airship Op. Manual	Recall airship — pressure height / dampers / position *7219*
PLT158	Goodyear Airship Op. Manual	Recall airship — pressure height / manometers *6851*
PLT160	Goodyear Airship Op. Manual	Recall airship — stability / control / positive superheat *6639, 6852*

Learning Statement Code	FAA Reference	Subject Description (or *Topic*) *Content*) *Specific* classification) Question Numbers
PLT161	14 CFR 91 AIM	Airspace 〉 Controlled 〉 Class A; Class C; Class D; Class E; Communications Airspace 〉 Uncontrolled 〉 Class D Regulations 〉 14 CFR Part 91 〉 ATC Transponder and Altitude Reporting Equipment Regulations 〉 Airspace Classes 〉 Limitations; Minimum Visibility, VFR Requirements; Visibility and Cloud Clearance Regulations 〉 Class B Airspace 〉 Maximum Indicated Airspeed Regulations 〉 Class D Airspace 〉 Communications; Maximum Indicated Airspeed Regulations 〉 Weather Minimums 〉 Special VFR *6422, 6423, 6424, 6425, 6436, 6437, 6438, 6439, 6440, 6448, 6451, 6478, 6479, 6480, 6481, 6928, 6929, 6931, 6932, 6959, 6960, 6964, 6965, 6966*
PLT162	14 CFR 91 AIM	Airspace 〉 Uncontrolled 〉 Class D Airspace Regulations 〉 Airspace Classes 〉 Maximum Indicated Airspeed Regulations 〉 Class B Airspace 〉 Maximum Indicated Airspeed *6456, 6457, 6459, 6930*
PLT163	14 CFR 91	Regulations 〉 14 CFR Part 91 〉 Distance from Clouds; Special VFR Regulations 〉 Airspace Classes 〉 Minimum Flight Visibility Regulations 〉 Weather Minimums 〉 Visibility; Special VFR *6445, 6446, 6447, 6449, 6450, 6452, 6453, 6454, 6455*
PLT165	FAA-H-8083-25	Aircraft Systems 〉 Pitot/Static 〉 Altimeter *6681*
PLT166	FAA-H-8083-15	Recall altimeter — settings / setting procedures *4850-1*
PLT167	FAA-H-8083-25	Aircraft Systems 〉 Pitot/Static 〉 Altimeter *6682*
PLT168	FAA-H-8083-3 FAA-H-8083-25	Aerodynamics 〉 Principles of Flight 〉 Forces Acting on Aircraft; Lift; Pitch Attitude; Stalls *6515, 6533, 6534, 6535, 6536, 6558*
PLT170	FAA-H-8083-3 FAA-H-8083-13 FAA-H-8083-21	Flight Operations 〉 Approach 〉 Go Around; Normal Approach/Landing; Short Field Approach/Landing Flight Operations 〉 Landing 〉 Crosswind Approach/Landing; Off-Field Landing; Roundout (Flare); Running Landing; Short Field Approach/Landing Flight Operations 〉 Maneuvers 〉 Advanced Flight Operation 〉 Soaring Techniques 〉 Approach and Landing *6992, 6993, 6994, 6995, 6997, 6999, 7000, 7001, 7004, 7005, 7006, 7007, 7053, 7091, 7186, 7187, 7193, 7224*
PLT172	14 CFR 91	Regulations 〉 Airspace Classes 〉 Transponder/Altitude Reporting Equipment *6477*
PLT173	AC 00-6	Weather 〉 Meteorology 〉 Stability *6187*
PLT175	FAA-H-8083-21	Aerodynamics 〉 Flight Characteristics 〉 Physics Aerodynamics 〉 Principles of Flight 〉 Helicopter Emergencies Flight Operations 〉 Emergency Procedures 〉 Autorotation *4849, 6607-2, 6607-3, 7078-1, 7078-2*

Learning Statement Code	FAA Reference	Subject Description (or Topic ⟩ Content ⟩ Specific classification) / Question Numbers
PLT177	Balloon Digest Balloon Ground School	Recall balloon — flight operations *6626, 7206*
PLT179	Balloon Ground School	Recall balloon — ground weigh-off / static equilibrium / load *6629*
PLT180	Balloon Ground School Powerline Excerpts	Recall balloon — hot air / lift / false lift / characteristics *6630, 6631, 7201, 7202, 7203*
PLT183	Balloon Ground School FAA-H-8083-11 How to Fly a Balloon	Recall balloon flight operations — ascent / descent *6628, 6632, 7198, 7204, 7209*
PLT184	Balloon Ground School	Recall balloon flight operations — launch / landing *6726, 7197, 7211, 7212, 7213, 7214*
PLT185	FAA-H-8083-15	Recall basic instrument flying — fundamental skills *4840, 4850-2, 4851, 4853, 4858, 4859, 4862, 4865, 4874, 4906, 4907, 7099, 7099-1*
PLT186	FAA-H-8083-15	Aircraft Systems ⟩ Flight Instruments ⟩ Attitude Instrument Flying *4872, 4876, 4899, 7100, 7100-1*
PLT187	FAA-H-8083-15	Recall basic instrument flying — turn coordinator / turn and slip indicator *4838, 4839, 4847, 4856, 4818-2, 4882, 4883, 4904, 4905, 4921*
PLT189	FAA-H-8083-25	Recall carburetor — effects of carburetor heat / heat control *7290*
PLT190	FAA-H-8083-21 FAA-H-8083-25	Aircraft Systems ⟩ Deicing/Anti-icing ⟩ Carburetor Air Temperature Aircraft Systems ⟩ Powerplant ⟩ Carburetor Icing *6658, 6659, 6660, 6661, 6662, 6704, 7244, 7248, 7254, 7280, 7291, 7292*
PLT191	FAA-H-8083-25	Aircraft Systems ⟩ Powerplant ⟩ Carburetor Systems *6656, 6657*
PLT192	AC 00-6	Weather ⟩ Hazardous ⟩ Thunderstorms Weather ⟩ Meteorology ⟩ Air Masses; Clouds *6188, 6189, 6190, 6191, 6193, 6200, 6218, 6242, 6245*
PLT194	AIM	Human Factors ⟩ Aeromedical Factors ⟩ Fitness for Flight; Visual Illusions *7148, 7149, 7172, 7174*
PLT195	AC 90-48 FAA-H-8083-3	Flight Operations ⟩ Approach ⟩ Normal Approach/Landing Flight Operations ⟩ Collision Avoidance ⟩ Pilot's Role *7002, 7173*
PLT196	AIM	Airport Operations ⟩ Tower Controlled ⟩ ATIS *7120, 7121*
PLT197	FAA-H-8083-21	Aerodynamics ⟩ Principles of Flight ⟩ Coriolis Effect *6608-2*

Learning Statement Code	FAA Reference	Subject Description (or *Topic* ⟩ *Content* ⟩ *Specific* classification) Question Numbers
PLT198	FAA-H-8083-25	Navigation ⟩ Dead Reckoning ⟩ Calculations *6882, 6883, 6884*
PLT199	FAA-H-8083-21	Recall cyclic control pressure — characteristics *6599-1*
PLT202	AIM FAA-H-8083-15	Navigation ⟩ Radio ⟩ DME; VOR *6911, 6912, 6926*
PLT203	AC 00-6	Weather ⟩ Meteorology ⟩ Temperature *6161, 6163*
PLT204	FAA-H-8083-9	Fundamentals of Instructing ⟩ Effective Communication ⟩ Developing Communication Skills Instructional Guidelines ⟩ Effective Communication ⟩ Testing Process *6056, 6057, 6058, 6059, 6060, 6061, 6062, 6063, 6064*
PLT206	AC 00-6 FAA-H-8083-25	Aircraft Performance ⟩ Atmospheric Effects ⟩ Determining Density Altitude Weather ⟩ Meteorology ⟩ Density Altitude *6170, 6173*
PLT207	FAA-H-8083-25	Aircraft Systems ⟩ Electrical ⟩ Electrical System Failure *6668, 6705, 7259*
PLT208	14 CFR 91 FAA-H-8083-3 FAA-H-8083-15 FAA-H-8083-21	Flight Operations ⟩ Emergency Procedures ⟩ Autorotation; Takeoff; Pilot-Induced Oscillation (PIO) Flight Operations ⟩ Landing ⟩ Emergency Approaches/Landings (Actual) Navigation ⟩ Dead Reckoning ⟩ Calculations Regulations ⟩ Equipment ⟩ Locator Transmitter *6466, 6734, 6996, 7068-1, 7068-2, 7069, 7097-2, 7097-3, 7097-4, 7101, 7101-1, 7102, 7102-1, 7199, 7207, 7215*
PLT211	FAA-H-8083-9	Fundamentals of Instruction ⟩ Critique/Evaluation ⟩ Evaluation Instructional Guidelines ⟩ Critique/Evaluation ⟩ Assessment Instructional Guidelines ⟩ Instructional Aids/Training Technologies ⟩ Teaching Aids Instructional Guidelines ⟩ Instructor Responsibilities/Professionalism ⟩ Evaluation; Pre-solo Requirements Instructional Guidelines ⟩ Teaching Process ⟩ Assessment *6069, 6098-2, 6124-2, 6124-3, 6127, 6129-2, 6129-3*
PLT213	FAA-H-8083-21	Aerodynamics ⟩ Stability/Control ⟩ Horizontal Stabilizer; Longitudinal *6699-2*
PLT214	FAA-H-8083-3 FAA-H-8083-13 FAA-H-8083-25	Aerodynamics ⟩ Load Factor ⟩ Maneuvering Speed Aerodynamics ⟩ Principles of Flight ⟩ Forces Acting on Aircraft; Subsonic Planform *6566, 6572, 6573, 6574, 6575, 6576*
PLT215	FAA-H-8083-25	Aircraft Systems ⟩ Flight Instruments ⟩ Acceleration Error; Compass; Deviation Error *4832, 6670, 6671, 6672, 6673, 6674, 6675*
PLT216	FAA-H-8083-31	Aircraft Systems ⟩ Flight Instruments ⟩ Total Energy Compensators *6716, 6717*
PLT217	FAA-H-8083-21	Flight Operations ⟩ Maneuvers ⟩ Advanced *7085, 7086, 7087*

Learning Statement Code	FAA Reference	Subject Description (or Topic 〉 Content 〉 Specific classification) Question Numbers
PLT219	FAA-H-8083-3 FAA-H-8083-21	Flight Operations 〉 Maneuvers 〉 Advanced; Basic; Ground Reference; Skids/ Slips; Stalls/Spins; Turns *6834, 6980, 6981, 6982, 6983, 6984, 6985, 7010, 7011, 7012, 7013, 7014, 7021, 7023, 7024, 7024-1, 7025, 7026, 7030, 7031, 7034, 7036, 7037, 7038, 7039, 7040, 7041, 7042, 7043, 7044, 7045, 7046, 7047, 7048, 7049*
PLT220	14 CFR 91	Regulations 〉 Operational Procedures 〉 Right of Way *6417, 6471*
PLT221	FAA-H-8083-3	Flight Operations 〉 Landing 〉 Normal Approach/Landing *7217, 7223*
PLT222	FAA-H-8083-3 FAA-H-8083-21	Aircraft Performance 〉 Atmospheric Effects 〉 Soft-Field Takeoff/Climb Flight Operations 〉 Emergency Procedures 〉 Approach/Landing Flight Operations 〉 Maneuvers 〉 Basic Flight Operations 〉 Takeoff 〉 Soft Field *6618-1, 7003*
PLT223	FAA-H-8083-3	Aircraft Performance 〉 Limitations 〉 Airspeeds Aircraft Systems 〉 Powerplant 〉 Performance Loss Flight Operations 〉 Positive Aircraft Control 〉 VMC *6808, 6810, 6812, 6813*
PLT225	AIM	Navigation 〉 Pilotage 〉 Aircraft Suffixes *6444, 7131, 7134*
PLT226	AC 00-6	Weather 〉 Meteorology 〉 Fog *6185, 6224, 6225, 6226, 6227, 6229*
PLT227	FAA-H-8083-9	Fundamentals of Instructing 〉 Techniques-Flight Instruction 〉 Integrated Flight Instruction Instructional Guidelines 〉 Techniques-Flight Instruction 〉 Integrated Flight Instruction *6135, 6136, 6137, 6138, 6138-1*
PLT228	FAA-H-8038-9	Instructional Guidelines 〉 Effective Communication 〉 Teaching Process Instructional Guidelines 〉 Learning Process 〉 Learning Transfer; Perceptions Instructional Guidelines 〉 Planning Instructional Activity 〉 Instructor Resources; Lesson Plan; Practice *6040-1, 6144-1, 6148, 6149, 6150-1, 6150-2, 6150-3, 6151, 6152, 6153, 6153- 1,6154, 6155, 6156, 6157, 6158, 6159, 6160*
PLT229	FAA-H-8083-9	Fundamentals of Instructing 〉 Learning Process 〉 Learning Theory Fundamentals of Instructing 〉 Techniques-Flight Instruction 〉 Instructor Responsibilities Instructional Guidelines 〉 Instructor Responsibilities/Professionalism 〉 Professionalism *6123-1, 6123-2, 6123-3*
PLT230	FAA-H-8083-9	Fundamentals of Instructing 〉 Techniques-Flight Instruction 〉 Instructor Responsibilities Instructional Guidelines 〉 Instructor Responsibilities/Professionalism 〉 Evaluation *6128, 6129-4, 6129-5, 6129-6, 6129-7, 6129-8, 6129-9, 6129-10*
PLT231	FAA-H-8083-9	Instructional Guidelines 〉 Human Behavior 〉 Anxiety; Stress *6130, 6131, 6132, 6132-1, 6133, 6133-1, 6133-3, 6133-3, 6133-4, 6133-5, 6143-1, 6143-2*

Learning Statement Code	FAA Reference	Subject Description (or Topic ⟩ Content ⟩ Specific classification) / Question Numbers
PLT232	FAA-H-8083-9	Instructional Guidelines ⟩ Human Behavior ⟩ Defense Mechanisms Instructional Guidelines ⟩ Instructor Responsibilities/Professionalism ⟩ Professionalism *6125, 6126, 6129-1, 7227-2*
PLT233	FAA-H-8083-9	Fundamentals of Instructing ⟩ Human Behavior ⟩ Defense Mechanisms Instructional Guidelines ⟩ Human Behavior ⟩ Defense Mechanisms *6044, 6049, 6049-1, 6049-2*
PLT234	FAA-H-8083-25	Aerodynamics ⟩ Principles of Flight ⟩ Axes *6505*
PLT235	FAA-H-8083-21 FAA-H-8083-25	Aerodynamics ⟩ Principles of Flight ⟩ Buntover; Definition; Forces Acting on Aircraft *6508, 6514, 6516, 6522, 6615-1, 6615-2, 6616*
PLT236	FAA-H-8083-21 FAA-H-8083-25	Aerodynamics ⟩ Principles of Flight ⟩ Airfoil; Airfoil Design; Forces Acting on Aircraft; Pressure Distribution Aerodynamics ⟩ Stability/Control ⟩ Design Characteristics *6512, 6531, 6562, 6570, 6597-1, 6622, 6624*
PLT237	FAA-H-8083-25	Aerodynamics ⟩ Principles of Flight ⟩ Forces Acting on Aircraft; Lift; Physics *6504, 6524, 6526, 6814*
PLT238	FAA-H-8083-13	Aerodynamics ⟩ Principles of Flight ⟩ Aspect Ratio; Definition *6577, 6578, 6579, 6580, 6581, 6582, 6583, 7329*
PLT239	Goodyear Airship Op. Manual	Recall forces acting on aircraft — buoyancy/drag/gravity/thrust *6637*
PLT240	FAA-H-8083-1 FAA-H-8083-21 FAA-H-8083-25	Aerodynamics ⟩ Principles of Flight ⟩ Physics Aerodynamics ⟩ Stability/Control ⟩ Adverse Balance; Aft CG; Destabilizing Effect; Indicated Airspeed; Performance Characteristics; Physics; Stability and Balance Control; Stall and Spin Recovery Weight and Balance ⟩ Center of Gravity ⟩ CG Location; CG Aft of Aft Limit; Insufficient Forward Cyclic Control *6571, 6610-2, 6816, 6818, 6819, 6820, 6821, 6822, 6823, 6824, 6825, 6827-1, 6827-3, 6827-4, 6828, 6829, 6835-3*
PLT241	FAA-H-8083-25	Aerodynamics ⟩ Principles of Flight ⟩ Forces Acting on Aircraft *6517, 6523, 6525, 6527*
PLT242	FAA-H-8083-3 FAA-H-8083-21 FAA-H-8083-25	Aerodynamics ⟩ Principles of Flight ⟩ Dissymmetry of Lift; Forces Acting on Aircraft; Pressure Distribution; Translational Lift *6507, 6513, 6521, 6605, 6613-3, 6760, 7075, 7274*
PLT244	FAA-H-8083-3 FAA-H-8083-25	Aerodynamics ⟩ Stability/Control ⟩ Buntover; Design Characteristics; Divergent Oscillations; Pilot Induced Oscillation (PIO); Power Pushover; Rolling; Spiral Instability Flight Operations ⟩ Landing ⟩ Normal Approach/Landing *6561, 6567, 6613-1, 6833-2, 6835-2, 6998, 7285*
PLT245	FAA-H-8083-3 FAA-H-8083-13 FAA-H-8083-25	Aerodynamics ⟩ Principles of Flight ⟩ Accelerated Stall; Forces Acting on Aircraft; Spins; Stalls/Spins; Steep Spiral Flight Operations ⟩ Maneuvers ⟩ Stalls/Spins *6511, 6806, 6826, 7032, 7035*

Learning Statement Code	FAA Reference	Subject Description (or *Topic* ⟩ *Content* ⟩ *Specific* classification) Question Numbers
PLT246	FAA-H-8083-25	Aerodynamics ⟩ Principles of Flight ⟩ Forces Acting on Aircraft *6518, 6519, 6529*
PLT247	FAA-H-8083-25	Recall forces acting on aircraft — thrust/drag/weight/lift *6528*
PLT248	FAA-H-8083-25	Aerodynamics ⟩ Principles of Flight ⟩ Level Turns; Turns Flight Operations ⟩ Maneuvers ⟩ Basic *6509, 6510, 6530, 6532, 6986, 6987*
PLT249	FAA-H-8083-25	Aircraft Systems ⟩ Powerplant ⟩ Mixture Control *6650, 6652, 7302, 7303, 7304*
PLT250	FAA-H-8083-25	Aircraft Systems ⟩ Fuel/Oil ⟩ Condensation *6644, 6647*
PLT251	AC 20-43 Balloon Digest Balloon Ground School	Recall fuel characteristics/contaminants/additives/leaks *6706, 6727, 6847, 6849, 7262*
PLT253	FAA-H-8083-25	Aircraft Systems ⟩ Fuel/Oil ⟩ Fuel System Preflight; Mixture Control; Tanks Aircraft Systems ⟩ Powerplant ⟩ Exhaust Gas Temperature Gauge; Fuel Injection System; Fuel Injectors; Mixture Control *6643, 6645, 6646, 6648, 6649, 6651, 6655, 6721, 6723, 6724, 6725, 6728, 6729, 6730, 6848, 6850, 7196-1, 7249, 7250, 7251, 7271, 7294, 7305*
PLT254	Balloon Digest Balloon Ground School Powered Parachute Bible	Recall fuel tank — components/operating principles/characteristics *6722, 7196, 7205*
PLT257	FAA-H-8083-13	Aerodynamics ⟩ Principles of Flight ⟩ Lift/Drag Devices Flight Operations ⟩ Soaring Techniques ⟩ Airspeed *6623, 7177*
PLT258	FAA-H-8083-3	Flight Operations ⟩ Maneuvers ⟩ Ground Reference *7009, 7015, 7016, 7017, 7018, 7019, 7020, 7022*
PLT259	FAA-H-8083-21	Aerodynamics ⟩ Flight Characteristics ⟩ Physics *7061*
PLT260	FAA-H-8083-21	Aircraft Systems ⟩ Rotor ⟩ Blade Flap *6700-2, 6835-1, 7093-1, 7093-2, 7095*
PLT261	AC 00-6	Weather ⟩ Hazardous ⟩ Thunderstorms *6221, 6222, 6223*
PLT263	AC 00-6	Weather ⟩ Meteorology ⟩ Fog *6211, 6213, 6228*
PLT264	FAA-H-8083-21	Flight Operations ⟩ Emergency Procedures ⟩ Recovery; Settling-with-Power *7063, 7064, 7065*
PLT265	FAA-H-8083-21	Recall helicopter takeoff/landing — ground resonance action required *7062*

Learning Statement Code	FAA Reference	Subject Description (or Topic 〉 Content 〉 Specific classification) Question Numbers
PLT267	Powerline Excerpts	Recall hot air balloon — weigh-off procedure *6627, 7200*
PLT268	FAA-H-8083-21	Flight Operations 〉 Approach 〉 Hovering Flight Operations 〉 Landing 〉 Hovering *7067*
PLT269	FAA-H-8083-9	Instructional Guidelines 〉 Human Behavior 〉 Defense Mechanisms; Repression *6045, 6046, 6047, 6048, 6050, 6051, 6051-1*
PLT270	FAA-H-8083-9	Instructional Guidelines 〉 Human Behavior 〉 Human Needs *6041, 6041-1, 6042, 6043, 6098-4, 6098-5, 6098-7, 6098-8, 7227-1*
PLT271	AC 60-22 FAA-H-8083-2	Human Factors 〉 ADM 〉 Risk Management *7230-3*
PLT272	FAA-H-8083-9	Instructional Guidelines 〉 Human Behavior 〉 Defense Mechanisms *7230-1, 7230-2*
PLT276	FAA-H-8083-25	Navigation 〉 Radio 〉 VOR *6900, 6901, 6902, 6903, 6904*
PLT278	FAA-H-8083-15 FAA-H-8083-25	Aircraft Systems 〉 Pitot/Static 〉 Airspeed Indicator Aircraft Systems 〉 Flight Instruments 〉 Attitude Instrument Flying *4836, 4837, 4845-1, 4845-2, 4848, 4863, 4900, 4920, 6482, 6683, 6736-1*
PLT280	AIM	Human Factors 〉 Aeromedical Factors 〉 Visual Illusions *7146*
PLT282	14 CFR 121	Regulations 〉 Documentation 〉 Certificate Holder's Manual *6494-2*
PLT283	AC 00-45	Recall information on a Constant Pressure Analysis Chart *6311, 6312*
PLT287	AC 00-45	Weather 〉 Charts/Maps 〉 Surface Analysis Charts *6281, 6283, 6283-1, 6284, 6284-1*
PLT288	AC 00-45	Recall information on a Terminal Aerodrome Forecast (TAF) *6262-1, 7327, 7328*
PLT290	AC 00-45	Weather 〉 Aeronautical Weather Forecasts 〉 Data Dissemination *6267, 6268, 6275, 6276, 6277, 6277-1*
PLT295	AC 61-67 FAA-H-8083-9	Fundamentals of Instructing 〉 Learning Process 〉 Skill Acquisition Fundamentals of Instructing 〉 Planning Instructional Activity 〉 Objectives Instructional Guidelines 〉 Instructor Responsibilities/Professionalism 〉 Demo Stalls; Professionalism Instructional Guidelines 〉 Learning Process 〉 Learning Transfer Instructional Guidelines 〉 Planning Instructional Activity 〉 Blocks of Learning Instructional Guidelines 〉 Techniques-Flight Instruction 〉 Apathy; Distractions; Fatigue; Obstacles to Learning During Flight Instruction *6038, 6139, 6139-1, 6140, 6141, 6142, 6143, 6145, 6147, 7168, 7168-1*
PLT297	FAA-H-8083-15	Recall instrument procedures — unusual attitude/unusual attitude recovery *4873-2, 4875-1, 4875-2, 4927*

Learning Statement Code	FAA Reference	Subject Description (or Topic 〉 Content 〉 Specific classification) Question Numbers
PLT300	AIM	Navigation 〉 Radio 〉 VOR; VORTAC; VOT *6922, 6923, 6924*
PLT301	AC 00-6	Weather 〉 Meteorology 〉 Temperature *6164, 6165*
PLT303	FAA-H-8083-13	Aerodynamics 〉 Principles of Flight 〉 Forces Acting on Aircraft; Physics *6836, 7191*
PLT304	FAA-H-8083-13	Flight Operations 〉 Launch Procedures 〉 Auto Launch; Autotow; CG Hook; Computations; Ground Launch; Landing; Tow Ring Strike; Winch Launch *6714, 6732, 7178, 7179, 7180, 7181, 7182, 7183, 7184, 7185*
PLT305	FAA-H-8083-25	Aerodynamics 〉 Principles of Flight 〉 Pitch Attitude Aircraft Systems 〉 Flight Controls/Secondary 〉 Flaps *6501, 6692*
PLT306	FAA-H-8083-9	Fundamentals of Instructing 〉 Learning Process 〉 Levels of Learning Instructional Guidelines 〉 Learning Process 〉 Learning Characteristics; Learning Theory; Learning Transfer *6003, 6027, 6027-1, 6027-2, 6027-3, 6027-4, 6027-5, 6029, 6030, 6033-5,* *6033-6, 6033-7, 6033-8, 6033-9, 6033-10, 6033-11, 6033-12, 6033-13, 6033-14,* *6033-15, 6035, 6035-1, 6037, 6039-1, 6040-5, 6040-6, 6040-7, 6040-12,* *6040-13, 6044-1, 6091-5, 6103-3, 6140-3, 7317, 7320, 7321*
PLT307	FAA-H-8083-9	Instructional Guidelines 〉 Critique/Evaluation 〉 Oral Assessment Instructional Guidelines 〉 Learning Process 〉 Learning Theory; Memory *6034, 6036, 6039-2, 6039-3, 6039-4, 6039-5, 6039-8, 6039-9, 6039-10, 6039-11*

PLT308	FAA-H-8083-9	Fundamentals of Instructing 〉 Learning Process 〉 Definitions of Learning;
		    Domains of Learning; Learning Plateau; Learning Theory; Principles of
		    Learning; Skill Acquisition
		Instructional Guidelines 〉 Learning Process 〉 Insights; Learning Characteristics;
		    Learning Theory; Perceptions
		
		6001, 6002, 6002-1, 6004, 6005, 6005-1, 6006, 6007, 6008, 6009, 6010, 6011,
		6012, 6013, 6014, 6015, 6016, 6017, 6018, 6019, 6020, 6020-1, 6021, 6022,
		6033, 6033-1,6033-2, 6033-3, 6033-4, 6040-2, 6040-3, 6040-4, 6040-11, 7319

PLT309	FAA-H-8083-21	Aerodynamics 〉 Principles of Flight 〉 Load Factor *6542, 6625*
PLT312	FAA-H-8083-25	Aerodynamics 〉 Stability/Control 〉 Stalling Speed *6817, 6988*
PLT314	FAA-H-8083-1	Weight and Balance 〉 Center of Gravity 〉 Formulas *6804, 6991*
PLT317	AIM	Weather 〉 Hazardous 〉 Microburst Weather 〉 Meteorology 〉 Microburst *6313, 6314*
PLT319	FAA-H-8083-25	Recall navigation — celestial *6905*
PLT320	FAA-H-8083-25	Navigation 〉 Dead Reckoning 〉 Aeronautical Charts; Calculations *6885*

Learning Statement Code	FAA Reference	Subject Description (or Topic 〉 Content 〉 Specific classification) Question Numbers
PLT322	AIM	Navigations 〉 Radio 〉 VORTAC *6925*
PLT323	AIM	Navigation 〉 Pilotage 〉 NOTAMS *7129, 7130*
PLT324	AC 91-13	Aircraft Systems 〉 Powerplant 〉 Oil System *6711, 7261, 7306, 7307*
PLT326	AC 61-107	Aircraft Systems 〉 Environmental 〉 Oxygen Systems *6708, 6709, 6718*
PLT328	FAA-H-8083-13	Weight and Balance 〉 Aircraft Loading 〉 Ballast *6838, 7309*
PLT329	FAA-H-8083-25	Recall physiological factors — cabin pressure *7165, 7166*
PLT330	AIM	Human Factors 〉 Aeromedical Factors 〉 Physiological *7157, 7158, 7170, 7171*
PLT331	AIM	Human Factors 〉 Aeromedical Factors 〉 Smoking *7163*
PLT332	AIM	Human Factors 〉 Aeromedical Factors 〉 Physiological *7160, 7161, 7162*
PLT333	FAA-H-8083-3	Recall physiological factors — night vision *7164*
PLT334	AIM FAA-H-8083-25	Human Factors 〉 Aeromedical Factors 〉 Physiological; Spatial Disorientation *7145, 7147*
PLT336	FAA-H-8083-15 FAA-H-8083-21	Aircraft Systems 〉 Pitot/Static 〉 Altimeter Flight Operations 〉 Landing 〉 Slope Operations Flight Operations 〉 Maneuvers 〉 Basic *4871, 7081, 7082, 7083, 7084, 7098, 7098-1*
PLT337	AC 91-43 FAA-H-8083-25	Aircraft Systems 〉 Pitot/Static 〉 Airspeed Indicator; Blockage *6677, 6678, 6679, 6680, 6712, 7289*
PLT342	FAA-H-8083-25 FAA-H-8083-29	Recall powerplant — controlling engine temperature *7256, 7293*
PLT343	FAA-H-8083-25	Aircraft Systems 〉 Powerplant 〉 Cooling; High Altitude Performance; Power; Reciprocating Engines *6641, 6642, 6667, 7054, 7210, 7252, 7253, 7255, 7257, 7258, 7263*
PLT344	AC 00-6	Weather 〉 Meteorology 〉 Moisture *6183, 6184, 7311*
PLT346	FAA-H-8083-3 FAA-H-8083-25	Aerodynamics 〉 Principles of Flight 〉 Forces Acting on Aircraft *6584, 6585, 6586, 7056, 7066, 7247, 7272, 7281*
PLT347	FAA-H-8083-3	Aircraft Systems 〉 Propeller 〉 The Critical Engine *6594, 6595, 6596*
PLT349	FAA-H-8083-21	Flight Operations 〉 Maneuvers 〉 Advanced *7090*

Learning Statement Code	FAA Reference	Subject Description (or Topic) Content) Specific classification) Question Numbers
PLT350	FAA-H-8083-25	Recall propeller operations — constant / variable speed
		6685
PLT351	FAA-H-8083-25	Aircraft Systems) Propeller) Blade Angle; Constant-Speed Propeller; Effective Pitch; Geometric Pitch; Propeller Slippage
		6588, 6589, 6590, 6592, 6664, 6665, 6666, 7308
PLT366	49 CFR 830	Regulations) NTSB Part 830) Reporting
		6496, 6497, 6498, 6499, 6500
PLT370	AIM	Flight Operations) Collision Avoidance) Ground Track
		7122
PLT372	14 CFR 91	Regulations) Aircraft Inspections) 100 Hour Inspection; Expiration Regulations) Aircraft Maintenance) Documentation
		6486, 6488, 6489, 6490
PLT373	14 CFR 91	Regulations) Documentation) Operating Limitations
		6410, 6746-1, 7195
PLT374	14 CFR 91	Regulations) Aircraft Maintenance) Responsibilities
		6484, 6485
PLT376	AIM	Airspace) Other) Wild Life Refuges
		6973-1
PLT377	14 CFR 91	Regulations) Aircraft Maintenance) Documentation
		6462
PLT384	14 CFR 91	Regulations) Pilot in Command) Passenger Briefing/Seatbelt Usage
		6414
PLT386	14 CFR 61	Regulations) Student Certificate) Expiration
		6404, 6404-1
PLT387	14 CFR 61	Recall regulations — change of address
		6355, 6356
PLT388	14 CFR 121	Regulations) Documentation) Cockpit Voice Recorder
		6494-3
PLT393	AIM	Airspace) Communications) Restricted Airspace Airspace) Special Use) Military Training Route; MOA; Warning Areas
		6969, 6970, 6971, 6972, 6973, 6975
PLT395	49 CFR 830	Regulations) NTSB Part 830) Definition
		6316-2, 6495
PLT401	FAA-H-8083-13	Recall regulations — dropping / aerial application / towing restrictions
		7175
PLT403	14 CFR 91	Regulations) 14 CFR Part 91) Emergency-Priority
		6430
PLT404	14 CFR 91	Regulations) Equipment) Locator Transmitter
		6467-2, 6483

Learning Statement Code	FAA Reference	Subject Description (or Topic 〉 Content 〉 Specific classification) Question Numbers
PLT405	14 CFR 61	Regulations 〉 Airspace Classes 〉 Transponder/Altitude Reporting Equipment Regulations 〉 Eligibility 〉 Practical Test Regulations 〉 Equipment 〉 Minimum Equipment Regulations 〉 Flight Instructor 〉 Application During Suspension Regulations 〉 Student Pilot 〉 Eligibility *6319, 6379, 6463, 6465, 6467-1, 6474, 6476*
PLT407	14 CFR 61	Regulations 〉 14 CFR 61 〉 Regulatory Requirement Regulations 〉 Additional Category Ratings 〉 Requirements Regulations 〉 Eligibility 〉 Flight Time; Practical Test Regulations 〉 Flight Review 〉 Proficiency Check; Training Requirements Regulations 〉 Flight Training 〉 Previous Foreign Instruction; Towing Gliders Regulations 〉 Knowledge/Practical Test 〉 Cheating Regulations 〉 Operating Pressurized Aircraft 〉 Training Requirements Regulations 〉 Student Pilot 〉 Eligibility Regulations 〉 Type Rating 〉 Additional Training *6326-1, 6327, 6328, 6329-1, 6329-2, 6336, 6344, 6347, 6348, 6349, 6350, 6352, 6353, 6357, 6358, 6359, 6363, 6368, 6380, 6390, 6402, 7313, 7316*
PLT409	14 CFR 61	Regulations 〉 14 CFR Part 61 〉 Eligibility Regulations 〉 Commercial Pilot 〉 Logging Flight Time Regulations 〉 Eligibility 〉 Flight Time Regulations 〉 Flight Instructor 〉 Training Regulations 〉 Second in Command 〉 Logging Flight Time *6345, 6346-2, 6383, 6394-2, 6399*
PLT411	14 CFR 61	Regulations 〉 Flight Instructor 〉 Certificate Renewal/Duration; Endorsements; Limitations; Restrictions; Requirements; Qualifications Training *6322, 6395, 6396, 6398, 6403*
PLT413	14 CFR 91	Regulations 〉 Fuel 〉 Minimum Requirements *6441, 6442, 6443*
PLT414	14 CFR 91	Regulations 〉 14 CFR Part 91 〉 Airship; Right of Way Rotorcraft Regulations 〉 Operational Procedures 〉 Right of Way *6418, 6419, 6420, 6421*
PLT418	14 CFR 61	Regulations 〉 14 CFR Part 61 〉 Knowledge Test-Retesting Regulations 〉 FAA Certificates 〉 Advanced/Basic Ground Instructor Limitations Regulations 〉 Flight Instructor 〉 Endorsements Regulations 〉 Student Pilot 〉 Logging Training Time *6339, 6405-1, 6405-2, 6405-3, 6405-4, 6405-5*
PLT419	FAA-H-8083-9	Instructional Guidelines 〉 Effective Communication 〉 Teaching Process Instructional Guidelines 〉 Instructor Responsibilities/Professionalism 〉 Professionalism *6039-6, 6055, 6055-1, 6342, 6366*
PLT425	14 CFR 91	Regulations 〉 Aircraft Maintenance 〉 Documentation; Rebuilt Engine Requirements *6487, 6493, 6494-1*
PLT427	14 CFR 61	Regulations 〉 Type Rating 〉 Medical Certificate Required *6333*

Learning Statement Code	FAA Reference	Subject Description (or Topic ⟩ Content ⟩ Specific classification) Question Numbers
PLT428	14 CFR 91	Recall regulations — minimum equipment list *6475*
PLT430	14 CFR 91	Regulations ⟩ Flight Altitude ⟩ VFR Regulations ⟩ Minimum Safe Altitude ⟩ Congested Areas; Definition; Helicopter; Other Than Congested Areas *6426, 6427, 6428, 6429, 6460, 6461*
PLT432	14 CFR 1	Regulations ⟩ 14 CFR Part 1 ⟩ Operational Control *6316-3*
PLT435	AIM	Airport Operations ⟩ Communications ⟩ CTAF; Unicom Frequency *7117, 7118, 7119*
PLT437	14 CFR 91	Regulations ⟩ Equipment ⟩ Over Water *6464*
PLT438	14 CFR 91	Regulations ⟩ Pressure Altitude ⟩ Supplemental Oxygen *6472, 6473, 6707, 7169*
PLT442	14 CFR 61	Regulations ⟩ Flight Review ⟩ Currency Requirements Regulations ⟩ Pilot in Command ⟩ Recent Flight Experience Regulations ⟩ Private Pilot ⟩ Currency Requirements Regulations ⟩ Type Rating ⟩ Training Requirements *6354*
PLT443	14 CFR 61	Regulations ⟩ 14 CFR Part 61 ⟩ Flight Review Regulations ⟩ Type Rating ⟩ Training Requirements *6318, 6326-2, 6351, 6387, 6391*
PLT444	14 CFR 91	Regulations ⟩ Pilot in Command ⟩ Emergency Responsibility *6406*
PLT445	14 CFR 91	Regulations ⟩ Pre-Flight ⟩ Requirements *6412, 6413*
PLT447	14 CFR 61	Regulations ⟩ 14 CFR Part 61 ⟩ Duration of Medical Certificate Regulations ⟩ Medical Certificate ⟩ Validity Period *6323, 6324, 6325*
PLT448	14 CFR 61	Regulations ⟩ 14 CFR Part 61 ⟩ Change of Address; Suspended/Revoked Regulations ⟩ Eligibility ⟩ Flight Time Regulations ⟩ FAA Certificates ⟩ Change of Address; Safety Pilot Requirements; Rec Pilot Privileges Regulations ⟩ Student Certificate ⟩ Endorsements; Expiration; Limitations *6332, 6369, 6376, 6377, 6385, 6386, 6415*
PLT451	14 CFR 61	Regulations ⟩ Additional Category Ratings ⟩ Requirements Regulations ⟩ Commercial Pilot ⟩ Limitations; Requirements Regulations ⟩ Eligibility ⟩ Flight Time Regulations ⟩ Flight Instructor ⟩ Endorsements Regulations ⟩ Student Pilot ⟩ Experience Requirements *6378, 6381, 6382, 6384, 6388, 6389, 6392, 6393, 6394-1, 7314, 7314-1, 7315, 7315-1*

Learning Statement Code	FAA Reference	Subject Description (or Topic) Content) Specific classification) Question Numbers
PLT457	14 CFR 61	Instructional Guidelines) Instructor Responsibilities/Professionalism) Pre-solo Requirements Regulations) 14 CFR Part 61) Endorsements; Flight Instructor Records Regulations) Student Certificate) Endorsements; Limitations Regulations) Student Pilot) Endorsements *6321, 6334, 6346-1, 6360, 6361, 6362, 6371, 6372, 6373, 6374, 6375, 6397, 6400, 6401*
PLT461	14 CFR 91	Regulations) 14 CFR Part 91) Aircraft Lights *6468, 6469, 6470*
PLT463	14 CFR 61	Regulations) FAA Certificates) Suspension/Revocation *6320, 6407, 6408, 6409*
PLT467	14 CFR 91	Regulations) Class B Airspace) Student Pilot Requirements Regulations) Flight Altitude) VFR Regulations) Weather Minimums) Special VFR *6458*
PLT470	FAA-H-8083-21	Aerodynamics) Principles of Flight) Autorotation; Blade Tip Stall; Coning; Coriolis Effect; Definition; Dissymmetry of Lift; Driving Region; Forces Acting on Aircraft; Forward Flight; Limitations; Main Rotor System; Negative G Maneuver; Physics; Prerotation; Pitch Attitude; Rotor Force; Rotor Lift; Translating Tendency or Drift Aerodynamics) Stability/Control) High Forward Airspeed; Translating Tendency or Drift Aircraft Systems) Rotor) Autorotation; Vibration Flight Operations) Emergency Procedures) Autorotation; Loss of Tail Rotor Effectiveness; Recovery from Low Rotor RPM Flight Operations) Maneuvers) Helicopter Emergencies *6503, 6597-2, 6598, 6599-2, 6600, 6601-1, 6601-2, 6602-1, 6602-2, 6603-1, 6603-2, 6604, 6606, 6607-1, 6607-4, 6608-1, 6608-3, 6609, 6610-1, 6611, 6612, 6613-2, 6614, 6617-1, 6617-2, 6617-3, 6617-4, 6619, 6620, 6621-1, 6621-2, 6694, 6695, 6696, 6827-2, 7055-1, 7055-2, 7057, 7058, 7059, 7088, 7089, 7089-1, 7097-1*
PLT471	FAA-H-8083-21	Aircraft Systems) Transmission) Engine Starting; Freewheeling Unit *6697, 6698*
PLT472	FAA-H-8083-21	Aerodynamics) Principles of Flight) Forward Flight; Transverse Flow Aircraft Systems) Rotor) Improperly Rigged Tail rotor; Vibration Aircraft Systems) Transmission) Vibration *6613-4, 6699-1, 6700-1, 6701, 6702, 6703, 7060*
PLT473	FAA-H-8083-13 FAA-H-8083-25	Aircraft Systems) Flight Controls/Secondary) Flaps; Spoilers *6688, 6689, 6690, 6691, 6693, 6715*
PLT474	AC 00-6	Weather) Meteorology) Mountain Wave Soaring; Soaring Weather *6232, 7189, 7190, 7192, 7194*
PLT475	AC 00-6	Recall squall lines — formation/characteristics/resulting weather *6219*

Learning Statement Code	FAA Reference	Subject Description (or Topic ⟩ Content ⟩ Specific classification) Question Numbers
PLT477	FAA-H-8083-3 FAA-H-8083-25	Aerodynamics ⟩ Principles of Flight ⟩ Longitudinal Stability Aircraft Performance ⟩ Limitations ⟩ Airspeeds Instructional Guidelines ⟩ Instructor Responsibilities/Professionalism ⟩ Demo Stalls Flight Operations ⟩ Maneuvers ⟩ Stalls/Spins *6506, 6543, 6833-1, 7029, 7033*
PLT478	FAA-H-8083-25 FAA-H-8083-29	Recall starter/ignition system — types/components/operating principles/characteristics *6669, 6687, 7242, 7243, 7260, 7297, 7300*
PLT479	FAA-H-8083-25	Recall starter system — starting procedures *7299*
PLT480	FAA-H-8083-25	Aerodynamics ⟩ Principles of Flight ⟩ Design Characteristics Aerodynamics ⟩ Stability/Control ⟩ Basic Concepts of Stability; Negative Static Stability; Positive Dynamics Stability *6502, 6563, 6564, 6565, 6568*
PLT481	FAA-H-8083-9	Fundamentals of Instructing ⟩ Critique/Evaluation ⟩ Evaluation Fundamentals of Instructing ⟩ Effective Communication ⟩ Developing Communication Skills Fundamentals of Instructing ⟩ Learning Process ⟩ Learning Plateau *6028, 6065, 6098-3, 6098-9, 7167-2*

PLT482	FAA-H-8083-9	Instructional Guidelines ⟩ Critique/Evaluation ⟩ Assessment; Oral Assessment;
		  Oral Quizzing; Test Questions; Written
		Instructional Guidelines ⟩ Instructor Responsibilities/Professionalism ⟩
		  Professionalism
		Instructional Guidelines ⟩ Teaching Methods ⟩ Assessment
		Instructional Guidelines ⟩ Teaching Process ⟩ Assessment
		
		6052, 6067, 6070, 6092, 6092-1, 6093, 6094, 6095, 6096, 6097, 6098-1, 6099,
		6100, 6101, 6102, 6103, 6103-1, 6103-2, 6103-4, 6104, 6105, 6106, 6107, 6108,
		6109, 6110, 6111, 6112, 6113, 6114, 6115, 6116, 6117, 6118, 6122-1, 6122-2,
		6330, 6331, 6335, 6337, 6338, 6340, 6341, 6343, 6343-1, 6367

PLT484	14 CFR 1	Regulations ⟩ 14 CFR Part 1 ⟩ V_S *6316-1*
PLT486	FAA-H-8083-3 FAA-H-8083-21	Flight Operations ⟩ Takeoff ⟩ Crosswind; Running/Rolling Takeoff; Soft Field *6979, 6989, 6990, 7080*
PLT487	FAA-H-8083-9	Instructional Guidelines ⟩ Instructional Aids/Training Technologies ⟩ Teaching Aids Instructional Guidelines ⟩ Teaching Methods ⟩ Demonstration/Performance Instructional Guidelines ⟩ Techniques-Flight Instruction ⟩ Demonstration/ Performance *6031, 6032, 6066, 6089, 6090, 6091-1, 6134, 7225*
PLT488	FAA-H-8083-9	Instructional Guidelines ⟩ Teaching Methods ⟩ Group Learning; Guided Discussion; Lecture *6068, 6076, 6077, 6077-1, 6078, 6079, 6080, 6081, 6082-1, 6082-2, 6082-3,* *6082-4, 6082-5, 6083, 6084, 6085, 6086, 6087, 6088*
PLT489	FAA-H-8083-9	Fundamentals of Instructing ⟩ Learning Process ⟩ Teaching Process *6074*

Learning Statement Code	FAA Reference	Subject Description (or Topic ⟩ Content ⟩ Specific classification) / Question Numbers
PLT490	FAA-H-8083-9	Instructional Guidelines ⟩ Instructor Responsibilities/Professionalism ⟩ Professionalism Instructional Guidelines ⟩ Learning Process ⟩ Learning Theory *6023, 6024, 6025, 6026, 6053, 6054, 6054-1, 6124-1*
PLT491	FAA-H-8083-9	Fundamentals of Instructing ⟩ Critique/Evaluation ⟩ Evaluation Fundamentals of Instructing ⟩ Learning Process ⟩ Teaching Process Fundamentals of Instructing ⟩ Planning Instructional Activity ⟩ Objectives Instructional Guidelines ⟩ Planning Instructional Activity ⟩ Blocks of Learning Instructional Guidelines ⟩ Teaching Methods ⟩ Lecture; Lesson Preparation *6071, 6072, 6073, 6075, 6133-2, 6144, 6146*
PLT492	AC 00-6	Weather ⟩ Meteorology ⟩ Clouds; Pressure; Temperature *6162, 6166, 6167, 6181*
PLT493	AC 00-6	Weather ⟩ Hazardous ⟩ Icing *6212, 7240*
PLT494	AC 00-6 FAA-H-8083-13	Weather ⟩ Charts/Maps ⟩ Thermal Soaring Weather ⟩ Meteorology ⟩ Clouds; Pressure; Thermal Soaring *6234, 6236, 6237, 6238, 6241, 7176, 7188*
PLT495	AC 00-6	Weather ⟩ Hazardous ⟩ Thunderstorms *6214, 6215, 6216, 6217, 6220*
PLT496	FAA-H-8083-13	Flight Operations ⟩ Launch Procedures ⟩ Crosswind Procedures *6719, 6720*
PLT497	AIM	Aircraft Systems ⟩ Avionics ⟩ Aircraft Codes *7123, 7123-1*
PLT499	FAA-H-8083-25	Recall turbine engines — components/operational characteristics/associated instruments *6684, 6686*
PLT501	AC 00-6	Weather ⟩ Hazardous ⟩ Mountain Flying Weather ⟩ Meteorology ⟩ Mountain Wave Soaring; Unstable Air *6208, 6233, 6235*
PLT502	14 CFR 91 AIM	Airport Operations ⟩ Tower Controlled ⟩ Light Signals Regulations ⟩ 14 CFR Part 91 ⟩ ATC Light Signals Regulations ⟩ Universal Signals ⟩ Control tower Signals *6431, 6432, 6433, 7124*
PLT503	AIM	Human Factors ⟩ Aeromedical Factors ⟩ Alcohol *7142*
PLT504	FAA-H-8083-9	Instructional Guidelines ⟩ Instructional Aids/Training Technologies ⟩ Teaching Aids *6119*
PLT505	FAA-H-8083-9	Fundamentals of Instructing ⟩ Teaching Methods ⟩ Computer-Based Training Method Instructional Guidelines ⟩ Instructional Aids/Training Technologies ⟩ Teaching Aids Instructional Guidelines ⟩ Teaching Methods ⟩ CAL *6091-2, 6091-3, 6091-4, 6091-6, 6120, 6121, 6122, 6122-3, 6122-5*

Learning Statement Code	FAA Reference	Subject Description (or Topic 〉 Content 〉 Specific classification) Question Numbers
PLT508	14 CFR 91	Regulations 〉 14 CFR Part 91 〉 91.413(a)
		6491, 6492
PLT509	AIM	Airport Operations 〉 Wake Turbulence 〉 Separation; Wake Turbulence Avoidance
		7135, 7136, 7137, 7138, 7139, 7140
PLT510	AC 00-6	Weather〉 Meteorology 〉 Circulation; Thermal Soaring
		6180, 6239, 6240
PLT511	AC 00-6	Weather 〉 Hazardous 〉 Icing; Mountain Flying Weather 〉 Meteorology 〉 Air Masses; Frontal Soaring; Fronts
		6194, 6195, 6196, 6197, 6198, 6199, 6201, 6202, 6203, 6204, 6205, 6206, 6207, 6231
PLT512	AC 00-6	Weather 〉 Meteorology 〉 Moisture
		6167-1, 6167-2, 6182, 6186
PLT516	AC 00-6	Weather 〉 Meteorology 〉 Air Masses; Atmospheric Circulation; Circulation; Sea Breeze Soaring
		6174, 6175, 6176
PLT517	AC 00-6	Weather 〉 Meteorology 〉 Circulation
		6177, 6178, 6179
PLT518	AC 00-6	Weather 〉 Hazardous 〉 Turbulence; Wind shear Weather 〉 Meteorology 〉 Microburst
		6209, 6210, 6230, 6243, 6244, 6315

Notes

Notes

Virtual flight school.

Flight Maneuvers Virtual Test Prep DVD Flight School

Over 3 hours of high-definition in-flight video, 3D and animated graphics, special effects, and experienced flight instructors work together to help pilots prepare for their flight training, checkride, or flight review. Covers all of the maneuvers required for Private, Sport, Commercial, and Instructor (CFI) pilot certification. Both DVD and Blu-ray disks are included.

Also Available as Video Segment Downloads

Lessons taken directly from the Virtual Test Prep Flight Maneuvers DVD and Blu-ray disc set. Segments include: Introduction, Airport Operations & Takeoffs, Landings, Maneuvers, Stalls & Emergencies, and Test Preparation.

On demand. On the go.

Get there faster with ASA Prepware and Checkride Apps

Prepware apps for Apple and Android devices are the perfect supplement when preparing for an FAA knowledge exam. Study or take practice tests anywhere, anytime.

Checkride apps list the questions most likely to be asked by examiners during the oral exam, and provide succinct, ready responses to help students prepare. Available for Apple and Android operating systems.

ONLINE GROUND SCHOOL

Prepare for the **FAA Knowledge Exam** *and* **the Cockpit.** From the cloud, to you. Anytime. Anywhere. On any internet-connected device.

Free app, free ebooks, free yourself...

The ASA Reader App
Aviation's Premier eLearning Solution

With access to over 100 titles and the flexibility to accommodate ebooks from other publishers, the ASA Reader puts your aviation library in the palm of your hand. Download for FREE at the app store.

How do you like to study?

Preparation is an aviator's most valuable asset. Our aviation test prep products have been helping aspiring aviators achieve their goals for more than 75 years. In print or on the go — **Test Prep wherever, whenever you want.**

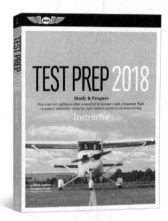

Test Prep Books

Also available in eBook PDF format. Includes 5 FREE practice tests at Prepware.com

Prepware Software

Compatible with PC or Mac. Includes a 2-year subscription to Prepware.com, accessible from any internet-connected device.

Test Prep Bundles

Includes Test Prep book, Prepware software, AND a 2-year subscription to Prepware.com, accessible from any internet-connected device.

Prepware Apps

Supplement your study with Prepware apps for Apple and Android devices.

You've passed your written, now get ready for the checkride.

Certified Flight Instructor Oral Exam Guide

This book lists the questions most likely to be asked by examiners and provides succinct, ready responses. Pilots will find these Guides indispensable tools in both planning for what to expect during the airplane checkride, and mastering the subject matter. This edition for CFI applicants includes "Fundamentals of Instruction" questions covering the subjects from the FAA's *Aviation Instructor's Handbook* (FAA-H-8083-9). Also available as an App and an eBook!

Flight Instructor Airplane Practical Test Standards

The Practical Test Standards are a guide for students, instructors, and FAA-designated examiners to know what is expected of pilots in a checkride, with details on the knowledge and skills pilots must demonstrate to earn a flight instructor certificate.

Practical Guide to the CFI Checkride

This *Practical Guide to the CFI Checkride* includes the CFI Practical Test Standards (Airplane, Single-Engine) and goes on to explain and clarify in "plain language" exactly what flight instructor applicants must know and demonstrate during the oral portion of the FAA Practical Exam, eliminating any surprise about examiner expectations. This book will help you prioritize information, consolidating the FAA guidance materials into language you can understand, remember, and quickly reference.

AVIATION SUPPLIES & ACADEMICS, INC.
Quality & Service You Can Depend On

Training Starts Here.

See our complete line of study aids, textbooks, pilot supplies and more at your local airport and in bookstores nationwide.   www.asa2fly.com | 425-235-1500

Airman Knowledge Testing Supplement for Flight Instructor, Ground Instructor, and Sport Pilot Instructor

2016

U.S. Department of Transportation
FEDERAL AVIATION ADMINISTRATION
Flight Standards Service

Preface

This testing supplement supersedes FAA-CT-8080-5F, Airman Knowledge Testing Supplement for Flight Instructor, Ground Instructor, and Sport Pilot Instructor, dated 2014. This Airman Knowledge Testing Supplement is designed by the Federal Aviation Administration (FAA) Flight Standards Service. It is intended for use by Airman Knowledge Testing (AKT) Organization Designation Authorization (ODA) Holders and other entities approved and/or authorized to administer airman knowledge tests on behalf of the FAA in the following knowledge areas:

FOI Fundamentals of Instructing
BGI Ground Instructor–Basic
AGI Ground Instructor–Advanced
FIA Flight Instructor–Airplane
FRH Flight Instructor–Helicopter
FRG Flight Instructor–Gyroplane
FIG Flight Instructor–Glider
AFA Flight Instructor–Airplane (Added Rating)
HFA Flight Instructor–Helicopter (Added Rating)
GFA Flight Instructor–Gyroplane (Added Rating)
AFG Flight Instructor–Glider (Added Rating)
MCI Military Competence Instructor

SIA Flight Instructor–Sport Pilot–Airplane
SIB Flight Instructor–Sport Pilot–Balloon
SIG Flight Instructor–Sport Pilot–Glider
SIL Flight Instructor–Sport Pilot–Lighter-Than-Air (Airship)
SIP Flight Instructor–Sport Pilot–Powered Parachute
SIR Flight Instructor–Sport Pilot–Gyroplane
SIW Flight Instructor–Sport Pilot–Weight-Shift Control

Comments regarding this supplement, or any AFS-630 publication, should be sent, in email form, to the following address:

AFS630comments@faa.gov

Contents

| LESSON | Ground reference maneuvers | STUDENT | | DATE | / / |

A _____ To develop the student's skill in planning and following a pattern over the ground compensating for wind drift at varying angles.

B _____ Use of ground references to control path
Observation and control of wind effect
Control of airplane attitude, altitude, and heading

C _____
Preflight discussion	:10
Instructor demonstrations	:25
Student practice	:45
Postflight critque	:10

D _____ Chalkboard for preflight discussion
IFR visor for maneuvers reviewed

E _____ Preflight—discuss lesson objective. Diagram "S" turns, eight along a road, and rectangular course on a chalkboard.

Inflight—demonstrate elements.
Demonstrate following a road, "S" turns, eights along a road, and rectangular course, coach student practice.

Postflight—critique student performance and make study assignment.

F _____ Preflight—discuss lesson objective and resolve questions.

Inflight—review previous maneuvers including power-off stalls and flight at minimum controllable airspeed. Perform each new maneuver as directed.

Postflight—ask pertinent questions.

G _____ Student should demonstrate competency in maintaining orientation, airspeed within 10 knots, altitude within 100 feet, and headings within 10 degrees, and in making proper correction for wind drift.

FIGURE 1.—Lesson Plan.

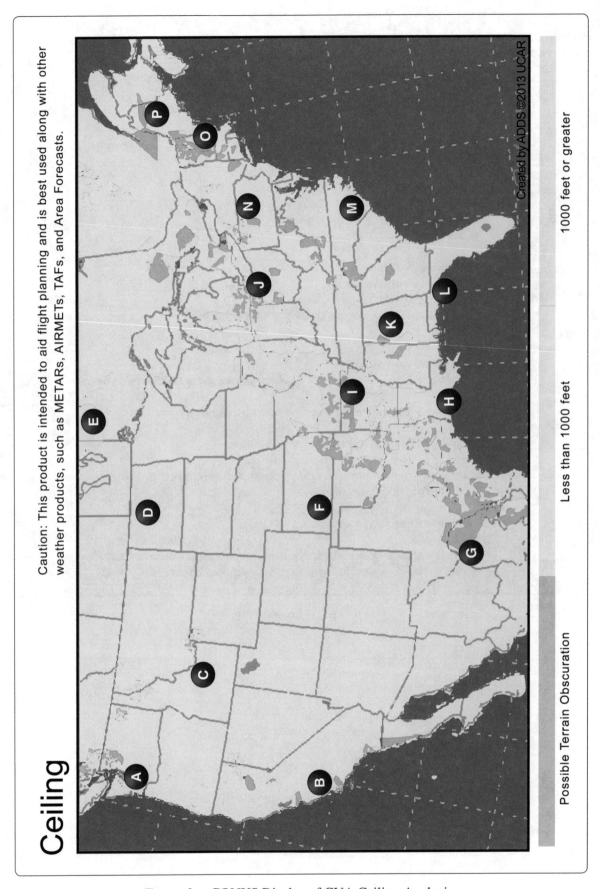

FIGURE 2.—CONUS Display of CVA Ceiling Analysis.

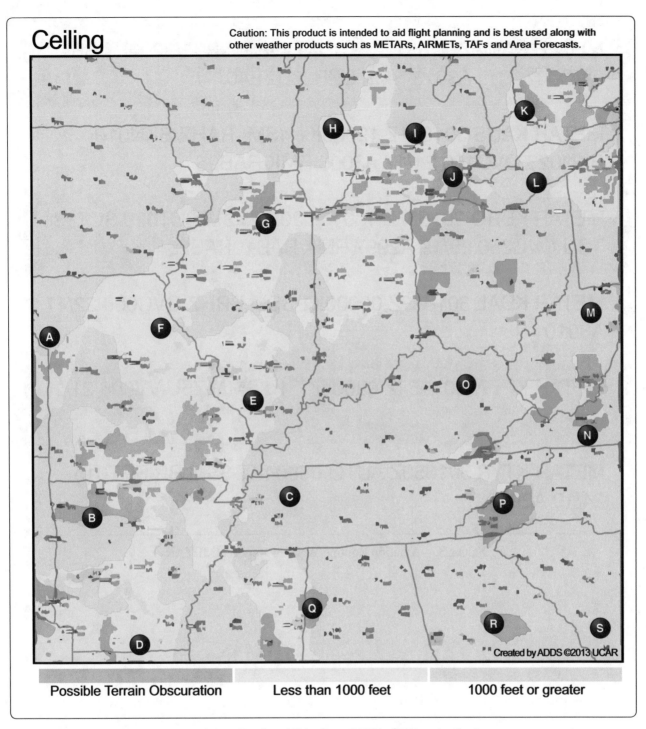

FIGURE 2A.—Regional Display of CVA Ceiling Analysis.

METAR KAMA 301651Z 05016KT 5/8SM R04/3000FT BR OVC007 11/9 A3013 RMK DZB26DZE40

METAR KAUS 301651Z 12008KT 4SM -RAHZ BKN010 BKN023 OVC160 21/17 A3005 RMK RAB25

METAR KBRO 301655Z 15015G20KT 7SM SCT020 SCT130 TCU OVC250 29/19 A2997 RMK RAB19RAE25

METAR KDAL 301649Z 00000KT 3SM BRHZ OVC009 22/17 A3010

METAR KFTW 301654Z 09004KT 1/2SM HZFU VV006 21/17 A3010

METAR KTYR 301650Z AUTO 08004KT 3SM BR SCT015 24/19 A2999

FIGURE 3.—Aviation Routine Weather Reports (METAR).

UA/OV KOKC-KTUL/TM 1800/FL120/TP BE90//SK BKN0 18-TOP055/OVC072-TOP089/CLR ABV/TA M7/WV 08021/ TB LGT 055-072/IC LGT-MOD RIME 072-089

FIGURE 4.—Pilot Weather Report.

TAF

KMEM 121720Z 121818 20012KT 5SM HZ BKN030 PROB40 2022 1SM TSRA OVC008CB
    FM2200 33015G20KT P6SM BKN015 OVC025 PROB40 2202 3SM SHRA
    FM0200 35012KT OVC008 PROB40 0205 2SM-RASN BECMG 0608 02008KT BKN012
    BECMG 1012 00000KT 3SM BR SKC TEMPO 1214 1/2SM FG
    FM1600 VRB06KT P6SM SKC=

KOKC 051130Z 051212 14008KT 5SM BR BKN030 TEMPO 1316 1 1/2SM BR
    FM1600 18010KT P6SM SKC BECMG 2224 20013G20KT 4SM SHRA OVC020
    PROB40 0006 2SM TSRA OVC008CB BECMG 0608 21015KT P6SM SCT040=

FIGURE 5.—Terminal Aerodome Forecasts (TAF).

6

```
BOSC FA 241845
SYNOPSIS AND VFR CLDS/WX
SYNOPSIS VALID UNTIL 251300
CLDS/WX VALID UNTIL 250700...OTLK VALID 250700-251300
ME NH VT MA RI CT NY LO NJ PA OH LE WV MD DC DE VA AND CSTL WTRS

.
SEE AIRMET SIERRA FOR IFR CONDS AND MTN OBSCN.
TS IMPLY SEV OR GTR TURB SEV ICE LLWS AND IFR CONDS.
NON MSL HGTS DENOTED BY AGL OR CIG.

.
SYNOPSIS...19Z CDFNT ALG A 16NE ACK-ENE LN...CONTG AS A QSTNRY
FNT ALG AN END-50SW MSS LN. BY 13Z...CDFNT ALG A 140ESE ACK-HTO
LN...CONTG AS A QSTNRY FNT ALG A HTO-SYR-YYZ LN. TROF ACRS CNTRL
PA INTO NRN VA. ...REYNOLDS...

.
OH LE
NRN HLF OH LE...SCT-BKN025 OVC045. CLDS LYRD 150. SCT SHRA. WDLY
    SCT TSRA. CB TOPS FL350. 23-01Z OVC020-030. VIS 3SM BR. OCNL-
    RA. OTLK...IFR CIG BR FG.
SWRN QTR OH...BKN050-060 TOPS 100. OTLK...MVFR BR.
SERN QTR OH...SCT-BKN040 BKN070 TOPS 120. WDLY SCT-TSRA. 00Z
    SCT-BKN030 OVC050. WDLY SCT-TSRA. CB TOPS FL350. OTLK...VFR
    SHRA.

.
CHIC FA 241945
SYNOPSIS AND VFR CLDS/WX
SYNOPSIS VALID UNTIL 251400
CLDS/WX VALID UNTIL 250800...OTLK VALID 250800-251400
ND SD NE KS MN IA MO WI LM LS MI LH IL IN KY

.
SEE AIRMET AIERRA DOR IFR CONDS AND MTN OBSCN.
TS IMPLY SEV OR GTR TURB SEV ICE LLWS AND IFR CONDS.
NON MSL HGTS DENOTED BY AGL OR CIG.

.
SYNOPSIS...LOW PRES AREA 20Z CNTRD OVR SERN WI FCST MOV NEWD INTO
LH BY 12Z AND WKN. LOW PRES FCST DEEPEN OVR ERN CO DURG PD AND
MOV NR WRN KS BORDER BY 14Z. DVLPG CDFNT WL MOV EWD INTO S CNTRL
NE-CNTRL KS BY 14Z. ...SMITH..

.
UPR MI LS
WRN PTNS...AGL SCT030 SCT 030 SCT-BKN050. TOPS 080. 02-05Z BECMG CIG
    OVC010 VIS 3-5SM BR. OTLK...IFR CIG BR.
ERN PTNS...CIG BKN020 OVC040. OCNL VIS 3-5SM -RA BR. TOPS FL200.
    23Z CIG OVC010 VIS 3-5SM -RA BR. OTLK...IFR CIG BR.

.
LWR MI LM LH
CNTRL/NRN PTNS...CIG OVC010 VIS 3-5SM -RA BR. TOPS FL200
    OTLK...IFR CIG BR.

.
SRN THIRD...CIG OVC015-025. SCT -SHRA. TOPS 150. 00-02Z BECMG CIG
    OVC010 VIS 3-5SM BR. TOPS 060. OTLK...IFR CIG BR.

.
IN
NRN HALF...CIG BKN035 BKN080. TOPS FL200. SCT -SHRA. 00Z CIG
    BKN-SCT040 BKN-SCT080. TOPS 120. 06Z AGL SCT-BKN030. TOPS 080.
    OCNL VIS 3-5SM BR. OTLK...MVFR CIG BR.
SRN HALF...AGL SCT050 SCT-BKN100. TOPS 120. 07Z AGL SCT 030
    SCT100. OTLK...VFR
```

FIGURE 6.—Aviation Area Forecast (FA).

FB WBC 151745 DATA BASED ON 151200Z VALID 1600Z FOR USE 1800-0300Z. TEMPS NEG ABV 24000									
FT	3000	6000	9000	12000	18000	24000	30000	34000	39000
ALS			2420	2635-08	2535-18	2444-30	245945	246755	246862
AMA		2714	2725+00	2625-04	2531-15	2542-27	265842	256352	256762
DEN			2321-04	2532-08	2434-19	2441-31	235347	236056	236262
HLC		1707-01	2113-03	2219-07	2330-17	2435-30	244145	244854	245561
MKC	0507	2006+03	2215-01	2322-06	2338-17	2348-29	236143	237252	238160
STL	2113	2325+7	2332+02	2339-04	2356-16	2373-27	239440	730649	731960

FIGURE 7.—Winds and Temperatures Aloft Forecast (FB).

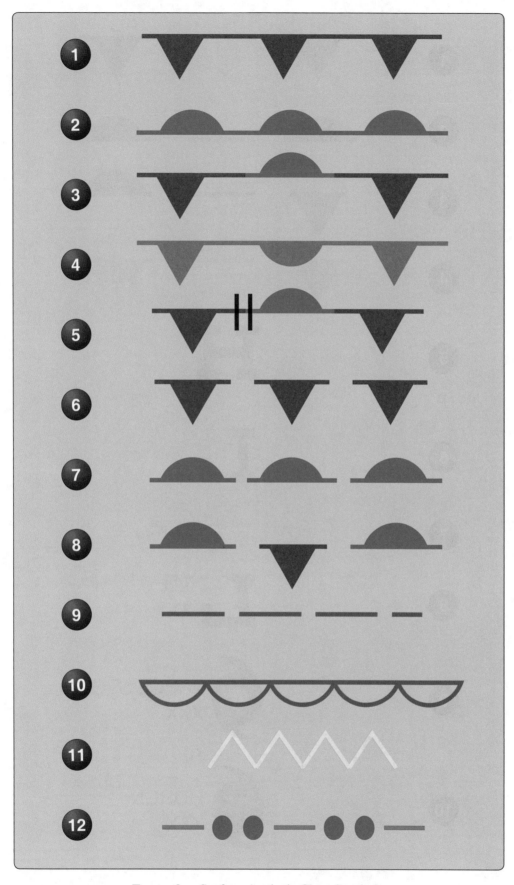

FIGURE 8.—Surface Analysis Chart Symbols.

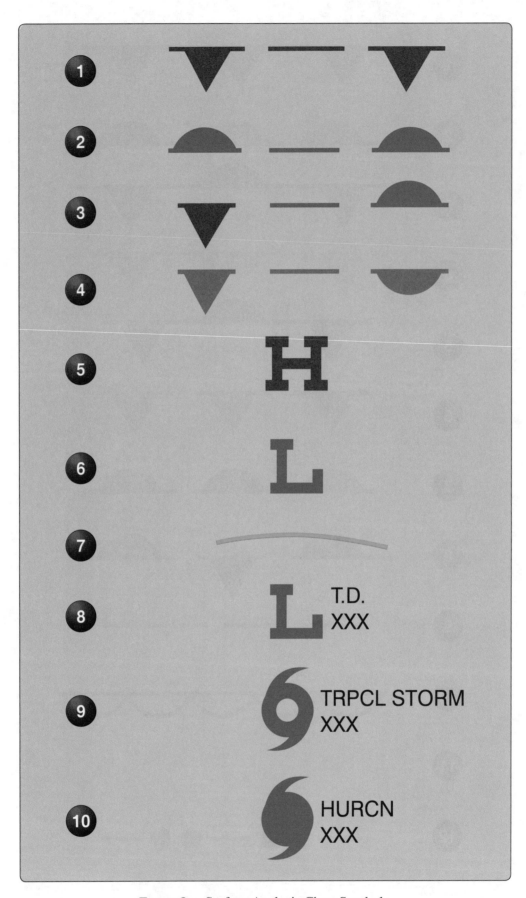

FIGURE 9.—Surface Analysis Chart Symbols.

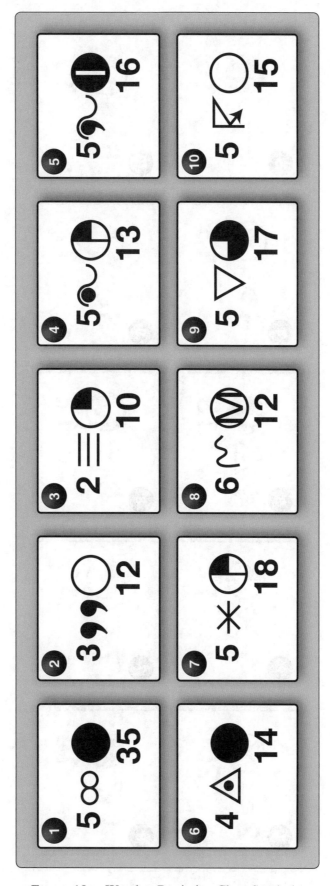

FIGURE 10.—Weather Depiction Chart Symbols.

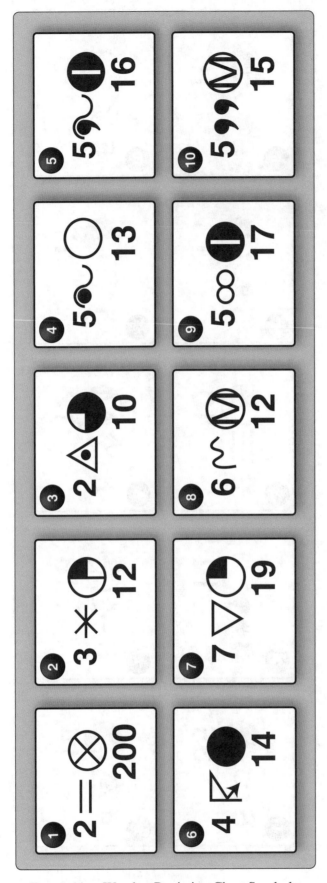

FIGURE 11.—Weather Depiction Chart Symbols.

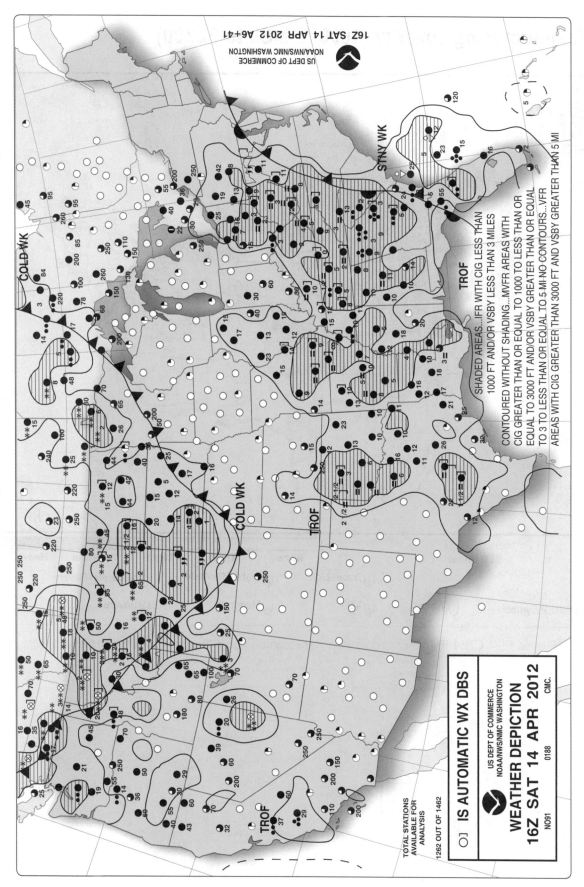

FIGURE 12.—Weather Depiction Chart.

Maximum icing severity (1000 ft. MSL to FL300)

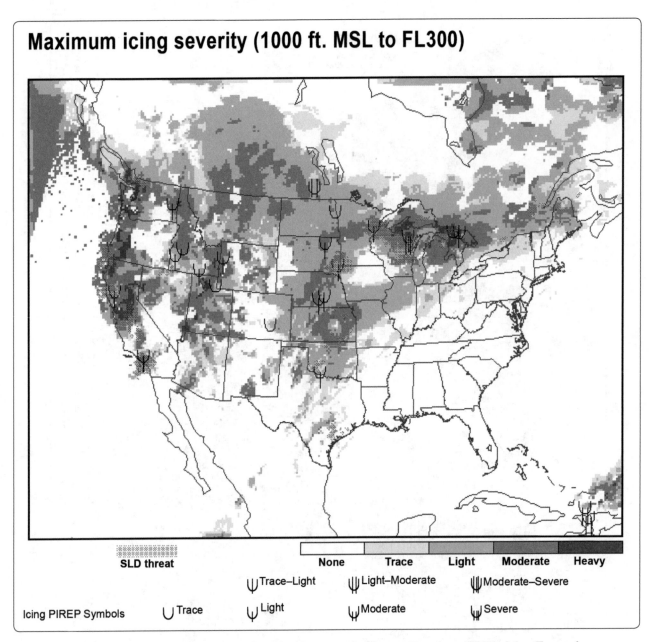

FIGURE 13.—CIP/FIP Icing Severity Plus Supercooled Large Droplets (SLD)–Max Example.

GTG2 - Maximum turbulence intensity (10000 ft. MSL to FL450)

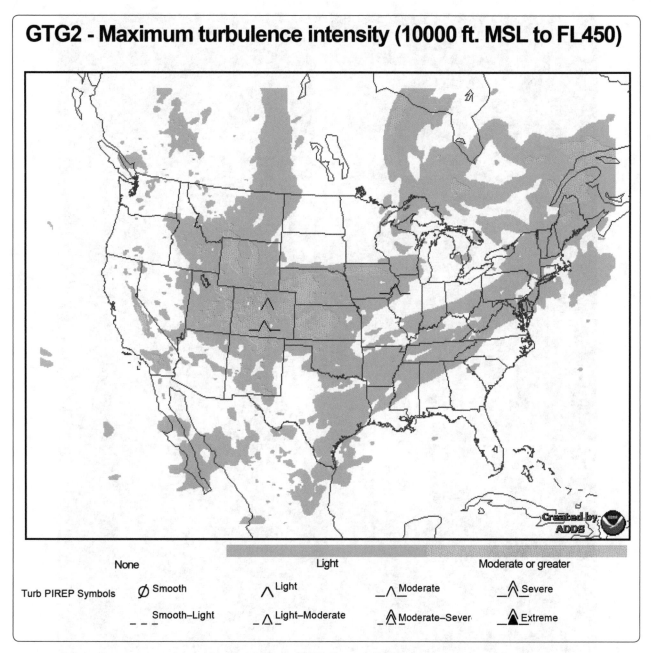

FIGURE 13A.—GTG Composite Example.

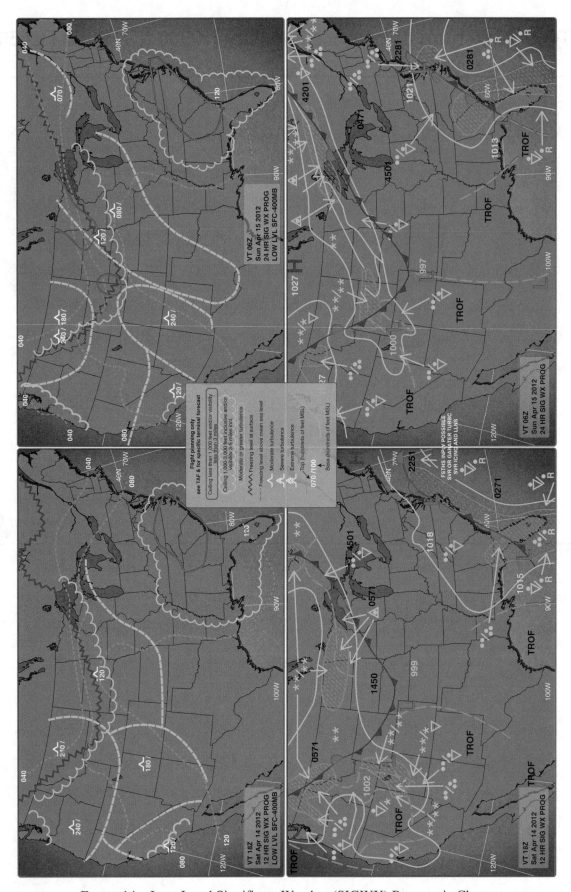

FIGURE 14—Low-Level Significant Weather (SIGWX) Prognostic Charts.

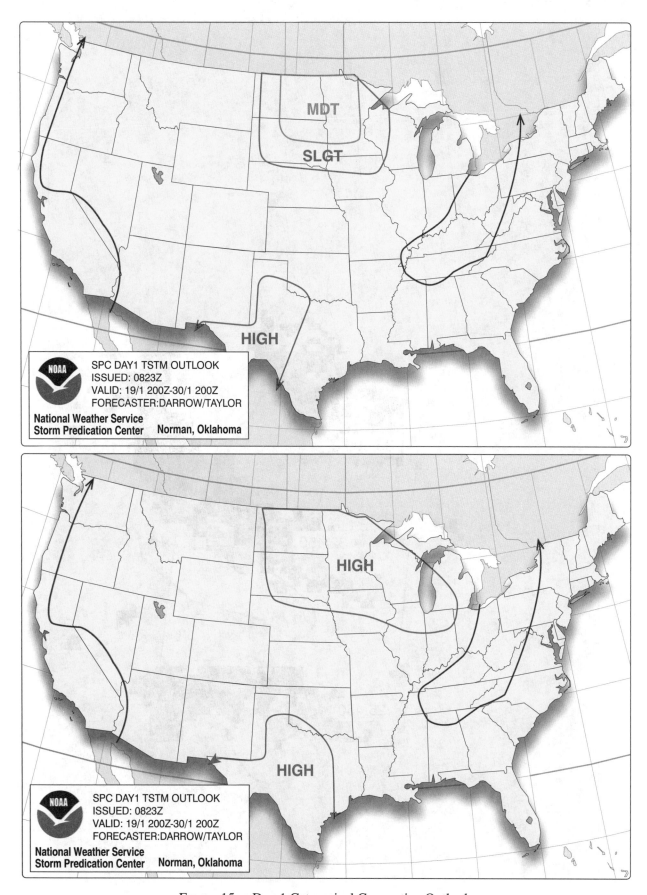

SPC DAY1 TSTM OUTLOOK
ISSUED: 0823Z
VALID: 19/1 200Z-30/1 200Z
FORECASTER:DARROW/TAYLOR

National Weather Service
Storm Predication Center   Norman, Oklahoma

SPC DAY1 TSTM OUTLOOK
ISSUED: 0823Z
VALID: 19/1 200Z-30/1 200Z
FORECASTER:DARROW/TAYLOR

National Weather Service
Storm Predication Center   Norman, Oklahoma

FIGURE 15.—Day 1 Categorical Convective Outlook.

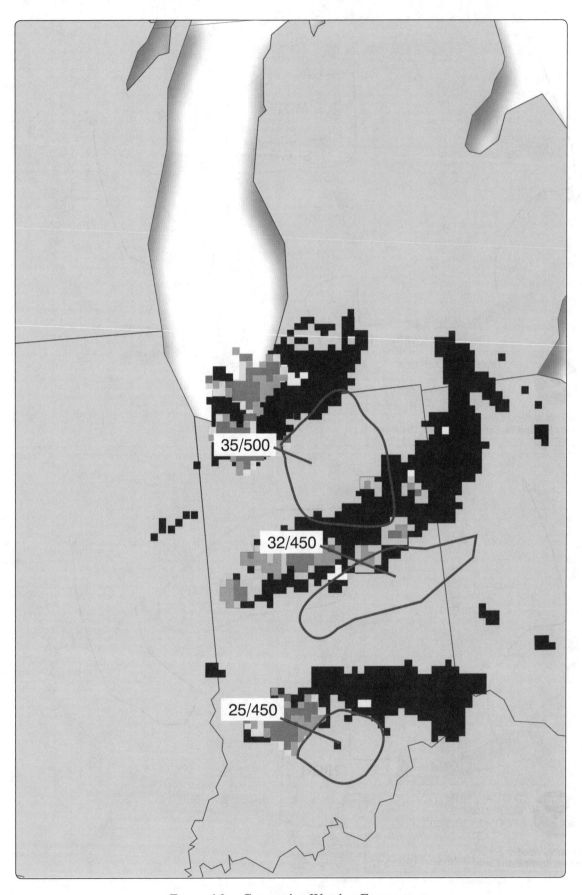

FIGURE 16.—Convective Weather Forecast.

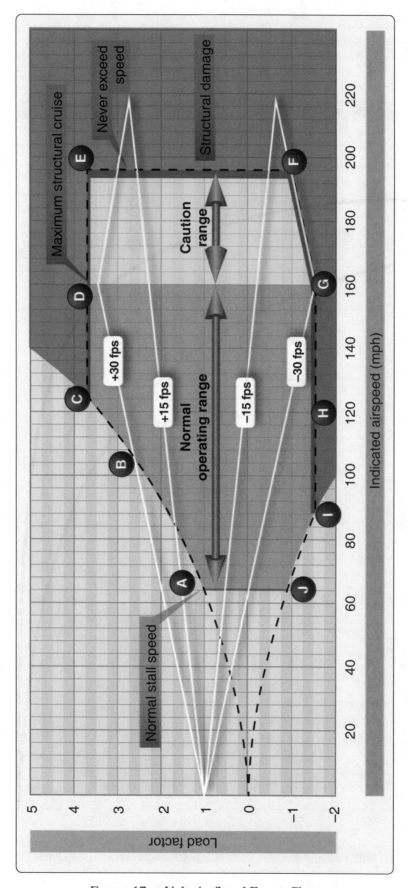

FIGURE 17.—Velocity/Load Factor Chart.

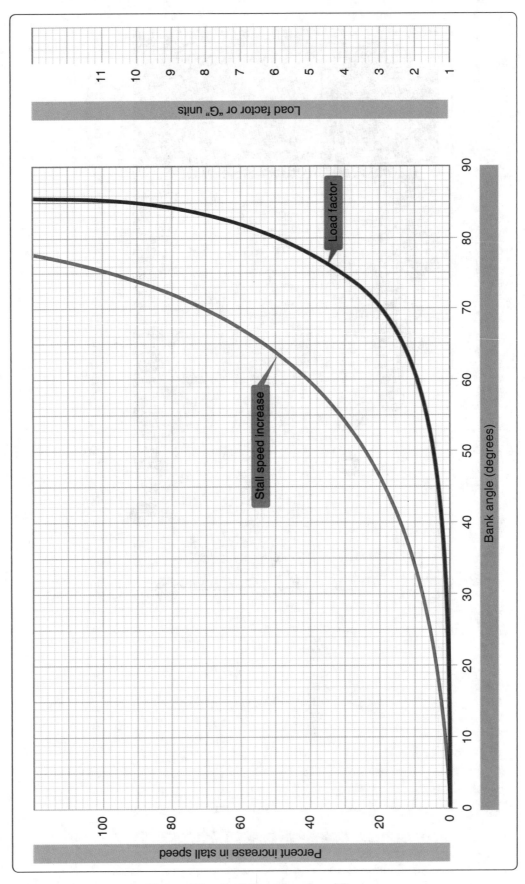

FIGURE 18.—Stall Speed vs. Load Factor.

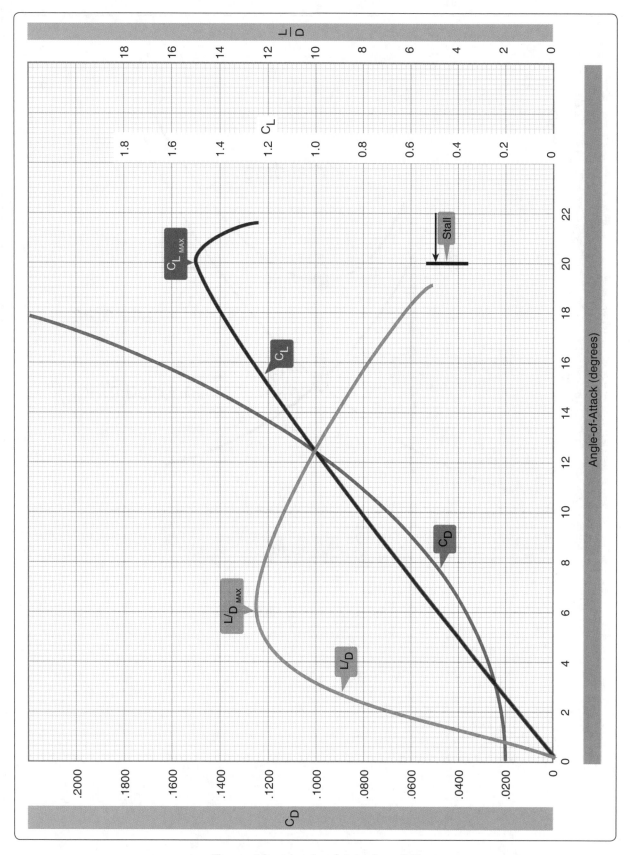

FIGURE 19.—Angle-of-Attack vs. Lift

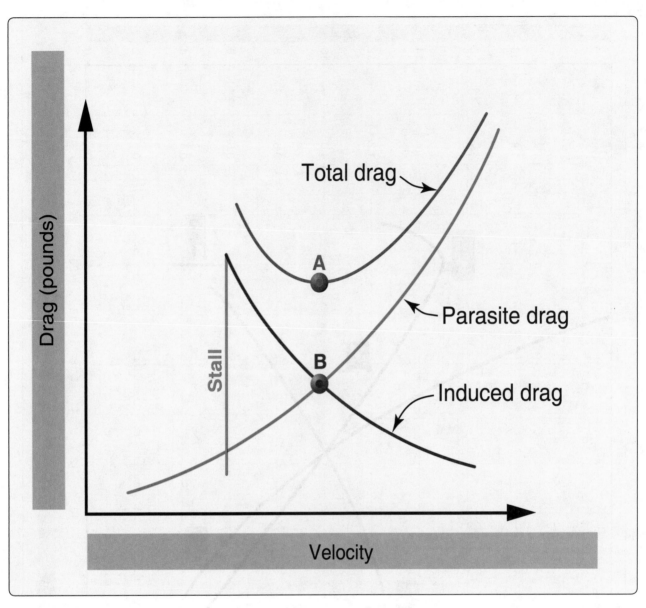

Figure 20.—Drag Chart.

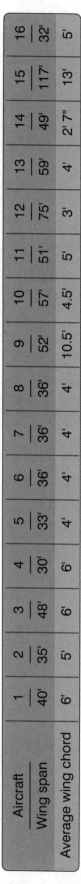

Aircraft	1	2	3	4	5	6	7	8	9	10	11	12	13	14	15	16
Wing span	40'	35'	48'	30'	33'	36'	36'	36'	52'	57'	51'	75'	59'	49'	117'	32'
Average wing chord	6'	5'	6'	6'	4'	4'	4'	4'	10.5'	4.5'	5'	3'	4'	2' 7"	13'	5'

FIGURE 21.—Aspect Ratio.

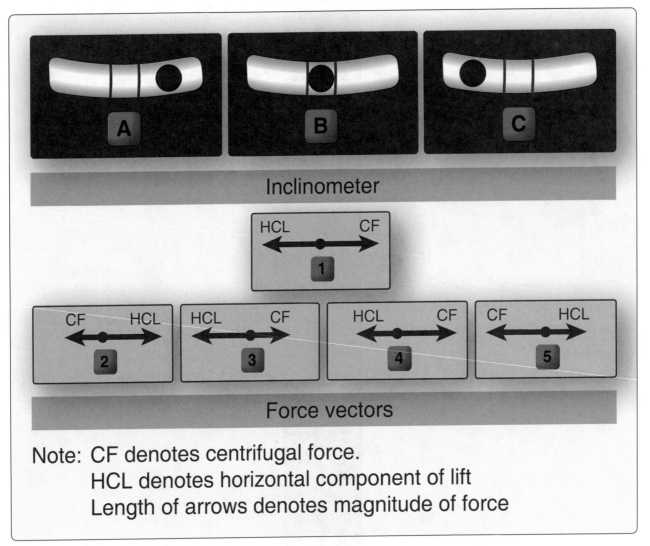

FIGURE 22.—Force Vectors.

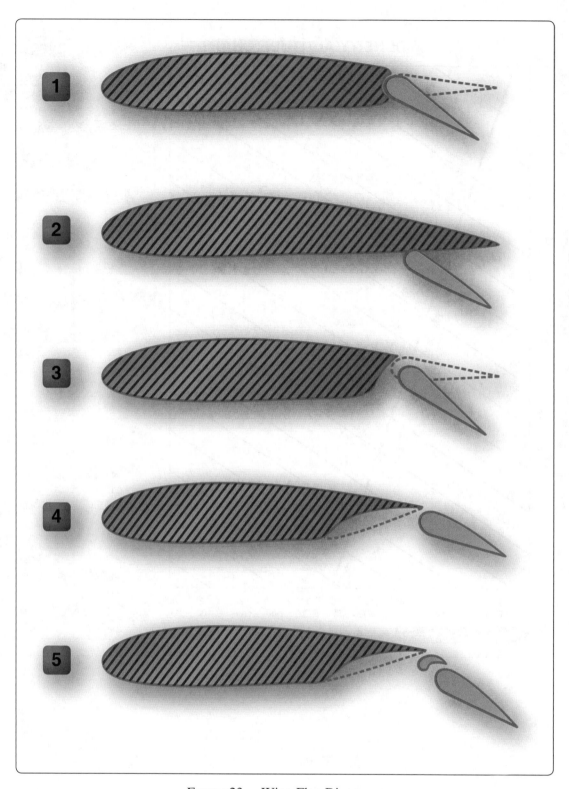

FIGURE 23.—Wing Flap Diagrams.

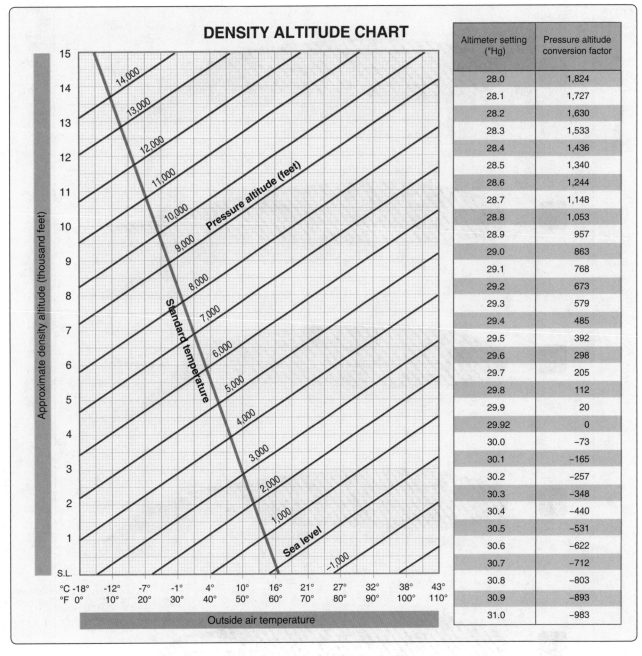

FIGURE 24.—Density Altitude Chart.

Airspeed calibration—Normal system

Flaps 0°		Flaps 15°		Flaps 45°	
KIAS	KCAS	KIAS	KCAS	KIAS	KCAS
80	84	70	79	70	76
100	102	80	86	80	84
120	122	90	94	90	93
140	141	100	103	100	102
160	161	110	112	110	111
180	181	120	121	120	120
200	201	130	131	130	129
220	221	140	141	140	138
240	242	150	151		

KIAS—indicated airspeed in knots
KCAS—calibrated airspeed in knots

Stall speeds—KCAS   4,600 lb gross weight

Configuration	Angle of bank			
	0°	20°	40°	60°
Gear and flaps up	84	87	97	119
Gear down and flaps 15°	80	83	92	113
Gear down and flaps 45°	76	79	87	108

FIGURE 25.—Airspeed Calibration Stalls/Speeds Chart.

Takeoff data

Takeoff distance with 10° flaps from hard-surfaced runway

Gross weight LB	KIAS at 50 feet	Head wind KTS	At sea level & 15 °C		At 2,500 feet & 10 °C		At 5,000 feet & 5 °C		At 7,500 feet & 0 °C	
			Ground roll	Total to clear 50' OBS	Ground roll	Total to clear 50' OBS	Ground roll	Total to clear 50' OBS	Ground roll	Total to clear 50' OBS
2200	55	0	345	680	405	770	480	885	580	1040
		15	205	460	245	525	295	615	365	725
		30	100	275	120	320	155	380	195	460
2600	60	0	500	915	585	1045	705	1230	855	1470
		15	310	635	370	735	455	870	560	1055
		30	165	395	200	465	255	565	325	695
3000	64	0	695	1210	820	1405	990	1675	1205	2045
		15	450	855	535	1005	660	1215	815	1505
		30	250	555	310	665	390	820	500	1030

Note: Increase distances 10% for each 14 °C above standard temperature for particular altitude.

FIGURE 26.—Takeoff Data Chart.

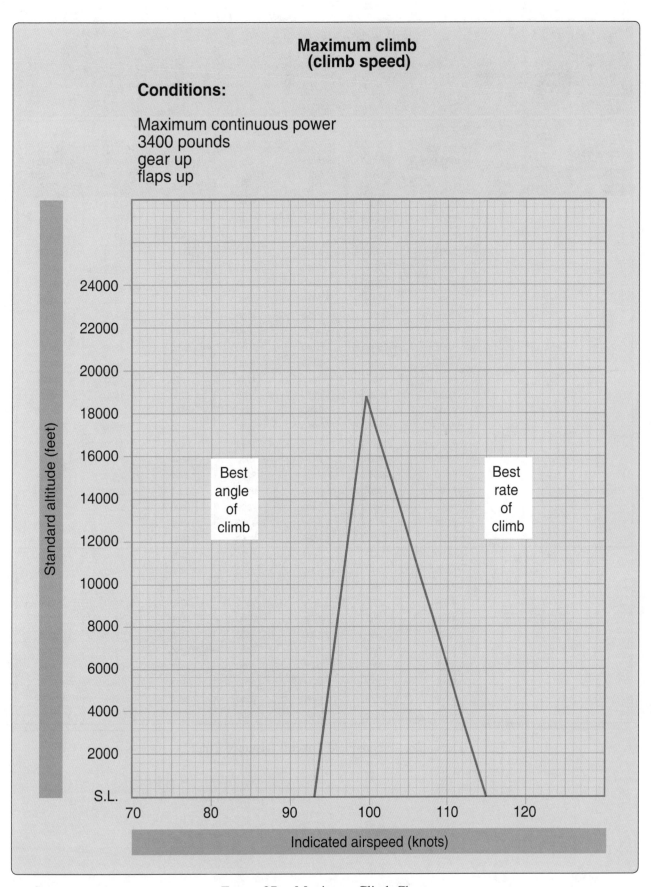

FIGURE 27.—Maximum Climb Chart.

Short-field takeoff distance

Conditions:
1. Power—FULL THROTTLE and 2700 rpm before releasing breaks.
2. Mixtures—LEAN for field elevation.
3. Cow flaps—OPEN.
4. Wing flaps—UP.
5. Level, dry, hard-surface runway.

Note:
1. Increase total distance 8% for operation on dry, sod runway.
2. Decrease total distance 7% for each 10 knots of headwind.
3. Increase total distance 5% for each 2 knots of tailwind.

Weight LB	Takeoff to 50 foot obstacle speed KIAS	Pressure altitude feet	20 °C		30 °C		40 °C	
			Ground roll feet	Total distance to clear 50' OBS	Ground roll feet	Total distance to clear 50' OBS	Ground roll feet	Total distance to clear 50' OBS
5500	82	Sea level	1390	1760	1490	1890	1590	2020
		1,000	1530	1950	1640	2080	1760	2230
		2,000	1680	2150	1810	2300	1940	2470
		3,000	1860	2380	2000	2550	2150	2750
		4,000	2060	2650	2220	2850	2380	3070
		5,000	2280	2950	2460	3190	2640	3450
		6,000	2530	3310	2730	3590	2950	3900
		7,000	2830	3750	3160	4190	3410	4570
		8,000	3280	4420	3540	4840	3830	5330
		9,000	3690	5170	4000	5730	4330	6420
		10,000	4150	6140	4500	6980	4880	8130
5100	78	Sea level	1160	1470	1240	1570	1330	1680
		1,000	1280	1620	1370	1730	1470	1850
		2,000	1400	1780	1500	1910	1610	2040
		3,000	1550	1960	1660	2100	1780	2260
		4,000	1710	2180	1840	2340	1970	2510
		5,000	1890	2410	2030	2590	2180	2790
		6,000	2090	2690	2250	2890	2420	3120
		7,000	2330	3010	2510	3250	2700	3520
		8,000	2600	3400	2800	3690	3030	4010
		9,000	2920	3890	3270	4360	3530	4760
		10,000	3390	4580	3660	5030	3960	5560
4700	75	Sea level	960	1220	1020	1300	1090	1380
		1,000	1050	1340	1120	1430	1200	1520
		2,000	1150	1460	1230	1560	1320	1670
		3,000	1270	1610	1360	1720	1460	1840
		4,000	1400	1770	1500	1900	1610	2030
		5,000	1540	1960	1650	2100	1780	2250
		6,000	1700	2170	1830	2330	1970	2500
		7,000	1890	2410	2030	2590	2190	2790
		8,000	2100	2700	2260	2910	2440	3140
		9,000	2350	3040	2540	3290	2730	3570
		10,000	2620	3430	2830	3730	3060	4060

FIGURE 28.—Short-Field Takeoff Distance Chart.

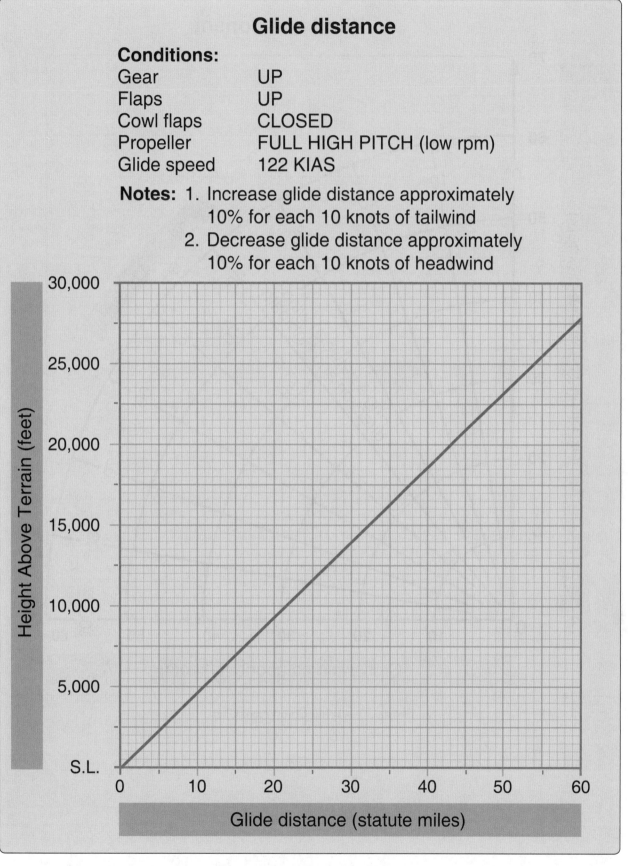

FIGURE 29.—Glide Distance Chart.

Wind component

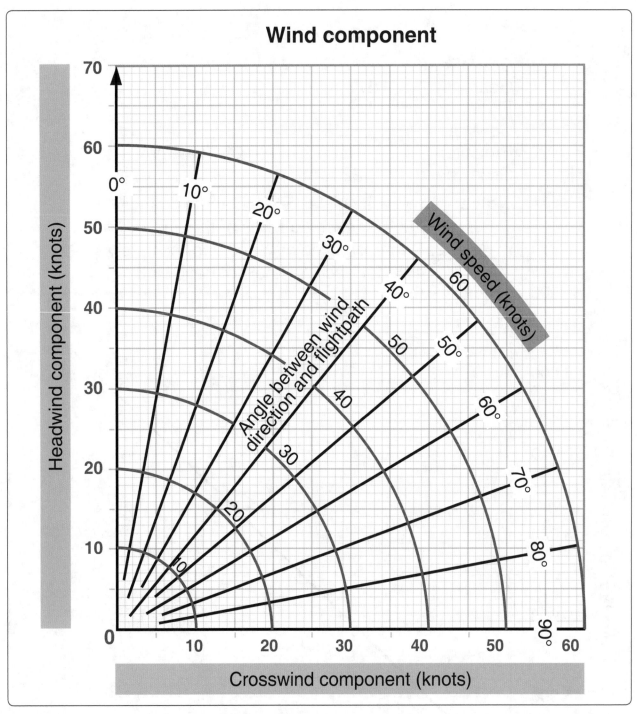

FIGURE 30.—Wind Component Chart.

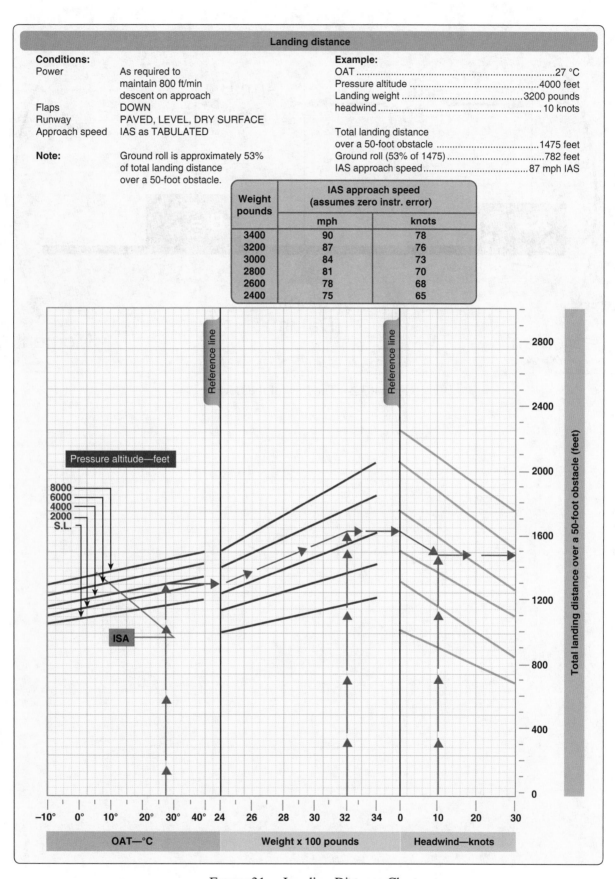

FIGURE 31.—Landing Distance Chart.

33

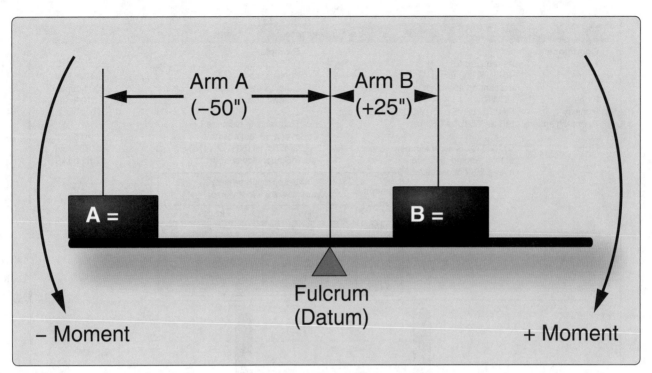

FIGURE 32.—The Law of the Lever.

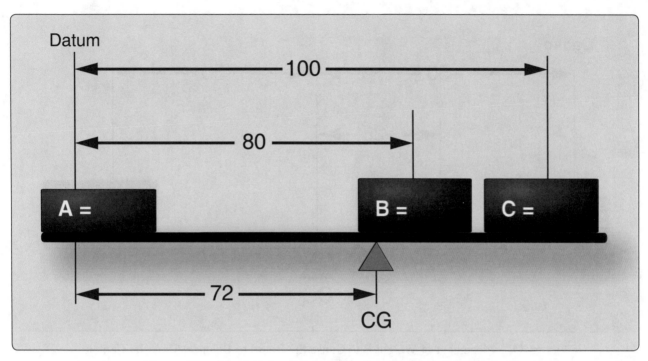

FIGURE 33.—Moving the CG of a Board by Shifting the Weights.

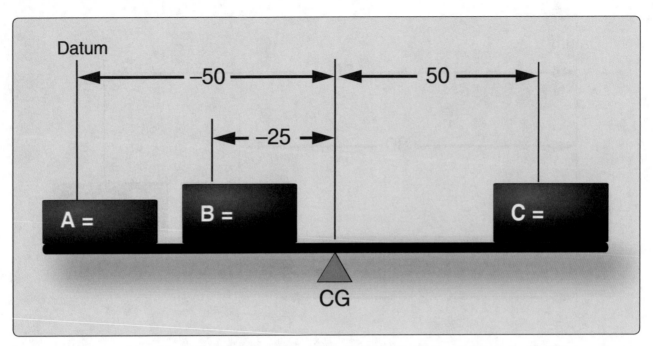

FIGURE 34.—Placement of Weight B to Cause the Board to Balance About Its Center.

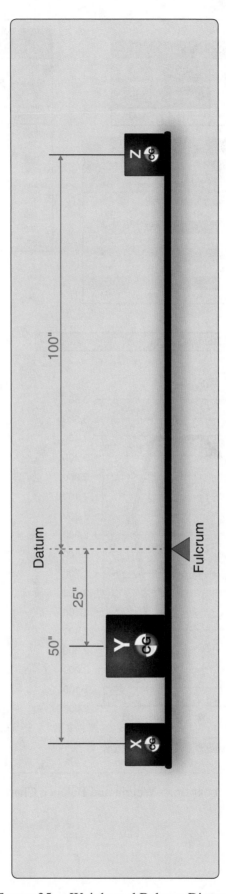

FIGURE 35.—Weight and Balance Diagram.

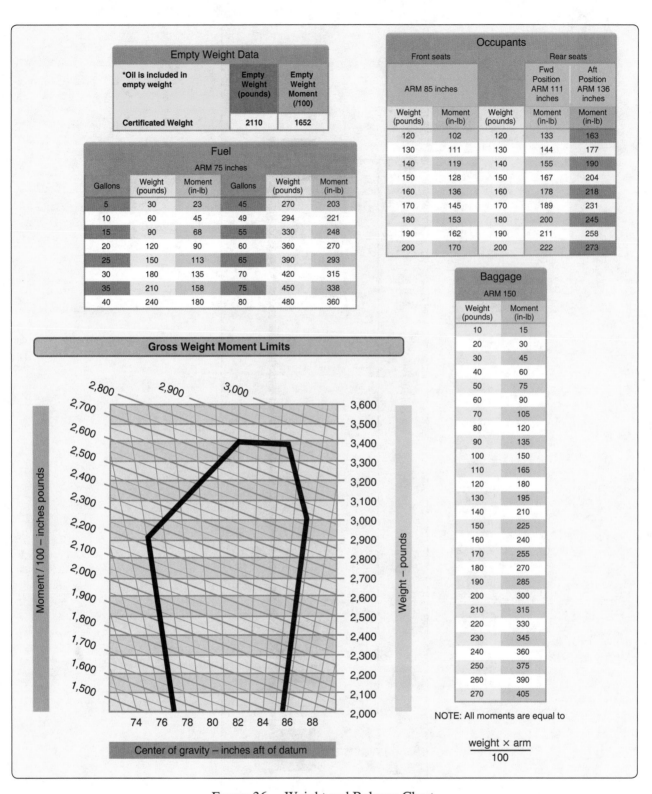

Empty Weight Data

*Oil is included in empty weight	Empty Weight (pounds)	Empty Weight Moment (/100)
Certificated Weight	2110	1652

Fuel

ARM 75 inches

Gallons	Weight (pounds)	Moment (in-lb)	Gallons	Weight (pounds)	Moment (in-lb)
5	30	23	45	270	203
10	60	45	49	294	221
15	90	68	55	330	248
20	120	90	60	360	270
25	150	113	65	390	293
30	180	135	70	420	315
35	210	158	75	450	338
40	240	180	80	480	360

Occupants

Front seats		Rear seats		
ARM 85 inches			Fwd Position ARM 111 inches	Aft Position ARM 136 inches
Weight (pounds)	Moment (in-lb)	Weight (pounds)	Moment (in-lb)	Moment (in-lb)
120	102	120	133	163
130	111	130	144	177
140	119	140	155	190
150	128	150	167	204
160	136	160	178	218
170	145	170	189	231
180	153	180	200	245
190	162	190	211	258
200	170	200	222	273

Baggage

ARM 150

Weight (pounds)	Moment (in-lb)
10	15
20	30
30	45
40	60
50	75
60	90
70	105
80	120
90	135
100	150
110	165
120	180
130	195
140	210
150	225
160	240
170	255
180	270
190	285
200	300
210	315
220	330
230	345
240	360
250	375
260	390
270	405

NOTE: All moments are equal to

$$\frac{weight \times arm}{100}$$

Gross Weight Moment Limits

Moment / 100 – inches pounds

Weight – pounds

Center of gravity – inches aft of datum

FIGURE 36.—Weight and Balance Chart.

FIGURE 37.—Rotor Blade Positions.

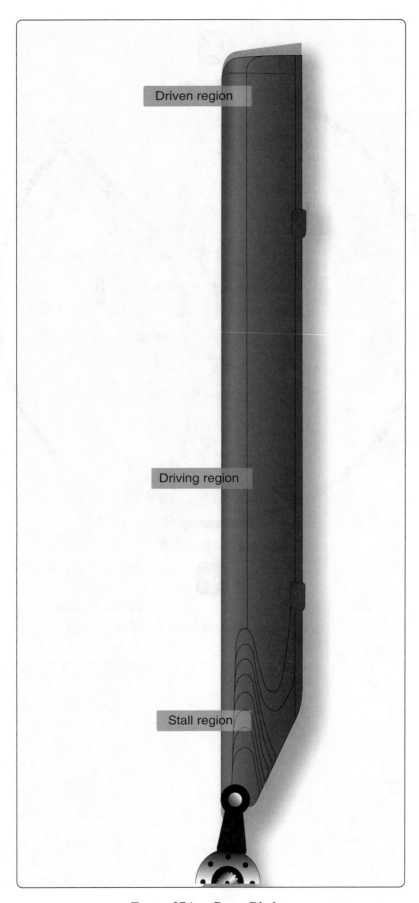

FIGURE 37A.—Rotor Blade.

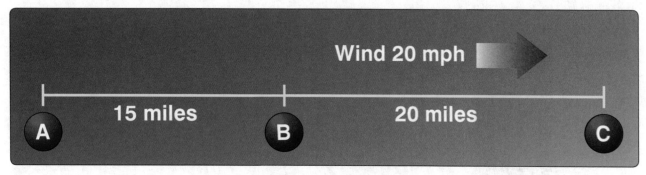

FIGURE 38.—Cross-Country.

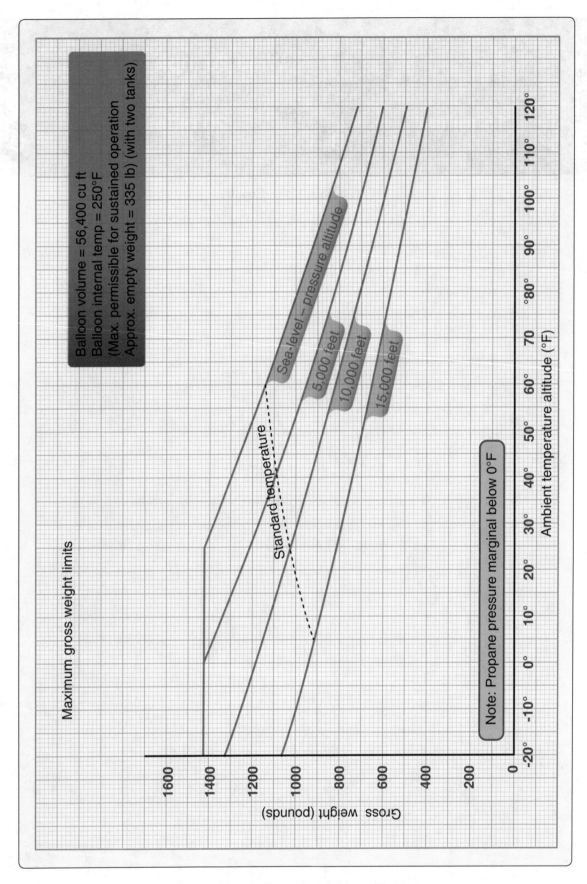

FIGURE 39.—Balloon Performance Graph.

42

Figure 40.—Wind Triangle.

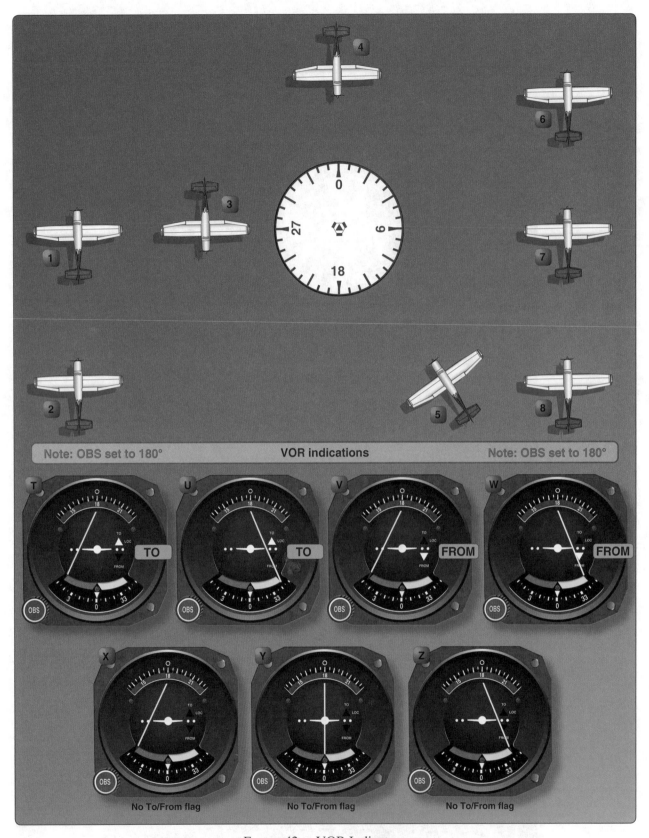

FIGURE 42.—VOR Indicators.

44

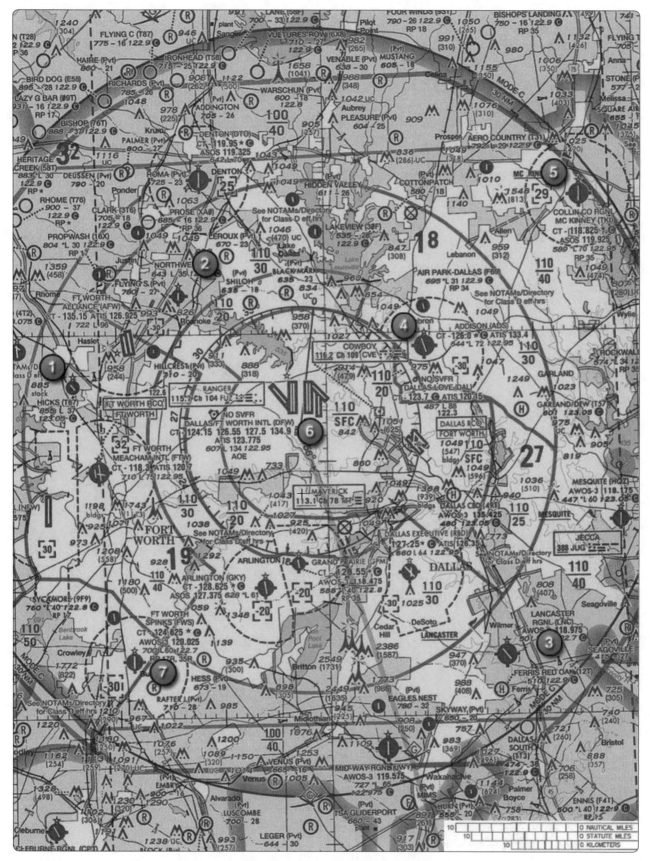

FIGURE 44.—Sectional Chart Excerpt.
NOTE: Chart is not to scale and should not be used for navigation. Use associated scale.

45

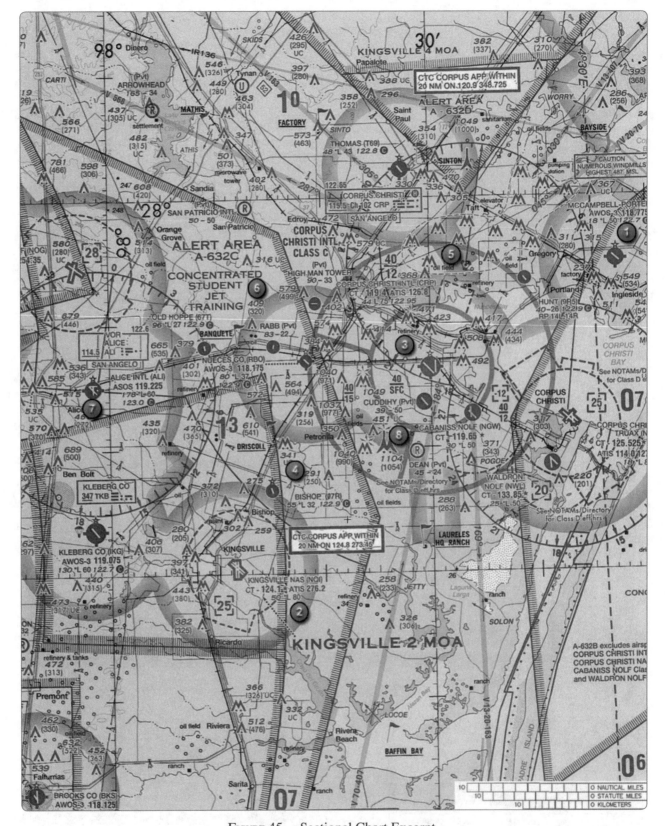

FIGURE 45.—Sectional Chart Excerpt.
NOTE: Chart is not to scale and should not be used for navigation. Use associated scale.

46

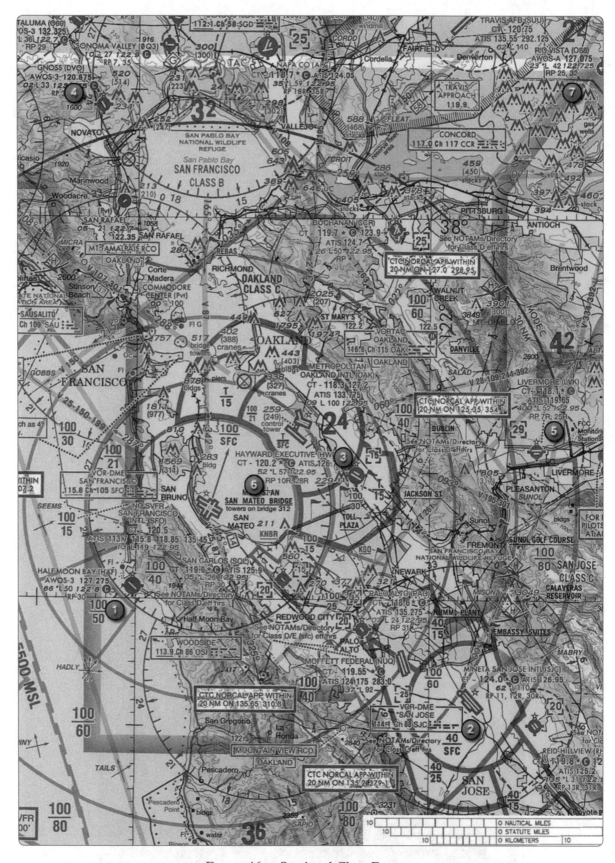

FIGURE 46.—Sectional Chart Excerpt.
NOTE: Chart is not to scale and should not be used for navigation. Use associated scale.

47

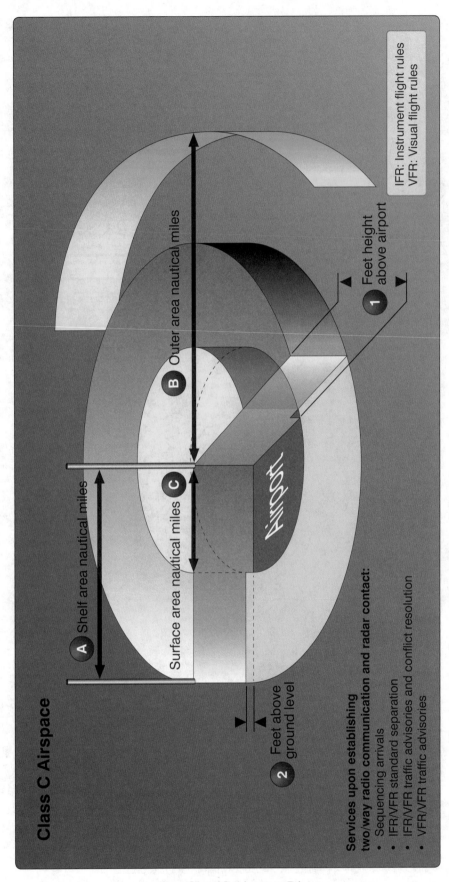

FIGURE 47.—Class C Airspace Diagram.

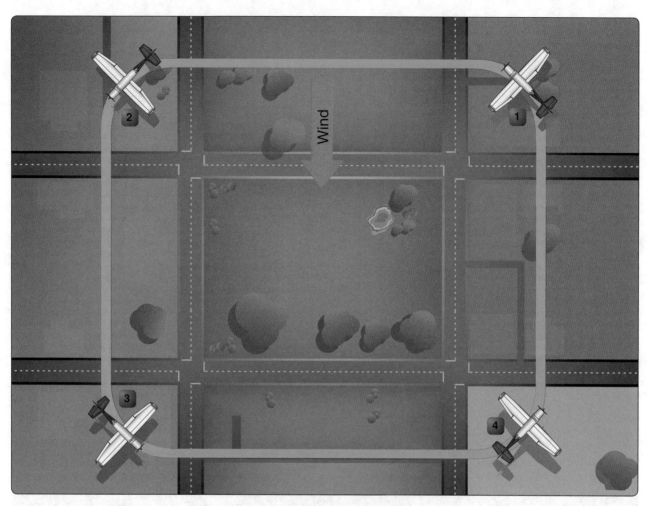

FIGURE 48.—Rectangular Course.

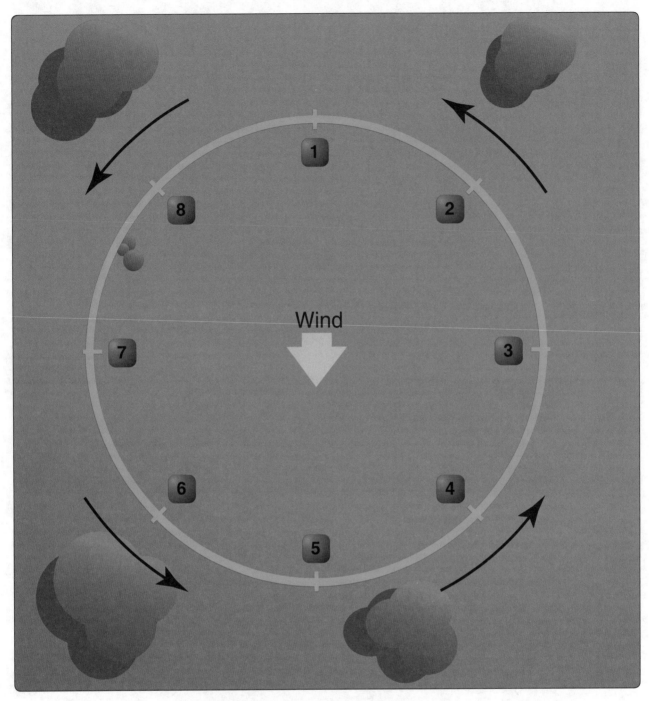

FIGURE 49.—Ground Track Maneuver Diagram.

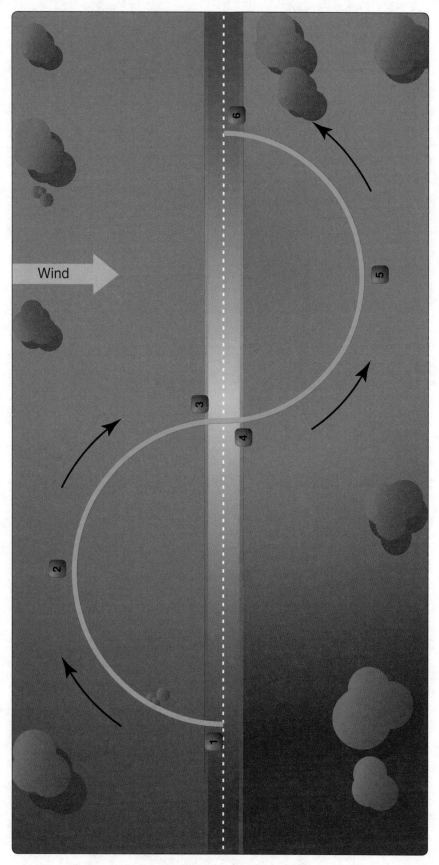

FIGURE 50.—S-Turn Diagram.

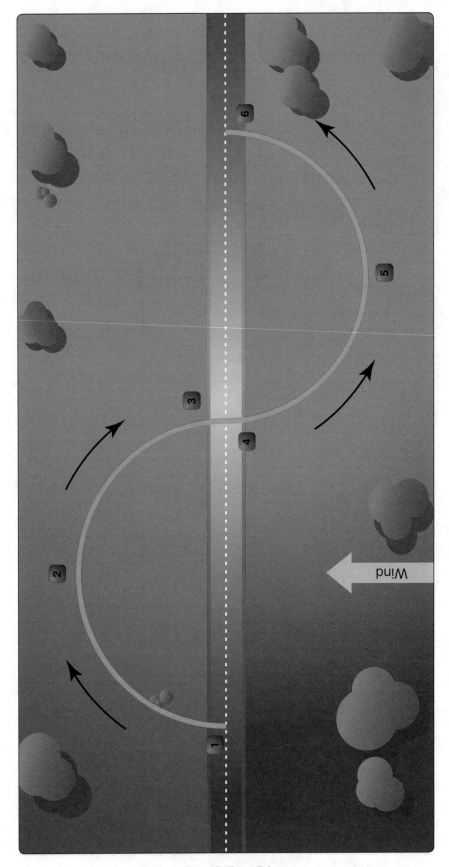

FIGURE 51.—S-Turn Diagram.

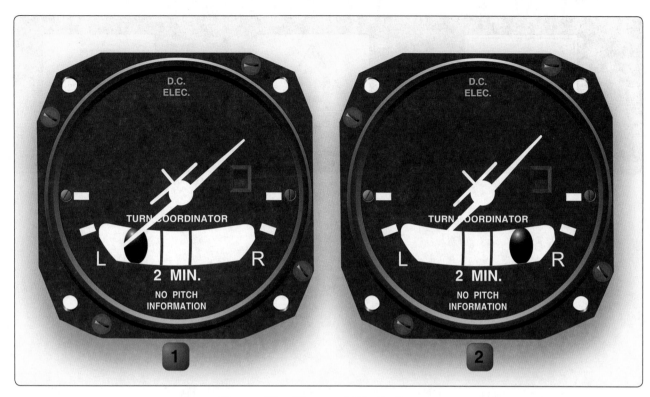

FIGURE 52.—Turn-and-Slip Indicators.

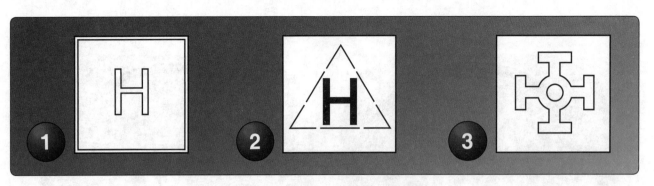

FIGURE 53.—Heliport Markings.

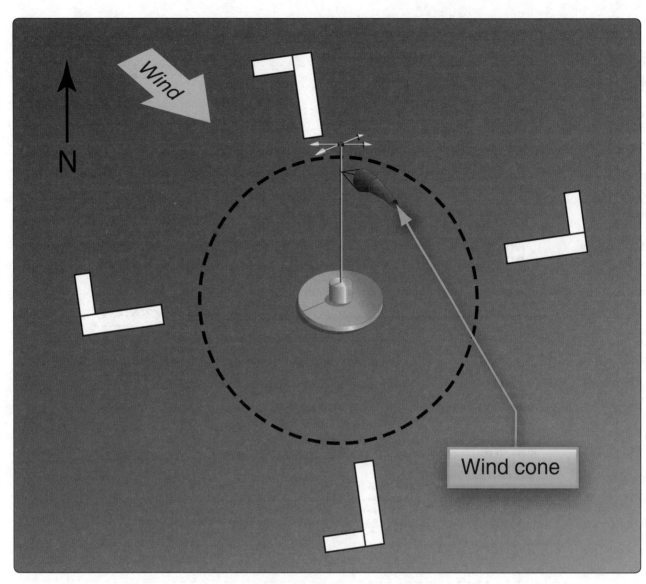

FIGURE 54.—Traffic Pattern Indicator.

DALLAS LOVE FLD (DAL) 5 NW UTC−6(−5DT) N32°50.83′ W96°51.11′ DALLAS−FT. WORTH

487 B S4 **FUEL** 100LL, JET A OX 1, 2, 3, 4 LRA Class I, ARFF Index B **COPTER**

NOTAM FILE DAL H−6H, L−17C, A

RWY 13R−31L: H8800X150 (CONC−GRVD) S−100, D−200, 2S−175, 2D−350 HIRL CL IAP, AD

RWY 13R: PAPI(P4R)—GA 3.0° TCH 52′. Thld dsplcd 490′. Rgt tfc.

RWY 31L: MALSR. TDZL. Building.

RWY 13L−31R: H7752X150 (CONC−GRVD) S−100, D−200, 2S−175,

2D−350 HIRL CL

RWY 13L: MALSR. TDZL.

RWY 31R: MALSR. PAPI(P4L)—GA 3.0° TCH 49′. Pole. Rgt tfc.

RWY 18−36: H6147X150 (ASPH) S−50, D−74, 2S−93, 2D−138

HIRL

RWY 18: VASI(V4L)—GA 3.0° TCH 52′. Tree. Rgt tfc.

RWY 36: VASI(V4L)—GA 3.0° TCH 52′. REIL. Rgt tfc.

RUNWAY DECLARED DISTANCE INFORMATION

RWY 13L: TORA−7752 TODA−7752 ASDA−7752 LDA−7752

RWY 13R: TORA−8800 TODA−8800 ASDA−8800 LDA−8310

RWY 18: TORA−6147 TODA−6147 ASDA−6147 LDA−6147

RWY 31L: TORA−8800 TODA−8800 ASDA−8000 LDA−8000

RWY 31R: TORA−7752 TODA−7752 ASDA−7752 LDA−7752

RWY 36: TORA−6147 TODA−6147 ASDA−6147 LDA−6147

AIRPORT REMARKS: Attended continuously. Birds on and invof arpt. Ldg

Rwy 18 & takeoff Rwy 36 not authorized to acft over 60,000 lbs

gross weight unless crosswind NW−SE rwys exceed acft safe operating capability. Rwy 13R, 13L, 31L and Rwy

31R runway visual range touchdown avbl. Noise sensitive areas all quadrants, noise abatement procedures in

effect for fixed and rotary wing tfc, for information call arpt ops 214−670−6610. Private pilot certificate or better

required to takeoff or land. No student solo flights permitted. Twy K clsd thru traffic. Twy L clsd indef. PAPI Rwy

31R unusable byd 7° either side of centerline. Flight Notification Service (ADCUS) available.

WEATHER DATA SOURCES: ASOS (214) 904−0251.

COMMUNICATIONS: D−ATIS 120.15 (214) 358−5355 **UNICOM** 122.95

DALLAS RCO 122.3 (FORT WORTH RADIO)

Ⓡ **RGNL APP CON** 125.2 (South) 124.3 (North)

LOVE TOWER 123.7 118.7 **GND CON** 121.75 **CLNC DEL** 127.9

Ⓡ **RGNL DEP CON** 124.3 (North Props) 125.2 (South Props) 125.125 118.55 (Turbojets)

AIRSPACE: CLASS B See VFR Terminal Area Chart.

RADIO AIDS TO NAVIGATION: NOTAM FILE FTW.

COWBOY (H) VORW/DME 116.2 CVE Chan 109 N32°53.42′ W96°54.24′ 128° 3.7 NM to fld. 450/6E.

ILS/DME 111.5 I−DAL Chan 52 Rwy 13L. Class IT. LOC unusable byd 20° right of centerline.

ILS/DME 111.1 I−DPX Chan 48 Rwy 13R. Class IT. LOC unusable beyond 25° right side of course.

ILS/DME 111.1 I−LVF Chan 48 Rwy 31L. Class IB. LOC unusable byd 20° right of course.

ILS/DME 111.5 I−OVW Chan 52 Rwy 31R. Class IE. Glide slope unusable for coupled apchs blo

636′ MSL.

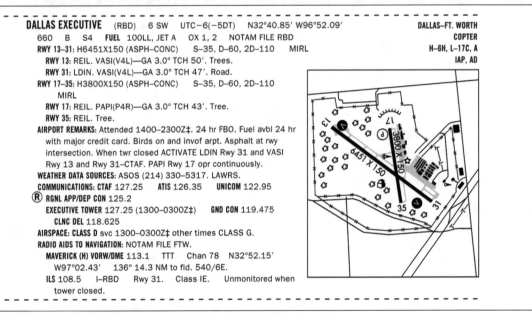

DALLAS EXECUTIVE (RBD) 6 SW UTC−6(−5DT) N32°40.85′ W96°52.09′ DALLAS−FT. WORTH

660 B S4 **FUEL** 100LL, JET A OX 1, 2 NOTAM FILE RBD **COPTER**

RWY 13−31: H6451X150 (ASPH−CONC) S−35, D−60, 2D−110 MIRL H−6H, L−17C, A

RWY 13: REIL. VASI(V4L)—GA 3.0° TCH 50′. Trees. IAP, AD

RWY 31: LDIN. VASI(V4L)—GA 3.0° TCH 47′. Road.

RWY 17−35: H3800X150 (ASPH−CONC) S−35, D−60, 2D−110

MIRL

RWY 17: REIL. PAPI(P4R)—GA 3.0° TCH 43′. Tree.

RWY 35: REIL. Tree.

AIRPORT REMARKS: Attended 1400−2300Z‡. 24 hr FBO. Fuel avbl 24 hr

with major credit card. Birds on and invof arpt. Asphalt at rwy

intersection. When twr closed ACTIVATE LDIN Rwy 31 and VASI

Rwy 13 and Rwy 31−CTAF. PAPI Rwy 17 opr continuously.

WEATHER DATA SOURCES: ASOS (214) 330−5317. LAWRS.

COMMUNICATIONS: CTAF 127.25 ATIS 126.35 **UNICOM** 122.95

Ⓡ **RGNL APP/DEP CON** 125.2

EXECUTIVE TOWER 127.25 (1300−0300Z‡) **GND CON** 119.475

CLNC DEL 118.625

AIRSPACE: CLASS D svc 1300−0300Z‡ other times CLASS G.

RADIO AIDS TO NAVIGATION: NOTAM FILE FTW.

MAVERICK (H) VORW/DME 113.1 TTT Chan 78 N32°52.15′

W97°02.43′ 136° 14.3 NM to fld. 540/6E.

ILS 108.5 I−RBD Rwy 31. Class IE. Unmonitored when

tower closed.

FIGURE 55.—Chart Supplements U.S. (formerly Airport/Facility Directory).

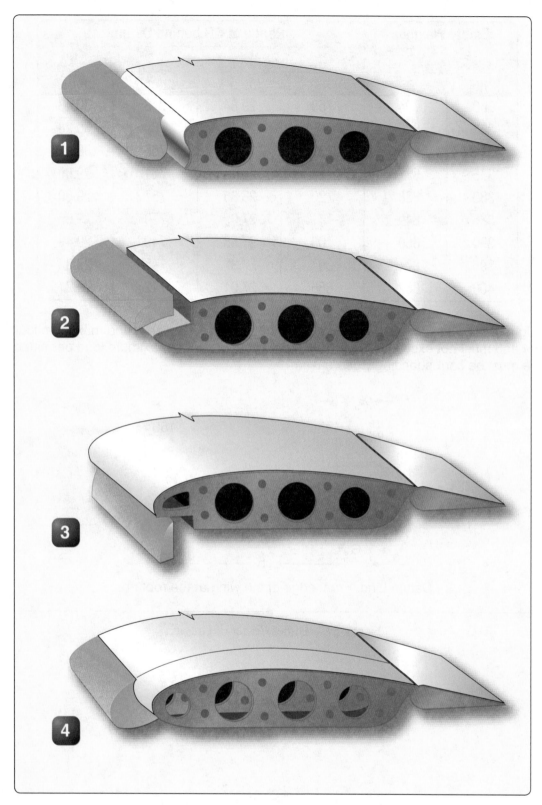

Figure 56.—Leading Edge High Lift Devices.

Empty Weight		Range of CG behind Datum			
		Forward		Aft	
kg	lbs	mm	inches	mm	inches
360	794	758	29.84	773	30.43
365	805	748	29.45	769	30.28
370	816	739	29.09	765	30.12
375	827	729	28.70	761	29.96
380	838	720	28.35	757	29.80
385	849	711	27.99	753	29.65
390	860	703	27.68	749	29.49
395	871	694	27.32	745	29.33
400	882	686	27.01	742	29.21

The weight of the non-lifting parts is the sum of the fuselage, tailplane, and maximum load in the fuselage and must not exceed 400 kgs (882 lbs). Otherwise, the maximum load permitted in the fuselage must be correspondingly decreased.

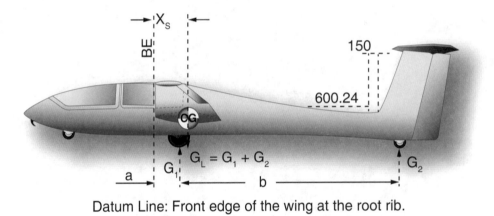

Datum Line: Front edge of the wing at the root rib.

FIGURE 57.—Glider Center of Gravity.

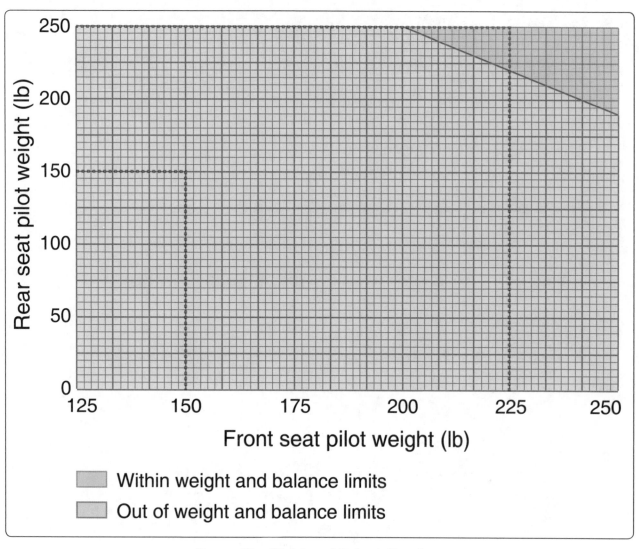

FIGURE 58.—Weight and Balance Envelope.